BRITISH WRITERS

BRITISH WRITERS

JAY PARINI

Editor

SUPPLEMENT VII

Charles Scribner's Sons
an imprint of the Gale Group
New York • Detroit • San Francisco • London • Boston • Woodbridge, CT

Charles Scribner's Sons
an imprint of The Gale Group
27500 Drake Rd.
Farmington Hills, MI 483331-3535

Library of Congress Cataloging-in-Publication Data

British Writers. supplement VII/Jay Parini, editor in chief.
    p. cm.
    Includes bibliographical references and index.
    ISBN 0-684-80655-X(alk. paper)
    1.English literature—Bio-bibliography. 2. English
literature—History and criticism. 3. Authors, English—
Biography. I Parini, Jay.

PR85.B688 Suppl.7
820.9—dc21
[B]   2001020992

Acknowledgments

Acknowledgment is gratefully made to those publishers and
individuals who permitted the use of the following materials in copyright:

BASIL BUNTING Excerpts from *The Complete Poems*. Copyright © 2000 by The Estate of Basil Bunting. Reprinted with the permission of Bloodaxe Books Ltd.

GAVIN EWART Excerpts from *The Collected Ewart, 1933-1980* (London: Hutchinson, 1980) and *Collected Poems, 1980-1990* (London: Hutchinson, 1991), excerpt from "No Smoking" from *Like It Or Not* (London: The Bodley Head, 1993). Copyright © 1980, 1991, 1993 by Gavin Ewart. All reprinted with the permission of M. A. Ewart. E. Clerihew Bentley, clerihew / from *The Complete Clerihews of E. Clerihew Bentley*, edited by Gavin Ewart (New York: Oxford University Press, 1981). Copyright © 1981 by E. C. Bentley. Reprinted with the permission of Curtis Brown Group, Ltd., on behalf of the Estate of E. C. Bentley.

MICHAEL FRAYN Excerpts from *Sweet Dreams* (London: Collins, 1973). Copyright © 1973 by Michael Frayn. Reprinted with the permission of Greene & Heaton, Ltd.

ROY FULLER Excerpts from *New and Collected Poems 1934-1984*. Copyright © 1985 by Roy Fuller. Excerpts from "Ambiguities" from *Brutus's Orchard*. Copyright © 1957 by Roy Fuller. Excerpt from "Images" from *Subsequent to Summer* (Edinburgh: Salamander Press, 1985). Copyright © 1985 by Roy Fuller. Excerpts from "Lessons of the Summer," "A Disc's Defects," "The Surgeon's Hand," and "Postscript" from *Available for Dreams* (London: Collins Harvill, 1989). Copyright © 1989 by Roy Fuller. Excerpts from "The Story" from *Last Poems*. Copyright © 1993. All reprinted with the permission of John Fuller.

W. S. GRAHAM Excerpts from "Enter Cloud" from *Implements in Their Places* (London: Faber & Faber, 1977). Copyright © 1977 by W. S. Graham. "What Is the Language Using Us For?," "A Note to the Difficult One," "Dear Bryan Wynter," and "Implements in Their Places" from *Implements in Their Places*. Copyright © 1977 by W. S. Graham. excerpts from *Cage Without Grievance* (Glasgow: Parton Press, 1942). Copyright 1942 by The Estate of W. S. Graham. Excerpts from "The First Journey" and "The Sixth Journey" from *The*

Seven Journeys. Copyright 1944 by W. S. Graham. Excerpts from "The Bright Building" and "The Crowd of Birds and Children" from *2nd Poems*. Copyright 1945 by W. S. Graham. Excerpt from "Shian Bay" from *The White Threshold*. Copyright 1949 by W. S. Graham. Excerpts from "The Nightfishing" and "Seven Letters" from *The Nightfishing*. Copyright © 1955 by W. S. Graham. Excerpts from "Malcolm Mooney's Land," "The Thermal Stair," and "The Dark Dialogues" from *Malcolm Mooney's Land*. Copyright © 1970 by W. S. Graham. All reprinted with the permission of Michael and Margaret Snow, Literary Executors for the W. S. Graham Estate. W. H. Auden, excerpt from "In Memory of W.B. Yeats" from *W. B. Auden: Collected Poems*, edited by Edward Mendelson. Copyright 1940, 1941, 1951, 1952 and renewed © 1968, 1969 by W. H. Auden. Copyright © 1976 by Edward Mendelson, William Meredith, and Monroe K. Spears. Reprinted with the permission of Random House, Inc. and Faber and Faber, Ltd.

L. P. HARTLEY Excerpts from "Simonetta Perkins" from *The Complete Short Stories* (London: Hamish Hamilton, 1973), excerpts from *Eustace and Hilda: A Trilogy*. Copyright © 1958 by L. P. Hartley. Excerpts from *The Hireling* (London: Hamish Hamilton, 1957). Copyright © 1957 by L. P. Hartley. All reprinted with the permission of The Society of Authors as the Literary Representative of the Estate of L. P. Hartley. The Concise Scots Dictionary, definition for "bellieflaucht" from *The Concise Scots Dictionary*, edited by Mairi Robinson. Reprinted with the permission of Chambers Harrup Publishers, Ltd.

A. D. HOPE Excerpts from "Ascent into Hell," "The Wandering Islands," "Invocation," and "Imperial Adam" from *The Wandering Islands*. Copyright © 1955 by A. D. Hope. Excerpts from "The Return from the Freudian Islands," "The End of a Journey," "An Epistle: Edward Sackville to Venetia Digby," and "Australia" from *Collected Poems 1930-1965*. Copyright © 1965 by A. D. Hope. Christopher Marlowe, excerpts from *The Tragical History of Doctor Faustus*, purged and amended by A. D. Hope. Copyright © 1982 by A. D. Hope. All reprinted with the permission of Curtis Brown (Aust) Pty Ltd.

ACKNOWLEDGMENTS

DAVID JONES Excerpts from *In Parenthesis*. Copyright 1937 by David Jones. Excerpts from *Anathemata*. Copyright 1952 by David Jones. Excerpts from *The Sleeping Lord and Other Fragments*. Copyright © 1974 by David Jones. All reprinted with the permission of Faber & Faber, Ltd.

PATRICK KAVANAGH Excerpts from "The Great Hunger," "April," "Inniskeen Road: July Evening," "Stony Grey Soil," "Spraying the Potatoes," "Art Mc-Cooey," "The Paddiad," "Pegasus," "Father Mat," "A Christmas Childhood," "Having Confessed," "Auditors In," "Prelude," "Canal Bank Walk," and "The Hospital" from *Patrick Kavanagh: Collected Poems*. Copyright © 1964 by Patrick Kavanagh. Reprinted with the permission of DevinAdair Publishers, Inc. Excerpts from *Lough Derg* (The Curragh, Ireland: Goldsmith Press, 1978). Reprinted with permission. Excerpts from "Personal Problem" from *Complete Poems* (The Curragh, Ireland: Goldsmith Press, 1990). Copyright © 1978 by Patrick Kavanagh. Reprinted with permission.

JAMAICA KINCAID Excerpts from "On Seeing England for the First Time" from Transition 51(1991). Copyright © 1991 by Jamaica Kincaid. Reprinted with the permission of The Wylie Agency, Inc. Kay Bonetti, excerpts from "An Interview with Jamaica Kincaid" from The Missouri Review 15, No. 2 (1992). Collected in Kay Bonetti, *Conversations with American Novelists: The Best Interviews from The Missouri Review and the American Audio Prose Library*. Copyright © 1997 by the Curators of the University of Missouri. Reprinted with the permission of the University of Missouri Press.

ANDREW MOTION Excerpts from "Skating," "A Dying Race," and "Open Secrets" from *Dangerous Play: Poems 1974-1984* (Edinburgh: Salamander Press, 1984). Copyright © 1984 by Andrew Motion. Excerpts from "Writing," "The Whole Truth," and "A Lyrical Ballad" from *Secret Narratives* (Edinburgh: Salamander Press, 1983). Copyright © 1983 by Andrew Motion. Excerpts from "The Dancing Hippo," "Natural Causes," "Afternoons," and "Firing Practice" from *Natural Causes* (London: Chatto & Windus, 1987). Copyright © 1987 by Andrew Motion. All reprinted with the permission of The Peters Fraser and Dunlop Group Limited on behalf of Andrew Motion. Excerpts from "Run" and "Look" from *Love in a Life*. Copyright © 1991 by Andrew Motion. Excerpts from "Leaving Belfast" from *Selected Poems 1976-1997*. Copyright © 1997 by Andrew Motion. Excerpts from "Lines of Desire," "Reading the Elephant," and "Joe Soap" from *The Price of Everything*. Copyright © 1994 by Andrew Motion. All reprinted with the permission of Faber and Faber, Ltd.

LES MURRAY Excerpts from "Joker as Told," "Letters to the Winner," "The Grandmother's Story," and "Bat's Ultrasound" from *The Daylight Moon and Other Poems*. Copyright © 1987 by Les Murray. Reprinted with the permission of Persea Books, Inc., Carcanet Press, Ltd., and Margaret Connolly & Associates. Excerpts from *The Rabbiter's Bounty: Collected Poems*. Copyright © 1991 by Les Murray. Excerpts from "The Past Ever Present," "The Fall of Aphrodite Street," and "The Emerald Dove" from *The Dog Fox Field*. Copyright © 1990 by Les Murray. Excerpts from "Goose to Donkey," "Pigs," and "Eagle Pair" from *Translations of the Natural World*. Copyright © 1992 by Les Murray. Excerpts from "The Cows on Killing Day" from *Dog Fox Field*. Collected in *Translations of the Natural World* and *Learning Human: Selected Prose*. Copyright © 1990 by Les Murray. Excerpts from "The Last Hellos," "Burning Want," "Demo," and "The Devil" from *Subhuman Redneck Poems*. Copyright © 1996 by Les Murray. Excerpts from *Freddy Neptune*. Copyright © 1998 by Les Murray. All reprinted with the permission of Farrar, Straus & Giroux, LLC., Carcanet Press, Ltd., and Margaret Connolly & Associates. Excerpt from "The Disorderly" from *Conscious and Verbal*. Copyright © 1999 by Les Murray. Reprinted with the permission of Carcanet Press, Ltd. and Margaret Connolly & Associates.

ALASTAIR REID Excerpts from "Weathering," "Curiosity," "Daedalus," and "What Gets Lost / *Lo Que Se Pierde*" from *Weathering: Poems and Translations* (New York: Dutton, 1978). Copyright © 1978 by Alastair Reid. Jacket notes and excerpts from "The Figures on the Frieze" and "Spiral" from *Passwords: Places, Poems, Preoccupations* (Boston: Little, Brown, 1963). Copyright © 1963 by Alastair Reid. Excerpts from "A Lesson in Music" from *An Alastair Reid Reader* (Middlebury College Press, 1994). Copyright © 1994 by Alastair Reid. "Autobiography" and excerpts from "Poem for My Father," "Lay for New Lovers," "The Village," "Not Now for My Sin's Sake," "Song for Four Seasons," "The Question in the Cobweb," "The Waterglass," and "Directions for a Map" from *To Lighten My House* (Scarsdale: Morgan and Morgan, 1953). Copyright 1953 by Alastair Reid. Excerpts from *Oddments Inklings Omens Moments* (Boston: Little, Brown, 1959). Copyright © 1959 by Alastair Reid. All reprinted with the permission of the author. Pablo Neruda, excerpts from "Forget about me," and "The great tablecloth" from *Extravagaria*, translated by Alastair Reid. Translation copyright © 1974 by Alastair Reid. Reprinted with the permission of Farrar, Straus & Giroux, LLC. and John Johnson, Author's Agent, Ltd. Jorge Luis Borges, excerpts from "The Other Tiger," translated by Alastair Reid, from *Selected Poems*. Copyright © 1999 by Alastair Reid. Reprinted with the permission of Viking Penguin, a division of Penguin Putnam Inc.

ACKNOWLEDGMENTS

BARRY UNSWORTH Excerpts from interviews in The (London) Sunday Times February 23, 1992 and July 29, 1999. Copyright © 1992, 1999. Reprinted with permission. Excerpts from *Pascali's Island*. Published in the United States as *The Idol Hunter*. Copyright © 1980 by Barry Unsworth. Reprinted with the permission of W. W. Norton & Company, Inc. and Michael Joseph, Ltd. Excerpts from *Sugar and Rum*. Copyright © 1988 by Barry Unsworth. Reprinted with the permission of W. W. Norton & Company, Inc. and Hamish Hamilton, Ltd.

SYLVIA TOWNSEND WARNER Excerpts from "The Loudest Lay," "Opus 7," "Benicasim," "Drawing you, heavy with sleep," and "Red Front" from *Collected Poems*. Reprinted with the permission of Carcanet Press, Ltd. Excerpt from "Since the first toss of gale ..." from *Whether a Dove or a Seagull* (New York: Viking, 1933). Copyright 1933 by Sylvia Townsend Warner. Reprinted with the permission of The Estate of Sylvia Townsend Warner. Excerpts from "But at the Stroke of Midnight" from *The Innocent and the Guilty*. Copyright © 1971 by Sylvia Townsend Warner. Reprinted with the permission of Chatto & Windus/ The Random House Group, Ltd.

Editorial and Production Staff

Project Editor
PAMELA PARKINSON

Contributing Editor
KEN WACHSBERGER

Copyeditors
JANET BYRNE
GINA MISIROGLU

Proofreader
GREG TEAGUE

Indexer
NOEL GNADINGER

Permission Researcher
FRED COURTRIGHT

Production Manager
EVI SEOUD

Buyer
STACY MELSON

Associate Publisher
TIMOTHY DEWERFF

Publisher
FRANK MENCHACA

Contents

Introduction

An ample range of article on British, Irish, and Angophone authors will be found in *British Writers, Supplement VII*. None of these authors has yet been discussed in previous volumes in the series, yet all of them are worthy of inclusion here. The range of subjects covered stretches from the anonymous poet who wrote *Sir Gawain and the Green Knight* —a great Anglo-Saxon masterwork—to such contemporary novelists and poets as Jamaica Kincaid, Andrew Motion, and Barry Unsworth, each of whom has added meaningfully to the growing body of literature in English.

British Writers was originally modeled on *American Writers* (1974–), another series published by Charles Scribner's Sons (an imprint of the Gale Group). In the original set of *British Writers*, published between 1979 and 1984, seven volumes were published, each of them an anthology that featured articles on the lives and works of well-known poets, novelists, playwrights, essayists and autobiographers from the AngloSaxon era to the present. This set was followed by six supplemental volumes that covered authors who, for various reasons, had been neglected.

Throughout the series, we have attempted to provide transparent, knowledgeable essays aimed at the general, literate reader. Most of the critics writing for this supplement, as in the previous volumes, are professionals: teachers, scholars, and writers. As anyone glancing through this anthology will see, the critics have held to the highest standards of scholarship and writing. Their work often rises to a high level of craft and critical vision as they survey the life and work of a writer who has made a genuine impact on the course of British, Irish, or Anglophone literature. The biographical context for works is provided so that readers can appreciate the historical ground beneath the texts under discussion. The essays each conclude with a select bibliography intended to direct the reading of those should want to pursue the subject in greater detail.

This volume looks at a number of modern or contemporary writers, most of whom have received little sustained attention from critics. For example, Anna Kavan, Michael Frayn, Sylvia Townsend Warner, and Barry Unsworth have been written about in the review pages of newspapers and magazines, but their work has yet to attract significant scholarship. The essays included here constitute a beginning.

The poets discussed here, such as Roy Fuller, Gavin Ewart, W.S. Graham, A.D. Hope, Les Murray, Alastair Reid, are well known in the world of contemporary poetry, and their work has in each case been widely admired by readers of poetry, but the real work of assimilation, of discovering the true place of each writer in the larger traditions of modern poetry, has only begun. In each case, these poets are treated by critics who are themselves established poets, and the depth and eloquence of their essays should be obvious even to casual readers.

We also include essays on long-established authors, such as the Gawain poet, Robert Henryson, Thomas More, Sydney Smith, Charles Darwin, John Henry Newman, Basil Bunting, L.P. Hartley, David Johnes, and Patrick Kavanagh. These authors, for various reasons, were neglected in previous volumes and supplements. In future volumes, we intend to revisit some of the canonical authors discussed in earlier essays, since scholarship on these writers continues to shift and grow, and since the work of culture involves the continuous assessment and reassessment of major texts produced by its finest writers. In Supplement VII, we offer dependable and lively introductions to nearly two dozen authors — some extremely well known, others less so. Each of them deserves this kind of critical attention.

JAY PARINI

Chronology

1272–1307	**Reign of Edward I**
1276	The prince of North Wales, Llewelyn II, refuses to pay homage to England's Edward I, who invades North Wales and forces Llewelyn to surrender
1282	Llewelyn II leads a second attack against Edward and fails; Wales falls to English rule
1297	William Wallace (Bravehart) leads attacks against British troops in an attempt for Scottish sovereignty
1305	William Wallace is captured, tried, and hanged
1307–1327	**Reign of Edward II**
ca. 1325	John Wycliffe born
	John Gower born
1327–1377	**Reign of Edward III**
ca. 1332	William Langland born
1337	Beginning of the Hundred Years' War
ca. 1340	Geoffrey Chaucer born
1346	The Battle of Crécy
1348	The Black Death (further outbreaks in 1361 and 1369)
ca. 1350	Boccaccio's *Decameron*
	Langland's *Piers Plowman*
1351	The Statute of Laborers pegs laborers' wages at rates in effect preceding the plague
1356	The Battle of Poitiers
1360	The Treaty of Brétigny: end of the first phase of the Hundred Years' War
1362	Pleadings in the law courts conducted in English
	Parliaments opened by speeches in English
1369	Chaucer's *The Book of the Duchess*, an elegy to Blanche of Lancaster, wife of John of Gaunt
1369–1377	Victorious French campaigns under du Guesclin

ca. 1370	John Lydgate born
1371	Sir John Mandeville's *Travels*
1372	Chaucer travels to Italy
1372–1382	Wycliffe active in Oxford
1373–1393	William of Wykeham founds Winchester College and New College, Oxford
ca. 1375–1400	*Sir Gawain and the Green Knight*
1376	Death of Edward the Black Prince
1377–1399	**Reign of Richard II**
ca. 1379	Gower's *Vox clamantis*
ca. 1380	Chaucer's *Troilus and Criseyde*
1381	The Peasants' Revolt
1386	Chaucer's *Canterbury Tales* begun
	Chaucer sits in Parliament
	Gower's *Confessio amantis*
1399–1413	**Reign of Henry IV**
ca. 1400	Death of William Langland
1400	Death of Geoffrey Chaucer
1408	Death of John Gower
1412–1420	Lydgate's *Troy Book*
1413–1422	**Reign of Henry V**
1415	The Battle of Agincourt
***ca.* 1420**	**Robert Henryson born**
1422–1461	**Reign of Henry VI**
1431	François Villon born
	Joan of Arc burned at Rouen
1440–1441	Henry VI founds Eton College and King's College, Cambridge
1444	Truce of Tours
1450	Jack Cade's rebellion
ca. 1451	Death of John Lydgate
1453	End of the Hundred Years' War
	The fall of Constantinople
1455–1485	The Wars of the Roses
ca. 1460	John Skelton born
1461–1470	**Reign of Edward IV**
1470–1471	**Reign of Henry VI**
1471	Death of Sir Thomas Malory
1471–1483	**Reign of Edward IV**

CHRONOLOGY

1557	Tottel's *Miscellany*, including the poems of Wyatt and Surrey, published
ca. 1558	Thomas Kyd born
1558	Calais, the last English possession in France, is lost
	Mary I dies
1558–1603	**Reign of Elizabeth I**
1559	John Knox arrives in Scotland
	Rebellion against the French regent
ca. 1559	George Chapman born
1561	Mary Queen of Scots (Mary Stuart) arrives in Edinburgh
	Thomas Hoby's translation of Castiglione's *The Courtier Gorboduc*, the first English play in blank verse
	Francis Bacon born
1562	Civil war in France
	English expedition sent to support the Huguenots
1562–1568	Sir John Hawkins' voyages to Africa
1564	Births of Christopher Marlowe and William Shakespeare
1565	Mary Queen of Scots marries Lord Darnley
1566	William Painter's *Palace of Pleasure*, a miscellany of prose stories, the source of many dramatists' plots
1567	Darnley murdered at Kirk o'Field
	Mary Queen of Scots marries the earl of Bothwell
1569	Rebellion of the English northern earls suppressed
1570	Roger Ascham's *The Schoolmaster*
1571	Defeat of the Turkish fleet at Lepanto
ca. 1572	Ben Jonson born
1572	St. Bartholomew's Day massacre
	John Donne born
1574	The earl of Leicester's theater company formed
1576	The Theater, the first permanent theater building in London, opened
	The first Blackfriars Theater opened with performances by the Children of St. Paul's
	John Marston born
1576–1578	Martin Frobisher's voyages to Labrador and the northwest
1577–1580	Sir Francis Drake sails around the world
1577	Holinshed's *Chronicles of England, Scotlande, and Irelande*
1579	John Lyly's *Euphues: The Anatomy of Wit*
	Thomas North's translation of *Plutarch's Lives*
1581	The Levant Company founded
	Seneca's *Ten Tragedies* translated
1582	Richard Hakluyt's *Divers Voyages Touching the Discoverie of America*
1584–1585	Sir John Davis' first voyage to Greenland
1585	First English settlement in America, the "Lost Colony" comprising 108 men under Ralph Lane, founded at Roanoke Island, off the coast of North Carolina
1586	Kyd's *Spanish Tragedy*
	Marlowe's *Tamburlaine*
	William Camden's *Britannia*
	The Babington conspiracy against Queen Elizabeth
	Death of Sir Philip Sidney
1587	Mary Queen of Scots executed
	Birth of Virginia Dare, first English child born in America, at Roanoke Island
1588	Defeat of the Spanish Armada
	Marlowe's *Dr. Faustus*
1590	Spenser's *The Faerie Queen*, Cantos 1–3
1592	Outbreak of plague in London; the theaters closed
	Henry King born
1593	Death of Christopher Marlowe
1594	The Lord Chamberlain's Men, the company to which Shakespeare belonged, founded
	The Swan Theater opened
	Death of Thomas Kyd
1595	Ralegh's expedition to Guiana
	Sidney's *Apology for Poetry*
1596	The earl of Essex's expedition captures Cadiz
	The second Blackfriars Theater opened
ca. 1597	Death of George Peele
1597	Bacon's first collection of *Essays*
1598	Jonson's *Every Man in His Humor*

CHRONOLOGY

CHRONOLOGY

The monarchy and the House of Lords abolished

The Commonwealth proclaimed

Cromwell invades Ireland and defeats the royalist Catholic forces

Death of Richard Crashaw

1650 Cromwell defeats the Scots at Dunbar

1651 Charles II crowned king of the Scots, at Scone

Charles II invades England, is defeated at Worcester, escapes to France

Thomas Hobbes's *Leviathan*

1652 War with Holland

1653 The Rump Parliament dissolved by the army

A new Parliament and council of state nominated; Cromwell becomes Lord Protector

Walton's *The Compleat Angler*

1654 Peace concluded with Holland

War against Spain

1655 Parliament attempts to reduce the army and is dissolved

Rule of the major-generals

1656 Sir William Davenant produces *The Siege of Rhodes*, one of the first English operas

1657 Second Parliament of the Protectorate

Cromwell is offered and declines the throne

Death of Richard Lovelace

1658 Death of Oliver Cromwell

Richard Cromwell succeeds as Protector

1659 Conflict between Parliament and the army

1660 General Monck negotiates with Charles II

Charles II offers the conciliatory Declaration of Breda and accepts Parliament's invitation to return

Will's Coffee House established

Sir William Davenant and Thomas Killigrew licensed to set up two companies of players, the Duke of York's and the King's Servants, including actors and actresses

Pepys's *Diary* begun

1660–1685   Reign of Charles II

1661 Parliament passes the Act of Uniformity, enjoining the use of the Book of Common Prayer; many Puritan and dissenting clergy leave their livings

1662 Peace Treaty with Spain

King Charles II marries Catherine of Braganza

The Royal Society incorporated (founded in 1660)

1664 War against Holland

New Amsterdam captured and becomes New York

John Vanbrugh born

1665 The Great Plague

Newton discovers the binomial theorem and invents the integral and differential calculus, at Cambridge

1666 The Great Fire of London

Bunyan's *Grace Abounding*

London Gazette founded

1667 The Dutch fleet sails up the Medway and burns English ships

The war with Holland ended by the Treaty of Breda

Milton's *Paradise Lost*

Thomas Sprat's *History of the Royal Society*

Death of Abraham Cowley

1668 Sir Christopher Wren begins to rebuild St. Paul's Cathedral

Triple Alliance formed with Holland and Sweden against France

Dryden's *Essay of Dramatick Poesy*

1670 Alliance formed with France through the secret Treaty of Dover

Pascal's *Pensées*

The Hudson's Bay Company founded

William Congreve born

1671 Milton's *Samson Agonistes* and *Paradise Regained*

1672 War against Holland

Wycherley's *The Country Wife*

King Charles issues the Declaration of Indulgence, suspending penal laws against Nonconformists and Catholics

1673 Parliament passes the Test Act, making acceptance of the doctrines of

CHRONOLOGY

CHRONOLOGY

1740 War of the Austrian Succession, 1740–1748 (King George's War in America, 1744–1748)

George Anson begins his circumnavigation of the world (1740–1744)

Frederick the Great becomes king of Prussia (1740–1786)

Richardson's *Pamela* (1740–1741)

James Boswell born

1742 Fielding's *Joseph Andrews*

Edward Young's *Night Thoughts* (1742–1745)

Pope's *The New Dunciad* (Book 4)

1744 Johnson's *Life of Mr. Richard Savage*

Death of Alexander Pope

1745 Second Jacobite rebellion, led by Charles Edward, the Young Pretender

Death of Jonathan Swift

1746 The Young Pretender defeated at Culloden

Collins' *Odes on Several Descriptive and Allegorical Subjects*

1747 Richardson's *Clarissa Harlowe* (1747–1748)

Franklin's experiments with electricity announced

Voltaire's *Essai sur les moeurs*

1748 War of the Austrian Succession ended by the Peace of Aix-la-Chapelle

Smollett's *Adventures of Roderick Random*

David Hume's *Enquiry Concerning Human Understanding*

Montesquieu's *L'Esprit des lois*

1749 Fielding's *Tom Jones*

Johnson's *The Vanity of Human Wishes*

Bolingbroke's *Idea of a Patriot King*

1750 The *Rambler* founded (1750–1752)

1751 Gray's *Elegy Written in a Country Churchyard*

Fielding's *Amelia*

Smollett's *Adventures of Peregrine Pickle*

Denis Diderot and Jean le Rond d'Alembert begin to publish the *Encyclopédie* (1751–1765)

Richard Brinsley Sheridan born

1752 Frances Burney and Thomas Chatterton born

1753 Richardson's *History of Sir Charles Grandison* (1753–1754)

Smollett's *The Adventures of Ferdinand Count Fathom*

1754 Hume's *History of England* (1754–1762)

Death of Henry Fielding

George Crabbe born

1755 Lisbon destroyed by earthquake

Fielding's *Journal of a Voyage to Lisbon* published posthumously

Johnson's *Dictionary of the English Language*

1756 The Seven Years' War against France, 1756–1763 (the French and Indian War in America, 1755–1760)

William Pitt the elder becomes prime minister

Johnson's proposal for an edition of Shakespeare

1757 Robert Clive wins the battle of Plassey, in India

Gray's "The Progress of Poesy" and "The Bard"

Burke's *Philosophical Enquiry into the Origin of Our Ideas of the Sublime and Beautiful*

Hume's *Natural History of Religion*

William Blake born

1758 The *Idler* founded (1758–1760)

1759 Capture of Quebec by General James Wolfe

Johnson's *History of Rasselas, Prince of Abyssinia*

Voltaire's *Candide*

The British Museum opens

Sterne's *The Life and Opinions of Tristram Shandy* (1759–1767)

Death of William Collins

Mary Wollstonecraft born

Robert Burns born

1760–1820 **Reign of George III**

1760 James Macpherson's *Fragments of Ancient Poetry Collected in the Highlands of Scotland*

William Beckford born

1761 Jean-Jacques Rousseau's *Julie, ou la nouvelle Héloïse*

Death of Samuel Richardson

1762 Rousseau's *Du Contrat social* and *Émile*

CHRONOLOGY

Catherine the Great becomes czarina of Russia (1762–1796)
1763 The Seven Years' War ended by the Peace of Paris
Smart's *A Song to David*
1764 James Hargreaves invents the spinning jenny
1765 Parliament passes the Stamp Act to tax the American colonies
Johnson's edition of Shakespeare
Walpole's *The Castle of Otranto*
Thomas Percy's *Reliques of Ancient English Poetry*
Blackstone's *Commentaries on the Laws of England* (1765–1769)
1766 The Stamp Act repealed
Swift's *Journal to Stella* first published in a collection of his letters
Goldsmith's *The Vicar of Wakefield*
Smollett's *Travels Through France and Italy*
Lessing's *Laokoon*
Rousseau in England (1766–1767)
1768 Sterne's *A Sentimental Journey Through France and Italy*
The Royal Academy founded by George III
First edition of the *Encyclopaedia Britannica*
Maria Edgeworth born
Death of Laurence Sterne
1769 David Garrick organizes the Shakespeare Jubilee at Stratford-upon-Avon
Sir Joshua Reynolds' *Discourses* (1769–1790)
Richard Arkwright invents the spinning water frame
1770 Boston Massacre
Burke's *Thoughts on the Cause of the Present Discontents*
Oliver Goldsmith's *The Deserted Village*
Death of Thomas Chatterton
William Wordsworth born
1771 Arkwright's first spinning mill founded
Deaths of Thomas Gray and Tobias Smollett
Sydney Smith born
1772 Samuel Taylor Coleridge born

1773 Boston Tea Party
Goldsmith's *She Stoops to Conquer*
Johann Wolfgang von Goethe's *Götz von Berlichingen*
1774 The first Continental Congress meets in Philadelphia
Goethe's *Sorrows of Young Werther*
Death of Oliver Goldsmith
Robert Southey born
1775 Burke's speech on American taxation
American War of Independence begins with the battles of Lexington and Concord
Samuel Johnson's *Journey to the Western Islands of Scotland*
Richard Brinsley Sheridan's *The Rivals* and *The Duenna*
Beaumarchais's *Le Barbier de Séville*
James Watt and Matthew Boulton begin building steam engines in England
Births of Jane Austen, Charles Lamb, Walter Savage Landor, and Matthew Lewis
1776 American Declaration of Independence
Edward Gibbon's *Decline and Fall of the Roman Empire* (1776–1788)
Adam Smith's *Inquiry into the Nature & Causes of the Wealth of Nations*
Thomas Paine's *Common Sense*
Death of David Hume
1777 Maurice Morgann's *Essay on the Dramatic Character of Sir John Falstaff*
Sheridan's *The School for Scandal* first performed (published 1780)
General Burgoyne surrenders at Saratoga
1778 The American colonies allied with France
Britain and France at war
Captain James Cook discovers Hawaii
Death of William Pitt, first earl of Chatham
Deaths of Jean Jacques Rousseau and Voltaire
William Hazlitt born
1779 Johnson's *Prefaces to the Works of the English Poets* (1779–1781); reissued

in 1781 as *The Lives of the Most Eminent English Poets*

Sheridan's *The Critic*

Samuel Crompton invents the spinning mule

Death of David Garrick

1780   The Gordon Riots in London

1781   Charles Cornwallis surrenders at Yorktown

Immanuel Kant's *Critique of Pure Reason*

Friedrich von Schiller's *Die Räuber*

1782   William Cowper's "The Journey of John Gilpin" published in the *Public Advertiser*

Choderlos de Laclos's *Les Liaisons dangereuses*

Rousseau's *Confessions* published posthumously

1783   American War of Independence ended by the Definitive Treaty of Peace, signed at Paris

William Blake's *Poetical Sketches*

George Crabbe's *The Village*

William Pitt the younger becomes prime minister

Henri Beyle (Stendhal) born

1784   Beaumarchais's *Le Mariage de Figaro* first performed (published 1785)

Death of Samuel Johnson

1785   Warren Hastings returns to England from India

James Boswell's *The Journey of a Tour of the Hebrides, with Samuel Johnson, LL.D.*

Cowper's *The Task*

Edmund Cartwright invents the power loom

Thomas De Quincey born

Thomas Love Peacock born

1786   William Beckford's *Vathek* published in English (originally written in French in 1782)

Robert Burns's *Poems Chiefly in the Scottish Dialect*

Wolfgang Amadeus Mozart's *The Marriage of Figaro*

Death of Frederick the Great

1787   The Committee for the Abolition of the Slave Trade founded in England

The Constitutional Convention meets at Philadelphia; the Constitution is signed

1788   The trial of Hastings begins on charges of corruption of the government in India

The Estates-General of France summoned

U.S. Constitution is ratified

George Washington elected president of the United States

Giovanni Casanova's *Histoire de ma fuite* (first manuscript of his memoirs)

The *Daily Universal Register* becomes the *Times* (London)

George Gordon, Lord Byron born

1789   The Estates-General meets at Versailles

The National Assembly (Assemblée Nationale) convened

The fall of the Bastille marks the beginning of the French Revolution

The National Assembly draws up the Declaration of Rights of Man and of the Citizen

First U.S. Congress meets in New York

Blake's *Songs of Innocence*

Jeremy Bentham's *Introduction to the Principles of Morals and Legislation* introduces the theory of utilitarianism

Gilbert White's *Natural History of Selborne*

1790   Congress sets permanent capital city site on the Potomac River

First U.S. Census

Burke's *Reflections on the Revolution in France*

Blake's *The Marriage of Heaven and Hell*

Edmund Malone's edition of Shakespeare

Wollstonecraft's *A Vindication of the Rights of Man*

Death of Benjamin Franklin

1791   French royal family's flight from Paris and capture at Varennes; imprisonment in the Tuileries

Bill of Rights is ratified
Paine's *The Rights of Man* (1791–1792)
Boswell's *The Life of Johnson*
Burns's *Tam o' Shanter*
The *Observer* founded

1792 The Prussians invade France and are repulsed at Valmy September massacres
The National Convention declares royalty abolished in France
Washington reelected president of the United States
New York Stock Exchange opens
Mary Wollstonecraft's *Vindication of the Rights of Woman*
William Bligh's voyage to the South Sea in H.M.S. *Bounty*
Percy Bysshe Shelley born

1793 Trial and execution of Louis XVI and Marie-Antoinette
France declares war against England
The Committee of Public Safety (Comité de Salut Public) established
Eli Whitney devises the cotton gin
William Godwin's *An Enquiry Concerning Political Justice*
Blake's *Visions of the Daughters of Albion and America*
Wordsworth's *An Evening Walk* and *Descriptive Sketches*

1794 Execution of Georges Danton and Maximilien de Robespierre
Paine's *The Age of Reason* (1794–1796)
Blake's *Songs of Experience*
Ann Radcliffe's *The Mysteries of Udolpho*
Death of Edward Gibbon

1795 The government of the Directory established (1795–1799)
Hastings acquitted
Landor's *Poems*
Death of James Boswell
John Keats born
Thomas Carlyle born

1796 Napoleon Bonaparte takes command in Italy
Matthew Lewis' *The Monk*
John Adams elected president of the United States
Death of Robert Burns

1797 The peace of Campo Formio: extinction of the Venetian Republic XYZ Affair
Mutinies in the Royal Navy at Spithead and the Nore
Blake's *Vala, Or the Four Zoas* (first version)
Mary Shelley born
Deaths of Edmund Burke, Mary Wollstonecraft, and Horace Walpole

1798 Napoleon invades Egypt
Horatio Nelson wins the battle of the Nile
Wordsworth's and Coleridge's *Lyrical Ballads*
Landor's *Gebir*
Thomas Malthus' *Essay on the Principle of Population*

1799 Napoleon becomes first consul
Pitt introduces first income tax in Great Britain
Sheridan's *Pizarro*
Honoré de Balzac born
Thomas Hood born
Alexander Pushkin born

1800 Thomas Jefferson elected president of the United States
Alessandro Volta produces electricity from a cell
Library of Congress established
Thomas Babington Macaulay born

1801 First census taken in England
John Henry Newman born

1802 The Treaty of Amiens marks the end of the French Revolutionary War
The *Edinburgh Review* founded

1803 England's war with France renewed
The Louisiana Purchase
Robert Fulton propels a boat by steam power on the Seine

1804 Napoleon crowned emperor of the French
Jefferson reelected president of the United States
Blake's *Milton* (1804–1808) and *Jerusalem*
The Code Napoleon promulgated in France
Beethoven's *Eroica* Symphony
Schiller's *Wilhelm Tell*

CHRONOLOGY

Benjamin Disraeli born

1805 Napoleon plans the invasion of England

Battle of Trafalgar

Battle of Austerlitz

Beethoven's *Fidelio* first produced

Scott's *Lay of the Last Minstrel*

1806 Scott's *Marmion*

Death of William Pitt

Death of Charles James Fox

Elizabeth Barrett born

1807 France invades Portugal

Aaron Burr tried for treason and acquitted

Byron's *Hours of Idleness*

Charles and Mary Lamb's *Tales from Shakespeare*

Thomas Moore's *Irish Melodies*

Wordsworth's *Ode on the Intimations of Immortality*

1808 National uprising in Spain against the French invasion

The Peninsular War begins

James Madison elected president of the United States

Covent Garden theater burned down

Goethe's *Faust* (Part 1)

Beethoven's Fifth Symphony completed

Lamb's *Specimens of English Dramatic Poets*

1809 Drury Lane theater burned down and rebuilt

The *Quarterly Review* founded

Byron's *English Bards and Scotch Reviewers*

Byron sails for the Mediterranean

Goya's *Los Desastres de la guerra* (1809–1814)

Alfred Tennyson born

Charles Darwin born

1810 Crabbe's *The Borough*

Scott's *The Lady of the Lake*

Elizabeth Gaskell born

1811–1820 Regency of George IV

1811 Luddite Riots begin

Coleridge's *Lectures on Shakespeare* (1811–1814)

Jane Austen's *Sense and Sensibility*

Shelley's *The Necessity of Atheism*

John Constable's *Dedham Vale*

William Makepeace Thackeray born

1812 Napoleon invades Russia; captures and retreats from Moscow

United States declares war against England

Henry Bell's steamship *Comet* is launched on the Clyde river

Madison reelected president of the United States

Byron's *Childe Harold* (Cantos 1–2)

The Brothers Grimm's *Fairy Tales* (1812–1815)

Hegel's *Science of Logic*

Robert Browning born

Charles Dickens born

1813 Wellington wins the battle of Vitoria and enters France

Jane Austen's *Pride and Prejudice*

Byron's *The Giaour* and *The Bride of Abydos*

Shelley's *Queen Mab*

Southey's *Life of Nelson*

1814 Napoleon abdicates and is exiled to Elba; Bourbon restoration with Louis XVIII

Treaty of Ghent ends the war between Britain and the United States

Jane Austen's *Mansfield Park*

Byron's *The Corsair* and *Lara*

Scott's *Waverley*

Wordsworth's *The Excursion*

1815 Napoleon returns to France (the Hundred Days); is defeated at Waterloo and exiled to St. Helena

U.S.S. *Fulton*, the first steam warship, built

Scott's *Guy Mannering*

Schlegel's *Lectures on Dramatic Art and Literature* translated

Wordsworth's *The White Doe of Rylstone*

Anthony Trollope born

1816 Byron leaves England permanently

The Elgin Marbles exhibited in the British Museum

James Monroe elected president of the United States

Jane Austen's *Emma*

Byron's *Childe Harold* (Canto 3)

Coleridge's *Christabel, Kubla Khan: A Vision, The Pains of Sleep*

CHRONOLOGY

Benjamin Constant's *Adolphe*
Goethe's *Italienische Reise*
Peacock's *Headlong Hall*
Scott's *The Antiquary*
Shelley's *Alastor*
Rossini's *Il Barbiere di Siviglia*
Death of Richard Brinsley Sheridan
Charlotte Brontë born

1817 *Blackwood's Edinburgh* magazine founded
Jane Austen's *Northanger Abbey* and *Persuasion*
Byron's *Manfred*
Coleridge's *Biographia Literaria*
Hazlitt's *The Characters of Shakespeare's Plays* and *The Round Table*
Keats's *Poems*
Peacock's *Melincourt*
David Ricardo's *Principles of Political Economy and Taxation*
Death of Jane Austen
Death of Mme de Staël
Branwell Brontë born
Henry David Thoreau born

1818 Byron's *Childe Harold* (Canto 4), and *Beppo*
Hazlitt's *Lectures on the English Poets*
Keats's *Endymion*
Peacock's *Nightmare Abbey*
Scott's *Rob Roy* and *The Heart of Mid-Lothian*
Mary Shelley's *Frankenstein*
Percy Shelley's *The Revolt of Islam*
Emily Brontë born
Karl Marx born
Ivan Sergeyevich Turgenev born

1819 The *Savannah* becomes the first steamship to cross the Atlantic (in 26 days)
Peterloo massacre in Manchester
Byron's *Don Juan* (1819–1824) and *Mazeppa*
Crabbe's *Tales of the Hall*
Géricault's *Raft of the Medusa*
Hazlitt's *Lectures on the English Comic Writers*
Arthur Schopenhauer's *Die Welt als Wille und Vorstellung (The World as Will and Idea)*
Scott's *The Bride of Lammermoor* and *A Legend of Montrose*

Shelley's *The Cenci*, "The Masque of Anarchy," and "Ode to the West Wind"
Wordsworth's *Peter Bell*
Queen Victoria born
George Eliot born

1820–1830 **Reign of George IV**
1820 Trial of Queen Caroline
Cato Street Conspiracy suppressed; Arthur Thistlewood hanged
Monroe reelected president of the United States
Missouri Compromise
The *London* magazine founded
Keats's *Lamia, Isabella, The Eve of St. Agnes, and Other Poems*
Hazlitt's *Lectures Chiefly on the Dramatic Literature of the Age of Elizabeth*
Charles Maturin's *Melmoth the Wanderer*
Scott's *Ivanhoe* and *The Monastery*
Shelley's *Prometheus Unbound*
Anne Brontë born

1821 Greek War of Independence begins
Liberia founded as a colony for freed slaves
Byron's *Cain, Marino Faliero, The Two Foscari*, and *Sardanapalus*
Hazlitt's *Table Talk* (1821–1822)
Scott's *Kenilworth*
Shelley's *Adonais* and *Epipsychidion*
Death of John Keats
Death of Napoleon
Charles Baudelaire born
Feodor Dostoyevsky born
Gustave Flaubert born

1822 The Massacres of Chios (Greeks rebel against Turkish rule)
Byron's *The Vision of Judgment*
De Quincey's *Confessions of an English Opium-Eater*
Peacock's *Maid Marian*
Scott's *Peveril of the Peak*
Shelley's *Hellas*
Death of Percy Bysshe Shelley
Matthew Arnold born

1823 Monroe Doctrine proclaimed
Byron's *The Age of Bronze* and *The Island*
Lamb's *Essays of Elia*

Scott's *Quentin Durward*

1824 The National Gallery opened in London

John Quincy Adams elected president of the United States

The *Westminster Review* founded

Beethoven's Ninth Symphony first performed

William (Wilkie) Collins born

James Hogg's *The Private Memoirs and Confessions of a Justified Sinner*

Landor's *Imaginary Conversations* (1824–1829)

Scott's *Redgauntlet*

Death of George Gordon, Lord Byron

1825 Inauguration of steam-powered passenger and freight service on the Stockton and Darlington railway Bolivia and Brazil become independent Alessandro Manzoni's *I Promessi Sposi* (1825–1826)

1826 André-Marie Ampère's *Mémoire sur la théorie mathématique des phénomènes électrodynamiques*

James Fenimore Cooper's *The Last of the Mohicans*

Disraeli's *Vivian Grey* (1826–1827)

Scott's *Woodstock*

1827 The battle of Navarino ensures the independence of Greece

Josef Ressel obtains patent for the screw propeller for steamships

Heinrich Heine's *Buch der Lieder*

Death of William Blake

1828 Andrew Jackson elected president of the United States

Henrik Ibsen born

George Meredith born

Dante Gabriel Rossetti born

Leo Tolstoy born

1829 The Catholic Emancipation Act

Robert Peel establishes the metropolitan police force

Greek independence recognized by Turkey

Balzac begins *La Comédie humaine* (1829–1848)

Peacock's *The Misfortunes of Elphin*

J. M. W. Turner's *Ulysses Deriding Polyphemus*

1830–1837 Reign of William IV

1830 Charles X of France abdicates and is succeeded by Louis-Philippe

The Liverpool-Manchester railway opened

Tennyson's *Poems, Chiefly Lyrical*

Death of William Hazlitt

Christina Rossetti born

1831 Michael Faraday discovers electromagnetic induction

Charles Darwin's voyage on H.M.S. *Beagle* begins (1831–1836)

The Barbizon school of artists' first exhibition

Nat Turner slave revolt crushed in Virginia

Peacock's *Crotchet Castle*

Stendhal's *Le Rouge et le noir*

Edward Trelawny's *The Adventures of a Younger Son*

1832 The first Reform Bill

Samuel Morse invents the telegraph

Jackson reelected president of the United States

Disraeli's *Contarini Fleming*

Goethe's *Faust* (Part 2)

Tennyson's *Poems, Chiefly Lyrical*, including "The Lotus-Eaters" and "The Lady of Shalott"

Death of Johann Wolfgang von Goethe

Death of Sir Walter Scott

Lewis Carroll born

1833 Robert Browning's *Pauline*

John Keble launches the Oxford Movement

American Anti-Slavery Society founded

Lamb's *Last Essays of Elia*

Carlyle's *Sartor Resartus* (1833–1834)

Pushkin's *Eugene Onegin*

Mendelssohn's *Italian Symphony* first performed

1834 Abolition of slavery in the British Empire

Louis Braille's alphabet for the blind

Balzac's *Le Père Goriot*

Nikolai Gogol's *Dead Souls* (Part 1, 1834–1842)

Death of Samuel Taylor Coleridge

Death of Charles Lamb

William Morris born

CHRONOLOGY

1835 Hans Christian Andersen's *Fairy Tales* (1st ser.)
Robert Browning's *Paracelsus*
Samuel Butler born
Alexis de Tocqueville's *De la Democratie en Amerique* (1835–1840)

1836 Martin Van Buren elected president of the United States
Dickens' *Sketches by Boz* (1836–1837)
Landor's *Pericles and Aspasia*

1837–1901 Reign of Queen Victoria

1837 Carlyle's *The French Revolution*
Dickens' *Oliver Twist* (1837–1838) and *Pickwick Papers*
Disraeli's *Venetia* and *Henrietta Temple*

1838 Chartist movement in England
National Gallery in London opened
Elizabeth Barrett Browning's *The Seraphim and Other Poems*
Dickens' *Nicholas Nickleby* (1838–1839)

1839 Louis Daguerre perfects process for producing an image on a silver-coated copper plate Faraday's *Experimental Researches in Electricity* (1839–1855)
First Chartist riots
Opium War between Great Britain and China
Carlyle's *Chartism*

1840 Canadian Act of Union
Queen Victoria marries Prince Albert
Charles Barry begins construction of the Houses of Parliament (1840–1852)
William Henry Harrison elected president of the United States
Robert Browning's *Sordello*
Thomas Hardy born

1841 New Zealand proclaimed a British colony
James Clark Ross discovers the Antarctic continent
Punch founded
John Tyler succeeds to the presidency after the death of Harrison
Carlyle's *Heroes and Hero-Worship*
Dickens' *The Old Curiosity Shop*

1842 Chartist riots
Income tax revived in Great Britain
The Mines Act, forbidding work underground by women or by children under the age of ten
Charles Edward Mudie's Lending Library founded in London
Dickens visits America
Robert Browning's *Dramatic Lyrics*
Macaulay's *Lays of Ancient Rome*
Tennyson's *Poems*, including "Morte d'Arthur," "St. Simeon Stylites," and "Ulysses"
Wordsworth's *Poems*

1843 Marc Isambard Brunel's Thames tunnel opened
The Economist founded
Carlyle's *Past and Present*
Dickens' *A Christmas Carol*
John Stuart Mill's *Logic*
Macaulay's *Critical and Historical Essays*
John Ruskin's *Modern Painters* (1843–1860)

1844 Rochdale Society of Equitable Pioneers, one of the first consumers' cooperatives, founded by twenty-eight Lancashire weavers
James K. Polk elected president of the United States
Elizabeth Barrett Browning's *Poems*, including "The Cry of the Children"
Dickens' *Martin Chuzzlewit*
Disraeli's *Coningsby*
Turner's *Rain, Steam and Speed*
Gerard Manley Hopkins born

1845 The great potato famine in Ireland begins (1845–1849)
Disraeli's *Sybil*

1846 Repeal of the Corn Laws
The *Daily News* founded (edited by Dickens the first three weeks)
Standard-gauge railway introduced in Britain
The Brontës' pseudonymous *Poems by Currer, Ellis and Acton Bell*
Lear's *Book of Nonsense*

1847 The Ten Hours Factory Act
James Simpson uses chloroform as an anesthetic
Anne Brontë's *Agnes Grey*
Charlotte Brontë's *Jane Eyre*

CHRONOLOGY

Emily Brontë's *Wuthering Heights*
Bram Stoker born
Tennyson's *The Princess*

1848 The year of revolutions in France, Germany, Italy, Hungary, Poland
Marx and Engels issue *The Communist Manifesto*
The Chartist Petition
The Pre-Raphaelite Brotherhood founded
Zachary Taylor elected president of the United States
Anne Brontë's *The Tenant of Wildfell Hall*
Dickens' *Dombey and Son*
Elizabeth Gaskell's *Mary Barton*
Macaulay's *History of England* (1848–1861)
Mill's *Principles of Political Economy*
Thackeray's *Vanity Fair*
Death of Emily Brontë

1849 Bedford College for women founded
Arnold's *The Strayed Reveller*
Charlotte Brontë's *Shirley*
Ruskin's *The Seven Lamps of Architecture*
Death of Anne Brontë

1850 The Public Libraries Act
First submarine telegraph cable laid between Dover and Calais
Millard Fillmore succeeds to the presidency after the death of Taylor
Elizabeth Barrett Browning's *Sonnets from the Portuguese*
Carlyle's *Latter-Day Pamphlets*
Dickens' *Household Words* (1850–1859) and *David Copperfield*
Charles Kingsley's *Alton Locke*
The Pre-Raphaelites publish the *Germ*
Tennyson's *In Memoriam*
Thackeray's *The History of Pendennis*
Wordsworth's *The Prelude* is published posthumously

1851 The Great Exhibition opens at the Crystal Palace in Hyde Park
Louis Napoleon seizes power in France
Gold strike in Victoria incites Australian gold rush

Elizabeth Gaskell's *Cranford* (1851–1853)
Meredith's *Poems*
Ruskin's *The Stones of Venice* (1851–1853)

1852 The Second Empire proclaimed with Napoleon III as emperor
David Livingstone begins to explore the Zambezi (1852–1856)
Franklin Pierce elected president of the United States
Arnold's *Empedocles on Etna*
Thackeray's *The History of Henry Esmond, Esq.*

1853 Crimean War (1853–1856)
Arnold's *Poems*, including "The Scholar Gypsy" and "Sohrab and Rustum"
Charlotte Brontë's *Villette*
Elizabeth Gaskell's *Crawford and Ruth*

1854 Frederick D. Maurice's Working Men's College founded in London with more than 130 pupils
Battle of Balaklava
Dickens' *Hard Times*
James George Frazer born
Theodor Mommsen's *History of Rome* (1854–1856)
Tennyson's "The Charge of the Light Brigade"
Florence Nightingale in the Crimea (1854–1856)
Oscar Wilde born

1855 David Livingstone discovers the Victoria Falls
Robert Browning's *Men and Women*
Elizabeth Gaskell's *North and South*
Olive Schreiner born
Tennyson's *Maud*
Thackeray's *The Newcomes*
Trollope's *The Warden*
Death of Charlotte Brontë

1856 The Treaty of Paris ends the Crimean War
Henry Bessemer's steel process invented
James Buchanan elected president of the United States
H. Rider Haggard born

1857 The Indian Mutiny begins; crushed in 1858
The Matrimonial Causes Act
Charlotte Brontë's *The Professor*
Elizabeth Barrett Browning's *Aurora Leigh*
Dickens' *Little Dorritt*
Elizabeth Gaskell's *The Life of Charlotte Brontë*
Thomas Hughes's *Tom Brown's School Days*
Trollope's *Barchester Towers*

1858 Carlyle's *History of Frederick the Great* (1858–1865)
George Eliot's *Scenes of Clerical Life*
Morris' *The Defense of Guinevere*
Trollope's *Dr. Thorne*

1859 Charles Darwin's *The Origin of Species*
Dickens' *A Tale of Two Cities*
Arthur Conan Doyle born
George Eliot's *Adam Bede*
Fitzgerald's *The Rubaiyat of Omar Khayyám*
Meredith's *The Ordeal of Richard Feverel*
Mill's *On Liberty*
Samuel Smiles's *Self-Help*
Tennyson's *Idylls of the King*

1860 Abraham Lincoln elected president of the United States
The *Cornhill* magazine founded with Thackeray as editor
James M. Barrie born
William Wilkie Collins' *The Woman in White*
George Eliot's *The Mill on the Floss*

1861 American Civil War begins
Louis Pasteur presents the germ theory of disease
Arnold's *Lectures on Translating Homer*
Dickens' *Great Expectations*
George Eliot's *Silas Marner*
Meredith's *Evan Harrington*
Francis Turner Palgrave's *The Golden Treasury*
Trollope's *Framley Parsonage*
Peacock's *Gryll Grange*
Death of Prince Albert

1862 George Eliot's *Romola*
Meredith's *Modern Love*
Christina Rossetti's *Goblin Market*

Ruskin's *Unto This Last*
Trollope's *Orley Farm*

1863 Thomas Huxley's *Man's Place in Nature*

1864 The Geneva Red Cross Convention signed by twelve nations
Lincoln reelected president of the United States
Robert Browning's *Dramatis Personae*
John Henry Newman's *Apologia pro vita sua*
Tennyson's *Enoch Arden*
Trollope's *The Small House at Allington*

1865 Assassination of Lincoln; Andrew Johnson succeeds to the presidency
Arnold's *Essays in Criticism* (1st ser.)
Carroll's *Alice's Adventures in Wonderland*
Dickens' *Our Mutual Friend*
Meredith's *Rhoda Fleming*
A. C. Swinburne's *Atalanta in Calydon*

1866 First successful transatlantic telegraph cable laid
George Eliot's *Felix Holt, the Radical*
Elizabeth Gaskell's *Wives and Daughters*
Beatrix Potter born
Swinburne's *Poems and Ballads*

1867 The second Reform Bill
Arnold's *New Poems*
Bagehot's *The English Constitution*
Carlyle's *Shooting Niagara*
Marx's *Das Kapital* (vol. 1)
Trollope's *The Last Chronicle of Barset*

1868 Gladstone becomes prime minister (1868–1874)
Johnson impeached by House of Representatives; acquitted by Senate
Ulysses S. Grant elected president of the United States
Robert Browning's *The Ring and the Book* (1868–1869)
Collins' *The Moonstone*

1869 The Suez Canal opened
Girton College, Cambridge, founded
Arnold's *Culture and Anarchy*
Mill's *The Subjection of Women*
Trollope's *Phineas Finn*

CHRONOLOGY

1870 The Elementary Education Act establishes schools under the aegis of local boards
Dickens' *Edwin Drood*
Disraeli's *Lothair*
Morris' *The Earthly Paradise*
Dante Gabriel Rossetti's *Poems*
Saki born

1871 Trade unions legalized
Newnham College, Cambridge, founded for women students
Carroll's *Through the Looking Glass*
Darwin's *The Descent of Man*
Meredith's *The Adventures of Harry Richmond*
Swinburne's *Songs Before Sunrise*

1872 Max Beerbohm born
Samuel Butler's *Erewhon*
George Eliot's *Middlemarch*
Grant reelected president of the United States
Hardy's *Under the Greenwood Tree*

1873 Arnold's *Literature and Dogma*
Mill's *Autobiography*
Pater's *Studies in the History of the Renaissance*
Trollope's *The Eustace Diamonds*

1874 Disraeli becomes prime minister
Hardy's *Far from the Madding Crowd*
James Thomson's *The City of Dreadful Night*

1875 Britain buys Suez Canal shares
Trollope's *The Way We Live Now*

1876 F. H. Bradley's *Ethical Studies*
George Eliot's *Daniel Deronda*
Henry James's *Roderick Hudson*
Meredith's *Beauchamp's Career*
Morris' *Sigurd the Volsung*
Trollope's *The Prime Minister*

1877 Rutherford B. Hayes elected president of the United States after Electoral Commission awards him disputed votes
Henry James's *The American*

1878 Electric street lighting introduced in London
Hardy's *The Return of the Native*
Swinburne's *Poems and Ballads* (2d ser.)
Edward Thomas born

1879 Somerville College and Lady Margaret Hall opened at Oxford for women
The London telephone exchange built
Gladstone's Midlothian campaign (1879–1880)
Browning's *Dramatic Idyls*
Meredith's *The Egoist*

1880 Gladstone's second term as prime minister (1880–1885)
James A. Garfield elected president of the United States
Browning's *Dramatic Idyls Second Series*
Disraeli's *Endymion*
Radclyffe Hall born
Hardy's *The Trumpet-Major*
Lytton Strachey born

1881 Garfield assassinated; Chester A. Arthur succeeds to the presidency
Henry James's *The Portrait of a Lady* and *Washington Square*
D. G. Rossetti's *Ballads and Sonnets*
P. G. Wodehouse born

1882 Triple Alliance formed between German empire, Austrian empire, and Italy
Leslie Stephen begins to edit the *Dictionary of National Biography*
Married Women's Property Act passed in Britain
Britain occupies Egypt and the Sudan

1883 Uprising of the Mahdi: Britain evacuates the Sudan
Royal College of Music opens
T. H. Green's *Ethics*
T. E. Hulme born
Stevenson's *Treasure Island*

1884 The Mahdi captures Omdurman: General Gordon appointed to command the garrison of Khartoum
Grover Cleveland elected president of the United States
The *Oxford English Dictionary* begins publishing
The Fabian Society founded
Hiram Maxim's recoil-operated machine gun invented

1885 The Mahdi captures Khartoum: General Gordon killed
Haggard's *King Solomon's Mines*

CHRONOLOGY

Marx's *Das Kapital* (vol. 2)
Meredith's *Diana of the Crossways*
Pater's *Marius the Epicurean*
1886 The Canadian Pacific Railway completed
Gold discovered in the Transvaal
Ronald Firbank born
Henry James's *The Bostonians* and *The Princess Casamassima*
Stevenson's *The Strange Case of Dr. Jekyll and Mr. Hyde*
1887 Queen Victoria's Golden Jubilee
Rupert Brooke born
Haggard's *Allan Quatermain* and *She*
Hardy's *The Woodlanders*
Edwin Muir born
1888 Benjamin Harrison elected president of the United States
Henry James's *The Aspern Papers*
Kipling's *Plain Tales from the Hills*
T. E. Lawrence born
1889 Yeats's *The Wanderings of Oisin*
Death of Robert Browning
1890 Morris founds the Kelmscott Press
Agatha Christie born
Frazer's *The Golden Bough* (1st ed.)
Henry James's *The Tragic Muse*
Morris' *News From Nowhere*
Jean Rhys born
1891 Gissing's *New Grub Street*
Hardy's *Tess of the d'Urbervilles*
Wilde's *The Picture of Dorian Gray*
1892 Grover Cleveland elected president of the United States
Conan Doyle's *The Adventures of Sherlock Holmes*
Shaw's *Widower's Houses*
J. R. R. Tolkien born
Rebecca West born
Wilde's *Lady Windermere's Fan*
1893 Wilde's *A Woman of No Importance* and *Salomé*
Sylvia Townsend Warner born
1894 Kipling's *The Jungle Book*
Marx's *Das Kapital* (vol. 3)
Audrey Beardsley's *The Yellow Book* begins to appear quarterly
Shaw's *Arms and the Man*
1895 Trial and imprisonment of Oscar Wilde

William Ramsay announces discovery of helium
The National Trust founded
L. P. Hartley born
David Jones born
Hardy's *Jude the Obscure*
Wells's *The Time Machine*
Wilde's *The Importance of Being Earnest*
1896 William McKinley elected president of the United States
Failure of the Jameson Raid on the Transvaal
Housman's *A Shropshire Lad*
1897 Queen Victoria's Diamond Jubilee
Conrad's *The Nigger of the Narcissus*
Havelock Ellis' *Studies in the Psychology of Sex* begins publication
Henry James's *The Spoils of Poynton* and *What Maisie Knew*
Kipling's *Captains Courageous*
Shaw's *Candida*
Stoker's *Dracula*
Wells's *The Invisible Man*
1898 Kitchener defeats the Mahdist forces at Omdurman: the Sudan reoccupied
Hardy's *Wessex Poems*
Henry James's *The Turn of the Screw*
C. S. Lewis born
Shaw's *Caesar and Cleopatra* and *You Never Can Tell*
Alec Waugh born
Wells's *The War of the Worlds*
Wilde's *The Ballad of Reading Gaol*
1899 The Boer War begins
Elizabeth Bowen born
Noël Coward born
Elgar's *Enigma Variations*
Kipling's *Stalky and Co.*
1900 McKinley reelected president of the United States
British Labour party founded
Boxer Rebellion in China
Reginald A. Fessenden transmits speech by wireless
First Zeppelin trial flight
Max Planck presents his first paper on the quantum theory
Conrad's *Lord Jim*
Elgar's *The Dream of Gerontius*

CHRONOLOGY

Sigmund Freud's *The Interpretation of Dreams*
Basil Bunting born
William Butler Yeats's *The Shadowy Waters*

901–1910   **Reign of King Edward VII**

1901   William McKinley assassinated; Theodore Roosevelt succeeds to the presidency
First transatlantic wireless telegraph signal transmitted
Chekhov's *Three Sisters*
Freud's *Psychopathology of Everyday Life*
Rudyard Kipling's *Kim*
Thomas Mann's *Buddenbrooks*
Anna Kavan born
Shaw's *Captain Brassbound's Conversion*
August Strindberg's *The Dance of Death*

1902   Barrie's *The Admirable Crichton*
Arnold Bennett's *Anna of the Five Towns*
Cézanne's *Le Lac D'Annecy*
Conrad's *Heart of Darkness*
Henry James's *The Wings of the Dove*
William James's *The Varieties of Religious Experience*
Kipling's *Just So Stories*
Maugham's *Mrs. Cradock*
Stevie Smith born
Times Literary Supplement begins publishing

1903   At its London congress the Russian Social Democratic Party divides into Mensheviks, led by Plekhanov, and Bolsheviks, led by Lenin
The treaty of Panama places the Canal Zone in U.S. hands for a nominal rent
Motor cars regulated in Britain to a 20-mile-per-hour limit
The Wright brothers make a successful flight in the United States
Burlington magazine founded
Samuel Butler's *The Way of All Flesh* published posthumously
Cyril Connolly born
George Gissing's *The Private Papers of Henry Ryecroft*

Thomas Hardy's *The Dynasts*
Henry James's *The Ambassadors*
Alan Paton born
Shaw's *Man and Superman*
Synge's *Riders to the Sea* produced in Dublin
Yeats's *In the Seven Woods* and *On Baile's Strand*

1904   Roosevelt elected president of the United States
Russo-Japanese war (1904–1905)
Construction of the Panama Canal begins
The ultraviolet lamp invented
The engineering firm of Rolls Royce founded
Barrie's *Peter Pan* first performed
Cecil Day Lewis born
Chekhov's *The Cherry Orchard*
Conrad's *Nostromo*
Henry James's *The Golden Bowl*
Kipling's *Traffics and Discoveries*
Georges Rouault's *Head of a Tragic Clown*
G. M. Trevelyan's *England Under the Stuarts*
Puccini's *Madame Butterfly*
First Shaw-Granville Barker season at the Royal Court Theatre
The Abbey Theatre founded in Dublin

1905   Russian sailors on the battleship Potemkin mutiny
After riots and a general strike the czar concedes demands by the Duma for legislative powers, a wider franchise, and civil liberties
Albert Einstein publishes his first theory of relativity
The Austin Motor Company founded
Bennett's *Tales of the Five Towns*
Claude Debussy's *La Mer*
E. M. Forster's *Where Angels Fear to Tread*
Henry Green born
Richard Strauss's *Salome*
H. G. Wells's *Kipps*
Oscar Wilde's *De Profundis*

1906   Liberals win a landslide victory in the British general election

The Trades Disputes Act legitimizes peaceful picketing in Britain

Captain Dreyfus rehabilitated in France

J. J. Thomson begins research on gamma rays

The U.S. Pure Food and Drug Act passed

Churchill's *Lord Randolph Churchill*

William Empson born

Galsworthy's *The Man of Property*

Kipling's *Puck of Pook's Hill*

Shaw's *The Doctor's Dilemma*

Yeats's *Poems* 1899–1905

1907 Exhibition of cubist paintings in Paris

Henry Adams' *The Education of Henry Adams*

Henri Bergson's *Creative Evolution*

Conrad's *The Secret Agent*

A. D. Hope born

Forster's *The Longest Journey*

Christopher Fry born

André Gide's *La Porte étroite*

Shaw's *John Bull's Other Island* and *Major Barbara*

Synge's *The Playboy of the Western World*

Trevelyan's *Garibaldi's Defence of the Roman Republic*

1908 Herbert Asquith becomes prime minister

David Lloyd George becomes chancellor of the exchequer

William Howard Taft elected president of the United States

The Young Turks seize power in Istanbul

Henry Ford's Model T car produced

Bennett's *The Old Wives' Tale*

Pierre Bonnard's *Nude Against the Light*

Georges Braque's *House at L'Estaque*

Chesterton's *The Man Who Was Thursday*

Jacob Epstein's *Figures* erected in London

Forster's *A Room with a View*

Anatole France's *L'Ile des Pingouins*

Henri Matisse's *Bonheur de Vivre*

Elgar's First Symphony

Ford Madox Ford founds the *English Review*

1909 The Young Turks depose Sultan Abdul Hamid

The Anglo-Persian Oil Company formed

Louis Bleriot crosses the English Channel from France by monoplane

Admiral Robert Peary reaches the North Pole

Freud lectures at Clark University (Worcester, Mass.) on psychoanalysis

Serge Diaghilev's Ballets Russes opens in Paris

Galsworthy's *Strife*

Hardy's *Time's Laughingstocks*

Malcolm Lowry born

Claude Monet's *Water Lilies*

Stephen Spender born

Trevelyan's *Garibaldi and the Thousand*

Wells's *Tono-Bungay* first published (book form, 1909)

1910–1936 **Reign of King George V**

1910 The Liberals win the British general election

Marie Curie's *Treatise on Radiography*

Arthur Evans excavates Knossos

Edouard Manet and the first post-impressionist exhibition in London

Filippo Marinetti publishes "Manifesto of the Futurist Painters"

Norman Angell's *The Great Illusion*

Bennett's *Clayhanger*

Forster's *Howards End*

Galsworthy's *Justice* and *The Silver Box*

Kipling's *Rewards and Fairies*

Rimsky-Korsakov's *Le Coq d'or*

Stravinsky's *The Firebird*

Vaughan Williams' *A Sea Symphony*

Wells's *The History of Mr. Polly*

Wells's *The New Machiavelli* first published (in book form, 1911)

1911 Lloyd George introduces National Health Insurance Bill

Suffragette riots in Whitehall

Roald Amundsen reaches the South Pole

CHRONOLOGY

Terrence Rattigan born
Bennett's *The Card*
Chagall's *Self Portrait with Seven Fingers*
Conrad's *Under Western Eyes*
D. H. Lawrence's *The White Peacock*
Katherine Mansfield's *In a German Pension*
Edward Marsh edits *Georgian Poetry*
Moore's *Hail and Farewell* (1911–1914)
Flann O'Brien born
Strauss's *Der Rosenkavalier*
Stravinsky's *Petrouchka*
Trevelyan's *Garibaldi and the Making of Italy*
Wells's *The New Machiavelli*
Mahler's *Das Lied von der Erde*

1912   Woodrow Wilson elected president of the United States
SS *Titanic* sinks on its maiden voyage
Five million Americans go to the movies daily; London has four hundred movie theaters
Second post-impressionist exhibition in London
Bennett's and Edward Knoblock's *Milestones*
Roy Fuller born
Constantin Brancusi's *Maiastra*
Wassily Kandinsky's *Black Lines*
D. H. Lawrence's *The Trespasser*

1913   Second Balkan War begins
Henry Ford pioneers factory assembly technique through conveyor belts
Epstein's *Tomb of Oscar Wilde*
New York Armory Show introduces modern art to the world
Alain Fournier's *Le Grand Meaulnes*
Freud's *Totem and Tabu*
D. H. Lawrence's *Sons and Lovers*
Mann's *Death in Venice*
Proust's *Du Côté de chez Swann* (first volume of *Á la recherche du temps perdu*, 1913–1922)
Barbara Pym born
Ravel's *Daphnis and Chloé*

1914   The Panama Canal opens (formal dedication on 12 July 1920)
Irish Home Rule Bill passed in the House of Commons

Archduke Franz Ferdinand assassinated at Sarajevo
World War I begins
Battles of the Marne, Masurian Lakes, and Falkland Islands
Joyce's *Dubliners*
Shaw's *Pygmalion* and *Androcles and the Lion*
Yeats's *Responsibilities*
Wyndham Lewis publishes *Blast* magazine and *The Vorticist Manifesto*

1915   The Dardanelles campaign begins
Britain and Germany begin naval and submarine blockades
The *Lusitania* is sunk
Hugo Junkers manufactures the first fighter aircraft
Poison gas used for the first time
First Zeppelin raid in London
Brooke's *1914: Five Sonnets*
Norman Douglas' *Old Calabria*
D. W. Griffith's *The Birth of a Nation*
Gustav Holst's *The Planets*
D. H. Lawrence's *The Rainbow*
Wyndham Lewis's *The Crowd*
Maugham's *Of Human Bondage*
Pablo Picasso's *Harlequin*
Sibelius' Fifth Symphony

1916   Evacuation of Gallipoli and the Dardanelles
Battles of the Somme, Jutland, and Verdun
Britain introduces conscription
The Easter Rebellion in Dublin
Asquith resigns and David Lloyd George becomes prime minister
The Sykes-Picot agreement on the partition of Turkey
First military tanks used
Wilson reelected president president of the United States
Gavin Ewart born
Griffith's *Intolerance*
Joyce's *Portrait of the Artist as a Young Man*
Jung's *Psychology of the Unconscious*
Moore's *The Brook Kerith*
Edith Sitwell edits *Wheels* (1916–1921)
Wells's *Mr. Britling Sees It Through*

1917   United States enters World War I
Czar Nicholas II abdicates

CHRONOLOGY

The Balfour Declaration on a Jewish national home in Palestine

The Bolshevik Revolution

Georges Clemenceau elected prime minister of France

Lenin appointed chief commissar; Trotsky appointed minister of foreign affairs

Conrad's *The Shadow-Line*

Douglas' *South Wind*

Eliot's *Prufrock and Other Observations*

Modigliani's *Nude with Necklace*

Sassoon's *The Old Huntsman*

Prokofiev's *Classical Symphony*

Yeats's *The Wild Swans at Coole*

1918 Wilson puts forward Fourteen Points for World Peace

Central Powers and Russia sign the Treaty of Brest-Litovsk

Execution of Czar Nicholas II and his family

Kaiser Wilhelm II abdicates

The Armistice signed

Women granted the vote at age thirty in Britain

Rupert Brooke's *Collected Poems*

Gerard Manley Hopkins' *Poems*

Joyce's *Exiles*

W. S. Graham born

Sassoon's *Counter-Attack*

Oswald Spengler's *The Decline of the West*

Strachey's *Eminent Victorians*

Béla Bartók's *Bluebeard's Castle*

Charlie Chaplin's *Shoulder Arms*

1919 The Versailles Peace Treaty signed

J. W. Alcock and A. W. Brown make first transatlantic flight

Ross Smith flies from London to Australia

National Socialist party founded in Germany

Benito Mussolini founds the Fascist party in Italy

Sinn Fein Congress adopts declaration of independence in Dublin

Eamon De Valera elected president of Sinn Fein party

Communist Third International founded

Lady Astor elected first woman Member of Parliament

Prohibition in the United States

John Maynard Keynes's *The Economic Consequences of the Peace*

Eliot's *Poems*

Maugham's *The Moon and Sixpence*

Shaw's *Heartbreak House*

The Bauhaus school of design, building, and crafts founded by Walter Gropius

Amedeo Modigliani's *Self-Portrait*

1920 The League of Nations established

Warren G. Harding elected president of the United States

Senate votes against joining the League and rejects the Treaty of Versailles

The Nineteenth Amendment gives women the right to vote

White Russian forces of Denikin and Kolchak defeated by the Bolsheviks

Karel Čapek's *R.U.R.*

Galsworthy's *In Chancery* and *The Skin Game*

Sinclair Lewis' *Main Street*

Katherine Mansfield's *Bliss*

Matisse's *Odalisques* (1920–1925)

Ezra Pound's *Hugh Selwyn Mauberly*

Paul Valéry's *Le Cimetière Marin*

Yeats's *Michael Robartes and the Dancer*

1921 Britain signs peace with Ireland

First medium-wave radio broadcast in the United States

The British Broadcasting Corporation founded

Braque's *Still Life with Guitar*

Chaplin's *The Kid*

Aldous Huxley's *Crome Yellow*

Paul Klee's *The Fish*

D. H. Lawrence's *Women in Love*

John McTaggart's *The Nature of Existence* (vol. 1)

Moore's *Héloïse and Abélard*

Eugene O'Neill's *The Emperor Jones*

Luigi Pirandello's *Six Characters in Search of an Author*

Shaw's *Back to Methuselah*

Strachey's *Queen Victoria*

George Mackay Brown born

CHRONOLOGY

1922 Lloyd George's Coalition government succeeded by Bonar Law's Conservative government

Benito Mussolini marches on Rome and forms a government

William Cosgrave elected president of the Irish Free State

The BBC begins broadcasting in London

Lord Carnarvon and Howard Carter discover Tutankhamen's tomb

The PEN club founded in London

The *Criterion* founded with T. S. Eliot as editor

Kingsley Amis born

Eliot's *The Waste Land*

A. E. Housman's *Last Poems*

Joyce's *Ulysses*

D. H. Lawrence's *Aaron's Rod* and *England, My England*

Sinclair Lewis's *Babbitt*

O'Neill's *Anna Christie*

Pirandello's *Henry IV*

Edith Sitwell's *Façade*

Virginia Woolf's *Jacob's Room*

Yeats's *The Trembling of the Veil*

Donald Davie born

1923 The Union of Soviet Socialist Republics established

French and Belgian troops occupy the Ruhr in consequence of Germany's failure to pay reparations

Mustafa Kemal (Ataturk) proclaims Turkey a republic and is elected president

Warren G. Harding dies; Calvin Coolidge becomes president

Stanley Baldwin succeeds Bonar Law as prime minister

Adolf Hitler's attempted coup in Munich fails

Time magazine begins publishing

E. N. da C. Andrade's *The Structure of the Atom*

Brendan Behan born

Bennett's *Riceyman Steps*

Churchill's *The World Crisis* (1923–1927)

J. E. Flecker's *Hassan* produced

Nadine Gordimer born

Paul Klee's *Magic Theatre*

Lawrence's *Kangaroo*

Rainer Maria Rilke's *Duino Elegies* and *Sonnets to Orpheus*

Sibelius' *Sixth Symphony*

Picasso's *Seated Woman*

William Walton's *Façade*

1924 Ramsay MacDonald forms first Labour government, loses general election, and is succeeded by Stanley Baldwin

Calvin Coolidge elected president of the United States

Noël Coward's *The Vortex*

Forster's *A Passage to India*

Mann's *The Magic Mountain*

Shaw's *St. Joan*

1925 Reza Khan becomes shah of Iran

First surrealist exhibition held in Paris

Alban Berg's *Wozzeck*

Chaplin's *The Gold Rush*

John Dos Passos' *Manhattan Transfer*

Theodore Dreiser's *An American Tragedy*

Sergei Eisenstein's *Battleship Potemkin*

F. Scott Fitzgerald's *The Great Gatsby*

André Gide's *Les Faux Monnayeurs*

Hardy's *Human Shows and Far Phantasies*

Huxley's *Those Barren Leaves*

Kafka's *The Trial*

O'Casey's *Juno and the Paycock*

Virginia Woolf's *Mrs. Dalloway* and *The Common Reader*

Brancusi's *Bird in Space*

Shostakovich's *First Symphony*

Sibelius' *Tapiola*

1926 Ford's *A Man Could Stand Up*

Alastair Reid born

Hemingway's *The Sun also Rises*

Kafka's *The Castle*

D. H. Lawrence's *The Plumed Serpent*

T. E. Lawrence's *Seven Pillars of Wisdom* privately circulated

Maugham's *The Casuarina Tree*

O'Casey's *The Plough and the Stars*

Puccini's *Turandot*

1927 General Chiang Kai-shek becomes prime minister in China

Trotsky expelled by the Communist party as a deviationist; Stalin

CHRONOLOGY

becomes leader of the party and dictator of the Soviet Union

Charles Lindbergh flies from New York to Paris

J. W. Dunne's *An Experiment with Time*

Freud's *Autobiography* translated into English

Albert Giacometti's *Observing Head*

Ernest Hemingway's *Men Without Women*

Fritz Lang's *Metropolis*

Wyndham Lewis' *Time and Western Man*

F. W. Murnau's *Sunrise*

Proust's *Le Temps retrouvé* posthumously published

Stravinsky's *Oedipus Rex*

Virginia Woolf's *To the Lighthouse*

1928   The Kellogg-Briand Pact, outlawing war and providing for peaceful settlement of disputes, signed in Paris by sixty-two nations, including the Soviet Union

Herbert Hoover elected president of the United States

Women's suffrage granted at age twenty-one in Britain

Alexander Fleming discovers penicillin

Bertolt Brecht and Kurt Weill's *The Three-Penny Opera*

Eisenstein's *October*

Huxley's *Point Counter Point*

Christopher Isherwood's *All the Conspirators*

D. H. Lawrence's *Lady Chatterley's Lover*

Wyndham Lewis' *The Childermass*

Matisse's *Seated Odalisque*

Munch's *Girl on a Sofa*

Shaw's *Intelligent Woman's Guide to Socialism*

Virginia Woolf's *Orlando*

Yeats's *The Tower*

1929   The Labour party wins British general election

Trotsky expelled from the Soviet Union

Museum of Modern Art opens in New York

Collapse of U.S. stock exchange begins world economic crisis

Robert Bridges's *The Testament of Beauty*

William Faulkner's *The Sound and the Fury*

Robert Graves's *Goodbye to All That*

Hemingway's *A Farewell to Arms*

Ernst Junger's *The Storm of Steel*

Hugo von Hoffmansthal's *Poems*

Henry Moore's *Reclining Figure*

J. B. Priestley's *The Good Companions*

Erich Maria Remarque's *All Quiet on the Western Front*

Shaw's *The Applecart*

R. C. Sheriff's *Journey's End*

Edith Sitwell's *Gold Coast Customs*

Thomas Wolfe's *Look Homeward, Angel*

Virginia Woolf's *A Room of One's Own*

Yeats's *The Winding Stair*

Second surrealist manifesto; Salvador Dali joins the surrealists

Epstein's *Night and Day*

Mondrian's *Composition with Yellow Blue*

1930   Allied occupation of the Rhineland ends

Mohandas Gandhi opens civil disobedience campaign in India

The *Daily Worker*, journal of the British Communist party, begins publishing

J. W. Reppe makes artificial fabrics from an acetylene base

Barry Unsworth born

Auden's *Poems*

Coward's *Private Lives*

Eliot's *Ash Wednesday*

Wyndham Lewis's *The Apes of God*

Maugham's *Cakes and Ale*

Ezra Pound's *XXX Cantos*

Evelyn Waugh's *Vile Bodies*

1931   The failure of the Credit Anstalt in Austria starts a financial collapse in Central Europe

Britain abandons the gold standard; the pound falls by twenty-five percent

Mutiny in the Royal Navy at Invergordon over pay cuts

Ramsay MacDonald resigns, splits the Cabinet, and is expelled by the Labour party; in the general election the National Government wins by a majority of five hundred seats

The Statute of Westminster defines dominion status

Ninette de Valois founds the Vic-Wells Ballet (eventually the Royal Ballet)

Patrick Kavanagh born

Dali's The *Persistence of Memory*

John le Carré born

O'Neill's *Mourning Becomes Electra*

Anthony Powell's *Afternoon Men*

Antoine de Saint-Exupéry's *Vol de nuit*

Walton's *Belshazzar's Feast*

Virginia Woolf's *The Waves*

1932 Franklin D. Roosevelt elected president of the United States

Paul von Hindenburg elected president of Germany; Franz von Papen elected chancellor

Sir Oswald Mosley founds British Union of Fascists

The BBC takes over development of television from J. L. Baird's company

Basic English of 850 words designed as a prospective international language

The Folger Library opens in Washington, D.C.

The Shakespeare Memorial Theatre opens in Stratford-upon-Avon

Faulkner's *Light in August*

Huxley's *Brave New World*

F. R. Leavis' *New Bearings in English Poetry*

Boris Pasternak's *Second Birth*

Ravel's *Concerto for Left Hand*

Peter Redgrove born

Rouault's *Christ Mocked by Soldiers*

Waugh's *Black Mischief*

Yeats's *Words for Music Perhaps*

1933 Roosevelt inaugurates the New Deal

Hitler becomes chancellor of Germany

The Reichstag set on fire

Hitler suspends civil liberties and freedom of the press; German trade unions suppressed

George Balanchine and Lincoln Kirstein found the School of American Ballet

Michael Frayn born

Lowry's *Ultramarine*

André Malraux's *La Condition humaine*

Orwell's *Down and Out in Paris and London*

Gertrude Stein's *The Autobiography of Alice B. Toklas*

Anne Stevenson born

1934 The League Disarmament Conference ends in failure

The Soviet Union admitted to the League

Hitler becomes Führer

Civil war in Austria; Engelbert Dollfuss assassinated in attempted Nazi coup

Frédéric Joliot and Irene Joliot-Curie discover artificial (induced) radioactivity

Einstein's *My Philosophy*

Fitzgerald's *Tender Is the Night*

Graves's *I, Claudius* and *Claudius the God*

Toynbee's *A Study of History* begins publication (1934–1954)

Waugh's *A Handful of Dust*

1935 Grigori Zinoviev and other Soviet leaders convicted of treason

Stanley Baldwin becomes prime minister in National Government; National Government wins general election in Britain

Italy invades Abyssinia

Germany repudiates disarmament clauses of Treaty of Versailles

Germany reintroduces compulsory military service and outlaws the Jews

Robert Watson-Watt builds first practical radar equipment

Karl Jaspers' *Suffering and Existence*

André Brink born

Ivy Compton-Burnett's *A House and Its Head*

Eliot's *Murder in the Cathedral*

CHRONOLOGY

Barbara Hepworth's *Three Forms*
George Gershwin's *Porgy and Bess*
Greene's *England Made Me*
Isherwood's *Mr. Norris Changes Trains*
Malraux's *Le Temps du mépris*
Yeats's *Dramatis Personae*
Klee's *Child Consecrated to Suffering*
Benedict Nicholson's *White Relief*

1936 Edward VII accedes to the throne in January; abdicates in December

1936–1952 Reign of George VI

1936 German troops occupy the Rhineland

Ninety-nine percent of German electorate vote for Nazi candidates

The Popular Front wins general election in France; Léon Blum becomes prime minister

Roosevelt reelected president of the United States

The Popular Front wins general election in Spain

Spanish Civil War begins

Italian troops occupy Addis Ababa; Abyssinia annexed by Italy

BBC begins television service from Alexandra Palace

Auden's *Look, Stranger!*

Auden and Isherwood's *The Ascent of F-6*

A. J. Ayer's *Language, Truth and Logic*

Chaplin's *Modern Times*

Greene's *A Gun for Sale*

Huxley's *Eyeless in Gaza*

Keynes's *General Theory of Employment*

F. R. Leavis' *Revaluation*

Mondrian's *Composition in Red and Blue*

Dylan Thomas' *Twenty-five Poems*

Wells's *The Shape of Things to Come* filmed

1937 Trial of Karl Radek and other Soviet leaders

Neville Chamberlain succeeds Stanley Baldwin as prime minister

China and Japan at war

Frank Whittle designs jet engine

Picasso's *Guernica*

Shostakovich's Fifth Symphony

Magritte's *La Reproduction interdite*
Hemingway's *To Have and Have Not*
Malraux's *L'Espoir*
Orwell's *The Road to Wigan Pier*
Priestley's *Time and the Conways*
Virginia Woolf's *The Years*

1938 Trial of Nikolai Bukharin and other Soviet political leaders

Austria occupied by German troops and declared part of the Reich

Hitler states his determination to annex Sudetenland from Czechoslovakia

Britain, France, Germany, and Italy sign the Munich agreement

German troops occupy Sudetenland

Edward Hulton founds *Picture Post*

Cyril Connolly's *Enemies of Promise*

Les Murray born

Faulkner's *The Unvanquished*

Graham Greene's *Brighton Rock*

Hindemith's *Mathis der Maler*

Jean Renoir's *La Grande Illusion*

Jean-Paul Sartre's *La Nausée*

Yeats's *New Poems*

Anthony Asquith's *Pygmalion* and Walt Disney's *Snow White*

1939 German troops occupy Bohemia and Moravia; Czechoslovakia incorporated into Third Reich

Madrid surrenders to General Franco; the Spanish Civil War ends

Italy invades Albania

Spain joins Germany, Italy, and Japan in anti-Comintern Pact

Britain and France pledge support to Poland, Romania, and Greece

The Soviet Union proposes defensive alliance with Britain; British military mission visits Moscow

The Soviet Union and Germany sign nonaggression treaty, secretly providing for partition of Poland between them

Germany invades Poland; Britain, France, and Germany at war

The Soviet Union invades Finland

New York World's Fair opens

Eliot's *The Family Reunion*

Seamus Heaney born

Isherwood's *Good-bye to Berlin*

xlii

CHRONOLOGY

Joyce's *Finnegans Wake* (1922–1939)

MacNeice's *Autumn Journal*

Powell's *What's Become of Waring?*

1940 Churchill becomes prime minister

Italy declares war on France, Britain, and Greece

General de Gaulle founds Free French Movement

The Battle of Britain and the bombing of London

Roosevelt reelected president of the United States for third term

Betjeman's *Old Lights for New Chancels*

Angela Carter born

Chaplin's *The Great Dictator*

J. M. Coetzee born

Disney's *Fantasia*

Greene's *The Power and the Glory*

Hemingway's *For Whom the Bell Tolls*

C. P. Snow's *Strangers and Brothers* (retitled *George Passant* in 1970, when entire sequence of ten novels, published 1940–1970, was entitled *Strangers and Brothers*)

1941 German forces occupy Yugoslavia, Greece, and Crete, and invade the Soviet Union

Lend-Lease agreement between the United States and Britain

President Roosevelt and Winston Churchill sign the Atlantic Charter

Japanese forces attack Pearl Harbor; United States declares war on Japan, Germany, Italy; Britain on Japan

Auden's *New Year Letter*

James Burnham's *The Managerial Revolution*

F. Scott Fitzgerald's *The Last Tycoon*

Huxley's *Grey Eminence*

Derek Mahon born

Shostakovich's *Seventh Symphony*

Tippett's *A Child of Our Time*

Orson Welles's *Citizen Kane*

Virginia Woolf's *Between the Acts*

1942 Japanese forces capture Singapore, Hong Kong, Bataan, Manila

German forces capture Tobruk

U.S. fleet defeats the Japanese in the Coral Sea, captures Guadalcanal

Battle of El Alamein

Allied forces land in French North Africa

Atom first split at University of Chicago

William Beveridge's *Social Insurance and Allied Services*

Albert Camus's *L'Étranger*

Joyce Cary's *To Be a Pilgrim*

Edith Sitwell's *Street Songs*

Waugh's *Put Out More Flags*

1943 German forces surrender at Stalingrad

German and Italian forces surrender in North Africa

Italy surrenders to Allies and declares war on Germany

Cairo conference between Roosevelt, Churchill, Chiang Kai-shek

Teheran conference between Roosevelt, Churchill, Stalin

Eliot's *Four Quartets*

Henry Moore's *Madonna and Child*

Sartre's *Les Mouches*

Vaughan Williams' *Fifth Symphony*

1944 Allied forces land in Normandy and southern France

Allied forces enter Rome

Attempted assassination of Hitler fails

Liberation of Paris

U.S. forces land in Philippines

German offensive in the Ardennes halted

Roosevelt reelected president of the United States for fourth term

Education Act passed in Britain

Pay-as-You-Earn income tax introduced

Beveridge's *Full Employment in a Free Society*

Cary's *The Horse's Mouth*

Huxley's *Time Must Have a Stop*

Maugham's *The Razor's Edge*

Sartre's *Huis Clos*

Edith Sitwell's *Green Song and Other Poems*

Graham Sutherland's *Christ on the Cross*

Trevelyan's *English Social History*

1945 British and Indian forces open offensive in Burma

CHRONOLOGY

Yalta conference between Roosevelt, Churchill, Stalin

Mussolini executed by Italian partisans

Roosevelt dies; Harry S. Truman becomes president

Hitler commits suicide; German forces surrender

The Potsdam Peace Conference

The United Nations Charter ratified in San Francisco

The Labour Party wins British General Election

Atomic bombs dropped on Hiroshima and Nagasaki

Surrender of Japanese forces ends World War II

Trial of Nazi war criminals opens at Nuremberg

All-India Congress demands British withdrawal from India

De Gaulle elected president of French Provisional Government; resigns the next year

Betjeman's *New Bats in Old Belfries*

Britten's *Peter Grimes*

Orwell's *Animal Farm*

Russell's *History of Western Philosophy*

Sartre's *The Age of Reason*

Edith Sitwell's *The Song of the Cold*

Waugh's *Brideshead Revisited*

1946   Bills to nationalize railways, coal mines, and the Bank of England passed in Britain

Nuremberg Trials concluded

United Nations General Assembly meets in New York as its permanent headquarters

The Arab Council inaugurated in Britain

Frederick Ashton's *Symphonic Variations*

Britten's *The Rape of Lucretia*

David Lean's *Great Expectations*

O'Neill's *The Iceman Cometh*

Roberto Rosselini's *Paisà*

Dylan Thomas' *Deaths and Entrances*

1947   President Truman announces program of aid to Greece and Turkey and outlines the "Truman Doctrine"

Independence of India proclaimed; partition between India and Pakistan, and communal strife between Hindus and Moslems follows

General Marshall calls for a European recovery program

First supersonic air flight

Britain's first atomic pile at Harwell comes into operation

Edinburgh festival established

Discovery of the Dead Sea Scrolls in Palestine

Princess Elizabeth marries Philip Mountbatten, duke of Edinburgh

Auden's *Age of Anxiety*

Camus's *La Peste*

Chaplin's *Monsieur Verdoux*

Lowry's *Under the Volcano*

Priestley's *An Inspector Calls*

Edith Sitwell's *The Shadow of Cain*

Waugh's *Scott-King's Modern Europe*

1948   Gandhi assassinated

Czech Communist Party seizes power

Pan-European movement (1948–1958) begins with the formation of the permanent Organization for European Economic Cooperation (OEEC)

Berlin airlift begins as the Soviet Union halts road and rail traffic to the city

British mandate in Palestine ends; Israeli provisional government formed

Yugoslavia expelled from Soviet bloc

Columbia Records introduces the long-playing record

Truman elected of the United States for second term

Greene's *The Heart of the Matter*

Huxley's *Ape and Essence*

Leavis' *The Great Tradition*

Pound's *Cantos*

Priestley's *The Linden Tree*

Waugh's *The Loved One*

1949   North Atlantic Treaty Organization established with headquarters in Brussels

Berlin blockade lifted

German Federal Republic recognized; capital established at Bonn

CHRONOLOGY

Konrad Adenauer becomes German chancellor

Mao Tse-tung becomes chairman of the People's Republic of China following Communist victory over the Nationalists

Jamaica Kincaid born

Simone de Beauvoir's *The Second Sex*

Cary's *A Fearful Joy*

Arthur Miller's *Death of a Salesman*

Orwell's *Nineteen Eighty-four*

1950   Korean War breaks out

Nobel Prize for literature awarded to Bertrand Russell

R. H. S. Crossman's *The God That Failed*

T. S. Eliot's *The Cocktail Party*

Fry's *Venus Observed*

Doris Lessing's *The Grass Is Singing*

C. S. Lewis' *The Chronicles of Narnia* (1950–1956)

Wyndham Lewis' *Rude Assignment*

George Orwell's *Shooting an Elephant*

Carol Reed's *The Third Man*

Dylan Thomas' *Twenty-six Poems*

A. N. Wilson born

1951   Guy Burgess and Donald Maclean defect from Britain to the Soviet Union

The Conservative party under Winston Churchill wins British general election

The Festival of Britain celebrates both the centenary of the Crystal Palace Exhibition and British postwar recovery

Electric power is produced by atomic energy at Arcon, Idaho

W. H. Auden's *Nones*

Samuel Beckett's *Molloy* and *Malone Dies*

Benjamin Britten's *Billy Budd*

Greene's *The End of the Affair*

Akira Kurosawa's *Rashomon*

Wyndham Lewis' *Rotting Hill*

Anthony Powell's *A Question of Upbringing* (first volume of *A Dance to the Music of Time*, 1951–1975)

J. D. Salinger's *The Catcher in the Rye*

C. P. Snow's *The Masters*

Igor Stravinsky's *The Rake's Progress*

1952–   **Reign of Elizabeth II**

At Eniwetok Atoll the United States detonates the first hydrogen bomb

The European Coal and Steel Community comes into being

Radiocarbon dating introduced to archaeology

Michael Ventris deciphers Linear B script

Dwight D. Eisenhower elected president of the United States

Beckett's *Waiting for Godot*

Andrew Motion born

Ernest Hemingway's *The Old Man and the Sea*

Arthur Koestler's *Arrow in the Blue*

F. R. Leavis' *The Common Pursuit*

Lessing's *Martha Quest* (first volume of *The Children of Violence*, 1952–1965)

C. S. Lewis' *Mere Christianity*

Thomas' *Collected Poems*

Evelyn Waugh's *Men at Arms* (first volume of *Sword of Honour*, 1952–1961)

Angus Wilson's *Hemlock and After*

1953   Constitution for a European political community drafted

Julius and Ethel Rosenberg executed for passing U.S. secrets to the Soviet Union

Cease-fire declared in Korea

Edmund Hillary and his Sherpa guide, Tenzing Norkay, scale Mt. Everest

Nobel Prize for literature awarded to Winston Churchill

General Mohammed Naguib proclaims Egypt a republic

Beckett's *Watt*

Joyce Cary's *Except the Lord*

Robert Graves's *Poems 1953*

1954   First atomic submarine, *Nautilus*, is launched by the United States

Dien Bien Phu captured by the Vietminh

Geneva Conference ends French dominion over Indochina

U.S. Supreme Court declares racial segregation in schools unconstitutional

CHRONOLOGY

Nasser becomes president of Egypt

Nobel Prize for literature awarded to Ernest Hemingway

Kingsley Amis' *Lucky Jim*

John Betjeman's *A Few Late Chrysanthemums*

William Golding's *Lord of the Flies*

Christopher Isherwood's *The World in the Evening*

Koestler's *The Invisible Writing*

Iris Murdoch's *Under the Net*

C. P. Snow's *The New Men*

Thomas' *Under Milk Wood* published posthumously

1955 Warsaw Pact signed

West Germany enters NATO as Allied occupation ends

The Conservative party under Anthony Eden wins British general election

Cary's *Not Honour More*

Greene's *The Quiet American*

Philip Larkin's *The Less Deceived*

F. R. Leavis' *D. H. Lawrence, Novelist*

Vladimir Nabokov's *Lolita*

Patrick White's *The Tree of Man*

1956 Nasser's nationalization of the Suez Canal leads to Israeli, British, and French armed intervention

Uprising in Hungary suppressed by Soviet troops

Khrushchev denounces Stalin at Twentieth Communist Party Congress

Eisenhower reelected president of the United States

Anthony Burgess' *Time for a Tiger*

Golding's *Pincher Martin*

Murdoch's *Flight from the Enchanter*

John Osborne's *Look Back in Anger*

Snow's *Homecomings*

Edmund Wilson's *Anglo-Saxon Attitudes*

1957 The Soviet Union launches the first artificial earth satellite, *Sputnik I*

Eden succeeded by Harold Macmillan

Suez Canal reopened

Eisenhower Doctrine formulated

Parliament receives the Wolfenden Report on Homosexuality and Prostitution

Nobel Prize for literature awarded to Albert Camus

Beckett's *Endgame* and *All That Fall*

Lawrence Durrell's *Justine* (first volume of *The Alexandria Quartet*, 1957–1960)

Ted Hughes's *The Hawk in the Rain*

Murdoch's *The Sandcastle*

V. S. Naipaul's *The Mystic Masseur*

Eugene O'Neill's *Long Day's Journey into Night*

Osborne's *The Entertainer*

Muriel Spark's *The Comforters*

White's *Voss*

1958 European Economic Community established

Khrushchev succeeds Bulganin as Soviet premier

Charles de Gaulle becomes head of France's newly constituted Fifth Republic

The United Arab Republic formed by Egypt and Syria

The United States sends troops into Lebanon

First U.S. satellite, *Explorer 1*, launched

Nobel Prize for literature awarded to Boris Pasternak

Beckett's *Krapp's Last Tape*

John Kenneth Galbraith's *The Affluent Society*

Greene's *Our Man in Havana*

Murdoch's *The Bell*

Pasternak's *Dr. Zhivago*

Snow's *The Conscience of the Rich*

1959 Fidel Castro assumes power in Cuba

St. Lawrence Seaway opens

The European Free Trade Association founded

Alaska and Hawaii become the forty-ninth and fiftieth states

The Conservative party under Harold Macmillan wins British general election

Brendan Behan's *The Hostage*

Golding's *Free Fall*

Graves's *Collected Poems*

CHRONOLOGY

Koestler's *The Sleepwalkers*
Harold Pinter's *The Birthday Party*
Snow's *The Two Cultures and the Scientific Revolution*
Spark's *Memento Mori*

1960 South Africa bans the African National Congress and Pan-African Congress
The Congo achieves independence
John F. Kennedy elected president of the United States
The U.S. bathyscaphe *Trieste* descends to 35,800 feet
Publication of the unexpurgated *Lady Chatterley's Lover* permitted by court
Auden's *Hommage to Clio*
Betjeman's *Summoned by Bells*
Pinter's *The Caretaker*
Snow's *The Affair*
David Storey's *This Sporting Life*

1961 South Africa leaves the British Commonwealth
Sierra Leone and Tanganyika achieve independence
The Berlin Wall erected
The New English Bible published
Beckett's *How It Is*
Greene's *A Burnt-Out Case*
Koestler's *The Lotus and the Robot*
Murdoch's *A Severed Head*
Naipaul's *A House for Mr Biswas*
Osborne's *Luther*
Spark's *The Prime of Miss Jean Brodie*
White's *Riders in the Chariot*

1962 John Glenn becomes first U.S. astronaut to orbit earth
The United States launches the spacecraft *Mariner* to explore Venus
Algeria achieves independence
Cuban missile crisis ends in withdrawal of Soviet missiles from Cuba
Adolf Eichmann executed in Israel for Nazi war crimes
Second Vatican Council convened by Pope John XXIII
Nobel Prize for literature awarded to John Steinbeck
Edward Albee's *Who's Afraid of Virginia Woolf?*
Beckett's *Happy Days*

Anthony Burgess' *A Clockwork Orange* and *The Wanting Seed*
Aldous Huxley's *Island*
Isherwood's *Down There on a Visit*
Lessing's *The Golden Notebook*
Nabokov's *Pale Fire*
Aleksandr Solzhenitsyn's *One Day in the Life of Ivan Denisovich*

1963 Britain, the United States, and the Soviet Union sign a test-ban treaty
Britain refused entry to the European Economic Community
The Soviet Union puts into orbit the first woman astronaut, Valentina Tereshkova
Paul VI becomes pope
President Kennedy assassinated; Lyndon B. Johnson assumes office
Nobel Prize for literature awarded to George Seferis
Britten's *War Requiem*
John Fowles's *The Collector*
Murdoch's *The Unicorn*
Spark's *The Girls of Slender Means*
Storey's *Radcliffe*
John Updike's *The Centaur*

1964 Tonkin Gulf incident leads to retaliatory strikes by U.S. aircraft against North Vietnam
Greece and Turkey contend for control of Cyprus
Britain grants licenses to drill for oil in the North Sea
The Shakespeare Quatercentenary celebrated
Lyndon Johnson elected president of the United States
The Labour party under Harold Wilson wins British general election
Nobel Prize for literature awarded to Jean-Paul Sartre
Saul Bellow's *Herzog*
Burgess' *Nothing Like the Sun*
Golding's *The Spire*
Isherwood's *A Single Man*
Stanley Kubrick's *Dr. Strangelove*
Larkin's *The Whitsun Weddings*
Naipaul's *An Area of Darkness*
Peter Shaffer's *The Royal Hunt of the Sun*
Snow's *Corridors of Power*

CHRONOLOGY

1965   The first U.S. combat forces land in
       Vietnam
       The U.S. spacecraft Mariner trans-
       mits photographs of Mars
       British Petroleum Company finds oil
       in the North Sea
       War breaks out between India and
       Pakistan
       Rhodesia declares its independence
       Ontario power failure blacks out the
       Canadian and U.S. east coasts
       Nobel Prize for literature awarded to
       Mikhail Sholokhov
       Robert Lowell's *For the Union Dead*
       Norman Mailer's *An American Dream*
       Osborne's *Inadmissible Evidence*
       Pinter's *The Homecoming*
       Spark's *The Mandelbaum Gate*

1966   The Labour party under Harold Wil-
       son wins British general election
       The Archbishop of Canterbury visits
       Pope Paul VI
       Florence, Italy, severely damaged by
       floods
       Paris exhibition celebrates Picasso's
       eighty-fifth birthday
       Fowles's *The Magus*
       Greene's *The Comedians*
       Osborne's *A Patriot for Me*
       Paul Scott's *The Jewel in the Crown*
       (first volume of *The Raj Quartet,*
       1966–1975)
       White's *The Solid Mandala*

1967   Thurgood Marshall becomes first
       black U.S. Supreme Court justice
       Six-Day War pits Israel against
       Egypt and Syria
       Biafra's secession from Nigeria leads
       to civil war
       Francis Chichester completes solo
       circumnavigation of the globe
       Dr. Christiaan Barnard performs first
       heart transplant operation, in
       South Africa
       China explodes its first hydrogen
       bomb
       Golding's *The Pyramid*
       Hughes's *Wodwo*
       Isherwood's *A Meeting by the River*
       Naipaul's *The Mimic Men*

       Tom Stoppard's *Rosencrantz and*
       Guildenstern Are Dead
       Orson Welles's *Chimes at Midnight*
       Angus Wilson's *No Laughing Matter*

1968   Violent student protests erupt in
       France and West Germany
       Warsaw Pact troops occupy Czecho-
       slovakia
       Violence in Northern Ireland causes
       Britain to send in troops
       Tet offensive by Communist forces
       launched against South Vietnam's
       cities
       Theater censorship ended in Britain
       Robert Kennedy and Martin Luther
       King Jr. assassinated
       Richard M. Nixon elected president
       of the United States
       Booker Prize for fiction established
       Durrell's *Tunc*
       Graves's *Poems 1965–1968*
       Osborne's *The Hotel in Amsterdam*
       Snow's *The Sleep of Reason*
       Solzhenitsyn's *The First Circle* and
       Cancer Ward
       Spark's *The Public Image*

1969   Humans set foot on the moon for the
       first time when astronauts descend
       to its surface in a landing vehicle
       from the U.S. spacecraft *Apollo 11*
       The Soviet unmanned spacecraft
       Venus V lands on Venus
       Capital punishment abolished in
       Britain
       Colonel Muammar Qaddafi seizes
       power in Libya
       Solzhenitsyn expelled from the Sovi-
       et Union
       Nobel Prize for literature awarded to
       Samuel Beckett
       Carter's *The Magic Toyshop*
       Fowles's *The French Lieutenant's*
       Woman
       Storey's *The Contractor*

1970   Civil war in Nigeria ends with
       Biafra's surrender
       U.S. planes bomb Cambodia
       The Conservative party under Ed-
       ward Heath wins British general
       election

CHRONOLOGY

Nobel Prize for literature awarded to Aleksandr Solzhenitsyn

Durrell's *Nunquam*

Hughes's *Crow*

F. R. Leavis and Q. D. Leavis' *Dickens the Novelist*

Snow's *Last Things*

Spark's *The Driver's Seat*

1971 Communist China given Nationalist China's UN seat

Decimal currency introduced to Britain

Indira Gandhi becomes India's prime minister

Nobel Prize for literature awarded to Heinrich Böll

Bond's *The Pope's Wedding*

Naipaul's *In a Free State*

Pinter's *Old Times*

Spark's *Not to Disturb*

1972 The civil strife of "Bloody Sunday" causes Northern Ireland to come under the direct rule of Westminster

Nixon becomes the first U.S. president to visit Moscow and Beijing

The Watergate break-in precipitates scandal in the United States

Eleven Israeli athletes killed by terrorists at Munich Olympics

Nixon reelected president of the United States

Bond's *Lear*

Snow's *The Malcontents*

Stoppard's *Jumpers*

1973 Britain, Ireland, and Denmark enter European Economic Community

Egypt and Syria attack Israel in the Yom Kippur War

Energy crisis in Britain reduces production to a three-day week

Nobel Prize for literature awarded to Patrick White

Bond's *The Sea*

Greene's *The Honorary Consul*

Lessing's *The Summer Before the Dark*

Murdoch's *The Black Prince*

Shaffer's *Equus*

White's *The Eye of the Storm*

1974 Miners strike in Britain

Greece's military junta overthrown

Emperor Haile Selassie of Ethiopia deposed

President Makarios of Cyprus replaced by military coup

Nixon resigns as U.S. president and is succeeded by Gerald R. Ford

Betjeman's *A Nip in the Air*

Bond's *Bingo*

Durrell's *Monsieur* (first volume of *The Avignon Quintet*, 1974–1985)

Larkin's *The High Windows*

Solzhenitsyn's *The Gulag Archipelago*

Spark's *The Abbess of Crewe*

1975 The U.S. *Apollo* and Soviet *Soyuz* spacecrafts rendezvous in space

The Helsinki Accords on human rights signed

U.S. forces leave Vietnam

King Juan Carlos succeeds Franco as Spain's head of state

Nobel Prize for literature awarded to Eugenio Montale

1976 New U.S. copyright law goes into effect

Israeli commandos free hostages from hijacked plane at Entebbe, Uganda

British and French SST Concordes make first regularly scheduled commercial flights

The United States celebrates its bicentennial

Jimmy Carter elected president of the United States

Byron and Shelley manuscripts discovered in Barclay's Bank, Pall Mall

Hughes's *Seasons' Songs*

Koestler's *The Thirteenth Tribe*

Scott's *Staying On*

Spark's *The Take-over*

White's *A Fringe of Leaves*

1977 Silver jubilee of Queen Elizabeth II celebrated

Egyptian president Anwar el-Sadat visits Israel

"Gang of Four" expelled from Chinese Communist party

First woman ordained in the U.S. Episcopal church

CHRONOLOGY

After twenty-nine years in power, Israel's Labour party is defeated by the Likud party

Fowles's *Daniel Martin*

Hughes's *Gaudete*

1978 Treaty between Israel and Egypt negotiated at Camp David

Pope John Paul I dies a month after his coronation and is succeeded by Karol Cardinal Wojtyla, who takes the name John Paul II

Former Italian premier Aldo Moro murdered by left-wing terrorists

Nobel Prize for literature awarded to Isaac Bashevis Singer

Greene's *The Human Factor*

Hughes's *Cave Birds*

Murdoch's *The Sea, The Sea*

1979 The United States and China establish diplomatic relations

Ayatollah Khomeini takes power in Iran and his supporters hold U.S. embassy staff hostage in Teheran

Rhodesia becomes Zimbabwe

Earl Mountbatten assassinated

The Soviet Union invades Afghanistan

The Conservative party under Margaret Thatcher wins British general election

Nobel Prize for literature awarded to Odysseus Elytis

Golding's *Darkness Visible*

Hughes's *Moortown*

Lessing's *Shikasta* (first volume of *Canopus in Argos, Archives*)

Naipaul's *A Bend in the River*

Spark's *Territorial Rights*

White's *The Twyborn Affair*

1980 Iran-Iraq war begins

Strikes in Gdansk give rise to the Solidarity movement

Mt. St. Helen's erupts in Washington State

British steelworkers strike for the first time since 1926

More than fifty nations boycott Moscow Olympics

Ronald Reagan elected president of the United States

Burgess's *Earthly Powers*

Golding's *Rites of Passage*

Shaffer's *Amadeus*

Storey's *A Prodigal Child*

Angus Wilson's *Setting the World on Fire*

1981 Greece admitted to the European Economic Community

Iran hostage crisis ends with release of U.S. embassy staff

Twelve Labour MPs and nine peers found British Social Democratic party

Socialist party under François Mitterand wins French general election

Rupert Murdoch buys *The Times* of London

Turkish gunman wounds Pope John Paul II in assassination attempt

U.S. gunman wounds President Reagan in assassination attempt

President Sadat of Egypt assassinated

Nobel Prize for literature awarded to Elias Canetti

Spark's *Loitering with Intent*

1982 Britain drives Argentina's invasion force out of the Falkland Islands

U.S. space shuttle makes first successful trip

Yuri Andropov becomes general secretary of the Central Committee of the Soviet Communist party

Israel invades Lebanon

First artificial heart implanted at Salt Lake City hospital

Bellow's *The Dean's December*

Greene's *Monsignor Quixote*

1983 South Korean airliner with 269 aboard shot down after straying into Soviet airspace

U.S. forces invade Grenada following left-wing coup

Widespread protests erupt over placement of nuclear missiles in Europe

The £1 coin comes into circulation in Britain

Australia wins the America's Cup

Nobel Prize for literature awarded to William Golding

CHRONOLOGY

Hughes's *River*

Murdoch's *The Philosopher's Pupil*

1984 Konstantin Chernenko becomes general secretary of the Central Committee of the Soviet Communist party

Prime Minister Indira Gandhi of India assassinated by Sikh bodyguards

Reagan reelected president of the United States

Toxic gas leak at Bhopal, India, plant kills 2,000

British miners go on strike

Irish Republican Army attempts to kill Prime Minister Thatcher with bomb detonated at a Brighton hotel

World Court holds against U.S. mining of Nicaraguan harbors

Golding's *The Paper Men*

Lessing's *The Diary of Jane Somers*

Spark's *The Only Problem*

1985 United States deploys cruise missiles in Europe

Mikhail Gorbachev becomes general secretary of the Soviet Communist party following death of Konstantin Chernenko

Riots break out in Handsworth district (Birmingham) and Brixton

Republic of Ireland gains consultative role in Northern Ireland

State of emergency is declared in South Africa

Nobel Prize for literature awarded to Claude Simon

A. N. Wilson's *Gentlemen in England*

Lessing's *The Good Terrorist*

Murdoch's *The Good Apprentice*

Fowles's *A Maggot*

1986 U.S. space shuttle *Challenger* explodes

United States attacks Libya

Atomic power plant at Chernobyl destroyed in accident

Corazon Aquino becomes president of the Philippines

Giotto spacecraft encounters Comet Halley

Nobel Prize for literature awarded to Wole Soyinka

Final volume of *Oxford English Dictionary* supplement published

Amis's *The Old Devils*

Ishiguro's *An Artist of the Floating World*

A. N. Wilson's *Love Unknown*

Powell's *The Fisher King*

1987 Gorbachev begins reform of Communist party of the Soviet Union

Stock market collapses

Iran-contra affair reveals that Reagan administration used money from arms sales to Iran to fund Nicaraguan rebels

Palestinian uprising begins in Israeli-occupied territories

Nobel Prize for literature awarded to Joseph Brodsky

Golding's *Close Quarters*

Burgess's *Little Wilson and Big God*

Drabble's *The Radiant Way*

1988 Soviet Union begins withdrawing troops from Afghanistan

Iranian airliner shot down by U.S. Navy over Persian Gulf

War between Iran and Iraq ends

George Bush elected president of the United States

Pan American flight 103 destroyed over Lockerbie, Scotland

Nobel Prize for literature awarded to Naguib Mafouz

Greene's *The Captain and the Enemy*

Amis's *Difficulties with Girls*

Rushdie's *Satanic Verses*

1989 Ayatollah Khomeini pronounces death sentence on Salman Rushdie; Great Britain and Iran sever diplomatic relations

F. W. de Klerk becomes president of South Africa

Chinese government crushes student demonstration in Tiananmen Square

Communist regimes are weakened or abolished in Poland, Czechoslovakia, Hungary, East Germany, and Romania

Lithuania nullifies its inclusion in Soviet Union

Nobel Prize for literature awarded to José Cela

Second edition of *Oxford English Dictionary* published

Drabble's *A Natural Curiosity*

Murdoch's *The Message to the Planet*

Amis's *London Fields*

Ishiguro's *The Remains of the Day*

1990 Communist monopoly ends in Bulgaria

Riots break out against community charge in England

First women ordained priests in Church of England

Civil war breaks out in Yugoslavia; Croatia and Slovenia declare independence

Bush and Gorbachev sign START agreement to reduce nuclear-weapons arsenals

President Jean-Baptiste Aristide overthrown by military in Haiti

Boris Yeltsin elected president of Russia

Dissolution of the Soviet Union

Nobel Prize for literature awarded to Nadine Gordimer

1992 U.N. Conference on Environment and Development (the "Earth Summit") meets in Rio de Janeiro

Prince and Princess of Wales separate

War in Bosnia-Herzegovina intensifies

Bill Clinton elected president of the United States in three-way race with Bush and independent candidate H. Ross Perot

Nobel Prize for literature awarded to Derek Walcott

1993 Czechoslovakia divides into the Czech Republic and Slovakia; playwright Vaclav Havel elected president of the Czech Republic

Britain ratifies Treaty on European Union (the "Maastricht Treaty")

U.S. troops provide humanitarian aid amid famine in Somalia

United States, Canada, and Mexico sign North American Free Trade Agreement

Nobel Prize for literature awarded to Toni Morrison

1994 Nelson Mandela elected president in South Africa's first post-apartheid election

Jean-Baptiste Aristide restored to presidency of Haiti

Clinton health care reforms rejected by Congress

Civil war in Rwanda

Republicans win control of both houses of Congress for first time in forty years

Prime Minister Albert Reynolds of Ireland meets with Gerry Adams, president of Sinn Fein

Nobel Prize for literature awarded to Kenzaburo Õe

Amis's *You Can't Do Both*

Naipaul's *A Way in the World*

1995 Britain and Irish Republican Army engage in diplomatic talks

Barings Bank forced into bankruptcy as a result of a maverick bond trader's losses

United States restores full diplomatic relations with Vietnam

NATO initiates air strikes in Bosnia

Death of Stephen Spender

Israeli Prime Minister Yitzhak Rabin assassinated

Nobel Prize for literature awarded to Seamus Heaney

1996 IRA breaks cease-fire; Sein Fein representatives barred from Northern Ireland peace talks

Prince and Princess of Wales divorce

Cease-fire agreement in Chechnia; Russian forces begin to withdraw

Boris Yeltsin reelected president of Russia

Bill Clinton reelected president of the United States

Nobel Prize for literature awarded to Wislawa Szymborska

1996 British government destroys around 100,000 cows suspected of infection with Creutzfeldt-Jakob, or "mad cow" disease

1997 Diana, Princess of Wales, dies in an automobile accident

CHRONOLOGY

Unveiling of first fully-cloned adult animal, a sheep named Dolly

Booker McConnell Prize for fiction awarded to Arundhati Roy

1998   United States renews bombing of Bagdad, Iraq

Independent legislature and Parliaments return to Scotland and Wales

Ted Hughes, Symbolist poet and husband of Sylvia Plath, dies

Booker McConnell Prize for fiction awarded to Ian McEwan

Nobel Prize for literature awarded to Jose Saramago

1999   King Hussein of Jordan dies

United Nations responds militarily to Serbian President Slobodan Milosevic's escalation of crisis in Kosovo

Booker McConnell Prize for fiction awarded to J. M. Coetzee

Nobel Prize for literature awarded to Günter Grass

2000   Penelope Fitzgerald dies

J. K. Rowling's *Harry Potter and the Goblet of Fire* sells more than 300,000 copies in its first day

Oil blockades by fuel haulers protesting high oil taxes bring much of Britain to a standstill

Slobodan Milosevic loses Serbian general election to Vojislav Kostunica

Death of Scotland's First Minister, Donald Dewar

Nobel Prize for literature awarded to Gao Xingjian

Booker McConnell Prize for fiction awarded to Margaret Atwood

George W. Bush, son of former president George Bush, becomes president of the United States after Supreme Court halts recount of closest election in history

Death of former Canadian Prime Minister Pierre Elliot Trudeau

Human Genome Project researchers announce that they have a complete map of the genetic code of a human chromosome

Vladimir Putin succeeds Boris Yeltsin as president of Russia

British Prime Minister Tony Blair's son Leo is born, making him the first child born to a sitting prime minister in 152 years

2001   In Britain, the House of Lords passes legislation that legalizes the creation of cloned human embryos

British Prime Minister Tony Blair wins second term

List of Contributors

SCOTT ASHLEY Sir James Knott Research Fellow in history at the University of Newcastle Upon Tyne. He has published on medieval and modern literary history and is currently researching the relationship between elite and popular culture in the middle ages. **David Jones**

ALAN BELL Librarian of The London Library since 1993. Previously held senior positions at libraries in Oxford and Edinburgh. He is author of *Sydney Smith* (1980) and editor of Leslie Stephen's autobiography, *The Mausoleum Book* (1978). He was for several years a regular contributor to *The Times Literary Supplement* and is now an advisory editor of *The New Dictionary of National Biography*. **Sydney Smith**

JOHN A. BERTOLINI Ellis Professor of the Liberal Arts and Chair of the English Department at Middlebury College, Vermont. He has written *The Playwrighting Self of Bernard Shaw*, edited Shaw and Other Playwrights, and published articles on Renaissance drama, modern British drama, and Alfred Hitchcock. He is currently working on a study of Terence Rattigan's plays. **Terence Rattigan**

DAVID BREITHAUPT Full-time writer. His fiction and poetry have appeared in numerous magazines, including volume 2 of Andrei Codrescu's *Thus Spake the Corpse (Best of the Exquisite Corpse)*. He contributed an essay on James Purdy for Scribner's *American Writers* series and edited an anthology of poet Charles Plymell's work called *Hand on the Doorknob* (2000). Breithaupt has also worked as an archivist for poet and writer Allen Ginsberg. He lives in Gambier, Ohio with his family while working a variety of odd jobs to supplement his income from freelance writing. He has traveled widely but never left the planet. **Anna Kavan**

ALAN BROWNJOHN Poet and lecturer of creative writing at the University of North London. Born in Catford, South-East London in 1931. Graduated from Oxford University in 1953. Author of ten books of poetry, including *Collected Poems* (1988) and most recently *The Cat Without E-mail* (2001). His three novels are *The Way You Tell Them (1990), The Long Shadows* (1997) and *A Funny Old Year* (2001). He has been a reviewer, mainly of poetry, for the *New Statesman*, the *Times Literary Supplement*, and *Encounter*, and currently is joint poetry critic, with Sean O'Brien, for the *Sunday Times*. He has also translated for the stage *Torquato Tasso* (Goethe) and *Horace* (Corneille), both published by Angel Books. **Gavin Ewart**

GERRY CAMBRIDGE Poet and editor of the Scottish-American poetry magazine, *The Dark Horse*. His own books of verse include *The Shell House* (1995), *"Nothing But Heather!": Scottish Nature in Poems, Photographs and Prose* (1999), illustrated with his own natural history photographs, and *The Praise of Swans* (2000). Cambridge was the 1997&ndash1999 Brownsbank Fellow, based at Hugh MacDiarmid's former home, Brownsbank Cottage, near Biggar in Scotland. **Les Murray**

RICHARD DAVENPORT-HINES Historian and biographer. Fellow of the Royal Historical Society, and a past winner of the Wolfson Prize for History and Biography. He also serves on the Committee of the London Library. Publications include *Dudley Docker* (1985), *Sex, Death and Punishment* (1990), *The Macmillans* (1992), *Vice* (1993), *Auden* (1995) and *Gothic* (1998). *The Pursuit of Oblivion: A Global History of Narcotics 1500–2000* will be published in Fall 2001. **Charles Darwin**

LIST OF CONTRIBUTORS

LAURIE DENNETT Freelance writer and scholar. She divides her time between London and a small village in Spain. A graduate of the University of Toronto, she has recently published two books, *A Hug For the Apostle*–a personal memoir and travel book–and a history of the British Prudential Insurance Company. **John Henry Newman**

CLAIRE HARMAN Freelance writer. Coordinating editor of the literary magazine *PN Review* in the 1980s. Published biographies of poet Sylvia Townsend Warner (1989) and eighteenth century novelist Fanny Burney (2000). She is currently engaged in writing a life of Robert Louis Stevenson, whose *Essays and Poems* and *Selected Stories* she has edited for Everyman Editions. She has also edited Sylvia Townsend Warner's *Collected Poems* and *Diaries* and reviews regularly in the British literary press. **Sylvia Townsend Warner**

JOHN HEADLEY Distinguished Professor in the History Department at the University of North Carolina, Chapel Hill. Teaches the Renaissance, Reformation, and Seventeenth-Century Europe. Publications include works on Martin Luther and Thomas More (Volume 5 of the Yale Edition). Research interests include questions of world empire that have led him to global history in the period 1450 to 1700. **Thomas More**

DEVIN JOHNSTON Assistant professor of English at Saint Louis University. Author of *Precipitations*, a study of American poetry and the occult, forthcoming from Wesleyan University Press in 2002. He has also published a book of poetry entitled *Telepathy* (2001). From 1995 to 2000 he worked as poetry editor for *Chicago Review*, and he currently co-directs a small press called Flood Editions. **Basil Bunting**

PETER KEMP Fiction editor and chief fiction reviewer of the *London Sunday Times*. Publications include *Muriel Spark* (1974), *H.G. Wells and the Culminating Ape* (1982, revised 1996) and *The Oxford Dictionary of Literary Quotations* (edited 1997). **Barry Unsworth**

ERIK KONGSHAUG Novelist and essayist. Teacher of fiction and composition at the University of California, Irvine. Author of *The Path*, a novel; essays on community, politics, and literature. **Jamaica Kincaid**

JAY PARINI Axinn Professor of English at Middlebury College. A poet, novelist, and biographer, his most recent books are *House Of Days*, a volume of poems, and *Robert Frost: A Life*. His sixth novel, *The Apprentice Lover*, will appear in 2002. **Alistair Reid**

PETER PARKER Writer. Fellow of the Royal Society of Literature. Author of *The Old Lie: The Great War and the Public-School Ethos* (1987) and a biography of J.R. Ackerley (1989). The editor of *A Reader's Guide to the Twentieth-Century Novel* (1994) and *A Reader's Guide to Twentieth-Century Writers* (1995), he also writes about books, authors, and gardening for various newspapers and periodicals in England. He is currently writing the authorized biography of Christopher Isherwood and is an associate editor of the forthcoming *New Dictionary of National Biography*. **L. P. Hartley**

ROBERT POTTS Politics editor of the *Times Literary Supplement*, and poetry critic for the *Guardian*. **Andrew Motion**

NEIL POWELL Poet, biographer, editor, and lecturer. His books include five collections of poetry—*At the Edge* (1977), *A Season of Calm Weather (1982)*, *True Colours* (1991), *The Stones on Thorpeness Beach* (1994), and *Selected Poems* (1998)as well as *Carpenters of Light* (1979), *Roy Fuller: Writer and Society* (1995), and *The Language of Jazz* (1997). He lives in Suffolk, England and is working on a biography of George Crabbe. **Roy Fuller**

JOHN REDMOND Professor and poet. Took his doctorate at St. Hugh's College, Oxford, and has taught at Queen Mary and Westfield College, London. His main research interests are Irish Studies and Twentieth century poetry. His first collection of poems, *Thumb's Width* was published by Carcanet Press, Manchester, 2001. **W. S. Graham**

LIST OF CONTRIBUTORS

N. S. THOMPSON Lecturer in English at Christ Church, Oxford. His publications include *Chaucer, Boccaccio and the Debate of Love* (1997), a comparative study of the *Decameron* and the *Canterbury Tales*, as well as academic and critical articles on medieval and modern poetry and regular reviews for the *Times Literary Supplement*. **The Gawain Poet**

ROBERT WELCH Dean of the Faculty of Arts at the University of Ulster. He joined the University in 1984 as Professor of English, having previously taught at the University of Leeds, and the University of Ife (Nigeria). A native of Cork, he was educated at UCC and Leeds; he is married to Angela and has four children. A novelist and poet as well as a critic and editor, he published *The Oxford Companion to Irish Literature* in 1996. Other publications include: *Irish Poetry from Moore to Yeats* (1980), *Changing States* (1993), *The Kilcolman Notebook* (novel, 1994), *Secret Societies* (poems, 1994), *Groundwork* (novel, 1997), *The Blue Formica Table* (poems, 1997), and *The Abbey Theatre 1899–1999* (1999). His novel *The Kings Are Out* appears in 2002. His ambition is to build a Japanese garden in the wilds of Donegal. **Patrick Kavanagh**

JOHN WILDERS Emeritus Fellow of Worcester College, Oxford and Emeritus Professor of the Humanities at Middlebury College, Vermont. He has also taught at the University of Bristol, Princeton University, and the University of California, Santa Barbara and was visiting Research Fellow at the Australian National University in Canberra. He has published books on Shakespeare and was literary consultant for the BBC Television productions of the complete plays of Shakespeare. **Michael Frayn**

GRACE WILSON College English teacher in Elizabeth City, North Carolina. She has published articles on Chaucer, Pitscottie, and other early Scottish writers. **Robert Henryson**

ANDREW ZAWACKI Writer and Co-editor of *Verse*. His criticism has appeared in the *Times Literary Supplement*, *Boston Review*, *The Kenyon Review*, *Australian Book Review* and elsewhere. His first book of poetry, *By Reason of Breakings*, is forthcoming from the University of Georgia Press. A former fellow of the Slovenian Writers' Association, he edited the anthology *Afterwards: Slovenian Writing 1945–1995* (1999). He was a 2000–2001 Fulbright Scholar in the Centre for Comparative Literature and Cultural Studies at Monash University in Melbourne, Australia. **A. D. Hope**

BASIL BUNTING

(1900–1985)

Devin Johnston

IN MANY RESPECTS, Basil Bunting represents the road not taken in twentieth-century British poetry, in which modernism has had an uneasy presence. Those who proved distinctively modernist, such as David Jones, Hugh MacDiarmid, and Bunting, were largely from outer regions (Wales, Scotland, and Northumberland, respectively) rather than the publishing center of London and have thus suffered from relative neglect. The Bloomsbury group (consisting of Virginia Woolf and E. M. Forster, among others) are an obvious exception; yet Bunting felt excluded from their London society by his class background and covertly satirized their gentility in his early verse. Until recently, Bunting's reputation depended upon his association with the American poet Ezra Pound, and his readership consisted primarily of fellow poets. Thus, while a select few have hailed his *Briggflatts* as one of the finest long poems of the century, Bunting cultivated little English audience for his work in his own lifetime. His writing is temperamentally at odds with most British poetry of its time and devoid of the irony and cautiousness that mark the attitude of much of the poetry written after the First World War. While his style and concerns are largely modernist—reflecting his contact with Ezra Pound and Louis Zukofsky—his widest publication did not occur until the early 1960s. In contrast to Movement poets such as Thom Gunn and Ted Hughes, who were then coming into prominence, his difficult and adventuresome style seemed belated.

In keeping with his modernist predecessors, Bunting's poetry exhibits remarkable sophistication in terms of influence. His slim volume of collected poems includes translations of Latin and Persian, adaptations of French and Japanese poetry, as well as the more pervasive presence of Thomas Wyatt, William Wordsworth, and Walt Whitman. Yet despite such erudition, much of his poetry takes its structure from commonplace subjects, including sensory pleasures and the hardships of poverty. In a typically self-effacing manner, Bunting has described his own concerns as "cottage wisdom." Yet the phrase is revealing: his verse could be characterized in terms of a modernist sensibility very much grounded in place and wedded to a pastoral tradition. Through this cottage wisdom, his aesthetics and ethics are closely related: he consistently advocates condensation and coherence in his approach to both verse and life. His poetry often addresses the need for artists to live frugally and independently, outside the structures of power, and does so with considerable economy. It was Bunting who discovered, in a German-Italian dictionary, the equivalence that became Pound's slogan: "dichten = condensare" (to compose is to condense).

In his scattered and reluctant critical statements, Bunting describes poetry as "lines and patterns of sound" and suggests that the experience of poetry should approach that of music. While the application of music to poetry is notoriously elusive (and Bunting did little to clarify his terms), the analogy highlights some important aspects of his writing. At the level of the line, he considered meter not as an abstract pattern to be fulfilled but as an evolving and flexible rhythm that unfolds in time. While interested in developing "subtle and unsteady" rhythmic motifs, he disparaged the pervasive use of iambic pentameter as both predictable and unresponsive to the meaning and texture of words. He felt that the aural component of poems should ideally reflect the experience described, and his poems are therefore rich in onomatopoeia. In "Silver blades of surf / fall crisp on rustling grit" (*Complete Poems*, 2000, p. 79), for instance, one can hear the surf in the alliteration of /s/ sounds. His poetry is full of such dense patterns of assonance and alliteration. In a more general sense, Bunting organized his longer poems according to musical structures, and particularly the sonata (a composition consisting of several sections varying in mood, key, and tempo). Such an analogy allowed him to attend closely to the repetition of themes (whether of sound or meaning) and to conceive of his poems in terms of the shape of their development. As a result, in contrast to the irregularity and incompletion that characterize most modernist long poems, Bunting's "sonatas" (as he referred to his extended writings) have a remarkable unity. *Briggflatts* is the culmination of his experiments with musical form: his success is evident in the coherent shape he gives to a rich diversity of stylist effects.

LIFE

BUNTING had strong objections to the work of scholars and was often quoted as saying that there is no excuse for literary criticism, and that he did not believe in biography. He destroyed all the letters he received after reading them and encouraged his correspondents to do the same (a request that has been irregularly honored). His dislike for biography derived from his belief that it distracts the reader from the experience of the poetry itself, which should require no explanatory apparatus or critical elaboration. This attitude accompanied a general resistance to social definition: despite his strong sense of place, Bunting thought of himself (and more generally, the poet) as an outsider or spy. He considered neglect prerequisite to the pursuit of craft. Indeed, Bunting lived in relative poverty and freedom most of his life.

Bunting was born on 1 March 1900, in Scotswood-on-Tyne, Northumberland—a region of England on the border of Scotland that once constituted one of the Anglo-Saxon kingdoms. His mother was the daughter of a local mine manager and related to many Border families. His father was a doctor who had received a gold medal in Edinburgh for his thesis on the histol-

ogy of lymphatic glands. He later shifted to radiology and worked as a general practitioner to the miners at Montagu Pit at Scotswood until his death. With these roots, Bunting's interest in working-class politics persisted throughout his life and distinguished him from most British modernists.

In addition to being a skilled mountainclimber and a supporter of the socialist Fabian Society, Dr. Bunting had considerable literary interests and moved in social circles of several contemporary poets. He was a friend of Joseph Skipsey, a nineteenth-century miner-poet, and Algernon Charles Swinburne was apparently an acquaintance. Beyond this pre-Raphaelite context, his father's enthusiasm for Wordsworth had a lasting impact. While other modernists such as Ezra Pound and T. S. Eliot tended to disparage Wordsworth for prolixity, Bunting admired his use of the common speech of Northern England. Wordsworth's emphasis on the daily life of the region, his precise observations of nature, and his structural subtlety were chief influences on Bunting's development as a poet.

Walt Whitman's poetry soon presented another formative influence on his emergence as a writer. Following the Quaker interests of an uncle, Bunting was sent in 1912 to a Quaker school in Yorkshire. There, at the age of sixteen, he discovered an early edition of Whitman's *Leaves of Grass* in the recesses of the school library. In his enthusiasm for the work, he wrote an essay on Whitman that won a national prize for Quaker schools. When the award was announced, Whitman's close friend Edward Carpenter rode on his bike from Sheffield to meet Bunting. Called from Latin class, he went into town to have a vegetarian meal with Carpenter. It was as a pantheistic visionary, with a strong emphasis on the natural cycles of life, that Whitman's thinking can be discerned in poems such as *Briggflatts*.

In 1916 Bunting transferred to another Quaker school, Leighton Park in Berkshire. When the First World War began, he objected (in an essay society paper) to the loss of personal liberty under British conscription law. He soon declared himself a conscientious objector and was arrested shortly before his eighteenth birthday for refusing service. Despite the Quaker atmosphere in which he was raised, he seems to have received little support in his decision from family or community. His decision was particularly principled, given that it coincided with the end of the war, and he further declared himself an *absolutist conchie*, meaning that—beyond his refusal to fight—he would not aid the war effort in any way. Much of his time in Wormwood Scrubs was spent without the opportunity to converse or the means to write, and he spent several days in isolation without clothes or food. Eventually, Bunting chose to begin a hunger strike, during which the prison authorities left a freshly roasted chicken in his cell each day to tempt him (an anecdote recalled in Pound's Canto LXXIV). After eleven days without food, he was released from prison on a pass in late 1919.

Bunting spent the following two years at the London School of Economics, during which time he contributed supporting evidence to a book by Graham Wallas (a founder of the Fabian Society) advocating prison reform. Bored with his course of studies, however, he never completed his degree. In 1920, he tried to visit Russia—apparently with the intention of converting Lenin and Trotsky to pacifism—but he was turned back at the border of Scandinavia. During this period he began writing poetry in earnest and first encountered the work of Ezra Pound and T. S. Eliot. Eager for the intellectual climate reflected in such literature, he left for Paris in 1922, and initially earned his living there as a road worker, artist's model, and barkeeper. He soon fell in with avant-gardists such as Philippe Soupault and Tristan Tzara and began working as secretary to the novelist Ford Madox Ford sub-editing the *Transatlantic Review*. The varied and rich intellectual climate of Paris at this time confirmed Bunting's sense of himself as a poet.

It was during this period that he met Ezra Pound, and their friendship was established through an incident that has become anecdotally famous. Bunting was arrested for assaulting a policeman when, quite drunk, he tried to batter his way into the wrong lodging. Pound somehow discovered his circumstances and perjured himself in the courts in order to rescue him. When he came to see him in his holding tank, Bunting was reading a pocket edition of François Villon's poetry—and was, in fact, probably confined to the same room that Villon had been nearly fivehundred years earlier. Given their mutual affection for the author, Pound was delighted when Bunting captured his experiences in English and French prisons by drafting *Villon*—his first longer poem, which incorporated sections of translation from Villon's own writings. In keeping with Pound's strident editorial practices (most famously in evidence in his paring of Eliot's *The Waste Land* [1922]), he cut it down to a highly charged if discursively truncated shape. Beyond such a direct editorial intervention, Pound's influence on Bunting during this period—in terms of both aesthetic principles and enthusiasm—was considerable. In its range of cultural reference and condensation, Bunting's writing during this time often resembles works such as *Cathay* (1915), *Homage to Sextus Propertius* (1917), and *Hugh Selwyn Mauberley* (1920). Between 1924 and 1932, which coincided with his closest relations with Pound—as well as the relative freedom of youth—he produced three long poems and twenty-five odes, constituting his most intense period of productivity.

In 1924 Bunting followed Pound to Rapallo, Italy, where he worked as a sailor, but was soon recalled to England by his father's death. For the next few years he tried to find satisfactory employment in London without much success. Meanwhile, when discontent among miners reached a head in the spring of 1926, general strike was declared by the Trade Union Congress in May. Bunting actively supported the strike and sabotaged strikebreaking busdrivers by sticking knives in their tires; he also chaired a meeting for miners' leaders. In 1927 his employment situation improved and he began writing music reviews for a respected journal called *Outlook*. Although this experience lasted only until May of the following year, the results constitute some of the only critical statements that Bunting chose to publish. When the journal folded, a wealthy acquaintance named Margaret de Silver offered to support him while he wrote poetry, which she did for the next two years. Bunting immediately moved north to a small cottage in Northumberland. Yet the relative isolation and quiet did little for his creative production, and he left for Germany after six months. The notable result of this visit was a poem entitled *Aus dem Zweiten Reich* [*From the Second Reich*], which offers a distinctly modernist satire of what he perceived as the sterility of both creative and sexual activity in modern Germany. In its critique of contemporary consumer culture, it recalls the jazz-inflected moments of T. S. Eliot: "efficiently whipped cream, / efficiently metropolitan chatter and snap, / transparent glistening wrapper / for a candy pack" (*Complete Poems*, 2000, p. 36).

Bunting soon returned to Rapallo, and on a trip to Venice met Marian Gray Culver, a Wisconsin native on holiday who was to become his first wife. In March of 1930 he had his first collection of poems (dating from 1924–1929) privately printed in Milan under the title *Redimiculum Matellarum* [*A Necklace of Chamberpots*]. Despite the creative advantages of Rapallo, finances forced Bunting to return to London for a brief period; he then traveled to America to rejoin Marian with hopes of better employment prospects there (based in part on his letters of introduction from Pound). Despite disappointment in that regard—as well as a general dislike for America—he formed valuable friendships with the poets William Carlos Williams and Louis Zukofsky. The latter, in particular, became a lifelong literary ally. Soon thereafter, when Zukofsky edited a special issue of *Poetry* magazine, he included Bunting's writing under his banner of "the Objectivists' movement." Though the definition of Objectivism—with its emphasis on precision, sincerity, and the poem as object—has been the subject of considerable dispute, the company and exposure were valuable for Bunting. He married Marian in the summer of 1930 and had returned to Rapallo by spring of the following year.

For the next two years, Basil and Marian lived in the company of the Pounds, W. B. Yeats, and a lively rotation of visitors. When they had their first child, a daughter named Bourtai (after the nine-year-old wife of Genghis Khan), the fifty-

dollar Lyric Prize from *Poetry* magazine arrived in time to pay the hospital bills. A few stray articles provided some income, and Margaret de Silver sent a check after Bourtai's birth—which Bunting used to purchase a small sailboat. Soon after his return to Rapallo, he composed *Chomei at Toyama*, which appeared in *Poetry* in September of 1933 and again in Pound's *Active Anthology* (published the following month by Faber & Faber). The latter was dedicated to both Bunting and Zukofsky, "strugglers in the desert," and marked a high point in Bunting's visibility.

Yet his creative productivity soon began to taper off, and insolvency forced the family to move to Tenerife, the largest of the Canary Islands (which lie off the coast of Spanish Sahara in the Atlantic Ocean). Bunting's depression during this period is reflected in the gloomy and obscure *The Well of Lycopolis* (1935), an ironic, anti-erotic poem in four sections. It concerns creative failure or impotence—a frequent theme in Bunting's poetry—and features an "ageing, bedraggled" Venus and a prostituted Polymnia as companions to the abject poet. In a manner recalling Pound's *Hugh Selwyn Mauberley*, the poem satirizes Eliot, Bloomsbury, Bunting himself, and the spirit of the age. The Buntings soon moved to an equally remote region of southern Portugal, where their second daughter was born. Bunting had been learning Persian, at Pound's prompting, and named his daughter Roudaba after a figure in a Persian epic. As political tensions in Spain escalated, the Buntings followed events closely, sympathizing with the Popular Front and attending political meetings. Shortly before the beginning of the Spanish Civil War in June of 1936, they returned to England, and Bunting set to work writing an article, "The Roots of the Spanish Civil War," for *The Spectator* based on his close observations. The family settled near Hampstead Heath, and Bunting secured some reviews for *The Spectator, The New English Weekly*, and *The Criterion* (of which T. S. Eliot was the editor). But financial hardships continued, and in despair—pregnant with her third child—Marian took custody of the children and returned to Wisconsin. Her departure left Bunting in deep depression, and he wrote almost no poetry for the next seventeen years. In the absence of family and poetry, he worked on fishing boats, and enrolled in a nautical academy to improve his sailing skills. From April 1938 until the beginning of the Second World War he worked on ships in New York and Los Angeles, drifting.

With Britain's entry into the Second World War, Bunting rushed home from California to Northumberland in order to enlist. He waited over a year for an appointment but was finally accepted as a balloon-man for the Royal Air Force. He then volunteered to be an interpreter for a squadron going to Persia—and was accepted, based on his cursory reading knowledge of ancient Persian. With remarkable aptitude, however, he picked up the spoken language. In the whirlwind of the war years, he accompanied a convoy from Baghdad across the desert to Tripoli, witnessed the last days of the siege of Malta, and briefly returned to England in time for his squadron to cover the invasion of Normandy in 1944. Soon thereafter, he returned to Persia as a squadron leader himself. He then served as vice-consul at Isfahan, working with the nomadic mountain tribes and acting as head of political intelligence in Persia, Iraq, and Saudia Arabia (one of his chief responsibilities was the cartography of tribal boundaries). By his own account, he led a life of excitement and unfamiliar luxury in the Middle East, with servants, a horse, and fine collections of whiskey and Persian literature. In 1948, Bunting fell in love with Sima Alladallian, a young Persian woman from a prominent family. Apparently as a result of this relationship, he was retired from the Information Department, and after returning briefly to London, took the post of *Times* correspondent to Tehran. Though the Foreign Office files on Bunting remain closed, there has been some speculation that Bunting continued to serve the Foreign Office for the next two years through his work as a journalist. During this time, Sima gave birth to a daughter, Maria. Through the auspices of an admirer of Pound, *Poems 1950* was published in Texas. It was Bunting's first full-length volume since 1930. In April 1952, the Iranian government refused to renew his visa—in the first stage of what was to

become a thorough expulsion of the British presence there.

He was given one more assignment by the *Times* in Italy; thereafter, for reasons not entirely clear, he could find employment through neither the *Times* nor the Foreign Office. His varied and unusual work experience did not effectively translate into a civilian context. He therefore gave up on London and returned to Northumberland in June of 1953—the date given for *The Spoils*, the sonata that proved the culmination of his Persian experiences. Yet he had little time or energy for poetry during these years, and earned a living as a proofreader for various papers. Bunting's sense of isolation was increased when Rustam—his son by Marian, and whom he never met—died of polio in October of 1953.

This fallow period came to an end in 1963. An aspiring Newcastle poet named Tom Pickard, then in his teens, sought critical advice from the poet and publisher Jonathan Williams, who directed him to Bunting. When Pickard arrived on his doorstep with a clutch of poems in hand, Bunting gave him *The Spoils* to publish through his fledgling press (after a twelve-year silence). Pickard also helped to arrange a reading for Bunting in the Morden Tower series, which proved a positive exposure to a younger readership. From 1963 to 1965, Bunting wrote eight odes and his greatest poem, *Briggflatts*. The following two years witnessed prolific publication: in addition to the publication of *The Spoils*, Fulcrum Press brought out the *First Book of Odes, Briggflatts*, and *Loquituri* within a few months. The latter collected all of the poems that Bunting eventually chose to preserve, with the exception of four short poems he had yet to write.

He received an Art Council Bursary in 1966 and quit his newspaper job to take a visiting lectureship at the University of California, Santa Barbara. With the rise of his reputation during the 1960s—particularly among American devotees of experimental modernism—opportunities began to present themselves with increasing frequency: he returned often over the next few years for readings, and taught at the University of British Columbia and the University of Vancouver. In England, he read at the Royal Albert

Hall International Poetry Festival and became president of the Poetry Society in 1972. Although this activity did not produce further poems, he edited the selected poems of Ford Madox Ford in 1972 and those of Joseph Skipsey in 1976. Oxford University Press issued the *Collected Poems* in 1977 (published in America by Moyer Bell in 1985). By 1980 Bunting was separated from his second wife and moved to a cottage near Bellingham (along the Tyne) with the intention of retiring from readings and teaching stints. Yet he continued to give irregular readings in London and elsewhere for money. A few years later, his small income forced him to move to more affordable lodgings at Fox Cottage near Hexham, where he died in 1985.

CHOMEI AT TOYAMA

EZRA Pound repeatedly advised younger poets to begin with translation and then proceed to original composition. An emphasis on translation, Pound believed, not only allows the young poet to discover what has already been accomplished but also provides a subject matter that he or she may otherwise lack. As one of Pound's most attentive students, Bunting followed this proscription closely in his early work: many of his odes, as well as both *Villon* and *Chomei at Toyama*, have translation or adaptation as their basis. In the case of the latter, Bunting was following the precedent of *Cathay*, which Pound based on the eighth-century Chinese of Li Po despite his lack of familiarity with the source language. Just as *Cathay* translates the political and social turbulence of classical China in the context of the First World War, *Chomei at Toyama* translates the social upheavals of thirteenth-century Japan in the uncertainties of Europe between the wars.

Bunting had run across Marcello Muccioli's Italian translation of Kamo no Chomei's *Hojoki* [*Record of the Ten-Foot-Square Hut*]—one of the masterpieces of Japanese literature—sometime after its publication in 1930. Chomei was active in the court of Go-Toba in the early thirteenth century but retired to a secluded hut, where he wrote his prose apologia for the meditative life in

1212. *Hojoki* follows in a tradition of Buddhist memoirs of the simple life that would include, most prominently, the T'ang poet Po Chü-I's *Record of the Thatched Hall on Mount Lu* as well as the eighth-century *Record of the Pond Pavilion* by the Japanese official Yoshinge no Yasutane. Like these, Chomei takes his secluded dwelling as the occasion for a meditation on the transience of the world and the minimal requirements for pleasure. He begins by musing on the impermanence of human beings and their habitations and turns to a series of disasters that have impressed upon him the ephemerality of the world (including a fire, whirlwind, the relocation of the capital, drought, flood, and an earthquake). He then discusses his own disappointments and frustrations and the circumstances of his retirement to Mount Hino. He describes the simplicity of his domestic arrangements and routines, the Buddhist devotion and pleasures he derives from his surroundings.

In his adaptation of Chomei's record, Bunting adheres fairly closely to both the narrative structure and the tone (though rendering the prose as verse). He begins with a condensed image of ceaseless change: "Swirl, sleeping in the waterfall! / On motionless pools scum appearing / disappearing!" (*Complete Poems*, 2000, p. 85). He then quickly locates this theme in human dwellings, observing "Housebreakers clamber about, / builders raising floor upon floor / at the corner sites, replacing / gardens by bungalows." Metaphysical questions concerning the evanescence of experience are thus immediately grounded in examples of disasters, a sequence of which commences with the statement, "I have been noting events forty years" (p. 85). Bunting's strength in the catalogue that follows is his ability to translate the original into a modern idiom that avoids *japonoiserie*, or fetishizing stylistic markers of Japanese culture. In some instances, he accomplishes this by transposing twelfth-century Kyoto onto twentieth-century London and New York: "Dead stank / on the curb, lay so thick on / Riverside Drive a car couldnt pass" (p. 87). He had learned this technique from Pound's *Homage to Sextus Propertius*, in which a Frigidaire (notoriously) crops up in ancient Rome.

Elsewhere, in a more subtle fashion, Bunting finds a modern equivalence for Chomei's language in a terse, plain style that modulates ethical imperatives into worldly wisdom: "Men are fools to invest in real estate" (p. 86). As a result of this plain style, *Chomei at Toyama* is more prosaic that most of Bunting's poetry; though its language and imagery are condensed, its lyricism is more muted than that of *Briggflatts*.

In roughly the second half of the poem, Bunting has Chomei describe how he became saddened with "idealistic philosophies" and withdrew into the mountains: "I have built my last house, or hovel, / a hunter's bivouac, an old / silkworm's cocoon: / ten feet by ten, seven high" (p. 89). The following descriptions of simple domesticity, and specific observations on the changing seasons, are some of the strongest passages in the poem. For instance, Bunting's Chomei specifies the limits to what his household requires: "I have gathered stones, fitted / stones for a cistern, laid bamboo / pipes. No woodstack, / wood enough in the thicket" (p. 90). Though this hut is ostensibly a spiritual retreat, Bunting downplays that aspect in his own version. The speaker wryly observes his own continued pleasure in domesticity; nonetheless, he has accepted its transience: "Oh! There's nothing to complain about. / Buddha says: 'None of the world is good.' / I am fond of my hut." (p. 94). Bunting's Chomei is thus no ascetic but rather an advocate of simple and available pleasures under an acceptance of chaos and impermanence.

Chomei's attitudes toward pleasure and impermanence in this sense closely reflect Bunting's own. Indeed, it is worth observing those moments when he diverges from the original in order to approach more closely his own views. For instance, Chomei does not himself refer to "idealistic philosophies" as a depressive force that impelled his retreat from the world. By adding the phrase, Bunting makes clear his own advocacy of empirical knowledge and embodiment over abstract idealism. In autobiographical terms, Chomei's preference for a ten-foot hut over larger structures may reflect Bunting's distrust of structural thinking, and his reliance on common sense and specificity as fundamental to his poetics. *Chomei at Toyama* concludes with a series of aphoristic statements that further reveal his sense of the role of the poet: "Friends fancy a rich man's riches, / friends suck up to a man in high office. / If you keep straight you will have no friends / but catgut and blossom in season" (p. 92). An appreciation for the productions of art and nature offer some compensation for the poet's necessary exile from power and privilege, according to Bunting. However, in a characteristic gesture of disavowal—and one not explicitly made in Chomei's record—he parenthetically qualifies such assertions: "Let it be quite understood, / all this is merely personal. / I am not preaching the simple life / to those who enjoy being rich" (p. 93).

THE SPOILS

THE Spoils marks the exception to several decades of meager creative output, yet it reads as a bridge in continuity between Bunting's early writing and *Briggflatts*. In subject matter and imagery, it draws on his extensive experience of the Middle East, which had begun—imaginatively, at least—with his learning to read Persian epics in the early 1930s. In its cultural references, the poem is thus exceptional to Bunting's oeuvre, which is primarily situated in the north of England, London, Paris, or Italy. Yet the poem's themes prove consistent with those that carry through nearly all of his writing: the function of ethics and aesthetics in the face of the impermanence. Such concerns are evident in the title itself, which derives from an Arabic epigraph from the Qur'an meaning "the spoils are to God." The emphasis on uncertainty one finds in *Chomei at Toyama* takes an apocalyptic turn in *The Spoils*, which traces attitudes toward death in Islamic culture. As the poem's bold opening states, "Man's life so little worth / do we fear to take or lose it? / No ill companion on a journey, Death / lays his purse on the table and opens the wine" (p. 47).

The poem has three parts or movements, the first of which illustrates what Bunting takes to be an Eastern view of life as a journey on which material wealth is an impediment. He conveys this view through a mosaic of four contrasting voices, which are attributed to the sons of Shem (and whose names appear in Genesis 10:22). The physical detail within each passage, and the contrasts explored within each, initially prove confusing; yet he offers these contrasts as analogous to mosaic complexity within a simple pattern. The first to speak is Asshur, a Bedouin clerk detailing transactions "As I sat at my counting frame to assess the people [...]" (p. 47). The exchange of goods confirms their interchangeability and fleeting quality—as well as the avarice of those involved. It is worth noting the deftness with which Bunting's lines suggest the repetition and variation of the clerk's activity: "with Abdoel squatting before piled pence, / counting and calling the sum, / ringing and weighing coin, / casting one out, four or five of a score, / calling the deficit; / one stood in the door / scorning our occupation [...]" (p. 47). The second speaker is Lud, who represents the city-dweller in his description of the hardships of life in Baghdad. He begins with the flooding of the Tigris, which results in "Dead camels, dead Kurds, / unmanageable rafts of logs" (p. 48) (which are brought together in close alliteration). Arpachshad, the third son, offers a slightly more carefree view of the life of an Arab tribesman. He catalogues the simple pleasures and dignities available: though without books or elevated conversation, his simple meals and evening recitations of sacred poetry cause him to conclude, "What's to dismay us?" (p. 49). The fourth speaker parodies Psalm 137 in his complaint concerning the life available to him as a Jew in Arab society: "By the dategroves of Babylon / there we sat down and sulked / while they were seeking to hire us / to a repugnant trade" (p. 49). The speakers continue, in two more rounds of comments, to make grievances against those who live for wealth, and then to register their attitudes toward pleasure. In each case, sensual pleasure is a transitory compensation in the face of loss.

While the first section ends with the rhetorical question, "What's begotten on a journey but souvenirs?" (p. 50), the opening to the second provides a strong contrast in its rich description of the architecture of a mosque. While the first section offered various expressions of *vita breve*, what follows are examples of *ars longa*—and the relative durability of human constructions. In this sense, the poem's meditation on evanescence is thus expanded from the individual life to that of a culture. After detailing the structural perfection of the Friday Mosque in Isfahan, Bunting moves on to a celebration of Eastern poetry and miniature painting; he declares, "Their passion's body was bricks and its soul algebra" (p. 51). Yet the creative perfection of Seljuk culture, historically tenuous, began to unravel—according to Bunting—as it became slack and aesthete: "Poetry / they remembered / too much, too well" (p. 51). The aesthetic clarity that characterized the mosque seems to have been lost, and lines that were once fine are repeated "heavily, languidly." In this historical critique, Bunting echoes Pound's advocacy of early Renaissance art over late (or William Blake's preference for a "wiry bounding line"). Yet Bunting concedes the relative merits of Seljuk culture: "For all that, the Seljuks avoided / Roman exaggeration and the leaden mind of Egypt / and withered precariously on the bough / with patience and public spirit. / O public spirit!" (p. 52). The ironic tone of this passage signals his sense of futility: whereas Pound takes such historical cycles as an instigation to cultural and political reform, Bunting sees such cycles of loss as inevitable (if depressing). After a lovely passage of pastoral description—intended to characterize those elements of grace and aesthetic pleasure that persist in Persian life—the poem returns to the general issue of loss and change: "Have you seen a falcon stoop / accurate, unforseen / and absolute, between / wind-ripples over harvest? Dread / of what's to be, is and has been— / were we not better dead?" (p. 53). While such endless alterations prove dreadful, the sections concludes with the suggestion that "dazzle rebuts our stare, / wonder our fright" (p. 54).

The final movement of *The Spoils* concerns the chaotic continuance of life under the awareness established in the first two sections. It opens with a discussion of baffled ambition: the speaker expresses a desire to pursue a traditional life of farming, yet asks, "How shall wheat sprout / through a shingle of Lydian pebbles / that turn the harrow's points?" (p. 55). These pebbles, one gathers, are not only literal but also represent the bureaucratic complexities that accompany such endeavors. In modern life, civic improvements (as we have seen, derived from "public spirit") prove constraining and—in an echo of Dante—infernal: "Let no one drink unchlorinated / living water but taxed tap, sterile, / or seek his contraband mouthful / in bog, under thicket [...]" (p. 55). This complaint against treated water recalls Pound's frequent citations of flavorless bread and uncomfortable chairs as the products of modernization. Just as the "artesian gush" invokes the fount of the Muses on Mount Helicon in classical mythology, the poem considers the fate of modern poets who must drink at its polluted stream. Pound, who was arrested and institutionalized for his radio broadcasts in support of Mussolini, is himself recognizable as "One cribbed in a madhouse / set about with diagnoses" (p. 55). Abruptly, the poem then shifts to a battle in the desert (based on Bunting's own experience accompanying a convoy from Baghdad to Tripoli). An acceptance of futility, one gathers, leads directly to the exercising of faculties in war. Here, Bunting accumulates vivid examples of material destruction, including "a new-painted recognisance / on a fragment of fuselage, sand drifting into dumps, / a tank's turret twisted skyward [...]" (p. 56). Through its chaos, war requires a Homeric acceptance of mortality—and is in this sense revelatory of our true condition. The poem ends with a touch of bravado:

From Largo Law look down,
moon and dry weather, look down
on convoy marshalled, filing between mines.
Cold northern clear sea-gardens
between Lofoten and Spitzbergen,
as good a grave as any, earth or water.
What else do we live for and take part,
we who would share the spoils?

(p. 58)

There is a slight ambiguity concerning the antecedent to *what* in this final rhetorical question. It may refer to the grave itself, suggesting that we live only to die, despite our desire to "share the spoils." More compellingly, it may also refer to the glimpse of activity described in the passage. For Bunting, aesthetic pleasures are themselves transitory, if worth grasping.

The Spoils is remarkable for its intricate formal patterning, which is exceeded in his oeuvre only by the complexity of *Briggflatts*. As critics such as Peter Makin have observed, the first section is particularly rich in its repetition of key terms such as *bread, pipes, bronze, kettles*, and *vulture*. Such imagistic echoes structure the poem according to an abstract, subtle pattern that Bunting was inclined to compare to Celtic manuscripts or—in this case, more topically—Middle Eastern carpets. Yet the most striking passages in the poem capture the unpredictability and swiftness of the instant, and follow the structure of an event in an imitative fashion. In fact, the richness of such details at times threaten to overwhelm one's awareness of the poem's structure. The third section, which is particularly dense, tends to sacrifice clear development in order to achieve its remarkable condensation. Such problems of scale may partially account for Bunting's thirteen-year silence after composing *The Spoils*.

BRIGGFLATTS

DESPITE the excellence of his prior publications, *Briggflatts* has proved the basis for Bunting's critical reputation. In contrast to his previous extended poems, it adheres to a simplicity of theme and structure that effectively offsets the density of its language and imagery. Moreover, despite the infrequency of first-person pronouns, its subject matter is grounded in the poet's own life and the landscape of Northern England (as indicated by the poem's subtitle, "An Autobiography"). As an admirer of William Wordsworth, Bunting may have had *The Prelude* as a model when composing his own "growth of the poet's mind" (as Wordsworth subtitled his poem). It is not merely the facts of a life but the aesthetic experiences and scattered memories which the poetic autobiography records. The two poets were not far removed in geographical terms, and Bunting followed the Romantic poet in exploring his personal development in relation to place. In *Briggflatts*, Bunting draws heavily on the Northumbrian dialect familiar to him from childhood. Like Wordsworth, he attends particularly closely to the natural environment in relation to individual consciousness. Just as the five sections of *Briggflatts* chart stages of the poet's life, four of the five also reflect the changing seasons of a year. Modernism is generally characterized as international in its outlook and urban in its concerns; as a pastoral poem largely concerned with Northumberland, *Briggflatts* is exceptional.

When considering the poem's concern for place, it is worth recalling the circumstances of its composition. Bunting had begun writing again with the encouragement of Tom Pickard, a young poet also native to the Northumbrian region. There was, in fact, a regional arts movement under way in the early 1960s, and arts funding for programs such as the Morden Tower reading series—which Pickard hosted, and in which Bunting read—reflected local interest. This audience may in part account for his attention to Northumbrian history and culture in the poem, which weaves in references to figures such as the Viking Eric Bloodaxe, who conquered the area and was killed there. Having returned to Northumberland in 1953, Bunting was also influenced by memories of his youth in composing the poem. In particular, he recollected his visits to Brigflatts (as it is usually spelled) at the invitation of a school friend at Ackworth between 1912 and 1916. Brigflatts was a small Quaker community on the edge of the Lake District, along the Rawthey River. It was there that he met Peggy Greenbank, the first love to whom the poem is dedicated. The breaking off of this relationship—and his failure to return to Brigflatts after the First World War—establishes the poem's elegiac tone. This lost love results in a mourning requiring a form of expression the poet can never realize. Thus the poem often turns to various forms of *impossibilia*, a rhetorical figure that gestures toward something for which there is no adequate expression.

The first section consists of twelve stanzas of thirteen lines—each of which ends with a rhym-ing couplet—and concerns the young lovers as they travel in late spring to Brigflatts to stay with Peggy's family. It opens with the image of a bull along the Rawthey, and then describes a mason at work on a gravestone, "till the stone spells a name / naming none, / a man abolished" (p. 61). The theme of mortality is thus quickly established, and even the spring hawthorn's blossoms (or *may*) pave "the slowworm's way." The slowworm is a limbless European lizard that serves Bunting as a symbol of the interrelation of life and death; it quietly takes part in decay or destruction but also expression. Thus the mason chiseling "name and date" (p. 64) is an apt figure for the poet, whose function is essentially elegiac. Beyond his symbolic role, the mason is Peggy's father, and the young couple ride to her home on a wagon, atop the gravestone. In his description of the journey, Bunting's knotty diction and alliteration of hard consonants vividly evoke sensory details: "Under sacks on the stone / two children lie, / hear the horse stale, / the mason whistle, / harness mutter to shaft, / felloe to axle squeak, / rut thud the rim, / crushed grit" (p. 62). That evening, after her parents have gone to bed, the young couple make love, and in the following passage, his penis is itself described as a slowworm—part of the cycle of creation and destruction. When the mason rises to work, the narration breaks off: "The mason stirs: / Words! / Pens are too light. / Take a chisel to write" (p. 63). The remainder of the section expresses guilt at ending the relationship, and the poet's inability to give adequate expression to his emotions. For the melancholic, the most vivid recollection fails to do justice to experience, and the movement thus ends on a mournful note.

The second section opens in summer some years later: Bunting is now a poet by self-definition, and living in London. As he struggles to register his perceptions, his sense of the poet's necessary exile develops, and he becomes "Secret, solitary, a spy" (p. 65). Yet his earlier betrayal of love leaves him "self-hating" and, in Bunting's harsh self-judgment, "mating / beauty with squalor to beget lines still-born" (p. 65). Following the middleyears of Bunting's life in an impressionistic fashion, the section continues in a manner both stylistically and geographically ranging. In dense nautical terminology, he describes his experiences as a sailor in the north and the south. His own impressions merge with a larger, historical consciousness as his ship becomes that of the Viking Eric Bloodaxe, who was destroyed in part by his own falsehoods. As an erasure of lived experience, it is this falseness with which Bunting identifies. It compromises even the catalogue of rich sensual pleasures he recalls from his time in Italy: "It looks well on the page, but never / well enough. Something is lost / when wind, sun, sea upbraid / justly an unconvinced deserter" (p. 67). Clearly, Bunting is a deserter for abandoning his first love, and his guilt is only aggravated through the experience of sensual beauty. Moreover, as a poet, he deserts sensual experience for its representation: in his efforts to become an artist, he is thus divided from the immediacy of pleasure. The movement ends with a lament against decay and failure—or more specifically, the failure to find clear form. Such odd creatures as the starfish and the Asian vulture are celebrated for their own distinctive versions of gracefulness; "But who will entune a bogged orchard, / its blossom gone, / fruit unformed, where hunger and / damp hush the hive? / A disappointed July full of codling / moth and ragged lettuces?" (p. 69). In an anti-pastoral image of the half-formed and overrun, Bunting identifies the summer of his autobiography as a creative failure.

As the poem's center, the third section departs from the autobiographical mode of the first two sections and instead narrates a nightmarish account of Alexander the Great's journey to the end of the earth (borrowed from the Persian epic *Shahnameh* of Firdosi). The legend concerns Alexander's wandering route to the mountains of Gog and Magog, where he encounters an angel with his lips to his trumpet, prepared to put an end to the world. The section opens with a Dantean passage describing Alexander's encounters with eaters of excrement, a commodity in the market. In their errant course, he and his men pass marshes of rotting corpses and disease. Particularly in its excremental imagery, these grotesqueries recall Ezra Pound's own account of

Hell in Canto XIV. And as in Canto XX, which addresses the fate of Odysseus's crew, the speaker in this section is not Alexander but one of his soldiers. They refuse to accompany Alexander to the mountaintop: "But we desired Macedonia, / the rocky meadows, horses, barley pancakes, / incest and familiar games, / to end in our place by our own wars, / and deemed the peak unscaleable" (p. 72). Alexander alone witnesses the angel preparing for apocalypse and, when he recovers from his vision, returns in peace to Macedonia. Yet on the homeward journey, everything in nature speaks to him of the cycle of decay and transformation: "Thorns prance in a gale. / In air snow flickers, / twigs tap, / elms drip" (p. 74). As the section concludes, in a more prosaic statement, "So he rose and led home silently through clean woodland / where every bough repeated the slowworm's song" (p. 74). The legend of Alexander allows Bunting to explore apocalypse, which appears to be the culmination of a vision of human corruption through greed. Through the extremity of Alexander's vision, Bunting suggests, he comes to an acceptance of the life cycle: whereas the angel prepares for an end to time, the slowworm participates in the temporal world through both decay and creation. While this section makes no reference to Bunting himself, one may interpolate its function in a poem subtitled "An Autobiography." The dismay at the manner in which a market determines value was Bunting's own through the 1930s, as he found it increasingly difficult to support his family while writing poetry. Furthermore, the apocalypse at the world's end echoes Bunting's experiences in the Middle East during the Second World War and, more generally, its massive destruction.

Just as Alexander returns to Macedonia after his vision of the angel, the fourth section of *Briggflatts* returns to Northumberland. The poet has come home, in late middle age, to observe that the "height" of what has occurred—in terms of history, autobiography, and the dramatic arc of the poem—"has subsided" (p. 75). The present has the instability of a house built on marsh: history is in this sense not progressive but precariously balanced above what has preceded it. As historical associations come flooding back, the subject becomes the complex interdependence of past and present, for which the rich brocade of Anglo-Saxon saints serves as metaphor. Yet the chaotic web of events is untraceable, the poet has found, and so the section turns to simplicity as an equally valid emphasis in his art. He considers Scarlatti as a model in this regard, who fulfills Bunting's own aesthetic aim of achieving condensation while maintaining clarity—"with never a crabbed turn or congested cadence, / never a boast or a see-here" (p. 76). Likewise, he returns to the theme of his first love as a tonic in its emotional directness and simplicity. In one of Bunting's finest passages, he returns in imagination to the first movement of the poem, and after considering the life he might have had with Peggy, asks, "What breeze will fill that sleeve limp on the line? / A boy's jet steams from the wall, time from the year, / care from deed and undoing" (p. 76). As a result of his betrayal long ago, his homecoming is imaginative rather than actual. The section ends with a contrasting account of his real and present difficulties: "Where rats go go I, / accustomed to penury, / filth, disgust and fury" (p. 77). Tonally, the movement is predominantly minor key, which proves suitable for its autumnal imagery—which slips into winter in the final stanzas. Likewise, the long lines of section four involve less elision and follow a more conventional syntax than do the previous sections; in this sense, the tempo could be described as andante—in keeping with the model of a sonata.

In autobiographical terms, the fourth section of the poem leads up to the composition of *Briggflatts* itself—which is reflected in its muster of Bunting's principle themes and historical references. The fifth section therefore moves into the present of winter and old age with more muted emotion. In a dense tissue of sound, rich in internal rhyme, Bunting offers an extended description of the present landscape and moment. There is an undertow of nostalgia in what is described: "Mist sets lace of frost / on rock for the tide to mangle. / Day is wreathed in what the summer lost" (p. 78). Yet the old poet does not give in to sentimental reflections; in an echo of Matthew 6:28 (in which the lilies "toil not,

neither do they spin") he suggests a peaceful acceptance: "Conger skimped at the ebb, lobster, / neither will I take, nor troll / roe of its like for salmon" (p. 78). The slow erosion of the seashore is compared to the mason's work, and "the river praises itself"—implying that the operations of nature are sufficient to themselves, without the poet's praise. In a phrase that could apply to Briggflatt's Quaker meetinghouse as well as to the Northumbrian landscape it more immediately describes, "silence by silence sits / and Then is diffused in Now" (p. 79). The latter line returns to a principle theme of *Briggflatts*, which is repeated and varied throughout: the interdependence of past and present. Thoughts of time turn to the stars, which unite observers far removed in time, though their light often reaches us long after the stars themselves are gone:

Furthest, fairest things, stars, free of our humbug,
each his own, the longer known the more alone,
wrapt in emphatic fire roaring out to a black flue.
Each spark trills on a tone beyond chronological compass,
yet in a sextant's bubble present and firm
places a surveyor's stone or steadies a tiller.
Then is Now. The star you steer by is gone [...]
(p. 80)

The sense of memory and experience that Bunting has arrived at can only be captured in a final paradox: "Fifty years a letter unanswered; / a visit postponed for fifty years. // She has been with me fifty years" (p. 80). Despite his preference for empirical data over abstraction, and "cottage wisdom" over philosophical speculation, such expressions approach a form of mysticism. Indeed, much of the poem's power derives from the contrast between expressions of harsh disappointment and those of peaceful understanding.

The slowworm is a central metaphor for Bunting's ambivalence in *Briggflatts*. It feeds off decay, and thus takes part in both creation and destruction. A phallic or erotic image, it also serves as a reminder of the betrayal of love and the destructive potential of passion. Like Whitman's leaves of grass, the slowworm is cause for celebration at nature's perpetual self-renewal. Such renewal, however, involves a temporality that does not always accord with human affection and memory. In other words, Bunting acknowledges personal loss in what Whitman calls "the amplitude of time." As Peter Makin has observed, not only Whitman but Lucretius and Darwin stand behind such considerations. Bunting proceeds from detailed observations and takes an interest in minutiae of nature. He captures the discontinuities as well as the continuities of creation: *Briggflatts* is largely concerned with this tension.

Bunting tended to frame his accomplishment in *Briggflatts* in terms of structure and musicality rather than thematic concerns. Indeed, it is well worth attending to the complex pattern of words and images woven into the fabric of the poem. One could, for instance, point to repeated motifs such as the mason, waves, historical figures (including Bloodaxe, Alexander, and the hermit Cuthbert), and a beastiary of bull, lark, rat, and of course, the slowworm. Equally, his use of the sonata form as a structuring principle determines the poem's variety of pace and form. He had Domenico Scarlatti's B minor fugato sonata L. 33 (K.87) in mind while writing the poem, and his quick tonal shifts parallel those in Scarlatti's virtuosic harpsichord pieces. Though scholars have debated the specific application of the sonata to *Briggflatts*, it would seem that Bunting intended a "marriage" of contrasting themes—namely, death and generation—such as one finds in the musical form. In any case, such a model encouraged him to seek rich diversity within a coherent and flowing structure, which is indeed one of the remarkable aspects of the poem. In keeping with its autobiographical framework, the very quest for such formal accomplishment is a central theme, and thus the poem often provides its own instructions for reading. Yet despite his aesthetic ambition, he conceives of the poet's role in remarkably modest terms. The rigorous economy of his poetics reflects the poet's need for stoic resolve in the face of neglect. Likewise, *Briggflatts* suggests, the poet's proper aim is not cultural revolution or political influence but some resolution with memory and time.

ODES

IN his final edition of *Collected Poems*, Bunting retained forty-nine shorter poems organized as two books of odes, which span a half century as well as a remarkable range of styles and subjects. *First Book of Odes*, issued by Fulcrum in 1965, included poems that had been published as "Carmina" in *Poems 1950*. Both titles are revealing in their references to Roman poetry, and specifically the *Carmina* of Catullus or Propertius and the *Odes* of Horace. Bunting sought the formal variety of such classical models as well as their ability to capture a broad spectrum of emotional life in language ranging from elevated to demotic. Though he organized his publications on a strictly chronological basis, the odes might well be grouped according to the varieties of classical elegy, including funereal, erotic, and satiric (or combinations thereof). Though a few of the odes feel like exercises toward the composition of longer poems, the best of them have a lyrical simplicity—combined with a rich awareness of lyrical traditions—which proves rare in modern poetry.

Though separated by forty years, the poems beginning both books of odes strike a mournful note. The first (I.1), written when Bunting was twenty-four, describes the onset of spring as a weary and repetitious cycle: "Weeping oaks grieve, chestnuts raise / mournful candles. Sad is spring / to perpetuate, sad to trace / immortalities never changing" (p. 97). The poem's emphasis on "merciless reiteration" reverses our expectations of pastoral elegy, and there is an oblique echo of T. S. Eliot's description of spring as a painful awakening in *The Waste Land*. Spring is finally characterized as "everlasting resurrection," and the poem is thus tinged with a cultural or religious weariness as the source of its exhaustion. The first poem in the *Second Book of Odes* similarly reverses our expectations of pastoralism. It describes what the thrush means by its song and responds ironically to the literary tradition in which John Keats's "Ode to a Nightingale" (1819) stands, and for which birdsong is transporting and otherworldly. In this case, the bird's difficulties are not far removed from the human realm; Bunting's pastoralism is in this sense not

Romantic but realist: "Death thrusts hard. My sons / by hawk's beak, by stones, / trusting weak wings / by cat and weasel, die" (p. 135). The poignancy of this poem is enhanced by the directness of the language, which avoids poetic diction in its approach to a traditional subject. Likewise, it achieves a delicate imitation of the thrush's song through slightly irregular rhymes and varied repetition of "Hunger ruffles my wings, fear, / lust, familiar things" as "From a shaken bush I / list familiar things, / fear, hunger, lust."

The melancholy tone of these two poems, and their emphasis on the relentlessness of nature, is offset by the erotic ecstasy of I.3—one of Bunting's most celebrated lyrics. The poem describes the movement of the tides from low to high to low again as an analogue to the cycle of sexual passion. As the poem begins, the poet declares, "I am agog for foam. Tumultuous come / with teeming sweetness to the bitter shore / tidelong unrinsed and midday parched and numb / with expectation" (p. 99). The sea's indifference arouses a complex response of envy, hostility, and impotence which is only relieved by the return of waves "braceletted with foam." The poem's psychological argument is perhaps less significant than its vivid mood and pacing, which stretches low tide over seventeen lines before arriving at high tide. Indeed, the syntax often demands unraveling, with unpredictable enjambments. In several instances, Bunting ends lines with "come," playing on the nominative possibility of orgasm before the next line suggests its more proper usage; in this manner he captures perfectly the charged expectation he describes. Written in a swift iambic pentameter with alternating endrhymes, Bunting imitates both the ebb and flow of the waves and the speaker's restless emotions. As in much of his poetry, such formal sophistication serves to render not an intellectual perception but rather a sensory experience and palpable mood.

The odes include a virtuosic—and perhaps unparalleled—range of forms and idioms. In a number of the early poems, Bunting experimented with the use of complex metrical patterns imported from classical poetry (translating long vowels into stresses, and vice versa). It may be worth observing his use of two such measures (derived from Greek sources through Horace) in I.5: "Empty vast days built in the waste memory seem a jail for / thoughts grown stale in the mind, tardy of birth, rank and inflexible" (p. 101). The first line corresponds to Sapphic Major

$$- \smile - \smile - \smile - \smile - \smile - \smile -$$
$$- \qquad\qquad\qquad -$$

while the second is a Greater Asclepiadean:

$$\smile - \smile - \smile - - \smile - - \smile - \smile - \smile -$$
$$- -$$

In contrast to such complex forms, many of the odes adopt ballad forms to accompany a folk idiom. Both "Gin the Goodwife Stint" (I.14) and "The Complaint of the Morpethshire Farmer" (I.18) are written in Northumbrian dialect and comment on the hardships of rural life and class injustices in a manner recalling John Clare. Much of the variety one finds in the odes is due to Bunting's deep sense of tradition, and his ability to write in the manner of earlier poetry with freshness and directness. While translations proper appear separately in his books as "Overdrafts," the lines between translation, imitation, and tradition are blurred throughout his writing. As a final example, take the brief lyric I.29, which begins: "Southwind, tell her what / wont sadden her, / not how wretched / I am" (p. 124). Despite its simplicity, the poem gains power through its echo of the anonymous fifteenth-century "Western Wind": "Western wind, when wilt thou blow, / The small rain down can rain? / Christ if my love were in my arms / And I in my bed again!" In Bunting's adaptation here, as in many of the odes, there is little that is strikingly modern in terms of style or reference. What is modern, rather, is the poet's sense of freedom in ransacking the past for material—which Bunting did with considerable success.

CONCLUSION

BUNTING has a reputation for difficulty, which is justified in several senses. In the first place, his range of reference is often unfamiliar, particularly to American readers. The breadth of literature which informs the poems draws from a variety of sources—including Persian—outside the scope of most Western canons. His poems often make passing reference to specificities of place, Northumbrian history and mythology, or nautical terminology. While such accuracies fulfilled his demand for poetic precision, they sometimes require just the sort of secondary research and commentary that he sought to avoid. Likewise, Bunting's emphasis on condensation and economy at times results in syntactic difficulties; while he celebrates Scarlatti for condensing "so much music into so few bars / with never a crabbed turn or congested cadence," his verse occasionally exhibits such failings.

Ironically, however, his thematic simplicity has perhaps proved the greatest stumbling block for critics, who have found in his poetry little of the thematic complexity that has propelled numerous critical studies of modernists such as Pound and Eliot. Indeed, some commentators have sensed a paucity of idea beneath the density of his language. It is this same quality, however, that Pound himself (among others) celebrated as a deep concern with basic human problems. Furthermore, this thematic simplicity leaves room for his remarkable sonic effects and formal concerns, which would be impossible within a more discursive framework. Though his subtlety in this regard exceeds our analytic vocabulary, and falls outside current critical concerns, it continues to offer to younger poets a model for craftsmanship. In this sense, it is fair to characterize his reception—until quite recently—as that of a "poet's poet." Bunting greeted an audience of poets—and relative neglect by critics—with equanimity; he generally preferred discussions of craft and history to those of theory. He was firmly opposed to theoretical abstractions and felt that all poetry (and discussions of it) should be grounded in observable phenomena. In his resolute empiricism, he often criticized English poets for a bookishness and inexperience that resulted in a narrowness of content. He championed Sir Walter Raleigh as an adventurer who

also composed poetry, and approximated such a life. As a result, his collected poems are slender but lively, and his best poetry has a chiseled quality born of sharp observation and meticulous craft.

SELECTED BIBLIOGRAPHY

I. COLLECTED WORKS. *Collected Poems* (London, 1968); *Collected Poems (Oxford, 1978); Collected Poems* (Mt. Kisco, New York, 1985); *Uncollected Poems* (Oxford and New York, 1991); *Complete Poems* (Oxford and New York, 1994); *Complete Poems* (Newcastle upon Tyne, 2000).

II. POETRY. *Redimiculum Matellarum* (Milan, 1930); *Poems 1950* (Galveston, Texas, 1950); *Loquitur* (London, 1965); *First Book of Odes* (London, 1965); *The Spoils* (Newcastle upon Tyne, 1965); *Briggflatts* (London, 1966).

III. POSTHUMOUS PROSE. *A Note on Briggflatts* (Durham, 1989); *Three Essays* (Durham, 1994); *Basil Bunting on Poetry* (Baltimore and London, 1999).

IV. AS EDITOR. *Selected Poems of Ford Madox Ford* (Cambridge, Mass., 1971); *Selected Poems of Joseph Skipsey* (Sunderland, 1976).

V. INTERVIEWS. Jonathan Williams, *Descant on Rawthey's Madrigal: Conversations with Basil Bunting* (Lexington, Ky., 1968); Jonathan Williams, "An Interview with Basil Bunting," in Conjunctions 5 (1983).

VI. CRITICAL STUDIES. Charles Tomlinson, "Experience into Music: The Poetry of Basil Bunting," in *Agenda* 4, no. 3 (Autumn 1966); *Basil Bunting: Man and Poet (Orono, Maine, 1981); Michael Heyward, "Aspects of Briggflatts,"* in Scripsi 1, nos. 3 and 4 (April 1982); Hilary Clark, "Briggflatts and the Cadence of Memory," in Sagetrieb 8, nos. 1 and 2 (Spring and Fall 1989); Donald Davie, *Under Briggflatts: A History of Poetry in Great Britain 1960–1988* (Manchester, 1989); Andrew Lawson, "Basil Bunting and English Modernism," in *Sagetrieb* 9, nos. 1 and 2 (Spring and Fall 1990); Richard Price and James McGonigal, *The Star You Steer By: Basil Bunting and British Modernism* (Amsterdam and New York, 1990); Peter Quartermain, *Basil Bunting: Poet of the North* (Durham, 1990); Victoria Forde, *The Poetry of Basil Bunting* (Newcastle upon Tyne, 1991); Peter Makin, *Basil Bunting: The Shaping of His Verse* (Oxford, 1992); Richard Caddel, ed., *Sharp Study and Long Toil: Basil Bunting Special Issue of Durham University Journal* (Durham, 1995); Ronald Johnson, "Take a Chisel to Write: Key to Briggflatts," in *Sagetrieb* 14, no. 3 (Winter 1995); Richard Caddel and Anthony Flowers, *Basil Bunting: A Northern Life* (Newcastle upon Tyne, 1997); Tom Pickard, "Sketches from My Voice Locked In: The Lives of Basil Bunting," in *Chicago Review 44, nos. 3 and 4* (1998); John Seed, "An English Objectivist? Basil Bunting's Other England," in *Chicago Review* 44, nos. 3 and 4 (1998); Carroll F. Terrell, ed., Keith Tuma, "Briggflatts, Melancholy, Northumbria," in *Fishing by Obstinate Isles: Modern and Postmodern British Poetry and American Readers* (Evanston, Ill., 1998); Keith Alldritt, *The Poet as Spy: The Life and Wild Times of Basil Bunting* (London, 1999).

CHARLES DARWIN

(1809–1882)

Richard Davenport-Hines

CHARLES DARWIN, AUTHOR of *The Origin of the Species* and *The Descent of Man*, was England's foremost nineteenth-century scientist and one of the greatest revolutionaries in the history of ideas. He worked a revolution not only in the natural sciences but in every branch of human thought. His books provided the most novel answer of the millennium to the great existential question: "Why are there people?" He conceived a theory of evolution that rested on accident and chance rather than the design of God. It stated that species naturally transmutated. In his lifetime his views were almost universally accepted by expert opinion in Europe and much of the United States. By the time of his death, Darwin was recognized as "the greatest intellect of the nineteenth century" by the London magazine *The Athenaeum*, which had earlier opposed his ideas. "The importance of Mr. Darwin's discoveries to science and the fact that his views have revolutionized many of its branches and strongly affected them all have long been recognized," its obituary proclaimed. "His influence has modified in the most momentous manner the whole thought and feeling of the civilized world. It is impossible to estimate at present the magnitude of the effect which he has produced and will produce. His great theory grows in strength day by day, receives daily wider and wider allegiance, and steadily extends its influence everywhere" (*The Athenaeum*, 29 April 1882).

EARLY LIFE

CHARLES Robert Darwin was born in Shrewsbury, a prosperous English country town, on 12 February 1809, the fifth child and second son of Robert Waring Darwin (1766–1848), a Shropshire physician and fellow of the Royal Society.

Dr. Darwin was a shrewd financier as well as a successful and energetic medical man. He provided mortgages and loans to several families involved in the burgeoning enterprises of the West Midlands during a crucial phase of England's Industrial Revolution. The success of these investments meant that his son Charles had a comfortable private income throughout his life. Dr. Darwin's business contacts were doubtless aided by his wife's connections: Susannah Darwin (1765–1817) was the favorite daughter of Josiah Wedgwood, owner of a famous pottery factory and historically one of the more important figures in the industrialization of England. She died when Charles Darwin was eight years old. His father was a man of overpowering personality who dominated conversations with exhausting monologues; in his misery after his wife's death, his wit soured into sarcasm. Charles Darwin revered his father, who was a highly intelligent, well-read, and generous man. However, partly as a result of his father's irritability, he became a self-critical little boy, who continued as an adult to reproach himself for exaggerated or imaginary failings. He lived at times in a reverie, inventing elaborate stories, which characteristically he later condemned as lies.

It was painful to him, and disappointing to his father, that his schoolmarks were consistently middling, for the family was educationally high achieving. Charles Darwin went to Edinburgh University in 1825 to study medicine but was disgusted by dissecting bodies, worried by sick people and horrified by witnessing two gruesome operations conducted without anesthesia. He despised his complacent lecturer on human anatomy, who sometimes read to the students of the 1820s from his own grandfather's lecture notes. Accordingly, after two years, Dr. Darwin decided that his son should become a clergyman, and in 1828 Charles was sent to Christ's College, Cambridge, where he took his degree in 1831. Overall, Darwin believed "that education and environment produce only a small effect on the mind of anyone, and that most of our qualities are innate" (*Life and Letters*, p. 22).

As a youth he was a keen sportsman but also a serious geologist and naturalist. The British government in 1831 commissioned a small ship, the H.M.S. *Beagle*, captained by Robert FitzRoy, to survey the coasts of South America. FitzRoy (who pioneered the barometer and founded weather forecasting) was willing to share his cabin with a young man who would act as his unpaid companion on the voyage and work as a naturalist. In the early nineteenth century phrenology and physiognomy (the supposedly scientific study of human character from head shapes and facial expressions) proposed deterministic views of human nature. These were so influential that Darwin was nearly rejected by FitzRoy as a companion because his nose signified lack of energy. At short notice, Darwin joined the expedition, which was scheduled to last for two years but continued for nearly five. After visiting Cape Verde and other Atlantic islands, the expedition surveyed the South American coast, including the Galapagos Islands. It afterward visited Tahiti, New Zealand, Australia, Tasmania, Keeling Island, the Maldives, Mauritius and St. Helena before returning to England in October 1836 via Brazil and the Azores. Although he later likened his notes from the voyage to those of "an *ignorant schoolboy*," they were the preparation for his life work (*Correspondence*, IV, p. 307). He regarded his explorations on FitzRoy's expedition as more of an education than school or university; his minute and careful observations of geology and other branches of natural history were the real training of his mind. He never again left Britain after 1836.

Between 1837 and 1839 Darwin wrote about nine hundred pages of notes in which he laid out the theory of evolution with which his name is associated. These notebooks do not suggest an orderly process of accumulating facts about animals and plants. Nor was he systematic in

rationalizing their meanings. Instead, they show an eruption of blazing creative ideas, which he wrote down in an almost disordered fashion. His creativity at this time, and his periods of depression in later life, suggested to the distinguished surgeon Sir Geoffrey Keynes, who married Darwin's granddaughter, that he suffered from bipolar disorder (manic depression). After the creative chaos of 1837–1839, Darwin was thoroughly systematic in his work. When preparing each of his books, he had a special set of shelves standing near his writing table, a shelf being devoted to the material that was destined to form each chapter. He wrote a thirty-five-page "sketch" of the theory in 1842 and a longer essay in 1844 but published neither. Instead, he continued collecting evidence and studying his specimens. He preferred observing to writing; but he was also deterred from publishing by his knowledge of the strong existing opposition to the idea of natural transmutation of species, and by the hostility of early Victorian scientists to theoretical schematizing. His intention was to draw on normalized scientific knowledge but then to organize it so as to construct a highly unconventional theory. He was uncomfortable with the knowledge that his views would seem heretical.

His father was so pleased with his achievements that he endowed him with an independent income in 1837; Darwin took a close personal interest in his investments and prospered for the rest of his days. Indeed, his skill in financial matters, and the commercial sales of his books, meant that by the end of his life he was an affluent man. Moreover, once his theories had been publicized, an unknown admirer—appropriately named Mr. Rich—left him a fortune.

Darwin's *Journal of Researches into the Geology and Natural History of the various countries visited by HMS Beagle* (1839) made his name familiar among many English readers. He prided himself on this engrossing, erudite, and amusing book. He described earthquakes, volcanic eruptions, icebergs, and striking geological features as well as the habits of ants, wasps, beetles, spiders, fish, reptiles, birds, and quadrupeds and the human inhabitants of the places he visited. Darwin's *Journal* conveyed the romance of the

Beagle's voyage to imaginative Victorians. In 1842 Darwin advanced a brilliant theory of the origin and distribution of coral reefs in his treatise *On the Structure and Distribution of Coral Reefs*, which secured his high reputation as a geologist. The processes of adaptive change that he described in coral reefs had their counterparts in his wider evolution theory. He also wrote a convincing and authoritative account of the rapid land elevation that was still forming the Andes Mountains.

His patience was inexhaustible. In 1842 he laid a layer of chalk on a patch of ground to study the interaction of vegetable mold and earthworms. He did not start work on the results until 1871. His last book, published in 1881, was on this subject. It is a rare type of human who can write books entitled *Origin of Species* and *Descent of Man* and then be satisfied watching worms. But it was typical of Darwin that he liked to make connections between very small phenomena and very great theoretical principles. From the time of the *Beagle* voyage, he developed his minute observations (whether of South American geology or the natives of Tierra del Fuega) into generalizations that were global and universal in their applications. This required the most concentrated, strenuous, and persistent effort of scientific imagination. He was so full of brilliant ideas, and worked so steadily, with such mature experience, that he gained for the world an astonishing amount and variety of new knowledge.

HOME LIFE AND CHARACTER

IN 1839 Darwin married his first cousin and lifelong friend Emma Wedgwood (1808–1896), having written to her before the wedding, "I think you will humanize me, and soon teach me there is greater happiness, than building theories, and accumulating facts in silence and solitude" (*Correspondence*, II, p. 166). Their marriage was devoted. They had six sons (of whom the youngest was born when his mother was aged forty-eight, had Down Syndrome, and died of scarlet fever at the age of eighteen months) and four daughters (the second of whom died aged three

weeks). From 1842 he lived the life of a country gentleman at a house called Down, southwest of London, near Bromley, in Kent. He was a respectable, cautious neighbor who disliked shocking or upsetting people; in 1857 he became a magistrate. Although many of his contemporaries assumed that the illustrious man was a professor, he never fulfilled any formal educational duties.

His first breakdown in health occurred in 1839, three days before the birth of his son William. He was incapable of serious work for eighteen months. Thereafter he suffered from dyspepsia, eczema, anxiety, and vertigo. He complained of palpitations, extreme flatulence, vomiting, sometimes preceded by trembling or hysterical weeping. Another medical crisis occurred in 1848–1849 during his father's terminal illness and after his death. A final serious breakdown followed in 1863–1864. During the last year or so of his life, he suffered angina attacks, eventually dying from one. It is possible that his ailments were caused by Chagas's Disease, a common infection in South America transmitted by a bug bite. Other twentieth-century writers suggested that the palpitations and some other symptoms were attributable to Da Costa's Syndrome, now better known as hyperventilation. This, in other words, means that he suffered panic attacks caused by anxiety. Darwin's father recognized that his illnesses were stress-related and tried to minimize the trouble. As Darwin complained on one occasion, "I told him of my dreadful numbness in my finger ends, & all the sympathy I could get, was 'yes yes exactly—tut-tut, neuralgic, exactly yes yes'—nor will he sympathise about money, 'stuff & nonsense' is all he says to my fears of ruin" (*Correspondence*, II, p. 399). For nearly forty years his life was one long struggle against the weariness and the strain of sickness. In the later years of his life, Emma Darwin never left him for a night and planned her days so that she could shield him from stress and weariness.

Although Darwin sometimes used medical sedatives to surmount his anxiety-related illnesses, his most effective escape from anxiety and depression was in concentrated thought. Overworking gave him the relaxation or emotional oblivion that other contemporaries sought in opiate drugs. He was "never comfortable except when at work," he wrote in 1861. "The word Holiday is written in a dead language for me, & much I grieve at it" (*Correspondence*, IX, p. 20). After his serious psychosomatic breakdown in 1863 he wrote, "Unless I can work a little, I hope my life may be very short; for to lie on a sofa all day & do nothing, but give trouble to the best & kindest of wives & good dear children is dreadful" (*Correspondence*, XI, p. 666). His anxiety and ailments meant that for periods of his life he was almost a recluse. "All excitement & fatigue brings on such dreadful flatulence; that in fact I can go nowhere," he explained, "I live a very retired life in the country, & for months together see no one out of my own large family" (*Correspondence*, V, pp. 91, 100). Even guests in the house upset his routine. "I have had the House full of visitors, & when I talk I can do absolutely nothing else" (*Correspondence*, V, p. 20). Living as a semi-invalid, but developing evolutionary theories about the survival of the fittest, "it has been a bitter mortification for me to digest the conclusion that 'the race is for the strong'" (*Correspondence*, II, p. 298). As an invalid, incapable of traveling, he devoured the travel books of other writers, and bombarded them with detailed questions about the geology, plants and creatures of places he could never visit. "I feel a great interest about Australia, and read every book I can get hold of," he declared in 1853 (*Correspondence*, V, p. 164). His imaginative life was rich and powerful: he liked to fantasize about leaving Kent to live somewhere more exotic and distant. "I am always building veritable castles-in the air about emigrating, & Tasmania has been my head quarters of late," he wrote in 1854 (*Correspondence*, V, pp. 180–181).

Darwin was a tender, affectionate parent. He was unusual among Victorian men in being actively involved in the birth of his children. At a time when many Victorians cited Genesis III: 316 ("In pain you shall bring forth your children") in opposition to the use of anesthesia in childbirth, Darwin was a pioneer of the practice. In 1850 he proudly administered chloroform before

the doctor came and kept his wife unconscious to protect her from pain when their fourth son was born. Darwin enjoyed kissing his babies, delighted in romping with them, and, unlike most Victorian fathers, bathed his children when they were small. He studied the physical and mental development of his son William meticulously, and scrutinized both his expressions and the apparent differences between instinctual and learned behavior. On one occasion he sneezed loudly next to the baby and made him cry; on another occasion Darwin started loud snoring noises as a test, which also made William cry. "This is curious considering the wondrous number of strange noises, & stranger grimaces I have made at him & which he has always taken as a good joke. I repeated the experiment" (Browne, *Darwin*, I, p. 430).

His love for his children influenced his development of evolution theory. In 1851 his eldest daughter and favorite child Annie became fatally ill. He nursed her through this illness (his wife was absent) with great tenderness. Annie rallied briefly—"I was foolish with delight & pictured her to myself making custards"—but after ten days, exhausted by vomiting and diarrhea, she died (*Correspondence*, V, p. 20). Her parents' grief was intense. Darwin's sisters had insisted that no reference could be made to their mother after her death, and he revived this stressful practice after Annie's death. This repressive way of coping with grief may have aggravated his tendency to anxiety attacks. The fact that he believed that Annie had inherited her physical weaknesses from him, and had failed to evolve from them, added a painful urgency to his thoughts on human evolution. His mother had died of gastric illness (possibly stomach cancer) and he was obsessed with his own digestive difficulties. "My dread is hereditary ill-health," he wrote a year after Annie's death. Even when "all the chicks" were "right well," he still worried about their fitness to survive: "the worst of my bugbears, is hereditary weakness" (*Correspondence*, V, pp. 84, 100). The illness of Annie's surviving siblings persistently disturbed and distracted him. "For the last ten days our darling little fellow Lenny's health has failed, *exactly* as three of our children's have done before," he wrote in near panic in 1857. "It makes life very bitter." The anxiety had made him ill, too (*Correspondence*, VI, p. 460).

His constant self-criticism, though it sometimes resulted in unjustifiable self-despising, helped him to be a wonderfully flexible thinker. The positive counterpart of being so anxious was that he was never smug about himself, his ideas, or his achievements. He was willing to renounce any pet notion as soon as facts became irreconcilable to it. His "golden rule" was to put every fact opposed to his preconceived opinions in the strongest light. He was also willing to explore any hypothesis. During his last years he investigated whether plants could hear a bassoon. His minute and painstaking researches seem to have dulled what he called his "higher tastes," or aesthetic senses. "My mind seems to have become a kind of machine for grinding general laws out of large collections of facts." Until the age of thirty, the poetry of Milton, Gray, Byron, Wordsworth, Coleridge and Shelley "gave me great pleasure, and even as a schoolboy I took intense delight in Shakespeare," he recalled. "But now for many years I cannot endure to read a line of poetry; I have tried lately to read Shakespeare and found it so intolerably dull that it nauseated me." He had also lost his early taste for pictures and music. "Music generally sets me thinking too energetically on what I have been at work on, instead of giving me pleasure" (*Autobiography*, pp. 138–139).

While continuing to accumulate information on evolution theory, Darwin also spent eight years on a different research project classifying the marine crustacea known as barnacles. This was an immense project, which was published during the early 1850s but had little bearing on his main work. As he wrote in 1848, when he was engaged on the barnacle work, "there exists, & I feel within me, an instinct for truth, or knowledge or discovery, of something the same nature as the instinct of virtue, & that our having such an instinct is reason enough for scientific researches, without any practical results *ever* ensuing from them" (*Correspondence*, IV, p. 128). His methods were slow, painstaking, and methodical.

In the 1850s he fancied settling in the midwest of the United States. The republic and its democratic politics interested him greatly. "I wish to God, though at the loss of millions of lives, that the North would proclaim a crusade against Slavery," he wrote in 1861. "A million horrid deaths would be amply repaid in the cause of humanity. What wonderful times we live in" (*Correspondence*, IX, p. 163). He regretted the political tensions between Great Britain and the United States. "For many years," he wrote in 1863 to his American friend Asa Gray (professor of natural history at Harvard), "your Government delighted in making us eat dirt, & this has greatly checked all sympathy with you." Reading a pamphlet about slavery "made me wish honestly for the North." He thought "it dreadful that the South, with its accursed Slavery, should triumph, & spread the evil" (*Correspondence*, XI, pp. 166–167).

This lovable man inspired great devotion in his friends. He persuaded an extraordinarily diverse number of people to collect specimens for his researches. One of his friends, the vicar of a Suffolk village, recruited the little girls of his parish into a botanical club supplying him with seeds. He also enlisted his butler, country squires, professors, colonial governors, high diplomats, and other international celebrities into obtaining specimens or information for him. Even his own household pets were enlisted to further his study of evolution. Altogether he had a talent for writing flattering or deferential letters to august figures, and to other great scientists, intended to extract information, advice, and specimens to use in his research. He had a wonderful network of friends and admirers in the community of science—partly because he did not crave celebrity. He had a humility that derived from constant, sometimes crippling self-criticism. Although he enjoyed his achievements, he was not vain, and he was shocked when scientific disagreements became personalized or vindictive. "What wretched doings come from the ardor of fame; the love of truth alone would never make one man attack another bitterly" (*Correspondence*, IV, p. 140).

CHARLES DARWIN

EVOLUTION THEORY

DARWIN did not invent evolutionary ideas. The Scottish judge Lord Monboddo had become a laughingstock for suggesting in 1773 that humankind were of the same species as the orangutan, and that humanity was gradually elevating itself from an animal condition, partly by its use of complex language. Other thinkers, notably the French naturalist Jean-Baptiste Lamarck, argued that humans had evolved from animal life forms, and that species were mutable rather than unchanging. Lamarck, though, insisted in his *Zoological Philosophy* (1809) on the "perfection" of "the established order" ordained by the creator. "What appears to be disorder, confusion, anomaly, incessantly passes again into the general order, and even contributes to it; everywhere and always, the will of the Sublime Author of nature and of everything that exists is invariably carried out" (Hawkins, *Social Darwinism*, p. 42). The theories of Lamarck and Monboddo, however, failed to satisfy scientific workers. It had been known by *savants* for some time that the fossils found in the earliest geological strata were of simple organisms, that later strata contained fossils of increasing complexity, and that mammals were only found in the most recent strata. Moreover, many fossilized species had become extinct. In Darwin's youth, the distinguished geologist Sir Charles Lyell discredited the orthodox view of the present as a geologically static period in contradistinction to the past as a formative period in which geological processes had sculpted the earth over a huge period of time. Lyell showed that geological processes were continuously operating. Such observations seemed hard to reconcile with the prevalent Christian view that the world, and its species, had been created by God in a week—according to one archbishop's calculations, in 4004 B.C. Several theories had been advanced to explain geologists' new fossil observations. These rested on the idea of a sudden catastrophe leading to an abrupt and drastic change in fauna. Among intellectuals interested in such subjects, it was assumed that each species was distinct and unchanging from every other species, and that all changes were part of a steady progression toward perfection: humankind was generally regarded as the apotheosis of creation.

During his voyage, probably in 1834, Darwin began pondering the species problem. In the Galapagos Islands he found a variety of different bird species only slightly differing from one another. On returning to England he confirmed in 1837 that there were three different species of mockingbird, each confined to its own island in the Galapagos archipelago, and that these species were closely related to the prevalent species on the nearest mainland, South America. From these facts, he deduced that all three Galapagos species descended from birds that had arrived from South America: species were therefore not unchanging. Moreover, the fact that the differences among the three species were slight indicated that the evolution of species was not sudden or caused by an abrupt catastrophic change but gradual. The Galapagos evidence indicated to Darwin that the isolation of populations from one another was conducive to change.

Sir Charles Lyell had raised the idea of the gradual extinction of species (rather than their abrupt death in major natural catastrophes or by sudden climate changes). Darwin wondered whether the birth of species might also be gradual. Arguably the most decisive literary influence on his evolution theory was his reading in 1838 of the Reverend Thomas Malthus' *Essay on the Principle of Population* (1798). Malthus was an English economist who noted that population increased geometrically while food levels increased mathematically. He concluded that as human population levels would outgrow the means of subsistence, humankind was doomed to suffer the miseries of overpopulation. Darwin, who was already convinced of the struggle for existence, was stimulated by Malthus' book to rethink the meaning of the facts he had accumulated. The numbers of each species do not increase nearly as much as the numbers of young each produces. Only a few of each generation live to breed successfully; hunger and predators kill the majority. Under these breeding conditions, he concluded, favorable variations would tend to be preserved and unfavorable ones destroyed. Nature was thus in a perpetual state of war. The successful few were clearly better adapted to survive in their environment. The result would be the formation of a new species. Having had these insights, he was appalled by the difficulties of convincing other people and did not hurry into print. Instead he collected evidence for twenty years before resolving to write up his ideas. In his efforts to explain the variation and origin of species, he began working in the 1850s on pigeons, poultry, ducks, and rabbits. He bought all the races of pigeons so as to watch them living and study their skeletons when dead. His researches were facilitated by the improved communication systems of the Victorian world. He was able, for example, to obtain live pigeons and fowl from Gambia in 1856.

He pondered the success of European breeders during the last fifty years in breeding advanced strains of animals, birds, and plants. Their method was to select types of special quality or with outstanding properties, and breed from them. He became convinced that such selective breeding had operated since ancient times as each race of people preserved and bred from individual animals that would be most useful to their circumstances. For example, humans bred one type of sheep for carpets and another to grow the wool for clothes. This sort of selective breeding enabled the different human races to adapt other living creatures, as well as plants, to their needs. Darwin's theory of evolution was a complete break from the evolutionary ideas of Lamarck or Monboddo because it rejected every precedent. In particular, three observations seemed to him incompatible with the story of creation in Genesis. Fossils from South America were related to the living fauna of that continent rather than to contemporaneous fossils of other continents; moreover, the fauna of different South American climatic zones were related to each other rather than to those of the same climatic zones of different continents. But most important of all, the fauna of the Galapagos Islands and the Falkland Islands were related to those of the nearest mainland, South America, while distinct but related species occur on different islands of the same archipelago.

While Darwin was laboriously investigating evolution in his gentle, unassuming way, the reading public was impressed by a flamboyant, scientifically reckless book, *Vestiges of the Natural History of Creation* (1844) written by a Scottish journalist. *Vestiges* had such success that the fashionable novelist and future prime minister Benjamin Disraeli parodied its arguments in *Tancred* (1847). One of the novel's sillier characters, Lady Constance Rawleigh, discusses a new book called *Revelations of Chaos*. "First, there was nothing, then there was something; there were shells, then fishes; then we came we are a link in the chain, as inferior animals were that preceded us: we in turn shall be inferior. We had fins; we may have wings" (*Tancred*, pp. 109–110). Then in 1858 Darwin was sent a manuscript written by Alfred Russel Wallace (1823–1913), a young researcher working in Borneo. On reading it, he saw that Wallace had independently developed the same theory of variation and natural selection as his own. It was decided to read Wallace's essay together with extracts from Darwin's work to a meeting of a learned biological society in London on 1 July 1858. This may be regarded as the birthdate of Darwinian theory. Although in retrospect this meeting in 1858 was arguably the most momentous of any learned society in history, it did not cause any immediate intellectual convulsion. In his disappointment, Darwin immediately began writing a book which was published in 1859 as *The Origin of the Species by Means of Natural Selection, or the Preservation of Favoured Races in the Struggle for Life.*

The first edition sold out on the first day. Darwin was delighted by its commercial success. The book had tremendous impact because it was elegantly conceived, authoritatively argued, ambitious, and contentious. Its author's extreme anxiety, and his dislike of uncertainty, contributed to his deep respect for authority, including the laws of nature, and this struck a chord with contemporary readers. His intentions were not reductive: he marveled at the wonderful diversity of nature. He thought that every living species was in the process of evolution and that most species would eventually become extinct. He predicted that common, widely dispersed species would prevail and procreate new dominant species. In Darwin's creed, as one reviewer uneasily summarized it, "Man in his view was born yesterday—he will perish to-morrow. In place of being immortal, we are only temporary, and, as it were, incidental" (*The Athenaeum*, 19 November 1859, p. 659). He seemed to discredit absolute morality and absolute truth. Darwin's revelations led the influential philosopher and critic Walter Pater to comment in 1866, "To the modern spirit nothing is, or rightly can be known, except relatively" (Matthew, *The Nineteenth Century*, p. 214).

Darwin argued that the different forms of life had gradually developed from common ancestry. He believed that animals were descended from only four or five progenitors, and plants from an equal or lesser number. By analogy, he further argued that all animals and plants descended from one prototype. Every species was striving to the utmost to increase in numbers: they survived if they were strong and well adapted to their conditions but perished if weak or ill adapted. Heavy destruction fell either on the young or old, during each generation or at recurrent intervals, for otherwise the species would procreate so prolifically as to overrun the world. Every species possessed a capacity of variation in more or less degree. If such variation gave an advantage over its fellows or its neighbors, it was likelier to survive. There was a disposition to propagate such modification of form or structure to the offspring—Herbert Spencer's descriptive phrase "the survival of the fittest" helped to spread a clear understanding of his theory. The change was often very slight, but it gradually tended, if really advantageous to the animal, to become more and more marked in successive generations; and at length a being had evolved that was so different from the original stock as to merit the name of a new species. Domesticated animals were usually more variable than wild animals because natural selection tended to fix the type according to local conditions, so that individual divergences were soon lost, while artificial selection abolished the struggle for existence and permitted new forms to be preserved. Darwin reveled in the variety and energy of the species

without idealizing perfection or design. He celebrated the unique, the aberrant, the deviant, and the grotesque. He accepted calmly the sovereignty of chance in the world. Although order existed in the natural world, it did so randomly; there were patterns, but these had been formed by a very long sequence of accidents. The appearance of purpose in the intricate design of living things, as well as their adaptation to their environment, seemed to him illusory. Human life and human society were heavily influenced, if not ruled, by biological factors.

Darwin's theory of evolution contradicted the biblical story of creation, and he lost any belief in Genesis. Against the previous view of natural theology, he taught that nature was without purpose, teleology, or choice. Human beings, accordingly, had no free will whatsoever. The existence of natural laws did not imply, for him, a lawgiver or a purpose to be served. He found it exhilarating rather than scary that throughout nature there were surprises, aberrations, and exceptions to the rule. His theories were vehemently preached against and reviled. Cardinal Henry Manning, archbishop of Westminster and leader of the Roman Catholic community in England, denounced him for relieving God of the "labour of creation," and the historian and moralist Thomas Carlyle for propagating "A Gospel of Dirt." At a meeting in Oxford of the British Association for the Advancement of Science in 1860, Samuel Wilberforce, bishop of Oxford, denounced Darwinian theory in wild and blustering language. The gifted young anatomist Thomas Huxley, who had become a fervent protector of Darwin's ideas and reputation, answered the bishop in a famous speech, which added to the momentum of evolution theory. Later, at another Oxford meeting, Benjamin Disraeli, by now the Conservative prime minister, attacked the "glib assurance" of Darwinism. "The question is this—is a man an ape or an angel? *I am on the side of the angels.* I repudiate with indignation and abhorrence these new-fangled theories" (*Wit and Wisdom of Benjamin Disraeli, Earl of Beaconsfield* [1883], p. 309). During twelve years of fierce controversy between 1860 and 1872 Huxley continued to protect Darwin. Although Darwin was perplexed by the tone of some opponents, he was amused when he arrived to receive an honorary degree from Oxford University and undergraduates dangled a monkey from the roof of the Senate House. He started featuring as a character in fashionable novels. He is Professor Long, author of *Researches into the Natural History of Limpets*, in Edward Bulwer-Lytton's *What will he do with it?* (1858). Roger Hamley, the romantic hero of Elizabeth Gaskell's *Wives and Daughters* (1864), was partly inspired by Darwin.

Despite his detractors, for many educated nineteenth-century Europeans the first reading of *The Origin of Species* was tantamount to an intellectual birth. In the United States, too, it was influential. Henry Adams recalled his reaction to Darwinism after the American Civil War. "Unbroken Evolution under uniform conditions pleased everyone—except curates and bishops; it was the best substitute for religion; a safe, conservative, practical, thoroughly Common-law deity." Darwin's "working system for the universe," according to Adams, "was only too seductive in its perfection; it had the charm of art" (*Education*, p. 926). By 1872 Darwin felt that his evolutionary theory had been largely accepted. He lived to see the remodeling not merely of zoology and botany but of literary imagination, psychology, political history, and social thought as a result. By giving evolution of the species priority over evolution of the individual, Darwinian theory installed chance and accident as the primary movers of human experience and reduced the importance of human will or desire. The plots of such leading nineteenth-century novelists as George Eliot, Anthony Trollope, and Thomas Hardy were influenced by his ideas of order without design. The decisive power of chance, not providence, in determining rewards for virtue and retribution for vice invalidated the Christian conception of rewards and punishments. Moreover, the intellectual impact of *Origin* seemed to reduce the standing of theology as a key to human behavior, and it enhanced the status of historians. Victorians increasingly sought an understanding of the human condition somewhat less from clergy in their pulpits and rather more from scholars tracing the patterns, and conceivably learning the lessons, of the past.

Darwin was so keen to convince readers of *Origin* of his argument about transmutation of species that he skirted the question of humankind's place in evolutionary theory. Initially, he left friends such as Huxley and Lyell to discuss the implications of Darwinian theory for the origins of mankind. For over a decade after the publication of *Origin* he concentrated on defending transmutation, and only when satisfied that he had converted the scientific community to his views was he willing to satisfy public interest with a full and formal account of his views on human origins. Finally, in *The Descent of Man, and Selection in Relation to Sex* (1871), he presented the anatomical evidence for human-kind's animal origins. As a young species, differentiated into several geographically distinct races, humankind provided strong supporting evidence for the theory of transmutation. He regarded his own species as only one among many to be studied: he rejected the prevalent orthodoxy that humanity possessed unique characteristics defying scientific analysis. His view of humanity derived from his encounter, on the *Beagle* in 1832, with the inhabitants of Tierra del Fuego. They were naked, daubed in paint, with long, tangled hair, mouths frothing excitedly, and savage in all their ways. Their signs and expressions seemed less intelligible to him than those of domesticated animals, and he felt that the difference between a savage and civilized man was greater than that between wild and domesticated animals. Seeing a primitive people in its native environment was as exciting for him as watching a tiger tearing into its prey in the jungle—and as significant. In *The Descent of Man* he arrayed a mass of detail indicating that higher apes had a closer resemblance to humans than they did to the lower primates. Humans and higher apes carried the same parasites and reacted similarly to different drugs. It was hubris to deny that mankind and other vertebrates were constructed on the same general model.

Darwin liked to interpret humans and animals in terms of one another. He believed that the English aristocracy, by its selective breeding, tended to be more handsome than the middle class. He had no intention of insulting the middle class: for him the duke of Buckingham and Chandos (with a long pedigree reflected in his surname, Temple-Nugent-Chandos-Brydges-Grenville) was on the same level as a carefully bred greyhound. Darwin's intention was to humanize nature and break down the demarcation between humans and other creatures. Humans were not exempt from the natural laws that governed the rest of earthly life. His object was to show that there was no fundamental difference between the mental faculties of mankind and the higher mammals. His processes were anthropomorphic. Thus he compared the appearance of a family dog, Squib, after it had clambered on a table to eat some meat, to that of a criminal who has stolen; he thought they evinced similar shame. He considered the attraction of the peahen to the peacock similar to that of a woman to a handsome man made attractive by his nose or his whiskers. In *Descent* he even drew an analogy between a dog's love for its master and a human's devotion to his God. If, as Darwin believed, dogs were capable of spirituality, and the belief system of primitive peoples was ignorant and fearful superstition, the status of Christianity and other great world religions seemed to be reduced.

In *The Descent of Man*, Darwin also examined the part that sexual selection played in evolution. He believed that some female animals chose their mates, or changed their mates, on the basis of individually subjective attraction: he wrote of sexual choice as a question of fashion. If women selected their mates according to attractive physical or mental characteristics, then the children they bred would change over generations toward that ideal; unconsciously, the human race was changing its breeding patterns, and therefore human characteristics were adapting. His account of sexual selection was framed to stress the similarities between humans and other creatures, including birds. His views on sexual selection disconcerted his Victorian readers and remain provocative in the twenty-first century to Christians and feminists alike. Later readers may be offended by another argument in the book. It criticized civilized people for trying to reduce the

impact of natural selection by building asylums for the mad or mentally retarded, rest homes for the maimed, and convalescent hospitals for the chronically ill. He faulted physicians for trying to save the life of everyone to the last moment. As a result, civilized societies were enabling the weak and defective to propagate their kind, which was highly injurious to humanity, as breeders of domestic animals well knew.

The arguments and evidence in *The Descent of Man* had a sequel in another book published by Darwin a year later. His new book was his most explicit account of human origins and, in some respects, his most personal book. Its research had begun more than thirty years earlier. The birth of his eldest child William in 1839 had prompted Darwin to study the boy's emergent emotional expressions. The behavior, emotions, voluntary, and involuntary actions of Annie and the other children were similarly scrutinized. He filled notebooks with speculations about human behavior, instinct, and will. As his biographer Janet Browne has written, "Darwin responded to fatherhood in the same distinctive way that he responded to all new phenomena—by sitting down and recording the baby's development as if it were a barnacle or a primrose, turning his private life into a scientific essay, his family into facts" (Kohn, *Darwinian Heritage*, p. 307). In January 1868 he sent a questionnaire about expressions to Huxley with a message for his wife: "Give Mrs. Huxley the enclosed, and ask her to look out when one of the children is struggling and just going to burst out crying." He was interested in the movement and shape of the Huxley children's eyebrows when they were distressed. "A dear young lady near here plagued a very young child for my sake, till it cried, and saw the eyebrows for a second or two beautifully oblique, just before the torrent of tears began" (Sir Francis Darwin and A. C. Seward, eds., *More Letters of Charles Darwin*, I [1903], p. 287). Children's faces displayed the smallest emotional changes in emphatic and apparently uncomplicated ways, but he also set out to compare the gestures and expressions of human beings across the world. Eventually he was ready to publish his conclu-

CHARLES DARWIN

sions in *The Expression of the Emotions in Man and Animals* (1872).

This extraordinary book extended his argument that humans were not an utterly separate creation from animals and provided the material for a revolution in attitudes to nonhuman animals—although this revolution did not occur. Darwin discussed with a welter of detail the facial expressions, posture, and gestures of human beings and the commoner animals. He analyzed how cats purr with pleasure, dogs wag their tails, and how humans, dogs, and cats can all bite as a way of expressing affection. Darwin's detailed scrutiny of animal behavior is written with an attractive sense of wonder at the variety of the animal kingdom. He showed that animals were capable of love, memory, curiosity, and sympathy. He liked to list pleasant characteristics in animals—the great Scottish novelist Sir Walter Scott, for example, had a greyhound called Maida, which grinned with happiness, and Darwin reports that this habit was common in terriers and had been seen in spitzes and sheepdogs (he might have added Labradors and Dalmatians, too). The way humans purse their lips when concentrating or remembering, and expose their canine teeth when angry, were among many other subjects of comparison and analysis. Some human expressions, such as the bristling of the hair when terrified, or the uncovering of the teeth when enraged, were incomprehensible to him except on the belief that humans previously existed in a much lower animal-like condition. The similarities of certain expressions in distinct though allied species, including the movements of facial muscles during laughter by humans and various monkeys, supported belief in their descent from a common progenitor. Darwin cited the cases of horses, setters, pointers, pigeons, and humans to argue that movements are inherited. He recounted the case of a man with a large nose who used to hit it vigorously when asleep. The man's son inherited this idiosyncrasy, as did the son's daughter.

Darwin reproduced more than two hundred photographs in his text to illustrate his arguments. He particularly scrutinized the facial expressions of sorrow and of joy. Eyes and eyelids, he thought, were the key to understanding these emotional expressions. In the course of his delightful chapter entitled "Joy, High Spirits, Love," Darwin noted: "Mr. B. F. Hartshorne states in the most positive manner that the Weddas of Ceylon never laugh. Every conceivable incitive to laughter was used in vain. When asked whether they ever laughed, they replied, 'No, what is there to laugh at?'" (*Expression*, p. 208). He concluded that laughter was fundamental to the origin of happy expressions but that weeping was superfluous to the expression of sorrow. Whereas expressions of sorrow or grief could be faked, joyous facial expressions were always authentic. Everyone could recognize a false smile for what it was; sham expressions of joy looked insincere or unconvincing. This was because a laughing mouth meant nothing without accompanying crinkled eyelids. Darwin obtained information on Australian aborigines and on the inmates of lunatic asylums. But because of the random dispersal of African Americans in the United States, and the interbreeding of white Americans from different European races, he largely excluded consideration of the U.S. population, which he considered contaminated for his particular purpose. He concluded that neither emotions nor expressions were unique to human beings; some animals share certain human emotions, and some animal expressions resemble human expressions. Human gestures (mainly hand movements) were not universal but acquired by imitation and learning, rather like spoken language. From these observations Darwin concluded that expressions were innate, not learned, and could therefore be incorporated into the service of evolution theory. He attempted to show that all the chief gestures and expressions of emotion exhibited by humankind were universal throughout the world, which supported the notion that they were descended from a single stock, and that in many important examples, these expressions resembled the movements and gestures of animals.

"Blushing is the most peculiar and the most human of all expressions," Darwin wrote. "Monkeys redden from passion, but it would require an overwhelming amount of evidence to make us believe that any animal could blush." He noted, as apparently no one had done before, that although "infants at an early age redden with passion," they never blush until between the ages of two and three (*Expression*, pp. 310–311). He collected examples from numerous cultures of "blushing—whether due to shyness—to shame from a breach of the laws of etiquette—to modesty from humility—to modesty from an indelicacy." Blushing distinguished humans from animals. He quoted Christian authorities who believed that blushing "was designed by the Creator in 'order that the soul might have sovereign power of displaying in the cheeks the various internal emotions of the moral feelings' [Burgess, *The Physiology or Mechanism of Blushing*, 1927 ed., p. 49]; so as to serve as a check on ourselves, and as a sign to others, that we were violating rules which ought to be held sacred." Darwin could not believe that any deity had "*specially* designed" blushing. It was so useless, especially among people with dark skins. "No doubt a slight blush adds to the beauty of a maiden's face; and the Circassian women who are capable of blushing, invariably fetch a higher price in the seraglio [harem] of the Sultan than less susceptible women. But the firmest believer in the efficacy of Sexual Selection will hardly suppose that blushing was acquired as a sexual ornament" (*Expression*, pp. 334–336). According to physicians whom Darwin consulted, blood vessels relaxed and filled with bright red arterial blood when attention was directed to any part of the human body. The face receives more attention than other bodily parts, and accordingly became progressively more susceptible to blushing. Because humans think that people are looking at their faces, their "self-attention" induces blushing. He wanted to compare blushing with sexual erections but realized that this would be too shocking to Victorian readers.

AFTERMATH

DARWIN'S ideas have filtered into every part of western culture. Edith Wharton considered her reading of Darwin at the age of twenty-two as the primary intellectual experience of her life. It provided her with a secular vision to replace her religious faith. As a result, according to a close friend, "the world was more wonderful, the problem more interesting, the moral obligation more stern and ennobling." She explained "the key" to her great novel *The House of Mirth* (1905) in Darwinian metaphors. "Nature, always apparently wasteful, and apparently compelled to create dozens of stupid people in order to produce a single genius, seems to reverse the process in manufacturing the shallow and the idle" (Preston, *Wharton's Register*, pp. 52–53, 55). The life of Lily Bart, the doomed heroine of *The House of Mirth*, is ruined by accidents, coincidences, or other people's expedience but never by their calculated or willed acts. Her attempts to adapt to a hostile environment fail. As another example, in Theodore Dreiser's novel *The Financier* (1912) Frank Cowperwood is inspired in his ruthless business career by watching a lobster and a squid competing with one another in a fishmonger's tank. Over the course of weeks the lobster takes nips from the squid until finally it dies. Cowperwood decides that this duel exemplifies the survival of the fittest and is analogous to all forms of life. Just as lobsters live on squids so strong men prey on the weak. The novel ends with another fish, the black grouper, which can adapt and camouflage itself to its surroundings. Its powers suggest, according to Dreiser, "that a beatific, beneficent, creative, overruling power" sometimes wills things that are "either tricky or deceptive"—or else that our faith in such a power is illusory (*The Financier*, 1927 ed., p. 510).

As Dreiser's novel showed, Darwinian evolutionary theory came to be presented as a sort of biological economics under free market conditions. The idea that human society could be perfected or human nature could be radically improved by human agencies seemed to be discredited by Darwinian theory. The agents for change had nothing to do with human intelligence or conscious acts. Evolution theory, under the guise of Social Darwinism, was enlisted to transfer the blame for social injustice and material inequality from society to nature and thus act as a bulwark of capitalism. People who prospered were held up as vindicating the principle of the survival of the fittest; poor and ill people proved their unfitness by failing. The randomness of natural evolution involved much wastage, as some mutations proved non-viable and others proved superfluous. So it was with humans in capitalist society.

Darwinism inspired the French novelist Émile Zola to write the twenty novels of the Rougon-Macquart series tracing the effects of hereditary traits passing down through different branches and generations of the same family. The most explicitly Darwinian of these novels is *Au bonheur des dames* [*The Ladies' Paradise*] (1883). Its central character, Octave Mouret, the highly competitive department store owner who is driving smaller retailers out of business, explains his driving power. "It's the wish to act," he exclaims. "You have an idea; you fight for it, you hammer it into people's heads, and you see it triumph" (*The Ladies' Paradise*, 1992 ed., p. 61). Mouret had many real-life counterparts in American big business. The multimillionaire Andrew Carnegie of the U.S. Steel Corporation acknowledged that ruthless competition "may be sometimes hard for the individual" but justified it as "best for the race, because it ensures the survival of the fittest in every department" (Andrew Carnegie, "Wealth," in *North American Review* 148 [1889], p. 655). John D. Rockefeller of Standard Oil used Darwinian ideas as an excuse for trusts and big corporations. "The growth of a large business is merely the survival of the fittest," he declared. "This is not an evil tendency in business. It is merely the working out of a law of Nature and a law of God." Others have tried to draw ethical ideas from the biological nature of humanity—usually implausibly. L. Ron Hubbard devised Dianetics as a program of personal salvation that has as its first law "the dynamic principle of existence is: survive!"

Darwin's cousin Sir Francis Galton took up the cause of eugenics from the 1880s. Eugenics was a middle-class program to apply the selective breeding techniques used on agricultural livestock to human beings. Supporters urged governments to improve the genetic condition of the human race by selective breeding. In the thirty years after Darwin's death, eugenics attracted many intellectuals and administrators in Europe and the United States who wanted to breed out the physically weak or the mentally backward. Several of the early twentieth-century pioneers of contraception were involved in the eugenics movement. Subsequently, eugenics was used as a vile racial pseudo-science by Adolf Hitler and the Nazis. In the 1880s the German philosopher Friedrich Nietzsche had propounded a variant of Darwinism whereby all human behavior was reduced to a single impulse, the will to power. Nietzsche believed that humankind must strive to re-create and perfect itself until it had accomplished a new race of "superman" who would dominate their human inferiors just as humankind dominated and exploited animals. His ideas were also later adopted, unscrupulously and inaccurately, by the Nazis. In addition, the German general Friedrich von Bernhardi in his book *Deutschland und der nächste Kreig* [*Germany and the Next War*] (1912) argued that the survival of the fittest could be ensured by conquering inferior races and by waging war against rival states in a sort of military "natural selection." Such sentiments raised the international tension in Europe in the prelude to the First World War.

As natural selection worked solely by and for the good of each being, it carried a tendency toward physical and mental perfection. Accordingly, Darwinism became an idealistic secular faith. "To other Darwinians—except Darwin—Natural Selection seemed a dogma," wrote Henry Adams. "It was a form of religious hope; a promise of ultimate perfection" (*Education*, p. 931). In the twentieth century, this trend in the Darwinian temper led to a robust counter-reaction in the United States (although not in Europe). A World Bible Conference held in Philadelphia in 1919 led to an intense campaign by Christian fundamentalists asserting the literal truth of the Bible in matters of science and history. In response to this lobbying, the Tennessee State Legislature in 1925 by a vote of 95-11 passed a new law stating that it was "unlawful for any teacher in any of the universities, normals and all other public schools of the state, to teach any theory which denies the story of the divine creation of man as taught in the Bible, and to teach instead that man has descended from a lower order of animals." (Mississippi in 1926, Arkansas in 1928, and Texas in 1929 passed similar legislation.) In a test case of July 1925, Thomas Scopes, a science teacher at Rhea High School in Dayton, Tennessee, was prosecuted for violating this law. The southern populist politician William Jennings Bryan came to Dayton to help the local prosecutor. Clarence Darrow, the most famous criminal lawyer of his generation, led the defense team in a case followed by millions of Europeans and Americans. Scopes was convicted and fined $100; Bryan received such a grueling cross-examination from Darrow on fundamentalist attitudes to biblical authority that he died a few days later.

Many Americans have continued to reject evolutionary theory. The Beat poet Gregory Corso felt like vomiting over Darwinian theory, as he wrote in his poem on the Kennedy assassination of 1963. In the U.S. presidential race of 1980, the two leading contenders, Jimmy Carter and Ronald Reagan, vied with each other in public declarations of their belief in the literal truth of the biblical story of creation. A Gallup opinion poll of 1991 in the United States found that 46 percent of respondents believed that "God created man pretty much in his present form at one time within the last 10,000 years." Forty percent believed that "Man has developed over millions of years from less advanced forms of life, but God guided this process, including man's creation." Nine percent believed "Man has developed over millions of years from less advanced forms of life. God had no part in this process." Five percent did not endorse any opinion. By contrast, a poll conducted in 2000 by Harris Interactive found that only 20 percent of the British people believe the human race was created by God (half the world average), and 80 percent subscribe to Darwinian evolution theory.

The new science of genetics is thought to be providing final clarification of some of the most difficult aspects of Darwinian theory. Until the 1960s many biological scientists subscribed to the idea that evolution tended to "the greater good." This notion that evolution is inherently progressive, "good," or "right" has since been generally discarded. Others still assert that an

interpretation of human nature based on evolution theory can help to identify appropriate social goals or the means to achieve them. As one example, the Canadian psychologists Martin Daly and Margo Wilson in *The Truth About Cinderella: A Darwinian View of Parental Love* note that the abused stepchild is a stock character in folklore. A wide variety of (mainly male) vertebrate and invertebrate animals kill the young of their deposed predecessors. Daly and Wilson use this knowledge to interpret their findings that in the United States a child in the 1980s had about one hundred times greater chances of being abused or killed by a stepparent than a genetic parent.

It is fairest to let Darwin speak for himself by quoting from one of his letters to Asa Gray:

With respect to the theological view of the question, this is always painful to me. I am bewildered. I had no intention to write atheistically. But I own that I cannot see, as plainly as others do, and as I should wish to do, evidence of design and benefice on all sides of us. There seems to me too much misery in the world. I cannot persuade myself that a beneficent and omnipotent God would have designedly created the Ichneumonidae [parasitic insects] with the express intention of their feeding within the living body of caterpillars, or that a cat should play with mice. On the other hand I cannot anyhow be contented to view this wonderful universe & especially the nature of man, & to conclude that everything is the result of brute force. I feel most profoundly that the subject is too profound for the human intellect. A dog might as well speculate on the mind of Newton.

(*Correspondence*, VIII, p. 224).

SELECTED BIBLIOGRAPHY

I. First Editions of Major Works. *Journals and Remarks, 1832–36* (London, 1839); *Zoology of the Voyage of H.M.S. "Beagle"* (London, 1840); *The Structure and Distribution of Coral Reefs* (London, 1842); *Geological Observations on the Volcanic Islands* (London, 1844); *Geological Observations on South America* (London, 1846); *On the Origin of Species by Means of Natural Selection, or the Preservation of Favoured Races in the Struggle for Life* (London, 1859); *The Variation of Animals and Plants under Domestication* (London, 1868); *The Descent of Man, and Selection in Relation to Sex* (London, 1871); *The Expression of the Emotions in Man and Animals* (London, 1872).

II. MODERN EDITION OF COLLECTED WORKS. Paul H. Barrett and R. B. Freeman, eds., *The Works of Charles Darwin*, volumes 1 to 10 (London, 1986), volumes 11 to 20 (London, 1988), volumes 21 to 29 (London, 1989).

III. MODERN EDITIONS OF INDIVIDUAL WORKS. Lady Barlow, ed., *The Autobiography of Charles Darwin, 1809–1882* (London, 1958); Robert Stauffer, ed., *Charles Darwin's Natural Selection* (1975); Paul H. Barrett, ed., *The Collected Papers of Charles Darwin*, 2 volumes (London, 1977); Richard Darwin Keynes, ed., *Charles Darwin's "Beagle" Diary* (London, 1988); Gillian Beer, ed., *The Origin of Species* (London, 1996); Harriet Ritvo, ed., *Variation of Animals and Plants under Domestication* (Baltimore, Md., 1998); *The Expression of the Emotions in Man and Animals*, third ed. with an introduction, afterword, and commentaries by Paul Ekman (London, 1998); Richard Darwin Keynes, ed., *Charles Darwin's Zoology Notes and Specimen Lists from HMS "Beagle"* (London, 2000).

IV. MODERN SELECTIONS OF HIS WORKS. Duncan M. Porter and Peter W. Graham, eds., *The Portable Darwin* (London, 1993); Mark Ridley, ed., *A Darwin Selection* (London, 1994); Frederick H. Burkhardt, ed., *Charles Darwin's Letters: A Selection 1825–1859* (London, 1996).

V. BIOGRAPHIES. Francis Darwin, *The Life and Letters of Charles Darwin* (London, 1887); Ralph Colp, *To Be an Invalid* (Chicago, 1977); Peter Brent, *Charles Darwin* (London, 1981); Frederick H. Burkhardt and S. Smith, eds., *The Correspondence of Charles Darwin*, 11 volumes (London, 1983–1999, still in progress); Edna Healey, *Wives of Fame* (London, 1986); John Bowlby, *Charles Darwin* (London, 1990); Michael White and John Gribbin, *Darwin, A Life in Science* (London, 1995); Janet Browne, *Charles Darwin*, vol. I (London, 1995), vol. II (London, 2002).

VI. CRITICAL STUDIES. Richard Hofstadter, *Social Darwinism in American Thought* (Boston, 1964); Gillian Beer, *Darwin's Plots* (London, 1983); David Kohn ed., *The Darwinian Heritage* (London, 1985); George Levine, *Darwin and the Novelists* (Chicago, 1991); Jerome Barkow, Leda Cosmides, and John Tooby, eds., *The Adapted Mind: Evolutionary Psychology and the Generation of Culture* (London, 1992); Paul Crook, *Darwinism, War and History* (London, 1994); Mike Hawkins, *Social Darwinism in European and American Thought 1860–1945* (London, 1997); Martin Daly and Margo Wilson, *The Truth about Cinderella: A Darwinian View of Parental Love* (London, 1998); Claire Preston, *Edith Wharton's Social Register* (New York, 2000).

GAVIN EWART

(1916–1995)

Alan Brownjohn

THERE IS PERENNIAL uncertainty about the precise status of "light verse" in the literary canon, the confusion beginning with how to define the term. When we see the words "Comic Verse" in the title of an anthology we think we know what it means: something patently funny and ridiculous (and probably harmless) that is designed to produce laughter, audible or silent; "Comic and Curious" suggests an added ingredient of oddity. "Naughty" or, less coyly, "Bawdy" verse we would similarly expect to be light; but we would realize that the words are telling us to expect a less or more shocking concentration on one particular area of human experience. On the other hand, "Humorous" Verse would appear to be making fewer demands on our experience or sensitivity; the contents of such a collection would surely have a wide and comfortable appeal.

Musical analogies might assist in this context. Mozart's *La Nozze di Figaro* is not a "light" opera in the sense that Donizetti's *L'Elisir d'Amore* is, nor is it a "light opera" or "operetta" like Offenbach's *Orpheus in the Underworld*. In each of the three a different degree of "lightness" is used in the treatment of a serious theme. They are all diverting, but they are also something more. With poetry, many of the greatest minds have shown a serene lightness of spirit when that is appropriate. And the finest practitioners of light verse have raised it above the level of easy diversion: they ask us not just to be entertained but to consider the message and register the craftsmanship. They know they deserve a reputation better than that of passing entertainers. Gavin Ewart's poetry is playful on the surface, sometimes wholly frivolous, often shocking and scandalously funny (a critic once complimented him on "growing old disgracefully"). But there is an underlying seriousness of intention. He writes books filled with poems—in an astonishing variety of forms—which for all the lubricious humor are compassionate and affirmative about the human condition.

The bulk of his writing came comparatively late. After a faltering start (checked by the Second World War) Ewart published well over a thousand pages of remarkable verse, most of it in the last third of a life of seventy-nine years. He perpetually crosses and recrosses the boundary between the absurd and the momentous: at one moment he deploys a formidable gift for parody or wicked burlesque, at the next his readers find a poem of moving personal candor and surprising innocence. Lecherous reverie and hilarious wordplay may give way to tenderness about married love and his children, and a poignant fear of aging and death. His many books and numerous smaller publications (hugely prolific, he never lost an opportunity to publish, in formats ranging from fine limited editions to ephemeral pamphlets) were collected in two immense collected editions, published in 1980 and 1990. Reading them is to feel awe at his youthful talent, shock at his explicitness, empathy with the sincerity of the personal poems, admiration at the skill of the pasticheur. But plain broad-minded delight was the reaction of most reviewers and ordinary readers when the books appeared.

He had an undisguised ambition to write as well as his masters (chief among them W. H. Auden) and be recognized, for all the ordinariness of some of his subjects, as a serious poet. He continually found fresh sources of inspiration in his reading of new verse, whether it was the patrician confessional poetry of Robert Lowell (see *85 Poems*, p. 11) or the calculatedly limp doggerel of "E. J. Thribb" (in the satirical magazine *Private Eye*), a specialist in the gentle deflation of reputations with jocular obituary tributes. But in the end Ewart's is a unique talent. The Scottish solemnity of his ancestors combined with the English rationality and gentlemanliness of his upbringing to produce a poetry that rebelled with mischievous originality against both. Neither of those cultures believed that pleasure was very respectable; Ewart made readers' enjoyment the principal purpose of his writing.

GAVIN Buchanan Ewart was born in London on 4 February 1916 to parents who were first cousins. His father was an agnostic Scottish gynecological surgeon and his mother (whose own father was also a surgeon) came from an English family with some Scottish ancestors. Ewart described himself on the jacket of his book *The New Ewart: Poems 1980–82* as being "of mainly Scottish descent." His paternal grandfather was a Darwinian, a professor of natural history at the University of Edinburgh: so a vein of unconventionality ran in the family. The father was later disappointed that his only son (there were two sisters) did not choose a career in medicine.

London remained Ewart's home all his life, and he came to seem wholly, even quintessentially, English. In dress, as photographs attest, he was formal with a touch of the bohemian. In manner he was infallibly gentle and courteous, though he had a reserve, or shyness, that could make him seem slightly severe at a distance. Throughout his life he spoke, slowly and deliberately, an immaculate standard English with no trace of a Scottish accent.

He wrote no memoirs or prose recollections of any length. Given the number of his celebrated literary friends and acquaintances, that was a pity. But the range and vigor of his poetry (where occasional reminiscences do in fact occur) more than compensates for the lack of them; that was where almost all his creative energy went. In conversation he enjoyed recalling the famous writers he had encountered (including W. B. Yeats and W. H. Auden), but he had no considerable stock of cherished anecdotes about them, and

little inclination to express opinions about their personalities. It was the work that mattered.

Ewart's education was of a traditional English upper middle-class, fee-paying kind, in a preparatory school in Kent between the ages of eight and thirteen and after that at Wellington College, a prestigious public school, until he went up to Cambridge University in 1934. At seventeen he was already writing accomplished and witty, distinctly daring, poetry, publishing some in the small but notable magazine *New Verse*, edited by Geoffrey Grigson, and, even more impressively, the BBC weekly journal the *Listener*. At Cambridge he was a scholar at Christ's College, for two years reading classics and then switching to English. He attended the lectures of I. A. Richards and his supervisor was F. R. Leavis, but he avoided the influence of the strenuous disciplines favored by these distinguished figures. He graduated in 1937 with a second-class degree, resolving to make his name as a poet. Literary connections (including an early friendship with the poet Stephen Spender) helped him to earn a living by working first as a seller of lithographs and then as a proofreader for Penguin Books. In his spare time he prepared a first volume, *Poems and Songs*, which appeared from R. A. Caton's somewhat notorious Fortune Press in 1939; but the outbreak of the Second World War drastically delayed the fulfillment of his early promise as a writer.

In 1940 he was conscripted into the Royal Artillery and stayed in the army until his demobilization in 1946. He saw service in North Africa and Italy, places that featured vividly in the British war poetry of the period, and rose to the rank of captain. But he was moved to produce very little verse in those years, and in an obituary tribute published when he died (in the *Daily Telegraph* in London), he is quoted as saying that he was incapable of "rushing about in a tank like [the poet] Keith Douglas writing poems between battles."

When his military service ended he obtained employment as a manager in the production of the books published by Editions Poetry London under its founder, the colorfully enthusiastic and erratic M. J. Tambimuttu. More secure and better-

GAVIN EWART

paid employment followed when Ewart joined the staff of the British Council. There he worked in an educational capacity, advising on books to be sent to the Council's centers overseas, and he continued to contribute to its journal for some years after he left in 1952 to join the first of four advertising agencies for which he worked over the next nineteen years. In 1956 he married Margaret ("Margo") Bennett; their children, Jane and Julian, were born in 1956 and 1958.

If Ewart's poetic production had ceased altogether with the war and the subsequent need to reconstruct his life after six years in the army, his work, reposing in one short and relatively obscure volume, would probably have been forgotten. But although he published virtually nothing during the years 1946 to 1963, his job provided contact with other writers then employed in advertising—notably the poets Peter Porter and Edwin Brock and the novelist William Trevor— and their literary colleagues.

Ewart is reported to have been writing some poems of his own in slack periods in the office. However, it was only when the poet Alan Ross, editor of the monthly *London Magazine*, urged him to produce a complete manuscript that he set to work seriously and finished *Londoners*, which appeared from Heinemann in 1964. It proved to be the first of a long and brilliant series of books and pamphlets: the reticent copywriter had suddenly become the unstoppable composer of exuberant, scandalous, and often touching light verse, rigorously crafted in a vast variety of poetic forms.

In 1971 he was made redundant without compensation from his last advertising agency, J. Walter Thompson, and, at fifty-five years old, resolved to live thereafter as a freelance author. The receipt of a Cholmondeley Award for Poetry in that year was financially helpful and provided timely encouragement. He supplemented his income with posts teaching senior students in a boys' school, at a college of continuing education, and as a writer-in-residence at Maria Grey College in Middlesex, and he reviewed for various newspapers. In 1981 he was made a Fellow of the Royal Society of Literature. In his sixties and seventies he derived great pleasure from tours abroad, particularly in Australia and the United States; in 1993 he wrote, "the award of which I am most proud is the Michael Braude Award for Light Verse that I was given in 1991 by the American Academy." He regarded the writing of light verse as a high vocation.

Ewart always encouraged the efforts of his peers and younger poets, regularly attending readings, an unobtrusive figure in the middle of the audience. He advised literary committees and served as chairman of the Poetry Society in 1978–1979. An attempt to become Oxford Professor of Poetry in 1984 failed. The professor is chosen by Oxford M.A.s, who have to attend in person to cast their votes, and both Peter Levi (the winner) and James Fenton (elected in 1994) secured much greater support from an electorate that prefers a local or an establishment incumbent.

Ewart never thrust his personal opinions on his public or on his friends; only those particularly determined to find out discovered that he remained all his life a moderate supporter of the left in politics, and was an agnostic, gratified to have been appointed an honorary associate of the Rationalist Press Association in 1993. All of the poems contained in his many books, with the exception of his verse for children and one later work, are included in the two large volumes, *The Collected Ewart, 1933–1980* and *Collected Poems 1980–1990*; the last, uncollected, volume is the substantial *85 Poems* of 1993. When he died, on 2 October 1995, he left a wide circle of readers and friends enriched by the published products of a fecund and resourceful talent. There would be even more riches for a future editor to unearth in the unpublished poems he sent out in his correspondence and preserved in his personal archive.

EARLY POEMS

IN a brief introduction to *The Collected Ewart, 1933–1980*, the poet declared that he had "aimed at completeness," omitting only the assemblage of short poems published the same year and called *All My Little Ones*. It is thus likely that the first three poems he includes, dating from when he was seventeen and eighteen years old, are among the first he ever wrote. One, "Phallus in Wonderland," is certainly the first he ever published (it appeared in *New Verse*), and a second, "Characters of the First Fifteen," would at least have had the limited circulation of an item in his school magazine if the master of Wellington College had not "vetoed it."

"Phallus in Wonderland" (the title is an arbitrary joke, having no apparent connection with the content of the poem) is a series of short statements or reflections in the mouths of a "Grammarian," an "Ancient," a "Sapient Man," a "Poet of the Generation," and others. The Poet praises one of the young Ewart's acknowledged influences, T. S. Eliot:

He gave us a voice, straightened each limb,
Set us a few mental exercises
And left us to our own devices.
(The Collected Ewart, 1933–1980, p. 14)

But the two-hundred line poem, has the form and the rueful erudition of another influence its author admits, the Hugh Selwyn Mauberley sequence of Ezra Pound. It is, frankly, a straight imitation of Pound, but in its sustained cleverness and technical confidence it can lay claim to being one of the most impressive juvenile exercises by any modern poet; it also anticipates many of Ewart's later themes.

One of his teachers at Wellington at this time was the critic, novelist, and memoirist T. C. Worsley. Worsley introduced him to the poetry of W. H. Auden, who by this time (at the age of twenty-seven) had published just three short books but provided a mesmerizing stylistic example for his young contemporaries. An Audenesque tone was already present in Ewart's "Characters of the First Fifteen," which fancifully celebrated the prowess of the school's rugby team. The full influence of the older poet became clear in Ewart's first book.

Poems and Songs came out in 1939 from the Fortune Press. Its director, a landlord and publishing entrepreneur called R. A. Caton, had secured the rights to Dylan Thomas' first volume, *18*

Poems (1934), and was later to number among his poets future celebrities such as C. Day Lewis, Roy Fuller, Kingsley Amis, and Philip Larkin; though none of these stayed with his firm beyond one early book. Caton also published books with dubious and hinting titles, which bordered on the pornographic while keeping just within the rigorous anti-obscenity laws in effect in Britain at the time. Ewart's volume, collecting work produced in his teens and early twenties, contains thirty-eight poems; they are all given Roman numerals, with twenty-four also having simple titles: "Song," "Sentimental Blues," "Political Poem," "Cambridge," and so forth. They proclaim their author a faithful follower of Auden in most of his moods and registers while suggesting (as with the Pound imitation) that he possesses a genuine talent of his own. Auden's emotionally charged yet cryptic vein is detectable in poem IV, titled "No Flowers by Request," which begins: "The thing finished is perfect. / Death perfects in point of fact / And I am always a fraction / Of my coming perfection" (p. 22). The relaxed informal Auden manner is apparent in VIII, a scandalous piece called, "The Fourth of May," about his "dear old school," which resulted in Ewart's being advised not to revisit Wellington College for at least three years (p. 6n). XIX, "Dollfuss Day, 1935," about a demonstration commemorating the first anniversary of the murder of the anti-Nazi Austrian chancellor Englebert Dollfuss, is reminiscent of the political verse of Stephen Spender, who had befriended and encouraged the younger poet. Ewart returns to the Auden manner with an unusual and successful ballad, "The English Wife" (XVII, ibid., pp. 45–47). "Miss Twye," the little comic poem that was later to become one of his most famous, appears in *Poems and Songs* (XXXIV). That is closest of all to Ewart's later style and runs, in its entirety:

Miss Twye was soaping her breasts in her bath
When she heard behind her a meaning laugh
And to her amazement she discovered
A wicked man in the bathroom cupboard.
(p. 64)

The most prominent poems are two that adopt Auden's style so exuberantly that they might

GAVIN EWART

almost be taken as affectionate parodies. "Audenesque for an Initiation" (V, pp. 23–25) is written in rhyming couplets (each line having eight stresses), which Auden himself borrowed, for a poem in his own first book, from Tennyson's "Locksley Hall." Auden's poem describes ruined industrial landscapes in the depression years and ends with a call for change and new kinds of thinking. Ewart's poem lacks Auden's lyric skill and the mysterious power of his serious, rhetorical passages, but it is technically adroit and jauntily entertaining in its use of deliberately Audenesque notions and references:

We've destroyed the rotting signposts, made holes in
all the pleasure boats;
We'll pull down ancestral castles when we've time to
swim the moats.

When we've practised we shall beat you with our
Third or Fourth Fifteen,
In spite of Royalists on the touchline. "Oh, well
played, Sir!" "Keep it clean!"

(pp. 23–25)

The second of these, the longest poem in *Poems and Songs*, has the general title *"Verse from an Opera—The Village Dragon."* It was a twelve-page libretto for a jazz opera for which the music was barely started (XXXIII pp. 52–63). Ewart acknowledges in a footnote that the work was "heavily in debt to Auden and Isherwood's play *The Dog Beneath the Skin*," but it shows little attempt at characterization and no attempt at all at creating dramatic action. It consists instead of a series of free-standing songs and lyrics, given principally to the villainous but plausible dragon, Sir Percy, Giles the hero, and his love, "a girl called H." There is also a chorus. The theme, so far as one is discernible, is the contest between an innocent and adventurous young love and the conventional temptations and corruptions offered by the dragon. The background is a bourgeois society where "the shadow on the floor / Is the longest shadow, cast by war." If the music had ever been provided it might have made a vaguely topical and satirical jazz cantata, but it is hardly a stageable opera.

By any standards *Poems and Songs* shows lively promise, but the outbreak of war seemed to cut Ewart short. In 1980 he could only find two further poems from this period to include in the *Collected*, under the heading "Other Pre-War Poems." One is a further exercise in efficient pastiche, "John Betjeman's Brighton," the other a diatribe against "Home" written, he recounts, while unemployed and "full of adolescent rebelliousness and bad temper":

How awful to see the same faces each day
So full of self-pity, disgust and dismay,
    To hear the same voices that say the same things
    And the dog having fits every time the bell rings

(p. 69)

It too is Betjemanesque, but with a touch of Ewartesque indignation. The section War Poems (1940–1946) contains just nine pieces. The prevailing mood is one of impotent anger and frustration, expressed either in the neo-romantic style of the time (the influence of Spender is again apparent in four sonnets done in traditional sonnet form) or in brisk accounts of the stupidity of human behavior, in "Officers' Mess" and "Oxford Leave"; observations of wartime atmosphere that fully anticipate Ewart's later vein of rueful comedy. The only war poem to which he returned frequently in later readings of his work was one that employs chilling understatement. "When a Beau Goes In" is about witnessing the standard British fighter aircraft of the Second World War crashing into the sea. Neither of the two Beaufighter crew survived these disasters.

Do you suppose *they* care?

You shouldn't cry
Or say a prayer or sigh.
In the cold sea, in the dark,
It isn't a lark
But it isn't Original Sin—
It's just a Beau going in.

(p. 78)

Ewart here cites the resignation and tight-lipped calm with which the prospect of violent death in war was required to be contemplated. It was another eighteen years before he felt he had enough conviction of his talent, and enough new poems, to venture a second book.

A SECOND BEGINNING

IF the six years of his army service resulted in only nine poems, Ewart was even less productive in the next eighteen years, writing only a further nine (*The Collected Ewart, 1933–1980*, pp. 79–85); though this is not counting one intriguing omission from his total: the lines he supplied in answer to an appeal for new words for the Song of the World Association of Girl Guides and Girl Scouts, to music by Jean Sibelius ("Our way is clear as we march on ..."). Nevertheless, the small postwar crop of verse anticipates, in its variety and technical adeptness, several of the numerous preoccupations explored in the flood of poems that came after 1964. "Young Blades," subtitled "A religious poem" (p. 79), pretends with deadpan wit to be pleading for help in resisting sexual temptation:

With curly heads they rampage through my thouqhts,
Full bosomed in their sweaters and their shorts ...

Protect me, Lord, from these desires of flesh,
Keep me from evil in Thy pastures fresh,

So that I may not fall, by lakes or ponds,
Into such sinful thoughts about young blondes!

By contrast, "Hymn to Proust" shows Ewart the lover of great works of literature, listing some of the master's major characters in poised quatrains that offer a perceptive appreciation of his themes. And "British Guiana" ("this piece of imaginary nostalgia," as he calls it in a footnote) sees him engaged in a favorite later activity: playing a poetic game, here involving the borrowing of colorful images deriving entirely from another work, a novel by the Jamaican writer Edgar Mittelholzer. Yet these interim pieces only partly prepare readers for the four books, rapidly published between 1964 and 1971, with which Ewart established a firm reputation.

It all began with the exercise he undertook in producing the sequence *Londoners* with the encouragement of Alan Ross now publishing books under the imprint bearing his name; this was to be his second book, and first mature volume, at the age of forty-seven. The collection has a misleading title: the poet is much less concerned with past or present denizens of the city than with places, taking the reader on visits to fourteen well-known London districts or institutions. In the great museums and churches of South Kensington, in Soho and Earls Court ("a bourgeois slum"), and at Hyde Park Corner, he is an amusing and observant, but uncharacteristically solemn, guide, speaking in a leisurely free verse. Occasionally the images take fire, as when he mourns the death of one form of transport familiar all his life until not long before:

Trams of nostalgia! So lately with us, now
One with the Giant Tortoise, Dodo and Great Auk.
Locomotives unnaturally preserved,
As mammoths in their thick Siberian ice.

(p. 116)

But *Londoners* leaves an impression of a challenging commission punctiliously (and indeed, wittily) executed, rather than a set of poems written out of spontaneous creative excitement. Only with the next book does the recognizable Ewart finally emerge, a versatile light verse writer who can frequently be obscenely funny and yet remain compassionate and even curiously moral in his outlook.

Pleasures of the Flesh followed two years after *Londoners*, in 1966, and shows a sudden new variety of form and subject matter, a cheerful spontaneity, and considerable underlying craft. There is also (this title *is* to be taken literally) a much greater degree of daring. The context of these poems is the day-to-day urban existence of a moderately well-paid, solidly middle-aged office employee, with wife and young children ("his dream, that he is still attractive," p. 126), who feels trapped between the peremptory demands of his work and the pull of his true vocation: poetry. "War-time" begins on a grim note (of a kind never far away in Ewart's writing) with a description of a drowned woman brought ashore in wartime Italy; it culminates in a bitter parallel between army existence and civilian occupation:

Twenty years later, in the offices,
The typists tread out the wine,
Pounding with sharp stiletto heels,
Working a money mine.

GAVIN EWART

It's a milder war, but it is one;
It's death by other means.
And I'm in the battle with them,
The soft recruits in their teens.

(p. 145)

Ewart hates his vain, piratical directors ("I shall stop my ears / When they fire an old copywriter from a cannon" (p. 128)), resents the attractiveness of female colleagues, manages to survive partly on nostalgia and partly through the spinning of comic fantasies—something the very nature of his work encourages. He can make splendid, accurate fun of this world, as for example in his much-anthologized poem "Office Friendships." But in "The Middle Years," he feels himself to be "an emotional dwarf" enduring a sad, unfulfilled kind of life:

Between the romantic lover
And the sordid dirty old man
Lies the fruitful wasted lifetime
Of the years that also ran.

("The Middle Years," p. 128.)

The best he can defiantly dare to hope for is possible recognition as "A Secular Saint" (p. 133): "Tell / How he was sacked in the takeover city ... / How his goodness was never recognised, / How he died and was translated." Most of the poems in the book are short. In two longer sequences, "Eight Awful Animals" and "A Handful of people," he employs the irregular and ridiculous rhyming couplets favored by Scotland's most celebrated talentless poet, William McGonagall, whose gravest sentiments end in bathos. The broad humor of the first sequence (which invents mythical creatures such as the Panteebra and The Stuffalo) is less subtle and discerning than the social observations of the second, which consists of a group of scabrous character sketches, though both sets are somewhat too heavily joky, unendearing exercises in a form to which he only occasionally returned. The next book, *The Deceptive Grin of the Gravel Porters* (1968), brings a conscious change of approach, a shift toward experimentation with poetic forms and language. But experiment does not mean the committed avant-gardism of the poets who were working with radical new patterns of words on the page, or with sound or found poetry. Between sections titled "The Life" and "The Others," Ewart has a batch of eighteen short poems labeled "The Cryptics," nearly all of which explore a theme ("Hands," "Falls," "Gnomes") in a group of single lines or couplets. "The Eight Suits" ends with:

An evening suit dark as nighttime,
the mourner at the feast.

A white protective suit of science,
at home among the poisons.

(p. 189)

This is relatively modest experimentation. The form of these "cryptics" suggests nothing more than a collecting together of the fleeting ideas and fragments that most poets will jot down and probably leave as jottings; W. H. Auden arranged his own as "Shorts." The satirical-sinister note is prominent in Ewart, and so is the enthusiasm for word play found in a twenty-six-line poem called "The Statements," where every letter of the alphabet begins an alliterated line of nonsense that sometimes verges on meaning:

Restless rovers are rarely repentant.
Soles slide sideways in silent seas.
Terrible tornadoes torture the terrain
Under umbrellas the uncles take umbrage.

(p. 188)

The two sections enclosing "The Cryptics" show his fantasies and resentments about working life turning more surreal or despairing. Poems in "The Life" variously depict his two feet pulling him in different directions (p. 168), tell of a "rock face" nightmare in which he realizes that "in advertising a man of fifty is expendable" (p. 169), and offer a bleak vision of how, "wishes grow like weeds / Hemming you in till you can't see the sky" ("A Cup Too Low"). The mood of "A Cup Too Low" uncharacteristically turns dark:

It's everything, not just the mind, that's ill.
Perhaps if all experience were pooled

39

GAVIN EWART

The house of life would not be quite so haunted?
And happiness grow from these sick weeds?

(pp. 172–173)

If most of the poems here are fantasies or games with poetic forms, many of them contain an autobiographical undercurrent of unease about the nature of his day-to-day working existence. The last section of the book, "The Others," includes poems attempting more extravagant, even Joycean, word play ("His lafe was spant. A less! Oh sod / To no thet promise never march filfulled" (p. 194)) though in the end they are outnumbered by more conventional (and very adroit) jokes and fantasies.

The Deceptive Grin of the Gravel Porters was produced in the attractive format adopted by Alan Ross's new publishing venture London Magazine Editions, paperback books described by a critic in the London *Times* as having "a sensible, healthy look like wholemeal sandwiches cut narrow for the traveller's pocket." The style attracted Ewart, who was subsequently pleased to have his work published in small editions, as long as they were agreeably designed. His next complete volume, *The Gavin Ewart Show* (1971), came out in an inexpensive hardback edition from the Trigram Press run by the poet and artist Asa Benveniste, who collaborated in its design. Its dedication to "H[omo] Ludens," echoes a similar enthusiasm for games playing in poetry present in the contemporary work of Ewart's fellow poet and friend George MacBeth (1932–1992). The first twelve poems in the book, fables, satires, and love poems in elaborately rhyming stanzas (there is no connection with the title), appeared originally as a booklet called *Twelve Apostles*, from Ulsterman Publications in Belfast, Northern Ireland. Pastiche and formal inventiveness had become Ewart's hallmarks as a poet. He emulated A. R. Ammons by producing not "a long thin poem" in the style of the American but "The Short Fat Poem." He adopts the style of the eighteenth-century master of satirical disgust, Jonathan Swift, for a poem in six rhyming couplets, "Dean Swift Watches Some Cows," about the natural functions of the cattle. A sequence of fourteen "So-called Sonnets," a term

Ewart often used later, consists of "rough and unrhyming" variants on the form. They display a remarkable variety of moods and registers, from the deliberately shocking though rueful reflection on why he comes to write poetry—

> Blood is in the ink,
> but it's a kind of homeopathic cure.
> Casting the runes on demons. Exorcised!

(p. 234)

to the tenderness of a sonnet contemplating "The Last Things" ("The last meeting with a friend. The last / stroking of the last cat, the last sight of a son or daughter"). Two poems in *The Gavin Ewart Show* reveal more about their author than almost any he had written to date. "The Sentimental Education" returns to the "Locksley Hall" couplets for an aggrieved account of his life thus far: upper-middle-class childhood and schooling, war, publishing, advertising, and then

> It's not pretty when they throw you, screaming, in the empty sack,
> Filled with nothing but the cries of wives and children screaming back ...

> All you learn—and from a lifetime—is that that's the way it goes.
> That's the crumbling of the cookie, till the turning up of toes.

(pp. 220–224)

Ewart is as forthright as usual with this reaction to losing his job; he knows that most people have to weather worse situations, but his principle is to express in poetry, with honesty, whatever he may be feeling and thinking. With "2001: The Tennyson / Hardy Poem" he is more jocularly positive, imagining a future in which "my lightest verse will seem quite weighty." For all the indignities to be endured in old age, he will ultimately enjoy the compensation of knowing that he is thought of as "a thesis" and "a classic," and:

> Simply because I have no seniors
> The literati will raise the cry:
> Ewart's a genius!

(pp. 226–227)

GAVIN EWART

That last modesty is genuine, but so is the latent aspiration to the status of a major talent.

EWART set himself to write a lot of verse and to explore as many different forms as possible. Even with so dexterous a practitioner this involved the risk of producing some weaker work. He was aware that some poems he wrote were not satisfactory and should not see the light of day in print. But if he himself had confidence in a poem, he would submit it to editors and reserve it for a future collection whether they accepted it or not. Those in his second Ulsterman Publications pamphlet, *An Imaginary Love Affair* (1974), often rely on the comic effect of an awkward, self-mocking rhyme:

> although the love was true—
> if I were more romantic I would say sublime—
> it was not a love that lasted until closing time.
> ("Memory Man," *The Collected Ewart, 1933–1980*,
> p. 252)

Here (and in other places) he jokes with himself and readers about the problems of making rhyme convincing and avoiding banality. For fun, Ewart is ready to accept the vocabulary of the popular songs of his youth; every kind of "high or low" art in verse was grist for his mill. The poems of this period, up to the publication of the first large collected edition, appeared in three books, *Be my Guest!* (1975), *No Fool Like an Old Fool* (1976), and *Or Where a Young Penguin Lies Screaming* (1977), and one smaller booklet, *The First Eleven* (1977). They show an ever-increasing range of forms and themes, and the Ewart voice—slightly formal and incongruously polite, whether he is being grimly serious or indecently comic—is unmistakable throughout.

It will be convenient, given the multiplicity of Ewart's concerns, to examine this large number of mainly short poems under a few broad headings, since his approach to the composition of verse did not vary for the rest of his writing life; nor does his work undergo any striking developments or transformations. Affectionate parody is one of his favorite modes, and among his victims in the 1970s were Philip Larkin, W. H. Auden, Samuel Richardson, William McGonagall, Anglo-Saxon verse, Byron, Rudyard Kipling, and Ella Wheeler Wilcox. He is never out to undermine or belittle another writer in these exercises; rather, he is adopting his or her manner for purposes of his own. "The Larkin Automatic Car Wash" (*The Collected Ewart, 1933—1980*, pp. 254–256) is a tour de force, a description of the sensation of sitting in a car while "the pliant / Great brushes whirred and closed. Like yellow fern / One blurred the windscreen." The poem is written in a bulky (here a ten-line) stanza similar to those Larkin employed for his more extended poems. But the voice is unlike Larkin's. It is audibly Ewart's own voice relishing a shot at imitating Larkin. "The Clarissa Harlowe Poem" imagines an address, in intricately rhymed stanzas, by the villain of Richardson's *Clarissa* to its virtuous heroine (p. 297). In "The Gods of the Copybook Headings," which takes its title from a poem by Rudyard Kipling, he firmly tells that celebrity not to expect to be remembered any more than some other writers who have fallen into obscurity (in May 1976, he explains, a class of thirteen British students of English had never even heard of Kipling!):

> You can write the Great Short Stories, on the sentimental side,
> With the politics pleasing to Tories, and lament how the loved ones died.
> You can fill them with genuine feeling (and dialect), all your skill
> Won't make them much more appealing to Time, as he moves on still.
> (pp. 367–368)

In "The Ella Wheeler Wilcox Woo" his wicked versatility takes him closer to her style than to some others' ("I could match with an ardent soul / Your longings to hold me close" (pp. 374–375); but in reverential imitation of Auden's elegy for Yeats Ewart writes a comparably moving tribute to Auden himself on the occasion of his death:

> Talent such as his is rare
> and our singing branch is bare,

where shall we find such an one
now the feeling voice has done?

                    ("To the Slow Drum," pp. 275–277)

If the shape of the stanza Ewart uses for "The Gentle Sex (1974)" (pp. 348–352) seems familiar to readers of nineteenth-century English poetry, that is because it is a serious imitation of the stanza used by Gerard Manley Hopkins in "The Wreck of the Deutschland." "The Gentle Sex" is an example of pastiche overlapping with a kind of poem that forms another broad group in Ewart's work: those that tell alarming or extravagant stories. His purpose in "The Gentle Sex" is to relate a modern story of the brutal persecution and murder of one of their comrades by Protestant loyalist women in Belfast. The cruelty dwelt on in the poem was profoundly shocking to readers who had enjoyed this poet's wild comedy but missed the hints of terror in a number of poems in earlier books. It seemed that Ewart wished to be taken seriously for his darker poems as well as applauded for his humor, and a deft handling of scary narrative is certainly apparent in "A Passionate Woman," based on a real happening (p. 365) and "The Price of Things" (pp. 363–364), a fiction. "Charles Augustus Milverton" retells as black comedy a frightening Conan Doyle story from *The Return of Sherlock Holmes* in a ramshackle-looking structure of nineteen stanzas with lines of varying length and a complex rhyme scheme, the poet reveling in the ridiculous challenge he has set himself:

Oh who's purloined these letters but Augustus
        Milverton?
        and who
's asking seven thousand pounds the lot, each sprightly
        one?
        What can
        Holmes do?
Though he looks like Mr Pickwick, he's a
fiend—and she's undone!
        A man
        who knew

no compunction for his victims ...

                    (pp. 292–293)

The tone immediately identifies the poem as humorous pastiche, for all the underlying grim-ness of the tale, and Ewart's openly comic verse narratives show his talents at their most extraordinary and entertaining.

"Fiction: The House Party" (p. 270) sends a group of incompatible persons to Lord Vintage's castle for a weekend of frustrated love and mutual incomprehension on the social level. This sort of extravaganza was a stock-in-trade for Ewart, and one of the finest examples is "Perchance a Jealous Foe," a verse parody of the standard novel featuring an indigent governess working for a dominating employer in a rich household. In charge of a wealthy aristocrat's daughter, Myfanwy, at Stoatswold, the young Annabel meets Sebastian Anchovy, "a sophisticated novelist / and a member of another old County family," and falls in love with him. They meet secretly on cycle rides and in a teashop, and even share a joint in the bathroom. One evening her master, the choleric widower Sir Norman Stoatswold, who has taken too much cowslip wine, drops and breaks his pipe, loses his temper, accuses Annabel of meeting Sebastian in the rhododendrons, and realizes he is in love with her. Next day he proposes marriage, which she of course accepts. Here, as elsewhere, Ewart delightfully sends up a social milieu with which he was acquainted through his own upper-middle-class upbringing, also its ludicrous portrayal in popular fiction. Such satire was beloved of cabaret artists and the stuff of a particular kind of English stage and film comedy. There is a sense in which very many of Ewart's poems could be regarded as games, but games with poetic forms and with language itself acquire an increasing attraction for him. Ewart's recreational pieces range from a poem "found" in *McCall's* magazine

Sharing their entertaining ideas and their recipes
are these five Washington hostesses.

Everything from cheesecake to moose meat

                    (p. 266)

to "The Afterflu Afterlife," in which each of the eight stanzas has a rhyme sound used five times:

To cross the ice before the ice can crack,
To tighten muscles now deformed and slack,

To straighten the curved-in bedridden back,
To run once more with the commuting pack?
To stumble with the hack? The answer's black ...

(pp. 259–260)

His attempt to translate four of the Odes of Horace into English verse while retaining the word order of the original was not as extreme as Louis Zukofsky's rendering of all the poems of Catullus into an English that sounded the same as the Latin, yet the game contributed little to the appreciation of great classic poems. Ewart contrived an inspired, zany invention in the form of the semantic limerick, in which every eligible word of the original rhyme is replaced by its dictionary definitions. Following this method, he wrote a mildly obscene but unobjectionable limerick beginning "There was a young man of St John's" using the Shorter Oxford Dictionary:

There existed an adult male person who had lived a relatively short time, belonging or pertaining to St John's ...

He continued in this style for fifteen lines of ponderously meticulous prose, then repeated the exercise using another dictionary, Dr. Johnson's, expanding the limerick to nineteen lines. Soon after this experiment, he varied and extended the technique with a burlesque called "Variations and Excerpts," providing three of his own paraphrases for every repetition of lines in the old comic song "Barnacle Bill the Sailor" ("Ballocky Bill" in his, and the vernacular, version). Thus, " 'Who's that knocking at my door?' / Cried the fair young maiden" becomes:

Who's that crepitating with his knuckledusters on my
   portico?
Who's the man aggresifying his digits on my door-
   box?
Who is the person terrifying the nightwood with his
   fistfuls?
      cried the beauteous young virgin
      (called the youthful female winner of Beauty Prizes)
      (enunciated the scarcely mature attractve lady)

The point here is the purely nonsensical character of such excursions, which Ewart now pursued with appealing enthusiasm and energy. By 1980, when he had enough material for the immense *Collected Ewart*, comprising work produced over forty-seven years (but most of it in the last twenty-five), he had won a late but wide admiration as a senior poet of outstanding gifts. He was the acknowledged master of exaggerated comic effects; but that was not the whole story. Distributed among the outrageously funny verses were not only gravely serious items (often with topical reference) but also poems of disconcerting personal candor and vulnerability. Those form another important category in his last years; and perceptive readers increasingly declined to endorse Ewart's modest conclusion to his 1980 *Collected*:

         already the children
are born who will commit the next century's murders,
my love so transient it's pathetic. They'll say (if I'm
   lucky):
He wrote some silly poems, and some of them were
   funny.

(pp. 405–406)

POEMS, 1980–1995

ONLY at the very end did illness slow Ewart's composition of verse. Before that he was awesomely productive, the number of poems he wrote and published in the last fifteen years of his writing life easily exceeding the number he produced in the first forty-five. Five substantial individual books and a shorter illustrated volume make up the crowded *Collected Poems 1980–1990*. In this ten-year period he also wrote three small collections of poetry for children, compiled two children's anthologies of poems, edited the *Penguin Book of Light Verse* and assembled the *Complete Clerihews of Edward Clerihew Bentley*.

At the same time he gave numerous performances and broadcasts of his work in England and abroad. As a reader, he gave an impression of diffidence, appearing embarrassed and shy when audiences laughed and applauded. In fact, he delighted in the acclaim and the affection. The modesty and agreeableness of his public persona played a significant part in accustoming readers to the bawdiness of many poems. After a reading, he frequently offered a dry apology in case he had caused offense, this often resulting in further laughter. His more delicate listeners and readers forgave him, because there might then follow a wholly serious poem, about death in war, or love, or family and children, in which the depth and genuineness of feeling was patent. Admirers accepted Ewart's talent as a whole without objection to the scandalous content; but they could hardly have complained without rejecting his achievement as a whole, the bawdiness being inherent to his vision.

The title of *The New Ewart: Poems 1980–1982* refers to the arrival of the book, not to any change in the poet. This is still the Ewart who juxtaposes jests and games with poems, mourning dead friends, recalling family incidents, or musing on his affection for animals. The pastiches become steadily more sustained and impressive. The dignified "Ode" is a fine tribute to the late Auden's ruminative style, ending on an Audenesque note of reserved affirmation:

> As with weather, to forecast or hope
> that our hearts grow perceptibly warmer
> is more or less all we can do—
>
> not giving up hope is the thing,
> in the old-fashioned phrase, to be sanguine
> is the must for us creatures of blood.
> (*Collected Poems 1980–1990*, p. 9)

Elsewhere in the book there are cheerful parodies of Sir Thomas Wyatt, Christopher Smart ("Jubilate Matteo," addressed to Ewart's cat, exactly catches Smart's engaging tendency to ramble), and *Patience Strong*, and a wicked prose skit on John Cowper Powys. Gradually, more about war emerges in his poems, usually in the form of recollections—raw and alarming, as in "War Death in a Low Key" (Collected Poems 1980–1990, pp. l7–18) or honest but slightly too solemn, as in "A Contemporary Film of Lancasters in Action" (p. 29). He continues to find his "so-called sonnets" a suitable vehicle for a

variety of briefer reflections, or memories, or items of bizarre comedy.

In one of the sonnets (*Collected Poems 1980–1990*, p. 63) he answers a challenge (implicitly his wife's) that his poems dwell too much on the dark side of marriage. He denies that, and then states a personal principle about writing poetry:

but in any case poems are general and not to be interpreted literally and they're also a kind of cure for the bad parts of life.

The notion of poetry as therapy alone certainly did not appeal to him. However, the idea that poems should compensate for the frustrations of daily life (and record its pleasures) was one he thoroughly supported. To fulfil that role, poetry should neglect virtually nothing. In a poem called "Preserved" (*Collected Poems 1980–1990*, p. 70) he cites a recurrent blurb phrase used by the publishers of "the slim volumes":

"These are all the poems that Mr Stringfellow wishes to preserve."

This ran utterly contrary to Ewart's own practice of preserving in books "all the poems of any merit (in the author's opinion)." Of "Mr Stringfellow" he goes on to observe:

> In fact there may be as much difference
> between real living experience and his verse
> as there is between the fresh beautiful raspberries
> and the artificiality of jam.

The Ewart Quarto, a short illustrated book published in 1984, is notable for a sardonic look at poets' jaundiced views of their contemporaries ("Graves, an engine in a siding— shunted there by Laura Riding— / thouqht all Auden's verse was 'fake' / and Willie Yeats a big mistake" (*Collected Poems 1980–1990*, pp. 111–113); and for a leisurely narrative poem, informally rhymed in couplets, in a manner of which he became fond. This is a six-page Pindaric Ode about a famous English victory at cricket over Australia in 1981, almost a sports short story in verse (*Collected Poems 1980–1990*, pp. 101–106). It was "real living experience" to cricket enthusiasts, but was it poetry? Ewart insisted, on the jacket of *The New Ewart*, that "doggerel, if it is used with intelligence, is a legitimate medium for poetry; and may, for certain subject matter, be the most suitable." He is, in Peter Porter's phrase, an "adapter of rules."

One year later came *The Young Pobble's Guide to His Toes* (1985), largest of all his individual volumes and his most energetic, outspoken, and varied collection. Alongside poems registering his resentment of old age and death ("In Another Country," "Deathbeds") are protests at human cruelty, doubts about the brassy patriotism of Margaret Thatcher during the Falklands War ("Three Weeks to Argentina") and a weird verse transcription of a sequence in a novel by A. E. W. Mason ("The Black Mass"). A poem called "Liqhts Out" provides a key to his mood:

With each new book the old poet thinks:
Will this be the last?
Biros, pencils, typewriters, pens and inks
Whisper to him: Get going! Move!
Get it out fast!

... shout it out, coming too soon you've
got silence enough!
               (*Collected Poems 1980–1990*, pp. 121–122)

The book suggests that now Ewart felt he could "shout out" anything he wished to. With a distinguished reputation firmly established he could take joyful liberties, rendering into verse what no one else would attempt (he himself being inimitable). One poem is lengthily titled "The Bob Hope Classic Show (ITV) and 'Shelley Among the Ruins,' Lecture by Professor Timothy Webb—both Saturday evening, 26.9.81." The two halves of the evening stand in fortuitous contrast. With the Bob Hope show

Money is the Cleopatra
that seduces Frank Sinatra—
fat and ugly women too,
all Republicans, all who
(lookalikes of old Liz Taylor)
never dug mad Norman Mailer.
               (*Collected Poems 1980–1990*, pp. 139–141)

At the quiet lecture in Keats House, London, that same evening, the poet learns that Shelley liked

ruins and drew "hope so tall" from them (is that an *accidental* allusion to Bob?) not because they were picturesque but because they showed how, in the end, bad regimes "all vanished in thin air." The daring explicit poems and outright jokes are fewer in this book, though a friendly parody of Philip Larkin in the expectation that he might become poet laureate is a brilliant exception (*Collected Poems 1980–1990*, p. 222), and "Lexicography" is a hilarious account of how Ewart tried, with the aid of the reading glass provided, to find in the Compact Edition of the OED an obscene term as if he were a lepidopterist looking for a "wonderful butterfly"—and failed to find it.

The center section of the 1990 *Collected* is the *Complete Little Ones* (1980), eighty pages of the tiny poems he had regularly been dashing off on any subject at all. Some reach as much as twenty lines, the best being "The Sad Widow," written as an exercise with creative writing students. Others are more of his surreal one-liners, haiku, nonsense limericks, mini-parodies: "Who is Circe? what is she, / That all these swine commend her?" (*Collected Poems 1980–1990*, p. 282). Were the Little Ones worth inclusion? Perhaps only for the sake of completeness. In general, the longer a Little One is, the better it turns out. Ewart was not an epigrammatist, though there are places where he comes near to being one with, for example, a harsh verdict contained in "T. S. Eliot and Ezra Pound":

Eliot loved the music halls
(and probably the pantos).
Pound took the rubbish out of *The Waste Land*
and put it all into the *Cantos*.
               (*Collected Poems 1980–1990*, p. 306)

The poet John Betjeman called a book published in his forties *A Few Late Chrysanthemums*. The titles Ewart used for the two volumes that complete the *Collected Poems 1980–1990* truly suggest the compositions of later years; and "few" the poems are not. *Late Pickings* (1987) and *Penultimate Poems* (1989) reach 126 and 125 pages respectively. In each the note of mortality sounds recurrently. In the former volume "The Sadness of Cricket" abandons his favorite theme of the endless fascination of the game and lists famous players whose lives culminated in failure, suicide, even in one case two acts of murder. Numerous poems about old age and death are barely balanced by lighter ones. Yet the parodies and extravaganzas are as brilliant as ever. He ventures a Shakespearean sonnet, weighs once again into Rudyard Kipling, and writes a scabrous but rueful variation on Edward Fitzgerald, "Rubaiyat of the Prostate":

I dreamed that Dawn's Left Hand was in my Fly
And lighted was the Candle, burning high!
    But waking, saw with disappointed Gaze
That Light a flicker, and about to die.

(*Collected Poems 1980–1990*, p. 376)

The poem's delicate *in*delicacy is complemented by an increased personal tenderness in other places, most deliberately and innocently vulnerable in "24th March 1986," written to mark the thirtieth anniversary of his marriage. "Lovers in Pairs" resumes the theme and mood:

When old ones lie side by side
what's real at last has a look-in.
    The breathing *could* surely stop—
    and with it the warmth of love.
It's the penultimate bed
before the one with the gravestone.
    This is what each one thinks—
    a thought sad, loving and warm.

(ibid., p. 329)

The book title *Penultimate Poems* did not appear to signify any intention of planning an end to the publication of books of verse (although it happened that there was only one more to come). For the first time, Ewart divided the "Heavier" from the "Lighter" poems, sandwiching six more "So-called Sonnets" between them. In his final volume, *85 Poems* (1993), he repeated the separation with sections of "Serious" and "Frivolous" poems. A foreword in the former book explains how he had attempted to make classical meters (no doubt absorbed at Wellington and Cambridge) fit the English language. It shows in an incidental way how important he considered detailed craftsmanship, whether applied to "light" or "heavy" subjects. Each of these last two books has poems that are finely crafted, whether they are grave and thoughtful, or set out to shock, or just wickedly funny. All chosen targets are hit with precision: see his "Thomas Hardy Section" or his discourse on English detective stories in the manner of Ogden Nash (*85 Poems*, pp. 75–78 and 96).

The poem "Modest Proposal" (*Collected Poems 1980–1990*, p. 447) is the ultimate key to his personal practice. He insists that "good light verse is better than bad heavy verse any day of the week"; also that it ought to be "responsible," "insouciant," "civilised," and "calm." The words represent Ewart's governing principles, and he keeps to them assiduously. Up to the very last pages of *85 Poems*, in which he ranges over all the old preoccupations (and some new ones) with undiminished zest, his immensely readable verse combines all the attributes that "Modest Proposal" prescribes.

OTHER WORKS

In 1981 Ewart edited a reissue of the *Complete Clerihews* of E. Clerihew Bentley, following his earlier anthology of *Other People's Clerihews*, a choice of work by the best Bentley imitators. The book sold well enough to justify a revised edition in 1993, which added the extra clerihews, by Bentley and teenage friends, subsequently discovered in a school notebook. Ewart enjoyed and (mainly in A Cluster of Clerihews [1985]) had had his own shots at, these inconsequential four-liners about famous persons, exemplified by Bentley on Sherman:

"No, sir," said General Sherman,
"I did *not* enjoy the sermon;
Nor did I git any
Kick outa the Litany."

(*The Complete Clerihews*, p. 116)

He appreciated the clever word play demonstrated by the most accomplished clerihews and appreciated that the form could lend itself to epigrammatic joking and satire. As was the case with earlier comprehensive editions, however, page on page of these little verses can be tedious, suggesting that Bentley's reputation as a comic versifier owes much to the wit of his various distinguished illustrators.

Another editing enterprise was a more formidable and fruitful assignment: to assemble a *Penguin Book of Light Verse* (published in 1980). Ewart introduces it only briefly (declining to enter a labyrinth of "conflicting definitions") with remarks on what can and cannot be regarded as light verse. It should

> never deal in strong emotion (love—but not tragic love); or matters of life and death. It should not have distressing content (unless this is humorously intended ...)
>
> It may be humorous, or partly humorous. ... It may be nonsense. ... It may also, of course, be obscene.
>
> (*The Penguin Book of Light Verse*, p. 27)

Not unexpectedly, the book resolves no confusions. Spanning poetry from Anglo-Saxon riddles to the doggerel of the pseudonymous "E. J. Thribb," it is a fascinating reflection of its editor's own practice as a poet. The scholarship and wide reading, the knowledge of popular song, an eye for the relaxed verse of the more serious poets (Coleridge, Housman, Frost), a frank enthusiasm for outrightly bawdy verse are all there. Only one inclusion, the anonymous rugby song known as "The Soldier's Tale," brought hostile comment from one reviewer.

Ewart directed readers who thought some of the contents of the book unsuitable for the young to his *Batsford Book of Light Verse for Children*, which complemented his earlier *Batsford Book of Verse for Children*. As might be expected from his editing of these anthologies and his prolific production of light verse for adults, he turned his own hand also, in his later years, to writing poems for children. It brought out his didactic side. *The Learned Hippopotamus* (1986), dedicated to his daughter and his two cats, is subtitled "Poems Conveying Useful Information About Animals Ordinary and Extraordinary." He deliv-

ers the information rather dryly, though with humor and charm (and footnotes); his second attempt, *Caterpillar Stew* (1990), is more confident and entertaining:

> When it comes to Cats
> I don't like the aristocrats!
> I have an aversion
> To the pampered Persian.
>
> (*Caterpillar Stew*, p. 19)

The last of these collections, *Like It Or Not* (1992), is addressed to younger children, slipping in occasional instructions on suitable behavior and hints about the environment, as with one nonsmoking creature:

> ... the beaver's not a puffer,
> he does *not* pollute the skies.
> He does *not* make others suffer.
> The beaver's very wise.
>
> ("No Smoking," *Like It Or Not*, p. 54)

AFTERWORD

MANY "serious" poets of great distinction have produced commendable examples of light verse. But can someone who is wholly or predominantly an excellent producer of light verse ever be classed as a poet of distinction? When the claim is made on behalf of one or another candidate, it is often accompanied by a suggestion that there are some good serious poems in the corpus. And then we are told that, anyway, the jokes are not the only point: some or all of the work in question conceals an element of seriousness behind the joking. Or the poetry is serious in its own way.

Well, so it should be. To be genuinely good a body of light verse needs to be leavened by seriousness just as tragedy, in the hands of the best dramatists, is relieved—perhaps intensified?—by moments of comic relief. The best practitioners of light verse leave their readers with something beyond the humor: a few graver thoughts to take away. It is therefore desirable for them to have produced a quantity of good material, enough for the flashes of wisdom or the realization of unexpected depths to come as a surprise when the credentials of the comedian have already been fully established. In the cases, for example, of Edward Lear, Lewis Carroll, W. S. Gilbert and Ogden Nash, all preeminently "light" writers, we first find a substantial body of work that is splendidly (on occasions, scarily) entertaining. And then we sense that, as Kent said after noting several sallies of King Lear's jester, it is "not altogether fool." The verse of these writers thus gradually acquires a particular kind of status in our esteem: as the work of light poets who rightly discerned that the world was not always a light place. The name of Gavin Ewart richly deserves to be added to this special list.

Of course, much of Ewart's poetry *is* "fool," of the most varied and virtuoso kind, and can be enjoyed as such; most of it hopes to raise laughter. But as soon as you have read a few of the books other considerations begin to suggest themselves. And here it helps to recall the situation of light verse when Ewart was hitting his stride in the 1960s. It seemed to have become largely the preserve of exhibitionist platform comics. It had become restricted to minimalist squibs and a small range of topics and emotions. Intelligent, undemonstrative poets did not appear to write it. But Ewart soon proved that you did not have to be wildly extrovert to be uproariously funny. He gave new life to an English comedy of understatement that depended on an urbane and precise use of language, even when his poems were filled with his own kind of absurdist bawdy. Page on page of extraordinary humor and fantasy, diversified by his abundant versatility, showed that light verse could still be written in all the traditional forms, in a variety of new ones that he invented, and, for that matter, in any complex pattern of verse he chose to try. And believing that poetry could and should be about almost anything, he turned himself, with truly daunting dedication, into one of the most inclusive English poets of his century, serious or light.

His reward came in the shape of critical admiration from his most eminent contemporaries and wide popularity with audiences for his many readings. They responded to the urbanity of his performances and the craftsmanship with which the poems were composed. Were they also finding in this skilful and hilarious poetry some of the lightness of spirit that irradiates many considerable works of art? It will not have mattered if they did not—the delight was sufficient—but the question should be asked again at some future time. Ewart's work requires further attention from critics and scholars who will analyze its spirit, relate it in detail to the poetry of his time, and decide on the status it finally merits. They would not lack for entertainment in facing the task.

SELECTED BIBLIOGRAPHY

I. COLLECTED WORKS. *The Collected Ewart, 1933–1980* (London, 1980); *The Complete Little Ones* (London, 1986); *Collected Poems 1980–1990* (London, 1990).

II. POEMS. *Poems and Songs* (London, 1936); *Londoners* (London, 1964); *Pleasures of the Flesh* (London, 1966); *The Deceptive Grin of the Gravel Porters* (London, 1968); *Twelve Apostles* (Belfast, Ire., 1970); *The Gavin Ewart Show* (London, 1971); *An Imaginary Love Affair* (Belfast, Ire., 1974); *Penguin Modern Poets 25*, with Zulfikar Ghose and B. S. Johnson (Harmondsworth, U.K., 1975); *Be My Guest!* (London, 1975); *No Fool Like an Old Fool* (London, 1976); *The First Eleven* (Hatch End, Middlesex, U.K., 1977); *Or Where a Young Penguin Lies Screaming* (London, 1977); *All My Little Ones* (London, 1978); *The New Ewart* (London, 1982); *More Little Ones* (London, 1983); *The Ewart Quarto* (London, 1984); *A Cluster of Clerihews* (Leamington Spa, U.K., 1985); *The Young Pobble's Guide to His Toes* (London, 1985); *Nine New Poems* (Cleveland, Ohio, 1986); *Late Pickings* (London, 1987); *Penultimate Poems* (London, 1989); *Poems from Putney* (Brockport, N.Y., 1990); *85 Poems* (London, 1993); *Selected Poems 1933–1993* (London, 1996).

III. FOR CHILDREN (POEMS). *The Learned Hippopotamus* (London, 1986); *Caterpillar Stew* (London, 1990); *Like It or Not* (London, 1993).

IV. AS EDITOR. *Forty Years On: An Anthology of School Songs* (London, 1976); *The Batsford Book of Verse for Children* (London, 1976); *The Batsford Book of Light Verse for Children* (London, 1978); *The Penguin Book of Light Verse* (Harmondsworth, U.K., 1980); *The Complete Clerihews of E. Clerihew Bentley* (Oxford, 1981, rev. 1983); *Other People's Clerihews* (Oxford, 1983).

V. CRITICAL STUDIES. Anthony Thwaite, *Times Literary Supplement*, reviewing *No Fool Like an Old Fool* (10 December 1976); Anthony Thwaite, *Times Literary Supplement*, reviewing *Or Where a Young Penguin Lies Screaming* (14 April 1978); Philip Larkin, *Quarto*, reviewing *The New Ewart* (May 1982; rep. in *Further Requirements*, ed. by Anthony Thwaite, London, 2001); Julian Symons, *Oxford*

Companion to Twentieth Century Poetry, ed. by Ian Hamilton (Oxford, U.K., 1994); anonymous, the *Reader's Companion to Twentieth Century Writers*, ed. by Peter Parker, pp. 224–225 (London, 1995); Anthony Thwaite: *Poetry Today: A Critical Guide to British Poetry 1960–1995*, pp. 35–37 (London, 1996); John Press, *Contemporary Poets* (6th ed., Detroit, 1996); Anthony Thwaite, obituary of Gavin Ewart, *Independent* (24 October 1995); obituary (anonymous), *The Times* (25 October 1995); Alan Brownjohn, obituary, *Daily Telegraph* (25 October 1995); Peter Porter, "A Last Lunch with a Genius," *Guardian* (29 October 1995); Simon Rae, *An Exuberant Subversive*, obituary, *Guardian* (24 October 1995).

MICHAEL FRAYN

(1933–   )

John Wilders

MICHAEL FRAYN IS an extremely productive writer. Between 1965 and 1999 he published eight novels, eleven plays, nine translations, most of them from Chekhov, six film and television scripts, and a philosophical work, *Constructions*. His plays, like those of his contemporary Tom Stoppard, are not political and carry no message, no comment on the state of society. "So far as I can see," he said, "all these plays are attempts to show something about the world, not to change it or promote any particular idea of it. That's not to say there are no ideas in them." He does, however, have a recognizable and consistent view of human experience, and in particular promotes the idea that our perception of the world is unreliable and cannot be verified. He is also preoccupied with the craft of writing and seems to have regarded each new work as a fresh challenge to his powers, a new beginning. He has never tried merely to repeat his previous successes.

Frayn was born on 8 September 1933 outside London. On leaving grammar school, he did his national service in the army and, after basic training, was sent to Emmanuel College, Cambridge, to learn Russian. When he returned to Cambridge as an undergraduate, he studied Russian for a year but subsequently changed to philosophy. He wrote frequently for *Varsity*, the student newspaper, and in his final year wrote the script for the annual revue put on by the Footlights, a student dramatic society that specializes in comic and satirical sketches. In 1960, he married Gillian Palmer. They had three daughters but in 1981 he became separated from his wife. He now lives with the biographer Claire Tomalin. His first professional work was as a journalist for the *Manchester Guardian*, for which he wrote news stories, reviews of plays, films, and books, and articles, mostly humorous. Later he wrote a regular weekly humorous column for the *Observer* (collected in *The Original Michael Frayn*, chosen and introduced by James Fenton). All these early experiences are reflected in his writings.

EARLY NOVELS

HIS first novel, *The Tin Men* (1965), is a satire that grew out of his humorous newspaper articles. It is set in the William Morris Institute for Automation Research, an opportunity for Frayn to ridicule research in statistics, automation, sociology, and the creation of elaborate machines to perform tasks hitherto carried out by human beings. In the Newspaper Department, for example, a team of researchers collects data in order to demonstrate that a digital computer can be programmed to produce newspapers with "all the variety and news sense of the old hand-made article." They work their way through stacks of newspaper cuttings, identifying the patterns of the stories and filing them under different headings. In the file marked "Child Told Dress Unsuitable by Teacher" there are ninety-five cuttings divided by variables consisting of "clothing objected to (high heels/petticoat/frilly knickers)," "whether child also smokes and/or uses lipstick" and "whether child alleged by parents to be humiliated by having clothing inspected before whole school." Similarly in the "They Think British Is Wonderful" file, the variables consist of the people who think so—American tourists, Danish *au pair* girls, and so forth. The frequency of occurrence is then recorded and, by using such data, a computer can be programmed to create newspapers that are indistinguishable from regular publications without the effort of investigating the "raw, messy, offendable real world." A program has also been created that allows all the bingo games in the country to be organized simultaneously from one central computer; another is being planned for automating football results and thereby making it unnecessary for games to be played. The experts even foresee a time when computers will write pornographic novels, since they are all "permutations of a very small range of variables," and will conduct religious services without the necessity of having a priest or congregation.

The Tin Men belongs to a tradition of English satire originated by Jonathan Swift in *Gulliver's Travels*, whose hero visits the Grand Academy of Lagado (a thinly disguised portrait of the newly formed Royal Society). A member "had been eight years upon a project for extracting sunbeams out of cucumbers, which were to be put into vials hermetically sealed, and let out to warm the air in inclement summers." Another member, "a most ingenious architect," has contrived "a new method for building houses, by beginning with the roof and working down to the foundation." *The Tin Men* is not so much a novel, however, as a series of satirical sketches. The characters are cardboard cutouts, and, although there is a plot involving the opening of a new wing at the Institute by the Queen, it is taken up only intermittently. The royal visit, with which *The Tin Men* ends, is nevertheless a brilliantly contrived fiasco.

Frayn's next novel was of an entirely different kind. Whereas *The Tin Men* resembles the satire of Swift and was compared by reviewers to the novels of Evelyn Waugh, *The Russian Interpreter* (1966) belongs to the world of John Le Carré. It is set in Moscow and the plot depends on suspicions of espionage. There are official diplomatic receptions, a character is mysteriously followed at night in the streets, and two of them are seized as political prisoners and placed in solitary confinement. In his accounts of the urban landscape of Moscow, Frayn revealed for the first time his gifts as a descriptive writer. The predominant impression is of solitary individuals dwarfed by the hugeness of their surroundings:

He crossed the great empty plaza in front of the university, watched impassively by the gigantic gimcrack statues thirty floors above of women grasping hammers and cog-wheels. Everything seemed enormous and out of scale. Beyond the plaza, in the formal vista of the ornamental gardens, solitary pedestrians moved like bedouin, separated from one another by Saharas of empty brown flower-bed and drying tarmacadam. They were so small they seemed to be merely an infestation. He walked through the gardens. The air was mild. On the marble benches here and there the old women gardeners lay asleep in the sun, their rakes and forks propped up beside them. Manning found the sight of them curiously moving.

(*The Russian Interpreter*, p. 9)

Manning is the Russian interpreter of the title, a young graduate student from England who is writing a thesis and is temporarily attached to the university. He is a good-natured man who speaks Russian and is familiar with the streets of the city but knows nothing about what goes on under the surface. His often thwarted attempts to understand the people he meets and the events that affect him create the tensions that hold the novel compellingly together.

The first significant event is his meeting with another Englishman, Gordon Proctor-Gould, the most substantial character in the book. Manning becomes closely involved in Proctor-Gould's life, since Proctor-Gould speaks no Russian and needs Manning as an interpreter. His face is "large and lugubrious" with "eyes as soft as a spaniel's," and he immediately strikes Manning as "seedy." His seediness extends to his dark, lofty hotel room in a large pre-Revolutionary hotel. It is in total disarray, with an open suitcase lying on the floor, a heap of possessions scattered over the carpet, and wet shirts and socks suspended on plastic coat hangers from the furniture. He makes Nescafe in plastic cups. He claims to be engaged in arranging for Russian citizens to visit England—not politicians or celebrities but "real, flesh and blood ordinary people," and thereby improving Anglo-Soviet relations. He is a rather formal, pompous man, eager to make speeches at parties and receptions, but, though he is perfectly friendly, he is also mysterious and reveals little of his inner life. His hotel room is full of English books, which, he explains, he brings as goodwill presents for the Russians. Manning is suspicious of him and wonders if he is secretly involved in intelligence work but is assured that he is not.

Proctor-Gould begins to behave oddly when he meets Raya, a beautiful, vivacious young woman whom Manning has met on a visit to the country and with whom he has become intimate. Manning thinks she may be working for the K.G.B., but she ridicules the idea. What he does not foresee is that Proctor-Gould should also become fascinated by her and, more surprisingly, that she should apparently be attracted to Proctor-Gould. Eventually she moves into the latter's hotel room, goes to bed with him, and comes to dominate his life. She becomes more of a problem when she starts to steal his belongings—tins of Nescafe, gifts presented to Proctor-Gould by the Russians, and quantities of his books. As the plot develops, it becomes steadily more mysterious. We are not sure whether or not Proctor-Gould is engaged in espionage, we are unable to understand Raya's apparent attraction to him, and we do not know the motive for her thefts. Moreover, our inability to understand exactly what is happening is characteristic of Russian life in general. As one character explains, "We know nothing worth knowing about what goes on outside our frontiers. Worse—we know very little more about what goes on within them. Beyond the light of one's own personal experience—darkness. What are people thinking? What are they feeling? How do they behave? ... We live like animals, in ignorance of the world around us" (*The Russian Interpreter*, p. 152). It is the accumulating mysteries and the unanswered questions they provoke that hold the attention of the reader and bind the novel together. Manning is employed as an interpreter, but, more fundamentally, he is trying to interpret his experience of Russia.

The theme of the novel is the universal desire we have to understand the world around us and to discover patterns and explanations for it that may or, more often, may not correspond to reality. As Frayn wrote in *Constructions*, the collection of philosophical observations which he published eight years later, "We are significance-

seeking organisms. We seek out significance from our environment as we seek out food. ...We look at the taciturn, inscrutable universe, and cry, 'Speak to me!'" The novel also appeals to this need in the reader and is the element that holds our attention until the truth is finally, though only partially, revealed. If we read it a second time, knowing in advance why the characters behave as they do, everything becomes obvious and the tension relaxes. As Frayn said in *Constructions*, "The most interesting concealed truths we are offered are about what lies plainly in our view. And this is why the forbidden exercises us so much—we feel it's being kept hidden from us." Repeated readings show that "once we have tasted the apple, and found it tastes just like any other apple, the charm vanishes."

In his third novel, *Towards the End of the Morning* (1967), published in America under the title *Against Entropy*, Frayn drew on his experience as a journalist. It is set mostly in the office of the features editor of a national newspaper, a place that is evoked in great detail. A confused pile of papers is heaped up on the editor's desk—copy waiting to be edited, galley proofs waiting to be corrected—messengers arrive with further work to be done, the telephone rings all the time, invitations are received to plays no one wants to see and to free trips from travel companies hoping for favorable publicity. There is a constant sense of urgency to complete everything in time for the next edition. Dyson, the features editor, is responsible for all this. "I toil all the hours God made at this job," he sighs, "and somehow I never quite get on top of it. It's like trying to fill a bottomless bucket."

Dyson believes that "a journalist's finished at forty" and now that he is thirty-seven he feels he is "towards the end of the morning" and will not last much longer. Occasional excitement occurs when he is asked to speak on the radio or appear on television, opportunities he seizes eagerly because they open up the prospect of a more glamorous, better-paid career. "I think I'm really competitive by nature," he confides to Bob, his assistant. "I have a tremendous fundamental urge to get out and make my way in the world." Asked to take part in a television discussion about race relations with several well-known personalities, he goes into the studio full of self-confidence, speaks frequently, sometimes interrupting the other members of the panel, and returns home elated. In fact, he has said nothing of any significance, and as he lies in bed awake he realizes with shame that his performance has been a failure and that he is no more than "an insignificant speck of human nothingness trampled on indifferently by every passer-by."

For the first time in the novel, he realizes that his belief in his own abilities is unfounded and that his imagined prospects have been nothing like the experience itself. His second discovery is much more prolonged and more deeply disillusioning. He accepts an offer from a travel company of a free trip to the Trucial Riviera, whose shores are "washed by the warm, sparkling waters of the Persian Gulf, and rich in all the Arabian Nights romance of the Middle East." At the airport, he sees himself as International Airport Man, "neat, sophisticated, compact, a wearer of lightweight suits and silky blue showercoats; moving over the surface of the earth like some free-floating spirit." The plane is two hours late for departure, lands in Paris where it is further delayed, then Amsterdam where the passengers have to spend the night, then Beirut where they land to refuel but are further delayed by a technical fault in the plane and have to spend two more nights. They never reach their destination but have to return to Amsterdam, breaking down in Yugoslavia on the way. The series of disasters is, naturally, exhausting, and the condition of the passengers is worsened by their consumption of the free drinks with which, not untypically, the travel company tries to console them. At daybreak in Amsterdam, on the last chilly morning, Dyson gazes at a field of weeds and a windowless little building, forgets the failure of the expedition, and thinks about his own failure: "He was a rather silly man ... vain and splenetic—passionately devoted to futile objectives," and he laughs aloud at "the optimistic presumption of the universe." Whereas in *The Russian Interpreter* the central character, Manning, changes his perception of other people, Dyson twice alters his view of himself.

Dyson's wife, Jannie, welcomes the prospect of being alone while her husband is away on his trip, and she looks forward to spending the time constructively—reading good books, making clothes for the children, rearranging the living room furniture. In fact she does none of these things. She continually watches television with a growing sense of waste and guilt; she is unable to sleep and gets up in the morning exhausted. She then realizes how dependent she is on her husband and wonders how some women can bear to be alone for years on end. She is appalled at "the world of desolation she had stumbled on, and ashamed that she had thought of it only because she herself had been left on her own for four days." The narrative switches between Jannie's recognition of the miseries of the world and Dyson's self-discovery on his catastrophic journey; together, the two points of view form a commentary on the ways people delude themselves and human expectations are thwarted.

Although much of the novel consists of repeated, sad self-discoveries, it is by no means depressing, and reviewers found it entertaining. The *New York Times* declared Frayn "probably England's funniest writer." Although he portrayed his characters sympathetically, he also did so ironically, juxtaposing his characters' naive, excessive hopes with their discovery that these hopes are unfounded. As Frayn said of Chekhov, he is interested not in "the inexorable tolling of fate, but the absurdity of human intentions."

A Very Private Life (1968) is written in yet another tradition. Like George Orwell's *1984* and Aldous Huxley's *Brave New World*, it is a futuristic novel, a description of life as it might be lived in the future, but unlike Orwell's novel it is not in the least political, and unlike Huxley's it is not satirical. Frayn simply describes the experiences of the central character and records her reactions to them. Her name is Uncumber (perhaps because she is not encumbered by other people), and she lives in a distant future when the world is divided between "inside" and "outside" people. As an insider, Uncumber lives with her parents and younger brother in a closed, windowless house that no one enters or leaves. All their requirements—food, medicine, clothing, toys—are transmitted into the house through a network of tubes, wires, and electromagnetic beams: "Out along the wires and beams their wishes go. Back, by return, will come the fulfillment of them." They see their friends and relatives not in person but in special reception chambers, reproduced by holovision, a kind of two- way television system, which also provides them with educational programs and vacations. Since the air is perfectly sterile, they suffer no infections and live for hundreds of years. Their lives are totally private and under their own control.

Uncumber is dissatisfied, however, and intrigued by the world outside. She breaks out into it and is terrified to find herself surrounded by animate, organic life, a windswept landscape of trees and undergrowth that gives off a rank, vegetable smell. Although she is rescued and brought inside again, she still longs for fresh experience beyond her enclosed, private world. One day she dials a wrong number on the holovision and, instead of receiving her Archaic Botany program, sees a small, bald, wrinkled man with gentle brown eyes, who smiles at her affectionately and tries to kiss her through the screen. He speaks a different language from hers, but before he disappears she manages to find out his number and learns that his name is Noli. Incidentally, the long-lived insiders presumably do not go bald and have no wrinkles.

She becomes wholly preoccupied with Noli and, determined to see him again, escapes from home and embarks on a long, bewildering journey by rocket to the remote part of the world where he lives. Finally she arrives in a crumbling, dirty palace by the sea, filled with people, one of whom is Noli. She is given revolting food, which she can scarcely eat, and catches a fever. As she begins to recover, she looks at the filthy room, full of bodies and noise: "The complex life of the room first bores and then disgusts her. Always this talk! Always these bodies cluttering the room! Always the arguments, laughter, tensions, slaps, sullen silences, yawns, belches!"

She recalls her room at home with its quiet, well-ordered life and realizes that "she has escaped from the privacy of the inside world only to find on the outside a world more totally private than ever—a world entirely enclosed by the limits of her own mind," and she sets off to walk to the rocketport and return home again. The journey is much harder than she had expected, but after several days struggling through the forest, aching with cold and hunger, captured by bandits (who speak French!), she is rescued by Kind People in a traveling house who place her inside a home of her own. From there she is reunited by holovision with her family—who are not particularly interested to see her. For a while she is relieved and content to be back in her former way of life, but, as the novel concludes, she again begins to feel restless and dissatisfied.

A Very Private Life is an extraordinary, wholly original work. Frayn's imagination creates two utterly different worlds—the sterile, dehumanized world in which Uncumber grows up and the messy, disintegrating, chaotic world of Noli and his people. He has visualized the sensations of a girl who has been sealed off from all forms of natural life, and when she enters the living, organic world for the first time, he conveys to the reader the familiar sensations of trees, wind, rain, and animal life as they would strike someone who had never known them before:

> She makes a surprising discovery. The unchanging elements of the scene are not unchanging at all if you look at them closely; the earth, the trees, the rocks, the boulders on the beach are all crawling with life.... The whole world suddenly takes on the aspect of a heaving mass of maggots, which appears still and solid only if you stand far enough off from it. So this is what she has been protected from for all these years!
>
> (A Very Private Life, p. 96)

Neither of these worlds is entirely fantastic. "The 'inside world'," commented a reviewer in the Observer, "is a logical projection into the future of our present increasing skill at shutting out uncomfortable realities," and Frayn himself explained that "the insulated houses owe something to those of middle-class America, and in particular to those farmhouses in deepest Connecticut, abandoned when the farmers went west, surrounded by forest, and now being bought by city people to be alone." Frayn abandoned his former comic, satirical style and withheld authorial comment, but since Uncumber is the only major character, an innocent, we do see her experiences through her eyes, and her discoveries appear to be Frayn's. In creating a wholly sanitized, comfortable life, we lose contact with the world of nature and human warmth and spontaneity. The alternative, however, is no more tolerable. If an ideal, perfect life exists, we are unable to create it.

PLAYS

FRAYN returned to this idea in a different mode in his next novel, *Sweet Dreams*, published five years later, but in the interim he put aside the writing of novels and embarked on a series of plays. The first, *Jamie on a Flying Visit*, was written for television and broadcast in January 1968. Essentially a farce, its comic effects arise not from dialogue but from physical action and depend on the separation between the world of the play and the world of the audience, who are shown a series of catastrophic events they are powerless to intervene in or stop.

Jamie is a large, wealthy, loud, tactless but well-intentioned man who, on an impulse, calls on Lois, whom he knew well when they were students at Oxford but has not seen for seven years. She lives in a very small, semi-detached house with her husband, Ian, a schoolteacher, and their three children. The house has steep, narrow stairs and is so filled with worn furniture, a disused pram, and children's toys that it is almost impossible to move in it. Most of the action consists of frequent collisions not so much between Jamie and the other characters as between Jamie and the house. "The running visual theme," said Frayn "is the unending contrast between the smallness of the house and the largeness of Jamie—his physical size and the general expansiveness of his behavior and character."

His destructiveness begins from the moment he arrives. Greeting Lois effusively from the next-door garden, he steps into a flower bed and, attempting to vault over the hedge, lands in the middle and smashes it down. Entering the house,

he knocks an ornament off a shelf and, trying to be friendly to one of the children, makes him recoil and knock over a bottle of milk. He walks around the lawn on his hands to amuse the children but falls into a flower bed and flattens the lupins. Persuaded by Lois to stay for the night, he insists on helping her to move a divan bed, which falls down the stairs, smashes the banisters, and breaks Jamie's leg. To add to the confusion, he calls a number of his friends, who arrive in their expensive cars and fill the house to overflowing. Throughout this chaos, Lois's schoolteacher husband struggles to grade his students' papers and, trying to offer drinks to Jamie's smart guests, finds that he has nothing but a half-empty bottle of sherry. By the time Jamie leaves, he has backed up his sports car into a lamp post and crashed into the back of Ian's battered compact car.

Like most farces, *Jamie on a Flying Visit* provokes laughter through an increasingly violent series of social embarrassments that have a cumulative effect. The audience waits in suspense for the next disaster and laughs when it occurs. We are embarrassed on behalf of Jamie, who is always apologizing but is unable to mend his ways. He is not intentionally destructive but creates most of the disasters while trying to clear up the previous ones. He is genuinely affectionate toward Lois, with whom he seems to have had a close friendship in earlier days, and he slowly realizes how dull and impoverished her daily life is. "Sometimes," she confesses, "I'd just like to lie down on my bed and cry. I feel as if I'm ... *walled in.* ...Every day—the same toys to be cleared up, the same plates to be washed. The same scenes with the children over the same things." His response is to propose various impossible escapes for her—to take her on a vacation to North Africa or cruising on a yacht in the Mediterranean. His intentions are generous, but he has no comprehension of the differences between his life and hers or of the impossibility of her breaking out of it. The damage he does is partly the result of the social and economic gulf that separates them, which Lois entirely understands but he is too insensitive to notice.

The farce is heightened by the playwright's detachment from the central character. He is not detached from Lois, however, and, as Jamie leaves in the final moments, Lois closes the front door, and "a light catches the shining trail of a tear down each cheek." Is she crying because of the destruction done to the house, or because Jamie represents a way of life that she might have had but now never can? The play, like much of Frayn's work, is both ridiculous and touching.

The comedy of *Birthday*, which Frayn wrote for television about a year later, also depends on the incompatibility of the characters, but their differences from one another are not social but temperamental. Liz, in whose rented London flat most of the action takes place, is making a survey of welfare services, and her roommate, Willa, is a medical social worker. Their disagreements are of the harmless kind that occur when any two people are living at close quarters. It is a Sunday morning and Liz is first seen tidying the living room in preparation for her birthday lunch. As she does so Willa, just out of bed, leaves her clothes lying around the room. The tensions develop further when Jess, Liz's sister, arrives for lunch. Married, with three children, she is heavily pregnant with a fourth. She talks unstoppably, mostly about her pregnancies and her children, in whom the other two have no interest. Willa attempts to psychoanalyze her, much to the annoyance of Jess. The situation is complicated by the presence of Bernie, Willa's boyfriend, who spends much of the play drifting around in pajamas and scattering newspapers, and the arrival of Neil, a highly conventional, nervous man, who appears in a Sunday suit, carrying an umbrella and a bunch of flowers. The stage is now set for a crisis. It develops when Jess realizes that she is about to give birth and, as she lies in bed with contractions, the already crowded flat is further confused by the arrival of a doctor (a young woman), the midwife (a tough West Indian), and a nurse, who, accustomed to this kind of thing, sits placidly knitting.

Each character reacts to the situation differently. Willa gives practical instructions to Jess, who, having already produced three children, is understandably furious; Liz is alarmed by the prospect of a baby arriving in the world in her flat, Bernie escapes to a party, and Neil tries ineffectually to be helpful by bringing glasses of water and searching for the basins, jam jars, and salt needed by the midwife for the delivery. When it happens, the childbirth has unexpected consequences for Liz and Neil, who, emotionally stirred by the event, are drawn to each other and slowly embrace. Everyone is seized by hunger, and they begin to eat the meat originally cooked for Liz's birthday but now eaten at another birthday. Jess, once the birth is over, resumes her former chatter about her children. The final scene is of a heap of Liz's birthday cards with a photograph of herself as a baby lying on top of them. It recalls her earlier remark to Neil: "It's ridiculous when you come to think of it. One moment you're a baby. Next moment you're producing a baby in your turn, and then you've been finished with. The system's used you up. It scarcely seems worth being who you are." It would be mistaken, however, to assume that this is the "message" of the play. It is simply Liz's way of seeing things at that particular moment. The play shows how different people react to the same situation, and the incompatibility of their reactions is a source of the comedy.

In the year after *Birthday* was shown on television, Frayn's first play for the stage, *The Two of Us*, opened in London. A set of four short comedies, with two characters played by the same pair of actors, each deals with recognizable, English middle-class situations: in *Black and Silver*, a married couple return to the hotel in Venice where they had spent their honeymoon, this time bringing their small baby with them; in *The New Quixote* a professional woman is surprised to discover a young man in her house whom she recalls meeting at a party and inviting to spend the night; in *Mr. Foot*, a man and his wife sit reading but she is distracted by his uncontrollable habit of jiggling his foot; and in *Chinamen* a young couple entertain some friends at dinner.

Chinamen is the most complex and inventive. Stephen and Jo have invited two couples for the evening and, inadvertently, a fifth friend, Barney, not knowing that he recently separated from his wife, who now lives with another man, Alex, who has come with her. They spend most of the play trying to keep Barney and Alex from meeting each other. As in a great many farces, much play is made with the doors, of which there are three—one leading to the room where four of the guests are having dinner, another to the kitchen where Barney is kept apart from the others, and the third to the hall and front door. The hosts, Stephen and Jo, have to keep going in and out of the doors with food and drink, and trying to keep their guests in the rooms where they have been placed, but there are a great many nearly catastrophic entrances and exits before Barney confronts Alex, who, because of his long hair and extensive jewelry, Barney mistakes for an attractive woman. Finally, the hosts, realizing that there is no food left for themselves, escape to eat elsewhere, leaving their guests to sort out their own problems. Like the three other plays, *Chinamen* starts with an apparently innocuous situation, which Frayn gradually complicates until it reaches a ridiculous, bizarre climax. The plays are designed simply to entertain, and they do so successfully because of the ingenuity of their dramatic construction.

Frayn wrote another play for the theater, *The Sandboy*, which was produced at the Greenwich Theater in London the following year, but the script was later withdrawn and has not been published.

SWEET DREAMS

FRAYN returned to the form of the novel in 1973 with *Sweet Dreams*, which is divided between two worlds, one imaginary. Howard Baker is killed in a car accident in London and immediately finds himself driving in what appears to be heaven. Heaven is in many ways a familiar world with the features of both a modern American city—ten-lane expressways, skyscrapers and yellow cabs—and an old European city, with narrow alleys, terrace cafés, a renaissance palace, and, in the museums, the originals of all the world's great pictures. It is also a place, as Howard discovers, in which dreams are instantly realized: he finds he can fly, can speak all

languages, become whatever age he chooses, and can telephone his father who died long ago. All his friends are there because they want to be with him, and they give dinner parties just like the ones they used to give on earth. To begin with, his friends seem to him to emanate a kind of radiance, which is the manifestation of their virtues, and when they speak, their words emerge visibly in illuminated manuscript.

Naturally he finds it wonderfully exciting and enjoyable, though he does notice some imperfections: there are beggars in the streets, a black street sweeper makes him realize there is a "racial situation," and the newspapers report that there are political conflicts. Howard pays little attention to these details, however, and is delighted to be given a job in a research institute, the members of which are employed in planning the earth. One of them is designing man, another inspires John Donne to write his poems, another is advising medieval kings and nineteenth-century prime ministers, and Howard, formerly an architect, works with a team that is planning the Alps. He is thrilled to be given the task of designing the Matterhorn, an opportunity that makes him feel he is "the best mountain designer in the universe."

An old friend, Phil Schaffer, sees things differently. He insists that the whole place is really run as a conspiracy, and he reads out public notices sarcastically in a voice that makes them sound phony. Whereas Howard, whom Phil describes as "the collective imagination of the middle classes compressed into one pair of trousers," idealizes it, Phil, temperamentally skeptical and politically radical, sees it as essentially corrupt. Frayn is once more interested in the idea of perception, "the way in which we impose our ideas on the world around us." It is an idea he had presented in different forms in his previous work and had expressed in philosophical terms in *Constructions*.

Howard's view begins to change when he is told that people will try to climb the Matterhorn and will undoubtedly fall to their deaths. At that point "he has the feeling that the floor is dropping away beneath his feet, as if he is in an express lift," and he resolves to stop working on mountains. He considers going into rivers, but realizes that people can drown in them, and then considers working on forests but remembers that trees fall on people. The skeptical Phil expresses Howard's new discovery—that "there isn't anything that isn't going to cause trouble"—and Howard revisits London to write a report on the situation there. He finds London horrifying. Cancer is endemic, heart disease is raging, the streets are filthy, and, to make matters worse, the people believe they are happy. He calls on a leading dissident intellectual, who explains everything in terms of profit:

> There is a massive investment in disease and mortality which the system protects by distracting people's attention from it. It has a vested interest in brainwashing people into believing that they are happy, when in fact they are not and could not possibly be. It does this by drugging them with things which it persuades them to believe they want ... food, drink, sex, attractive clothing; labor-saving machines and mechanical transport ... so-called high culture—music, art, literature, etc.—and so-called pop culture—in which he includes the singing of old Tin Pan Alley songs, such as "Show Me the Way to Go Home," in public houses run by the big breweries.
>
> (*Sweet Dreams*, pp. 96–97)

Like the other characters, the dissident imposes his ideas on the world.

The report Howard writes proposes the kind of compromise a middle-class liberal would be expected to write. He recommends that in the redesigned earth, unhealthy, indoor causes of death, such as heart disease, should be abolished and replaced with facilities for outward-looking deaths in the fresh air, and he proposes the creation of carefully landscaped mountains, and waterless deserts stocked with carnivorous animals and poisonous reptiles. Realizing that suffering is unavoidable, he proposes that it should be hygienic and controlled. He then makes an even more troubling discovery: that he has himself been the cause of suffering. For some time he has been having an affair with a woman who, unknown to himself, is married to Phil, his closest friend. The realization that he can himself betray others and cause harm comes as a serious

shock. As his wife tells him, "You discover a complete new range of abilities in yourself. You find you can betray your friends, and suffer, and inflict suffering on others. You've unearthed a completely new range of possibilities in your character." Howard now sees that "the whole lovely complex crystal machine in which they live is built upon suffering and death." His reaction is to escape a world that he now believes to be irremediably flawed, and he and his family move to an old, ramshackle farmhouse in the country, where Howard begins to write articles about a perfect universe: the oceans are fresh enough to drink, bacteria the size of hamsters are kept in zoos, and all can be explored safely by a hiker with some sandwiches and a map.

Their simple life does not last long. His old friends come to stay for the weekend, and he converts his barns into guest houses and installs a swimming pool. Celebrated for the challenging articles he writes for the newspapers, he is introduced to God, a courteous, urbane, highly intelligent man whom Howard recalls meeting when they were both students at Cambridge. God makes Howard prime minister with a mandate to redesign the universe, and he sets out to create an environment that "offers its inhabitants the possibility of moral action; one which challenges its inhabitants to transcend it." This requires the presence of pain and suffering. There should be underwater rocks in the shipping lanes, sub-arctic regions where labor camps can be built and great writers developed, and a desert with just enough vegetation to support a group of nomadic tribes, and "exactly the right mix of privation to enable these tribes to develop a monotheistic religion." He believes that men should be offered "terms which are self-evidently unacceptable" and should be provided with "the harsh materials on which their imaginations can be exercised."

Obviously, *Sweet Dreams* is a philosophical novel. Its subject is the human condition and the widely differing views of what it is and what it should be. It is also sustainedly ironic, the irony created by Frayn's portrayal of the central character. Howard is consistently self-deceived, and each time he recognizes his self-deception, he radically changes his view of the world, but whenever he thinks he has finally seen the light, he has simply exchanged one false impression for another. What also makes him a ridiculous, laughable figure is his complacency, his certainty that he is right. As prime minister, he sees his whole life as "one long series of decisions taken with difficulty, of crises resolved. And in the process he has developed and grown. His intelligence and sensibility and compassion have been stretched." *Sweet Dreams* is one of Frayn's funniest, most thought-provoking novels.

COMEDIES, 1975–1985

In *Alphabetical Order*, a comedy first produced in 1975, Frayn again drew on his experience as journalist, setting the play in the library of a provincial newspaper. To begin with, the library is in complete confusion: shelves overflowing with brown envelopes, parcels, and old milk bottles, half-open filing cabinets, every surface covered with dusty, yellowing newspapers, open telephone directories and empty jam jars. The librarian, Lucy, incapable of organization, receives frequent phone calls asking for information, which she struggles with difficulty to track down. A number of journalists come and go, chatting inconsequentially, their conversation as disorganized as the room, but they create the impression that they know and like one another and that Lucy, for all her confusion, holds them all together. Lucy's new assistant, Leslie, arrives and, though at first hesitant and apologetic, manages by the opening of the second act to put all the files into "alphabetical order." The only real event occurs toward the end of the play, with its announcement that the newspaper is to close down immediately. Everyone now sees that the material Leslie has painstakingly organized is of no further use, and they spontaneously seize the papers from the files and fling them all over the room, making it even more chaotic than before. Leslie, undeterred, however, proposes that they should take over the newspaper and run it themselves, an idea to which the staff react with little enthusiasm. The staff's restoration of the office to its former chaos suggests that they actually preferred to be disorganized. Frayn explains,

"I think *Alphabetical Order* is about the interdependence of order and disorder—about how any excess of the one makes you long for the other—about how the very possibility of the one implies the existence of the other."

It was now almost twenty years since Frayn had graduated from Cambridge, and the setting for his next play, *Donkeys' Years* (1976), is "one of the lesser colleges at one of the older universities," to which a group of men have returned after twenty years' absence for a reunion dinner. Frayn creates the atmosphere in authentic detail—"the mulberry tree in the Fellows' Garden," "the smell of the river," and the Victorian bath house over which, in their student days, they used to climb into college when they were out after hours. He also reproduces the kind of inane, nervous conversation in which old friends engage when they meet after a long time—"You haven't changed at all," "I feel as if I'd never been away."

They behave as they used to twenty years earlier, getting drunk, throwing one of their number into the river, and singing the kind of bawdy songs Frayn had written for the Footlights. But the men are now respectable public figures—one is a junior government minister, another a successful surgeon and a third a clergyman. In his introduction, Frayn writes,

> In *Donkeys' Years* middle-aged men find themselves confronted by the perceptions they formed of each other—and of themselves—when they were young, and by the styles of being they adopted then to give themselves shape in each other's eyes, and in their own. In the ensuing years they have all, consciously or unconsciously, slipped out of these shells, and when for one night they try to reinhabit them the effect is as absurd as wearing outgrown clothes would be.
>
> (*Plays: I*, p. xiii)

The crisis of the play is precipitated by Lady Driver, a student contemporary of theirs who is married to the head of the college and has become a grand lady, sitting on committees and serving as a magistrate. She hopes at the reunion to see a former boyfriend with whom she is still half in love but who, unknown to her, is not present. She goes into what she believes are his rooms, but they are actually occupied by another man. Frayn has already established that, without her spectacles, her sight is poor, and has set the play up for a situation found in practically all farce—mistaken identity. She embarks on a long, emotional monologue, bursts into tears, and tries to explain herself, unaware she is addressing a perfect stranger. The comedy arises from the violation by almost all the characters of the normal conventions of social conduct.

In a novel such as *Sweet Dreams* Frayn expresses his interest in philosophical questions of the kind he presumably studied as an undergraduate. In his comedies, on the other hand, he drew on the experiences he had had as a child. He recalls, in his introduction to *Plays: I*, that his father wrote comic sketches that the family performed at Christmas, that he regularly listened to comic shows on the radio, and that he was taken to the local music halls, where he laughed uncontrollably at a conjurer "whose tricks went sublimely, perfectly wrong," and enjoyed the comic patter of the comedians. "This," he explains, "is the language that fed my dramatic imagination in the years to come."

The setting for *Clouds* (1976) consists of no more than a table and six chairs placed in front of a cyclorama. It depicts the journey of five characters through Cuba, table and chairs rearranged to serve as waiting room, hotel bedrooms, a restaurant, and the car in which they go on their bumpy journey. The changing cloud formations on the cyclorama suggest the changing relationships between the characters, which alternate between mistrust, open hostility, and love. The form of *Noises Off* is even more original and has much in common with the plays of Frayn's contemporary Alan Ayckbourn. It is about a seedy theatrical company touring the English provinces with a production of a mildly risqué comedy, *Nothing On*. In the first act, as they attempt to go through the final rehearsal, lines are forgotten, entrances missed, and properties mislaid. In the second act, the identical scene is shown from back stage, with various rows, crises, and disasters occurring as the actors, off stage, perform the play they had rehearsed in the first act. In *Look Look* (1990), the experiment is developed still further. The characters are members of an audience looking into the audito-

rium where a play is supposedly being performed. They behave as audiences usually do, arriving late, sitting in the wrong seats, coughing loudly, holding audibly whispered conversations, and showing little interest in the play they have ostensibly come to see.

During the period 1978–1988 Frayn translated Chekhov's last four plays, *The Cherry Orchard, The Three Sisters, The Sea Gull*, and *Uncle Vanya*, and adapted an untitled play by Chekhov sometimes known as *Platonov* but retitled *Wild Honey*. All were produced with great success and were subsequently published with an introduction by the translator. The introduction is particularly valuable for its insights into Chekhov and for the light it throws on Frayn's own work, especially its combination of the comic and the serious.

THE TRICK OF IT *AND* A LANDING ON THE SUN

THE Trick of It, an epistolary novel, consists of a series of letters all written by R. D., a young university lecturer in English. They are addressed to the same man, a lecturer in German at a university in Australia. The letters are often witty, and because they are frank and the recipient a close friend who lives thousands of miles away, we receive a full, intimate impression of the writer, who shows himself to be a naive, well-intentioned man, absurdly unpredictable, who acts impulsively and usually regrets his actions.

R. D. specializes in the work of a successful woman novelist who, at the beginning of the book, accepts his invitation to speak at the university. On her arrival, she turns out not to be at all as he had imagined her, and he is struck by how ordinary she is, "quietly spoken, slightly plumper than I expected, almost motherly." She is unwilling to talk to the students about books, least of all her own, and when asked directly about them, she seems perplexed, "as if she had found these volumes with her name on the title page lying on her bookshelves one day and couldn't account for their presence." What she does say about them is not at all revealing, but she has what R. D. calls "a wonderful dullness and brownness, like the linoleum in some old-fashioned public library." The students are disappointed by her inability to say anything significant about her own writings, "as if Moses had held up the tablets of stone and they had nothing on them but the bylaws of the Mount Sinai National Park." R. D.'s expectations of her are the first of many that turn out to be false, and, although he marries her, she remains both ordinary and inscrutable to the end. The only extraordinary thing about her is her work.

The two are thrown into closer contact when, on a sudden impulse, he resigns his post and accepts one in Abu Dhabi, where they know no one and he works in "an air-conditioned, viewless, well-sound-proofed office halfway down a long empty corridor in a largely uninhabited new concrete building," while she stays at home and devotes herself to the writing of a new novel. Their isolation does not bring them to a closer understanding of each other. On the contrary, they scarcely speak to each other for weeks on end, and he realizes that he has lost her. As she continues to write, he decides to produce a book himself, feeling that writing is simply "a trade that anyone can learn, not a Masonic mystery." He believes that he can see how it's done, that he sees "the trick of it." But whereas her novel is an international success, R. D. is unable even to start his. As the novel concludes, he realizes that the only thing he has created—unlike his friend and correspondent in Australia, who has produced a son—is his letters. They are "all that remains of my life." Yet, paradoxically, they are indeed what remains of his life, whereas his wife's novels are unknown to us.

A Landing on the Sun (1991) is set in the enclosed, private world of the British Civil Service, the administrators who work for the government. Brian Jessel, a young member of the Cabinet Office, is asked to enquire into the death of Stephen Summerchild, another civil servant, whose body was found on the ground outside the Ministry of Defense fifteen years earlier. Like *The Trick of It* it is about an attempt, in a very different context, to discover the truth. Since The whole process is narrated, in the present tense, by Jessel, in the dry, factual style a civil servant might be expected to use. He

consults the newspaper accounts of the inquest into Summerchild's death, where he reads that his injuries were consistent with a fall from an upper floor. The cause of the fall is unknown. Summerchild's former colleagues remember him as a quiet, depressive man who worked in a special unit, which has been disbanded. None of this information reveals much about Summerchild's character, but Jessel learns more about him when, in a tiny, dusty office at the top of the building, he comes across an old cardboard box containing the papers relating to the special unit. It emerges that Summerchild worked with a Dr. Serafin, whom Jessel first assumes to have been a man of Russian origin but who turns out to have been a woman who taught philosophy at Oxford. The unit, which consisted only of Summerchild and Serafin, had been asked by the prime minister, Harold Wilson, to enquire into the concept of "the quality of life," which the new government had declared it would improve.

Jessel realizes that he and Summerchild had much in common. Both worked in the same building, the Cabinet Office, both lived in the same suburb of London and traveled to and from work by the same train. Then Jessel recalls that he briefly met Summerchild and played in an orchestra with Summerchild's daughter. Jessel begins to identify himself with Summerchild to the extent of imagining the other man's movements, thoughts, and feelings, and he starts to confuse Summerchild with himself, as though he were living the other man's life. The novel is therefore in part an account given by Jessel of the transformation in his own personality from a dull, conscientious man into someone who is passionately caught up in the mind of someone who has apparently committed suicide. More central, however, is Jessel's discovery of the slow transformation in the relationship between Summerchild and Serafin. Initially they have nothing in common. She is intimately personal, loquacious, and illogical; he is restrained, impersonal, and scrupulously correct. But Jessel finds photographs of them, apparently taken by each other, and comes across dozens of tapes on which they have recorded their conversations. He is thus able to visualize their appearance, to listen to their voices as they continue to discuss "the quality of life," and to hear them in the very room in which they talked to each other. The material shows that their relationship became more personal, even domestic. Summerchild brings in a geranium and puts it on the window sill, hangs pictures on the wall, buys a teapot and mugs, a salad bowl, a can of soup, wine, and, finally, an airbed. They have, in effect, set up house together in an office on the top floor of the Cabinet Office, and the changes in the room reflect the changes—the growing intimacy—in their feelings for each other.

Their enquiry into the concept of "the quality of life" develops into an examination of the nature of happiness, which they analyze together at length, she playing her accustomed role as a college tutor asking questions, he willingly playing the role of student and answering them on the evidence of his own experience, no longer expressing himself in his usual clipped, restrained style but pouring out his feelings without restraint. "I should say," he suggests, "that happiness is being where one is and not wanting to be anywhere else," and, shortly afterward, "I suppose it's the feeling that comes from being with someone you love." As Jessel concludes, "These two set out on their preposterous search for human happiness—and, against the odds, they find it." Serafin remarks that the idea of happiness is surely the sun at the center of our planetary system. ... "It seems to me possible that here in this room we might between us just conceivably be able to make a first." Their mutual love is their landing on the sun.

With its two levels of narration—Jessel's and the conversations on the tapes—the structure of the novel is complex, and with its inquiries into the quality of life and the nature of happiness, it makes considerable demands on the reader. It is a melancholy story in that neither of the two characters has a satisfactory marriage, and their brief discovery of happiness is, with Summerchild's death, lost almost as soon as it is found. It is also a tense, exciting novel in which Jessel plays the role of detective, moving ever closer to solving the mystery—the reason for Summerchild's death (which, in the event, is not im-

portant). Moreover, as the two central characters furtively construct a life for themselves within the walls of the Cabinet Office, they become increasingly ridiculous. Frayn created a work simultaneously serious and absurd.

COPENHAGEN

THE characters in *Copenhagen*, which had its premiere at the Royal National Theater in 1998, are based on real people—the great Danish scientist Niels Bohr, his wife, Margrethe, and the German physicist Werner Heisenberg. The action—or, rather, the dialogue, for there is no action—takes place when all three are dead and look back on the association they had while they lived. Their minds wander through different periods—the time they first met, in 1924; the time when Bohr and Heisenberg worked together at the research institute in Copenhagen; wartime, when Denmark was occupied by the Germans; the time of the defeat of Germany, when the country was in ruins. Because the characters' recollections flow freely through most of their lives, the play seems to have no structure. In fact, as Frayn wrote of Chekhov, "The characters just seem to say what they feel, but in fact those plays are very tightly plotted and this is why they hold our attention. Every word ... is actually driving the play forward."

The play begins with a question: "Why did Heisenberg come to Copenhagen in 1941?" It is especially baffling because he came in the middle of a war in which the two countries were on opposite sides and Heisenberg must have had great difficulty in being allowed to leave Nazi Germany. The question keeps recurring like a *leitmotif*, and time and again the three characters recall those events of 1941: their scientific research; the nature of quantum mechanics; the tragedy that continues to haunt Bohr and his wife, the death of their son by drowning; the hikes around Denmark, especially to Elsinore, which the two men took together; Heisenberg's playing of Beethoven on the piano. Such recollections also recur like *leitmotifs*, which at the same time bind the play together and give it the appearance of shapelessness. They also provide the characters with pasts, which give them substance.

Margrethe asks, "What was this mysterious thing you said?" Heisenberg answers, "There's no mystery about it. There never was any mystery. I remember it absolutely clearly, because my life was at stake; and I chose my words very carefully. I simply asked you if as a physicist one had the moral right to work on the practical exploitation of atomic energy." Bohr replies, "I don't recall," and they begin to talk about other things. Their differences arise from a problem central to the play: the impossibility of perceiving motives or intentions, other people's and one's own. Bohr, for example, believes that he and Heisenberg spoke German, whereas Heisenberg insists it was Danish. Bohr recalls that Heisenberg conducted his first colloquium in Danish, to which Heisenberg replies, "That excellent Danish you heard was my first attempt at English." The two men reminisce affectionately about the research they did together, but Margrethe disagrees—"Not together. You didn't do any of those things together. ... Every single one of them you did when you were apart." Heisenberg exclaims, "How difficult it is to see even what's in front of one's eyes. All we possess is the present, and the present endlessly dissolves into the past."

Copenhagen is the most explicitly philosophical work Frayn had hitherto written, apart, of course, from *Constructions*. It is certainly his most philosophical work for the stage. Nevertheless, it has enjoyed long runs in England, Europe, and America, perhaps because it takes the form of a mystery—a mystery that the three characters attempt to penetrate, an exploration in which they take the audience along with them.

In *Headlong* (1999) Frayn returned again to the question of perception and the extent to which our impressions may or may not correspond to reality. Martin Clay, who teaches philosophy in London, his wife, Kate, an art historian, and their baby daughter come to stay at their cottage in the country so that Martin can finish writing a book. They receive a visit from neighbors, Tony and Laura Churt, who invite them to dinner. It transpires that Tony Churt wants Martin to assess the value of one of his pictures, which the latter finds unremarkable, but he is powerfully struck by another painting, which is being used to block up a fireplace. Although Martin merely catches a glimpse of it, he is instantly convinced that it is a missing picture by the sixteenth-century Flemish artist Pieter Brueghel. He becomes obsessed by it, dreams of owning it, of becoming celebrated for discovering it, and winning acclaim by giving it to the nation.

From then onward, Martin is determined to acquire the picture while concealing its value from the owner, and he tries to establish its authenticity by accumulating all the information he can about Brueghel—his life, his personality, his paintings, the politics of the Netherlands under Spanish domination, and the extent to which the political situation is reflected in his paintings. All Martin's researches are recorded in detail, so that the novel provides the reader with a long, full account of Breughel. The novel could have been a mere recital of facts, but it is charged with life because Martin pursues the painting in the hope of establishing his reputation and his fortune.

As his obsession grows, so does the pace of the action. Martin seizes the picture from Churt's house and is pursued as he tries to take it to London. During the car chase there is a violent accident in which the picture is destroyed; we never know whether it was a genuine Breughel or not. What matters, however, is not the genuineness of the picture but the extent to which it becomes Martin's "triumph and torment and downfall." Martin Clay is another Frayn character who ruins himself by pursuing an idea that exists only in his imagination.

CONCLUSION

FRAYN'S work encompasses a wide variety of locations, forms, and modes, from the purely satirical novel *The Tin Men* to the deeply serious play *Copenhagen*. His plays, which are mostly comic or farcical, do not have the subtlety or complexity of the novels. This is because the demands of the theater restrict the length of the plays and because the language of the plays, which is naturalistic and colloquial, does not admit the expressiveness of the novels. Although he is probably best known for his plays, the novels are, in fact, the greater achievement and allow for the subtle combination of humor and seriousness that is largely absent from the plays. The humor of the novels is created by irony. In several of them a central character, such as Dyson in *Towards the End of the Morning*, Howard Baker in *Sweet Dreams*, and Martin Clay in *Headlong*, sets out with high hopes but gradually and inevitably discovers that his expectations are unfounded and recognizes his former self-delusion. The irony derives from the inconsistency between the character's confident expectations and his ultimate disappointment. Hence such characters are shown to be both ridiculous and sad, a quality Frayn admired in the plays of Chekhov. To read his work chronologically from beginning to end cannot help but impress the reader with the breadth of his talent, his inventiveness, and the range of his imagination. It is impossible to guess what he may write next.

SELECTED BIBLIOGRAPHY

I. Novels. *The Tin Men* (London, 1965); *The Russian Interpreter* (London, 1966); *Towards the End of the Morning* (London, 1967), repub. as *Against Entropy* (New York, 1967); *A Very Private Life* (London, 1968); *Sweet Dreams* (London, 1973); *The Trick of It* (London, 1989); *A Landing on the Sun* (London, 1991); *Now You Know* (London, 1992); *Headlong* (London, 1999).

II. Plays. *The Two of Us* (four one-act plays: *Black and Silver, The New Quixote, Mr. Foot, Chinamen*, London, 1970); *Alphabetical Order* and *Donkeys' Years* (London, 1977); *Clouds (London, 1977); Make and Break* (London, 1980), *Noises Off (London, 1982; rev. ed., London, 1983); Benefactors* (London, 1984); *Balmoral* (London, 1987); *Look, Look* (London, 1990); *Now You Know* (London, 1992); *Here* (London, 1993); *Copenhagen* (London, 1998).

III. Television Plays. *Jamie on a Flying Visit* and *Birthday* (London, 1990); *First and Last* (London, 1989).

IV. Film. *Clockwise* (London, 1986).

V. Philosophy. *Constructions* (London, 1974).

Chekhov, *Plays* (London, 1988); Leo Tolstoy, *The Fruits of Enlightenment* (London, 1979); Anton Chekhov, *Three Sisters* (London, 1983), rev. in Chekhov, *Plays* (London, 1988); Anton Chekhov, *Wild Honey* (London, 1984); Jean Anouilh, *Number One* (London, 1985); Anton Chekhov, *The Seagull* (London, 1986); Anton Chekhov, *Uncle Vanya* (London, 1987); *The Sneeze* (four short plays: *The Evils of Tobacco, Swan Song, The Bear, The Proposal*, with adaptations of four stories by Chekhov, London, 1989); Yuri Trifonov, *Exchange* (London, 1990).

ROY FULLER

(1912–1991)

Neil Powell

ROY FULLER WAS fond of recalling a story told at the dinner to mark his retirement as a Governor of the BBC by its director-general, Ian Trethowan. Fuller had joined the board of governors at the same time as a businessman named Tony Morgan; and Trethowan said that, on first meeting the pair of them, he had "realized immediately which was which: the long-haired, trendily dressed chap was the poet, Roy Fuller; the businessman was the short-haired, cropped-moustached, conventionally garbed other" (*Spanner and Pen*, 1991, p. 116). The reverse was the case, of course; for Fuller was that most anachronistic of literary figures, a poet who looked exactly like (and indeed was) a solicitor, by that time legal director, with the Woolwich Equitable Building Society—a career that spanned almost fifty years and was only interrupted by his wartime service in the Royal Navy. Yet somehow he also found time to be a distinguished and prolific poet, as well as the author of eleven novels, four volumes of memoirs, two collections of Oxford lectures, and numerous articles and reviews; professor of poetry at Oxford; chairman of the Arts Council of Great Britain's Literature Panel; and BBC governor. As uneventful-looking lives go, Fuller's was a remarkably full one.

Roy Broadbent Fuller was born in Failsworth, near Manchester, on 11 February 1912. His father, Leopold Charles Fuller, had been brought up as an orphan in Caithness but had done well in the fast-growing industrial environment of Manchester, becoming a director of a mill that produced material for waterproof garments at Hollinwood; Roy's mother, Nellie Broadbent, was the daughter of a local alderman who would later serve as mayor of Oldham. But this conventional, conservative, and decently prosperous back-

ground was thrown into turmoil when Leopold Fuller died of cancer in 1920: "My father's death," wrote his son in *Souvenirs*, "shattered my mother's existence: it also caused his children to lead lives that were for many years divided and too narrow in scope" (p. 28).

Nellie Fuller and her two sons—Roy and his younger brother John—moved to Blackpool, where they lived in a series of lodgings and at Seacliffe, a hotel. Roy was sent as a boarder to the grandly named Blackpool High School, in reality a small private school in a state of terminal decline. Largely through his own avid reading, he acquired an adequate general education; he also developed lifelong interests in music and in the quirks of human nature. On leaving school in 1928, he joined a local firm of solicitors as an articled clerk; he qualified five years later but, failing to find employment in his home town, moved south early in 1936 to work as an assistant solicitor in Ashford, Kent. On 25 June 1936, he married Kathleen Smith, whom he had met seven years earlier; on 1 January 1937 she gave birth to a son, John Leopold—the poet and critic John Fuller.

Kent was a welcome escape from Blackpool, but Fuller had set his heart on London. In 1938 the *Law Society's Gazette* advertised an assistant solicitorship with a "large corporate body" in southeast London: this turned out to be the Woolwich Equitable Building Society, which Fuller joined on 1 December; in the same week the Fullers moved to the pleasant south London suburb of Blackheath. He had already begun to publish poetry in magazines, and his first book was in press; he had, in fact, skillfully positioned himself for a neatly integrated legal and literary life. Such plans were, however, soon to be disrupted by the outbreak of war. Kate and John returned to the greater safety of Blackpool, their Blackheath home suffered bomb damage, and Roy was eventually called up in April 1941. For twelve months the Royal Navy shunted him around Britain to assorted training camps, where he wrote his first mature poems. Eventually he was sent off as an air fitter on a troopship to Kenya.

Although Fuller spent only a year in East Africa, it would provide the setting for some of his best-known poems and the background for two novels: it is the one place outside England with which he remains inextricably associated. He arrived home late in 1943 "after a journey devised by The Admiralty in association with Kafka" (letter to Julian Symons, 10 November 1943). In the last years of the war he was appointed to a desk job at the Directorate of Naval Air Radio. At the same time, he was steadily becoming more involved in London's literary world. He had published two further collections of poetry, in 1942 and in 1944; he was reviewing regularly for the *Listener*; and he was on friendly terms with influential editors such as John Lehmann, J. R. Ackerley, and Edgell Rickword. When the war ended, he might reasonably have opted for a freelance literary career; instead, he returned to the Woolwich and to Blackheath, where he and Kate would spend the rest of their lives.

"When I think back to that decade following the war," he wrote in *Spanner and Pen*, "a sense of arduousness and discomfort comes to me" (p. 58). He suffered from enervating health problems—ulcers, hyperthyroidism, insomnia—and his professional life, though mostly congenial, threw up sharper conflicts of personality than he would openly admit (they can be guessed at from his 1956 novel *Image of a Society*); moreover, his youthful left-wing idealism was becoming tempered by the disenchantments of middle age. During the 1950s and early 1960s he nevertheless remained remarkably productive, even if he found his reputation overtaken by those of younger, postwar writers.

Appointed senior solicitor at the Woolwich in 1958 and legal director in 1969, Fuller might easily have coasted toward the close of a career in which his unquestionable distinction as a lawyer was the dominant feature; but this was far from the case. In 1968 he was elected professor of poetry at Oxford, a bracingly sensible choice at a moment when both universities and literary standards were in a frenetically unstable state. Four years later he became a governor of the BBC and in 1976 chairman of the Literature Panel at the Arts Council of Great Britain, a post he held for only a year before resigning in protest at the council's support of work he regarded as fashionable nonsense. Though he liked to describe himself in later years as an "old bull of the Right," this was characteristically both a tease and a mask for a serious point; estranged from the Labour Party, his political allegiance shifted only as far as the then newly formed Social Democratic Party, but he did believe, passionately and angrily, that the left had betrayed its commitment to cultural and educational excellence. His honors and prizes included the Queen's Gold Medal for Poetry in 1970 and an honorary degree of D. Litt. from the University of Kent in 1986.

Fuller reluctantly retired from the board of the Woolwich, as its rules decreed, on his seventy-fifth birthday in 1987. Despite deteriorating health, he continued to write prolifically in the last decade of his life; many regard his long sonnet sequence, *Available for Dreams* (1989), as his finest work. He died at home in Blackheath on 27 September 1991.

EARLY POEMS

ROY Fuller's first poems appeared in periodicals in 1933; his first collection, called (like Auden's) simply *Poems*, in 1939. Given these chronological facts and his poetic temperament—wry, rational, formalist—it is inevitable that he should have been regarded as an "Audenesque" writer. And so for a while he was. A stanza which opens with the lines "Aeroplanes softly landing / Beyond the willowed marsh ..." ("August 1938," *ew and Collected Poems 1934–84*, p. 19; otherwise unidentified page references are to this edition) betrays its ancestry in the juxtaposition of machine and nature and in the relaxed three-stress line. More Audenesque still—though, curiously, their closest resemblance is to a later Auden—are these lines from "End of the City," with their evocation of plumbing on the grand scale:

The shining aqueducts, elaborate drains,
Puffed fountains, cleanse a sheeted culture
Where the greatest movement is the soft
Wear of stone by water that leaves no trace
Of green, coming from static glaciers.

(p. 8)

Capable and effective as that is, from a young, untraveled poet it seems too effortfully literary.

The outbreak of war provided a lived-in concreteness that transformed his work; and the change was immediate and beneficial "First Winter of the War" teems with physical details of blacked-out London: "The last trains go earlier, stations are like aquaria, / The mauve-lit carriages are full of lust" (p. 34). "Autumn 1939," which opened his second collection, *The Middle of a War* (1942), conjures the landscape of suburban Kent, which he knew well: "Cigar-coloured bracken, the gloom between the trees, / The straight wet by-pass through the shaven clover" (p. 31). Once he had been called up he wrote salty, funny letters to his friend Julian Symons, who in turn invited him to contribute to an anthology of war poetry he was editing for Penguin; Fuller responded with "ABC of a Naval Trainee," which, recalling Auden's "The Airman's Alphabet," offers a surprisingly jaunty view of life at HMS *Ganges*, the Royal Navy's training establishment at Shotley in Suffolk:

A is the anger we hide with some danger,
Keeping it down like the thirteenth beer.
B is the boredom we feel in this bedlam.
C is the cautious and supervised cheer.

(p. 42)

After Shotley, Fuller was posted to Chatham, then to Aberdeen, and after that to HMS *Daedalus* at Lee-on-the-Solent, a dowdy and miserable place that produced his best pre-embarkation poems, "Royal Naval Air Station" (p. 48) and "The Middle of a War" (p. 50).

The latter poem, a sonnet, is remarkable for several reasons, not least of which is the calcu-

lated gamble of the title. Fuller enclosed it in a letter he wrote to Symons while on leave in Blackpool on 19 February 1942 and also sent a copy to John Lehmann, who published it in *Penguin New Writing* 13 (April–June 1942, p. 86); before the year was out, it had also become the titlepoem of his second collection. The timing was inspired and the poem, which begins with the author contemplating a photograph of his youthful self in naval uniform (it exists in two versions, somber in *Penguin New Writing* 17, April–June 1943, smiling in *Roy Fuller: Writer and Society*, catches the sense of personal change and of historical time passing rapidly that war creates:

My photograph already looks historic.
The promising youthful face, the matelot's collar,
Say "This one is remembered for a lyric.
His place and period—nothing could be duller."

(p. 50)

Toward the end, however, "The original [of the photograph] turns away" and reflects on the wider world in which "ridiculous empires break like biscuits." Fuller himself was soon to discover that world. *The Middle of a War* concludes with "Troopship," where "The hissing of the deep is silence, the / Only noise is our memories" (p. 55).

Appropriately for a book mostly written in a distant country, *A Lost Season* (1944) takes its title from Donne's twelfth elegy, "His Parting from Her." Among the Kenyan poems are some of Fuller's best-known pieces. What is striking about them is how little he has to adjust a characteristic tone that remains observant, unruffled, mildly skeptical. He is, after all, a serviceman doing a job, not a tourist, and he seems eager not to appear overimpressed. "The green, humped, wrinkled hills: with such a look / Of age (or youth) as to erect the hair" ("The Green Hills of Africa," p. 57) may be hair-raisingly surprising on one level, but on another they are merely green and humped and wrinkled, like the North Downs in Kent. As for "The Plains," though Fuller concedes that they are beautiful by night, he reports that by day their only blossoms "are black / And rubbery, the spiked spheres of the thorn, / And stuffed with ants" (p. 58). In "The Giraffes," his wariness is transferred to the animals themselves in an elegant paradox—"I think before they saw me the giraffes / Were watching me"—but the reader who expects this to develop into the nature poet's traditional gestures of empathy will be disappointed: giraffes, Fuller discovers without any particular regret, have "no desire for intercourse, or no / Capacity" (p. 58). Poems such as these, in which a familiar tone is relocated, have a curious air of being simultaneously in and entirely out of character; and they remind us that English poetry of the Second World War, unlike that of the First, tended to comprise either this sort of disillusioned travel writing or reportage from service establishments in Britain.

By the time he wrote the poems toward the end of *A Lost Season*, Fuller was back at just such a place—Bedhampton, "a new camp of Nissen huts along a bleak road out of Portsmouth" (*Home and Dry*, p. 94). The nine-sonnet sequence "Winter in Camp" (pp. 86–90) offers his most dourly authentic view of service life. His stance is alienated and withdrawn; he is the unnoticed eavesdropper, the invisible observer. The opening sonnet finds him in a drab pub:

A three-badge killick in the public bar
Voluptuously sups his beer. The girl
Behind the counter reads an early *Star*.
Suddenly from the radio is a whirl
Of classical emotion, and the drums
Precisely mark despair, the violin
Unending ferment. Some chrysanthemums
Outside the window, yellow, pale, burn thin.

(p. 86)

It is a scene of negative alchemy, in which music is reduced to "classical emotion" and even plump chrysanthemums become pallid and thin. Later, more desolate still, he listens to three of his colleagues talking around a stove. One—Fuller notices his "capable and rough" craftsman's hand—says, "The strikers should be shot"; the second, "Niggers and Jews I hate"; the third, "I hate / Nobody" (p. 88) yet he raises, "to gesticulate, / His arm in navy with a gun on it" (p. 88). Only the cinema provides a brief respite, yet

when he leaves it and goes to the canteen he is once more surrounded by "the poor anonymous swarm; / I am awake but everybody sleeps" (p. 86).

"Winter in Camp" is not an unqualified success (nor are Fuller's revisions of the original version, "Winter in England," in *A Lost Season*, (pp. 55–59). Some readers may find the stance unacceptably aloof. Nevertheless, the sequence was a candid and vulnerable attempt to define the feeling of exclusion that will recur in his work. Furthermore, we know—from other, jauntier poems, and from his letters—that part of him was more in tune with his fellows than might appear here. In short, the emerging theme in these important sonnets is the divided self, and we have not heard the last of it.

CRIME NOVELS

TOWARD the end of the war, restlessat the Directorate of Naval Air Radio, Fuller began to write a novel for children, or more particularly for his own child (it is dedicated "To Johnny"), set in Kenya: this was published as *Savage Gold* in 1946. It is a somewhat ironic variation on the classic children's adventure story, and Fuller was well aware that in writing it he was "gradually easing myself into fully-felt, and technically flexible, adult fiction" (*Home and Dry*, p. 131). He described his second novel, *With My Little Eye* (1948), as a mystery story for teenagers. (It was collected in his *Crime Omnibus* of 1988; unidentified page references to the crime novels are to this edition.) Its main concession to its original audience is its precocious adolescent narrator, Frederick French, who father is a county court judge; when he witnesses, and correctly reckons he can solve, a murder that takes place in his father's courtroom, he resolves: "Already I saw my future profession, not as hitherto, that of a novelist of genius, but as private detective. Or perhaps the two combined" (p. 32). He thus embodies a transposed version of his author's legal-literary duality, which perhaps excuses the book's hectic literary allusiveness: there is a Gothic subplot, a nod to Graham Greene's *Brigh-*

ton Rock (when Frederick loses all his money at Westsea races on a horse called Murder Most Foul) and even a merciless pastiche of an apocalyptic Welsh poet, here called Gryfydd Jones. The result is exuberant and hugely entertaining, though the narrator's tireless precocity prompts some sympathy with Frederick's father, here seeing off a departing dinner guest:

> The air was so still that the aroma of their cigars floated up to me. The Admiral's foreshortened figure, shaped like a dinghy, rowed itself off, and my father looked up and saw me.
>
> "What are you doing?" he called.
>
> "Making a list of suspects. Shall I add you?"
>
> My father tore his imaginary hair. "Go to bed. Go to bed."

(p. 74)

The dinghy-shaped admiral, a characteristic touch, must have given the former naval officer particular pleasure.

With My Little Eye is a delightful book, but *The Second Curtain* (1953) is an achievement of an altogether different order. Its central character, George Garner—who becomes entangled in a web of industrial espionage, sexual duplicity, and pursuit-induced paranoia worthy of Greene or, indeed, of Alfred Hitchcock—is essentially Roy Fuller's alter ego. A cultured though impoverished author and editor, thanklessly writing a book on Pope, he is exactly the sort of literary freelancer Fuller feared he might become had he not returned to Woolwich after the war. He has, moreover, a northern past, kept alive by correspondence with his childhood friend Widgery, whose industrial home town of Askington has to be visited early in the story. Traveling north by train, Garner "comforted himself with the thought that whatever happens to oneself, however extraordinary or painful, becomes eventually commonplace and bearable" (p. 177). This passage is partly the novelist's encoded warning of outlandish things to come, of course, but it is also an indication that Fuller is here meditating on human experience no less profoundly than in his poetry.

The Second Curtain's ludicrous plotness is mitigated by its truly funny allusions: Garner, in

a scene that surely recalls *The Third Man*, has to give a lecture called "Godwin to Greene: The Novel of Pursuit"; later the same evening, he returns home to think about a planned essay on Busoni—specifically his one-act opera *Arlecchino*. Fuller could not in 1953 have heard this work in performance (though, coincidentally, it was given at Glyndebourne in 1954, the year after *The Second Curtain* appeared), but Busoni was a deep-rooted interest, an enthusiasm inherited from his music teacher at Blackpool High School. *Arlecchino*, though unnamed, provides the novel's title and one of Garner's pivotal insights:

> When the curtain rose on the Busoni opera, he thought, it revealed another curtain. The second curtain rose on a puppet show. It was the grotesqueness and cruelty of puppets that Busoni saw as final reality: as well (Garner guessed) as their raw simplicity and symbolism which had fascinated him throughout his life. And yet (or rather, because of that) Busoni's masterpiece lacked genius: it was merely *about* genius. Artists of the second class knew all the rules for being a genius, but missed the final absorption in, acceptance of, life: they preferred art.

(p. 247)

This typically entwines a practical point about the construction of the novel—in which some characters become puppets and their manipulative puppeteer is called Perrott (with its harlequinesque echo of "Pierrot")—with a meditation on genius and second-class artists, which, one feels, Garner is articulating on his author's behalf. With its treatment of other dichotomies central to his life and work—North versus South, culture versus commerce—*The Second Curtain* is a great deal more than "a sort of thriller that has got wound up in the highbrow entrails of its hero," as Fuller self-deprecatingly described it to Symons (26 August 1952).

The third and darkest of Fuller's crime trilogy, *Fantasy and Fugue*, followed in 1954: this time, his description of it to Symons as "a clotted psychological thing, alas" (24 August 1954) seems just. It is another "novel of pursuit," again about doubleness, again set in literary London: Harry Sinton, who believes himself to be a

71

murderer, has a brother called Laurence, who is; both are directors of a publishing house. But it differs from *The Second Curtain* most notably in scope and in narrative technique: it is a single-strand, first-person narrative of claustrophobic introspection, describing an arc between two pairs of double images, which open and close the book. In the first of these, Harry finds in his wardrobe mirror "the portrait of a stranger whose deeply interesting reputation had preceded it" (p. 293); in the appropriately fugue-like finale, he opens the door of his former bedroom to find "a figure, not myself, who lowered the evening paper and said petulantly: 'Who are you?'" (p. 404). This particular doppelgänger turns out to be his brother's lover, Adrian Rossiter, a character of impeccable period campness who might have stepped from the pages of Angus Wilson's *Hemlock and After*: Fuller's treatment of homosexuality (on which he had already touched in *The Second Curtain*) is quite boldly sympathetic in the context of a 1950s crime novel, but the book remains dispiriting, glumly impressive though it may be.

POETRY: EPITAPHS AND OCCASIONS TO BUFF

"BETWEEN the bright eyes the bulbous nose: / Between the poetry the prose," wrote Fuller in the dedicatory verse (for John Lehmann) to *The Second Curtain* (p. 158); poetry, he added, was for "Enemies and lovers," prose "for all to recognize." He had the relatively rare knack of switching easily from poetry to prose and back when necessary; and the decade after the war, during which he wrote the crime novels, was his least successful period as a poet. The problems in *Epitaphs and Occasions* (1949) may look simple enough to diagnose now, but they must have been frustratingly difficult to solve then: the crucial one was the mismatch between his modified Audenesque tone, which had perfectly suited his wartime poetry, and the uneventfulness of postwar life. Two of the earliest poems in *Epitaphs and Occasions*, both dated 1945 (and both moved back into the wartime section of the *Collected Poems*), illustrate his dilemma with comical clarity. On the one hand there is bathos—"An

owl is hooting in the grove, / The moonlight makes the night air mauve" ("Winter Night," p. 91)—and on the other intolerable sententiousness: "Incredibly I lasted out a war, / Survived the unnatural, enormous danger" ("Epitaphs for Soldiers," p. 90). Amazingly, in "The Divided Life Re-Lived," Fuller seems fleetingly nostalgic for those elements of naval life he most disliked at the time: "Once and only once we were in touch with brutal, bloody life," he writes, whereas now "we have slipped into the same old world of cod, / Our companions Henry James or cats or God" (p. 101). No wonder he found himself turning to fiction.

Nevertheless, there are poems in *Epitaphs and Occasions* that provide hints emerging themes and styles—"On Hearing Bartok's Concerto for Orchestra" (p. 99), for instance, is the prelude to numerous later poems successfully based on specific pieces of music, while "Knole" looks forward to other meditative-descriptive poems about places and concludes with guarded optimism: "the spirits of earth and air still serve the passionate man" (p. 106). These are welcome exceptions to the tentative, interim air of *Epitaphs and Occasions*, which is largely dispelled in Fuller's next collection, *Counterparts* (1954); this book opens strongly with "Rhetoric of a Journey" (pp. 118–121) and "Ten Memorial Poems" (pp. 121–124), both occasioned by his mother's illness and death in 1949, closely followed by the still finer "Youth Revisited" (pp. 126–127). Alan Brownjohn has shrewdly called these "the first wholly successful poems in the 'high' Fuller manner" (*Roy Fuller: A Tribute*, p. 39); and though the gains could hardly be simpler—substantial themes and a more expansive style—they are enormous. In "Rhetoric of a Journey" he travels by train with a nineteenth-century novel for company, like George Garner in *The Second Curtain*, except that the novel here is not *Our Mutual Friend* but *The Eustace Diamonds*. He reflects on Trollope's money-driven world, where everything "revolves round the right to a necklace," "something is always missing," and "life is made tolerable" by processes of distancing and selection paralleled in his own writing:

I think of the poem I wrote on another visit—
A list of the poet's hoarded perceptions:
The net of walls thrown over waves of green,
The valleys clogged with villages, the cattle
Pink against the smoking mills—and only now
Experience what was delayed and omitted. (p. 119)

Though the conflicts between life and art continue to nag away at Fuller, art is in the most significant sense vindicated by the ease and fluency of the poem itself. "Youth Revisited" is a consciously Wordsworthian poem of return, with strong echoes of "Tintern Abbey": "A dozen years have gone since last I saw / This tiny church set on the parkland's edge ... " (p. 126), and during this time it has become—as if deliberately marking his absence—a ruin. The place revisited is East-well Park, near his prewar home in Kent, and he is accompanied by his adolescent son: "I wonder if my son completely fails / To grasp my halting reconstruction of / My youth" (p. 126). Time, place, mutability, memory: Fuller has discovered the great romantic themes and found a style to match them.Of course, not all of *Counterparts* is in this "high" manner. The dour domesticity of "The Image" (p. 130), about finding a spider in the bath, was to become more famous than its author might have wished; while a poem called "The Fifties" begins, dejectedly if memorably, "The wretched summers start again" (p. 141). However gloomy Fuller might have felt about aspects of life in the 1950s, he had found a new voice, which he carried triumphantly into *Brutus's Orchard* (1957); and it is a voice sufficiently confident to embrace echoes not only of Words-worth but of Yeats, as it very notably does at the start of another place-poem, "Newstead Abbey":

Birds on the lake; a distant waterfall:
Surrounded by its lawns, a vandyke shawl
Of woods, against the washed-in sky of March,
The abbey with its broken wall and arch,
Its scoured and yellow look, has power still
To move.

(p. 167)

Beyond Wordsworth and Yeats in *Brutus's Or-chard* stands Shakespeare. The poem at the heart of the book is "The Ides of March" (pp. 165–166), a blank verse meditation of fifty-five lines

that Brutus thinks to himself just as the conspira-tors enter his orchard in *Julius Caesar*, act 2, scene 1. It is an astonishingly bold combination of rhetoric and inwardness, beginning in fine de-clamatory style ("Fireballs and thunder augment the wailing wind"); moving through reflections on "Love and letters," loyalty and treachery, mar-riage and fatherhood; and ending as the "rather muffled figures" enter the garden with the "moon-like" dawn:

There still
Is time to send a servant with a message:
"Brutus is not at home"; time to postpone
Relief and fear. Yet, plucking nervously
The pregnant twigs, I stay. Good morning, comrades.

(p. 166)

The transition from the theatrical bombast of the opening to the troubled hesitancy of this conclu-sion is managed with extraordinary subtlety. "The Ides of March" is a poem that deserves and repays close reading (see *Roy Fuller: Writer and Society*, pp. 172–176).

Brutus's Orchard is both more confident and less domestic than its postwar predecessors. Its other large-scale pieces include "Expostulation and Inadequate Reply" (pp. 158–160), "Pleasure Drive" (pp. 161–162), "The Perturbations of Uranus" (pp. 171–172), "Amateur Film-Making" (pp. 172–173), "At a Warwickshire Mansion" (pp. 176–177) and "Mythological Sonnets" (pp. 181–189). All are poems of weight and serious-ness, and so too is "Ambiguities" (*Brutus's Or-chard*, pp. 28–29), which Fuller no doubt ex-cluded from *New and Collected Poems* because of its hectoring conclusion; in other ways, however, it is a fascinating poem. Images of quintessential 1950s disillusionment ("The age regards me from the summer sky / Where aircraft slowly chalk the blue with frost") occur in the elegiac domestic context thatis to become so familiar in his later work ("A blackbird, rather worn about the eyes, / Flaps down beside me as I clip the grass"). And yet, just as had happened a decade or so earlier, when Fuller's wartime mode quite suddenly ceased to work for him, the "high" middle-period manner was drawing to its close.

The late 1950s to mid-1960s represent the least productive period for verse in Fuller's writing career. The *Collected Poems* of 1962, published to mark his fiftieth birthday (which was, he later thought, far too early an occasion for it), contains only thirty-five pages of work uncollected since *Brutus's Orchard*; his next separate collection, *Buff* (1965), is relatively thin, too. Moreover, much of the substance here is provided by three semifictional sonnet sequences, "Meredithian Sonnets" (pp. 214–224), "To X" (pp. 227–236) and "The Historian" (pp. 254–264). They are in different ways profoundly and puzzlingly ambiguous. The first consists of twenty-one meditations, written in the third person and the present tense, on middle age, an unhappy marriage, unrealized affairs with younger women; the tone—simultaneously compressed and richly sonorous—owes less to Meredith than to Wallace Stevens (there are close resemblances to "Sunday Morning"). The distance between the author and his alter ego varies: he is plainly not the husband in Sonnet XV who sneaks away from his sleeping wife to visit the maid in the attic, for there was neither attic nor maid at his Blackheath home; whereas the insomniac reading at night about the habits of the owl is very like him. "To X," in which a first-person narrator describes his affair with a younger woman, seems at first glance much more autobiographical; and yet, troubled as Fuller's marriage was at times, not even his close friend Julian Symons could identify "X." We must trust the author himself, who in a lecture to the Royal Society of Literature described the sequence as "twenty-one rondels about an imaginary love affair—the precise number and form of the sequence called Pierrot Lunaire which Schoenberg once set to music" (*Essays by Divers Hands* XXXV, p. 79). In fact, from start ("To X") to finish ("The Historian"), *Buff* deals with the ambiguous hinterlands of fictional or mythical material, in which reality becomes distorted and blurred: the indecipherable "Logic of Dreams" that "contrive / To deposit one nude before mad girl-faced apes" (p. 241); the disembodied song of Orpheus in "Orpheus Beheaded" (p. 252). Another typically teasing piece, included at the end of the 1962 *Collected Poems* though in the spirit of *Buff*, ponders a hypothetical Shakespearean crux—"My love for you has faded" or "My love for you was fated"—which poses, with more immediate significance, "The question of what the poet really wrote / In the glum middle reaches of his life" (p. 208). The glumness is genuine enough, but it is continually tempered and deflected by irony. We shall do well to remember that *Buff*'s epigraph is from an "old forfeits game": "'Methinks Buff smiles.'" "'Buff neither laughs nor smiles.'"

THE SOCIAL NOVELS

BETWEEN the mid-1950s and the mid-1960s Fuller published five novels: *Image of a Society* (1956), *The Ruined Boys* (1959), *The Father's Comedy* (1961), *The Perfect Fool* (1963), and *My Child, My Sister* (1965). For all their diversity of setting and chronology, they each contain a central character who bears a partial resemblance to Fuller and they can all be seen as responses to those "glum middle reaches" of life.

The surprising catalyst for *Image of a Society* (as well as for *Brutus's Orchard*) may well have been Robert Graves, who, having read *Counterparts*, wrote to Fuller: "But what a world you live in! Stoicism seems the only possible attitude. The word 'love' does not occur even to be saluted with a witty Bronx cheer ... Your solicitor's job doesn't sound very thrilling" (quoted in *Spanner and Pen*, p. 12). Certainly this letter urged Fuller toward the more ambitious poems of *Brutus's Orchard*; possibly it persuaded him to attempt a "thrilling" novel about the fictional Saddleford Building Society. It is a mixed success. One problem is the lack of narrative focus: the single-character perspectives of the crime novels give way to a hazy authorial omniscience in which the viewpoint of Philip Witt—a building society solicitor with literary ambitions, who suffers from poor digestion and insomnia—predominates. Yet if Witt is a version of Fuller, he is not only a younger but a dimmer and less attractive one. The novel's dominant force is the Machiavellian Stuart Blackledge, the society's mortgage manager, who aspires to the imminently vacant general managership; yet he is too insistently scheming, just as Philip Witt is too uncertain, to function as a fully rounded character, while the affair between Philip and Stuart's wife, Rose, proceeds with all the implausible creakiness of a soap opera. Despite its faults, *Image of a Society* is redeemed—and made highly readable—by Fuller's careful attention to urban detail and by his peculiarly ambitious choice of subject: novels about office life are rare enough, but in this one a major strand of the plot turns on an improperly mortgaged property, which is not a field of expertise available to many writers. Indeed, so realistic was Fuller's Saddleford Building Society that its Woolwich origins were all too recognizable. Fuller received a formal warning from Sandy Meikle, the general manager and Blackledge's approximate counterpart.

In Image of a Society Fuller uses elements of his present, professional life; *The Ruined Boys* and *The Perfect Fool* are attempts to make sense of the past. The former is set in a small private boarding school called Seafolde House, closely modeled on Blackpool High School; its central character, Gerald Bracher, is given a distant South African background and a motherless (rather than a fatherless) home to explain his alienated insecurity. Near the start of the book, suffering from a toothache, Bracher worries: "A difficult period of his life stretched before him when he would have to discover, through his pain, the unknown procedure for obtaining permission to leave the school premises, for finding the dentist's surgery" (p. 14). The slightly pedantic, solicitorial prose is typical of Fuller, as is the way in which a day or two stretched into a "period of his life" (Fuller was fond of using the word "epoch" to describe any brief period of his own life), but the sense of the boy's helpless bafflement at the ways of an unfamiliar institution is utterly authentic. The chief interest of *The Ruined Boys*, in which with surely conscious irony the dénouement hinges once again on the fate of a mortgaged property (the school itself), is in Fuller's exploration of actual childhood influences—notably the master, called Mr Percy in the novel and Mr Treganza in the memoirs, who lends Gerald books and interests him in music.

Fuller himself thought *The Perfect Fool* his least successful work of fiction, and, despite its accumulation of evocative childhood detail, he was right. It tells the story of Alan Percival, a northern boy who, after the death of his father, spends much of his time with his maternal grandparents, Mr and Mrs Wrigley—an exact and largely affectionate portrait of Alderman Broadbent and his wife. Its focus, complementing *The Ruined Boys*, is on the child's domestic world rather than on his school life. Curiously, it then leaps over the adolescent years, which might be expected to provide the richest material in a novel about growing up, and pursues Alan's career as a trainee journalist. This, too, is adapted from Fuller's own experiences as a law student in London, when his closest friend was a journalist, Graham Miller, also from Blackpool. Even more than *The Ruined Boys*, *The Perfect Fool* is too close to a coded autobiography to come fully alive as fiction; both books are clarified, and to some extent superseded, by the volumes of memoirs Fuller began to publish in 1980.

The Father's Comedy opens in familiar territory. Harold Colmore is an accountant, a senior executive in a large organization (called simply, and with menacing imprecision, "the Authority") who lives comfortably enough with his wife, Dorothy, in suburban south London, while taking a pleasant interest in one of his son's girlfriends; the son, Giles, is meanwhile stationed in East Africa with the army, on National Service. Plainly this could be the start of a novel very like *Image of a Society*; but it is swiftly disrupted by a phone call from a reporter: Giles has been arrested for assaulting an officer. When Harold flies out he encounters a sequence of misleadingly helpful characters—a bigoted old tea planter, a radical Indian solicitor, a corporal who tempts him into a drunken evening of brothel visiting. But at the heart of the novel is a revelatory series of interviews between father and son, in which they move slowly from estrangement to empathy. This is a book about compromised ideologies, and the middle-aged man has most to learn. Harold has failed to admit how his own youthful principles were jettisoned for the sake of his career: "When did you relegate your own copies of Marx from your study shelves to the loft?" asks his son (p. 111). He is at last forced to confront his own "double life" (p. 123) and in disclosing his communist past at Giles's trial he both secures his son's acquittal and jeopardizes his own future with "the Authority." A beautifully poised conclusion suggests that while Harold has acquired some of his son's youthful anti-authoritarian honesty—"You've just got to be yourself. Don't knuckle under to anyone—or to any set of beliefs" (p. 168)—he knows that such reckless candor must have its limits in a complex social world.

In some ways, *My Child, My Sister* is a companion-piece to *The Father's Comedy*: both involve a journey from alienation to understanding between father and son and an ambiguous relationship between a girl and an older man. But whereas Harold Colmore is an accountant with a hidden ideological and cultural life, Albert Shore is a novelist and former Oxford don (whose style often parodies that of an actual Oxonian novelist, J. I. M. Stewart). "No doubt," he reflects at a crucial point in the novel, "there is something wrong with all of us, who practise the arts: whether or not it shows in our work is irrelevant to that" (p. 110); this inner "something wrong," a recurrent Fuller theme, is set against the fears of global annihilation prompted by the Cuban missile crisis of 1961–1962. Albert's midlife enlightenment comes partly from his son, Fabian (the name carries resonances both of left-wing politics and of *Twelfth Night*), and even more startlingly from Flip, "a young girl with a sad, innocent face" (p. 42) who is the daughter of Albert's ex-wife, Eve, and his old friend Christopher Leaf. Their first meeting occurs when Albert offers her a lift on a wet evening to her life class in Brunswick Square:

She said to the windscreen: "It sounds appropriate, doesn't it?"
"What does?"
"Life class. A class for learning about life."
"Unfortunately there aren't any such." How had we suddenly got on terms of these quite intimately foolish generalizations?
"No, I'd like to be taught how to be a real person."
"Most people are content not to be."
"I don't mean that. I mean I haven't any identity.

Everything you see now—isn't me."

(p. 48)

Albert's understandable, if temporary, mistake is to take this at face value—to assume that her lack of "identity" implies emptiness instead of masking a mass of internal conflicts. Later on, he takes her to an aggressively modernist exhibition at the Tate, which is not at all to his (and his author's) conservative taste, and begins to see that the gulf between them is paralleled by the division between an art that seeks to make sense of the world and one that offers a vision of unresolved chaos: between his way of seeing and hers. As the novel proceeds, Flip starts to deteriorate both physically and psychologically—at Fabian's wedding, she stubs out a cigarette on her hand—while Albert tries helplessly and affectionately to reach her. Yet the book closes with a remarkably affirmative epilogue, which recalls E. M. Forster's in *Howards End*: the human world will survive its global and personal crises, after all, symbolized by Albert's infant granddaughter, Freda: "I see that the mere fact of still not being destroyed represents a human triumph," he thinks. "One forgets how short a time needs to be rescued from the odds for happiness to constitute itself—for a new generation to establish itself in the very arena where its parents quarrelled" (p. 185).

THE OXFORD YEARS

NEW Poems (1968) had already been published when Fuller was elected Oxford professor of poetry—indeed, the book made a most persuasive advocate for his candidacy—so it is not strictly accurate to describe it as belonging to his Oxford years. Yet that is exactly where it does belong, as part of a creative and intellectual resurgence that seems to have convinced him, possibly for the first time, that poetry (writing it, thinking about it) was his primary vocation. "The springs of verse are flowing after a long / Spell of being bunged up" ("In Lambeth Palace Road," p. 293); and they were flowing in a new and distinctive way. Just as his adoption of a Shakespearean (or

Wordsworthian) iambic pentameter had given him a confident new voice in the early 1950s, so his transition to syllabic rather than accentual measures in the mid-1960s seems to have enabled ideas that had preoccupied him for years to find their properly fluent expression. Syllabics—and specifically the eleven-syllable line, which he especially liked—provide "an escape from iambic clichés, a chance of making a fresh music"; "the technique," he adds in his third Oxford lecture, "An Artifice of Versification," "can provide a way into the composition of a poem, particularly at the dry start of a period of poetic productiveness" (*Owls and Artificers*, p. 54).

He had discovered an altogether new sense of intellectual congruence, in which even that insistently nagging theme, the divided self or the double life, takes on an unexpectedly benign appearance:

No one could be more suspicious than I of
The sudden appearance of divinities
In middle-aged verse, but how else to describe
The double nature of nature in epochs
Of creative happiness?

("The Visitors," p. 298)

Nowhere is this sense of a poet at last feeling he can *manage* his creative world more evident than in the magnificent and difficult poem "Orders" (pp. 295–297), which is the grand centerpiece of *New Poems*. It begins, on a misleadingly complacent-looking note, with familiar suburban wildlife—"All through the summer a visiting quartet— / Father and daughter blackbird, pigeon, squirrel"—and then moves in a huge and gracefully ruminative arc through nature and nurture, Goethe and J. B. Bury, war and poetry, before finally coming to rest in a suspended rhetorical conclusion that is also a fine example of Fuller's eleven-syllable line at its most supple:

And what if ourselves became divine, and fell On the pitiful but attractive human,
Taking the temporary guise of a swan
Or a serpent: could we return to our more
Abstract designs untouched by the temporal;

Would we not afterwards try to get back those
Beautiful offspring, so mortal, so fated?

(p. 297)

Not all of *New Poems* is on this grand scale: "In Memory of my Cat, Domino" (p. 288), for instance, treats a perilous subject, the death of a pet, with a frank self-knowledge that is both tough-minded and touching; while "Last Sheet" (p. 310) invokes the consolatory furnishings of the "gloomy dripping world," a "blackbird visitor ... a disc of Debussy." It is the book in which Fuller, with blackbirds and Debussy, at last seems to feel at home.

Fuller's lectures during his tenure of the Oxford chair were collected in two volumes, *Owls and Artificers* (1971) and *Professors and Gods* (1973). Their witty and passionate denunciations of popular culture, which he scathingly describes as kitsch, caused a good deal of comment at the time; but their real value is in the insights they provide of a working poet's response to writers from Shakespeare to Wallace Stevens, their treatment of poetic technique (notably, syllabic meter) and their commitment to informed cultural debate. But there is at least as much about the nature of poetry in Fuller's penultimate novel, *The Carnal Island*, published in 1970, which has not always received the attention it deserves. The most subtle, compact, and carefully written of all his fictional works, it is set in a single weekend and concerns the visit of James Ross, a young poet, to Daniel House, an old and distinguished one (born in 1890), whom he hopes he might persuade to edit an anthology; the mutual learning of fathers and sons in *The Father's Comedy* and *My Child, My Sister* is thus translated into a specifically literary context. House shares certain aspects of his author's background—northern childhood, legal training—and in literary temperament he is very much his older, engagingly grumpier counterpart: "The poetic character is one of constant feigning" (p. 22) and "If only one's art hadn't always to be ironical" (p. 100) are House's *aperçus*, though they might as well be Fuller's. House lives at a carefully unspecified coastal home, and the novel's only action—such as it is—comprises a Saturday evening dinner party and an ultimately disastrous Sunday excursion to the "carnal island," where his illegitimate daughter and granddaughter live. The tone is autumnal, in keeping both with House's age—"He might very well not see another summer" (p. 33)—and with the actual season; and as the two begin their homeward journey across the river, aboard an ancient vessel steered by a Charon-like boatman, the conversation turns to the variable truths of obituary, autobiography, biography, poetry itself. Obituaries, says House, deal with "the worldly honours the obituarist despises, and the weak spots in your work he's so pleased with himself for finding." James replies:

> "Autobiographies also lie."
> "So do biographies," he said. "Though whether the thesis of the sympathetic biographer is any more inaccurate than the thesis the subject himself tries to embody may be doubted."
> "Even poetry lies."
> "But there," he said, "some truth may be found, if not the strictly factual narration biographically desirable."
> "Should poetry be read in that way? And who can do it?"
> "You, perhaps."
> "I shall certainly go back to yours with different eyes."
>
> (pp. 144–145)

Here, as elsewhere in this novel, one has a strong sense of Fuller speaking directly to his readers about the equivocal nature of poetry, his own, especially, included. All the novels have something of this—the disclosure of information that seems to bear on Fuller's more secretive poems—but *The Carnal Island* is unique in having as its central character a wholly convincing, and in the end deeply moving, literary figure.

Continuing, if only ironically, this new intimacy between poet and reader, the opening poem of Fuller's next collection, *Tiny Tears* (1973), is called "To an Unknown Reader." "You, too, are a poet, I guess, though lacking / Perhaps any public success ... " (p. 313). This imaginary reader may indeed be no more than "a private bathroom vocalist," but if so then he or she is at least spared "a whole lifetime's remorseful exposure / Of a talent falling short of its vision." That rueful note,

which is to become so predominant and so skillfully managed in Fuller's late poems, here almost verges on self-pity; *Tiny Tears* is a transitional book, in which his high and low styles start to fuse as intellectual and cultural life is continually juxtaposed with the curiosities of daily experience.

This, of course, is an inescapable consequence of growing older. Fuller had retired from full-time solicitorship soon after he was appointed to the Oxford chair, though he remained on the Woolwich board. His life became a more domestic one, interspersed with notable literary occasions, and this is accurately reflected in the poems. Auden's sixtieth birthday is commemorated, and there are memorials to Eliot, Max Born, Randall Swingler, Alan Rawsthorne; but the backdrop against which these are set is daily life in Blackheath where, in "Late Period," "discs of Brahms' / Late keyboard pieces" may assuage "The tenderness and sadness of keeping house" (p. 327), a tactful reference to Kate's poor health; or where, in "Magnolia," the repainting of his study, formerly "a sombre reddish brown," presages "a new creative period" (p. 329). The sadness, which approaches the rich autumnal melancholy of Daniel House, is indisputable, yet life's consolations are gratefully received, as a fine poem, "The Unremarkable Year," demonstrates:

But there is much to be said for a summer
Without alarms. The plum crop is modest,
The monarch has remained unchanged,
Small differences only in one's teeth and hair and verse-forms.

(p. 354)

It is a year defined by the absence of thrushes or by painting the garden shed; but it is also, Fuller concludes in a deft paradox, the year "of harmonies / That have made one's life and art for evermore off-key."

LATE POEMS

Tiny Tears ushers in the long Indian summer of Fuller's literary career, a spell of almost twenty years in which writing poetry came more easily to him than at any previous period of his life.

There were to be six further full-length books, or seven if one includes the "new" poems added to *New and Collected Poems 1934–84*. Three of them are extended sequences that attempt to work his increasingly journal-like subject matter into coherent forms: *From the Joke Shop* (1975), *Subsequent to Summer* (1985), and *Available for Dreams* (1989). The remaining three are *The Reign of Sparrows* (1980), *Consolations* (1987), and the posthumous *Last Poems* (1993). The common theme of these collections—one exactly complemented by the four volumes of memoirs he wrote during the same period—is his need to make sense of life: to embrace daily experience and remembered past, as well as the enthusiasms and anxieties of a highly civilized man at a time of perceived cultural decay.

From the Joke Shop comprises sixty-three poems, all in "Iambics that keep falling into threes" (p. 389), which run chronologically from the summer of 1973 to the spring of 1974. If the form seems at first glance constricting, the range of tone and subject is surprisingly wide. At one extreme, there is a sort of willful vagueness that finds him wondering, as he suns himself, whether he mightn't make "quite good material for compost" (p. 374) or meeting in the venerable chain drugstore Boots the Chemists and "oldish fellow" with a look of "semi-recognition, tinged with alarm." It is his reflection in a mirrored wall (p. 404). At the other, there are elegies for his uncle John Broadbent, Kenneth Allott, and—the greatest single influence on his own literary life—W. H. Auden, whose death on 29 September 1973 prompts Fuller to wonder, "Can we love retrospectively the dead / We never really knew?" (p. 390). Here, of course, the skittish and the elegiac are parallel strategies for dealing with the consequences of aging; yet the overwhelming impression of *From the Joke Shop* is affirmative, the earlier blackbirds and Debussy finding their equivalents in the February montage of snowdrops, rhubarb's "sore fingers," robin singing "in actual moonlight," Mozart and Poulenc of "The Future" (pp. 414–415).

In *The Reign of Sparrows*, the affirmation is as strong as ever, though the elderliness seems more embattled. The "Hedge-Sparrows and House-Sparrows," which are to "populate our homely area / With dashing aviators, tireless songsters" (p. 447), are an apt emblem of the former; so are the "Two Blond Flautists," a goldcrest and his granddaughter, who lead Fuller gratefully to acknowledge "How blest are those / Destiny has engardened and grand-daughtered!" (p. 456). Nature and music remain his abiding consolations, health and age his continuing worries. "Bits of me keep falling off," he writes in "The Old Toy" (p. 462), while in the bitter-sweet "Singing, 1977" he self-mockingly complains: "Of all my portraits I say: poor likeness. / 'Colonel (Retired)' or 'Disgusted' stares out" (p. 466). But the elderly mask can be a useful one for the poet, as Yeats or Robert Frost or the fictional Daniel House also illustrate; and it is Yeats who is clearly parodied when, buying trousers, Fuller describes himself as "An ageing man, a man without much waist" (p. 461; the allusion is to Yeats's "Sailing to Byzantium").

For most of his life, Fuller had suffered from insomnia, and in 1983 he was prescribed an antidepressant, Mianserin. The results were sleep, vivid dreams, and a series, "Mianserin Sonnets," which ends *New and Collected Poems 1934–84*; these often edgy and unkempt poems reach back into his childhood (his grandparents' house, for instance), recall old friends, and prompt him to wonder:

> Will chemicals renew
> One's life, and let one slumber through the birds,
> And wake and sleep again, and wake and view
> A day that fulfils the wishes of the night?
>
> (p. 533)

There was certainly still to be renewal. No sooner was the huge *Collected* finished than Fuller began work on another sonnet sequence, intended as a pamphlet, which swiftly grew to the book-length *Subsequent to Summer*; here he marveled anew "At the amazing pleasures of the human" (p. 58). This, too, was soon followed by a further collection of miscellaneous short poems, *Consolations*, organized into four loosely thematic sections. The first, "Age," includes instances of characteristic dottiness—the old buffer feeds chocolate drops to a dog, mistakes fox droppings for a mushroom—but also reaches back to the year of his birth ("Born 1912," pp. 9–10), to wartime Kenya ("Down Kaunda Street," pp. 3–4) and, in one deceptively modest-looking poem, across the whole span of his life: this is "Emperor's Tomb Found in China" (p. 7), a newspaper headline punningly deployed to describe the chance rediscovery of crockery handed down by his mother and thus forming a link between the present and "my infancy's mills and moors." The second and third sections—"Footnotes" and "Tenners" (not notes but truncated sonnets)—have a more randomly catch-all character, while the fourth, "Seasons," returns to a familiar though far from exhausted theme. These are the finest poems in the book, full of touching details the more effective for being so quietly stated: carving his wife's initial in peel while making marmalade, in the wryly titled "Preserving" (p. 44) or driving home after visiting her in the hospital ("Ward 1G," pp. 55–56), grateful for "Your scaffold-timed reprieve, that's also mine." By this time, Fuller's autumnal voice has become utterly distinctive, melancholic yet measured; in "Images" he once more invokes the modest consolations that give the book its title:

The creeper knows when it must start to blush.
As in a "magic" painting-book, the hose
Reveals an unsuspected spider's web.
Summer's about to end: let's hope to be
Inspired by rotten weather, like Debussy.

(p. 52)

That is very much the tone of *Available for Dreams*, a book formally a companion to the earlier sequences and thematically a continuation of *Consolations*. There are seven sections: the first and last ("Kitchen Sonnets" and "The Cancer Hospital") start from specific contexts; the second and sixth deal respectively with another progress through the seasons and with aspects of personal and social decay; while the central sections range over Fuller's familiar late themes—suburban domestic life, gardening, shopping, music, recollections. Of all his sequences, *Available for Dreams* benefits most from being read through as a quasi-narrative, its details resonating within an extended family of other details, its moments of

emotional power and of self-deflation skillfully balanced. For example, one poem in the sequence-within-a-sequence, "Lessons of the Summer," begins with the usual finely observed natural details, moves on to a glum reflection about the probably poor quality of 1986 red wine (he decides he won't survive to drink it), and concludes back in the garden with a witheringly reckless pun: "The annuals die like old folk in their beds" (p. 46). Conversely, in the last lesson of the summer, a delicate and almost sentimental series of images—an "empty evening sky, / Great calm, some robin-song" and a "demi-moon, beginning just to glow"—is brilliantly resolved on a note of high romantic eloquence: "If time stayed for emotion, what great tears / Might occupy the hours, and moons and years!" (p. 51).

Yet Fuller cheerfully claims, "I play—I am!—the Shakespearean daft old man" ("Sort of," p. 75); a little further on, he asks, "How did an old man's doings seem / Even remotely apt for poetry?" ("A Disc's Defects," p. 95). One answer is that in these late poems he makes a virtue of that duality—the divided self, the double man—that had been such a recurrent preoccupation in his earlier work. Part of him is indeed a representative old man who likes to grumble about the toughness of lettuces and the price of fish; who finds the times "rotten" ("Programme Note," p. 98) and, seeing "some winos" outside a "ruined cinema" through the window of a bus, desolately concludes, "Too much is wrong" ("Dans un Omnibus de Londre," p. 117). The other part of him, more introspective and eccentric, validates and qualifies the first's unhappiness, sustained as ever by intellectual life, the natural world, and, perhaps above all, by music. Mozart, Poulenc, Debussy, Delius, Franz Schmidt, Alan Rawsthorne, Gerald Finzi; jazz musicians—Sidney Bechet, Art Tatum, Bill Evans, and Ella Fitzgerald, with whom he proposes to "sigh" as she performs songs by Gershwin ("At the Ball," p. 66)—all figure in *Available for Dreams*. Both selves come together in the poems about Kate's further absence during her prolonged stay in the hospital, where the displacements of illness are treated with exemplary plainness of diction:

Back home, I have no doubt the door will be
Unlocked, because I expect you always there;
And have to search my pockets for the key;
And find the flattened bed and vacant chair.

("The Surgeon's Hand," p. 137)

The final poem, "Postscript," is an almost uncanny synthesis of themes. It combines domestic life and wartime service (his hands, "burnt through cooking, by roses scarred," remind him of the way he would "skin my fingers" in aircraft hangars); illness and insomnia; and, in the end, redemptive dreams: "Available for dreams: a mighty cast / Of all the dead and living of my life" (p. 151).

Those are, appropriately, the closing words from the last book of poems Fuller published in his lifetime. After his death, however, his son John discovered an extraordinary number of other poems, mostly written in the mid-1980s alongside *Consolations* and *Available for Dreams*, from which he drew the posthumous *Last Poems*. It is a rich, wise, and various book, mellow in its view of everyday life and stoical about old age and death: "Often I feel perhaps I don't mind death," he says in "The Story," although "I blench to think some moment in / The story I shan't be there to turn the page" (p. 83). No less remarkably, alongside these poems, Fuller had also been writing prose during this period: his last novel, *Stares* (1990), is a lightly characterized and somewhat Chekovian piece set in a convalescent home for the mentally ill; but his four volumes of memoirs are more substantial. The first three—*Souvenirs* (1980), *Vamp Till Ready* (1982), and *Home and Dry* (1984)—are really a continuous narrative, running from childhood to the end of the war; they were subsequently republished in one volume, regrettably in a slightly abbreviated form, as *The Strange and the Good* (1989). Teasingly evasive, written in a style influenced in equal measure by Fuller's legal training and by the novels of Anthony Powell, they are as quirkily engaging as one would hope; the second and third volumes, in particular, provide fascinating background to the poems written in wartime. A fourth volume, *Spanner and Pen* (1991), is less focused and too dominated by Fuller's "retired colonel" persona, though usefully informative on the workings of institutions such as the BBC, the Arts Council, and of course the Woolwich.

But it is the poems that matter, of course: the poems and, more than has been generally recognized, the fiction, particularly *The Second Curtain*, *The Father's Comedy*, *My Child, My Sister* and *The Carnal Island*. While some readers will think the poems' thematic range too limited or their verse forms too conventional; precisely the same could be said of Hardy. Indeed, in his ability to make major poems from ostensibly local themes, and in his transitions from poetry to variable though sometimes outstanding novels, Thomas Hardy is the writer whom Roy Fuller most resembles.

SELECTED BIBLIOGRAPHY

I. POETRY. *Poems* (London, 1939); *The Middle of a War* (London, 1942); *A Lost Season* (London, 1944); *Epitaphs and Occasions* (London, 1949); *Counterparts* (London, 1954); *Brutus's Orchard* (London, 1957); *Collected Poems 1936–1961* (London, 1962); *Buff* (London, 1965); *New Poems* (London, 1968); *Off Course* (London, 1969); *Tiny Tears* (London, 1973); *An Old War* (Edinburgh, 1974); *From the Joke Shop* (London, 1975); *The Joke Shop Annexe* (Edinburgh, 1975) *Re-treads* (Edinburgh, 1979); *The Reign of Sparrows* (London, 1980); *More about Tompkins, and Other Light Verse* (Edinburgh, 1981); *House and Shop* (Edinburgh, 1982); *The Individual and His Times* (ed. V. J. Lee) (London, 1982); *As from the Thirties* (Edinburgh, 1983); *Mianserin Sonnets* (Edinburgh, 1984); *New and Collected Poems 1934–1984* (London, 1985); *Subsequent to Summer* (Edinburgh, 1985); *Outside the Canon* (Edinburgh, 1986); *Consolations* (London, 1987); *Available for Dreams* (London, 1989); *Last Poems* (London, 1993).

II. FICTION. *With My Little Eye* (London, 1948); The Second Curtain (London, 1953); *Fantasy and Fugue* (London, 1954); *Image of a Society* (London, 1956); *The Ruined Boys* (London, 1959); *The Father's Comedy* (London, 1961); *The Perfect Fool* (London, 1963); *My Child, My Sister* (London, 1965); *The Carnal Island* (London, 1970); *Crime Omnibus* (Manchester, 1988); *Stares* (London, 1990).

III. MEMOIRS. "Living in London: IV," in *London Magazine*, New Series, 9, no. 10 (January 1970); *Souvenirs* (London, 1980); *Vamp Till Ready* (London, 1982); *Home and Dry* (London, 1984); *The Strange and the Good* (London, 1989); *Spanner and Pen* (London, 1991).

IV. CRITICISM. "Poetry in My Time," in *Essays by Divers Hands* XXXV, ed. Sheila Birkenhead (London, 1969); *Owls and Artificers* (London, 1971); *Professors and Gods* (London, 1973); "Boos of Different Durations," *Thames Poetry* 1, no. 1 (1975); "The Bum-Bum Game," *Thames Poetry* 1, no. 3 (1977); *Twelfth Night: A Personal View* (Edinburgh, 1985).

V. FOR CHILDREN. *Savage Gold* (London, 1946); *Catspaw* (London, 1966); *Seen Grandpa Lately?* (London, 1972); *Poor Roy* (London, 1977); *The World through the Window: Collected Poems for Children* (Glasgow, 1989).

VI. NONFICTION. *Questions and Answers in Building Society Law and Practice* (London, 1949).

VII. CRITICAL STUDIES. Allan Austin, *Roy Fuller* (Boston, 1979); Graham Martin, "Roy Fuller," in *The Modern Poet*, ed. Ian Hamilton (London, 1968); Neil Powell, *Roy Fuller: Writer and Society* (Manchester, 1995); Julian Symons, "Roy Fuller; After the Obituaries," *London Magazine*, New Series, 31, no. 12 (February/March 1992); A. T. Tolley, ed., *Roy Fuller: A Tribute* (Ottawa, 1993).

VIII. INTERVIEWS. "From Blackheath to Oxford," *London Magazine*, 8, no. 12 (March 1969); "Roy Fuller in Conversation with Brian Morton," *P. N. Review*, 50 (1986).

THE GAWAIN-POET

(ANONYMOUS, FOURTEENTH CENTURY)

N. S. Thompson

FOUR REMARKABLE WORKS of Middle English literature come to us in a single small manuscript (4¾" x 7¾"), written in the same Gothic minuscule hand, now preserved as MS Cotton Nero A.x in the British Library. In the manuscript order, these works are the dream vision *Pearl* (1,212 lines), the homiletic *Cleanness* (1,812 lines), the equally homiletic retelling of the Book of Jonah in *Patience* (531 lines) and the Arthurian romance *Sir Gawain and the Green Knight* (2,530 lines). All these titles were given by modern editors when the works were first published and do not appear in the manuscript. The works reflect the major genres of medieval literature and, internally, the concerns and conflicts of medieval chivalry and Christianity. On the basis of lexis, phrasing, and style, all four poems are generally taken to be by the same anonymous poet, here known as the *Gawain*-poet. It follows that all four poems are in the same northwest Midlands dialect, localized to an area of southwest Cheshire and northwest Staffordshire. The dating of the manuscript on the basis of palaeography is the second half of the fourteenth century. Unusual for such a small and otherwise plain manuscript is the presence of twelve colored illustrations (four each for *Pearl* and *Sir Gawain*, two for the others). They have expressive charm rather than finesse and add yet another question to the many posed by this unique surviving instance of what all critics agree are two masterpieces of medieval writing in *Pearl* and *Sir Gawain*. There is no mention of the works by other authors and no record of them having been read or otherwise noted. All interest in the texts stems from their first publication, either in the nineteenth or twentieth century, and from critical attention focused mainly in the latter half of the twentieth century.

In their own day, the poems were part of the movement known as the Alliterative Revival, a phenomenon associated mainly with northern texts, such as *Wynnere and Wastoure, William of Palerne, The Parlement of the Thre Ages, The Destruction of Troy*, and the Alliterative *Morte Arthure*, but also with the London-based texts of *St. Erkenwald* and William Langland's *Piers Plowman*. The variety of these works, together with the importance (and popularity) of *Piers Plowman*, tells us that it was not a parochial movement but one to which extremely sophisticated writers contributed, including the *Gawain*-poet himself. Why poets in the middle of the fourteenth century should have revived (if it had ever died out) the poetic meter of Old English is not clear. Nevertheless, these poets went back to the Anglo-Saxon method of composition, namely two verses (or half lines) linked on either side of a caesura by the repetition of rhyming consonants or even assonantal vowels. The alliterating words usually carry a semantic as well as a rhythmical stress, with two normally found before the caesura and one after (a a x a). They can be accompanied by an undetermined number of unstressed and non-alliterating words:

He cared for his cortaysye, lest craÞayn he were
    (*Sir Gawain and the Green Knight*, 1,773)

[He was concerned about his courtesy, lest he should appear churlish]

In *Sir Gawain and the Green Knight* this pattern is complicated by the fact that the lines are grouped into stanzas of varying length, which end in a rhyming dissyllabic "bob" and a four-line "wheel" (a b a b a). There are 101 stanzas, and, as many critics note, a numerological patterning is seen in the poem. A hybrid metrical/

alliterative structure is seen to a greater degree in *Pearl*. It, too, has 101 stanzas of 12 lines each, making the poem a significant 1,212 lines long (similarly *Sir Gawain and the Green Knight* is 2,525 lines, if the last bob and wheel are discounted). Its four-stress line exhibits variable alliteration but forms a complex rhyme scheme of a b a b a b a b b c b c. The poet also repeats a concluding word from one stanza in the opening line of the next, creating a rhetorical pattern known as *concatenatio* (concatenation), which has the effect of linking the stanzas together as a "string of pearls." *Patience* and *Cleanness* follow the standard alliterative line, some editors taking the manuscript's double virgule at every fourth line to mean the lines are organized into quatrains, while others do not.

Although alliterative style skews the lexical evidence, by necessitating certain alliterating words (as does the chivalric and biblical subject matter itself), the language exhibits the usual mixture of Germanic and Romance words for the time, with a smattering of Old Norse words. Although the style is highly literary, it vibrates with colloquial dialogue and details from everyday life. All four poems assume a sophisticated interpretative community, well versed in readings and interpretations of the Bible, as well as Arthurian romance.

SIR GAWAIN AND THE GREEN KNIGHT

INTRODUCTION. The great narrative of all chivalric tales is the quest. A single knight adventures against known and unknown odds to prove himself eventually to be worthy of his spurs and, sometimes, of the hand of a lady. The story of a quest is therefore the story of a test, namely the worthiness of a knight to be a knight. In this crucial aspect of a romance, *Sir Gawain and the Green Knight* conforms to all expectations, but after that to very little else. Being a romance, it is a popular tale of courtly exploits, but the attention to character, descriptive detail, finely interwoven plot, and its profound moral concerns take it many removes from what one would normally understand of Arthurian romance by reading Malory. Indeed, the only poet close in

subtlety and complexity to the *Gawain*-poet is Chrétien de Troyes, who flourished in the last quarter of the twelfth century, taking the "matter of Britain" (as Arthurian material was known) and shaping it into a series of wonderful tales that combine chivalric enterprise, marvels, and moral questions (*Erec and Enide*, *Cligés*, *Lancelot*, *Yvain*, and the incomplete *Perceval*).

In *Anatomy of Criticism* (1957), Northrop Frye notes:

> The complete form of the romance is clearly the successful quest, and such a completed form has three main stages: the stage of the perilous journey and the preliminary minor adventures; the crucial struggle, usually some kind of battle in which either the hero or his foe, or both, must die; the exaltation of the hero. We may call these three stages respectively, using Greek terms, the *agon* or conflict, the *pathos* or death-struggle, and the *anagnorisis* or discovery, the recognition of the hero, who has clearly proved himself to be a hero even if he does not survive the conflict.
>
> (p. 187)

On the basis of this simple scheme, which rightly alerts us to a vital triadic structure, we can see how the *Gawain*-poet transforms what is expected into something rich and strange. Firstly, suspense (and indeed the filling of time itself) was an essential ingredient of a medieval courtly entertainment, especially if we assume the poem was read aloud as part of a collective gathering; normally, preliminary minor adventures are no less important than the main plot in that a series of warm-up adventures proves the hero worthy of tackling the main quest. In this narrative, the poet dismisses them in one stanza of twenty seven lines (713–739) where the natural (bulls, bears, and boars) and supernatural (giants, wodwos, dragons) are clearly seen to be much less of a problem than the icy weather. "For werre wrathed hym not so much Þat wynter nas wors" (726): [For fighting troubled him not so much as the winter, which was worse].

Secondly, we find that the climactic meeting at the Green Chapel, where Sir Gawain keeps his promise to meet the Green Knight, is revealed not to be the central conflict after all but the place of discovery where Gawain learns the truth of the preceding testing by the Lady in the Castle of Hautdesert, which turns out to be the crucial struggle. Lastly, there is no clear distribution of praise and blame. Are Gawain's adversaries truly evil, or are they pawns in the game of the enchantress Morgan le Fay, who has apparently originated the whole plot (2,445–2,462)? And what of Gawain? His behavior is judged by the Green Knight, by himself, and by Camelot, each interpretation differing from the other. In addition, there is the reader's own view. It is thus what Umberto Eco calls an "open text": there is no one authorially given conclusion, simply a variety of possibilities, something akin to a "problem play" in the Shakespeare canon. The reader is meant to engage with the text and enter into a debate with it in order the more fully to appreciate its moral complexities. It is this latter aspect that takes the poem far away from the standard romance where a knight overcomes difficulties through physical prowess and moral courage and vanquishes forces of evil.

As Sir Gawain prepares to leave on his quest at the beginning of Fitt II, the poet warns: "A ȝere ȝernes ful ȝerne and ȝeldez never lyke; / þe forme to Þe fynisment foldez ful selden" (498–499: [A year runs very quickly and never yields the same (thing); the beginning and the end very seldom match]. These two lines suggest that not only did the poet know what he was doing in manipulating romance expectations, he was trying to make the narrative (however fabulous or imaginary) conform to some essential reality, perhaps his most surprising manipulation of all. We now look firstly at the narrative, then at the interpretation of its many ambiguous signs and symbols, before finally considering the nature of Sir Gawain's fault.

THE NARRATIVE

WE might expect King Arthur's court at Camelot to be splendid, but nothing as sparkling or magnificent as in the opening Christmas scene, which has more the atmosphere of a frivolous end-of-term party than a high religious feast for the birth of Christ. The court is a young one,

composed of "þe most kyd knyghtez" (51: [most renowned knights]), "Þe lovelokkest ladies" (52: [most beautiful ladies]), "al watz Þis fayre folk in her first age" (54: [all of these fair people were in their first age]). Arthur is no exception, his youthfulness modified by the fact that he is "sumquat childgered" (86: [somewhat boyish]) and has a "brayn wylde" (89: [restless mind]). Normally, a more venerable Arthur is seated at a great feast, such as Pentecost, to hear petitioners before the festivities commence. He then selects a knight who rides off to right the wrongs outlined by the petitioner. In *Sir Gawain and the Green Knight* this scene is transformed into a restless young monarch who will not eat until he has heard of "sum auenturus Þyng, an vncouÞe tale / Of sum mayn meruayle" (93–94: [some daring exploit, an unheard of tale of some great marvel]).

He gets more than he bargains for when, while he is out of his seat talking to some guests, there comes clattering into the hall one of the most incredible fusions of courtly and fantastic ever conceived in a romance, a huge kight and horse, both totally green. Thus into the dead season of winter rushes a summery, almost pagan figure, whose similarity to the enigmatic Green Man found in some churches is yoked to an ornament and style more at one with the extravagant courtliness of Camelot. Looking around, this fantastic figure's red eyes scan the assembled court for Arthur and in a less than courtly manner he demands abruptly, "Wher is ... þe gouenour of Þis gyng?" (224–225: [Where is ... the ruler of this company?]). He then offers the King a "Crystemas gomen" (283: [Christmas game]), which has been identified from other traditional narratives as a Beheading Game. An unusual challenger offers his head to a hero for decapitation, if the hero will accept to offer his own head at a later date. Naturally, the odds seem in favor of the hero, but the challenger is able to regain the head (and life), much to the chagrin of the hero, who must now submit his own head. The outcomes of the narratives vary, but all involve an education for the hero. In this particular case, the Green Knight goads the court with taunts about its renown and its pride until, in a rush of anger (and also, we feel, youthful rashness), Arthur accepts the Green Knight's challenge. It is at this point that Sir Gawain intervenes to beg for the task.

For reasons of dignity, and practicality, the king was the one man who could not fight; in real life, he had a champion to fight for him, his own life deemed too precious to put at risk (cf. the game of chess). On the other hand, Gawain cannot accuse his king of impetuosity, nor of foolhardiness, nor of being incompetent to fulfill the task. In a speech of great diplomacy (343–361) he acknowledges that both the assembled knights and the king are perfectly capable of dealing with this trivial matter (not that any other knight has stepped forward); then he says that he is the "wakkest ... of wyt feblest" (354: [weakest and feeblest of wit]), and thus would be the least missed; finally, seeing that he asked first and is the King's nephew, Arthur should grant him his wish. Camelot very quickly confers and agrees with the new proposal, which allows everyone to save face.

But as Gawain takes up Arthur's position, the Green Knight pauses and insists they "Refourme ... our forwardes" (378: [Restate ... our terms]). He has Gawain state his name, and the time and the place of the next meeting, even specifying that there be no witnesses. If the Green Knight is a strange mixture of wild green man and chivalric warrior, he appears an even stranger figure insisting here on what is a serious mercantile agreement. But only after Gawain has chopped his head off and he in turn has retrieved it from the horrified knights does he utter the concluding condition of the place where in one year's time they are to meet, namely the Green Chapel.

Toward the end of the next year Gawain has to depart on his quest to find this mysterious place. Much is passed over in favor of concentrating on the realistic details of weather and landscape that a real traveler would have had to battle. As he approaches Christmas in unknown territory, Gawain prays for lodging where he might offer thanks to God. Almost immediately, he perceives through the trees an elegant castle, so finely wrought it seems like a banquet decoration cut

out of paper. Inside, he is recognized and made much of by the company, who cannot wait to hear stories of his adventures in love. At the conclusion of the season's festivities, the lord of the castle (Sir Bertilak) insists on an Exchange of Winnings game with his remaining guest, establishing a compact whereby everything he gains out hunting will be exchanged for what Gawain "wins" indoors.

This second narrative topos from earlier tales leads up to the third, interwoven with it, namely the Temptation Scenes. A standard event in Arthurian romance, temptations are usually by maidens who turn out to be demons (for example, *The Quest of the Holy Grail*) but are also found in more comic narratives (see E. Brewer, 1992). On three consecutive days Sir Bertilak goes out hunting, while every morning the lady of the castle comes to Sir Gawain's room with the specific intention of offering herself to sleep with him. The knight's efforts to preserve his chastity in the face of so delightful a companion are highly amusing, especially if the reader remembers Gawain's reputation for "luf-talkyng" (927: [the artful conversation of love]) and, in other romances, for being an unprincipled lecher. The lady's assaults are not simply coquettish dalliance, mixed with direct invitation, but also a witty interpretation of the canon of chivlaric romance, which she says is more to do with the exploits of knights in lady's chambers than anything else (1,512–1,519). Although he is highly attracted to the young lady (there would be no point if he were not), Gawain is bound by his courtesy to the lord to refuse politely. On the first and second days he manages this by conceding a kiss, which he duly passes on to Sir Bertilak, much to the other's amusement, and receives the days' spoils of a deer and a wild boar. On the third day, however, Gawain also accepts a beautifully woven green silk girdle from the lady because, she tells him, it has magical properties that will help save his life. That evening, Gawain admits to three kisses received but retains the magical "lovelace." In return, he receives the "foule fox felle" (1,944: [dirty fox skin]) that was the lord's only gain at the hunt. If Gawain received good meat on the first two days for his honesty, on the third he receives the sly fox as an emblem of his own deception with the lady's gift. It is also symbolic of the skin he himself might lose.

Despite retaining the talisman, Gawain has a sleepless night before he must resume his quest, Sir Bertilak having told him earlier that the Green Chapel lies close by. A servant rides out with him and points him in the right direction, adding that if Gawain were simply to ride home, no one would be any the wiser. Gawain resists this further temptation. Very shortly, hearing a great scraping sound on a hillside, he sees a barrow on the ground and knows that he has found the so-called Green Chapel. Brandishing the great axe he has been sharpening, the Green Knight strides out of the woods ready to implement his side of the bargain, and Gawain dutifully kneels to receive the blow. But, as with the grinding noise, the Green Knight is a master of terror and suspense. Seeing Gawain flinch, he feints with two blows. On the third, with Gawain firmly convinced his head will fly, his adversary skilfully brings the axe up short so that it only nicks the flesh of Gawain's neck. Seeing his blood stain the snow, Gawain immediately lets the Green Knight know that he has had his chance and that he now stands ready for a real fight.

But the Green Knight calls a halt to proceedings and surprises both Gawain and reader by revealing that his is both Sir Bertilak and the Green Knight, and that he brought about his wife's wooing of Gawain, for whom he is full of admiration:

I sende hir to asay Þe, and soÞly me Þynkkez
On Þe fautlest freke Þat ever on fote ȝede.
As perle bi Þe quite pese is of prys more,
So is Gawayn, in god fayth, bi oÞer gay knyȝtez.
(2,362–2,365)

[I sent her to test you and truly it seems to me that you are the most faultless knight to walk the earth. As a pearl is worth more than a white pea, so—in good faith—Gawain is worth more than other fair knights.]

Although the Green Knight upbraids Sir Gawain for having kept the girdle, he knows Gawain did not covet it for being a fine piece of work, and only kept it because he thought it might save his life. The Green Knight does not therefore blame him. Moreover, by accepting the lady's girdle, Gawain was able to refuse her other charms and thus, we suppose, does not suffer decapitation, only a nick on the third blow in token of his failing on the third day of the temptations.

Gawain, however, is far from satisfied with the Green Knight's approval. He casts the girdle on the ground and launches into a catalogue of faults, which seems to encompass breaking a number of the pentangle virtues (see below) but culminates in an overwhelming commission of "vyse, Þat vertue dystryez" (2,375: [vice, that destroys virtue]). Once again, the Green Knight is sympathetic, and after Gawain's confession he assumes the role of a priest-confessor and absolves Gawain of any blame. Gawain is still far from satisfied with himself and seeks to find fault with the women who beguile men but concedes that if Adam, Solomon, Samson, and David were taken in, he might be the less to blame. Naturally, he declines the Green Knight's offer to stay at the castle again on his return to Camelot.

Wearing the girdle as a badge of his shame (2,488), Gawain is greeted as victorious, having upheld the virtue and renown of the Round Table. As for his shame, all decide to wear a green girdle, both to minimize the shame Gawain feels and to show that his failing is a human one shared by all. The poem ends, as it began, with a salute to the founding of Britain by the exiled Trojan warrior Brutus, leaving the reader to debate the three judgments on Gawain: by the Green Knight, Gawain himself, and Camelot.

SIGNS AND SYMBOLS

IN many ways, *Sir Gawain and the Green Knight* is a very modern text. Its "open" ending provides no moral closure in the way one would expect of a medieval text. Moreover, the work exhibits, on the one hand, enigmatic signs and symbols that complicate the reading process and, on the other, signs and symbols that are radically overdetermined and yet cause as much ambiguity as, say, the figure of the Green Knight.

Firstly, what are we to make of this strange figure, so tantalizingly real and yet so fantastically without precedent? He breaks into the poem indecorously but is gorgeously arrayed, sometimes courteous, sometimes bluff and belligerent, as he challenges the court to accept his deadly game. If one can rightly see his kinship with wild men of the woods, Green Men and the like, he has undergone several accretions of courtliness, manners and dress. When he enters the hall, he carries in one hand a "holyn bobbe" (206: [holly branch]) as a sign of peace and in the other his tremendous axe, an obvious sign of war. At the same time, and as he points out, he is not dressed for battle, having left his armor at home. Nevertheless, his game is a deadly one.

His effect on Camelot is not only a dumbfounded silence but also a shrewd appraisal of him as a man of war:

He loked as layt so ly3t —
So sayd al Þat hym sy3e.
Hit semed as no man mon my3t
Under his dynttez dry3e.

(199–202)

[His look was as swift as lightning, so said all who saw him. It seemed as if no man could survive under his great blows.]

This reductive, if entirely practical, reading of the Green Knight enhances his physical presence and his manliness. The knights put him on a par with themselves and see that this knight has advantages of size and strength they could not possibly equal. If we think of the Green Knight as a man bewitched (as, very possibly, he is), who has turned green for some reason, he swiftly enters the world of "faerie" when he retrieves his head after the blow and begins to speak. We are left wondering what kind of creature he is. When we later find out that he is also Sir Bertilak, this relates him to the shape shifters of Old Norse literature. But shape shifters were autonomous creatures, whereas the Green Knight admits that he was sent in that shape to Camelot by the enchantress Morgan le Fay (Arthur's half-sister and arch-enemy), who we realize is the lady's ancient companion in Hautdesert. At court he was to test Camelot's pride and also scare Guinevere to death (2,456–2,466). But he takes full responsibility for testing Gawain at his own castle (2,358–2,362). We are left to wonder which is the originary creature: Green Knight or Sir Bertilak? As with the exact "nature" of the Green Knight, there has been no satisfactory answer to the question.

What we can read with certainty is the complex role that the Green Knight/Sir Bertilak serves. In many ways, he does not have to be explained by outside reference, for there is enough in the text to give a poetic reading that is simple and yet not reductive. Other than his chivalry, the knight's most striking attribute is his greenness, accentuated by his great bushy beard and general hirsute appearance, and his red eyes looking perhaps like berries in a holly bush, all of which link him to nature. The fact that he can be decapitated and still survive links him even more to the cropping of vegetation and to myths of ceremony and ritual (for example, the famous John Barleycorn songs, associated with mumming). He arranges to meet Sir Gawain on the first day of the year, a significant stepping over into a new cycle (cf. 101 stanzas). Thus he represents a conceptual nature, everything that is "other" to humanity. Nature is multiple, it is larger than we are, and, of course, it can regenerate itself in its multiplicity, especially after pruning or cropping. It extends beyond the compass of the single individual conceptually, geographically and in time. It will go on "living" long after we are dead. These attributes make the Green Knight, for all his mystery, a satisfying character in the poem, such that we can accept him for what he is. He is what one would want conceptually, as well as dramatically, to test the limits of humanity, because he goes so far beyond them; indeed, he transcends them, such that some critics have tried to see in him a Christ figure. He puts all of man's pretensions to chivalry in perspective (especially its unavoidable urge to perfection) and is a fitting figure to test them. Ultimately, for all the fascination of the Green Knight, the poem is about humanity and its claims to virtue. When he comes to Camelot to find its "sourquydrye" (311: [pride]) and its renown for great deeds, he is not telling the half of it. If Camelot's pride appears here to be simply satisfaction at its own good name, the poem takes the claim much further. Chivalry's pretension to perfection is linked to the most fundamental sin, namely pride.

Against the Green Knight's taunts, Camelot musters its best shot in the figure of Gawain. As the superlative representative of Arthurian chivalry, Gawain sets out dressed emblematically in everything that Camelot and chivalry hold dear, including the spiritual blessing of Christianity. In the course of his quest, we see the superlatives buckle under the strain and learn there is no failsafe system of human perfection. As Christianity taught, only God was perfect. What, we might ask, was a medieval knight supposed to be? A bundle of roles that, in essence, were in conflict: a warrior, a courtly lover, a courtier (adviser, diplomat), and, above all, a Christian. The inherent tensions here had been long (and long continued to be) explored in Arthurian narrative, especially in the figure of Lancelot. As courtly lover, his romantic devotion (so perfect in its way) to Guinevere is flawed, she is the king's wife, and his actions are treasonable to the feudal lord to whom he also should be dutiful. As a warrior he is without equal, and yet this does not square with his duty to God. Indeed, as with any warrior, how is he to turn the other cheek? Certainly not on the field of battle. How can Lancelot hope to serve Arthur fully at the same time that he serves Guinevere, while he must defend himself (and his adultery) against accusations, and how does it all square again with his Christian faith? Yet Sir Lancelot is the flower of chivalry, able to support his transgression by his legendary prowess.

In this particular romance, the Lancelot-Guinevere-Arthur triangle becomes that of Gawain-the lady-Sir Bertilak. Indeed, in the figure of Gawain we are to assume much that pertains to chivalric perfection. Around his head he wears turtledoves and true-love-knots associated with courtly love; conversely, on the inner side of his shield, next to his heart, is the image of the Virgin Mary, both conflicting with his warrior's armor. If this conflict were not clear enough, on the outside of his shield (and on his surcoat) he wears the symbol of the pentangle, a complex sign that we learn is composed of five grouped elements of five (pentads), which together comprise and expound Gawain's "trawÞe" (626, 638–639). As many critics have noted, this is not the simple truth of Gawain's veracity but more the "whole truth," everything that he is supposed to stand for, spiritually as well as morally: a very high order of chivalry indeed. It will thus be convenient to retain the Middle English version of the word to mean precisely this valency. But again we can see the pentads in potential conflict. They represent his "five wits," "five fingers," "five wounds of Christ," "five joys of Mary," and a fifth pentad comprising the virtues of "fraunchuyse" [generosity], "felaȝschyp" [fellowship], "clannes" [purity], "cortaysye" [courtesy] and "pité" [pity or piety]. These physical, moral and spiritual virtues contain contradictions in the same way we have seen with regard to Lancelot. In a masterly comedy of manners, the *Gawain*-poet explores these tensions, pointing us gently toward the truth but not insisting on it himself, testing the efficacy of the pretensions (as they turn out to be) to the claim to "trawÞe." For what is this magnificent set of attributes if not tantamount to the sin of pride? How can any one man encompass so much? Every individual in the Middle Ages knew that perfection lay only in heaven, it was taken as foundational. Yet they still yearned for fictional perfection in romance. Today, perhaps, we innocently take the symbol of the pentangle at face value. A medieval audience should have been much more suspicious or circumspect. Certainly, the crucifix would have been a more orthodox symbol: it was essentially the locus of God's "trawÞe" for mankind; or the Virgin Mary, perhaps (here relegated to the underside of the shield). Instead of these, the poet substitutes the pentangle as the man-made symbol of a totalizing truth, going to great lengths to persuade his readers of its efficacy, blithely stating that this "endless knot" is known all over England. Why, then, does he describe its configuration in a symbolic twenty-five lines

(640–665) if his audience is so familiar with it? The simple answer is that, despite its heritage as Solomon's Seal, it was not well known at all at the time in England. There are no references to it or representations in contemporary manuscripts or anywhere else, except possibly one or two carvings. And certainly the moral configuration given to its five pentads is purely the poet's own.

GAWAIN'S FAULT

HEAPED with such a wealth of signification on the outside, what of Sir Gawain's inner self? This is a crucial question. The interplay of tensions in Sir Lancelot passes without the hero losing a single night's sleep (except for dreams or passion). There are no moral debates in the head of Sir Lancelot. Indeed, there is no "innerness" to the characters of Arthurian romance; they play out their roles on the surface, winning or losing as the case may be. The same cannot be said of Sir Gawain. We learn a good deal about what he thinks and feels and certainly share in his embarrassments over the lady's attentions, though we learn nothing of any qualms he may have had taking the lovelace. Despite his overdetermined set of symbols supposedly representing his inner qualities, Sir Gawain opts for a magical talisman taken from the supernatural world when his life is on the line. We might argue with the Green Knight that this is quite understandable under the circumstances. Why should Gawain not avail himself of such help when he has to face a magical figure? Except that it should remind him that he is not perfect and that it conflicts directly with his profession of faith, which, in the conspectus of the poem alone, we know to be an efficacious system: it protects him in the wilds and answers his prayer with the appearance of Hautdesert (however dubious a benefit), and the Virgin is seen to watch over his confrontation with the lady (1,668–1,669). Thus Gawain really has no excuse for taking the lovelace, except that receiving it as a favor was the only courteous thing to do when he was patently not accepting what else the lady was attempting to offer. But in keeping it, he breaks his word with Sir Bertilak.

An examination of the various aspects of Sir Gawain's fault is a critical issue central to a reading of the poem. As has been demonstrated, the complex of issues is not open to one single resolution. If Gawain fails to put his faith where it supremely belongs, we can side with the Green Knight, considering the pressure he was under at the time and the fact that, despite everything, he wanted to treat the lady courteously. Camelot, too, complements the knight on having survived both ordeals (he confesses everything to them), furthermore, they symbolically absorb him back into the common flawed humanity they all share by wearing the green girdle as a badge of shame. This simple, flexible fold of cloth replaces the magnificent golden pentangle as a more humble sign of Camelot, an acknowledgment of imperfection.

But what of Gawain himself? While being sensitive enough to the lady's advances to be acutely embarrassed by them, he appears supremely oblivious to the complexities outlined above. Indeed, he seems genuinely surprised and ashamed when the Green Knight reveals himself to be Sir Bertilak and unmasks Gawain's own deception in retaining the magic girdle—a small fault but, in the context of medieval chivalry, also a spiritual enormity. This never seems to occur to Gawain, who appears to have no inner sense of guilt. We learn that he confesses before leaving Hautdesert, but does he confess to taking the girdle? And when confronted by the fact, he seems genuinely at a loss as to what exactly he has done wrong. In dashing the lovelace to the ground, he seems to take elements of the pentangle virtues and test himself against each one, so that it comes to pieces in his speech. However, there is no one fault he can find with himself; he can only finish on the climactic "untrawÞe," the direct opposite of his "trawÞe."

Given the many mitigating circumstances, the reader feels that this is too much. In many ways, Gawain is like Superman suddenly finding himself in a "Peanuts" cartoon. He is playing by one set of rules, everyone else by another. Perhaps we feel that his judgment is simply too rigid, too absolute. Do we not prefer to side with the Green Knight or with Camelot? And yet here is the profound truth about the pentangle, and it explains the difficulty everyone has in pinpointing Gawain's fault. If the pentangle is broken at any one point, then it is broken everywhere: it is no longer perfect. But then who said the pentangle was "trawÞe"? It is, after all, a man-made symbol (the seal of Solomon) and hence, like all things human, fatally flawed. Gawain does not seem to see this, thinking that if he cannot be the perfect hero, he will be the perfect failure, along with other great heroes of the past. Gawain's ultimate fault is that, in his pride, he wants to be singular and different, and it is up to Camelot to remind him that, *sub specie aeternatis*, he is not. It is this deeply human lesson that stands at the heart of this remarkable poem.

PEARL

DOCTRINE and Debate. *Pearl* opens with an ambiguous lament for a lost precious pearl, described in such a way that it could almost be a courtly beloved, especially by the use of the feminine pronoun:

Oute of oryent, I hardyly saye,
Ne proued I neuer her precious pere.
So rounde, so reken in vche array,
So smal, so smoÞe her sydez were

(3–6)

[I can surely say that I never found her equal in value among (pearls of) the Orient. So round, so lovely in every setting, so slender and so smooth her sides were.]

This precious pearl has been lost in the earth. In his grief the first-person narrator (the Dreamer) lies down on the spot and falls asleep and has a marvelous dream (62–64). In it his spirit is taken to a paradise garden where, after a fulsome description of its delightful surroundings, he sees a maiden dressed in white pearls standing at the foot of a crystal cliff across a stream (157 ff.). He recognizes her, but the reader does not yet learn that she is the "Pearl" he has lost, although the line "So smoÞe, so smal, so seme sly3t" [190: [So smooth, so slender, so becomingly slim]) prepares us for the later identification (233). It turns out that the maiden is the Dreamer's daughter, a relationship on which critics have unanimously agreed, based on line 233: "Ho watz me nerre Þen aunte or nece" ([She was closer to me than aunt or niece]). The ambiguity of the relationship here allows readers to identify with the Dreamer's loss on the basis of any close bereavements they may have experienced themselves.

Seeing him, the Pearl Maiden takes off her crown with great solemnity, bows gracefully and with a word invites the Dreamer to speak. Overwhelmed at seeing her, the Dreamer asks if in this "paradys erde" (248: [earthly paradise]) she is the "Pearl" he has lost, leaving him a "joylez juelere" (252: [joyless jeweler]). Putting her crown back on, the Maiden picks up on the language of "pearls" and "jewels," replying with authority that the "jeweler" is mistaken to say that his "Pearl" is lost and that he is mad to mourn on account of it. What he lost was simply a rose "Þat flowred and fayled as kynde hyt gef" (270: [That flowered and died according to nature]). If she is eternally in the "cofer" (259: [casket]) of this paradise garden, she is truly a "precious pearl" and not a transitory earthly thing. The Dreamer begs the Maiden's pardon, saying that her words are jewels (of comfort) and that, having found her, he joyfully wishes to come and dwell with her. Once more the Maiden rebukes him rather sharply, telling him that he is mistaken in three things and does not even understand one of them:

Þou says Þou trawez me in Þis dene Becawse Þou may with y3en me se;
AnoÞer, Þou says in Þis countré
Þyself schal won with me ry3t here;
Þe Þrydde, to passe Þys water fre:
Þat may no joyful jueler.

(295–300)

[You say you believe me to be in this valley because you can see me with your eyes; another thing you say is that you shall come to live with me right here in this country; the third thing is that no joyful jeweler can cross this noble stream.]

It is clear that the Dreamer does not understand the nature of his evolving dream. It is partly his amazement and wonder at the vision, partly a dramatic ploy on the poet's part so that the Maiden has an opportunity to instruct. The Maiden expounds on the above three points, reminding the Dreamer explicitly that he is foolish only to believe what he can plainly see, and that he is guilty of pride and presumption if he thinks that he may dwell there, saying that he must be patient and wait until his time comes; indeed, that he must suffer death. Yet again, he must ask permission to dwell there, and this may not be granted. The Dreamer sorrowfully asks the Maiden if, having found her, he must now lose her once more. At this point she tells him explicitly that, even though she died so young, she is one of the blessed in heaven. The Dreamer marvels, wondering if this can be true, whereupon the Maiden expounds on the idea of the "cortayse" of heaven (section VIII), turning the meaning of courtly graciousness to signify a heavenly grace that will accept all suitable comers. The Dreamer finds this difficult to accept and tries to bring earthly reason to bear, protesting that the Maiden had barely done anything to justify her place in heaven:

þou lyfed not two ȝer in oure Þede;
þou cowÞez neuer God nauÞer plese ne pray,
Ne neuer nawÞer Pater ne Crede —
And quen mad on Þe fyrst day!

(483–486)

[You lived not two years in our company; you never knew how to please God, nor to pray to him, nor did you ever know your Paternoster or Creed—and yet made a queen on the first day!]

Having already stated that the crown she wears is common to all the blessed (447–448), who are made either a king or a queen, the Maiden further explains her position by repeating the parable of the vineyard from Matthew 20: 1–16 (section IX). If this analogy strains logic, as several critics have said, it makes perfect sense if one considers the length of service in the vineyard. Like the laborers of the eleventh hour, the Maiden was not long in the service of the Lord, yet she—like they—can enjoy the same reward for service as those who have laboured a good deal longer. It is not what we think of as earthly justice, but it is the nature of the divine economy. The Dreamer protests that this is unreasonable (590), and the Maiden expands further on heaven's generosity

in the next two sections (X and XI). God's grace is so great that it can extend to the death of an infant who has no justification by either works or faith but only innocence. Indeed, in section XI the last line in five of its six stanzas repeats the same refrain, reminding the Dreamer that there is a rightness and a justice to this: "Þe grace of God is gret innoghe" [The grace of God is great/ magnanimous enough]. Section XII also repeats the end of a stanza: "Þe innosent is ay saf by ryȝt" [The innocent are always saved by justification (through grace)]. In this section God is equated with Reason (665) specifically to counter the Dreamer's charge of "vnresounable" (590): "Bot Resoun, of ryȝt Þat con not raue, / Sauez euermore Þe innossent" (665–666: [But Reason, which cannot stray from justice, / will always save the innocent]). Contrary to the Dreamer's opinion, the Maiden explains that God is reasonable and is prepared to save two kinds of men:

Ryȝt Þus I knaw wel in Þis cas
Two men to saue is God—by skylle:
Þe ryȝtwys man schal se Hys face,
Þe harmelez haÞel schal com Hym tylle.

(673–676)

[Just so I knew well in this case / that God saves two kinds of men—by reason: the righteous man shall see his face, / the innocent man shall come to him.]

The lines have justification, of course, from the Beatitudes (Matthew 5). But the Maiden also says that although it is reasonable that the righteous man be saved, it is not a "right" (703). This was an important proviso to make in the fourteenth century, when there had been renewed interest in the Pelagian idea that a man can be saved by the accumulation of good works, a heresy that had long been refuted by Saint Augustine, who said that only God, through his grace, could decide whether the individual would be saved or not. After this point, the poem moves from an intellectual and moral debate between the Dreamer and the Maiden on the nature of salvation and reverts to the series of visionary images with which it began. It is significant that, despite the Maiden's efforts, the Dreamer does not state that he has understood her words and the reader therefore assumes that further instruction is necessary.

At the beginning of Section XIII, the Maiden reminds the Dreamer that no one can come to heaven except as a child (721–724); then the argument moves away from justifying the ways of heaven and returns to emphasizing its precious value with a reminder of Christ's parable of the "pearl of great price" in Matthew 13: 45–46, where a merchant sells everything he has to purchace the one pearl—that is, the kingdom of heaven. Instead of understanding the true import of the images, the Dreamer then begins to hymn the beauty of the Pearl Maiden once again, in a series of literary allusions ranging from the *Roman de la Rose* to the Song of Songs. We can see him ennumerating the different symbolic associations as he refers to three different pearls:

O maskelez perle in perlez pure,
þat berez', quoþ I, þe perle of prys,
Quo formed þe þy fayre fygure?'

(745–747)

[O matchless pearl in real pearls, / who bears, said I, the pearl of price, who shaped your fair figure?]

Although he can differentiate a variety of pearls here, from the maiden to her dress to the one great pearl she wears on her breast (symbolic of heaven and her salvation), the Dreamer's curiosity takes him away from the point the Maiden has been making. Using an allusion to the Song of Songs herself, she tells him that she has been chosen as a bride of the Lamb, who called to her after she died, crowned her, and dressed her in pearls. The Dreamer marvels at the nature of the Lamb who would take her above all others to be his bride. The Maiden says that she may be "maskelles" (unblemished), but she did not say "makelez" (matchless); she is simply one of the 140,000 blessed in heaven (the manuscript gives this figure rather than the 144,000 of Revelation), again reminding the Dreamer of the lack of differentiation in heaven among the saved (781–785). Rather than elaborate again on the nature of the blessed, with another apostrophe from the Song of Songs, the Maiden paraphrases Isaiah 53:7 as she describes the beauty of her spouse,

which is the Lamb, the image of Christ on earth. Still not satisfied, the Dreamer wants to know more details of the Maiden's life. He repeats his abject state and comes back to the image of the rose, which the Maiden has already informed him simply represents the transitory life on earth, reinterpreting it as the *rosa caritatis* (rose of charity) of Christian tradition:

I am bot mokke and mul among,
And þou so ryche a reken rose,
And bydez here by þys blysful bonc
þer lyuez lyste may neuer lose.

(905–908)

[I am only a mix of dirt and dust,/ and you so noble a lovely rose, / and live here beside this pleasant bank / where life's delight can never fade.]

A much humbler Dreamer is evident as he now beseeches the Maiden to respond to his "ruful bone" (916: [piteous prayer]) to know exactly where she dwells. He acknowledges that she has told him that Jerusalem is a "ryche ryalle" (919: [royal kingdom]), but he also sees that it cannot be "here" in the woods around them. In fact, as far as he knows, it is an actual city in Judea where David once lived (920–922). The inference here is: how can there be two Jerusalems? Rather surprisingly, the Maiden has to remind the Dreamer that the actual city is the "olde Jerusalem" (941), while where she dwells is the new Jerusalem spoken of in the Apocalypse (Revelation 21). Almost like a child (perhaps, appropriately), the Dreamer begs her for a sight of the heavenly city. The Maiden says that she is able to grant this by means of a special vision, granted by the Lamb (965–972) but that he may not enter, only look from the outside. Thus what the Dreamer sees is almost a vision within a vision, the heavenly city brought down, as it were, to the paradise garden for him to view at a distance. Sections XVII and XVIII then describe with full lapidary splendor the heavenly city as outlined with numerological symmetry in Revelation: it has twelve types of jewels layered in its foundations, twelve gates, and is twelve furlongs long (where Revelation 21:16 has twelve thousand), its walls are of jasper, and the streets are of a gold that shines like glass. The poet's descriptive powers are put to excellent use here, albeit based on the biblical original, and the Dreamer is suitably impressed by what he sees:

Anvnder mone so gret merwayle
No fleschly hert ne my3t endeure
As quen I blusched vpon þat baly,
So ferly þerof watz þe fasure.
I stod as stylle as dased quayle
For ferly of þat frech fygure,
þat felde I nawþer reste ne trauayle,
So watz I rauyste wyth glymme pure.

(1,081–1,088)

[Under the moon so great a marvel / no human heart could endure/ as when I gazed upon that castle wall, so wonderful was the form. *I stood as still as a dazed quail* (italics mine), out of amazement of that noble apparition, / so that I felt no bodily sensation, so was I ravished by (its) clear radiance.]

As the Dreamer's spirit stands mesmerized by the vision, the next section (XIX) recounts how he then sees a wondrous procession of young virgins dressed in the same way as his Pearl Maiden. He estimates there are a hundred thousand of them, led by the Lamb of Revelation, with seven golden horns and clothes like precious pearls; they are met by the twenty-four elders of the church (Revelation 4:4) and bands of angels as they move toward the Lamb's throne. The Dreamer's delight in this vision is evident, and the word forms the repeated refrain word from stanza to stanza. But the vision then focuses on the Lamb, which in one stanza modulates from splendor to pathos:

So worþly whyt wern wedez Hys,
Hys lokez symple, Hymself so gent.
Bot a wounde ful wyde and weete con wyse
Anende Hys hert, þur3 hyde torente.
Of His quyte side His blod outsprent.
Alas, þo3t I, who did þat spyt?

(1,133–1,138)

[So worthily white his clothes were, his looks simple, himself so gracious. But a very wide wound wet with blood showed close to his heart, through the cruely torn skin. Blood spurted out of his white side. Alas, I thought, who did that evil deed?]

If the Dreamer's delight is shattered in his sorrow for the pitiful but joyful Lamb, which remains unaffected by its wound, it rises again when he sees his "lyttel queen" among the company, so much so that he desires to cross the water dividing them. In the last section (XX) he confesses his foolishness in thinking that he could cross the divide between them. It was a fit of passion almost like that of a lover longing for his beloved. Nevertheless, he was going against the divine will and finds instead that he awakens on the grassy bank where he fell asleep. Sorrowfully, he now realizes the great difference there is between heaven and earth, a difference that is absolute. He takes consolation in the fact that he has received an assurance that his "Pearl" is saved and in heaven, but his joy is mingled with sadness when he realizes that he himself must still live out the rest of his life on earth before he may join her in bliss: " 'So wel is me in þys doeldoungoun /þat þou art to þat Prynsez paye' " (1,187–1,188: [It is well with me in this dungeon of sorrow / that you are in the Prince's pleasure]).

The poem ends ambiguously on the Dreamer's personal sorrow at his continued life on earth, his joy in the Maiden's salvation, and also his knowledge that humans are potential pearls for the Prince's pleasure (1,211–1,212).

HEAVEN IN FIGURES

As we have seen above, *Pearl* turns on the one hand on an axis of doctrine and of affective piety on the other. If the Dreamer does not understand rationally the difference between life on earth and the nature of heaven, he can at least feel sorrow, pity, and love for the sacrifice made for the world by God's own son—even if this does cause the Dreamer to attempt prematurely to join the blessed. Like Gawain's fault, it is one the reader can understand, sympathize with, and forgive all at the same time. The greatest difficulty is feeling sympathy for the Dreamer when he so patently cannot understand either his vision or what the Maiden is telling him. It might be thought that a fourteenth-century Christian would know certain things: the innocent are saved by divine justice; the blessed are all one; one cannot force oneself into heaven—whereas the Dreamer has difficulty believing in her salvation and in the nature of the blessed state. This is where the poem becomes a "poem" and not simply a doctrinal tract. In dramatizing the Dreamer's difficulties, the poet acts out the problems of belief that face all his potential readers. How do we cope with grief? How can a human being understand the scope of salvation? The poem portrays a man who is evidently far too locked into the things of this world, be they people, possessions, or ideas of right and wrong. Hence the things of this world are precious jewels to him, and he is their covetous jeweler. The Dreamer's identification of his daughter as a "pearl" shows how precious she was to him; but the very use of the signifier "pearl" shows how his valorization is expressed in material terms. It is the Maiden who has to take herself as metaphor and say that the casket that now surrounds her (heaven) is the one that will truly preserve her value. The Dreamer is still thinking of her value only to himself, not realizing her new, true value in heaven. If this is understandable, it is a lesson he must learn. But the poem is much more than an attempt at vicarious catharsis, although this should not be discounted as unimportant, especially for a time when infant (and other) mortality was high.

However much the poem concretizes a particular man as a jeweler who has lost a precious jewel, it is also a universal poem about loss. The "pearl" is so ambiguous, it could be any person precious to the reader. The courtly imagery allows identification with a mature woman, for example. Certainly, the Pearl Maiden does not speak as a child, and her severe tone with the Dreamer is reminiscent of the chastisement Dante receives from Mathilda and Beatrice when he sees them in the earthly paradise of *Purgatory* (28–29). Indeed, comparison has often been made between Dante's great vision and the no less noble vision of *Pearl*. Reading the two texts together enhances the understanding of both, even if the question of *Pearl*'s indebtedness (which is entirely possible) can never be resolved textually, because the poems have a different dramatic setting. Another source text suggested has been Boccaccio's Fourteenth Latin Eclogue, *Olympia*, which Gollancz published with his edition of the

poem in 1923. Here, the dream vision imitates a Classical elegy where the grieving shepherd Silvius sees a vision of his dead daughter Olympia, who reminds him of the virtues necessary to give him "wings" to get into heaven. The only problem to citing this as a definite source is the lack of substantive eveidence about manuscript transmission between Italy and England. Nevertheless, the parallels are highly suggestive, as with Dante, whose work was at least known to Chaucer. Where Dante and the poet of *Pearl* unite is in the very fact of trying to figure the divine. Not only do they want to give a shape to the ineffability of divinity, they also want to "figure" it out in the rhetorical sense. No doubt somewhat taken aback by Dante's supreme confidence in his imaginative creation of not only heaven but hell and purgatory also, Chaucer states with a certain irony in the opening lines to *The Legend of Good Women* (1–8):

A thousand tymes have I herd men telle
That ther ys joy in hevene and peyne in helle,
And I acorde wel that yt is so;
But, natheles, yet wot I wel also
That ther nis noon dwellyng in this contree
That eyther hath in hevene or helle ybe,
Ne may of hit noon other weyes witen
But as he hath heard seyd or founde it writen ...

The supreme fiction of Dante's persona in the *Divine Comedy* is that he did experience all of the events of the poem: it is not an allegory (although it has allegorical meanings within it). What Chaucer says above is that in reality this cannot be. The poet of *Pearl* is on better doctrinal ground for his invention in that it is based on what is written in Revelation. Like Dante's work, the poem is not an allegory as such; it is what it is: a dream vision by a real dreamer. Furthermore, the poet has circumscribed his vision so that it is not necessarily what is there but only what is afforded human eyes to see. Therefore, unlike Dante, the poem is a series of approximations, all concretely depicted, yet simply a pictorial interface of the ineffable, something that an ordinary mortal can witness without too much of a shock. And it will be remembered what a shock it was for the Dreamer to see the heavenly Jerusalem. The Maiden reminds the Dreamer that he only "thinks" he sees her standing on the bank; she also says that he may have a vision of the heavenly city, not experience it directly.

Therefore, the drama of the poem enacts another tension besides that between the earthly and the heavenly: how can we figure the divine when we have only earthly materials and an earthly vision? How can we go beyond this state of life and appreciate or anticipate the life to come? The answer is, of course, that we cannot, but also that we may try to use earthly imagery, however fallible the enterprise might be. And, of course, there is a biblical precedent; the things of heaven are there depicted in human terms, supremely so in Revelation but also in simpler form in Christ's parables—for example, Matthew 13: 44–48. But a further problem exists in the manner in which things are depicted. If we perceive heaven as distant, highly prized, altogether precious and perfect, then it is perhaps only natural to select from the repertoire of earthly imagery a signifier that represents those qualities (in earthly terms), as where Christ likens the desire for heaven to a merchant's desire for a pearl of great price.

Similarly, if there is a community of the blessed, safe and protected, perhaps it is likely that they come to be depicted as the fortunate retainers of a royal court, only more regal and more honored. It seems that there is a desperate need for hyperbole that can only be satisfied in terms of human hyperbole. Herein lies a danger, which the poem very cleverly uses to its advantage.

It should be remembered from the gospels that the life of Christ is one where he constantly rejects the divinity and honor people wish to invest in him. Born in a humble stable, he lives a simple life and enters Jerusalem not in triumphal military cavalcade but on an ass. Indeed, the only coronation he receives is the ignominy of the crown of thorns at the crucifixion. Medieval art and letters maintain this strain of humility, but gradually there coexists with it a courtly version, where Mary is not the mother "meek and mild" of the carols, but indeed a queen of heaven. Similarly, Christ also comes to be figured as a regal warrior, majestic, and powerful.

Pearl very cleverly opposes these two strains of imagery, the simple and the courtly, to enable another kind of didacticism to unfold, where the hyperbolic visions of glory are undercut by the sight of the simple, wounded Lamb. As the Dreamer's marvelous vision rises from an already ecstatic view of an earthly paradise to the overpowering beauty of the heavenly city, it is no wonder that he should stand there bewildered, "as stylle as dased quayle." Beneath the vast battlements, how could he feel anything but a tiny trembling bird that has been surprised before or upon capture? It is significant that he is not moved by the vision in any way; he feels simply diminished. Only when he sees the pathos of the bleeding Lamb, and all that glorious architecture becomes as nothing, is he actually, and literally, moved to want to become closer and cross the great divide between them. It is the magnitude of the sacrifice that so noble a being made that makes the real climax of the poem. Having been led through the succession of hyperbolic images, both Dreamer and reader suddenly find all the previous imagery undercut by the uncomfortable and upsetting sight of the wounded Lamb with "hyde torente." Hence this is the true center of the poem, not the search for the ineffable; that was simply a means to gain interest, to satisfy curiosity, in the same way that the Dreamer desires to know more and see more of the glorious life of the blessed. The final vision of the Lamb brings him and the reader back to the basis of what salvation means. If the poem can be seen as a search for the ineffable through earthly and biblical signs, and a debate on the nature of divine versus human ideas of justice and salvation, it comes to end on the sacrifice that made it all possible.

PATIENCE

USING the *exemplum* of the Old Testament story of Jonah, Patience opens as if it were a pious homiletic poem that will preach the virtue of the eighth beatitude (Matthew 5:10), long taken by the exegetical tradition to mean "patience." There are two immediate problems with this simplistic view. The first is that the narrative of

Jonah, unlike that of Job or, say, Griselda in Chaucer's *Clerk's Tale*, does not actually embody the virtue. The second is that, like *Pearl*, the poem does not so much preach as create a dramatic story of tension between opposing forces. In this case we have the will of Jonah opposing the will of God. As many commentators have noted, there is also a third problem in the idea of "patience" itself.

The virtue is a complex one, as the prologue of sixty lines reveals. The poet begins by saying that it is a beneficial everyday virtue, a remedy against troubles:

When heuy herttes ben hurt wyth heÞyng oÞer elles,
Suffraunce may aswagen hem and Þe swelme leÞe,
For ho quelles vche a qued and quenches malyce

(2–4)

[When sorrowful hearts are hurt by scorn or something else, / Sufferance may assuage them and ease the heat (of anger) / because it subdues all badness and chokes malice]

Perhaps a better identification of the virtue would be forebearance, a patient acceptance of circumstances, as seems to be implied by the Sermon on the Mount (Matthew 5:10), where the beatitudes are given: "Beati, qui persecutionem patiuntur propter justitiam: quoniam ipsorum est regnum coelorum (Vulgate)." [Blessed are those who are persecuted for the sake of righteousness: for theirs is the kingdom of heaven].

The poet says he has heard this uttered at a "hyȝe masse" and rehearses the eight beatitudes over four quatrains (13–28), each virtue introduced by the phrase "Þay ar happen ... " (Blessed are they ...). The poet then summarizes them all in a series of allegorical personifications, so that we know he understands the eight beatitude as "patience":

Dame Pouert, Dame Pitée, Dame Penaunce Þe
  Þrydde,
Dame Mekenesse, Dame Mercy and miry Clannesse,
And Þenne Dame Pes, and Pacyence put in Þerafter.

(31–33)

[Dame Poverty, Dame Pity, Dame Penance the third one, Dame Meekness, Dame Mercy and merry Purity, and then Dame Peace and Patience put in after.]

We also find that the application of patience applies to the poet: he says that poverty and patience are "nedes playferes" (45: [necessary playmates]) because the one must follow the other, and he applies this to his own case in life, a point he repeats at the end of the work. Finally, one should not forget that in the course of the narrative the virtue applies to God, who shows great forebearance with the Ninevites whom he had threatened to destroy.

All studies agree that the poet was working very closely with the Book of Jonah as given in the Vulgate, the standard Latin translation of the Bible used in the Middle Ages, originally made by Saint Jerome. Obviously, given new lexical knowledge of biblical texts, two key material components have changed: we now have a "great fish" instead of a "whale," and a "plant" instead of the poet's "woodbine" (as opposed to the Vulgate's "vine"). The narrative relates how God instructs the prophet Jonah to warn the citizens of Nineveh (capital of the Assyrian Empire) of their sins. Jonah instead takes ship for Tarshish, whereupon a violent storm erupts. Thinking that it is a sign of divine displeasure, the sailors cast lots to find out who the culprit might be and discover Jonah, who confesses he is fleeing from God and agrees to be cast overboard. As soon as he leaves the sailor's hands he is swallowed by the whale, in whose belly he stays three days and nights. When he repents of his action, God has the whale spew him out on shore and again asks him to go to Nineveh, which happens to be within reach. This time Jonah complies, the Ninevites repent, and God spares the city. Aggrieved that his prophecies of destruction were not fulfilled, Jonah justifies his flight by saying he knew that God would eventually be merciful and that is why he went off to Tarshish. Feeling so upset he wishes he were dead, he goes to a vantage point overlooking the city to await its fate. God appoints a plant to cover and shelter him, much to Jonah's pleasure. But then God commands a worm to destroy its roots, and the next day in the sun it withers. Again, Jonah is furious with God and asks that he might die. God then makes an analogy between Jonah's pity for the shade-giving plant, which he had no part in making, and his own pity for Nineveh, which God did create. Should not God be able to show pity on a great city full of people, just as Jonah expresses pity for the plant?

The true example of patience in the narrative is God, who shows forbearance with the sinful city and shows much more mercy than his vindictive prophet, who probably had no wish to save the iniquitous Assyrians in the first place. The fearful, querulous figure of the biblical Jonah became much softer by the Middle Ages, because of Christ's own identification with the prophet in Matthew 12:40–41 (Putter, 1996, pp. 96 ff.). However, the poet's amplification of Jonah remains true to the Old Testament character. Noteworthy is the prophet's imagining what tortures might happen to him at the hands of the Ninevites (a kind of crucifixion), and the poet's making a symmetry of the three sleeps in the ship, in the whale and under the plant, as symbolic of Jonah's lack of awareness. Other details range from the actuality of the boat and the storm to the amplification of the whale as a foul, infernal place, picking up on the later identification of the whale as the hell that Christ harrows during the three days after the crucifixion.

Thus the narrative is no perfunctory effort for the sake of the moral but is an extremely vivid account made real by the addition of vibrant detail. Everything is "seen" through the eyes of the poet or the characters, in the same way that *Sir Gawain and the Green Knight* is told. It relates a battle of wills between the prophet and God with much subtle amusement at Jonah's discomfiture. As an exemplum of obedience it teaches a direct lesson in the figure of Jonah, who has to learn to accept God's will. In the end, it is God who shows the virtue of his patient suffering of the Ninevites' sins, relenting when he sees their repentance. The ending is slightly problematical in that the voice expressing the final moral or application of the story has been disputed by editors. Some think that lines 524–527 are spoken by God, some by the narrator. All agree, however, that the final lines about suffering poverty with patience are the narrator's own.

CLEANNESS

IF *Patience* is a complex examination of the virtue, its interest enhanced by the negative example of a figure who fails to exhibit it, then *Cleanness*, although using a more complex series of negative examples, is overall much simpler in intention. It is more homiletic, with more direct preaching from the narrator, whose voice is often singleminded, impassioned, with no room for doubt, irony, or debate. At the end of the poem, the narrator says:

þus vpon Þrynne wyses I haf yow Þro schewed
þat vnclannes tocleues in corage dere
Of Þat wynnelych Lorde Þat wonyes in heuen,
Entyses Hym to be tene, teldes vp His wrake
(1,805–1,808)

[Thus in three ways have I shown you / that impurity cleaves apart the precious heart / of that gracious Lord who lives in heaven, / arousing him to anger, swelling him to vengeance.]

A more apt title would be "uncleanness" (or "impurity"), because the three narrative *exempla* are biblical narratives of God's vengeance on a sinful world, namely the Flood, the destruction of Sodom and Gomorrah, and Belshazzar's Feast. Interwoven into these three major narratives, which follow the Bible chronologically, is a series of minor examples, which do not have much to do with the immediate thrust of the whole argument; nor do the three main narratives build to an obvious climactic point. Indeed, the severest penalty God wreaks on man comes first in the story of the Flood. It is after this, the narrator says, in a striking addition to the Bible, that God decides to soften his judgment:

Hym rwed Þat He hem vprerde and raȝt hem lyflode;
And efte Þat He hem vndyd, hard hit Hym Þoȝt.
For quen Þe swemande sorȝe soȝt to His hert,
He knyt a couenande cortaysly with monkynde Þere,
In Þe mesure of His mode and meÞe of His wylle,
þat He schulde neuer for no syt smyte al at onez,
As to quelle alle quykez for qued Þat myȝt falle
(561–568)

[He regretted that he had raised them up and given them the means of life; / And likewise that he had destroyed them, which seemed to him harsh. / For when the grievous sorrow went to his heart, / he courteously made a covenant with mankind there, / in the moderation of his mood and mercy of his will, / that he should never for any grief smite all at the same time, / so as to kill all living creatures for any evil they might do]

If, taken in isolation, God's vengeance in the Flood seems harsh, the poet shows God's own repentance, but also carefully builds up to it by first telling the stories of the Fall of Lucifer (205–234) and the Fall of Adam (235–248). In this context, the Flood is better understood, and God's gentler attitude prepares for the greater discrimination in vengeance shown in the later narratives.

The second narrative is prepared for again by two introductory *exempla*, the stories of Abraham and Sarah and of Lot and his wife. The direct application of these to the destruction of the cities of the plain is not at first obvious. Abraham is a positive figure who receives three guests into his house, who later turn out to be the Trinity; while his wife Sarah is doubtful, even scornful, of the prophecy that she will have a child. The same contrast between obedience and disobedience is made between Lot and his wife. Contrary to God's will, she looks back to see what fate has befallen the cities and is turned into a pillar of salt. Thus the poet very cleverly sets up a sequence of domestic disobedience with which the audience can readily identify, only then to link the sins of doubt and disobedience with the carnal sins of the Sodomites, where fleshly pursuits in general can be read, not simply the sexual preferences of those particular citizens.

The third sequence moves to its main *exemplum* in a more direct fashion, reminding the reader that God's displeasure at the Jews resulted in Nebuchadnezzar's sacking of Jerusalem, his seizing the Temple vessels and taking the nation captive. The main narrative relates the later defiling of the holy vessels by Belshazzar, Nebuchadnezzar's son, who is visited by the mysterious writing on the wall at a feast. The only prophet who can interpret the words is Daniel, who relates the story of Nebuchadnezzar's conversion after exile and madness, but this fails to produce any repentance in his son, who is bat-

tered to death in his bed when his enemies invade and sack Babylon.

Given these *exempla*, we might ask: what type of purity is the poet trying to extoll? The introductory passage on the Beatitudes informs us that he refers to the "pure in heart" (23–48), following Matthew 5:8. Then the poet relates the story of the Wedding Feast from Matthew 22 and applies it to purity: the true soul must somehow clothe itself in fitting raiment (purity) if it seeks to be with the Lord. The poet is evasive, however, about how that raiment is to be achieved, as the poem is a series of negative examples of how not to be pure. Obviously, the second sequence has some immediately recognizable antifeminist satire at the expense of Sarah and Lot's wife, comparable to that in the medieval Mystery Plays over Mrs. Noah, which leads to the sexual excesses of Sodom and Gomorrah. If we are to take those as adherence to carnal pleasures in general, the poet is also careful to warn against the sexual preferences of those cities, showing how Lot could not get the men to turn heterosexual even when he offered them his virgin daughters (841–872), and includes a surprising courtly eulogy on heterosexual coupling from God himself without scrupling to limit this within the state of marriage (702–709).

In the third sequence, the sin is much more symbolic, despite the concrete nature of the example in the biblical narrative. As structured by the poet, the emphasis here is on the human being as a vessel that, like those of the Temple, has become defiled. This is about the only symbolic meaning in the poem, whose didacticism is overt and unambiguous. It has to be said, however, that its narration is again vivid, the biblical stories told as if original, with added detail, and the moralizing they receive is zealous to a fault. If not to the taste of present readers, as an example of its kind it rises well above the norm.

SELECTED BIBLIOGRAPHY

I. *PEARL*. Pearl, ed. by and trans. Sir I. Gollancz (London, 1891; second ed., with Boccaccio's *Olympia*, 1921); *The Pearl*, ed. by Charles G. Osgood (Boston and London, 1906); *Pearl*, ed. by E. V. Gordon (Oxford, 1953); The Pearl, ed. and trans. Sr Mary V. Hillman (New York, 1961; second ed., 1967).

II. CLEANNESS. *Purity*, ed. by Robert J. Menner (New Haven and London, 1920; rep. Hamden, Conn., 1970); *Cleanness*, ed. by Sir I. Gollancz (London, Part I, 1921; Part II, 1933; rep. as one volume with trans. D. S. Brewer, Cambridge and Totowa, 1974); *Cleanness*, ed. by J. J. Anderson (Manchester and New York, 1977).

III. PATIENCE. *Patience*, ed. by Hartley Bateson (Manchester, U.K., 1912; second ed., 1918); *Patience*, ed. by Sir I. Gollancz (London, 1913; second ed., 1924); *Patience*, ed. by J. J. Anderson (Manchester, U.K.; and New York, 1969).

IV. SIR GAWAIN AND THE GREEN KNIGHT. *Sir Gawayne and the Green Knight*, ed. by R. Morris (London, 1864; rev. Sir I. Gollancz, 1897 and 1912); *Sir Gawain and the Green Knight*, ed. by J. R. R. Tolkien and E. V. Gordon (Oxford, U.K., 1925; rev. Norman Davis, 1967); *Sir Gawain and the Green Knight*, ed. by R. A. Waldron (London, 1970); *Sir Gawain and the Green Knight*, ed. J. A. Burrow (Harmondsworth: 1972); *Sir Gawain and the Green Knight*, ed. by and trans. W. R. J. Barron (Manchester, U.K.; and New York, 1974); *Sir Gawain and the Green Knight*, ed. by Theodore Silverstein (Chicago and London, 1984).

V. COLLECTED EDITION. *The Poems of the Pearl Manuscript*, ed. by Malcom Andrew and Ronald Waldron (London, 1978; rev. and rep., Exeter, U.K., 1987, 1996). All quotations from this edition, translations by N. S. Thompson.

VI. TRANSLATIONS. *Sir Gawain and the Green Knight*, trans. Brian Stone (Harmondsworth, U.K., 1959); *Medieval English Verse*, trans. Brian Stone (Harmondsworth, U.K., 1964; contains *Patience* and *Pearl*); *The Complete Works of the Gawain Poet*, trans. John Gardner (Chicago, London, and Amsterdam, 1965); *Sir Gawain and the Green Knight*, trans. Marie Borroff (New York, 1967); *The Owl and the Nightingale; Cleanness; St Erkenwald*, trans. Brian Stone (Harmondsworth, U.K., 1971); *"Pearl": A New Verse Translation*, trans. Marie Borroff (New York and Toronto, 1977); *The Complete Works of the Pearl Poet*, trans. Casey Finch (Berkeley, Los Angeles, and Oxford, U.K., 1993).

VII. INDIVIDUAL CRITICAL STUDIES: *PEARL*. P. M. Kean, *The* Pearl: *An Interpretation* (London, 1967); Ian Bishop, *Pearl in Its Setting* (Oxford, U.K., 1968); John Conley, ed. *The Middle English "Pearl": Critical Essays* (Notre Dame and London, 1970); Edward Wilson, "Word Play and the Interpretation of *Pearl*," in *Medium Aevum* 40 (1971); Laurence Eldredge, "The State of *Pearl* Studies since 1933," in *Viator* 6 (1975); D. Horgan, "Justice in *The Pearl*," in *RES* 32 (1981); Elizabeth Petroff, "Landscape in *Pearl*: The Transformation of Nature," in *Chaucer Review* 16 (1981–1982), 181–193; Marie Borroff, "Pearl's Maynful Mone': Crux, Simile, and Structure," in Mary J. Carruthers and Elizabeth D. Kirk, eds., *Acts of Interpretation: The Text in Its Contexts, 700–1600* (Norman, OK, 1982); Theodore Bogdanos, Pearl: *Image of the Ineffable* (University Park and London, 1983); David Aers, "The Self Mourning: Reflections on *Pearl*," in *Speculum* 68 (1993); Jim Rhodes, "The Dreamer Redeemed: Exile and the Kingdom in the Middle English *Pearl*," in *SAC* 16 (1994).

VIII. INDIVIDUAL CRITICAL STUDIES: *CLEANNESS*. Charlotte C. Morse, "The Image of the Vessel in *Cleanness*," in *UTQ* 40 (1970–1971); Jonathan A. Glenn, "Dislocation of *kynde* in the Middle English *Cleanness*," in *Chaucer Review* 18 (1983–1984); William Vantuono, "A Triple-Three Structure for *Cleanness*," in *Manuscripta* 28 (1984); Ruth E. Hamilton, "Repeating Narrative and Anachrony in *Cleanness*," in *Style* 20 (1986); Monica Brzezinski, "Conscience and Covenant: The Sermon Structure of *Cleanness*," in *JEGP* 89 (1990).

IX. INDIVIDUAL CRITICAL STUDIES: *PATIENCE*. David Williams, "The Point of *Patience*," in *MP* 68 (1970–1971); William Vantuono, "The Question of Quatrains in *Patience*," in *Manuscripta* 16 (1972); S. L. Clark and Julian Wasserman, "Jonah and the Whale: Narrative Perspective in *Patience*," in *Orbis Litterarum* 35 (1980); Sandra Pierson Prior, "*Patience*—beyond Apocalypse," in *MP* 83 (1985–1986); Adam Brooke Davis, "What the Poet of *Patience* Really Did to the Book of Jonah," in *Viator* 22 (1991).

X. INDIVIDUAL CRITICAL STUDIES: *SIR GAWAIN AND THE GREEN KNIGHT*. Marie Borroff, *SGGK: A Stylistic and Metrical Study* (New Haven and London, 1962); Larry D. Benson, *Art and Tradition in SGGK* (New Brunswick, 1965); John Burrow, *A Reading of SGGK* (London, 1965); Gordon M. Shedd, "Knight in Tarnished Armour: The Meaning of *SGGK*," in *MLR* 62 (1967); Denton Fox, ed., *Twentieth Century Interpretations of SGGK* (Englewood Cliffs, N. J., 1968); Donald R. Howard and Christian K. Zacher, eds., *Critical Studies of SGGK* (Notre Dame and London, 1968); David Mills, "An Analysis of the Temptation Scenes in SGGK," in *JEGP* 67 (1968); W. R. J. Barron, *"Trawthe" and Treason: The Sin of Gawain Reconsidered* (Manchester, U.K., 1980); R. A. Shoaf, The Poem as Green Girdle: "Commercium" in SGGK (Gainesville, Fla., 1984); A. W. Astell, "*SGGK*: A Study in the Rhetoric of Romance," in *JEGP* 84 (1985); Ian Bishop, "Time and Tempo in *SGGK*," in *Neophilologus* 69 (1985); Wendy Clein, *Concepts of Chivalry in SGGK* (Norman, OK, 1987); Ross G. Arthur, *Medieval Sign Theory and SGGK* (Toronto, Buffalo, and London, 1987); Christopher Wrigley, "*SGGK*: The Underlying Myth," in D. Brewer, ed., *Studies in Medieval English Romances: Some New Approaches* (Cambridge, 1988); J. J. Anderson, "The Three Judgments and the Ethos of Chivalry in *SGGK*," in *Chaucer Review* 24 (1989–1990); Gerald Morgan, *SGGK and the Idea of Righteousness* (Blackrock, 1991); Harvey De Roo, "Undressing Lady Bertilak: Guilt and Denial in *SGGK*," in *Chaucer Review* 27 (1992–1993); Ad Putter, *SGGK and French Arthurian Romance* (Oxford, U.K., 1995); Piotr Sadowski, *The Knight on His Quest: Symbolic Patterns of Transition in SGGK* (Newark and London: 1996).

XI. THE GAWAIN-POET. Charles Moorman, *The* Pearl-*Poet* (New York, 1968); A. C. Spearing, *The Gawain-Poet: A Critical Study* (Cambridge: 1970); J. A. Burrow, *Ricardian Poetry: Chaucer, Gower, Langland and the "Gawain" Poet* (London, 1971); Edward Wilson, *The Gawain-Poet* (Leiden, 1976); W. A. Davenport, *The Art of the "Gawain"-Poet* (London, 1978); Lynn Staley Johnson, *The Voice of the "Gawain"-Poet* (Madison, 1984); J. Nicholls, *The Matter of Courtesy: A Study of Medieval Courtesy Books and the Gawain-Poet* (Cambridge, U.K., 1985); R. A. Cooper and D. A. Pearsall, "The *Gawain* Poems: A Statistical Approach to the Question of Common Authorship," in *RES* 39 (1988); Sarah Stanbury, *Seeing the "Gawain"-Poet: Description and the Act of Perception* (Philadelphia, 1991); Ad Putter, *An Introduction to the* Gawain-*Poet* (London and New York,

1996); Derek Brewer and Jonathan Gibson, eds., *A Companion to the* Gawain- *Poet* (Cambridge, 1997).

XII. REFERENCE. Barnet Kottler and Alan M. Markman, *A Concordance to Five Middle English Poems: Cleanness, St. Erkenwald, SGGK, Patience, Pearl* (Pittsburgh, 1966); Malcom Andrew, *The Gawain-Poet: An Annotated Bibliography*, 1839–1977 (New York and London, 1979); E.

Brewer, ed., *SGGK: Sources and Analogues* (Cambridge, 1992); Meg Stainsby, *SGGK: An Annotated Bibliography, 1979–1989* (New York and London, 1992).

ABBREVIATIONS: *JEGP, Journal of English and Germanic Philology; MLR, Modern Language Review; MP, Modern Philology; RES, Review of English Studies; SAC, Studies in the Age of Chaucer; UTQ, University of Toronto Quarterly.*

W. S. GRAHAM

1918–1986

John Redmond

WILLIAM SYDNEY GRAHAM has claims to being
one of the most important Scottish poets of the
twentieth century. His poetry is not at all well
known, even in Scotland, although he has gained
over the years a small but influential band of
admirers. He wrote about silence and being alone,
and he has been left alone by many readers. In a
century when many readers approach poets and
other artists via the label of a group or movement, Graham had no label. In a period when
writing was often politicized by writers and critics, he was not political. He lived his life—and
to some degree chose to live it—at the margins
of different, though ultimately interweaving,
kinds of power: economic, social and literary.
Self-conscious about his working-class roots, he
wrote poems that were self-conscious about being made up.

Graham, however, very much deserves to be
heard, and it is not necessary to take the work at
its own modest face value. His poems approach
subjects that may be discomforting, even depressing, but that are fundamental to our lives. They
listen for things we cannot quite hear and
describe states we cannot quite control and so
emphasize our comparative helplessness. In the
opening lines of "Enter a Cloud," a simple situation—a man lying on a hill looking at the sky—is
described with simple diction. Through the
sophistication of the syntax and the line breaks,
the poem creates a dizzying depth out of seemingly nothing:

Gently disintegrate me
Said nothing at all.

Is there still time to say
Said I myself lying
In a bower of bramble
Into which I have fallen.

Look through my eyes up
At blue with not anything
We could have ever arranged
Slowly taking place.

(*Implements in Their Places*, p. 33)

LIFE AND BACKGROUND

GRAHAM was born in Greenock in Renfrewshire,
Scotland, on 19 November 1918. Known to his
friends as Sydney, he was the son of Alexander
Graham, a journeyman engineer, and Margaret
McDermid. The family lived on the top floor of a
tenement building, which overlooked the
"winches and steel giants" of the dockyards.
Graham left school at the age of fourteen and
became a draftman's apprentice with a Glasgow
engineering firm.

The location of Greenock plays an influential
role in Graham's poetry. Glasgow, during the
period when it styled itself as the second city of
the British Empire, owed much of its economic
prosperity to the river Clyde. But deepwater
ships, coming from the west, had not always been
able to navigate the whole length of the river (it
was widened and deepened at various points in
its history) and sometimes would deliver their
cargo at more accessible locations. Greenock,
downriver of Glasgow to the west, is located at
the point where the Clyde widens dramatically
into its firth (or fjord) before flowing into the sea
proper, and it is easily in reach of deepwater shipping. Hence it was a place of traditional, labor-
intensive industries, of fishing and shipbuilding,
as well as being decidedly secondary in relation
to the major city it served, a place through which
traffic was always passing, a "threshold," to use
Graham's term, between Glasgow and the sea.

Graham, too, lived his life at the periphery. Like Greenock he lived downriver of the big city, whether that city was Glasgow, London, or New York. He could stay in such places for a short period of time but could never put down roots. Most of his life was lived in the relative seclusion of Cornwall, in the southwest corner of England, far removed from Scotland. His early years, like the ships and cargoes, passing through Greenock, had an itinerant, provisional quality, as he moved, always unsettled, and sometimes unsettling to others. His working-class background remained an issue, as he once said, jokingly: "Am I a poet? Or am I just a boy from Greenock?"

Graham's alcoholism, which played a considerable role in his life, also partly derives from a Clydeside background where hard drinking was common, the one easily available release for men from lower-class backgrounds. The pub, though, was more to Graham than a place where he could easily indulge himself. The culture of the pub was close to the center of his work, and a pub named Mooney's features numerous times in his later poetry, including the title of arguably his best book, Malcolm Mooney's Land. For Graham the pub was where views could be exhanged and roles tried out and tested and where free-flowing, heightened language was possible. He was fascinated by the pub scene in *The Waste Land*, with its slangy, side-of-the-mouth conversation. David Wright, his friend and fellow writer, has recorded examples of Graham's sometimes abrasive pubtalk. Once confronted by a literary bore, Graham burst out:

> In three days I will begin the novel of my life with—"Unlike my brother, the Grand Duke Ferdinand ...". There is no reply—You have to sit and be talked to—OK OK Reply reply if you dare. Well well eh? So what? You don't know eh?—Yeheeh—Alright?, lay cards on table—I thought so. No cards eh?
>
> (David Wright, "W. S. Graham in the Forties," in *Edinburgh Review* 75 [1987], p. 52.)

Perhaps one of the most puzzling aspects of Graham's character was how someone so voluble and gregarious could also write such delicate, quiet, almost self-erasing poems. It was a trait he shared with other poets of the periods, notably Dylan Thomas and Patrick Kavanagh, whose desire to become "characters" with the help of alcoholic inspiration masked fundamental sensitivity and shyness. A Celtic poet of the time could be expected, especially by an English audience, to play a bardic role, to play up to the stereotype of the mercurial, verbose, extravagant clown. Of course this role was also a trap

Most of Graham's life was lived in conditions that dipped in and out of poverty, and he was always dependent, to a greater or lesser extent, on others. From his teenage years, however, it was clear that he wished to improve himself, though in a nonmaterialistic way. To the consternation of his traditionally minded parents, he took evening classes in art appreciation and literature at Glasgow University and then, in 1938, began a year of study at Newbattle Abbey Adult Residential College. Unusually progressive for the time, Newbattle modeled itself on an Oxford College and was open to working students who were not from prosperous backgrounds. There Graham embarked on a mixed program of subjects, mainly concentrating on arts and philosophy. At this point he had already gained a reputation among his classmates for writing poetry, as well as for being something of a character or, more unkindly, a poseur. One of the students Graham met there was the woman he would eventually marry, Agnes Dunsmuir, who was known as Nessie.

Graham's mother was Irish and much of his work leans sympathetically toward the Irish culture of the singer John McCormack and the writers J. M. Synge, James Joyce, and Samuel Beckett. It was not surprising when, in 1939, seeking to avoid conscription into the armed forces, he went to Ireland, which was neutral during the Second World War, and sought work. The jobs he found were mixed—on a farm, with a fair, on the docks—and short-lived. He also drifted from place to place. Later, he returned to Scotland, where a medical examination revealed an ulcer, which made him unfit for military service. In a belated contribution to the war effort, he put his engineering skills to use in a torpedo factory.

All of these occupations tended to suck him back into the limited cultural expectations of his upbringing. More rewarding opportunities and contacts were to be gained through the artistic circles in which he was beginning to move. Graham's first book, *Cage Without Grievance*, was taken up by David Archer, who published it with his Parton Press in 1942. Archer, a literary philanthropist with many contacts, was one of a line of figures who played a generous, avuncular role in Graham's life, recognizing his talent and providing him, from time to time, with financial and moral support. Graham lived for a while in Archer's flat in Glasgow, and the circles of his artistic friends became significantly wider and more elevated. Through the cultural events Archer organized, Graham met the poets Hugh McDiarmid and Dylan Thomas and the painters Robert Colquhoun and Robert MacBryde.

These contacts also led further afield to London, where Graham moved in 1944. He became associated with the wartime literary community, especially the Fitzrovia scene, which was based around pubs in Soho in the center of London. That same year he had a daughter by Mary Harris. Pleading his unsuitability in the role, he gave up his responsibilities as a father. He had little contact with either daughter or her mother subsequently.

In late 1944, Graham moved with Nessie Dunsmuir to Cornwall. Initially they lived a spartan existence in a pair of vans. Graham is said to have worked as a casual laborer and fisherman during the early part of his residence while his wife supplemented their income with seasonal work for a local hotel.

In 1946, the couple moved into a cottage in Mevagissey, Cornwall. Soon thereafter, they separated for six years. Graham began a relationship with the American academic Vivienne Koch, which was to have a considerable influence on him. It led to his living in New York for a year, giving a series of lectures on literature at New York university, and winning an Atlantic Award in 1947. Koch obligingly wrote about his work in Sewanee Review, helping him to become better known. His cultural horizons broadened, and there is an evident deepening of his style in his collection *The White Threshold*, which was published in 1949.

Graham returned to England in 1948, briefly to Cornwall and then to London. His health was poor. Under pressure of an inadequate diet and, especially, the excessive drinking that was becoming a permanent feature of his life, he had agitated his ulcer. Some of Graham's contemporaries around this time remembered him as being difficult and prickly. Julian Maclaren-Ross, in his Memoirs of the Forties (London, 1963), draws a picture of Graham holding forth in the literary pubs and recalling how difficult it could be even to say hello to him. Except with close personal friends, Graham found communication stressful. In order to counteract his difficulty, he would fuel himself up with alcohol and treat each meeting as a performance, even a high-wire act. A reading, an interview or the most casual encounter became an adventure. However jovial his intentions, he tended to put his listeners, interlocutors, and, indeed, readers on edge—or, as he might have seen it, made them aware that the edge was where they had been all along. Edwin Morgan, in "W. S. Graham and Voice,'" records this kind of baiting in a 1978 interview with Graham by Penelope Mortimer, in *The Observer,* which is also a good example of Graham's humor:

PM: Tell me about your parents.
WSG: My dear. You must ask me something very small. Like "Why do you put capitals at the beginning of the lines of your verse?"
PM: Why do you put capitals at the beginning of the lines of your verse?
WSG: To make people realize it's poetry.

(p. 78)

Graham lived with a friend in London and then again with Vivienne Koch until their separation, in 1950. In the same year he worked briefly for an advertising agency. He was writing the long poem for which he would become best known, "The Nightfishing." By 1953 he had reunited with Nessie Dunsmuir, who had been living in Paris. In 1955, Graham moved back to Cornwall with Nessie as his wife (they had married the previous year). His first significant collection, *The Nightfishing*, was published in 1955.

W. S. GRAHAM

Graham developed friendships with many of the painters based around St. Ives, in Cornwall. In a setting he Graham found agreeable, St. Ives combined a traditional (if declining) fishing community with the bohemian atmosphere created by an influx of painters. The bombing of London in the Blitz meant that many were eager to escape the city. Property was going cheap in Cornwall, and painters went there attracted by the quality of the light, the chance to buy studio space, and the congenial presence of their peers. Graham met and made friends with many who would prove important to the history of postwar British painting—like Peter Lanyon, Roger Hilton, and Bryan Wynter—writing poems about all of them.

The subject and methods of Graham's approach to writing found echoes in the attitudes of the painters. The style of the primitive painter Alfred Wallis was a major influence in St. Ives, emphasizing an existential approach where the borderline between subject and object crumbled. The painting (or the poem) could now be seen as an experience, not so much a commentary on life as an extension of it, and therefore more appropriate to the way we actually live. As the St. Ives scene also represents the beginning of a coming to terms with Abstract Expressionism in British painting, Graham's position could be compared with the American poets Frank O'Hara and John Ashbery, of the New York School, who were coming to terms with Abstract Expressionism around the same time.

There is a synesthetic aspect to Graham's work—not only could he appreciate art forms other than poetry, he saturated himself in them. Graham's readings often became a dialogue between different kinds of art. Before a performance he would decorate a room with his own paintings and hangings, light the area with candles, and play music by Bartok or Mozart. The audience was encouraged to join in and make dramatic sounds (the noise of a storm perhaps), while different poems were read by different voices. Graham's sheer exuberance was striking; he sought in any given moment the transcendence that art can afford. As he once wrote, "I happen to feel most alive when I am trying to write poetry."

Such combinations were also a part of his working methods. When composing a poem over a long period Graham used a wall, rather as a painter uses a canvas, and pinned up phrases he found particularly resonant. His notebooks are composed in different inks, with lettering of different sizes, sometimes painted over with a wash of color. His letters often read like excerpts from Joyce's *Finnegans Wake*; a long list of puns and variations on words unwound, creating a playful, intoxicating effect.

Despite its being well received, Graham did not follow up The Nightfishing with a new collection for fifteen years, when *Malcolm Mooney's Land* was published in 1970. He seemed to disappear from the literary scene at the moment he should have been most visible. One of Graham's significant patrons during this bleak period in his life was the poet Robin Skelton (1925–1997), who had interceded with publishers on his behalf and who was interested in collecting Graham's manuscripts. Skelton notes the extent of Graham's vanishing in his introduction to an edition of Graham's notebooks: "When in the late sixties I asked Faber & Faber why they had not seen fit to bring out a new Graham book I was astonished to be told that they had lost touch with him and did not know he was still writing" (*Aimed at Nobody*, p. viii).

Faber may have forgotten about Graham simply because he went out of fashion. Partly, this was because the style of the Movement writers, dominant in the 1950s, was far removed from Graham's new style. The typical Movement poem was ironic, English, low key, and featured a lyric self acting in recognizable contemporary situations, whereas the typical Graham poem was contemplative, Scottish, and featured a fragmented self acting in metaphorical, psychologized landscapes. Philip Larkin's *The Less Deceived*, a popular triumph of the Movement style, was published in the same year as The Nightfishing and probably helped to overshadow it.

Nor did Graham receive his due from his homeland. He was never fully accepted by the Scottish Renaissance movement, which was at its height between the years 1920 and 1945. The movement laid heavy stress on the use of a literary version, or versions, of the Scots dialect, an emphasis with which Graham was out of sympathy. Graham, through his literary style and his decision to move away from Glasgow to Cornwall, was perhaps not obviously Scottish enough. Admittedly, to remove himself to Cornwall was to withdraw to the other end of the island of Britain. He could hardly get much further away. However, Graham never stopped seeing himself as Scottish. His fundamental stance, in any case, was of solitude—he did not exist for formal groups or alliances, and neither did they exist for him. During periods when it was fashionable to be explicitly political, particularly in the 1960s, he was obviously not so. Although poets in the late twentieth century usually didn't live off their poetry but from activities peripheral to it, Graham made no sustained effort to promote his works through, for example, broadcasting, reviewing, or lecturing. As much as anything else, this contributed to his neglect.

By 1958 Graham had started to supplement his income by selling some of his manuscripts. He remained in a precarious financial position, however, still reliant on friends for aid. In 1962, the Grahams stayed in a house lent by a friend, the painter Nancy Wynne-Jones, with whom they traveled in 1964 to Greece, a location that would feature later in his work. In 1968 they moved into a cottage she owned and were allowed to stay without paying rent. An arrangement was worked out whereby Graham received a regular if modest income in return for sending all his drafts and manuscripts to Skelton, who had moved to Canada and was teaching at the University of Victoria. In 1973 Graham visited Canada, where he gave a series of poetry readings at universities and colleges. The 1970s saw a reawakening of interest in his work, as he published two of his most important collections with Faber, an *American Selected Poems* in 1979, and in the same year his *Collected Poems* 1942–1977. Graham remained in demand for poetry readings through the 1980s, despite illness and the strain of traveling. He died, after a long battle with cancer, on 9 January 1986.

CAGE WITHOUT GRIEVANCE

THE advent of Graham's publishing career was not much appreciated by his family. David Wright records one of Graham's more rueful, and probably painful memories of *Cage Without Grievance*:

> My father gave 5 dozen copies away to the paper salvage people about 4 years ago. He just handed out the two packages which were unopened, straight from the printers. I had left them in the house when I went to Cornwall—thinking "well I'll always have those safe anyhow"—but there you are!

(David Wright, "W. S. Graham in the Forties," p. 54)

As a consequence of Graham's friendship with so many painters, his first book bore illustrations by Benjamin Crème and Robert Frame. This is significant in view of his later life, but the drawings do not help to elucidate the book. The first poem in *Cage Without Grievance* combines pastoral with industrial images:

Over the apparatus of Spring is drawn
A constructed festival of pulleys from sky.

(p. 7)

We must remember that Graham, like his father, trained to be an engineer in an area where engineering was a traditional activity. Although his later poetry has a somewhat pastoral appeal, it also draws much of its imagery from mechanical, technical activity. Fishing, of which Graham had firsthand experience, and which features so memorably in his long poem "The Nightfishing," was also an important traditional feature of the area. The Clydeside landscape where Graham grew up was indeed industrial, but it was within easy reach of some outstanding natural beauty. So Graham was combining a picture of natural beauty with an industrial, or increasingly postindustrial, landscape in an environment that featured this very combination. This opening poem concludes:

A derrick in flower swings evening values in
And wildernight or garden day frames government
For thieves in a prison of guilt. Birches erect

The ephemeral mechanism of welcoming.
And Spring conquests the law in a cuckoo's school.

(p. 7)

Most of the poems in the book confront us with a simple question: "What does this mean?" The sense of the passage above is difficult to catch, as the different levels of diction clash—the concrete "birches" seem to be operating on the same plane as the abstract "law," the pastoral and the industrial jostle with the administrative. We may gather that some kind of conflict is taking place along the lines of sexuality versus culture, in which presumably the former comes out on top. But it is not clear who the thieves are in the "prison of guilt" or what it is that constitutes "the cuckoo's school." Several influences are at work on Graham in this collection: Hopkins, Dylan Thomas, and W. H. Auden. These are influences to which much of Graham's generation responded. From Hopkins, Graham is taking the headlong rhythms, the compulsion to coin new words like "wildernight," and the packing of stresses in alliterative clusters ("garden day frames government"). From Auden he is taking the familiar psychologized landscape of 1930s British poetry, with its often-sinister combination of pastoral and industrial images. From Thomas, however, he takes the most. In his essay "W. S. Graham: Professor of Silence," Denis O'Driscoll draws attention to features of Dylan Thomas' style identified by John Berryman, the same features with which O'Driscoll notes Graham's poems become saturated:

> ... unusual epithets, compound words, notions of dichotomy, marine imagery. Graham seemed to seize on all of them without allowing words the breathing space which Thomas did.
>
> (The Constructed Space, p. 52)

Thomas' poems tend to place a hazily identified speaker, a kind of supercharged ego, within a network of conflicting and powerful associations: love, grief, guilt, spring, summer. In this vein, Graham's first poem mysteriously touches on "jealous agonies" and "funnels of fever." The poem makes a hymn out of this drama, as it measures the force of powerful feelings without defining them. The action of the poem has a surreal coloring; Graham rarely lingers to describe

any specific, recognizable state, such as a man walking down a street or a casual conversation. The collection as a whole depends on the inclusion of powerful ingredients, and when a poem fails it is usually through the inclusion of too many, rather than too few, of these ingredients.

A framework of sexuality and regeneration occasionally renders Graham's universal dramas, in which this self is so enigmatically engaged, a little more comprehensible. Again, the evocation is relatively hazy, and there is no attempt made to complicate the matter by delineating realistic but difficult emotional situations. This element, combined with some of the formal features (particularly the songlike rhythmical qualities), gives the ordinary reader something on which to fasten and with which he can identify.

Blood builds its platform on a love-me-not
And calculates from exile the seed's dominion.
Love cascades myrtle gospels from the nipple's hill.
Who, with a nettle forefinger sparking covenants
Will sting humanity and point the docken ground?

(Cage Without Grievance, p. 8)

Although the surface of this untitled poem is busy, one can pick out a basic thread of meaning. It is that love or desire creates the essential tension or conflict from which vital writing emerges. This was not a surprising position for Graham to hold; indeed, it is something of an adolescent commonplace. The language is unnecessarily twisted—the rather silly variation on "forget-me-not," portentous phrases like "seed's dominion," and the dubious personifications of "Blood" and "Love." The sexual imagery is straight out of the Dylan Thomas cosmology.

Although Graham's poetry changed profoundly over the course of his writing career—deliriously lush at the beginning, ascetically spare at the end—one feature remains constant. Each poem is treated as what we might call an existential field, that is to the say, the poem is not seen as removed, commenting on life. Each poem is inseparable from life. One of the ways of looking at how his poetry changed is to say that the poems themselves become ever more sharply aware of—and ever more self-conscious about—their experiential immediacy.

Graham's second book is really a pamphlet—its eight poems seldom exceed the length of a page and the book was issued as part of a Poetry Scotland series. Like his first book, it features artwork by Robert Frame. Graham advances a metaphor that will stay with him throughout his career: the journey. The seven journeys of the title are related to the reader in the breathless, Thomasesque rhetoric found in *Cage Without Grievance*. "The First Journey," for example, concludes:

Graham's second book is really a pamphlet—its eight poems seldom exceed the length of a page and the book was issued as part of a Poetry Scotland series. Like his first book, it features artwork by Robert Frame. Graham advances a metaphor that will stay with him throughout his career: the journey. The seven journeys of the title are related to the reader in the breathless, Thomasesque rhetoric found in *Cage Without Grievance*. "The First Journey," for example, concludes:

My flourishing prophet on cockhorse scatters the sun
Through dragonfly graves dark on my pith of travel.
SHEER I break AGAINST those EVERMORE GLIT-
TERING SEASONS.

(n.p.)

The poem conveys a sense of motion, if not exactly of journeying, through its active verbs ("spins," "scatters," "break"). The first word of the poem is "launched," and indeed we do have a sense of some tremendous energy, however indiscriminate, being released. The "I" of the poem is not so much an everyman as a super-man, and the material of the poem provides an appropriate backdrop, or stage, for his declarations. The speaker's actions are invested with power, and evidently there is a certain amount of wish fulfillment in this immature fantasy of assuming godlike status. The uppercase typography adds extra emphasis.

Some of the excesses of the collection's rhetoric are contained by the occasional hint that these journeys are not exercises of godlike power but poetic journeys within domestic spaces or spiritual journeys—that the project is seeing the universe, as Blake saw it, in a grain of sand. Such

moments anticipate developments in Graham's later work. In "The Third Journey" he says, "I build an iliad in a limpet dome." The poems exhibit a jumble of romantic protagonists: swains, clowns, saints, harlequins, acrobats, mermaids, and leopards. None stays in focus longer than it takes to register their elusive presence.

The burden of meaning seems to indicate that the poet is dependent on himself, not on institutionalized religion. "I call the ocean my faith," Graham writes in "The Sixth Journey," and he asks:

Who times my deity, defines my walking sin
In curfew inches on a chain of printed chimes?
What text is my breath on resurrected reefs
Where west records my teething bliss of helms?

(n.p.)

Most of the nouns in the poems are accompanied by unexpected adjectives, even in this passage, where the sense is clearer than usual. The passage seems to suggest that there is no law, no institution, that can anticipate the experience of any moment. Each moment is a new experience, and the definition of its spirituality remains open.

2ND POEMS

2ND Poems is a relatively short book of twenty-three poems. The rather obscure title refers in part to Graham's future wife—To (2) Nessie (N) Dunsmuir (D). The poems in this book are more carefully shaped than before—there is a noticeable use of refrain and a more restrained use of adjectives. The "I" of the poems is fractionally less impersonal and less supercharged than in the earlier work, and Graham settled on a recognizable northern coastal landscape. From this point on, the "temperature" of the environment in his poetry, almost Mediterranean in his first, overheated book, begins to lower, till it reaches the arctic conditions of *Malcolm Mooney's Land*. Graham also began to settle on the roughhewn diction associated with his later work, interspering his verse with some harshly accented, monosyllabic lines, as in "The Bright Building":

W. S. GRAHAM

You in a squad of dead pecked by the tides
Speak as likely as the sea rolls its stones

(2nd Poems, p. 18)

The objects with which the poems are furnished swing toward the recognizable. The volume also illustrates a tendency firmly established in his style: the use of compound nouns to create heavily stressed neologisms. Graham was particularly fond of coining compounds with the word "sea," such as "seanight" and "sealaw."

However, to adopt a phrase used by Seamus Heaney, Graham still had the veins bulging in his biro. The first five lines of "The Crowd of Birds and Children" illustrate some of the improvements in as well as the lingering vices of Graham's style:

Beginning to be very still
I know the country puffed green through the glens.
I see the tree's folly appleing into angels
Dress up the sun as my brother
And climb slow branches and religious miracles.

(2nd Poems, p. 27)

Here the opening line exhibits the syntactic ambiguity that also features at the start of "The Nightfishing." The subordinate clause of the first line might be referring to any, or even all, of the nouns in the next line. It could also be taken as a statement about itself, or even about the change that was taking place in Graham's poetry, which was beginning to be very still. The second line features the typically quirky adjective "puffed," which is just about successful, but the neologistic verb "appleing" in the third line is excessive, especially when surrounded by the portentous religious imagery. In later volumes, Graham retained the kind of dignity he achieves in the first two lines of "The Crowd of Birds and Children," but he progressively dropped the overheated rhetoric of the next three.

The more recognizable landscape of these poems is partly generated by Graham's use of names that refer to the Scottish landscape, such as Calder and Lanarkshire. Equally important, he used fewer exotic proper nouns drawn from books rather than from experience. The result was greater consistency in the texture of the verse.

THE WHITE THRESHOLD

THIS significant transitional volume was also the first of Graham's to be published by the preeminent British poetry firm Faber and Faber. The book was accepted for publication by T. S. Eliot. Eliot and Graham often met for lunch to discuss poetic form, a development that was immensely flattering to the young Scot.

An important feature of the book was Graham's adoption of the three-stress line. The tempo suited his contemplative style. Graham was reported to have trained himself in the form by using it to record every entry in one of his journals, an indication both of his ambitious formalism and of his singlemindedness. It is not just the three-stress line, however, that indicates a growing attention to form in his work of the period. The poems in *The White Threshold* are carefully shaped in a variety of ways with regular stanza forms, including ballad forms, tercets, quatrains, Yeatsian nine-line stanzas, and stanzas with patterned alterations of their line lengths. There are a vast number of compounds in this book based on the word "sea": "seawind," "sea-lamb," "sea-tombs," "seagreat," "seachanged," "sea-martyrdom," "seabraes," and "seabent"—a list that could readily be extended. The influence of the sea can even be felt in the titles: "Men Sign the Sea," "Night's Fall Unlocks the Dirge of the Sea," "Three Poems of Drowning," and "The Voyages of Alfred Wallis" (the latter significantly draws a parallel between voyaging and painting). Drowning is a major motif, eliciting comparisons to J. M. Synge's *Riders to the Sea* as will be discussed later. Such consistency of diction and subject matter allows the poems to speak to each other, and The White Threshold works well as a book. It ends with three letters to members of Graham's family—his brother, father, and mother—again demonstrating his fondness for the letter as a form.

The use of adjectives is markedly restrained, making descriptions crisper, and the diction becomes more harsh and clipped. This more measured style allows individual lines to stand out in a way they could never have in his earliest work, as in the last stanza of "Shian Bay":

Last gale washed five into the bay's stretched arms,
Four drowned men and a boy drowned into shelter.
The stones roll out to shelter in the sea.

(The White Threshold, p. 39)

The dignified finality of the last line, charged by the disturbing ambiguity of the word shelter marks a new, more powerful kind of effect in Graham's work. The diction is unforced and simple, and the effects are gained by the use of somber understatement. Since the book is so wholly given over to maritime influences, it is fitting that the poem ends with the word "sea." The use of the sea as a constant point of reference had become a fully established motif by the time of *The White Threshold*, although Graham had yet to make such startling use of it as later on.

The White Threshold (the title also refers to the sea) was an attempt at self-definition, through an analysis of the poet's environment—the geographical and social factors that shaped his community and himself. As such, it was the closest Graham came to the mainstream of postwar British poetry, which he subsequently approached only to pass far beyond. The style of the Movement (as it was colorlessly known) called for restrained diction, careful observations and description and, more negatively, avoidance of grandiose poses and statements or mystification of any kind. Since Graham was writing *The White Threshold* in the years before the Movement became established, he could not be said to be adhering to any program. Nevertheless, the book showed a temporary convergence with the cultural aims of some of his contemporaries, aims that would sharply diverge.

THE NIGHTFISHING

The Nightfishing is dominated by two sequences, the title poem and "Seven Letters." The epistolary sequence (an echo of *The Seven Journeys*) marked a significant advance in Graham's technique. The letters are addressed to his wife and are filled with his signature motifs, in particular the use of a landscape that is densely metaphorical and yet has recognizable features (the loch, the moor, the shore, a pub called Mooney's)

combined with an increasingly self-reflexive focus on language:

My love my love anywhere
Drifted away, listen.
From the dark rush under
Us comes our end. Endure
Each word as it breaks at last
To become our home here.
Who hears us now? Suddenly
In a stark flash the nerves
Of language broke. The sea
Cried out loud under the keel.
Listen. Now I fall.

(p. 62)

The use of the sea and the invocation to listen are prominent features of "The Nightfishing," Graham's first major work. The poem opens with sound, not a voice: the striking of a bell. The sound has qualities of command and strangeness, a solemnity that announces change. That the poem opens with a sound also reminds us of Graham's knowledge of, and love for, music. As a young man he was an enthusiast for choirs and singers and traveled into Glasgow whenever he could to hear the best of them. "The Nightfishing" has a markedly musical form, opening with a slow, dignified movement and gradually accelerating into the sonic storm of the long third section, until calming toward its conclusion. When reading this poem, Graham performed like a cross between an opera singer and a stage actor, as his friend Edwin Morgan has testified:

> I have his own copy of the programme he used for a reading at the Institute of Contemporary Arts in London on 26 November 1957, and the margins are spattered with handwritten commands to himself, almost in the manner of musical annotation, indicating exactly how particular lines are (or are not!) to be delivered. He writes: "as clearly enunciated as possible," "as formal and mechanical as possible," "slow easy conversational," "shock," "take it easy," "these words slow and separate," "don't ham this," "almost casual," "slay them."
>
> (Edwin Morgan, "W. S. Graham and Voice,'" in The Constructed Space, pp. 76–77)

The opening of "The Nightfishing" is a call to attention, reminding us of Graham's uneasy desire to make a connection with the listener. He treated the poem as a tour de force but began by starting slowly, recognizing the dramatic value of understatement.

> Very gently struck
> The quay night bell

The opening illustrates some of the enlivening syntactical ambiguity that operates in nearly all of Graham's poetry. It is not clear whether or not the inversion of the clause is party to an ellipsis. Is the bell striking or is it being struck? Is it the object or the subject? The opportunity to listen that the poem extends remains at the heart of his work from this collection onward. Uncertainty about who or what is acting or being acted upon permeates the work and is one of its most apparent themes. The adverbial opening, also characteristic of some of his work, asks us to pay attention not only to action but to that which qualifies it.

Although the poem is presented as a journey out to sea, the reader is less conscious of where the speaker is going than of what he is undergoing. We are not conscious of having arrived at a particular significant point; rather, we have a sense of rising and falling (particularly falling) within an ambiguous environment. "The Nightfishing" creates a poetics of the wave, the nature of its odyssey the oscillation. If there is progress then it is circular in nature, like Shakespeare's "waves which approach the pebbled shore, / each one changing place with that which went before."

When he was at college, Graham took part in a production of J. M. Synge's *Riders to the Sea*, a one-act tragedy that invokes the sea as a symbolic force while at the same time depicting the actual appalling conditions for fishermen on the west coast of Ireland. In his play, Synge effectively evokes the death of one of the fishermen, and anticipates the death of another, through the clothes retrieved from a drowned body. Although none of the action actually takes place on the sea, it figures as an immensely powerful offstage presence, with the islanders like prisoners encircled by its malevolence. The atmosphere is of doom and foreboding. In "The Nightfishing," the outlook is not as bleak, informed as it is by

Graham's energetic melancholy. Nevertheless, Graham uses clothing in a way similar to Synge; the sea is presented as an all-encompassing, all-penetrating entity, which has even worked its way into what the speaker wears:

> Here we dress up in a new grave,
> The fish-boots with their herring-scales
> Inlaid as silver of a good week,
> The jersey knitted close as nerves
> (*The Nightfishing*, p. 18)

This quote from section II of the poem follows the speaker's discussion of the material conditions in which he has grown up. Again, as in Synge, the encroaching symbolism of the sea as a force of nature is not allowed to obscure bald observations about how harsh living conditions are for the speaker. This kind of grounding is absent from Graham's first book, *Cage Without Grievance*. The use of clothing details is of a piece with points of technical authenticity ("tethers and springropes," "corks / And bladders") sprinkled throughout the text, from which the poem greatly benefits.

If Graham's poem is not a depiction of physical death, as in *Riders to the Sea*, it nevertheless anticipates and conveys a metaphysical death undergone by the speaker. The experience of the sea, which becomes a metaphor for all life-changing experience, focuses on the death of identity through experience—words are inadequate to convey what happens and need constantly to be renewed, as in the third section:

> This mingling element
> Gives up myself. Words travel from what they once
> Passed silence with. Here, in this intricate death,
> He goes as fixed on silence as ever he'll be.
> (*The Nightfishing*, p. 27)

Another point of connection between "The Nightfishing" and *Riders to the Sea* is the association of the grave with domestic space:

> I sat rested at the grave's table
> Saying his epitaph who shall

Saying his epitaph who shall
After me to shout farewell.

(The Nightfishing, p. 31)

Other antecedents of the poem include Pound's "The Seafarer," Nansen's *Far North*, and *Moby-Dick*. It also bears comparison with the maritime imagery and religious or quasi-religious existentialism in Robert Lowell's "The Quaker Graveyard at Nantucket," T. S. Eliot's "Little Gidding," and parts of David Jones's much longer modernist sequence, "The Anathemata."

MALCOLM MOONEY'S LAND

BEFORE embarking on a reading tour of Canada in 1973, when he was promoting *Malcolm Mooney's Land*, Graham wrote to a lecturer friend at the Calgary School of Art. Asking about the best approach to Canadian audiences, Graham revealed how he saw the relationship between his background and his poetry:

About the class thing. What shall I do? I suppose I am lower working class. Shall I be superior or inferior? How shall I behave? What shall I wear? I'm coming anyhow and I'll have to make the best of it fuckthem.

Graham's anxiety and self-consciousness were reflected in the stance he took in his poetry. Calvin Bedient, in *Eight Contemporary Poets*, speaks of Graham's style as "having gained the surprised ring of one who had never expected to hear himself speak" (p. 173). One might add that part of the pathos of his later poetry in particular is the articulation of a voice that does not assume it will be heard. In their varying ways, the more public poets of the 1960s, like Robert Lowell and Allen Ginsberg, wrote to command attention; an audience was readily assumed to exist. Graham never counted on an audience. The neglect of his writing must have hurt and it is mirrored by the startling isolation of the speakers in *Malcolm Mooney's Land*.

Graham's apprehensions about language come starkly into view in the book. They could be considered with reference to lines from W. H. Auden's elegy "In Memory of W. B. Yeats": "The words of a dead man / Are modified in the guts of the living." Graham could not be certain about his words once they had been digested by his readers, and this troubled him.

The volume opens spectacularly with the title poem, which introduces us to the frigid landscape of the whole book, a snowscape that in its emptiness, is even more uncompromisingly metaphorical than the seascapes of his earlier work. In the title poem, which is divided into five sections, we read, as if in a journal, the words of an arctic explorer who is trying to come to terms with the extreme conditions of his journey. Here, then, is the definitive Graham figure, a seeker thrown entirely on his own resources, desperate to connect with others, yet facing the obstacles of the definitive Graham landscape, the blinding, page-like whiteness of the snow. The seeker is surrounded by figures and memories that rise beguilingly out of the whiteness as if to mock him with their presence. From time to time, he hallucinates a surreal yet significant event:

Enough
Voices are with me here and more
The further I go. Yesterday
I heard the telephone ringing deep
Down in a blue crevasse.
I did not answer it and could
Hardly bear to pass.

(p. 12)

Commenting on his own book for a *Poetry Society Bulletin*, Graham wrote that he was aware that a poem was not like a telephone call, because you can never hear a voice speaking back. Thus the unanswered imaginary telephone in the ice of "Malcolm Mooney's Land" partly stands for a possibility that is closed to this explorer and to any poet.

Again indicating Graham's fondness for the epistolary form, the explorer in "Malcolm Mooney's Land" sometimes writes his journal as if it were a letter that has been found or is about to be found, like a message in a bottle. He dreamily addresses two figures in particular (not to be confused with any actual people in Graham's life) who may be his loved ones, "Elizabeth" (possibly his wife or lover) and "the boy" (possibly his son). Speaking of his expedition, the explorer urges Elizabeth to let the boy understand it in the form of a story:

Tell him I came across
An old sulphur bear
Sawing his log of sleep
Loud beneath the snow.
He puffed the powdered light
Up on to the page
And here his reek fell
In splinters among
These words.

(p. 15)

The attractive simplicity of these lines, with their almost reassuring tones, relates them to other forms we usually encounter in childhood, the fairytale, the beast fable, and the cartoon. With its imaginary creatures and its puzzling rules of behavior, the book's imaginary landscape often resembles the imaginary landscape of a child.

After the opening poem, the figure of the explorer is replaced by others who are engaged in similar existential struggles. These figures remain isolated; they are never seen as part of a cohesive group. Often, they are artists, though other figures that feature are the climber, the gambler, and the prisoner. Their lonely struggles, taken to an extreme, against conditions they may never overcome, are meant to be seen as parallel.

Given that the poems have started to consider themselves as literature, it is not surprising that other literary writings become prominent within them. One of the foremost presences in the book is Samuel Beckett, with whom Graham admitted he was fascinated. In his novels in particular, Beckett presented a solitary voice that fails to come to terms with its own existence, although it can see no alternative to the attempt. In his essay "Walls of Glass: The Poetry of W. S. Graham," Damian Grant lists the features that Beckett's novels have in common with Graham's later poetry:

The revolving obsession with identity, consciousness, and articulating the telling of stories to create the fiction of the self; the reliance on pun and illu-

sion as a literary method; the deepening (which this implies) as to the possibility of communication with our kind, and the admission of loneliness as one's ultimate condition ...

(*British Poetry Since 1970*, p. 28)

Although the poems in the book are self-conscious, they are not overwhelmingly cerebral or abstract. Graham does not allow us to forget that words are spoken by creatures of flesh and blood, especially in those poems that adopt the form of a letter. Characteristically, Graham's poems have a strong emotional tug; they remain human appeals from one person to an imagined other, although he is usually able to stop just the right side of sentimentality. These qualities are particularly sharply felt in "The Thermal Stair," his elegy for a painter friend, Peter Lanyon:

Uneasy, lovable man, give me your painting
Hand to steady me taking the word-road home.
Lanyon, why is it you're earlier away?
Remember me wherever you listen from.

(p. 27)

Childhood again appears in "The Dark Dialogues," a long poem at the center of the book that Graham, toward the end of his life, thought was his most successful. Here the landscape of the snow shifts into a ghostly evocation of Graham's own childhood, in which he daringly imagines being, and speaks in the voice of, his parents. He describes the Greenock flat where he grew up:

Here, this is the door
With the loud grain and the name
Unreadable in brass.
Knock, but a small knock,
The children are asleep.
I sit here at the fire
And the children are there
And in this poem I am,
Wherever elsewhere I am,
Their mother through his mother.

(p. 31)

Graham's use of pronouns, as in "The Nightfishing," unsettles easy identity. When we read this for the first time, we are not aware that the "I" here is not the "I" of the poem's other sections, that it is meant to be Graham's mother who is speaking. At least, the "I" is mainly Graham's mother, for the poem is too self-conscious not to admit the poet's presence himself within the mother, as in the next section he is a ghostly presence in his own father. At the same time, the poem traces a dizzying circle where Graham's mother is looking at the boy who will imagine being his mother looking at him.

Unlike his earliest work, where the poem was a kaleidoscopic field for any number of heterogeneous impressions, most of which were not arranged in any satisfactory relationship to each other, in *Malcolm Mooney's Land* the situations described and the memories revived are integrated, so that the poems behave like close relatives. The title of the collection is taken from the name of a chain of pubs, and it also has a distinctly Irish resonance. Christian names feature prominently and help to give an air of informality. The lunar associations of Mooney contribute to the evocation of a white, inhospitable landscape. In this book, consideration of language has become much more self-conscious, to an extent that some readers may feel uncomfortable. At a philosophical level, the poems have come to a point where they distrust the relationship between words and the realities to which they refer. The poems puzzle over the gaps between what is said and what was intended to be said.

IMPLEMENTS IN THEIR PLACES

To some extent *Implements in Their Places* is a book that speaks to its predecessor, despite the seven-year gap between dates of publication. The pair share a common territory and can usefully be studied side by side. *Implements in Their Places* is seen as Graham's most accessible book, which owes something to the frankness and directness of its approach to the reader; it was also to be his last. It begins with a poem in sections, "What Is the Language Using Us For?" In its first section, an explorer strikes out over the frozen wastes: "What is the language using us for? / Said Malcolm Mooney moving away / Slowly over the white language" (p. 11). The

opening question becomes a refrain in the poem and echoes throughout the rest of the book. Reflecting Eliot's use of everyday speech in parts of *The Waste Land,* the poem includes snatches of humdrum conversation. Language is seen as limiting description, just as the "sailing terms" of sailors condition their "inner-sailing thoughts." In the final section, Graham allows himself one of his swift, sudden addresses to the reader:

What is the language using us for?
I don't know. Have the words ever
Made anything of you, near a kind
Of truth you thought you were? Me
Neither.

(p. 15)

The word "flying" and the figure of flight arise often and unexpectedly after periods of direct and seemingly straightforward speech, dramatically heightening the tone and suggesting a lingering unreality. "Flying" describes woods both in "The Murdered Drinker" and "How Are the Children Robin" and jungles in "Language Ah Now You Have Me," and in each case it gives the poetry an eerie valedictory air. In the final stanza of "A Note to the Difficult One," the poet finishes addressing a mysterious other (himself? a friend? the reader?) who is trying to speak:

This morning I am ready if you are
To speak. The early quick rains
Of spring are drenching the window-glass.
Here in my words looking out
I see your face speaking flying
In a cloud wanting to say something.

(p. 20)

The image of flight crops up again in the book's concluding elegy, "Dear Bryan Wynter," where it seems to change the scene into something phantasmagorical: "The house and the whole moor / Is flying in the mist" (p. 84). This kind of consistent use of a term or image is common in Graham's poetry, although the device is probably overused here, consistent with a slight slackening of tension compared with Malcolm Mooney's Land.

The emphasis on flight might be paralleled with the late work of Seamus Heaney. In *Seeing*

W. S. GRAHAM

Things, Heaney reaches a state where he is engaged with the element of air. The quality of fading into a common substance serves as a poetic equivalent to being assumed into heaven. In Graham, if not in Heaney, the movement is often downward. Journeying still takes place without any progress. As fragment No. 68 in the title poem puts it:

The earth was flat. Always
The mind or earth wanderer's choice
Was up or down, a lonely vertical.

(p. 80)

The title poem marks something of a departure in Graham's work. A sequence of small fragments (there are seventy-four of them) that have not been worked into an obvious shape, it is the closest Graham came to a poetry of process. The poem resembles one of his workboards, where a set of vaguely interrelated pieces is pinned up. Graham wished to explore the possibilities of finishing a poem without applying the polish of complete finish. The difference is not just that he is writing about language but that he is writing, intermittently, about his own technique:

Nouns are the very devil. Once
When the good nicely chosen verb
Came up which was to very do,
The king noun took the huff and changed
To represent another object.
I was embarrassed but I said something
Else and kept the extravert verb.

(No. 26, p. 69)

The emphasis on technique, which is more than just friendly advice for other artists, is given a fuller treatment in the well-finished "Johann Joachim Quantz's Five Lessons," in which a teacher instructs his student in how to play the flute (only the first of these lessons had appeared in *Malcolm Mooney's Land*). Here the emphasis on technique has a philosophical basis. As Tony Lopez, in *The Poetry of W. S. Graham*, explains, the title poem includes:

the use of material from early Greek philosophy, the idea of language actively participating in the fullness of creation; that is, the whole matter of the poem is most likely derived from Heidegger.

(p. 106)

Graham seems to be examining how we come to know the world through the implements that we have, and the techniques that we have for employing them, a central concern in Heidegger's very influential book *Being And Time*. The fragments are what Graham makes his world out of—they are implements themselves.

Twenty of the poems Graham wrote after *Implements in Their Places* was published (plus a few not collected before) are to be found in the posthumously published *Uncollected Poems*. These are variable in quality, and some, such as "Look at the Children" and "To Leonard Clark," seem underwritten and sentimental. Tributes to other artists proliferate, including two for writers who were old drinking companions: "For John Heath-Stubbs" and "An Entertainment for David Wright on His Being Sixty." A few stand with his best work, including "I Will Lend You Malcolm" and "Look at the Cloud His Evening Playing Cards." Overall, we have a sense of a new collection in the making, perhaps a quarter of the way to being completed.

CONCLUSION

W. S. Graham does not deserve to be neglected. From *The Nightfishing* onward, he wrote poetry of unusual dexterity and originality. His stance and his style are very much his own, and *Malcolm Mooney's Land* is probably one of the five or six best individual collections from Britain since the Second World War. He is important because he showed British poetry an alternative to the conservative poetics of the Movement. Anticipating a linguistic turn in postmodern poetry, his work sees language as an obstacle and as a gift. Experience, for Graham, cannot be detached from the problems of language, nor can it be detached from the problems of where there is no language—and only silence.

W. S. GRAHAM

SELECTED BIBLIOGRAPHY

I. POETRY. *Cage Without Grievance* (Glasgow, 1942); *The Seven Journeys* (Glasgow, 1944); *2nd Poems* (London, 1945); *The White Threshold* (London, 1949); *The Nightfishing* (London, 1955); *Malcolm Mooney's Land* (London, 1970); *Implements in Their Places (London, 1977); Collected Poems 1942–1977* (London, 1979); *Selected Poems* (New York, 1979); *Uncollected Poems* (Warwick, 1990); *Aimed at Nobody: Poems from Notebooks* (London, 1993); *The Nightfisherman: Selected Letters of W. S. Graham,* ed. by Michael Snow and Margaret Snow (Manchester, U.K., 1999).

II. BIOGRAPHICAL AND CRITICAL STUDIES. Calvin Bedient, *Eight Contemporary Poets* (London, 1974); Damian Grant, "Walls of Glass; The Poetry of W. S. Graham," in Peter Jones and Michael Schmidt, eds., *British Poetry Since 1970* (Manchester, U.K., 1980); David Wright, "W. S. Graham in the Forties—Memoirs and Conversations," in *Edinburgh Review* 75 (1987), a special issue on Graham; Tony Lopez, *The Poetry of W. S. Graham* (Edinburgh, 1989); Ronnie Duncan and Jonathan Davidson, eds., *The Constructed Space: A Celebration of W. S. Graham* (Lincoln, U.K., 1994).

L. P. HARTLEY

(1895–1972)

Peter Parker

In discussing the work of Leslie Poles Hartley, there is a problem that must be faced at the outset. Although during his lifetime Hartley secured a reputation as one of England's most distinguished novelists, he wrote a great many bad books. Even Lord David Cecil, his staunchest champion, was obliged to concede (after Hartley was safely dead): "As a writer Hartley was unequal; his later books especially—though always marked by an individual flavor and sense of style—were sometimes disfigured by melodrama and improbability. Moreover his peculiar imaginative power only showed its full strength in his best-known works: the 'Eustace and Hilda' trilogy and *The Go-Between*" (*Dictionary of National Biography 1971–1980* [Oxford, 1986, p. 389). That said, these books are of sufficient quality to secure Hartley a place among important writers of the twentieth century, one that need not be undermined by a lengthy consideration of the work he produced when old, infirm, and, more often than not, drunk. *The Shrimp and the Anemone* (1944) and *The Go-Between* (1953) remain two of the twentieth century's most remarkable fictional evocations of childhood, and the latter is generally agreed to be a masterpiece.

Readers are nevertheless confronted by a writer whose output was extensive (eighteen novels and several volumes of short stories) but of such uneven quality that they might well be put off him altogether if they start in the wrong place. Consequently, this essay will concentrate on Hartley's best books, mentioning the inferior work only in passing or when relevant to the principal discussion.

THEMES AND INFLUENCES

For the epigraph of *The Shrimp and the Anemone*, Hartley chose two bleak lines of poetry:

I've known a hundred kinds of love,
All made the loved one rue.

These sound as if they ought to be by A. E. Housman, which would indeed be appropriate to Hartley's own case, but they are in fact by Emily Brontë, a writer Hartley had discovered at school and who remained one of his favorite authors. Hartley's fiction describes many kinds of love, and in almost every case they lead to regret—or worse.

Hartley is often discussed, with some justification, as an author of "symbolic novels" (as the subtitle of one critical study puts it), but the best of his work is also firmly grounded in the real world, where human actions are bound by social and sexual conventions. If Hartley's novels were merely concerned with signs and symbols, with working out patterns like crossword puzzles, they would be a good deal less involving than, at their best, they undoubtedly are. It is not simply that Hartley weaves his symbolism so seamlessly into the detailed social fabric of such novels as *The Go-Between* and the *Eustace and Hilda* trilogy but that he is as much concerned with feeling as he is with meaning. Symbolism is used to underscore the narrative, not stand in for it.

Apart from Brontë, the writers who most influenced Hartley were Nathaniel Hawthorne and Henry James, as he frequently acknowledged. In particular he admired their prose styles and was attracted to their concern with guilt and innocence, secrecy and exposure, sin and redemption. As a consequence, much has been written about Hartley's own moral universe and his notions of good and evil; but discussions of his work sometimes give the impression that he presents an uncomplicated fictional world in which opposing forces are neatly lined up to do battle one against the other.

119

In the first substantial critical study of Hartley, for example, Peter Bien states that one of the most obvious ways in which Hartley resembles James is in "the use of the theme of innocence exposed to evil," with the crucial difference that Hartley's "unique vision is not the conquering of evil by man's moral strength, but in the conquering of man by evil," a vision Bien discerns in both *The Go-Between* and the *Eustace and Hilda* trilogy (*L. P. Hartley*, pp. 24, 25). The young protagonists of these novels, Leo Colston and Eustace Cherrington, may be "vanquished," to use Leo's word, but not by anything that could be categorized as "evil." Bien compares Leo with the eponymous child in James's *What Maisie Knew* (1897), "since the childish consciousness of each is made to register adult depravity" (*L. P. Hartley*, p. 24). The adults surrounding Maisie are clearly supposed to be depraved, or at any rate morally corrupt, but Hartley is far too humane a writer not to treat the illicit affair in his novel between his characters Marian and Ted with some sympathy, even if this (as we shall see) was not his original intention. In his fiction Hartley portrays passion as destructive, but he does so with regret rather than with any sense of moral opprobrium. The reasons for this may be glimpsed in what we know about his life.

THE CENTRAL "MYSTERY" OF HARTLEY'S LIFE

HARTLEY'S understanding of human relationships came at considerable cost to himself, and although little of his best work is narrowly autobiographical, in order to appreciate it fully one needs to know something of his life. The central question about Hartley's life is prompted by *The Go-Between*, which is generally regarded as his most deeply felt novel. The plot concerns a schoolboy, Leo Colston, whose involvement in a sexual scandal scars him to such an extent that he is unable as an adult to form any sort of satisfactory relationship. "You flew too near the sun, and you were scorched," Leo tells his twelve-year-old self. "This cindery creature is what you made me" (p. 20). Hartley himself was a somewhat cindery creature and this has led to speculation as to whether he too underwent some

unwelcome experience as a child that permanently affected his life. In public Hartley was determined to reveal as little as possible about his personal circumstances. A standard reference book could do no better in 1955 than state: "L. P. Hartley is a man whose private life, at least as far as the public knows, is almost entirely absorbed by his literary life. Unmarried, he lives in Somerset, travels occasionally in France and Italy, and lists his recreations as rowing, swimming, and going for walks" (*Twentieth Century Authors: First Supplement*, ed. by Stanley J. Kunitz [New York, 1973], p. 416). In fact, it is possible to argue that Hartley covered his tracks so effectively that the psychological truth about him is indeed to be found in his books rather than in biographical investigation.

Speculation about Hartley's life was for many years firmly discouraged. After his death, his memory was fiercely guarded by his younger sister, Norah, and attempts to write his life were frustrated or abandoned until 1992, when Adrian Wright gained authorization and access to Hartley's papers, all of which were destroyed after Norah's death two years later. Wright's *Foreign Country: The Life of L. P. Hartley* (1996) is, therefore, the only biography we are likely to get; fortunately, it is an excellent account, genuinely sympathetic but not in the least uncritical.

Although his sister always insisted that *The Go-Between* was entirely fictional, Hartley himself provided clues that suggest otherwise. Like Leo, the young Hartley went to stay in the large country house of a school friend in Norfolk, although the visit took place in 1909 rather than 1900, the year in which Hartley symbolically sets his novel. The house was called Bradenham Hall, a name Hartley adapted only slightly for the novel to "Brandham Hall." One story has it that while there Hartley came across the diary of a young woman that described a love affair between two people from different social classes, and that this provided him with the basis of the relationship in the novel between the young lady of the house, Marian Maudsley, and the tenant farmer, Ted Burgess. When Joseph Losey started location work on his celebrated 1970 film version of the book, Hartley wrote in a letter that it was to be "'shot' near East Dereham, though not at the house where it happened" (*Foreign Country*, p. 253). Of the phrase "where it happened," Wright comments:

a slip of the pen or a careless confession that the book had its foundation in truth? What can the "it" that Hartley refers to be? If not the central plot of the novel, perhaps the trauma that so affected both Leo and Hartley? The unwanted learning about physical love, the dangers of adoration? For Hartley to have been so imprecise in his meaning as to have written of the place "where it happened" is perhaps unthinkable; this is at once the flimsiest, and most suggestible, evidence that may tell us that the running shadow that followed Hartley through his life had its true origins here.

(*Foreign Country*, p. 253)

Wright is referring here to what one of Hartley's fictional alter egos, Richard Mardick in *The Betrayal* (1966), calls "an unfortunate experience in youth. Something that cast a shadow—a running shadow," something that can pursue and blight an entire life (*The Betrayal*, p. 20).

Since the publication of Wright's book, a reference to *The Go-Between* has appeared in the posthumous diaries of the British writer James Lees-Milne, who knew Hartley well. "I remember Leslie telling me that the story was autobiographical," Lees-Milne wrote after seeing Losey's film. "The experience had a devastating effect upon him, and turned him away from women" (*Deep Romantic Chasm: Diaries, 1979–1981*, ed. by Michael Bloch [London, 2000], p. 65).

There is no way of knowing for certain how much of the novel is taken from life and how much is invented, but there is no doubt that as an adult Hartley was unable to sustain any sort of permanent relationship with a woman or a man, and this colored much of his writing. Hartley did, however, have what he believed to be one real chance of love. While an undergraduate at Oxford, he had met Lord David Cecil. The son of the Fourth Marquis of Salisbury, Cecil was seven years Hartley's junior, an aristocratic, delicate, dandyish figure who represented everything Hartley most desired in life. They embarked

on a friendship, which evidently went deeper for Hartley than it did for Cecil, and he was devastated when in 1932 his friend sent him a pointedly valedictory letter announcing his engagement. Hartley was not to be shaken off so easily, and the two men remained friends, Cecil becoming one of the most prominent—and most obfuscating—commentators on Hartley's work. Nevertheless, Hartley seems to have been deeply and permanently affected by Cecil's rejection, and thereafter cultivated friendships rather than romance, chiefly with elderly aristocratic women.

EARLY LIFE AND WORK

THE aristocracy was not Hartley's natural milieu. The son of a country solicitor who subsequently made a great deal of money as the director of a brickworks, he was born on 30 December 1895 at Whittlesey (sometimes spelled "Whittlesea"), a water-bound market town in the Cambridgeshire Fens. He had a hypochondriacal, overprotective mother and two sisters: Enid, born in 1892, and Norah, born in 1903. He was brought up as a Wesleyan Methodist and a liberal, and this marked him as different when he went to Harrow, one of Britain's leading public schools, where most of his fellow pupils were Church of England and Tory. An urge to conform, and perhaps to escape from his suffocating mother, led to his being confirmed into the Church of England at the age of sixteen.

Hartley went up to Balliol College, Oxford, to read modern history in 1915, but the university was severely depleted of both tutors and undergraduates, many of whom had marched away to the First World War. Hartley decided to follow suit in April 1916 but ended up doing all his war service in England. He enjoyed a spell of popularity at one army camp distributing the mail among his fellow soldiers. The sense of importance this gave him, and the gratitude of those receiving letters, would remain with him, resurfacing almost half a century later in *The Go-Between*.

Hartley had always suffered indifferent health—though not as indifferent as his cosseting mother believed—and was invalided out of the army in September 1918. He resumed his studies at Oxford the following year and started writing short stories, several of which were published in the *Oxford Outlook*, a leading undergraduate magazine of which he became a co-editor in 1920.

One of these stories attracted the interest of Lady Ottoline Morrell, whose home at Garsington Manor had long been a meeting place for writers, artists, and intellectuals. He was also introduced to the family of Herbert Asquith, the former prime minister, by his friend Clifford Kitchin, who was to make his reputation as a novelist and writer of detective fiction. Through these introductions, Hartley was launched into the social and literary world, and throughout his life he had a weakness for people with titles. Within months of leaving Oxford, he had started reviewing for the *Spectator*, and he subsequently wrote for many of the leading periodicals of the time.

Hartley was also fortunate in meeting Constant Huntington, the American publisher who ran the London office of Putnam & Co. Huntington offered to publish a collection of Hartley's stories, which had been appearing in such magazines as the *London Mercury* and the *Saturday Review*. The book was published in 1924 as *Night Fears*, and Huntington would energetically promote Hartley's career for many years. As its title suggests, *Night Fears* featured several tales of terror and the supernatural, a genre that continued to attract Hartley throughout his career. The book is, however, essentially an apprentice work.

Night Fears was followed by Hartley's first novel, *Simonetta Perkins* (1925), a brief tale set in Venice. He had first visited the city with Kitchin in 1922, and after graduating from Oxford with a second class degree, he began to spend the spring and autumn of each year there, often with Lord David Cecil. (The private income Hartley derived from the Whittlesea Central Brick Company, of which he eventually became a director, meant that he never had to earn a living and always enjoyed a comfortable *rentier* existence.) It took Hartley only a fortnight to write his novella: "I knew just what I wanted to

say and the technique for saying it came automatically," he recalled (*Foreign Country*, p. 85). That technique is very clearly derived from Henry James, as is the plot, in which American innocence is exposed to European worldliness. The protagonist is a young woman from Boston, Lavinia Johnstone, who becomes sexually obsessed by a gondolier while on holiday. Any sort of relationship between Lavinia and Emilio is, of course, out of the question, not only for social reasons but also because Lavinia is unable to accept her own sexual awakening. The book opens with the observation that "Love is the greatest of the passions, the first and the last," but it is significant that this sentiment is derived from a book Lavinia is reading, as if it is something that she—like Hartley—understands theoretically but is unable to experience in practice (*The Complete Short Stories*, p. 3). "The victim of the amorous passion has a holiday from himself," Lavinia reads on, but this is something of which she is incapable; as the narrator later comments: "the enmity of convention was outside her experience, for she had always been its ally, marched in its van" (*The Complete Short Stories*, p. 49).

Simonetta Perkins not only remains one of Hartley's most accomplished pieces of writing, it also introduces themes that will recur throughout his work: the conflict arising from warring feelings of attraction and repulsion over sex; the inadvisability or even impossibility of romantic or sexual relationships conducted across social or cultural divisions; the individual impulse defeated and crushed by convention; innocence confronted by experience. The descriptions of Venice are masterly, and the city will reappear in later books, most notably *Eustace and Hilda*. Venice not only provided Hartley with a second home and a new collection of friends among the Anglo-American community there; it also provided him with a useful metaphor. Venice is above all a city of water, of distorting reflections, where hidden depths lurk dangerously beneath the glittering surface of the canals, and, like much of Hartley's work, *Simonetta Perkins* is more revealing than the author perhaps intended or realized. Lavinia's half-fascinated, half-fearful appreciation of the *gondolieri*, and the sexual possibilities they offered, is evidently shared by Hartley himself.

Venice is also a place of corruption, as indicated in the reader's first glimpse of it, through Lavinia's eyes, which she lifts from her book to rest "on the grey dome of Santa Maria della Salute, rising like a blister out of the inflamed and suppurating stonework below" (*The Complete Short Stories*, p. 3). "How I hate Baroque" (*The Complete Short Stories*, p. 3), Lavinia exclaims, a prejudice she shares with Eustace Cherrington, both characters preferring (as Oscar Wilde put it) "the grey twilight of Gothic things" (*The Complete Letters of Oscar Wilde*, ed. by Merlin Holland and Rupert Hart-Davis [London, 2000], p. 544). The baroque, of course, is a style that originated in Italy and is noted for its exuberance and its emotional intensity, perhaps reaching its apogee in Bernini's distinctly erotic rendering of the *Ecstasy of St Theresa*. Both Lavinia and Eustace shy away from such feelings, unable to offer themselves up as Bernini's saint does.

Simonetta Perkins ends with an extraordinary scene in which Lavinia tries to overcome her reserve and declare herself to Emilio during an excursion along the canals. Having consulted her dictionary in order to get the vocabulary of love exactly right, she brings out "*Ti amo*," which the gondolier fails to hear the first time. She repeats the phrase: "This time he heard, and understood" (*The Complete Short Stories*, p. 54). There follows a description of the progress of the gondola, which is heavily sexual in its imagery:

Rapidly the gondola pressed its way alongside the Fondamenta delle Zattere. With each stroke it shivered and thrilled. They turned into a little canal, turned again into a smaller one, almost a ditch. The V-shaped ripple of the gondola clucked and sucked at the walls of the crumbling tenements. Ever and again the prow slapped the water with a clopping sound that, each time she heard it, stung Lavinia's nerves like a box on the ear. She was afraid to look back, but in her mind's eye she could see, repeated again and again, the arrested rocking movement of the gondolier. The alteration of stroke and recovery became dreadful to her, suggesting no more what was useful or romantic, but proclaiming a crude physical sufficiency, at once restless and unwilling.

It came to her overwhelmingly that physical energy was dangerous and cruel, just in so far as it was free; there flashed across her mind the straining bodies in Tiepolo and Tintoretto, one wielding an axe, another tugging at a rope, a third heaving the Cross aloft, a fourth turning his sword upon the Innocents. And Emilio with his hands clasping the oar was such another; a minister at her martyrdom.

She strove to rid her mind of symbols ...
(*The Complete Short Stories*, p. 54)

This proves impossible, however: "It suddenly seemed to Lavinia that she was going down a tunnel that grew smaller and smaller; something was after her. She ran, she crawled; she flung herself on her face, she wriggled" (*The Complete Short Stories*, p. 55). She orders Emilio to return to the hotel.

A second volume of short stories, *The Killing Bottle*, appeared in 1932, once again containing a number of ghost stories, some of which had been commissioned by Cynthia Asquith for the anthologies she edited. Although these are essentially genre pieces, stories such as "The Visitor from Down Under" are as interestingly oblique and suggestive as much of Hartley's other fiction. The bulk of these stories was subsequently reprinted in *The Travelling Grave* (1951), which gathered the best of Hartley's tales of terror, including "Podolo." Set in Venice, this story provides the reader with a genuine frisson of the sort generated in the work of M. R. James.

EUSTACE AND HILDA

ITALY had become a second home to Hartley, but when war broke out in 1939, he was obliged to return to England, renting a house on the river in the Wiltshire village of Lower Woodford. The river might have provided Hartley with a substitute for the canals of Venice. To his disgust, however, he discovered that he was forbidden to boat there, and this disappointment, festering into grievance against the local landowners, provided a plot for *The Boat* (1949), the most openly (and indeed almost libelously) autobiographical of his books. Meanwhile, he was delving into the past, drawing upon memories of childhood holidays on the beach at Hunstanton in Norfolk to write a novel about a brother and sister. *The Shrimp and the Anemone* had its origins in an early story, "Back to Cambo," which he developed over a long period of time until it became his first full-length novel and the first volume of a trilogy. It was published in 1944 (appearing under the title *The West Window* in the United States), and was followed by *The Sixth Heaven* (1946) and *Eustace and Hilda* (1947). The trilogy was subsequently published in a single volume with the first two novels linked by an additional chapter, "Hilda's Letter," which concerns Hilda's vain attempts to prevent her brother being sent away to boarding school.

It was *The Shrimp and the Anemone* that established Hartley's reputation, since his first three books had not attracted much attention. It remains one of his best novels, a vividly imagined (or perhaps remembered) account of childhood and of the relationship between a weak brother and a domineering sister. (The latter, despite Hartley's protests to the contrary, is based on his own elder sister, Enid.) It opens with one of Hartley's most arresting symbols, and one of the most haunting images in twentieth-century literature. Playing among rockpools at Anchorstone, nine-year-old Eustace Cherrington is upset to discover a sea anemone devouring a shrimp. Eustace wants to save the life of the shrimp but is worried about depriving the anemone of vital sustenance. His twelve-year-old sister, Hilda, has no such qualms and decisively pulls free the shrimp, which turns out to be already dead. In doing so, she partly disembowels the anemone. Eustace is horrified at this result, but Hilda tells him: "We had to do something. We couldn't let them go on like that." "Why couldn't we?" Eustace replies. "They didn't mean to hurt each other" (*Eustace and Hilda: A Trilogy* p. 19). This brief scene provides the reader with a shocking and resonant metaphor for the symbiotic yet destructive relationship between these siblings.

It is unclear whether or not Hartley consciously recognized that the insucking plumous anemone, which reappears in a dream at the end of the novel to take the dying Eustace's finger between its cold "lips," is also a type of *vagina dentata* (*Eustace and Hilda: A Trilogy*, p. 736). He would certainly not admit as much, informing an audience that he knew nothing about Freud, while knowledgeably discussing the influential psychoanalyst among friends in private. Like Lavinia Johnstone, like Hartley himself, Eustace is both attracted to but frightened of sex, and this alarming image of a fleshy, devouring sea creature opens, closes, and contains the entire trilogy.

The Cherringtons' mother died while giving birth to their baby sister, Barbara, and their genial father's rather forbidding sister has come to keep house for them. The puritanical Aunt Sarah is, however, much less maternal than the other member of the household, their beloved nanny, Minney, to whom Eustace is particularly attached, thus emphasizing his emotional dependence. Eustace has a weak heart, which is one of the reasons Hilda has taken it upon herself to oversee his life: she is genuinely concerned for his welfare, but this makes her intolerably priggish and overbearing. She is forever siding with the adults and making her brother do things for his own good, one of which is to talk to Miss Fothergill, an old woman in a wheelchair, whose sinister appearance terrifies the boy. This, ironically, does indeed turn out to be for his own good, though in a way Hilda cannot have predicted: Eustace becomes a regular visitor at Miss Fothergill's house, and when she dies she leaves him a substantial legacy. It is decided not to tell Eustace about his inheritance or about plans to send him to boarding school on the proceeds, so that when a carriage driver remarks, "I hear we shall be losing you before long," Eustace imagines that he is mortally ill. The confusion is eventually cleared up and the novel ends with Eustace and Hilda returning home from the beach, symbolically bound together by a handkerchief as if for a three-legged race.

Hartley evidently saw the novel as being principally about Eustace, a nervous, indecisive little boy with a vivid imagination, and he conveys the child's fears, doubts, and dreams with astonishing empathy. His delineation of the appallingly bossy Hilda is equally assured,

124

however. Although *The Shrimp and the Anemone* was, and continued to be, published separately, it almost demanded a sequel. "I keep adding new passages to Eustace's later history," Hartley told a friend, "but I don't feel very sure about them and wonder if it wouldn't be better to leave him undeveloped" (*Foreign Country*, pp. 135–136). The choice of adjective is an interesting one, since it might be argued that in spite of two further novels, which carry Eustace into adulthood, he does indeed remain undeveloped, never achieving emotional and psychological maturity. This, rather than his premature death, is his tragedy.

It was largely thanks to the encouragement of the aptly named Constant Huntington that Hartley continued with this project. In the first sequel, *The Sixth Heaven*, Eustace has come into his inheritance and is an undergraduate at Oxford. He has, as he promised in childhood he would, given Hilda half his legacy, and she is using it to expand a home for disabled children that she runs with characteristically ruthless efficiency. Although a beauty, Hilda has avoided romance, unlike her sister, Barbara, who marries a garage mechanic named Jimmy Crankshaw. The wedding, at which the bride's guests are heavily outnumbered by the groom's, provides Hartley with an opportunity to suggest Eustace and Hilda's self-sufficient sterility, one perhaps derived from his own family, since neither he nor his two sisters married:

> Hilda's friends were fellow-workers in whatever field of endeavor she was engaged, and were united to her by nothing more personal than a common aim. Eustace brought to the wedding one or two friends of old standing, but much the largest contribution to the bride's party came from the bride herself Y all told, the bride's contingent mustered hardly a score, several of whom were unknown to each other, whereas the bridegroom's following amounted to double that number, and gave the impression of being treble, so enormously did the exuberance of their personalities multiply the impact of their presence. Even in church, walking up the aisle with Barbara, buxom and bosomy, clinging to his arm, Eustace was aware of a blast of insurgent vitality, like an incitement to procreation, from the pews on his right, a shuffling, a rustling, a

turning and nodding of expectant faces; whereas from the thin ranks on the left there was no such demonstration, only a discreet slewing of the eyes and then the attitude proper to church.

> (pp. 286–287)

At Oxford, Eustace has re-encountered Dick Staveley, son of the "big house" at Anchorstone, and now a politician. Eustace had once disobeyed Hilda by taking part in a paper chase rather than visiting Miss Fothergill, and had nearly paid for it with his life. Caught in a storm, and having exceeded his strength, he had collapsed in the grounds of Anchorstone Hall and been rescued by Dick. Thereafter he had hero-worshipped Dick and attempted to get Hilda to return the young man's evident interest in her. This may be seen as a case of transference, for it is always through Eustace's eyes that Dick's sensual, masculine allure is described, while Hilda remains completely indifferent. It has been suggested that the trilogy would have been improved had Hartley made Eustace "overtly homosexual" (Martin Seymour-Smith, *Who's Who in Twentieth Century Literature* [London, 1976], p. 152), but this would have unbalanced the novels' overall design. Eustace's sexuality, like that of his sister, is severely repressed, and it hardly matters whether he is more drawn to men or women. That said, apart from a childhood crush on a flirtatious local girl, Nancy Steptoe, which Hilda does everything in her power to extinguish, Eustace does seem to be more responsive to masculinity than he is to femininity.

Still determined to promote some sort of match between Dick and Hilda, Eustace manages to persuade his unwilling sister to accompany him to a weekend house party as Anchorstone Hall. Hartley nicely balances the comedy of this episode (Eustace's exaggerated anxiety about making social gaffes, his hosts' familial banter) with genuine tension when Dick and Hilda are very late returning from a trip in his airplane. Eustace had watched anxiously as the airplane took off, but once it is safely airborne, he is ecstatic:

> Something he had launched had taken wing and was flying far beyond his control, with a strength which was not his, but which he had it in him to

release. Somewhere in his dull being, as in the messy cells of a battery, that dynamism had slumbered; now it was off to its native ether, not taking him with it—that could not be—but leaving him exalted and tingling with the energy of its discharge.

(p. 399)

As in *Simonetta Perkins*, the language Hartley uses here is sexually charged, but it is unclear where Eustace's vicarious "ecstasy" is focused: on Hilda or on Dick. Hartley allows the reader to suspect that Eustace is persuading his sister to have a relationship with Dick because he is unable to do so himself. His friend and fellow guest, Anthony Laschich, has earlier described visiting Dick's room in order to borrow a bow tie. "Would you have thought he had such a thick neck?" Anthony asks, finding the tie too long. "I suppose he's fairly big all round," replies Eustace, who has evidently given the matter his attention.

"He is," said Anthony. "When I went into his room he was stark naked, and his skin fits him like armour-plating—it's almost disgusting. His body is like a lethal weapon. There's something repellent in sheer masculinity."

(p. 353)

Repellent, but also dangerously attractive, and this description subsequently prompts Eustace to have a dream in which he attempts to creep into Hilda's room at night in order to enquire after the bruises she has received while playing a game of billiards-fives with Dick. (In this dangerous game players use their hands to propel billiard balls around the table, and it is impossible not to read Hilda's injuries as another sexual metaphor):

The handle turned easily and noiselessly, and he went in.

But could this be Hilda's room when Dick was sitting on the bed clad only in his pyjama trousers?

He rose from the bed and moved slowly towards Eustace, his eyes glittering in the moonlight.

"I was expecting you," he said. "I knew you'd come sneaking in."

"I'm looking for Hilda," said Eustace wildly. "Haven't you made a mistake? Isn't this her room?"

"It's you who've made the mistake," said Dick, coming nearer.

(p. 377)

No wonder Eustace awakes at this point "with a start," but it is characteristic of Hartley's method that the reader is left—one might almost say abandoned—to decide what that mistake is and how it is to be remedied. Whose room has Eustace strayed into? What threat, or promise, is the semi-naked Dick posing?

When Eustace watches Dick and Hilda take off in the plane, he is in his "sixth heaven," as Dick's worldly aunt, Lady Nelly, puts it, giving the novel its title. "I expect you always keep one in reserve," she explains, for she intuitively understands his inability to surrender entirely to pleasure (p. 409). She nevertheless invites him to stay with her in Venice, which is where the third volume of the trilogy opens. In attempting to describe Eustace to the gondolier who is to meet him at the station, Lady Nelly significantly finds herself unable to produce any sort of substantial likeness: "She was dismayed by the number of negatives that the idea of him conjured up, and began to wonder if he had any existence at all" (p. 447).

It is in Venice that Eustace meets his former childhood sweetheart, Nancy Steptoe, since married and separated from her husband. After a few too many stregas, Nancy attempts to seduce Eustace, who entirely misunderstands the situation and thus rejects the chance of sexual initiation. This outcome has already been signaled by his stated preference for the Gothic over the Baroque (p. 451) and by his initial reluctance to take part in a ritual communal bathe in the Adriatic on the Feast of the Redeemer, in which "the friendly waters of the ancient sea crept higher and higher up legs and thighs and stomachs, submerging warts and scars and birthmarks, omitting nothing from its intimate embrace" (p. 523).

News reaches him from England that Dick Staveley is engaged to another woman, and that on learning of this Hilda has had a nervous collapse and is now paralyzed, unable to talk. (Early in his life Hartley himself suffered a breakdown when he learned that a young woman to whom he had been unenthusiastically engaged had sensibly decided to marry someone else.) At first Eustace thinks, quite wrongly, that Lady Nelly had lured him to Venice to leave the way clear for Dick to seduce and then abandon Hilda. Then Dick turns up in Venice and gives his side of the story, which is confirmed by his sister Anne when Eustace returns to England. Dick had been in love with Hilda, but she had become unbearably possessive, trying to mold and manage him as she had Eustace, and so he was forced to disengage himself.

The Cherringtons have settled back into their old home at Anchorstone, where Eustace attempts to shock Hilda out of her paralysis by pretending to tip her out of her wheelchair while pushing her along the cliff path. He nearly does send her to her death when he is overcome by faintness, and loses control of the chair. It is, however, Hilda's fear upon seeing the unconscious Eustace that he has died in his effort to prevent the chair from hurtling over the cliff that galvanizes and cures her. Indeed, she is cured to such a degree that she immediately begins bullying Eustace once more, demanding that he shave off his newly grown mustache (reducing him once more to infantilism) and saying that although she blames him for putting her into Dick's "clutches," she has forgiven him (p. 721). Exhausted by the day's events, Eustace goes to bed, where he dreams that he is taking an exam, overseen by Hilda, who "inexorably" points out his mistakes (p. 734). Then, as he drifts toward death, he is back on the beach, gazing once more into the rockpool, searching for something to feed a sea anemone.

THE GO-BETWEEN

EUSTACE and Hilda is a major achievement, superbly structured and crafted, filled with hints and glances, its symbolism controlled and subsumed within the story. It is in an altogether different class from the two novels that followed it.

In its time *The Boat* (1949) was considered an important work. Both Peter Bien and Anne Maul-

keen devote substantial chapters to it, perhaps because it seems to deal with weighty issues: the Second World War and the individual's relationship with a community. The novel has not worn well, however: its protagonist is a bore, far too many of its other characters are stock, its comedy is labored, its central romance unconvincing, its conclusion melodramatic. The prose is clogged with cliché and cumbrous circumlocution, and its distinctly sluggish narrative pace is further slowed down by the inclusion of long letters to and from three of the protagonist's friends. A great big lumbering novel of over five hundred pages, it long outstays its welcome.

My Fellow Devils, which followed two years later, is no better, and is an example of what happened when Hartley tried to write allegorically. The novel concerns a respectable woman, Margaret Pennefather, who gives up what seems a perfectly suitable engagement to a barrister, Nick Burden, in order to marry a glamorous film actor, Colum McInnes. She soon realizes her mistake, since Colum turns out to be a criminal. She asks her former fiancé to sort things out, only to lose him to Colum. She consults a Roman Catholic priest in an attempt to find consolation through religious belief. The novel's chief distinction is that it introduces more overtly than before a subject close to Hartley's own life: homosexuality. In a letter to Peter Bien, Hartley wrote that this theme "is *in* the book, but I played it down as much as I could, because I didn't want to write a specifically 'homosexual novel', and I didn't want to suggest that Colum was wicked because of his homosexuality" (*L. P. Hartley*, p. 280). Even Bien, who felt that "contemporary English novels are so overpopulated with homosexuals" that Hartley's discretion might be thought "salutary," had to concede that the novel would have been improved by a little more plain speaking on the subject. Instead, Hartley proceeds to labor the point that Colum is the devil incarnate.

As with many of Hartley's inferior books, it is hard to believe that these two novels could have been written by the author of the *Eustace and Hilda* trilogy or the book that followed in 1953: *The Go-Between*. Hartley wrote best about things he had experienced, and *My Fellow Devils* makes it fairly clear that the film world and the Roman Catholic church were alien territory. Many details of *The Boat* were borrowed directly from Hartley's own life in the 1940s, but he is a writer who needed to distance himself from experience, and to approach it from an oblique angle, in order to transform it into art. It is surely significant that his best novels make no attempt to be contemporary but are set in the increasingly remote period of his own childhood. As the famous opening sentence of *The Go-Between* suggests: "The past is a foreign country: they do things differently there" (p. 7). And better, one is tempted to add.

The plot of *The Go-Between* is simple enough. Leo Colston, who lives with his widowed mother in modest circumstances, goes to spend the blazing hot July of 1900 at Brandham Hall, the large country house where the parents of his school friend, Marcus Maudsley, live as tenants. Also staying at Brandham is Viscount Trimingham, a professional soldier with a scarred face. Since he is heir to the Brandham estate, the forceful Mrs. Maudsley is determined that he should marry her beautiful daughter, Marian. Trimingham would like nothing better, but Marian is less enthusiastic. When Marcus develops measles, Leo is left to amuse himself, although Marian takes a kindly interest in him, taking him to Norwich to buy clothes more suitable to the weather. While exploring the Brandham estate, Leo meets Ted Burgess, a tenant farmer, who asks if he would take a message to "Miss Marian." Pleased to be of service, Leo does so, and soon becomes the go-between of the title, innocently believing that the secret love letters he carries concern business matters.

Without fully understanding its nature, Leo comes to recognize that the relationship between Ted and Marian is making people unhappy and, using his private magic, he puts a curse on the lovers in an attempt to avert disaster. The story reaches a climax on Leo's birthday, when Marian fails to appear at the celebratory tea party. Mrs. Maudsley has become aware that Marian harbors a secret to which Leo is privy, and drags the boy from the dining room to join her in a search. Ted and Marian are found having sex in an outhouse. "I think I was more mystified than horrified,"

Leo recalls; "it was Mrs Maudsley's screams that frightened me, and a shadow on the wall that opened and closed like an umbrella" (p. 262). As a result of this discovery, Ted shoots himself. Leo suffers some sort of breakdown and, as has already been suggested, never makes a full recovery.

The story is narrated by Leo, now in his sixties, his memory triggered by the rediscovery of his diary for 1900. In an epilogue, Leo revisits Brandham, where he meets the present Viscount Trimingham, a young man who bears a marked resemblance to Ted Burgess. It transpires that Trimingham had married Marian, even though she was bearing Ted's son, and that she has survived them both. Leo visits her and finds her wrapped in self-delusion about the events of that summer, having rewritten history in order to convince herself that nobody was hurt or betrayed by her actions. She asks Leo to perform one last message, one last "errand of love" (p. 279). Would he tell her estranged grandson that there was nothing shameful about the affair between her and Ted, that there is "no spell or curse except an unloving heart" (p. 280), and that he should feel free to marry? Older and wiser now, Leo recognizes Marian's self-deception but is nevertheless moved by what she has told him. "Why did I half wish that I could see it all as she did? And why should I go on this preposterous errand?" (p. 280). He nevertheless does so, which suggests that he too might escape "the running shadow."

The novel is set quite deliberately in 1900. "In my eyes the actors in my drama had been immortals, inheritors of the summer and of the coming glory of the twentieth century," Leo recalls with bitter irony (p. 264). The innocence of Leo is that of twentieth-century man, soon to be destroyed in the trenches of the First World War. It is there that both Marcus and his brother are killed in action, while Marian's son and daughter-in-law perish in the Second World War. Ted proved all too mortal, as does Trimingham, who also dies young.

Hartley underpins his narrative with a complex skein of allusiveness. Leo's innocence, his "greenness," is signaled by Marian's choice of green as an appropriate color for the clothes and the bicycle she buys him. In turn, Leo, who is a keen astrologer, identifies the sexually experienced Marian with Virgo, an ironic association also suggested by her Madonna-like name. More sinisterly, Marian is also associated with the deadly nightshade that grows around the outbuildings where her secret is eventually exposed. The botanical name for this plant, as Leo knows, is *Atropa belladonna: "atropa"* derived from the Greek word for the Three Fates, from whom there is no escape for man, *"belladonna"* ("beautiful woman") from the ancient practice of using a decoction from the plant to artificially enhance the beauty of women's eyes by enlarging the pupils. Leo himself bears an astrological name and is born under that star sign. Marian also dubs him "Mercury," because he is a messenger, but this also associates him with the summer heat; as the novel builds inexorably toward its tragic climax, the mercury in the thermometer, regularly monitored by Mr. Maudsley, continues to rise. The weather changes on Leo's birthday, storm clouds presaging the coming disaster.

It is a measure of Hartley's skill that these allusions and associations are to be found in the book for those who care to look, but do not usurp the narrative. His original intention was to make the novel much more straightforward, with "a proper segregation of sheep and goats":

> I did not know what was to become of Marian and Ted, but Leo was to be utterly demoralised [by which Hartley means robbed of any moral sense]: the little boy in [Henry James's] "The Turn of the Screw" would be an angel compared to what he was to become. And for this Ted and Marian would be completely to blame—not only by reason of their irresponsibility and selfishness, but by deliberately corrupting his tender mind, as the serpent corrupted Adam and Eve. There was to be no limit to their wickedness.
>
> (Bien, *L. P. Hartley*, p. 182)

This stern vision softened considerably during the writing of the book, since Hartley confessed that ideas "only really take shape when the pen is in my hand" (*L. P. Hartley*, p. 278). This is fortunate, since the novel is all the stronger, its tragedy all the greater, because Hartley makes

the two lovers characters with whom the reader can to some extent sympathize. Ted and Marian are not by any means blameless, but most readers will feel that if anyone is a villain it is the scheming, snobbish, and ruthless Mrs. Maudsley. The story is wholly involving, deeply moving, and beautifully written. By re-creating a classic English summer of "golden afternoons" (p. 102), with bathing parties of decorously clad swimmers in clear rivers and a keenly contested cricket match between the Hall and the village, Hartley provides an almost prelapsarian vision of Edwardian country life on the brink of being savagely extinguished.

LATER NOVELS

HARTLEY never wrote a better book than *The Go-Between*, and the remainder of his career was distinctly anti-climactic. He was fifty-eight, and it was almost as if he had said everything he wanted to say as a novelist. He kept writing, but, with one exception, his later books are largely undistinguished.

That exception is *The Hireling* (1957), which has a contemporary setting but once again deals with the impossibility—and the fatal consequences—of a relationship conducted across the class divide. The protagonist is Stephen Leadbitter, a man introduced to the reader with a cliché: "The car-hire driver was tall and dark and handsome" (p. 7). This would probably be how most of Leadbitter's clients would carelessly describe him, if indeed they deigned to notice him at all. In the first few pages of the novel, Hartley provides a brilliantly detailed physical and psychological profile of Leadbitter, demonstrating how the chauffeur has trained and honed himself to be scarcely distinguishable from the immaculate car he drives. Before taking this job, he had enjoyed a successful career as a soldier. "In the Army, he felt, a man was rated at his true value, he had nothing but himself to make him count. Recognition of his own value, by himself and others, was of paramount importance to the car-hire driver" (p. 13). It is the failure of people to recognize Leadbitter's own value that leads to disaster.

The army has also taught Leadbitter loyalty, discipline, and self-sufficiency. Deeply misogynistic, he is a solitary figure, living in a rented room, and has no emotional ties: "Next to his car, the telephone was the most important thing in Leadbitter's life, and perhaps his greatest friend; of all the sounds he heard, mechanical or human, its summons was the one he welcomed most" (p. 17). This is because it brings him work, the most important thing in his life. At the same time, there is a human being lurking within this carapace, one whose strong feelings are ruthlessly and dangerously suppressed.

When one of Leadbitter's customers, an attractive and wealthy young widow named Lady Franklin, insists upon sitting beside him in the front seat of his car and telling him about her guilt and unhappiness over her husband's death, a breach is made in the wall Leadbitter has built around himself. At first he listens impassively, interjecting the occasional noncommittal remark, although Hartley also supplies Leadbitter's cynical private commentary as an ironic counterpoint. When Lady Franklin asks Leadbitter whether he is married, his answer, like much of his professional behavior, is dictated by what he imagines will please a client most. He makes up a wife and three children, describing for Lady Franklin a wholly invented home life. The interest she takes in this domestic saga, in something outside herself, results in her emerging from the mantle of grief in which she has enfolded herself. Unshelled, these two creatures, the aristocrat and the servant, become highly vulnerable.

A less harmless deception takes place when Leadbitter claims that he is unable to meet the payment due on his car, which he has on lease. Lady Franklin immediately writes him a large check with which he is able to expand his business. At the same time as tricking her, he finds himself becoming attracted to her. Suspecting the attraction is mutual, he makes a pass at her, which she rejects. She subsequently becomes engaged to Hughie Cantrip, a portraitist Leadbitter thinks both unreliable and unsuitable.

Leadbitter, who has also acted as driver for Hughie and his mistress, Constance, whom the painter intends to go on seeing after his marriage, is quite right. He is also motivated by jealousy and protectiveness, however, since he has himself fallen in love with Lady Franklin. Lady Franklin's chief regret was that she never told her late husband that she loved him, and she had advised Leadbitter: "If there's ever anything you want to tell anyone, tell them. Don't wait till it's too late or it may spoil your life, as it has mine" (p. 27). He sends her an anonymous letter denouncing her fiancé and she calls off the wedding. When Hughie, who has discussed his plans with his mistress while being driven by Leadbitter, accuses her of sending the letter ("Well, who else is there?" he demands [p. 206]), the driver angrily confesses that he is the culprit. "You told *me*," he shouts at Hughie. "Do you think I'm deaf? What do you think I am? Do you think I'm just a bit of the car, or one of those damned bloody automatons? Do you think I can sit here without hearing all the poppycock you talk?" (p. 215). In the argument that follows, the car crashes and both Leadbitter and Hughie are killed. Leadbitter's last words, cut off by the impact, are: "Tell Lady Franklin that I—" (p. 219). After recovering in the hospital, Constance feels she must visit Lady Franklin to convey her condolences and deliver Leadbitter's last message, the last two words of which, "love her," she guesses correctly.

It is Hughie who, in anger, supplies the book with its resonant title. In response to Leadbitter's plea not to reveal to Lady Franklin that it was he who sent the letter, Hughie replies contemptuously: "What does it matter what she thinks of you—you're only a hireling!" (p. 219). And it is Leadbitter's angry response to this insult that results in the fatal, and possibly willed, accident. Leadbitter may repress his feelings, and be at pains to efface himself, hiding the sentient human being behind a mask of impersonal professionalism, but he is also too proud not to be offended when others judge him by this appearance, taking him at his own public estimation. "To 'them' Leadbitter was just part of the car's furniture, with as little personal feeling as the car had, perhaps less, for the car had its moods and might break down, whereas Leadbitter had no moods, or was supposed to have none, and couldn't break down, he couldn't afford to. For at least half his customers, Leadbitter didn't exist as a man" (p. 151).

Once again, this novel convinces the reader because Hartley has drawn upon his own life, his own most deeply held feelings—albeit carefully disguised. Hartley might have been thinking of himself when he wrote that Henry James "was not the only novelist whose life was given to his art and [who] seems to have had no important emotional experience outside it." Like James, and like Hartley himself, Leadbitter regards his work "as a substitute for life" (The Novelist's Responsibility, p. 181). Long after the moment had passed, Hartley persisted in describing Lord David Cecil as "the love of his life" (Foreign Country, p. 250), and he knew from bitter experience the price of not declaring oneself in matters of the heart. In the class-ridden interwar period he must have been acutely aware of the social difference between himself, a middle-class young man whose money came from "trade," and the aristocratic Cecil, and this is echoed, greatly exaggerated, in Leadbitter's undeclared love for Lady Franklin. In Hartley's novels, as in E. M. Forster's Howards End (1910), social divisions (such as the one between Helen Schlegel and Leonard Bast) can be understood to stand for sexual ones, an affair between people of different classes proving as dangerous as one between people of the same sex. Hartley's own attraction to working-class men such as his own "hirelings," a succession of untrustworthy manservants, is evident in his lovingly detailed descriptions of Leadbitter's face and physique.

The Hireling is as compact and as polished as its protagonist. It was, however, disliked by Hartley's British and American publishers. Hamish Hamilton published it reluctantly, while Knopf turned it down, and the reviews were distinctly mixed. Posterity rates it a great deal higher, and it is the only book of Hartley's, apart from The Go-Between and the Eustace and Hilda trilogy, to be frequently reprinted. The revival in its fortunes was sparked by a film version (directed by Alan Bridges from a screenplay by Wolf Mankowitz) released in 1973. Perhaps in a bid to capitalize on the success of Losey's The Go-Between (for which Harold Pinter had provided an extremely distinguished script), the film was given period treatment, set in the 1920s rather than the novel's 1950s, but it was a lackluster affair, in every way inferior to the earlier movie. The novel now stands on its own merits, which are considerable.

Hartley greeted the 1960s with a wholly uncharacteristic and unsatisfactory excursion into the science-fiction genre, Facial Justice, conceived as a satire on socialism. He returned, however, to what he knew best in The Brickfield and The Betrayal—in reality one novel published in two separate volumes. The principal interest of these books is in their relation to his major works and themes, dealing as they do with a writer who has been scarred by a trauma in his youth. The Brickfield, which is by far the better book, draws fruitfully upon Hartley's family background among the brickworks of Cambridgeshire, and describes a love affair between two teenagers in the early years of the century. This, as by now Hartley's readers might expect, ends in tragedy: the young girl drowns, either intentionally or by accident, after wrongly thinking she might be pregnant. Her young lover, Richard Mardick, escapes being implicated in her death but feels himself to be morally culpable. He subsequently becomes a well-known novelist, and the book takes the form of his recollections of this affair told to his young companion, Denys Aspin, whom he thinks might want to write a biography of him after he is dead. He has two reasons for telling the story: "One is that I don't like the idea of dying with a secret. And the other is that though you can't put it recognizably into the memoir, you can make its presence felt, just as you can describe the results of an accident without describing the accident itself. You can show me as the product of the experience" (p. 14). While not as "cindery" as Leo Colston, Mardick has failed to marry or form a properly homosexual attachment to Denys, whom people incorrectly but naturally enough assume to be his lover. A comparison with The Go-Between, however, is greatly to the later novel's disadvantage. The incidental detail and scene painting is well done, but the flashback is handled clumsily, interspersed with asides and interruptions, and the entire premise of the book seems little more than a half-hearted reprise of Leo's story. Although the story clearly demands some sort of sequel or resolution, the one Hartley provides in the all too obviously titled *The Betrayal* is highly implausible and is used largely to air Hartley's grievances against the working classes, whom (on the admittedly substantial evidence provided by his own servants) he characterizes as feckless and dishonest.

LAST YEARS

"Freudian critics, inparticular, will find much material for speculation in the more daring topics, including homosexuality, which Hartley touched on in his later years," Anne Mulkeen wrote in her critical study *Wild Thyme, Winter Lightning*, published two years after Hartley's death (p. 133). Readers will unfortunately find little else in the arid, slapdash novels that Hartley continued to produce long after his talent had exhausted itself and his concentration had been destroyed by heavy drinking. When Hartley dedicated *Poor Clare* (1968) "In gratitude to my friend Francis King, whose help has been invaluable to me," he was not exaggerating. Fuddled by drink, Hartley was beyond collating the various drafts of the novels he was writing and had to rely upon the good offices of literary friends. It did not much help matters that he was often trying to write several books at the same time. "I actually took more trouble over *The Harness Room* than over any of my novels," he claimed in a letter to his loyal secretary, Joan Hall (*Foreign Country*, p. 249). He presumably forgot that he had earlier handed Hall the manuscript of this potentially interesting story (in which a seventeen-year-old youth becomes infatuated with his father's chauffeur) with the words: "What I want to convey is the genuine love the boy feels for the man—you put it together and see what you can make of it" (*Foreign Country*, p. 247). Hall did her best, but when she returned her emended version of this preposterous and anachronistic sadomasochistic melodrama to

Hartley, he did not even bother to reread it before despatching it to his hapless publisher.

CONCLUSION

The *Go-Between* and the *Eustace and Hilda* trilogy are fine enough to allow Hartley, despite the dramatic decline in his powers later in his career, his place among the finest and most interesting British novelists of the mid-twentieth century. During his lifetime his work was generally treated with respect, even when books disappointed the critics; but he deserves better than that. Lord David Cecil's vague and high-flown introduction to the *Eustace and Hilda* trilogy, for example, fails signally to get to the heart of the matter, preferring to see the novel "in a grander context" (p. 8). To state, as Cecil does, that Hartley had "used the story of Eustace to express his vision of the spiritual laws governing human existence" (p. 9) does nothing at all to explain that story's enduring power to engage and unsettle the reader. It was precisely when Hartley aimed at "spiritual significance" (p. 10), rather than psychological truth—as in *My Fellow Devils*—that he was at his least convincing and compelling. As Hartley himself acknowledged in a lecture on "The Novelist's Responsibility" delivered to the Royal Society of Literature in 1963: "it is safer for a novelist to choose as his subject something he feels about than something he knows about, or has got to know about by study and conscious observation" (*Essays by Diverse Hands*, New Series, vol. 34, ed. by L. P. Hartley [London, 1966], pp. 78–79).

In this same lecture, Hartley quoted Goethe's confession that "All the things I have written are but fragments of a long confession" (p. 78). The same might be said of Hartley himself. However much he attempted to cover his tracks when alive, he evidently hoped that posterity would come to understand both him and his work. The Hartley-like writer in *The Brickfield* is surely speaking for his creator when he says:

I don't want to have to look back at my life as if it was a jig-saw puzzle with one piece of the pattern—the most important piece—always missing. I know what the piece is, but other people don't, and it isn't enough to see the jig-saw oneself, one wants other people to see it, after a fashion, anyhow. There are few people who do jig-saws for their own satisfaction, but most of us like a witness to our cleverness.

(pp. 13–14)

SELECTED BIBLIOGRAPHY

I. Novels, Stories, Lectures, and Essays. [If other than first editions are used for quotation, this is noted in square brackets.] *Night Fears and Other Stories* (London, 1924); *Simonetta Perkins* (London, 1925) *The Killing Bottle* (short stories; London, 1932); *The Shrimp and the Anemone* (London, 1944); *The Sixth Heaven* (London, 1946); *Eustace and Hilda* (London, 1947); *The Boat* (London, 1949); *The Travelling Grave* ([short stories; London, 1951); *My Fellow Devils* (London, 1951); *The Go-Between* (London, 1953) [1971]; *The White Wand and Other Stories* (London, 1954); *A Perfect Woman* (London, 1955); *The Hireling* (London, 1957) [1964]; *Eustace and Hilda: A Trilogy* (London, 1958) [1979]; *Facial Justice* (London, 1960); *Two for the River* (short stories; London, 1961); *The Brickfield* (London, 1964) [1969]; *The Betrayal* (London, 1966); *The Novelist's Responsibility: Lectures and Essays* (London, 1967); *The Collected Short Stories of L. P. Hartley* (London, 1968); *Poor Clare* (London, 1968); *The Love-Adept* (London, 1969); *My Sister's Keeper* (London, 1970); *The Harness Room* (London, 1971); *Mrs Carteret Receives and Other Stories* (London, 1971); *The Collections* (London, 1971); *The Will and the Way* (London, 1973); *The Complete Short Stories of L. P. Hartley* (London, 1973).

II. Critical and Biographical Studies. Peter Bien, *L. P. Hartley* (London, 1963); E. T. Jones, *L. P. Hartley* (Boston, 1978); Anne Mulkeen, *Wild Thyme, Winter Lightning: The Symbolic Novels of L. P. Hartley* (London, 1974); Adrian Wright, *Foreign Country: The Life of L. P. Hartley* (London, 1996).

ROBERT HENRYSON

(1420?–1505?)

Grace G. Wilson

LIFE AND TIMES

FOR A POET of his stature, Robert Henryson has left behind very few firm biographical details. Readers may feel they know him from his works, but documented facts are sparse. He must have been a university graduate because William Dunbar in his *Lament for the Makaris*, and others, refer to him as "Maister Robert Henrysoun," and he must have been dead by 1505 when that poem was written. Printers and others refer to him as a schoolmaster in Dunfermline, in Fife. He may have been a bachelor in canon law and a notary public and likely was old at the time of his death. He flourished probably in the 1470s. No manuscript or print of his works survives from his lifetime. The poems are undated; topical allusions and literary source relationships sometimes used in attempting to date them are mostly speculative and encourage circular arguments about dating.

From William Thynne's 1532 printing of *The Testament of Cresseid* to the middle of the twentieth century, Henryson's reputation may have suffered from the implied or stated label "Scottish Chaucerian." Any medieval poet familiar with Geoffrey Chaucer's works and writing in English or Scots could hardly have avoided being influenced by Chaucer. King James I, Gavin Douglas, "Blind Harry," and William Dunbar, although all affected by Chaucer's example, can stand as important poets on their own merits, as can Henryson.

For a writer whose surviving oeuvre amounts to only slightly over five thousand lines, Henryson commands a tremendous generic range and variety. At one moment he appears to be an easygoing rural observer, at another an austere pedant. His poetry is almost all of the highest quality. He combines great learning, usually very well assimilated and therefore often impossible to trace to its precise source, with mastery of the native alliterative tradition and of French and English verse forms. His Middle Scots is copious and flexible. Some of his poetry gives amusement and relatively simple pleasure, while some encourages meditation. Scholars find that however deeply they plumb his depths, they sooner or later suspect they have not gone far enough.

The years of Henryson's flourishing provided little political stability. In 1488, after a troubled reign of twenty-six years, James III met his death at Sauchieburn where his fifteen-year-old son, the future James IV, stood with the royal standard on the opposite side. According to Ranald Nicholson in *Scotland in the Later Middle Ages,* the plague ravaged Scotland in 1455, 1475–1476, and repeatedly from 1498 on. Loyalties clashed within and beyond Scotland: Henryson's period overlaps with Blind Harry's, whose *Wallace* (c. 1478), with its passion and blood, expresses a long history of political turmoil.

Intellectual ferment was part of the mix. Some scholars see Henryson as a humanist, but his connections with Italy are unproven, and his poetry works best when read as a late part of the long, rich medieval tradition that includes allegory and figural interpretation, encyclopedic collections of lore, applications of classical rhetoric, scholasticism, and popular preaching.

Henryson's language presents only a moderate challenge to the reader familiar with Chaucer. The recent teaching edition, Robert Kindrick's *The Poems of Robert Henryson*, assumes some knowledge of Chaucer, normalizes spelling, and glosses generously. The present study quotes Henryson from this edition. Beyond the standard differences from Middle English, such as "quh-" for "wh-" ("quhilk" for "which") and final "-is" for "-es" ("flouris" for "floures"), Henryson's large eclectic vocabulary and sometimes elliptical expression keep the reader alert. He is a poet's poet, but he has the common touch. Both qualities reward the effort to read his poems in the original.

Because Henryson's works are undated, their order of composition is unknown, but many editions and discussions, including the present one, follow a traditional order. First come *The Morall Fabillis of Esope the Phrygian*, varied and substantial, making up about fifty-eight percent of the surviving poetry. In scope and artistry they far surpass other fable collections, and any student of Henryson will keep coming back to them. Next is *The Testament of Cresseid*, well known for centuries and at times mistaken for Chaucer's work, which many readers consider to be Henryson's masterpiece. Enigmatic and multifaceted it stands, quite perfect. *Orpheus and Eurydice* is harder to place, possibly flawed, and intriguing. The twelve or thirteen "shorter poems" together are longer than *The Testament of Cresseid*.

THE MORALL FABILLIS OF ESOPE THE PHRYGIAN

PROLOGUE, The Cock and the Jasp, The Two Mice, The Cock and the Fox, The Fox and the Wolf, The Trial of the Fox, The Sheep and the Dog, The Lion and the Mouse, The Preaching of the Swallow, The Fox, the Wolf, and the Cadger, The Fox, the Wolf and the Husbandman, The Wolf and the Wether, the Wolf and the Lamb, The Paddock and the Mouse

Henryson's longest work is *The Morall Fabillis,* made up of a prologue and thirteen fables, each including a tale and a *moralitas*, or moral lesson. By the late fifteenth century, fables had long been used as school texts for rhetorical practice and as exempla for preachers; Henryson's fables draw on a tradition beginning back with Aesop in the sixth century B.C. and coming up through such authors as Phaedrus and Babrius by the end of the classical period. They incorporate much of the ironic spirit of the medieval *Roman de Renart*. Henryson's more immediate sources have proven very difficult to pin down but appear to include works by Gualterus Anglicus or Walter of England (early twelfth century), Odo of Cheriton (thirteenth century), Chaucer, probably John Lydgate, possibly William Caxton, and others. Both traditions, of Aesop and of Reynard, for centuries combined popular lore and scholarly depth and became extremely complicated. (Critics have noted a symmetry in the broad source relationships of Henryson's fables: the first two are Aesopian, the next three Reynardian, the middle three Aesopian, the next three Reynardian, and the final two Aesopian.) Henryson shows a command of both the popular and the learned registers and overall brings the form to a very high level of development.

The *Fabillis* vary widely but form a unified whole of 2,975 lines. Including their *moralitates* (plural of *moralitas*), they range in length from 98 lines (*The Cock and the Jasp*) to 350 (*The Trial of the Fox*) and are longer and better developed than their analogues. Some include human beings, and some of the human beings speak. Evil may be punished, ignored, or rewarded. The tone may be comic, tragic, ironic, or a combination. Some characters die. The lesson may seem obvious or obscure, and it may concern prudent personal behavior or political conditions or eternal salvation or damnation.

The *Prologue* resembles Walter of England's. It is sixty-three lines long, in rhyme royal, *ababbcc*. (Rhyme royal is used throughout the *Fabillis* except for a few spots, which are noted.) It presents the purpose behind this fable writing, to reprove our *misleving* or bad living by representing truth by a *figure*. Three famous similes follow: sweet moral meaning springs from poetry's subtle verse the way flowers and grain spring from the rough earth as it is worked diligently; a fictional story holds wise doctrine the way a nut's tough shell holds the sweet kernel; and the mind whose thought and study are always serious, unrelieved by merriment, will lose its spring like a bow that is always bent. The speaker will translate his or her source at the request of a lord. (The "lord" is probably a fiction.) The beasts by speaking and arguing will illustrate how human beings resemble beasts: no surprise, since people indulge in their pleasures until, completely habitual, those pleasures make the person a beast. Aesop ("Esope") wrote in metaphors to evade scorn.

The first fable, *The Cock and the Jasp*, expands greatly on Walter's version of the story. The tale tells of a cock, beautiful if poor, who finds a precious stone (jasp, jasper, or jacinth) while scraping in the rubbish heap for something to eat. The cock eloquently and respectfully addresses the jewel, regretting that the jasp does not have a proper rich setting and that it can provide the cock no sustenance. The moralitas comes as a surprise. A reader naturally thinks that a cock with the common sense to leave alone a jewel he cannot use is reasonable, even commendable. But, says the moralizer, the jewel represents learning and spiritual wisdom, the best thing anyone could desire. The cock, representing the fool, is like a sow on which precious stones would be wasted.

This fable presents early on the problem in Henryson of the counter-intuitive moralitas, the interpretation that few if any readers would come up with independently. Henryson did not invent this one; Walter's is similar. Douglas Gray's *Robert Henryson* makes a useful and often-cited distinction between "clear" moralitates, which readers can accept with little resistance, and "dark" moralitates, like the one in *The Cock and the Jasp*, hidden and not easy to accept even after learned exposition.

Such an abstruse lesson, coming so early in the fables, may well carry special emphasis. The cock not only misses the significance of the jewel, but could hardly have done otherwise. Our choices probably make as much sense to us: we reject wisdom because we are naturally unable to use it just as the cock is naturally unable to use the jasp. We will miss important meanings and find the fables tough nuts to crack.

The Two Mice, or *The Taill of the Uponlondis Mous and the Burges Mous*, is very well known and frequently anthologized. Its details and atmosphere convey a sense of everyday fifteenth-century Lowland Scottish life. Horace used the basic story in *Satires* II. Henryson's version seems closest to Walter's, but, as usual, is much more ambitious. The fable is middling in length, 235 lines; its relatively short moralitas is written not in rhyme royal but in the eight-line *ababbcbc* stanza, the *ballade* or *Monk's Tale* stanza.

Two mice are sisters. The elder lives in town, the younger in the country. In winter food is easier to come by in town, especially as the town mouse has burgh privileges, "Was gild-brother and made ane fre burges" (l. 172), with access to food stores. The town mouse visits her sister and decides that when it comes to eating, "My Gude Friday is better nor your Pace [Easter]" (l. 248). She persuades her rural sister to come home with her. They do eat well but are disturbed by the spencer, or butler. The country mouse recovers from that scare, only to be caught, toyed with, and almost killed by "Gib Hunter, our jolie cat" (l. 326). She returns to her quiet rural sufficiency as soon as she can.

Henryson's humorously observant touches in the treatment of small animals has been compared to Walt Disney's; the mice remain mice while they exercise social pretensions or talk about Easter. The fable has been praised for achieving broad universal appeal through particulars of time and place.

The moralitas does not disturb. It counsels a moderation that is perennially prudent: climbing high invites adversity, while contentment with modest possessions provides security. The recurring a-rhyme and the fourfold refrain reinforce the point.

The Cock and the Fox, or *The Taill of Schir Chantecleir and the Foxe*, appears to have been inspired quite directly by Chaucer's *Nun's Priest's Tale*, and the basic story was current in the *Roman de Renart* tradition. Chaucer's tale is 626 lines long; Henryson's fable is 217 lines, including the 28 lines of the moralitas.

Like *The Nun's Priest's Tale*, the fable includes the poor widow, the rooster and hens, and the fast-talking fox who appeals to the rooster's filial pride and rivalry. When Chantecleir falls into the trap of crowing with his eyes closed and is carried to the woods, the hens—Pertok, Sprutok, and Coppok—startlingly admit that they hope to find a better lover. But Chantecleir tricks the fox into speaking and so allows him to escape.

The moralitas makes immediate sense: the cock, representing the foolish, proud, vainglorious man, cannot help falling. The fox, representing flatterers, will ruin anyone who believes him.

Henryson picks up on some of Chaucer's major mock-heroic elements, particularly the widow's lament for her stolen bird and Pertok's first sorrowing speech. Henryson's tale does not have *The Nun's Priest's Tale*'s display of encyclopedic learning, especially on dreams, or its sense of riotous excess, but it keeps the animals more consistently in focus as animals.

The Fox and the Wolf, or *How this foirsaid Tod maid his Confession to Freir Wolf Waitskaith*, has some resemblances to a tale in Walter, to Caxton, and to the Reynard tradition generally, but scholars find it relatively original. Its satire on the hypocrisy of friars, particularly Franciscans, makes it especially Reynardian.

As the longer title indicates, this fox is the same one Chantecleir outsmarted in *The Cock and the Fox*. An astrological reading, elaborately described, warns him to beware, so he seeks a confessor, who turns out to be "Freir Wolf Waitskaith" ("do harm"). The parody of confession is pointed and compelling as the fox confesses chiefly regret that he has killed so few hens and lambs. Even a light penance is too much for the fox, who fishes no better than he fasts. In a parody of baptism, Henryson has the fox "baptizing" a kid as a salmon: "Ga doun, schir Kid, cum up, schir Salmond, agane" (l. 751). Basking in the sun, he says to himself that that moment would be a perfect one for "ane bolt" to pierce his full belly. Fatefully, the goatherd agrees, and stakes the fox to the earth with an arrow. Tale and moralitas have the same subject, the evil of false confession.

The Trial of the Fox, or *The Sone and Air of the Foirsaid Foxe, called Father wer: Alswa the Parliament of fourfuttit Beistis, halden be the Lyoun*, is the longest fable of all, 350 lines counting its 49-line moralitas. It too seems fairly original although related to the *Roman de Renart* and possibly Odo of Cheriton. The fox is the son of the one who flattered Chantecleir and who

was killed after "confessing." He is "Father-war" (l. 801), or worse than his father, as evidenced by his joy at finding his father's stripped corpse because he will inherit his poaching grounds. He dumps the body into a peat bog.

There follows one of the most stately and formal scenes in Henryson, the gathering of animals, including mythical and heraldic beasts, for a parliament. The autocratic lion requires peace within twenty miles. The fox, "the tod Lowrie," fears justice and tries to hide and disguise himself. The fox and wolf are chosen to visit a gray brood mare who has stayed away. She insists that the wolf read her excuse written "heir under my hufe" (l. 1018), then kicks him and knocks the top off his head. On the way back to the parliament, the fox kills a lamb. All are laughing at his mockery of the wolf when the lamb's mother comes to accuse the fox, who is found guilty and hanged.

A dark moralitas informs readers that wisdom can be as hard to win from figures as gold is for a miner to separate from lead. The lion represents the world. Emperor and king (the other animals?) bow down to the lion/world to increase their power, possessions, and gold. The mare represents contemplative clergy, withdrawn from the world and its corruptions. The wolf is sensuality, valuing the world. The mare's hoof is the thought of death, that can make sensuality flee away. The fox represents temptation of religious men, which will disappear when sensuality is struck down.

The Sheep and the Dog is half the length of *The Trial of the Fox*, and it seems far simpler and more unified. It has similarities to Walter especially, and Lydgate. It is thick with legal language, language of the "consistory" or church court (Henryson may have had legal training). The tale views the workings of the law with extreme disillusionment.

A dog is poor so sues a sheep for a loaf of bread. A "fraudful wolf" is the judge, with other predators as officers of the court. The sheep, with his legal knowledge, objects to the judge (as hostile), the time (evening), and the place (distant). Arbiters—bear and badger—say that the sheep must stand trial anyway. The judgment predictably goes against the sheep, who has to sell his wool to pay the five shillings the dog says he owes. He passes "naikit and bair" to the field (l. 1257). (In Lydgate, he perishes of cold.)

The moralitas is striking. It is the longest so far in the *Fabillis*, sixty-three lines. It is the first openly to protest contemporary legal and economic abuses. Only in this moralitas does an animal speak. He represents the poor common person, oppressed by tyrannous men intent on cheating him. The wolf is like a sheriff indicting everyone the false coroner indicts. Bribes are exacted from both sides and names changed in documents (ll. 1276–1278). In a cave to be out of the wind, he utters a memorable line: "O lord, quhy sleipis thow sa lang?" (l. 1295). This tale with its moralitas has been compared to *Piers Plowman* for taking the part of the "pure commounis" (l. 1259).

The Lion and the Mouse stands out in several ways. Quite a common story, the fable does not much resemble its closest Aesopian analogue in Walter. Several critics, notably George Gopen, cite Howard Henry Roerecke's unpublished dissertation for pointing out that the tale has a central position, number seven out of thirteen, taking up lines 1321–1621 of 2,975, with two hundred stanzas before it and two hundred after. The fable is unique in having its own prologue of eighty-four lines. The narrator arises one day in mid-June and falls asleep. A handsome well-dressed man approaches and reveals that he is "Esope." When the narrator requests a tale, Esope at first refuses because, with holy preaching being ignored, how can a fictional tale be of any use? The narrator responds that something useful may indeed be borne away from a story told "under the figure off ane brutall beist" (l. 1400), and Esope proceeds.

In the forest a tired lion falls asleep in the sun. Several mice dance around him and leap over him, then climb on him. The lion wakes and seizes the leader, a female, who fears swift death. The lion stands on his dignity. The mouse makes a case for mercy but is ordered to die on the gallows. Nevertheless, she continues. Justice requires mercy. A lion's victory over a little mouse could damage a noble reputation. Mouse meat is far less suitable than venison. And alive, a mouse

may be able to help a lion. The lion is swayed. Later, while hunting, he is caught in a net. He laments his fallen magnificence. The mouse-leader hears, then recognizes him; she summons her companions, and they chew him free.

The narrator asks Esope whether the fable has a moral. It does, one of broad political import. The lion stands for a ruler who sleeps when he should be watchful. The forest is the world and its deceptive pleasures. The mice are the common folk who need firm government and merciful handling of offenses. A low-ranking person may help or harm a higher-ranking one. After urging his pupil to solicit churchmen's prayers for faith, justice, and loyalty of lords to their king, Esope vanishes, and the narrator awakes.

This fable seems to ask to be read in light of contemporary politics. Is the lion James III? ("For he had nocht, bot levit on his pray"[l. 1511]). Critical opinion has been quite divided, but recently has leaned toward more apolitical readings. As Florence Ridley implies in her essay, "Middle Scots Writers," uncertainty might suit Henryson: political allegory criticizing a monarch should not be too clear.

If "haly preiching may na thing availl" (l. 1390), then the next fable, *The Preiching of the Swallow*, supports that pessimistic judgment. This fable is the weightiest of all and has attracted much critical admiration. Only *The Trial of the Fox* is longer. The first ninety-one lines make up a sermon on human ignorance contrasted with divine knowledge and wisdom. Nature shows God's intelligent plan. The progression of the seasons illustrates God's order in nature and introduces classical-style allusions to Flora, Phebus, Ceres, and others, examples of the fable's abundant and effective use of rhetorical devices.

A sober swallow begins preaching to carefree larks. In every line, the swallow quotes clerks and advises prudence, delivering with great urgency three pieces of advice, each at a particular stage of the growth and production of flax, the backdrop to the poem. First, the birds should scrape out and eat the seed before it grows. Startlingly, the larks reply with several proverbs stating the foolishness of borrowing trouble. Then in June, when the plants have grown tall enough to hide hares, the swallow urges the larks to pluck up the flax. The swallows counter that they look forward to eating the ripe flax seeds. The swallow is more specific: the farmer is a fowler, and the birds will end up on his spit.

Winter comes, and the fowler puts out nets baited with chaff. Even with the swallow preaching a third warning, the larks, desperate for food, cannot grasp the unwisdom of thinking only of present things, and they are taken in nets.

In an explicit and grisly scene, the swallow must watch the man butcher the birds as efficiently as he harvested the flax. The swallow then preaches briefly to the reader on the danger of not listening to warnings (ll. 1882–1887).

A dark moralitas follows. The peasant bondman represents the devil, sowing evil in the human soul, the earth, which, delighting in the idea of sin, encourages them to grow. Reason is overwhelmed by lustful habits. Sin ripens as the devil prepares his nets. The chaff represents worldly goods. The birds are vain, sinful people. The swallow signifies the holy preacher, giving warnings. But listeners do not hear, and their bodies go to the worm's kitchen, their souls to everlasting fire.

Any fable would seem less serious than *The Preiching of the Swallow* and *The Fox, the Wolf, and the Cadger*, or *The Wolf that gat the Nekhering throw the wrinkis of the Foxe that begylit the Cadgear*, certainly does so. It is almost as frequently anthologized as *The Two Mice*, and with good reason: it combines some of the best cruel ironic humor from the *Roman de Renart* tradition with sharp dialogue and an active, quite Scottish, human character (the first human character to speak within a fable), the cadger or fishmonger. In both *The Fox and the Wolf* and *The Trial of the Fox*, the fox is killed for his crimes; this fable, by contrast, has the more usual Reynardian outcome of the fox's outwitting the slower wolf and keeping all gains for himself.

The fox pretends to agree to help the wolf hunt. A cadger comes along singing. The fox plays dead; the cadger tosses him into the back of his wagon, for his pelt. The fox opens the cadger's creel and throws herring onto the ground, escaping when discovered. The wolf, impressed, is gulled by the fox with tales of a "nekhering," a huge salmon, in the creel. The fox advises the wolf to play dead and steal fish himself. The wolf takes a turn lying in the road, but the cadger beats him blind and deaf. The fox makes off with the fish.

According to the short and dark moralitas, the fox is like the world, the wolf a man, the cadger death. The world is steward to man, flattering him, allowing death to come up unannounced. The herring are gold, bringing destruction.

The Fox, the Wolf, and the Husbandman, or *The Foxe, that begylit the Wolf, in the Schadow of the Mone*, also belongs to the Reynardian tradition, apparently by way of Petrus Alfonsi. Again, the fox wins at the expense of the wolf. The farmer has a scare but does not suffer actual loss.

In the opening scene a farmer curses his inexperienced young oxen, saying the wolf may have them. The wolf, using eloquent legal language, comes to claim them, calling the fox as a witness. The fox arbitrates; he will save the man's oxen for the price of "six or seven" hens, "For God is gane to sleip, as for this nycht" (l. 2332) and won't see such a small thing. He then advises the wolf to take a large cheese or "cabok" in place of the oxen. The reflection of the moon in the well of a manor-house fortuitously (for the fox) provides the cheese. The fox asks for help lifting it, and the wolf finds himself in a bucket down the well.

Another dark moralitas ensues. The wolf stands for a wicked or oppressive man, the fox the devil, and the farmer a godly man tempted by the devil. The hens are works of faith that forestall the devil and send him back angry to the wicked man. The woods are riches, and the cheese is covetousness drawing a man to hell.

The Wolf and the Wether, possibly based on Caxton's *Aesop*, is the first in a short series of three fables that recount breathtaking cruelty and injustice triumphant. A shepherd's hard-working and very effective dog dies of sickness, and the shepherd fears ruin. A wether offers to take the dog's place if the shepherd will sew the dog's skin onto him. Surprisingly, the sheep does a fine job as substitute dog, driving the wolf to hungry frustration.

But the wether is not content merely to protect the sheep; he wants to catch the wolf, who is so frightened by the pursuit that he repeatedly befouls himself and the landscape. A briar bush tears the dog's skin off the wether, who, completely vulnerable, tells the wolf that he was only teasing. The wolf demonstrates that to him the chase was no game. Despite the wether's wise proverbial rejoinders, the wolf breaks his neck.

Readers sympathizing with the wether should look for no support from the moralitas. Briskly, it says that fine clothes and trappings can cause men to climb so high above their station that someone will upend them. They should not imitate, outdo, or disparage their betters; hall benches are slippery (l. 2608).

The Wolf and the Lamb, apparently based on Walter's tale and close to Lydgate's, seems from its title as if it will resemble *The Wolf and the Wether*; it does, in that both the wether and the lamb are ready talkers, and both are killed.

A wolf and a lamb are drinking, the lamb downstream from the wolf. The wolf accuses him of fouling the water. The lamb knows that water can't flow upstream and argues that his lips are pure, having touched only mother's milk, "richt naturall, sweit, and als delitious" (l. 2654). The wolf doesn't like verbal resistance: the lamb's father once outtalked him. The lamb replies that a son should not be punished for a father's fault, then asks to be tried in court. The wolf responds that the lamb wants to "intrude" reason where wrong and robbery should be in command, then kills the lamb, who "culd do na thing bot bleit" (l. 2700).

The narrator seems far more sympathetic to the lamb than to the wether. The last three lines of the tale request pity. The long (seventy lines) moralitas then resembles *The Sheep and the Dog*. The lamb represents the poor people—tenant farmers, merchants, and laborers—whose life is half a purgatory. The wolf stands for three kinds of oppressors: 1) perverters of the laws, who abuse justice for bribes; 2) men who dispossess small tenants by paying more for the land; and 3) the very large landowners who trick the tenant farmers into paying the same fine twice. The narrator believes that all such oppressors will suffer as if they had killed the poor with their own hands.

The final fable, *The Paddock and the Mouse,* expands Walter's and leaves a haunting sense of the cruelty of fate and the futility of the effort of creatures. A mouse wants to cross a stream to reach better food. A "paddock" (frog or toad) offers to swim her over. The mouse finds the toad's ugliness off-putting and cites clerks and a proverb in support of her reluctance to trust him. The toad utters learned counterexamples of mismatches between appearance and character.

The mouse, frightened at the prospect of being tied to the toad with a thread, demands that he swear the "murder oath." The toad does indeed try to drown her, and she fights back, but a bird of prey, a kite, seeing the struggle, silently snatches up the two, kills them, and flays them, as *The Concise Scots Dictionary* defines "bellieflaucht" (l. 2904), "by pulling the skin off whole over the head." Guts and all, the two make scarcely half a meal for the kite.

The narrator presents more than one moralitas. The first, in three ballade stanzas, is prudential: do not believe fair words too quickly, as they may mask evil intent. In addition, do not bind yourself when you can be free.

Then comes the figurative spiritual meaning. The toad represents mankind's body, suffering the vicissitudes of earthly life, or the river of the world. The mouse represents the soul, tied to the body by the thread of life and in danger of being drowned. The body wants to sink, the soul to rise. The kite is death, cutting the struggle short. Only good deeds can defend against death, which may strike at any time. The rest the narrator leaves to the friars.

The story ends starkly, and with it *The Morall Fabillis*. Some readers have noted that the tone darkens as the work proceeds. The deaths of innocent and well-meaning animals, even when caused by natural predators, bring pain. But on the human level, Henryson's readers have choices that his animals do not: the readers can mend their lives, have faith, and pray. Greed and brutality do overcome goodness and learning, but not as inevitably as wolves eat lambs. Despite Esope's reservations about holy preaching, the stories have deferred somewhat to preaching, after preparing the ground for it. The moralitates add weight to the lighter tales and hope to the more desperate. In the past, some readers felt that the lessons were a kind of tax paid to virtue for the amusement afforded by the tales. But the moralitates work neither as afterthoughts nor retractions, but as finishers and fulfillments of the tales. Douglas Gray says they are related somewhat as soul and body are. Most readers now interpret the tale and moralitas together.

THE TESTAMENT OF CRESSEID

HENRYSON'S *Testament of Cresseid* needs to be read in context. Probably few readers have come to the poem in isolation. It appears to have been first printed in 1532 as an attachment to Chaucer's *Troilus and Criseyde,* possibly, as Denton Fox says in his edition of the poems, because William Thynne, the printer, meant it to be taken as Chaucer's work (p. cii). Early on, the narrator refers the reader to Chaucer's poem: "I tuik ane quair . . . / Writtin be worthie Chaucer glorious / Of fair Creisseid and worthie Troylus" (ll. 40–42). Building as he does on Chaucer's characters, story, and perhaps narrative persona, and using mostly rhyme royal as Chaucer does, Henryson almost invites the label Scottish Chaucerian. But the very similarities point up the differences and Henryson's originality.

The poem's size is compelling, 616 lines, short enough to be read at a single sitting. The personable narrator, describing himself as an aged former devotee of Venus, draws the reader in. He takes "ane uthir quair," another book (probably a pretense), and, in the spirit of excusing Cresseid, tells of her final days.

As John MacQueen notes in *Robert Henryson,* the poem alternates the narration of events with descriptions or speeches, set-pieces. Lines 92–119, 344–406, 470–539, and 596–609 are narrative. Lines 92–119 recount Cresseid's solitary and disgraced return to the house of her father Calchas after Diomede, the Greek warrior for whom she'd left Troilus, had "all his appetyte, / And mair, fulfilled of" her and sent her away (ll.

71–72). Other amorous partners may have followed if indeed, as "sum men sayis," she "walkit up and doun . . . into the court commoun" (ll. 76–77). Her father, a priest of Venus (not Apollo, as in *Troilus and Criseyde*), welcomes her. Angry and self-absorbed, she spends lines 126–140 blaming Cupid and Venus for failing to maintain her as "the flour of luif in Troy."

This rebuke calls forth a remarkable scene: to Cresseid in a dream or vision appear Cupid and the seven "planets." The account of this formal procession strikingly combines fullness and focus. The whole scene, including the gods' judgment of Cresseid, constitutes one-third of the entire poem (lines 141–343). Saturn leads, old, cold, and hostile, and coming from farthest away, followed by Jupiter, a picture of health and good spirits, then angry Mars, glorious Phebus (horses and all), shifting Venus, sharp Mercury, and elusive Cynthia. These portraits sum up a long literary tradition and also introduce apparently original elements. Cupid particularly stands out: he is no boyish love god, shooting arrows, nor is he a planet, but rather a powerful and irate master of ceremonies. Cresseid seems almost to have called him into being by her curse.

By any account, the gods judge Cresseid very harshly. Mercury suggests Saturn and Cynthia, as the highest- and lowest-ranking planets, as judges. Both are negative, unlucky planets. They sentence Cresseid to melancholy, disease, and penury, specifically by infecting her with leprosy.

Readers rightly emphasize the horror of this affliction. Cresseid as leper is the strongest image in the poem, and she takes the story far from any path of Chaucer's. Scholars believe that Henryson most likely learned the symptoms of leprosy, which he conveys very accurately, from life. Some readers have suggested that leprosy was considered a venereal disease, or that Cresseid in fact has syphilis. Others say that leprosy is disease enough. Whatever the precise diagnosis, the corruption and the resulting shame and isolation serve Henryson's literary purposes.

The planetary parliament over, the narrative resumes for lines 344–406. The bad dream proves all too real. Cresseid stays closeted in her secret chapel (l. 120) until called to supper by a child who relates Calchas' supremely ironic message that Cresseid can stop praying because "The goddis wait [know] all your intent full weill" (l. 364). She sends for her father and tells him of her fate; "Thus was thair cair aneuch betuix thame twane" (l. 378). He helps her go out a back way to the "spittail house" half a mile away.

The narrative pauses again as Cresseid gives voice to her complaint (ll. 407–469). Its different stanza form (aabaabbab), the form of Chaucer's *Complaint of Anelida*, and its high style set it off. It gives classic expression to the *ubi sunt* theme, the asking where past joys and beauties have gone. But she cannot just lament; the "lipper lady" rightly tells Cresseid that she needs to "make vertew of ane neid," or make a virtue of necessity, and go begging, or "leif eftir the law of lipper leid," live according to the law of leper folk (ll. 478, 480). So the narrative resumes, in lines 470–539.

The Testament of Cresseid is not a sequel to Chaucer because Chaucer tells of the death of Troilus and his enlightenment, with his spirit laughing from high in the heavens at the futility of human vanity and effort, while Henryson shows Troilus still alive and even successful in battle. Leading his soldiers back to Troy after a victory, he responds to lepers' begging. He does not consciously recognize Cresseid, but her glance awakens an "idole . . . deip emprentit in the fantasy" that brings Cresseid's image before him (ll. 507–508). He throws the beggar a belt filled with gold and jewels. She asks her amazed friends who he is, and she faints at the answer.

Another complaint follows, on the theme "O fals Cresseid and trew knicht Troylus!" (l. 546). Troilus's faith and generosity have encompassed even an unfortunate beggar whom he didn't know he knew. Cresseid ends her lament with the line, "Nane but myself as now I will accuse" (l. 574). She then writes her will and testament: her body to worms and toads, her property to the lepers to pay for her burial, Troilus's ring back to him to inform him of her death, and her spirit "to Diane, quhair scho dwellis, / To walk with hir in waist woddis and wellis" (ll. 587–588). Death comes suddenly with the shattering recollection that Di-

omede has the brooch and belt Troilus gave Cresseid.

The poem winds up in three more stanzas. Troilus mourns and reportedly erects a tomb with a neutral inscription in gold. The final stanza takes a different direction: the narrator's voice breaks in to "monische and exhort" (l. 612) worthy women not to mix love with deception.

The Testament of Cresseid raises some major critical questions. One concerns its morality or justice. What laws has Cresseid broken? Is one single moral system at work? If so, what is it? Does a particular infraction draw a particular punishment? Is the system, if any, fair? What does the narrator think of it? Does it change Cresseid?

Some readers argue that the poem is fundamentally pagan, noting for example that Calchas is a priest of Venus, the pagan gods judge Cresseid after she curses them, and she leaves her spirit to Diana. References to such things as "oratur" (l. 120) and "beedes" (l. 363) are anachronisms. Cresseid has played Venus's game, and has finally lost. She, like Venus and Fortune and mirrors and some forms of love, is fickle or "brukill," but unlike them, she had a choice, and she must suffer. Cupid, rightly from his perspective, accuses Cresseid of blaspheming when she blames the gods for her own "leving unclene and lecherous" (ll. 274–287). Whether as divine judgment or as the consequence of human actions, leprosy follows infidelity and promiscuity. The allegory drives the narrative. The justice here shows no mercy; it obeys natural laws.

On the large question of Cresseid's inner development readers agree that she moves from self-pity and defiance, in which she blames others for her lot, to a genuine sorrow in which she accuses herself. She changes because Troilus's innate generosity convicts her of her guilt and of her folly in abandoning him. Some readers believe that Cresseid's informed remorse, her repentance, her taking of responsibility for her actions, lead to peace of mind and redemption in some sense. That reading perhaps sees a parallel with the final lofty unconcern of Chaucer's Troilus with worldly things. It may also be equating the planetary gods and their chastened worshiper with the Christian god and a repentant sinner. Some readers feel that Christianity is so deeply the grounding for all Henryson's poetry that a Christian meaning can be assumed. Probably the burden of proof is on readers who argue that Cresseid attains much more than self-knowledge and perhaps closure.

Henryson, living and writing in the late Middle Ages with its philosophical and artistic inclusiveness and its gift for synthesis, does not force readers to choose between "strict" paganism and orthodox Christianity. The literature of courtly love normally combines aspects of the pagan and the Christian, weighting and highlighting them with considerable freedom. Traditionally taking place outside marriage, courtly love cannot fully enter the church, but it has its own virtues and rituals, its own patron deities, and its own crimes. Insofar as the offenses and the punishments in *The Testament of Cresseid* occur on courtly ground, they have already traveled some distance from Hesiod's or Homer's or even Boethius's version of paganism.

Another and perhaps related question, also much debated, is the poem's status as tragedy. As A. C. Spearing writes in "Conciseness and *The Testament of Cresseid*," Chaucer has his Monk define the common medieval kind of tragedy, Senecan or Boethian, as the harm of those in "heigh degree" who fell so that nothing could help them out of their adversity (p.184). Cresseid has certainly fallen into adversity, where apparently nothing can help her.

Many readers feel without making a detailed analysis that *The Testament of Cresseid* comes close to classical tragedy. This opinion has some justification. Aristotelian unities of place, time, and action are largely present; they help give the poem its deserved reputation for concentration and intensity. Tragedy does require some plotted action, and while the amount of action in the poem is not great, the importance of the "recognition" scene shows a feel for the kind of plotting or construction that is central to Aristotelian tragedy. Recognition occurs as part of reversal: when Cresseid belatedly recognizes Troilus's faith and goodness and her fault, her blame changes direction.

As to whether Cresseid is a tragic protagonist, she conforms to Aristotelian guidelines in her high birth and in her fall from better fortune to much unhappiness. Aristotle may play down character, but readers do not, and Cresseid's "flaw" expresses itself in events. The poem conveys a sense basic to tragedy that punishment is greater than the offense but nevertheless deserved. A catharsis of pity and fear may not happen, even for Cresseid, but the action does come to a resolution or denouement.

Another major question about Cresseid is whether her character stands enough above the average, whether she has a sufficiently large soul, to gain tragic self-knowledge and acceptance. This remains a major critical issue. Tragic heroes transcend morality and cannot be used for a merely didactic purpose. Cresseid may not attain such stature.

Any tragic sense of *The Testament of Cresseid* is not enhanced by the narrator's comments. The narrator himself has come in for much attention, in part because Chaucer's narrator expresses such interest in the events of *Troilus and Criseyde*. Some readers consider Henryson's narrator a rather fatuous old man who would do more of Venus's work if he could. Others see him as a formerly unsuccessful servant of love who has come to terms with his age and incapacity and has realistically retired to his study. He undertakes to revise Chaucer's poem ("Quha wait gif all that Chaucer wrait was trew?" [l. 64]), apparently in light of the "uther quhair," which he considers to be true. But he will excuse Cresseid as far as he may (l. 87), blaming fortune and the gods. However, her fault comes through so clearly that readers suspect Henryson of treating his narrator with irony. The retired lover tells a story that is larger than he is. For most readers, the didactic final stanza seems an attempt to shrink the story to more nearly his own size.

Readers of *The Testament of Cresseid* can (and do) disagree on the philosophical underpinnings and generic tendencies of the poem and still consider it to be Henryson's masterpiece. Its poetic and emotional range, its conciseness, the Scottishness of its temper, its original handling of well-known material, its inevitability and wistful finality, all help justify the label.

ORPHEUS AND EURYDICE (THE TAILL OF ORPHEUS AND HIS WIF ERUDICES)

ANOTHER tale of lost love and regret is *Orpheus and Eurydice*. Henryson chose for his subject an old and widely adapted story. The tale of Orpheus, supreme musician, who loses his wife and finds her only to lose her again, had been told by Ovid in *Metamorphoses* VII, Virgil in *Georgics* II, Boethius in *De Consolatione Philosophiae* III, metrum 12, the Middle English *Sir Orfeo*, Boccaccio in *De Genealogia Deorum*, and others. It also attracted neoplatonic and scholastic commentaries. Henryson names his sources: Boethius for the fable, and Nicholas Trivet, a thirteenth-century Dominican friar, for the moralitas (ll. 415–424).

Henryson's poem runs to 633 lines, just seventeen more than *The Testament of Cresseid*. Like *The Morall Fabillis,* it contains a fable and a moralitas, the fable of fifty-two rhyme royal stanzas, plus five ten-line stanzas of Orpheus's complaint, rhymed *aabaabbcbc* (ll.134–183), and the moralitas not in stanzas but in 228 heroic couplets.

Orpheus is the son of Phebus and the muse Calliope, and the poem emphasizes the nobility of his lineage. Eurydice, queen of Thrace, loves him by reputation and demands that he marry her. They enjoy every happiness until, while fleeing across the meadow from a "busteous hird" (a rough shepherd) named Aristaeus, Eurydice is bitten by a serpent and taken away. Orpheus rages at the news and then composes a stunning lament, sometimes anthologized by itself. He ascends to the heavens and asks Jupiter, Mars, Phebus, Venus, and Mercury for help. Eurydice is not there, but from the heavenly spheres he learns new musical possibilities. He travels for twenty days and arrives at the gates of hell, where his music puts Cerberus and the Furies to sleep so that Ixion, Tantalus, and Tityus can rest from their torments. After descending to a place of despair and seeing many dead monarchs, popes, cardinals, and abbots, Orpheus approaches Pluto and sees Eurydice. A little cryptic conversation ensues. Orpheus's music wins his wife's conditional release, but, "blindit . . . with grit effectioun" (l. 388) he looks back, loses her for good, and rebukes love. A long complex moralitas follows.

Of Henryson's longer poems, *Orpheus and Eurydice* is most likely to leave a modern reader somewhat baffled, if curious. One puzzle is the apparent disjunction between the fable, with its romance characters and its human feeling, and the moralitas, which Trivet borrowed from William of Conches. In the moralitas, the allegory is uncompromising: Orpheus is "the pairte intellectyve / Of manis saule and undirstanding" separate from sensuality (ll. 428–430). Eurydice is the opposite, "our effectioun, / Be fantesy oft movit up and doun" (ll. 431–432). So far, so good: Orpheus as reason, and Eurydice as the passion that should attach itself to reason, may work as symbolism in narrative. For example, it is not in the heavens that Orpheus, as reason, would find his strayed affections. Affection may be provisionally trusted to follow reason. As Douglas Gray has noted, it is tragic but logical that the love that drew Orpheus to Eurydice would also separate them. Reason cannot keep affection always in check and by its side.

But the allegory becomes murkier with the question of just how Orpheus and Eurydice become separated once they are married. The moralitas states that Eurydice flees from virtue (Aristaeus, from the Greek "aristeus," or "best") through the world's vain pleasures to be stung by sin, which poisons and holds down the soul (ll. 435–443). The idea that a would-be rapist stands for "nocht bot gud vertew, / That bissy is to keip our myndis clene" (ll. 436–437) is too hard for most readers who are not neoplatonists. That the interpretation goes all the way back to Fulgentius' *Mythologiae* of the early sixth century helps only a little.

Once Aristaeus has set the reader digging around the poem, other questions present themselves. Philosophical and musical lore appear in the poem seemingly unannounced and perhaps not fully digested: see especially lines 226–239 and 369–370. Music learned from the heavenly spheres might well be difficult, though. The narrator professes not to understand it: "Off sic musik to wryt I do bot doit [deceive myself] . . . / For in my lyfe I cowth nevir sing a noit" (ll. 240, 242).

Other catalogues, such as that of the nine muses (ll. 29–63), help establish the poem's register. Some readers find overlong the allegorical treatment of the three major sinners, Ixion, Tantalus, and Tityus, as desire for the world's goods, greed and covetousness, and the desire to know things that only God should know (ll. 515–518, 531–558, 571–599).

The poem cries out for interpretation. Usually in Henryson's poetry, however erudite, the narrative and didactic aspects fit together fairly unobtrusively. *Orpheus and Eurydice* has more visible seams. Readers looking for an explanation traditionally have liked to think that *Orpheus and Eurydice* was an early work, perhaps almost apprentice work, showing marks of greatness but lacking full poetic control. The relatively close dependence on sources could support the apprentice-work theory.

But as the poem cannot be dated, other explanations for its apparent peculiarities must be considered. Denton Fox and Douglas Gray have pointed out the solid philosophical and structural base of the poem in its "interlocking system" of three kinds of music: instrumental; human, especially between the soul's rational and irrational parts; and the music of the spheres. Fox rightly suggests that the poem works better if read not as a verse romance but as an "encyclopedic and cosmological poem" that ascends to the spheres and descends into Hades and revels in a full panoply of rhetorical devices (1981, p. cix). Some readers find wit, irony, and paradox at many points. And, as Fox says, the poem is a defense of poetry, of the effort to bring heaven's eloquence to earth (pp. cix–cx).

Although there is little or no solid evidence that Henryson knew the Middle English romance *Sir Orfeo*, much of the charm of *Orpheus and Eurydice* derives from lines, phrasings, sentiments, and motifs that would be at home in a ballad or verse romance, sometimes shading into courtly romance. A setting on a May morning and a heroic quest appear in most romances. "Wedlingis Streit" ("Watling Street," l. 188) for the Milky Way is a traditional folk locution. Some lines, particularly ones that clinch a stanza, are sharp and pointed and sound like speech. Eurydice's maiden tells how her mistress disappeared: "Allace, Euridicess, your quene, is with the phary [faery] tane befoir my ene!" (ll. 118–119). See also lines 197, 245–246, and 288. Overall, the poem challenges with its combination of medieval learning, popular verse traditions, and apparently fresh interpretations.

Orpheus and Eurydice well repays a second reading. As Matthew McDiarmid in *Robert Henryson* says, the poem's interest "can even make us accept a reading procedure that delays understanding and expects a reconsideration" (p. 60). All told, however interpreted, the poem is something of an enigma that tends to grow in its appeal.

And likenesses to *The Testament of Cresseid* abound. A woman of passion dies or is dying, and her death gives rise to poetry. A Christian author presents classical gods at length. A glance has tremendous effect. Love is inevitable, but brings great loss, with all lovers finally bereft.

SHORTER POEMS

ROBENE and Makyne, The Want of Wyse Men, Against Hasty Credence, Sum Practysis of Medecyn, The Abbey Walk, The Ressoning betuix Deth and Man, The Ressoning betuix Aige and Yowth, The Praise of Age, The Thre Deid Pollis, The Garmont of Guid Ladeis, Ane Prayer for the Pest, The Annunciation, The Bludy Serk

The reader looking to Henryson's shorter poems for respite from some of the critical and literary uncertainties of the longer works will find some relief but also new questions. Twelve or thirteen shorter poems have been attributed to Henryson with varying degrees of certainty. (Denton Fox has dropped *The Want of Wyse Men* from the Henryson canon for lack of any "real evidence" that Henryson wrote it [p. cxvi].) Ranging in length from 32 to 128 lines, they add up to almost one-fifth of his oeuvre. As with his other works, no dates and therefore no chronological order can be assigned to the poems. Efforts have been made to link one poem or another with a particular event, but evidence remains inconclusive. About half the poems use the same meter, the eight-line ballade or *Monk's Tale* stanza, another three use the ballad meter, and the three remaining use three different meters. Alliteration can be quite heavy.

Most of the poems appear in the Bannatyne manuscript with varying kinds of testimony that Henryson wrote them. The case for the reliability of the attributions can be argued two opposite ways. Perhaps fairly local and contemporary tradition kept current the knowledge that Henryson was the author. Conversely, someone who liked Henryson's other work may have attributed to him something else pleasing, or similar in theme.

Scholars have traditionally classified the poems by subject: as Robert Kindrick in his edition puts it, poems on love, poems on religion, and poems on social themes and conventions. By this division, nine of the poems, a large majority, are primarily religious. Only one is purely about love, and two or three deal mainly with social matters. Two of the religious poems have to do with issues in society. Seven poems, over half, stand out as superior in quality. Each sets a standard for its type and is in some way a tour de force. Some bear almost no resemblance to Henryson's longer poems.

Robene and Makyne is the longest of the short poems (128 lines), the only one primarily about love, and the one most often included in anthologies. It is the best British example of the pastourelle, or exchange about love between a shepherd and a maid. It sports a lilting, alliterating ballad meter and uses stock phrases in a lively way. Its wit, irony, and human drama are pronounced. Makene, the maid, is in love with Robene and begs for his amorous attentions, but he has no interest and sends her away disappointed. Once he goes home, the situation is reversed: now he feels love for her, but she has recovered, and she dismisses him with, "The man that wil nocht quhen he may / Sall haif not

quhen he wald" (ll. 91–92), or the man who doesn't take what's offered will not have another chance at it.

Of the poems on social themes and conventions, *The Want of Wyse Men*, which may very well not be Henryson's, makes very broad and inclusive criticisms of corruption and foolishness and out-of-jointness in society because, as the refrain says, "Want of wyse men makes fulis sit on binkis [law-benches]."

Shorter and more focused is *Against Hasty Credence* [of *fals titlaris*, or gossips]. I. W. A. Jamieson in his article "The Minor Poems of Robert Henryson" notes that *The Cock and the Fox*, in lines 600–606, and *The Paddock and the Mouse*, in lines 2910–2925, also advise against hasty credence of false talkers, whether gossips, flatterers, or liars.

A very different work that apparently bears on society is *Sum Practysis of Medecyn*. The stanza—thirteen lines long, including a wheel, and strongly alliterative—is unique in Henryson's surviving work. So are the tone and content. The poem is a dramatic monologue that defends the prescription-writing powers of the speaker and includes four sample prescriptions. The first, mainly scatological, is for colic; another apparently purports to cure impotence; a third is for foolishness, and the fourth, also employing various animal parts and bodily waste, should cure hoarseness, coughing, and heartburn. The poem appears to be related to medical burlesques and flytings of the period. Who or what is the target of satire is debatable, but the antic excess is worthy of William Dunbar.

Henryson's more routine religious poems have some good points, though *The Abbey Walk*, fairly short and pleasant, might not stand out in a collection of poems on a similar theme. The same is true of *The Ressoning betuix Deth and Man. The Ressoning betuix Aige and Yowth* compels more attention through its greater length, the very strong alliteration, the spring morning setting, and the rival refrains of the youth and the aged man, "O yowth, be glaid in to thi flouris grene!" and "O yowth, thi flouris fedis fellone sone [fade horribly soon]!" The discussion of the speakers' relative virility is surprisingly frank.

A poem whose charms improve with acquaintance is *The Praise of Age*. At thirty-two lines, it is the shortest of the poems. Being general, it succeeds in expatiating upon and then distilling the main reason an aging Christian would happily look ahead: according to the refrain, "The more of age, the nerar hevynnis blis." Alliteration works effectively throughout.

The Thre Deid Pollis [Heads] is part of a well-established visual and verbal tradition in which skulls or corpses address the living. If the ideas are common, they are effectively dramatized.

Among the religious poems, four are small masterpieces: *The Garmont of Gud Ladeis, Ane Prayer for the Pest, The Annunciation,* and *The Bludy Serk.* All are distinctive, and all can stand up to extensive literary-critical analysis and still hold onto some of their secrets. *The Garmont of Gud Ladeis* includes some social commentary in prescribing the items of apparel a grand lady of the period would wear. The Bible, including 2 Timothy 2:9–10 and Ephesians 6:13–17, apparently inspired the allegorical matching of a virtue with a garment. The ballad meter, the steady progress through some fourteen pieces of clothing, the alliteration, the combination of seriousness and lightness, make the poem, though only forty lines long, very full.

Ane Prayer for the Pest has attracted much commentary. As social criticism, it says that if leaders would punish their people, the plague would not need to do it. It accuses the leaders of oppressing the people so much that God does not hear those leaders' prayers (ll. 57–64). The striking earnestness of the poem has persuaded some scholars that it marks a particular visitation of the plague. Some alliteration is very effective, and the aureate language in lines 65–80 is among the most pronounced in Henryson.

The Bludy Serk, written in ballad meter, has the feel of a ballad and seems shorter than its 120 lines. It tells of a beautiful princess stolen by a giant. A peerless prince fights and defeats the giant but sustains mortal wounds in the contest. He directs the princess to keep his bloody shirt ("bludy serk") before her eyes. The presence of an explicit moralitas, the only one in any of these shorter poems, recalls *The Morall Fabillis* and *Orpheus and Eurydice.* In the moralitas, the king is the Trinity, the lady is man's soul, the giant is Lucifer, and the knight is Jesus Christ. Some readers have proposed the *Gesta Romanorum* as a source, but the tale circulated in several versions. Critics do not agree on the extent to which Henryson was affecting a naïve style. Whatever the critical issues, the poem is a great artistic success.

From the arresting first line, "Forcy as death is likand lufe," or "Strong as death is pleasing love," *The Annunciation* reveals a master poetic hand. The poem startles by its overall complexity and beauty and finish. The seventy-two lines are in twelve-line stanzas, *ababbaabbaab*, with the *a* lines tetrameters and the *b* lines trimeters. Among other poetic praises of the Virgin, this one stands out. The paradox of the Immaculate Conception is explored historically, symbolically, and verbally, and the wit and wordplay of the treatment almost invite comparison with the Metaphysical poets.

The shorter poems are now usually approached through their generic characteristics. In the absence of dates and of known connections with history or Henryson's life, such a line of inquiry has the best chance of placing the poems in their literary-historical context.

CONCLUSION

HENRYSON'S poetry provides a touchstone to late medieval life, learning, and art. If a subject is important—sin, salvation, aspiration, failure, good government, common sense—the works will deal with it, briefly but in depth. The poems, like the man himself, seem solidly there, but become more mysterious on closer inspection. Some readers have called Henryson the greatest Scottish poet of any period. Given his command of form and verse music, his grounding in tradition and learning, and the inclusiveness of his work, they have a case.

SELECTED BIBLIOGRAPHY

I. MANUSCRIPTS AND EARLY PRINTS. The Chepman and Millar Print of part of *Orpheus and Eurydice* (1508) in facsimile ed. by William Beattie (Edinburgh, 1950); the Thynne edition of *The Testament of Cresseid* in *The Workes of Geffray Chaucer* (London, 1532); the Charteris edition of *The Morall Fabillis of Esope the Phrygian* (Edinburgh, 1570); the Bassandyne edition of *The Morall Fabillis of Esope the Phrygian* (Edinburgh, 1571); the Charteris edition of *The Testament of Cresseid* (Edinburgh, 1593); *The Maitland Folio Manuscript*, ed. by W. A. Craigie, 2 vols., Scottish Text Society new series nos. 7, 10 (Edinburgh, 1919–1927); *The Bannatyne Manuscript*, ed. by W. Tod Ritchie, 4 vols., Scottish Text Society new series nos. 22, 23, and 26; 3d series, no. 5 (Edinburgh, 1928–1934), and in facsimile, *The Bannatyne Manuscripts*, with an introduction by Denton Fox and William A. Ringler (London, 1980).

II. MODERN EDITIONS. G. Gregory Smith, ed. *The Poems of Robert Henryson*, 3 vols., Scottish Text Society nos. 55, 58, and 64 (Edinburgh, 1906, 1908, 1914); Denton Fox, ed., *The Testament of Cresseid* (London, 1968); Denton Fox, ed., *The Poems of Robert Henryson* (Oxford, 1981); George Gopen, ed. and trans., *The Moral Fables of Aesop* (Notre Dame, Ind., 1987); Robert L. Kindrick, ed., with Kristie A. Bixby, *The Poems of Robert Henryson* (Kalamazoo, Mich., 1997).

III. CRITICAL AND HISTORICAL STUDIES. Denton Fox, "The Scottish Chaucerians," in D. S. Brewer, ed., *Chaucer and Chaucerians* (Tuscaloosa, Ala., 1966); John MacQueen, *Robert Henryson* (Oxford, 1967); I. W. A. Jamieson, "The Minor Poems of Robert Henryson," in *Studies in Scottish Literature* 9, nos. 2–3 (Oct.–Jan. 1971–1972); A. C. Spearing, "Conciseness and *The Testament of Cresseid*," in his *Criticism and Medieval Poetry*, 2d ed. (London, 1972); Florence Ridley, "Middle Scots Writers," in Albert E. Hartung, ed., *A Manual of the Writings in Middle English 1050–1500*, vol. 4 (New Haven, Conn., 1973); Ranald Nicholson, *Scotland in the Later Middle Ages* (Edinburgh, 1974); Florence Ridley, "A Plea for the Middle Scots," in Larry D. Benson, ed., *The Learned and the Lewed* (Cambridge, Mass., 1974); Douglas Gray, *Robert Henryson* (Leiden, 1979); Matthew P. McDiarmid, *Robert Henryson* (Edinburgh, 1981); Marianne Powell, *Fabula docet* (Odense, Denmark, 1983); Gerald Baird, *The Poems of Robert Henryson*, Scotnotes no. 11 (Aberdeen, 1996).

IV. BIBLIOGRAPHIES. William Geddie, ed., *A Bibliography of Middle Scots Poets*, Scottish Text Society, no. 61 (Edinburgh, 1912); Louise O. Fradenburg, "Henryson Scholarship: The Recent Decades," in Robert F. Yeager, ed., *Fifteenth-Century Studies* (Hamden, Conn., 1984); Walter Scheps and J. Anna Looney, *Middle Scots Poets* (Boston, 1986); Various authors, "The Year's Work in Scottish Literary and Linguistic Studies," in issues of *The Scottish Literary Journal* from the 1980s and 1990s.

A. D. HOPE

(1907–2000)

Andrew Zawacki

EARLY LIFE, IDENTIFICATION, AND IDENTITY

ALEC DERWENT HOPE was born on 21 July 1907, in Cooma, New South Wales, Australia. His father Percival, a Presbyterian minister, enlisted as a chaplain in the Australian forces sent to France during the First World War. His mother Florence had trained to be a concert pianist. In 1911 the family moved to Campbelltown in Tasmania, where Hope was taught at home, Latin by his father and reading by his mother. Hope began writing verses in ballad meter around age seven or eight. In the essay "Meet Nurse!" in *Native Companions: Essays and Comments on Australian Literature 1936–1966* (1974), he described the first poem he could recall writing as a "pious rhyme in fifty-two stanzas—one for each week in the year—composed for my mother's birthday and designed to encourage her in her Christian duty." Hope recollected the "amusement and slight impatience with which she read it and gently suggested that I might perhaps consider improving my own conduct rather than hers" (pp. 4–5). While his father kept no volumes of Australian poetry on his shelves, by age nine Hope knew the work of Adam Lindsay Gordon as well as William Wordsworth, John Keats, and Percy Bysshe Shelley. Thus began what he would later recognize as the difficulty in marrying Romantic richness to an Australian idiom.

When Hope was fourteen the family returned to New South Wales, where he was educated at Bathurst High School and published his first poem, a rendering of Catullus, whose sexually explicit poems intrigued the youngster because they were considered off limits by his teachers. Thereafter, he fell under the sway of Robert Browning, who taught him that poetry need not be "poetical," and also Walt Whitman and Alger-

non Charles Swinburne, from whom he learned that poetry should possess at least the echo of the singing voice. Hope also claimed the early influence of William Shakespeare as well as the Authorized Version of the English Bible, "which was read to me over and over as a child till its language now forms a permanent substratum in my mind," as he wrote half a century later in *The New Cratylus: Notes on the Craft of Poetry* (1979, p. 8). He took up Italian at the Conservatorium of Music in order to read Dante in the original, thus beginning a lifelong commitment to learning languages other than English. The only real training in poetic craft that Hope was given he credited to Violet McKee, a young painter. Upon asking to see the aspiring poet's verses, she urged him to burn his early work, which she felt was burdened by secondhand emotion, and to write instead from experience by evoking objects, such as his kitchen, in the simplest, most concrete terms, without appealing to abstract ideas or emotion.

In 1924 he matriculated from Fort Street Boys' High School in Sydney, having been awarded an arts scholarship although he'd applied in medicine. He attended the University of Sydney, where he read philosophy and English, studying under the philosopher John Anderson. His one meeting with the poet Christopher Brennan occurred in a urinal, where Hope capriciously wrote part of a well-known, ribald Latin phrase on the wall, and then looked on as Brennan corrected his grammar and completed the sentence. Hope also spent time with John Le Gay Brereton, who spoke with Hope about his own favorite subject, Christopher Marlowe, and this served as the genesis of the book on Marlowe that Hope would publish over half a century later. In 1928 Hope was awarded the University Medal in Philosophy and received the James King of Irraway traveling scholarship to attend Oxford University, which had been a goal of his for many years. Quite apart from feeling alienated outside Australia, Hope later recalled in his memoir *Chance Encounters* (1992) that from the very first day in England he had felt "oddly at home, as though not observing a foreign country but returning from a long absence, picking up what I had always known" (p. 58). At Oxford he read in the Language School with hopes of becoming a linguist. He took up German, Old English, and Gothic, in addition to having enrolled in a Spanish course six months prior to term. His primary tutor was C. L. Wrenn, while he also studied under C. T. Onions, J. R. R. Tolkien, and C. S. Lewis. Hope fared poorly in his exams and left England with third-class honors. He would claim nearly sixty years later that he was still in disgrace over that event.

Hope returned to Australia in 1931 during the depression and spent a year unemployed. He trained at Sydney Teachers' College and taught in several secondary schools before working as a vocational psychologist in the Department of Labour and Industry from 1934 to 1936. During this time he began learning Russian. He was then employed as an educational researcher by the Department of Education, which in 1936 asked him to take charge of the Trades School in Canberra, where he met Penelope Robinson, a typist in the Prime Minister's office, whom he married the following year. He was subsequently appointed as lecturer in education at Sydney Teachers' College, where a year later he earned a lectureship in English. He became friendly with one of his students, James McAuley, who volunteered criticism of his teacher's poetry. McAuley would become one of Australia's major twentieth-century poets, and the two remained friends until McAuley's death in 1976. Hope's daughter Emily was born in 1940, and four years later twin sons, Andrew and Geoffrey, were born. In 1945 Hope was appointed senior lecturer in English at the University of Melbourne. Throughout the 1940s, he acted the character of "Anthony Inkwell" for a radio program broadcast daily by the Australian Broadcasting Corporation called "The Argo-

nauts," in which he encouraged and offered constructive criticism to young people who submitted their poems to be read on air.

The 1940s and early 1950s were a tumultuous and formative period in Australian letters. Hope cut his teeth on the central debates and sometimes found himself at their center. To begin with, he was privy to the secret plotting of the controversial Ern Malley poetry hoax. McAuley and James Stewart published intentionally poor surrealist poems, under a pseudonym, in the journal *Angry Penguins*, in order to expose what they believed to be the formally sloppy and intellectually vapid nature of avant-garde writing. Ern Malley was soon promoted by the magazine's editors, Max Harris and John Reid, to international status as a leading experimental writer. Hope supported the hoax, delighting in the embarrassment that its eventual disclosure brought to the aesthetic left wing. Soon after, national journals such as *Southerly* and the newly founded *Meanjin* provided Hope with outlets for articulating his critical positions more thoroughly and more publicly. He was extremely dismissive of the Jindyworobak movement, which rejected the English literary tradition and sought to naturalize Australian literature by including numerous references to indigenous objects and beliefs. Hope called the Jindyworobaks the "Boy Scout School of Poetry," claiming that "the poet who tries to write like a second-hand abo is no more likely to produce sincere work than the poet who writes like a second-hand Englishman." He was equally harsh toward Max Harris' novel *The Vegetative Eye* and, while generally laudatory of Patrick White's *The Tree of Man*, criticized it for its occasional "pretentious and illiterate verbal sludge" (*Native Companions*, pp. 45, 79).

Hope's reviews began earning him a reputation as a savage critic. Some in the literary world even felt that his positions indicated an antipathy toward Australian literature per se. The question of Australianness was a heated public preoccupation during the 1950s. In the tenth anniversary issue of *Meanjin* in 1950, the critic Arthur Phillips documented a "disease of the Australian mind" that he coined the "Cultural Cringe," or an inability of Australian writers and readers to escape comparisons with English culture (p. 299). Phillips claimed Australians were constantly assuming Australian art to be inferior to English aesthetics and taste. "Once the reader's mind begins to be nagged by the thought of how an Englishman might feel" about a given book, Phillips claimed, "he loses the fine edge of his Australian responsiveness." Phillips found this state of affairs absurd, arguing that it was part of the "distinctive virtue" of Australian novels "that no Englishman can fully understand them" (p. 300). In the public eye at least, Hope was perceived as conforming somewhat to the alienated Australian intellectual that Phillips had observed, one who claimed to be self-consciously most at home abroad. This perception stemmed from Hope's statements in various reviews. "This theory, that each country has its own standards by which its writers are to be judged, that a book is not simply a good book but a good Australian book," Hope wrote in one review, "is one of the common delusions of criticism in this country today" (*Native Companions*, p. 59). Hope would have agreed with Phillips that Australians' obsessive and insecure comparisons between English literature and their own were foolish and irrelevant. At the same time, however, Hope felt strongly that attempts to define a purely "Australian" literature were equally misguided. He made it clear in numerous essays that English literature would increasingly play for Australian literature the part played by the classics in English literature, namely, another country essential to defining the imagination and comprehension of one's own.

In 1951 Hope became professor of English at Canberra University College. The view that he disparaged Antipodean culture notwithstanding, Hope instituted the country's first course in Australian literature in spite of the fact that the University of Melbourne, of which Canberra College was a satellite, refused to recognize it for a degree. When the college became independent of Melbourne University, Australian literature became a degree course at the Australian National University under the general heading of English Studies. Hope often said that a university career had been necessary to his making a living but not one he enjoyed. He referred to teaching as a game, while his real work was writing poems. His own poetry circulated among friends and colleagues during the 1940s and found its way into print only sporadically in a few journals. Much of his early work had been destroyed in an accidental fire. Thus when his first full-length collection finally appeared in 1955, when Hope was forty-eight years old, it was quite an anticipated event.

THE WANDERING ISLANDS AND THE FREUDIAN ISLANDS

HOPE's debut collection *The Wandering Islands* contained poems written between 1938 and 1953. Dense, highly formal in style, and packed with poems containing references to biblical stories and Greek myths, the volume earned him the label "classicist." Unlike other prominent postwar poets such as McAuley, David Campbell, Douglas Stewart, and Judith Wright, Hope was "least influenced by distinctively Australian experience," Leonie Kramer wrote in one of the earliest studies of his work, *A. D. Hope* (p. 3). Indeed, the poem "Australia," while written in 1939, was not included in the volume and was only later gathered in *Collected Poems 1930–1965* (1966), perhaps because as one of the few early poems that Hope wrote about his native country, it would not have fit the arc of a collection. Its view of Australia as a barren desert might not have been palatable to readers, either. While a number of poems in *The Wandering Islands* address childhood and its landscapes both real and imagined, "Ascent into Hell" is one of the few that speaks explicitly of Hope's boyhood in Australia. Now in the middle of his life, like Dante in the *Divine Comedy*, the poet revisits Tasmania, "my receding childish island." Yet rather than describing the scene as an external geography with its own verifiable properties, he claims that its "prehistoric flora grows / within me." Hope likewise surveys a valley and its river, gum trees and poplars, but says the Western Tiers "make distance an emotion," as the poem becomes less an account of a specifically Australian terrain than an exploration of psychological states. He conceives memory as a sequence of islands, disconnected and full of despair, as he enters a world of panic and nightmare. The speaker then asserts that even the waking life "turns inward," and while he envisions his mother comforting him among terrors of lions and tigers, he is met with the stares of stone faces that remind him of Easter Island. Ultimately, the speaker feels divided even from himself, as an "unrecognized Other Voice speaks in my ear, / the voice of my fear, the voice of my unseen guide" (27–28).

The title poem dramatizes Hope's dual and even dueling conceptions of solitude and isolation. On the one hand, he quarrels with John Donne's assertion that no man is an island, arguing instead, in a manner akin to Virginia Woolf's recurring anxiety that nobody really knows anyone else, that people are always separated from each other, despite their most passionate attempts to be united:

You cannot build bridges between the wandering
  islands;
The Mind has no neighbours, and the unteachable
  heart
Announces its armistice time after time, but spends
Its love to draw them closer and closer apart.

                                                    (p. 15)

This distance of the individual from other human beings is experienced as an indifference endemic to life. The mind's attempt to end its loneliness occurs only intermittently and succeeds for a mere instant, as people furiously collide in sexual acts. Their mutual fulfillment quickly dissolves into the feeling that they are each, once again, castaways. The poem ends on the portentous note that no rescue for them, or for anyone, will occur, and that the heart will remain without companionship.

On the other hand, buried inside the poem is another, more subtle narrative that demonstrates the allure that solitude held for Hope. He claims the wandering islands can also be a refuge for the shipwrecked sailor. While the stranded sailor is described as masturbating—an image that Hope reprises as incest and sex with contraception elsewhere in the book to condemn the steril-

ity of his age—he is likewise an individual who bravely stands apart from a philistine society overly driven by a desire for productivity. In the opening "Flower Poem," Hope pits the transforming quality of poetry against "civilisation" (p. 11), while "The Brides" figures marriage as an assembly line. "The Lingam and the Yoni" characterizes how mortgages and rent turn love into banal arithmetic, and "The Explorers" mocks the way love is manifested as a cottage with a lawn and two people kissing at the gate as one leaves for the office. In "Observation Car" he likens the monotony of daily life to a train ride, holding the poet up as the person who may be capable of charting a new, more vigorous path by driving his own car.

An interesting tension arises between Hope's insistence on traditional forms and classical bases of poetry, and the Romantic aspirations he champions on behalf of the poet as a possible hero. "Pyramis or The House of Ascent" valorizes a "lone man digging" in the lineage of William Blake, John Milton, Jonathan Swift, and other builders of the "great work" (p. 38), among whom Hope also included William Butler Yeats, whom he praised for his "noble, candid speech" (p. 43), a phrase that ambiguously summons both the Irish poet's classical stature as well as his Romantic tendencies. "Invocation" promises that poets, like Shelley's unacknowledged legislators, "alone defend / That darkness out of which our light is won" (p. 42). The designations "classical" and "Romantic" became, in fact, the antithetical categories from which critics argued their positions about Hope's work. In the most famous early essay on Hope's poetry, "The Unknown Poet" (1957), Vincent Buckley asserted that Hope "is a classical poet whose material is Romantic," insofar as Hope often absorbs the world in an unbalanced or anarchistic fashion, only to stringently control its form and argumentation (Brooks, p. 43).

One way of considering the distinction between classicism and Romanticism in Hope's work is to examine his conflicting views on the doctrines of psychoanalysis and how they affect poetic creation. What Hope had found objectionable in neosurrealist poetry was its authors' unwillingness to subject the associative material of dreams to the sophisticated formal constraints that Hope believed serious poetry required. Hope's disapproval extended to much Modernist poetry as it was being practiced by T. S. Eliot and Ezra Pound especially, on the grounds that their often unrhymed, fragmented free verse neglected the rigorous demands of craft and technique. Hope claimed that free verse was merely prose arbitrarily divided into lines. In his essay "Free Verse: A Post-Mortem" in *The Cave and the Spring: Essays in Poetry* (1965) he stated: "The truth about free verse is that it is not free and it is not verse. It is not free because it has no discipline by which its freedom may be assessed. It is not verse because it has neither measure nor metre" (p. 45). Hope believed he detected too much of Sigmund Freud's unconscious at work in surrealism and indeed in many versions of Modernist poetry that did not appear to appeal to order so much as revel in chaos and contingency. Proponents of free verse seemed to him lazy, uninventive, and ultimately more confined by the formal restraints they refused to respect than they would have been by adhering to rhyme and meter.

Hope's condescension can be easily discerned in another poem he excluded from *The Wandering Islands* despite having written it in 1942, "The Return from the Freudian Islands." The poem is largely concerned to denigrate the father of psychoanalysis, whom Hope refers to caustically as Sigmund the Saviour, as well as to demote his theories, which center around an Analytic Eye. Hope imagines islands whose inhabitants adopt psychoanalysis as a new religion and who, in their fervor to expose their latent desires, thus strip their clothes and eventually peel their skin. A Brave Nude World is declared, in which love is rethought as nothing more than a common skin disease. The annual Fertility Festival is a mockery, of course, since people have been reduced to their sinews and no longer demonstrate any longing, now that The Sacred Id has been purged. The Holy Freud finally declares The Triumph of Analysis and awaits the crowd's applause, but nobody claps. All that's heard is a "faint, dry sound / As first a poet buttoned on his skin" (*Collected Poems*

1930–1965, p. 21). While more a satire on the hysterias of Freud's prescriptions than a discourse on poetic power and craft, "The Return from the Freudian Islands" expresses Hope's beliefs that only a poet can lead society out of its faddish but pernicious delusions, and that poetry involves not raw, unmediated experience but rather the clothing of experience in a semblance of form. In addition, it implies that the poet seeks not to exhibit his own private dramas and melodramas—his guts, in effect—but to fashion works of art that, while perhaps stemming from personal emotion or urgency, are created in mind of their status as public statements.

"The Return from the Freudian Islands" was made more widely public in 1966, when Hope included it in his *Collected Poems 1930–1965*. He never relinquished his conviction that poetry imposes order on a disorderly world, giving rhyme and reason to language that otherwise exhibits unruly tendencies. Nor did he ever concede that free verse was more than a "tedious shuffle," as he wrote in an essay called "Dream Work," or that most surrealist verse was anything less than "the incoherent vomit of that uncontrolled subconscious" (*The New Cratylus*, p. 28). However, Hope did begin to accommodate some of Freud's basic tenets as they applied to writing poems. The mechanism of devising poems, he said, is "a sort of controlled waking dreaming," an idea that clearly owes a debt to Freud's expositions of the creative processes involved in dreaming (p. 25). Hope claimed that poetry requires both dream work and craft work, the former an act of imagination proposing suggestions, the latter a practical concern for selecting and ordering those possibilities metrically and rhythmically. In this way poetry is "partly making and partly finding," and if the poet is serious, the elements of craft work will not only frame the dream work but also even stimulate it. Hence the principle of restraint actually doubles as a mode of freedom. Hope was not as far as he thought from T. S. Eliot's insistence that the ghost of meter must persist behind the arras of all free verse. Hope implied—perhaps unconsciously, against his intentions—that the ghost of free verse haunted every formally accomplished poem, and that the ghost, moreover, was often benign. "It has taken me half a century to learn," Hope admitted in the preface to his *Selected Poems* (1973), that "there is a sense in which poems must be allowed, indeed helped, to write themselves, just as there is another sense in which they must be controlled, disciplined and forced to meet the inexorable demands of the medium, if they are to achieve the possibilities latent in their mysterious intentions" (p. v). One reason that Hope had dismissed Freud so vehemently, Kevin Hart argues in *A. D. Hope*, is "because psychoanalysis and poetry contest the same space, the world of dreams and myths" (p. 105). Yet while dreams are the affair of an individual, often not fully understood by the dreamer himself, myths are shared accounts of the world held by a society at large.

MYTH

ANOTHER poem Hope excluded from *The Wandering Islands* although it had been written in 1930, was "The End of a Journey," which considers Odysseus' return home to Ithaca from his peripatetic adventures en route from the Trojan War. The poem was only the first of several accounts Hope would write about the Greek hero. It may be that Hope's own return to Australia from England had triggered an identification with the protagonist of Homer's epic. If that is the case, however, the picture he paints is not necessarily a pretty one. In any event, Hope chose to place the poem first in his *Collected Poems*, so that a paradoxical if not unsettling scenario is established, whereby a narrative about reaching the end—and, what's more, about being disillusioned by what one finds there—serves as the book's initial statement. This maneuver implies that the end is always lurking in every beginning.

The poem opens with Penelope being embraced by her long delayed husband. Rather than the celebrated connubial reunion in which Homer's tale rejoices, however, Hope's poem witnesses Penelope "Raped by a stranger in her sullen bed" (*Collected Poems*, p. 1). The poem emphasizes not the pleasures of reencounter, in the hope of which Penelope had for so many years kept her suitors at bay by unraveling each night the shawl

she wove by day, but instead focuses on the alienation that has grown up between her and her delayed husband during their separation. For his part, Odysseus thinks their first night together "tedious" and is depicted not as the conquering and contented king but as an "old man sleeping with his housekeeper." At dawn he walks outside to survey the carnage he and his followers wreaked when they first got back to find the court crawling with unwanted guests. Yet unlike the original story, where the political and marital usurpers to Odysseus' throne are presented, Hope's version evokes the women that Odysseus slew, each of them now strangled. There is a sense of sexual claustrophobia that permeates the poem. The glory of Odysseus' anticipated return is further diminished in Hope's poem by the memories the warrior rehearses of other women he'd slept with, such as Calypso and Circe, and of the ravages of the war he is now so far away from. Standing on the shore, he considers the sea not as the passage that has finally brought him home, but rather as an enemy that has unfortunately returned him to "the petty kingdom he called home." Instead of feeling that he has been blessed by the gods with safe return, he broods on the dark certainty that the gods have finally abandoned him. He has become, in effect, a lifeless embodiment of the same boredom and regret that many of Hope's other early poems characterized. In a concluding vision about the anticlimactic emptiness of conclusion, Odysseus imagines the Sirens singing to him again, though now the danger they present is not something he mortally dreads but is rather a peril he finds exhilarating. He realizes he has given up the life of a reckless wanderer, only to discover himself all too safely arrived. The song of the Sirens he hears now asks him what had deluded him into thinking he should return. Hope is candid about Odysseus' disillusionment. The hero is hardly a hero any longer but a mere "castaway" on a "cruel" shore, left to "prolong / Stale years and chew the cud of ancient wrong" (p. 2).

It is often the young poet's ploy to anticipate the disenchantment of old age. Eliot had done no less in "The Love Song of J. Alfred Prufrock" especially, written when he was in his early twenties, and in the slightly later "Gerontion." Interestingly, Hope more positively reprised his view of both old age and the Odysseus myth forty-four years later, in his poem "Spätlese," which concludes *A Late Picking: Poems 1965–1974* (1975). There he describes an old man sipping his wine and thinking that the next vintage "will not be too bad" (p. 87). The *spätlese* seems to possess some of the grace the speaker once aspired to as a lad. While he admits that "ripeness is not all," recalling fondly how young men seek perfection and transcendence in a way that older men can no longer fully emulate, he does take heart from the lessons inspired by youth. "Old men should be adventurous," he believes. While this sentiment may indeed be the way Odysseus feels in "The End of a Journey," the difference is that the speaker of "Spätlese" makes good on that sense of adventure—it is, after all, "what old age is really for," he reasons. Hope ends the poem and the book with the image of Ulysses hefting his oar, as if to signal that, whether he really sets out once again or does so only in imagination, the Greek hero has not lost his ardor for rowing into risk. The poem may call to mind Rainer Maria Rilke's observation that while the Bible says the prodigal son returned after years away, it never tells if he actually stayed at home or if he left again.

Hope repeatedly appealed to classical myths and biblical stories in his poems, including those of Apollo and Daphne, Persephone, Pygmalion, Orpheus, Adam and Eve, Lot and his daughters, and Susannah and the Elders. His theory about the significance and relevance of myths is most succinctly elaborated in the poem "An Epistle from Holofernes." The poem claims that myths were used in antiquity as the means for understanding both the universe and an individual's place within it. Myths were also how people renewed themselves, and hence Hope conceives myths as possible modes of salvation. The power of myth is that while it may attempt to account for the ordinary, it does so by recourse to the extraordinary. Consequently, humanity recognizes in mythology both its own mortal status as well as its potential for immortality. According to Hope, myth "confirms / The heart's conjectures"

and protects human emotion and aspiration from "the servile speech of compromise" and from those habits and customs that hide people from themselves (*Collected Poems*, pp. 59–60). Myth is thus a special kind of discourse: it reminds humans that they are human, while simultaneously encouraging them toward transformation. Because myth is an account of the world, and because the world is constantly changing, however, the myths as they have been handed down will not fit today's world without being adapted. Although the seed of each myth may still contain truths that are eternal, it is the poet's task, Hope believed, to recreate the fables and apply them to the present. By reimagining myths, the poet will not merely insure that the myths themselves continue to matter even centuries since they were devised, but he will also elevate his fellow human beings—as all good poetry, according to Aristotle, should do.

WOMEN, SEX, AND LOVE

HOPE has routinely been considered in certain quarters, however, as a poet who, rather than having uplifted his readers with noble subject matter, espoused views that were less than decent, especially regarding women, sex, and love. In "The Unknown Poet," Buckley had put his finger on the wider implications of Hope's divided and divisive poetry within the social climate of the mid-1950s. Buckley claimed that Hope's idiom was "of such a kind that members of the *avant-garde* may feel impelled to dismiss Hope as an incurable traditionalist, while people themselves incurably conservative (rather than traditionalist) may regard him as an experimentalist, a confirmed tamperer with the emotional status quo" (pp. 36–37). While Hope's passage between the intractably traditional and the unemotionally experimental stemmed in part from a few poems that seemed to put their verbal alacrity ahead of their impetus to make sense, Buckley was thinking mostly about the controversial views of sex put forward in *The Wandering Islands*. "The Cheek," for instance, depicts a woman's body, with her breasts, thighs, and straining hips described in unashamedly sensual terms, as a terrain for her lover's erotic explorations. The two-part "Lot and His Daughters" deals with the theme of incest, "Chorale" sees the speaker clasped by a woman who shudders as he joins with her, and "The Lamp and the Jar" witnesses a speaker drawing "from your loins this inexhaustible joy" (p. 54). The ironically titled "Conquistador" tells the more riotous tale of Henry Clay, a humdrum fellow who nonetheless picks up a woman in a bar, fantasizes about his genitals being stewed and eaten by six black virgins, and ends up getting literally squashed when the woman rolls over on him in bed. Perhaps most distressing to some was "Imperial Adam," one of Hope's most famous and anthologized poems. Eve is described as "Sly as the snake" who tempted her and as loosening her "sinuous thighs" to Adam, who takes her "from behind" in a manner similar to the beasts they live among (p. 35). His seed spurts into her, she becomes pregnant, and the final lines ominously announce, "Between her legs a pigmy face appear[s] / And the first murderer lay upon the earth" (p. 36). Though Hope claimed he was having a bit of fun with the ending, various commentators found the poem's trajectory to be nearly sacrilegious or at least unnecessarily shocking.

While Hope was considered lewd or misogynist by many reviewers, who resented his depiction of women as passive and depersonalized, apologists found him refreshingly unconventional and even courageous for putting aside provincial ideas about the modesty in sexual relations and for describing sex in all its physicality. His bawdy barroom catches such as "Three Songs for Monaro Pubs" could be interpreted as either the crass blatherings of a drunken bloke assumed to be Hope himself, or equally as Hope's gutsy rendition of tunes carried by a persona—someone other than the poet—in a raucous scene as it might actually occur. One of the most disputed poems was certainly "The Countess of Pembroke's Dream" from *A Late Picking*, which, as Hope explains in his notes to the volume, follows John Aubrey's account of the sexual exploits of the countess of Pembroke, sister of the poet Sir Philip Sidney. Aubrey's candid narration of

the countess' amorous habits had heretofore met with silence and prudery among literary scholars. In his poem, Hope is frank about the woman's desires and how she acts on them. Despite being brought up in what might be considered proper English fashion, the countess rejects the corseted sixteenth-century conservatism of courtly love sonnets, wondering instead, "What has become of the Prick and Balls?" (p. 30). In her vivid dream she becomes a centaur who is mounted from behind. As the male horse ejaculates, they both give thanks to Zeus for the consummation of their coupling. Hope insinuates that the instinct causing the countess to have such dreams is not an aberration or exception but derives from nature itself. Even Zeus, the poem points out, incarnated himself as a beast in order to participate in often violent sexual acts with mortals. The poem promotes the idea that everyone, despite appearances and the taboos set up by society, possesses animalistic drives. Whether people choose to display those drives or prefer to pretend they don't exist is another matter, but Hope—not unlike Freud—was clearly concerned to be honest about such urges. He saw them not as signs of moral decay but as means of participating in the natural, and naturally renewing, order.

Hope's attention to the relations between men and women, while often sexual, were not always quite so graphic, though, or so close to what some critics might label pornographic. In his 1974 essay, "The Image of Women in A. D. Hope's Poetry," John Docker argued that because older organic communities are no longer accessible due to technology, Hope instead "pitches his search for the analogies between man and the 'womb' of nature on a metaphysical and literary level," in which sexuality with women offers a primordial link to nature, otherwise lost in modernity (Brooks, p. 114). Women become both the way Hope communes with nature as well as how he stages a dialogue with European aesthetic traditions, since the women in his poems are often drawn from mythology or European artworks. According to Docker, women also represent for Hope a connection to both eternity and death. The reproductive cycles of women suggest the endless turn of the seasons, as the earth renews itself repeatedly. As such, they take on the aspect of the muse, source of the poet's creativity and transcendence. In "The School of Night," for instance, the speaker figures a woman's body as his book, and her bed as the nocturnal school in which he studies. The woman finally asks him to read all of her, "translate me to your tongue" (*Selected Poems*, p. 144), so that she becomes both his text as well as his inspiration for imagining further texts. To Hope, the sexual act is also a kind of death, however, or an entrance into oblivion, the end of which is a return to the earth, symbolized by women. The notion that women represent destruction can be gleaned from the title poem to *Antechinus: Poems 1975–1980* (1981), which depicts how the male marsupial *Antechinus stuartii* mates violently with a female counterpart for up to five hours, only to die soon after as a result. This death following such a rough display of life is an "irony no species quite escapes" (p. 18), according to Hope, who admits to recognizing himself in the male mouse's drama.

The major difference between men and women, Hope noted in a review of Judith Wright's *The Two Fires*, is that the experience of men is "that of a creature ephemeral, temporary and incidental in the biological process," while the experience of women is "fundamentally that of the continuity of the biological process" (*Native Companions*, p. 80). If the male poet intellectualizes the world and revolves it in his consciousness, as Judith Wright herself claimed Hope did, Hope believed he must likewise rely upon the vision of women to keep him grounded in reality so that his work would not become stale or wholly cerebral. Whether that is a masturbatory hallucination that gives women short intellectual shrift by framing them as mere vessels for men or as vehicles of sensuality, or whether it is the metaphysical truth Hope believed it to be, had commentators bristling for the better part of his career.

Hope was not unaware of the potential problems inherent in these notions, nor did he neglect to write several poems that problematized his beliefs. "The Double Looking Glass" from *Collected Poems*, for one, while portraying Susannah

as she bathes naked in a pool as the Elders watch her from behind bushes, essentially establishes poetry as an auto-erotic activity, as R. F. Brissenden claimed. The looking glass of the water, in which Susannah sees her reflection, is described as double because it represents both how the world actually is—Susannah in her nakedness—and how it is refracted and refashioned in her imagination. Yet the scene is also appropriated by the voyeuristic Elders, whom Hope implicitly despises for finally interrupting Susannah's solitary moment; for being bald and perhaps repressed compared to Susannah's comfort with her own sexuality, especially as it relates to the nature around her; and for the fact that they will eventually invent a story, as the Bible relates, to have her condemned. Likewise, in "The Damnation of Byron," the final poem Hope left out of *The Wandering Islands* although it had been composed twenty years earlier, he considers the Romantic lover at the end of his days of romancing, or at least at the end of writing about Don Juan's romances. Lord Byron, having exhausted himself on hundreds of women of all sorts, now discovers himself in hell, paying for his carousing with the closing in of sexual terrors and the condescension of all the women he'd known.

Hope believed strongly in both the power of love and the power of art. He attempted to resolve which is the greater in "An Epistle: Edward Sackville to Venetia Digby" from his *Collected Poems*. The two lovers are now separated, Sackville having been exiled, Digby having returned to her husband. Sackville writes to her, aware that his words may either exaggerate the experience of love in their attempt to make it beautiful in retrospect, or else fall flat in their effort to capture the beauty of love in the flesh. On the one hand, he asks her, "What care for silk or lute string who possess / The splendour of your nakedness [?]" (p. 160). No poem, photograph, letter, or work of art could ever do justice to his lover as she used to appear to him in reality. On the other hand, he is left with only memories and, like Hope, wants to trust that art is not useless, that its mystery and ordered arrangement can, in fact, provide consolation and even "Fresh modes of being, unguessed forms of bliss." He concludes that because both love and language come from the same source, Nature, they are related in their ability to dispel chaos and inspire "the comprehending heart" (p. 161). One tongue is for taste, he tells her, while the Speaking Tongue commemorates sensual experience. The two taken together enact a dance, an image that marries eroticism and art.

DRAMA

HOPE wrote two plays, each of them, in its own way, an implicit form of criticism as well as a dramatic narrative. In his preface to *Ladies from the Sea* (1987), Hope notes that Homer's *Odyssey*, while fascinating, has an unconvincing ending. First, Hope is skeptical that Odysseus, upon his return home, could defeat the numerous men hanging around his court in just a minor skirmish, with only a few followers to help, and so easily chase off a large band of angry, armed citizens. More importantly, because these suitors who had visited Penelope during the years her husband was absent were sons of leading princely chiefs in Ithaca and in nearby Greece, it is hard to believe, Hope says, that Odysseus' slaying of them caused so little turmoil in a society bound to the sacred duties of revenge. It seems unlikely that Odysseus would be able to resume his influence in Ithaca as if he'd never left. Hope set out to dramatize what he felt would be a more likely set of conflicts and circumstances confronting Odysseus.

The hero returns to find himself embroiled in a tempestuous political fray. No one in the army has been paid for years, so mutinies are fast becoming a dreadful prospect. A general economic ruin is imminent. Since Odysseus killed most of the women when he got back, there are few remaining to assist as servants. Most alarmingly, the kingdom is under threat from both domestic rebels and foreign attackers, and Odysseus is forced to resort to his wiles and cunning, devising elaborate strategies for preventing civil war and invasion. He spreads rumors, leaks information opportunely, and promises amnesty

for various parties under certain conditions. The play is in part a chance for Hope to recreate Homer's epic and, in doing so, to suggest ways in which the original poem might be improved. In general, it is clear that Homer's foundational myth of wandering, of departure and return, is problematized for Hope, who conceives homecoming less as triumphal than as a confrontation with an entirely new set of dilemmas.

Among those dilemmas for Odysseus is the unexpected visitation by three women whom he had met on his return voyage. Hope takes humorous liberties with the *Odyssey* by having first Calypso, then Circe, and eventually Nausicaa show up in Ithaca. Calypso is looking to reclaim her love and lust with "Oddy," as she calls him, and alienates Penelope by candidly telling her of her husband's infidelity. Since Calypso won't go away, Odysseus decides to advertise her as the queen of a distant state with whom he formed an alliance on his return trip and who has promised military help in case of war. Calypso, however, tries to assist Odysseus in remedying his political quandaries and ends up making a mess by accidentally revealing that she's not, in fact, in charge of a military and by casting spells that wreak havoc. No sooner does Circe arrive from Aiaia, where Odysseus had spent a year and a day. Her intentions are more mature regarding Odysseus, and while she manages to get rid of the ditzy Calypso to help him, it's not before she, too, informs Penelope that Odysseus has been unfaithful with her as well. Just as the coast is finally clear, Circe having lured Calypso away and the kingdom preparing to celebrate, it is announced that Nausicaa has arrived. Hope has added an element of romantic complication to Odysseus' life that was missing from the original version. Even before Nausicaa lands in Ithaca, Penelope has learned that it's what men don't say that is more important than what they do say, and the reader is left feeling that from here, Odysseus will embark on a new adventure to explain and perhaps even atone for his infidelities.

Hope's other play, *The Tragical History of Doctor Faustus* (1982), likewise doubles as a critical enterprise. The subtitle of the work notes that the play written by Christopher Marlowe has been "purged and amended by A. D. Hope." Hope's plan to attempt a restoration of those parts of Marlowe's text that have been damaged or lost began half a century earlier, around 1927, and he first began working on the project while jobless after returning to Australia from Oxford. Hope wanted to rescue the work from interpolators, especially Sir Walter Greg, author of the 1950 "A Conjectural Reconstruction," and supply instead a more likely representation of the original. Yet Hope states in his preface that the damage to the original has been so extensive that he can at best suggest possibilities of what it might have contained. The allure of the play for Hope was quite personal, his preface reveals, since as a young man he'd identified with Faustus in feeling he had wasted his life and misdirected his poetic gift. Yet as Kevin Hart noted in *A. D. Hope*, if the young and unemployed Hope found grounds for seeing himself as Faustean, he discovered different reasons for identifying with Faust as an older poet all too ensconced in an academic setting. By 1982 Hope had been appointed a Library Fellow of Australian National University, been awarded an OBE, been named a Companion of the Order of Australia, and become a member of several prominent literary boards.

Hope saw the play as less a critique of his own life, however, than a sad commentary on the evils and trivialities that too often beset intellectual ambition. Hope believed the play to be no less relevant to his own time period than to the sixteenth century in which it was written. As the chorus observes in act 2, Faustus "lusts to know the secret cause of things" (p. 25) and sells his soul to Lucifer in exchange for twenty-four years of knowledge and pleasure. Hope's series of notes at the end of his version explain that even after Faustus has made his bargain with the devil's messenger Mephostophilis, he continues to wrestle with good and evil. The play's dramatic tension, according to Hope, relies on Faustus' feisty and ever-active conscience, preventing him from actually enjoying any of the delights promised by Mephostophilis, which are in any case less extensive than Faustus had been led to believe. He is not, for instance, privy to knowledge of paradise or indeed of anything contrary

to the kingdom of hell. This is because, as Mephostophilis states in act 3, scene 5, ever since Adam was expelled from Eden for his transgression, nobody, "but he die the death, / May stand upon that blessed ground and live" (p. 62). Like Adam and Eve before him, Faustus has tasted the forbidden fruit, and as a result he is prevented from further access to divine mysteries unless he surrenders to God. Faustus does attempt repentance several times throughout the play, but as Hope's commentaries note, Faustus is too quickly and easily swayed away from hope of God's forgiveness by the threats Mephostophilis levels. Hope's intellectual interest in the play logically followed his preoccupation with John Milton's *Paradise Lost*, his own earlier poetic efforts to recast biblical narratives of pride and punishment, and his similar renditions, in poems like "Prometheus Unbound," of mythological hubris and damnation. His attention to the play also related to his poems such as "Toast for a Golden Age" that address even secular themes about the danger in—and the dismay caused by—seeking knowledge at any cost.

SATIRE AND CRITICISM

HOPE'S critical views on literature and culture and his comments on the state of contemporary criticism took more explicit and more vitriolic forms than those contained in *Faustus*. Hope was particularly fond of the genre of satire, especially as it had been practiced by Jonathan Swift and Alexander Pope, the eighteenth-century author of the mock epic *The Dunciad*. Hope's own "Dunciad Minimus" made the rounds among friends and associates in the 1950s after having been written as a private joke and as a mere exercise in a literary form he felt was no longer being taken seriously, but it was eventually revised and published as *Dunciad Minor: A Heroick Poem* in 1970. In his preface to that work, Hope explains that his idea for a satire originated when A. A. Phillips denigrated Pope's writing during one of the ABC's radio series of literary talks, "Standard Works I'd Like to Burn," a show on which Hope had also appeared. Hope considered Phillips a friend and generally admired him as a critic, pointing out, however, that whereas Phillips adopted the Romantic view, he himself inclined towards neoclassicism. But "we are both old-fashioned enough to take this debate seriously," Hope wrote (p. viii), and he felt he ought to repay the senior English master of Wesley College in kind. They corresponded over the matter of Hope answering Phillips with a satire, an idea Phillips encouraged. The work was ultimately dedicated to Phillips. Hope believed that despite their antithetical positions, each of them regarded their function as the service of literature, unlike other current critics that Hope would take to task in the work itself. Figures such as F. R. Leavis, William Empson, Northrop Frye, T. R. Henn, Kenneth Burke, Allen Tate, and others Hope felt treated literature as something to be exploited and drowned in extraneous material and deleterious explication. Hope admitted that his poem was perhaps "the protest of a poet against the arrogance of the professor who shares his body" (p. x).

Like Pope's *Dunciad*, Hope's *Dunciad Minor* is written in rhyming couplets, and he makes his attacks with the same degree of mockery. He establishes Arthur Angell Phillips, great grandson of one Ambrose Philips who had found his way into Pope's poem, as the long-lost Heir to Dullness. Hope even appends a foreword, purportedly written by Ambrose Philips, as well as annotations that Philips and Phillips supposedly collaborated in writing. The younger figure is constantly put in the position of having to ask his elder relation what certain phrases are references to or what they mean, so that a humorous sort of conversation develops within the footnotes. The mock hero is described as "dauntless and dumb" (p. 11), certainly not intelligent enough to pick up on the many allusions to *Paradise Lost*, the *Inferno, Absalom and Achitophel, King Lear*, and other Shakespearean plays, and the *Iliad, Aeneid*, and *Odyssey*. Eventually the Goddess of Dullness adopts Phillips as her own, directs the "epic ass" (p. 20) to blaspheme and act pedantically and rudely on a radio show, and finally allows him to ascend the Throne of Dullness, where he burns the work of Pope. Not before Hope, however, has dismantled the state of modern criticism. He

laments how the criticism once propounded by the likes of William Hazlitt, Walter Savage Landor, Samuel Johnson, Matthew Arnold, Walter Pater, John Ruskin, and others has been replaced by boorish and inferior movements such as New Criticism, Aestheticism, Realism, Psychology, Social Theory, Marxism, and Bibliography. Hope documents that criticism now puts the horse of endless irrelevant critical theories ahead of the cart of literature. The newer critics, who pursue Research at the expense of true scholarship and parade their academic regalia, are depicted as machinelike pseudoscientists and as vultures who feed on the carcasses of dead writers. The Funeral Games they play insure that "all authors, good or bad / Soon lose what meaning they might once have had" (p. 53).

Hope regretted that not only had an earlier stage of outstanding and upstanding criticism been overrun by what he considered to be faddish methods of approaching and denigrating literature, but also that satire itself, as a mode of poetry, had fallen by the wayside. Hope believed that the death of the so-called great poem had begun in the seventeenth century, with the advent of the novel, and that thereafter people's attention spans and tastes no longer attuned them to the epic, to tragedy, or to satire. Paralleling that downward slide, once poets had begun writing poetry purely concerned with their own private obsessions, with no thought given to its instructive components or to its noble history as the art that at one time had spoken for society, they soon lost all knowledge of the grand forms altogether. Hope documents this distressing scenario in his lengthy poem "Conversation with Calliope" from *Collected Poems*. A conversation between Hope and the epic muse, the poem charts the dissolution of the epic, which flourished during Homer's time as an instrument of teaching and leadership, but which began to fail in Milton's age. Daniel Defoe's invention of the novel drove away heroism and heroic diction, as an appreciation for poetic invention dwindled along with interest in long narratives. The "sacred truth" and "moral passion" upon which the epic had staked its reputation belonged to "former centuries" and have since been replaced by prose, which Calliope calls "the small beer of private lives" (p. 180). Hope, through the persona of Calliope, characterizes this waning of the epic as a Fall, claiming that it began when society ended its ancient covenant with the divine. Thereafter, no common faith remained. Hence epic had neither ground in which to take root nor an audience that would find it appealing.

Hope did find sustenance in the mock epic poetry of authors such as Pope and John Dryden, however. He admitted in his essay "The Satiric Muse" in *The Cave and the Spring* that satire may have less claim to being pure poetry than other types of poetry, since a poem is a poem not by virtue of what it sets out to do but by virtue of what it is, and satire sets out to criticize. Yet Hope felt that satire nonetheless had an extremely important role to play, not merely within the bounds of letters but pertaining to the world at large. Unabashedly aristocratic, satire does not shy away from telling truths that, while crucial to a society's moral and intellectual progress, are not always popular with society, since those truths can often be uncomfortable. Hope argued for a renewal of interest in satire on the grounds that it is a public poem that performs a public service. Satire "keeps the public conscience alert," he claimed, and "exposes absurdity for what it is and makes those who are inclined to adopt foolish or tasteless fashions aware that they are ridiculous" (p. 66). Rather than being a direct personal attack on individuals, however, satire "shows vice its own feature and makes it odious to others." Hope was certain that if absurdity could be adequately and appropriately depicted via the public forum that satire provides its properties would speak for themselves.

The decline in public sensibility for works of a public nature, Hope felt, also mirrored the hypertrophy of cultural consciousness in general. When Hope wrote in *Dunciad Minor* that the "climate of the mind at last had changed" (p. 31), he was not speaking solely of the way in which the great forms of poetry had been neglected over time, to be replaced by parochial concerns couched in undisciplined lines. He meant that a phenomenon had occurred whereby, alongside the "dissociation of sensibility" that T. S. Eliot had likewise detected in literature, society had begun to slide away from its moral imperatives and foundation in nature. What was once a golden age was now, according to Hope, reduced to mere culture, as Man is separated from men. Hope hinted at this in "Conversation with Calliope" when the epic muse warned that where once there had stood a vineyard, soon there would be a Coca-Cola factory.

DIONYSUS, APOLLO, AND ORPHEUS

WINE is the preferred drink of Dionysus, and certainly one angle of Hope's work has been considered Dionysian in its love of wine, women, and the mystery of the written word. This Romantic aspect of his poetry hailed largely from the English tradition. Among those to whom Hope owed a debt was Samuel Taylor Coleridge, whose facility for what he himself termed "esemplastic" power, or the ability to fuse and reintegrate disparate images through the imagination, Hope praised repeatedly. Hope likewise tipped his hat continually to Keats and particularly to the notion of "negative capability," or the poet's capacity for remaining in doubt and mystery and for making himself characterless in an effort to embody numerous characters. Chris Wallace-Crabbe has repeatedly called attention to Hope's negative capability, claiming it is one of the resources that make his poetry so spunky and unpredictable, if not one of the reasons responsible for the curious rub between Hope's sometimes bland criticism and his more violent poems. In his 1988 essay "True Tales and False A like Work by Suggestion," Wallace-Crabbe has also suggested a possible link between Hope's interest in negative capability and his problematic but fruitful relationship to Symbolism, since "The impersonality of the symbolists can attract him, but not their sustained indeterminacy" (Brooks, p. 214). Hope's various personae, especially Odysseus and Faustus, attest to an interest in negative capability, an impersonation act he learned also from Browning. Another of Hope's personae, of course, was Don Juan, the consummate cosmopolitan and lover, so that Byron, too, played a significant role in forming the Romantic impulses in Hope's work. In addition, Hope was drawn to the poetry of Yeats, who combined his Romantic flights of feeling with a public discourse that Hope found lacking, for instance, in Wordsworth. And while he would not have considered himself a visionary, Hope found a visionary model in Blake.

The curious relationship between Romanticism and Symbolism is one to which Hope devoted a good deal of thought. In *A Book of Answers* (1978), for instance, he was of two minds regarding Stephan Mallarmé. The nuance and descriptive indirectness of the nineteenth-century French Symbolist poet, he claimed, was a kind of mere puzzle or game that "led a whole generation of poets into a wasteland of rather pointless obscurity" (p. 73). On the other hand, Hope was willing to concede at the same time, "Nevertheless, a poet of genius can triumph over the most perverse theory and succeed in making it work, and it is perhaps the greatest of Mallarmé's gifts that he was able to do so." Hope's critical support of Romanticism, then, often redeemed what he perceived to be flaws in the Symbolist approach. Elsewhere, however, his championing of Romantic individuality took a back seat to his admiration for Eliot's theory of impersonality and for the chameleonic impersonations effected by writers such as Shakespeare and Emily Brontë. These sometimes contradictory dynamics aside, Hope broadly conceived both Romanticism and Symbolism together, as "the latest forms of a second great intellectual tradition in Western civilisation" (*Native Companions*, p. 151). Both were powerful and influential, he admitted, though neither could claim to be "the main tradition." The "minor" tradition they represent views humanity as having lost the knowledge and vision it once possessed, or as on its way to acquiring them.

Hope clearly saw himself as aligned more to the main tradition. Despite his penchant for inventing heroes, his belief in the strength of genius to improve society, and his conviction that art was a viable means of transcendence, Hope was less comfortable acknowledging his Romantic tendencies—and certainly less keen to claim more than a slim inheritance from the Symbol-

ists—than he was to privilege his neoclassical or Apollonian heritage. His poem "A Letter from Rome" is an overt statement of this allegiance to classical antiquity. Its speaker travels to Italy, called the "*fons et origo* of Western man," where he hopes to recover something since lost to humanity, namely, a sense of the timeless, especially as it manifests itself as a link with a primordial past (*Collected Poems*, p. 142). Yet even here Hope's assertions of the "single, sure, tradition" (p. 146) represented by the city of Rome are not without complications, since the search for a lost origin is precisely what Hope claimed was the provenance of the "minor" tradition in literature. Likewise, as Paul Kane has argued, there is nothing particularly un-Romantic about a search for origins, and Hope was most characteristically Romantic precisely when seeking origins through an exploration of myth, erotic love, art, and the self. Hope's various travels to Greece (Hope began learning Greek in 1973), Italy, France, England, Portugal, and Spain during the latter half of his life undoubtedly reconnected him to the European tradition in profound ways, however. His excursions to other countries, such as the United States, Canada, Egypt, India, Malaysia, and Pakistan, could only have served to bring the European tradition into greater relief, while also expanding his already enormous range of affinities for international writing. He had a particular interest in Russian poetry, having translated Osip Mandelstam and Anna Akhmatova, each in their own way representative of an Apollonian line.

Hope possessed enormous trust in the rational mind and its ability to order art beyond puzzles and games. He maintained likewise a sympathy for the intellectual endeavors of the Augustan Age and the Enlightenment, as his eleven narrative poems in *The Age of Reason* (1985) demonstrate. Some of those same poems, though, also evidence that the so-called Age of Reason was not always so much reasonable or rational as passionate and filled with foible, nor the Enlightenment as enlightened as it was possessed by the demon of progress. "Man Friday" and "Sir William Herschel's Long Year" warn against the dangers of ambition and the overconfidence that science can replace the visionary truths of myth with empiricism. Such hubris was as much a result of Romanticism and its Promethean desire to steal the fire of the gods, Hope believed, as it was indicative or constitutive of the Age of Reason itself. Hope argued in several essays that no poet could claim a synoptic or accurate view of the universe without taking into account the discoveries of modern science, though he also took pains to caution readers of the demises science can wreak upon nature.

Hope was not so much a natural conservationist, however, a title more befitting his contemporary Judith Wright, as a conservationist of the literary landscape. He often lamented the erosions he perceived within the fragile ecology of literature—an analogy he frequently employed—and in this way may be thought to have been conservative. Yet Hope maintained a radical faith in the ability of literature, no less than of nature itself, to undergo constant rejuvenation. He claimed he did not, for example, subscribe to prophecies of doom as he felt they'd been promulgated by Eliot and others. The more fitting characterization of Hope as a poet may be not classical/Apollonian or Romantic/Dionysian but, as Kevin Hart has suggested, Orphic. Hope's final collection, *Orpheus* (1991), published in his eighty-fifth year, speaks to the sense in which, as Hart puts it, poetry does not compete with science so much as make it possible. In Hope's conception, poetry does not merely protect nature or even add to its resources. Poetry, which comes from nature, also serves to complete the natural order. Moreover, poetry does so by creating a new order, a "fire-bird language" (p. 6). Hope's aspiration was that the poet would be set not apart from society but within it, so that he might change it for the better from inside. "[O]f all our poets," wrote Judith Wright, "Hope has thought most about the task of poetry" (Brooks, p. 89). This much is implied in "Australia," in which Hope begins by regretting his nation's lack of poetry, architecture, and history, but which ends with the speaker gladly returning home from Europe, away from the "learned doubt, the chatter of cultured apes / Which is called civilization over there" (*Collected Poems*, p. 13). Hope

recognized in Australia some "spirit" which escapes the clutter of modernity, a spirit grounded in the rivers and deserts of the land where he was born.

Hope died on 13 July 2000, in Canberra, at age ninety-two.

BIBLIOGRAPHY

I. POETRY. *The Wandering Islands* (Sydney, 1955); *Poems* (London, 1960; New York, 1961); *Collected Poems 1930–1965* (Sydney, 1966; New York, 1966); *New Poems 1965–1969* (Sydney, 1969; New York, 1970); *Dunciad Minor: An Heroick Poem* (Melbourne, 1970); *Collected Poems 1930–1970* (Sydney, 1972); *Selected Poems* (Sydney, 1973); *A Late Picking: Poems 1965–1974* (Sydney, 1975); *A Book of Answers* (Sydney, 1978); *The Drifting Continent and Other Poems* (Canberra, 1979), the text of this limited edition pamphlet, illustrated by Arthur Boyd, is reprinted in *Antechinus*, without the illustrations; *Antechinus: Poems 1975–1980* (Sydney, 1981); *The Age of Reason* (Melbourne, 1985); *Selected Poems*, ed. by Ruth Morse (Manchester, 1986); *Orpheus* (Sydney, 1991); *A. D. Hope: Selected Poetry and Prose*, ed. by David Brooks (Sydney, 2000).

II. DRAMA. *The Tragical History of Doctor Faustus: By Christopher Marlowe, Purged and Amended by A. D. Hope* (Canberra, 1982); *Ladies from the Sea: A Play in Three Acts* (Melbourne, 1987).

III. MEMOIR. *Chance Encounters (With a Memoir of A. D. Hope by Peter Ryan)* (Melbourne, 1992).

IV. CRITICISM. *The Structure of Verse and Prose* (Sydney, 1938); *Australian Literature 1950–1962* (Melbourne, 1963); *A Midsummer Eve's Dream: Variations on a Theme by William Dunbar* (Canberra, 1970; New York, 1970); *The Cave and the Spring: Essays in Poetry* (Adelaide, 1965; Sydney, 1974; Chicago, 1974); *Native Companions: Essays and Comments on Australian Literature 1936–1996* (Sydney, 1974), includes Hope's early reviews of Helen Heney's *Dark Moon* and Mary Gilmore's *Fourteen Men*, from the ABC, of Kenneth Slessor's *Poems* from *Bulletin*, of John Pengwerne Matthews' *Tradition in Exile* from *Dalhousie Review*, of Max Harris' *The Vegetative Eye* and Miles Franklin's *Joseph Furphy: The Legend of a Man and His Book* from *Meanjin Papers*, of John Ingamells' edited *Cultural Cross-section*, Victor Kennedy's *Flaunted Banners*, John Ingamells' and Rex Ingamells' *At a Boundary Gate*, and Ian Mudie's *This Is Australia* from *Southerly*, of David Martin's *From Life*, John Thompson's *Thirty Poems*, Nan McDonald's *The Lonely Fire*, Patrick White's *The Tree of Man*, Judith Wright's *The Two Fires*, and selected *A Book of Australian Verse*, and Roland Robinson's *The Feathered Serpent* from the *Sydney Morning Herald*; *Judith Wright* (Melbourne, 1975); *The Pack of Autolycus* (Canberra, 1978); *The New Cratylus: Notes on the Craft of Poetry* (Melbourne, 1979); *Directions in Australian Poetry* (Townsville, 1984).

V. INTERVIEWS. Peter Kuch and Paul Kavanaugh, "Daytime Thoughts about the Night Shift," *Southerly* 47, no. 2

(1986); Ruth Morse, *A. D. Hope. Selected Poems*, tape recording (Broadbottom, 1988).

VI. BOOKS, ESSAYS, AND REVIEWS CONCERNING A. D. HOPE. Arthur Phillips, "The Cultural Cringe," in *Meanjin* 4 (1950); Geoffrey H. Hartmann, "Beyond the Middle Style," in *Kenyon Review* 25, no. 4 (1963); Gustav Cross, "The Poetry of A. D. Hope," in Geoffrey Dutton, ed., *The Literature of Australia* (Middlesex, 1964); David Kalstone, "Two Poets," in *Partisan Review* (Fall 1967); Chris Wallace-Crabbe, "Three Faces of Hope," in *Meanjin* 26, no. 4 (1967); "Un-Australian Activities," review of *New Poems 1965–1969*, in *Times Literary Supplement* (23 July 1970); William Jay Smith, review of *New Poems 1965–1969*, in *American Scholar* (Winter 1970); R. F. Brissenden, review of *New Poems*, in *Southerly* 30, no. 2 (1970); John Hollander, review of *New Poems 1965–1969*, in *Harper's Magazine* (September 1970); Daniel Hoffman, "A Poet's Prose and Poetry," in *New York Times Book Review* (21 February 1971); Edwin Webb, "Dualities and Their Resolution in the Poetry of A. D. Hope," in *Southerly* 32, no. 3 (1972); Suzanne Graham, "Myth and the Poetry of A. D. Hope," *Australian Literary Studies* 7, no. 2 (1975); Ross Metzger, "Alienation and Prophecy: The Grotesque in the Poetry of A. D. Hope," in *Southerly* 36, no. 3 (1976); David Kirby, review of *A Late Picking*, in *Times Literary Supplement* (7 April 1978); Bruce King, "A. D. Hope and Australian Poetry," in *Sewanee Review* 87, no. 1 (1979); Leonie Kramer, *A. D. Hope* (Melbourne, 1979); A. L. McLeod, "Maturity in Australian Satire: The Poetry of A. D. Hope," in *Modern Language Studies* 10, no. 2 (1980); Noel Macainsh, "The Suburban Aristocrat: A. D. Hope and Classicism," in *Meridian* 4, no. 1 (1985); Neil Corcoran, review of *Selected Poems*, in *Times Literary Supplement* (22 August 1986); Paul Kane, review of *The Age of Reason*, in *Antipodes* 1, no. 1 (March 1987); Claude Rawson, review of *Selected Poems*, in *Times Literary Supplement* (24 July 1987); Vivian Smith, "Experiment and Renewal: A Missing Link in Modern Australian Poetry," in *Southerly* 47, no. 1 (1987); R. S. Gwynn, "A.D. Hope," in Frank N. Magill, ed., *Critical Survey of Poetry: Supplement* (Englewood Cliffs, N.J., 1987); Kevin Hart, *A. D. Hope* (Melbourne, 1992); Walter Tonetto, *A. D. Hope: Questions of Poetic Strength* (New Delhi, 1993); Paul Kane, "A. D. Hope and Romantic Displacement," in his *Australian Poetry: Romanticism and Negativity* (New York, 1996); Robert Darling, *A. D. Hope* (New York, 1997); David Brooks, ed., *The Double Looking Glass: New and Classic Essays on the Poetry of A. D. Hope* (Queensland, 2000), includes seminal essays or excerpts from larger works by Vincent Buckley (1957), S. L. Goldberg (1957), James McAuley (1961), Judith Wright (1965), R. F. Brissenden (1974), John Docker (1974), Humphrey McQueen (1979), David Malouf (1980), H. P. Heseltine (1988), Peter Steele (1988), Jennifer Strauss (1988), Chris Wallace-Crabbe (1988), Fay Zwicky (1988), Kevin Hart (1990), Ann McCulloch (1990), and David Brooks (1991); Chris Wallace-Crabbe, "Savage and Scarlet: A. D. Hope: Selected Poetry and Prose," in *Australian Book Review* 220 (May 2000).

VII. BIBLIOGRAPHIES. Patricia O'Brien, *A. D. Hope: A Bibliography* (Adelaide, 1968); Joy W. Hooten, *A. D. Hope* (Melbourne, 1979).

David Jones

(1895–1974)

Scott Ashley

ONE OF THE formal devices David Jones favored was that of the slowly unraveling and frequently rhetorical question. Readers new to the work often end up asking a couple of questions themselves. Are the two full-length books on which his reputation largely rests, *In Parenthesis* and *The Anathemata*, and the fragments collected in *The Sleeping Lord* and *The Roman Quarry* best described as poetry or prose? Because Jones is typically classified by critics, anthologists, and (perhaps most importantly) bookstores as a poet, the first-time reader of Jones can only be surprised to find that almost all of *In Parenthesis* (1937) and a significant part of *The Anathemata* (1952) is in prose. Or just what place does Jones occupy in the wider tradition of British and European writing in the twentieth century? In 1961 T. S. Eliot, Jones's friend and patron, hinted at some of the difficulties both critics and readers have had in placing the work of David Jones: "[it] has some affinity with that of James Joyce (both men seem to me to have the Celtic ear for the music of words) and with the later work of Ezra Pound, and with my own. I stress the affinity, as any possible influence seems to me slight and of no importance" (*In Parenthesis*, pp. vii–viii). But if critics and reviewers have accepted the first half of Eliot's reading and happily ushered Jones into the arms of "high modernism" (although Eliot's triad of affinities has been expanded to embrace a whole range of writers), the cautious note sounded in the second remains.

Thankfully, Jones himself provides plenty of information for preliminary answers. As to what kind of writer David Jones was, a reading of his reflections on the poetic art suggests that the terms are perhaps not quite the right ones. To understand his literary self-perception it is vital to bear in mind that Jones's original vocation had been as an artist, and that he retains a major reputation in Britain as a painter, illustrator, calligrapher and engraver at least equal to his poetic fame. Like the poets of late medieval Scotland, and particularly William Dunbar of whom he was especially fond, Jones liked to think of himself less as a writer than as a "maker," stressing the essential analogies between the literary side of his career and his activities in the visual arts. Profoundly influenced by the assumptions of the late Victorian and Edwardian arts and crafts movement mediated through the Christian ideas of his friend the sculptor Eric Gill, Jones transcended (or neatly sidestepped, depending on the perspective) the generic distinctions of "poetry" or "prose" in favor of the writing as object, seeing himself less as a writer than as a "carpenter of song," a suggestive phrase borrowed from the bards of medieval Wales and used in a radio lecture in 1954.

Which brings readers to the second of the preliminary questions: If Jones identified himself with medieval writers can he also be understood through traditions of twentieth-century writing? Something of Jones's originality and allusiveness can be discerned from the fact that real disagreement continues to divide critics, particularly about Jones's relationships to literary modernism. To many of his friends and personal admirers, Jones was an "original," a man whose work, as Eliot indicated, bore affinity with the modernist work of James Joyce, Ezra Pound, and Eliot himself, but which was largely created independently of it and achieved something different from it. Both the work itself and Jones's remarks on its making provide plenty of evidence to support this position. After *The Anathemata* was published Jones felt it necessary to send several explanatory letters correcting the assumptions of critics and reviewers that he owed a rather large debt to Pound and Joyce. Several readers (the most eminent of which was W. H. Auden) had related the new book to Pound's *Cantos*, while *In Parenthesis* had since the time of its publication been compared to Joyce's Ulysses. Jones responded, "I can *quite* see *why* chaps think *I. P.* and the *Anathemata* are based stylistically on Joyce and Pound, but it happens not to be historically true" (*Dai Greatcoat*, p. 189). Jones always insisted that prolonged exposure to Pound and Joyce had come after his own works, not before. Rather than influence, Jones preferred to think in terms of "the whole conditioning civilizational situation into which one was born that determines the 'form'" (p. 190).

But if Jones always felt himself to be somewhat outside the main trends of literary modernism few academic critics have had much doubt that his work firmly belongs in this august company. In his conception of his later work as a set of fragments, in the analogies he made between different branches of the arts and objectification of the poem or writing as "thing," in his use of masks, dialect and patois (particularly in the Cockney voices of his Roman and British soldiers) for the authorial persona to hide behind, in his suspicion rising to hatred of the modern world and its ways, critics have convincingly been able to talk of the author of *In Parenthesis* and *The Anathemata* in the same breath as William Carlos Williams, Hugh MacDiarmid, Basil Bunting, and Geoffrey Hill, never mind Pound and Eliot. In other words, Jones has, despite his own protestations, proved co-optable into the history of the long modernist poem or poetic sequence in the English language.

LIFE

Walter David Jones was born on 1 November 1895 in Brockley, Kent, of a Welsh father and an English mother. James Jones, a printer by trade, had been born in Holywell, Flintshire, in the northeastern corner of Wales in 1860, an area that through the early Middle Ages had been contested between the English kingdom of Mer-

cia and the Welsh princes. That it definitively ended up as a part of Wales after 1149 was of no small significance for David Jones (the Walter was soon dropped), as he was to note in 1954: "Had that twelfth-century recovery not occurred the area around Holywell would have remained within the Mercian zone of influence. In which case its inhabitants would, centuries since have become wholly English in tradition, nomenclature and feeling. ...You see by what close shaves some of us are what we are" (*Epoch and Artist*, p. 25). By the criteria of language, birth and cultural upbringing Jones was implacably English, yet during the course of his life he successfully reinvented himself as a Welsh writer, and it is with Wales that he is most often associated today. The accidental and provisional (and hence malleable) nature of national identity was clear to Jones from an early age.

In the early 1880s James Jones came to London, where in 1888 he married Alice Ann Bradshaw, the daughter of a mast and ship's block maker from Rotherhithe in Surrey. Although the elders of the Jones family had been Welsh speaking, James Jones had been encouraged to speak English by his family in Holywell and reportedly had only a weak grasp of the ancient language of Wales and was unable to pass on any knowledge of it to his three children. Yet as a child David Jones and his family seem to have regularly returned to Wales to visit relatives, visits which Jones was to remember many years later with affection. In his early years it was perhaps his mother who had the greatest impact, encouraging his evident skill at drawing animals (she herself had been an artist before her marriage) as a counterweight to his slowness in learning to read and his resultant backwardness in more academic subjects. In 1910 he was sent to the Camberwell School of Art, where he was introduced to the classics of the European visual tradition, including the originally third century B.C. statue of the Dying Gaul that was to become an important symbol in his personal mythology, as well as to some of the postimpressionist developments of modern art (his tutor had known both Vincent Van Gogh and Paul Gauguin).

Jones was reaching the end of his time at Camberwell and was pondering his future without much enthusiasm when Britain declared war on Germany. In January 1915 Jones joined the Royal Welsh Fusiliers and left for France in December of that year. His first experience of the western front was to the south of the Ypres Salient, before his division was moved in early 1916 to take part in the major offensive planned for the summer. Jones did not see action on the first day of the Battle of the Somme, 1 July, when the British army suffered sixty thousand casualties before the German wire, the most disastrous twenty-four hours in its history. But on 10 July, with casualties still averaging ten thousand a day, Jones's battalion was sent into action to capture the heavily defended Mametz Wood. Although the wood was taken, early the next day, during a German counterattack, he was badly wounded in the leg and evacuated to the rear and then back to England.

Jones returned to the trenches in October 1916 and would have seen action in the equally murderous Passchendaele offensive of 1917 had he not been temporarily posted to a reserve unit before the battle. In February 1918 he was invalided from France with severe trench fever and after a spell of service in the west of Ireland was demobilized in 1919. Initially, and perhaps surprisingly, he wished to re-enlist in the army as a professional soldier, but with parental encouragement eventually accepted a place at the Westminster School of Art, where he became increasingly influenced by postimpressionist art theory and Roman Catholicism. In 1921 he left the Church of England and became a Roman Catholic, before joining the spiritual-artistic community at Ditchling in Sussex under the aegis of the sculptor and theoretician of Catholic arts and crafts Eric Gill. It was at Ditchling and then at Capel-y-Ffin in the Black Mountains of Wales between 1924 and 1928 that Jones began to paint and draw seriously, met his life-long friend René Hague (Gill's son-in-law) and was introduced to the work of the Catholic philosophers Maurice de la Taille and Jacques Maritain that were to provide him with the basic tools for his own aesthetic theories linking the practice of the artist

with the Christian sacraments. In 1924 Jones was engaged to Gill's daughter, Petra, but it was broken off by her three years later and he never married. Jones's apparent lifelong celibacy has given rise to some speculation about his sexual tastes, and while his heterosexuality seems beyond any doubt, biographical investigations, especially by Thomas Dilworth, have seen a sexual, possibly oedipal, neurosis behind his two major breakdowns of 1933 and 1946–1947.

Although Jones continued to visit Gill and his extended kin group, based in Buckinghamshire after leaving Capel-y-Ffin, by the late 1920s he had achieved a level of success and artistic confidence independent of his sometimes-domineering mentor. In 1928 he was elected to the Seven and Five Society, whose membership boasted many of the talents of British avant-garde art, including Ben and Winifred Nicholson, Barbara Hepworth, Henry Moore, John Piper, and Christopher Wood. And in the same year (or perhaps slightly earlier), in a house rented by his parents at Portslade near Brighton, he began to write what would eventually become *In Parenthesis*. His circle of acquaintances broadened too, meeting several artistic patrons and a number of intellectual and politically engaged Catholics in London, including Harman Grisewood and Tom Burns who were to become two of his closest friends and confidantes. But in 1933, after a period of intense artistic and literary effort, he experienced the first of his major nervous breakdowns and was whisked away by Burns to Cairo and then to Jerusalem to convalesce. Although Jones's lassitude and hypochondria while in Palestine frustrated Eric Gill who happened to be in Jerusalem on a carving project (reportedly Jones laid in bed all day reading Anthony Trollope), it was there that he saw British soldiers patrolling the streets of the city evoking in his mind Roman legionaries at the time of the Crucifixion. This recognition of the past in the present laid the foundations for *The Anathemata* and indeed for all of Jones's later work.

Through a mixture of poverty and an inability to take decisive action concerning the direction of his own life (the two are not unconnected—he refused to sell many of the paintings that would have provided him with a good income) David Jones never lived in a house he could call his own. On his return to England in 1935 he moved to Sidmouth in Devon and began that ferrying between boarding houses, hotels, nursing homes, and friends that would characterize the rest of his life. The late 1930s proved to be intellectually fruitful for Jones, however, even if some of the directions taken look in retrospect naive, possibly dangerous. While *In Parenthesis* was finished around 1934 it was not published until 1937, to immediate success, winning the Hawthornden Prize in 1938. He began new work utilizing his experiences in Jerusalem, provisionally to be called *The Book of Balaam's Ass*, and he continued to draw, paint, and produce illustrations and engravings. But Jones's intimacy with the group of intellectual and radically conservative Catholics based around Tom Burns and his brother in Chelsea also encouraged political explorations. He became heavily influenced for a time by Oswald Spengler's *Decline of the West*, found good things to say about Adolf Hitler's *Mein Kampf* (although he was both alarmed and disturbed by the hatred he found there) and lauded what he and the "Chelsea group" saw as the anticapitalist stance of the Nazis in an essay, "Hitler," still unpublished in its entirety. While much of this was perhaps genuine ignorance and naïvete on the part of Jones and his friends, and he would admit his errors of political judgement after the war, the extent to which fascist ideologies continued to determine the content of the later poems is still a live subject among scholars and friends of Jones.

In June 1940 he made an odd choice and moved to London—odd because of the widespread bombing of the capital expected and experienced in that summer. Yet through the early 1940s he continued to be artistically productive, making some of his best-known paintings and inscriptions, writing a number of important essays and beginning the work that would lead to *The Anathemata*. But after bouts of illness over a number of years in 1946 he experienced the second and more serious of his nervous breakdowns and moved to Harrow, to the northwest of London, where he was to remain for the rest of his life. The causes of this collapse are being seriously investigated by scholars: it is often assumed that old traumas originating in the First World War came back to haunt Jones, but Dilworth has drawn attention to his therapeutic reading of Sigmund Freud's *Totem and Taboo* in 1947 and Jones's somewhat cryptic notes on his sexual crises.

Despite pronouncing himself cured after seven months, Jones became increasingly reclusive (though not by all accounts unsociable, continuing to make new friends), perhaps suffering from a mild form of agoraphobia. By 1952 *The Anathemata* had been quarried out of the vast meditation on the relationships between art and sacrament, past and present, that made of the later work one vast work-in-progress. Although the book found some good reviews and won the Russell Loines Memorial Award for poetry in the United States in 1954, poetic fashions in Britain were changing and it was less well received than *In Parenthesis*. While public honors came his way (a major retrospective of his art was organized at the National Library of Wales and the Tate Gallery in London in 1954–1955, he was made a Commander in the Order of the British Empire in 1955 and received an honorary D.Litt from the University of Wales in 1960), essays and radio broadcasts for the British Broadcasting Company, increasingly on Wales and the Welsh tradition, a selection of which appeared as *Epoch and Artist* in 1959, constituted Jones's main literary statement over the course of the next decade. But fragments of the work from which *The Anathemata* had come continued to appear and Jones the poet reemerged onto a wider scene in 1967 when William Cookson's *Agenda* magazine published their first David Jones special issue, collecting together six of the nine works that would make up *The Sleeping Lord and Other Fragments*. In 1970 Jones experienced a minor stroke and was moved to the Calvary Nursing Home in Harrow. He died on 28 October 1974, the same year *The Sleeping Lord* finally appeared in book form and he was made a Companion of Honor by the Queen Elizabeth II. Editing and publishing of Jones's manuscripts and occasional pieces has continued after his death, especially under the aegis of his friends Harman Grisewood and René Hague. The most important of these are *The Dying Gaul and Other Writings* in 1978, a selection of prose pieces, and *The Roman Quarry and Other Sequences* in 1981, containing the unpublished sections of the long-abandoned Book of Balaam's Ass and of the unfinished and probably unfinishable work-in-progress.

IN PARENTHESIS

DAVID Jones tells readers that in "1927 or '28 in a house at Portslade near Brighton, from the balcony of which I used to make paintings of the sea, I began to write down some sentences which turned out to be the initial passages of *In Parenthesis*" (*Epoch and Artist*, p. 30). A first draft of the book was complete by August 1932, and the final text essentially finished by 1934 when Jones experienced the first of his major breakdowns and was taken to Egypt and Palestine. It is this period that is in many ways more relevant to understanding the context of *In Parenthesis* than the moment at which it finally made its long-delayed public appearance. From the perspective of 1937 *In Parenthesis* appears to be a belated child of the vogue for war memoirs current a decade or so earlier, a work that looks back to an older war when a new one is already beginning to cast its shadow over Europe. Yet to see it as in essence a production of 1928 to 1932 is to place it among some august company indeed: Edmund Blunden's *Undertones of War* (1928); Robert Graves's *Goodbye to All That* (1929); Erich Maria Remarque's *All Quiet on the Western Front* (1929); and Siegfried Sassoon's *Memoirs of an Infantry Officer* (1930). It took about a decade for the experience of many of the soldiers who had fought in the First World War to be distilled into literature, to become available for memoir. But when it did become available the works came in profusion, and *In Parenthesis* was very much one of them.

But this is to assume that *In Parenthesis* is a book that takes Wilfred Owen's famous declaration as its own: "My subject is War, and the pity of War." And this is indeed the context in which the work has been read by a whole range of eminent critics from John H. Johnston to Paul Fussell and Jon Silkin. Yet David Jones himself suggested a very different way of understanding what he had written: "I did not intend this as a 'War Book'—it happens to be concerned with war. I should prefer it to be about a good kind of peace" (pp. xii–xiii). The book is about the war because it was his experience to be a private in an infantry regiment—he had not been part of a good kind of peace. If *In Parenthesis* is a war book it is one only by default, and Jones has other ambitions than to provide a realistic account of several months spent on the western front.

A bald summary of "what happens" in the book may obscure this central fact of *In Parenthesis*, structured as it is around the experiences of Private '01 Ball (a thinly disguised mask for Jones himself) between December 1915 and July 1916. On the surface the book follows Ball and his battalion from base camp in England, through the departure for France and journey into the trenches of the western front, to the climactic attack on Mametz Wood on the Somme where Ball is wounded in the legs as his comrades are killed around him. Within this broad narrative Jones details the language and everyday experiences of the infantryman in the First World War, from the secretive and clannish world of the battalion signalers to the local cafe with its menu of egg and chips and cheap beer, from the Cockney slang of the common soldier to the almost ritualistic quality of the words of command. This attachment to the locally real facilitates the reader's acceptance of the last lines of the book with its statement of its own truth and the veracity of its author: "The geste says this and the man who was on the field …and who wrote the book …the man who does not know this has not understood anything" (p. 187). But what truth has the man who was on the field and who wrote the book expressed? In one of the most controversial and best known critiques of *In Parenthesis*, Paul Fussell, in his *The Great War and Modern Memory*, has asserted the fact that the work fails, albeit honorably, to express anything at all of the shocking reality of the First World War: "The tradition to which the poem points holds suffering to be close to sacrifice and individual effort to end in heroism; it contains, unfortunately, no precedent for an understanding of war as a shambles and its participants as victims" (pp. 146–147).

Whether or not this reading happens to be true, Fussell's analysis draws attention to Jones's almost obsessive use of literary tradition in the work. For any plotline sketch fails to register the fact that the incomparably rich underlying geology of the book is formed around a dense series of references to other books, beginning with the Bible and Catholic liturgy, before running through a British (as opposed to an exclusively English or Welsh) literary tradition taking in the sixth-century epic, *Y Gododdin*, Sir Thomas Malory and Arthurian legend, through to Sir James Frazer's anthropological myth making in *The Golden Bough* and T. S. Eliot's *The Waste Land*. This literariness is seen with particular clarity in the boast of Dai Greatcoat in part 4 of *In Parenthesis*, when a veteran, a survivor from the old professional army of 1914, suddenly begins to speak in a mythic cadence, "articulating his English with an alien care":

My fathers were with the Black Prinse of Wales
at the passion of
the blind Bohemian king.
They served in these fields,
it is in the histories that you can read it, Corporal—boys
Gower, they were—it is writ down—yes.
    Wot about Methuselum, Taffy?
I was with Abel when his brother found him,
under the green tree.
I built a shit-house for Artaxerxes.
I was the spear in Balin's hand
            that made waste King Pellam's land.

(p. 79)

Dai Greatcoat then goes on to relate how he has served with King Saul of Israel, fought in Julius Caesar's invasion of Britain, campaigned with King Arthur across the island of Britain, provided guard duty with the Roman legions at the Crucifixion, "was in Michael's trench when bright Lucifer bulged his primal salient out" (p. 84). It is this literariness that provokes Fussell's irritation: in his eyes the First World War was qualitatively different from all wars that came before, and cannot be threaded into the braid of history no matter how skillful the weaver.

Whether the war fought between 1914 and 1918 was precedented or not is a question that must be left to historians to argue over. But Elizabeth Ward has countered Fussell by arguing that only if *In Parenthesis* is read primarily as a war book, which Jones preferred it not to be, might the traditional and epic elements prove problematic. Despite being written three years and a nervous breakdown after the completion of the main text, the 1937 preface to the work provides a clarificatory function, suggesting that Jones saw his real subject lying behind the war, as the malaise in modern civilization, with the war being merely its symptom. Jones saw his work as an act of resistance to the mechanization and impersonality of the modern age and an articulation of the dilemmas of a poetic language working within that modernity, for it "is not easy in considering a trench-mortar barrage to give praise for the proper action to chemicals—full though it may be of beauty" (p. xiv).

In the preface Jones is ironically close to Paul Fussell in regarding the war from mid-1916 as being wholly new, as being on the far shore of a rubicon crossed during the Somme campaign. Yet rather than writing about that newness, Jones instead concentrates on the months from December 1915 to July 1916 when he believed something could still be felt of earlier wars, of "a less exacting past," before the "wholesale slaughter of the later years, the conscripted levies filling the gaps in every file of four, knocked the bottom out of the intimate, continuing, domestic life of small contingents of men" (p. ix). Jones fought against the violent claims of modernity not by exposing them, as a Wilfred Owen or a Siegfried Sassoon might have done, but by showing how deep-rooted alternatives to transience and destruction existed, even within the nightmarish world of the trenches. As the Royal Welsh Fusiliers move into the front line at night, even then "like some unexpected benignity …you know the homing perfume of wood burned, at the termination of ways; and sense here near habitation, a folk-life here, a people, a culture already developed, already venerable and rooted" (pp. 48–49). It is the genealogy of this precarious folk-life that Dai Greatcoat recites at such length; but is already nearing its end, receiving its mortal wound on the field of battle at the end of the book. Although the end is not quite the end, for as Malory removed King Arthur to Avalon, so Jones has the Queen of the Woods, who covers the dead with boughs and berries, searching in vain for "Dai Greatcoat, she can't find him anywhere—she calls both high and low, she had a very special one for him" (p. 186).

The possibility of survival and hence renewal remains a possibility that in retrospect has come to assume a problematic tinge. For it is this dissatisfaction with the trends of Western industrial—capitalist civilization and the belief that the modern world could be redeemed in a millennial future by the organic spirituality and values of folkish communities that has led Elizabeth Ward to brand Jones's work as fascist. For along with the Chelsea group of Catholic intellectuals that Jones associated with during the writing of *In Parenthesis*, he undoubtedly saw Hitler and the Nazis in Germany as the political force most likely to bring about this revolution in European society. There have been several critics quick to defend Jones from these charges, most notably Thomas Dilworth, who has been able to show that Jones had plenty of personal doubts about Hitler and felt uneasy about what he saw as the racial obsessions and hatreds of the Nazis. He has also drawn attention to that fact that several of Jones's post–Second World War poems seem explicitly to criticize the Nazi regime, leading Dilworth to claim that Jones was never really interested in their essentially political solutions to what he saw as a cultural problem. Yet the critics are to some extent talking past each other: Ward does not accuse Jones of being a Nazi, but of being sympathetic to a naïve English Catholic perception of Italian and German fascisms as spiritual back-to-the-land movements, preferable to a British liberal democracy deeply complicit with capitalist power, undoubtedly linked in Jones's circle with "international Jewry." But while it is clear that *In Parenthesis* does favor

the local, the spiritual and the organic, and can replace empirical reality with aesthetic spectacle (a characteristic of totalitarian regimes throughout history), these elements are neither dominant nor unquestioned within the text. Despite its very real flirtations with fascist themes, *In Parenthesis* does not seem to be a fascist poem.

If an aestheticization of combat does indeed take place in *In Parenthesis* then it is precisely the Queen of the Woods episode that can be pointed to as a prime site where the process takes place. Yet an alternative perspective can be gained from reading historically the role played by woods in the work as deriving from Jones's interest in one of the central mythic books of the late nineteenth and early twentieth centuries: James Frazer's *The Golden Bough*. First published in 1890 and expanded to twelve volumes by 1913, Frazer's work provided a potent scheme for understanding the postwar world for a whole range of thinkers and writers, including T. S. Eliot, D. H. Lawrence, and William Butler Yeats. Encapsulated in the bloody central image of the ancient Italian priest-king who murdered his predecessor and would in turn be murdered in the holy wood of Nemi by the man who plucked the golden bough from the tree sacred to the goddess Diana, Frazer articulated a timely vision of violence and irrational savagery underlying civilized Europe.

As part of her critique of his entire works, Elizabeth Ward has seen in Jones less a coherent and informed historical consciousness than a simplistic application of abstract formulae to the diverse realities of the past. Jones's emotional acceptance of Frazer's myth in *The Golden Bough* might be seen as an example of this privileging of formulae over experience; yet the framework of the book also allowed Jones to develop a vision of the infantryman as victim, despite the claims of Paul Fussell that *In Parenthesis* lacks such an understanding. From the opening pages of the book, even before they see action, Private Ball and his comrades are represented as Frazerian scapegoats, ritual beings used to expiate the sins of the community as a whole, the fleece coats issued by the army for protection against the northern French winter turning them almost literally into lambs for the slaughter. The biblical texts that Jones placed on the last page of the book follow Frazer's anthropological vision, with the Lamb of God, the scapegoat of the ancient Israelites and the crucified Christ casting mythic shadows back over the dead of both sides. And it is in "the twisted wood beyond" that Ball observes through his periscope in the fourth part of the work that the sacrifice of Mametz Wood is foreshadowed: "Keep date with the genius of the place—come with a weapon or effectual branch—and here this winter copse might well be special to Diana's Jack, for none might attempt it, but by perilous bough-plucking" (p. 66). And in the final hallucinatory pages of the book, as the remnants of the Royal Welsh Fusiliers are bombarded by German artillery, Mametz Wood does indeed begin to metamorphose into the grove at Nemi:

in the tangled avenues
    fair Balder falleth everywhere
and thunder-besom breakings
bright the wood
and a Golden Bough for
Johnny and Jack
and blasted oaks for Jerry
and shrapnel the swift Jupiter for each expectant tree
(pp. 177–178)

The men who died in the wood, whether as ordinary soldiers or as the scapegoats of modernity, have their "bright boughs of various flowering" at last cut for them by the Queen of the Woods, the tutelary spirit of the place, their bodies crowned with the berries, flowers, and branches that crashed down on them as the bombardment shredded the trees.

But even if, despite humane intentions, such literary strategies do risk turning real human life into abstract formulae, if "Mr. X adjusting his box-respirator" is sometimes equated too insistently with Shakespeare's "young Harry with his beaver on" (p. xiv) as Fussell has argued, Jones never totally submitted to the seductions of his mythic method. He never forgot that when a soldier was gassed or blasted by shrapnel this was death that came with a speed and on a scale that the traditional forms, whether of the old

Welsh bards, of Sir Thomas Malory, or of the Christian Church, could not cope with, had no response to:

The First Field Dressing is futile as frantic seaman's
  shift bunged to
stoved bulwark, so soon the darking flood percolates
  and he dies in your
arms.
    And get back to that digging can't yer—
this aint a bloody Wake
            for these dead, who soon will have their dead
for burial clods heaped over.
      Nor time for halsing
nor to clip green wounds
nor weeping Maries bringing anointments
neither any word spoken
nor no decent nor appropriate sowing of this seed
nor remembrance of the harvesting
of the renascent cycle
and return
nor shaving of the head nor ritual incising for these
viriles under each
tree.
    No one sings: Lully lully
for the mate whose blood runs down.
(p. 174)

Apart from the Anna Livia section of James Joyce's *Finnegans Wake*, one of the few canonical modernist texts David Jones recognised as a direct influence on his own work was Eliot's *The Waste Land*, and there are references to this earlier poem throughout *In Parenthesis*. Jones first met Eliot in 1930 when *In Parenthesis* was already very much in progress, with the older poet coming to act as a patron and champion for the work. But it is the literary rather than the personal power of Eliot that remains of importance. For if *In Parenthesis* bursts out of the war book genre and has greater ambitions, those ambitions are at least partly those of *The Waste Land*. Both use a mixture of biblical, Arthurian, and anthropological texts to juxtapose past with present cultures, to indict the spiritual aridity and self-destructive character of modern civilization. And his incorporation of debris from these texts within his narrative surely owes something to the most famous line in the whole of Eliot's poem: "These fragments I have shored against my ruins."

But if *The Waste Land* towers over *In Parenthesis* both in its influence and reputation, Jones was able to inch out from under the shadow. For there is a hope of renewal in Jones; Dai Greatcoat escapes the slaughter. Mythic pasts do not only articulate the sterility of the modern wastelands of the western front and Western civilization. Rather, as Jon Silkin has noted in *Out of Battle*, Jones found himself "gathering deposits of understanding with which to withstand, and help others to withstand, the stresses of war and turn it into a better kind of peace" (p. 340). If no one sings Lully lully over the dying and if Dai Greatcoat has disappeared back into the legends from which he first emerged, the memory of them remains. Jones proves to be less a pupil of the Eliot of the early 1920s than a contemporary of the Eliot meditating *Four Quartets*.

THE ANATHEMATA

IN 1971 David Jones described to his friend, the Welsh nationalist and writer Saunders Lewis, the sights of Jerusalem that had most impressed him. After a space of some thirty-five years a glimpse of British soldiers in the city still remained vivid:

> "Gotta gasper, mate? ...Thanks, what a sod of a place." It might have been a rain-soaked Givenchy duck-board track-way instead of a sweltering Hierosolyma by-street .... [but] the riot-shields aligned to cover the left side and in each right fist the half-grip of a stout baton, evoked not the familiar things of less than two decades back, but rather of two millennia close on, and the ring of the hob-nailed service-boots on the stone sets and the sharp commands,—so they were a section from the Antonia, up for duties in Hierosolyma after all!
>
> (*Agenda* 12, no. 1, p. 23)

This imaginative alliance between soldiers of the British army engaged on police duties in twentieth-century Palestine and Roman legionaries engaged in police duties in first-century Judaea in some ways provides the key to an understanding of the whole of Jones's later work. For if *In Parenthesis* brought Arthurian knights and medieval Welsh heroes into the trenches of the western front, the work from *The Anathemata*

onward sought to abolish earthly temporal distinctions completely, fusing past and present together in a sacramental time focused on the sacrifice enacted by Christ on the cross and reenacted in the Catholic Mass. In poems like "The Wall," "The Dream of Private Clitus," "The Fatigue," and "The Tribune's Visitation" those Roman legionaries who are also, simultaneously, British Cockney squaddies come into their own; readers shall return to them in the next section. Yet as a near contemporary of these poems *The Anathemata* undoubtedly dramatizes the same kind of slippages between eras and places but on a vaster scale as befits the epithet most often bestowed on it: epic.

There is no doubt that *The Anathemata* is a difficult work; too difficult for many critics, who have both questioned its integrity as a project and generally regarded it as inferior work to *In Parenthesis*. This inverts Jones's own estimation of it as excelling the earlier book in the way the efforts of a mature master overshadow his own apprentice pieces. Opinion generally splits between those who knew Jones personally, or who have identified their poetic or critical careers closely with his work, who tend to see *The Anathemata* as the greater achievement, and those with more general interests who do not. But all agree that the work is difficult for the first-time reader, lacking the strong narrative thrust provided by the war in *In Parenthesis*; it also resists easy summary as to what it is actually "about," as Jones himself admitted. T. S. Eliot claimed that it would take at least three careful readings before making any kind of sense at all; it is no accident that almost every page comes with explanatory footnotes. The poet-critic Tony Conran has described the book as having the look of a work of academic scholarship, with explanatory glosses, plates, and critical introduction, and the analogy is a good one.

Jones makes it explicit in the subtitle that *The Anathemata* is merely made up from "fragments of an attempted writing"; what can now be read "represents parts, dislocated attempts, reshuffled and again rewritten intermittently between 1946 and 1951" (p. 15). Yet later in the same introduction Jones admits that the work "has themes and a theme even if it wanders far. If it has a unity it is that what goes before conditions what comes after and *vice versa*" (p. 33). Like many modernist works, such as Joyce's *Finnegans Wake* and Pound's *Cantos*, the internal movement is cyclical rather than linear. Despite Jones's independence from Pound the two works share much: both place sea voyagers in prominent positions, Pound beginning the whole work with the voyage of Odysseus, while Jones gives a central role to a number of voyagers to the island of Britain, including Phoenicians from the eastern Mediterranean and Anglo-Saxons from Denmark and northwestern Germany. Structurally both eschew narrative in favor of the periodic recurrence of a number of themes, some kind of coherence coming from their gradual emergence and complication as the book progresses. The disorientation this can induce in some readers means a description of the shape of the work, no matter how simplistic and selective this might appear to those more experienced in the complexities of Jones's poetics, is of primary importance.

Part 1 ("Rite and Fore-Time") begins with the figure of the Christian priest celebrating Mass, focusing in on the Crucifixion on the hill of Calvary of which the Mass is an act of *anamnesis*, or recalling. The notion of the hill shifts focus to other famous hills from the past, including Hissarlik on which stood the city of Troy, and the geological epochs that have laid low and will raise up the hills and mountains of the world. This primeval perspective opens up Jones's first main theme, that all humans, from as early as Neanderthal man and the first Homo sapiens, because of their facility as makers of art and users of signs (makers and users of "anathemata" in Jones's terminology, hence the title) are recalled and included within the grace of God shown forth in the Catholic Mass. For through all the geological layers in which their remains are fossilized:

From beyond all time
                       the New Light beams for them
and with eternal clarities
                   infulsit and athwart

the fore-times:

            era, period, epoch, hemera.
                          (pp. 73–74)

Part 2 ("Middle-Sea and Lear-Sea") moves from pre-history into the literary worlds of legend and history itself, with the Crucifixion again providing the axle around which historical time turns. A wide panorama of the ancient world narrows onto the first contacts between the Mediterranean cultures and that of the island of Britain in the shape of the sea voyage of a Phoenician merchant ship to the tin mines of southern Cornwall. In their devotion of the sailors to their maiden goddess the Phoenicians prefigure the community of the Christian Church. Part 3 ("Angle-Land") continues the theme of the foundational sea voyage, this time that of an Anglo-Saxon long ship into the mouth of the River Thames and up the eastern coast of a Britain poised between the last vestiges of the Roman Empire and a revived Celtic culture. Part 4 ("Redriff") shifts attention from the sailors to the men of the shore, specifically Eb Bradshaw, mast maker, David Jones's maternal grandfather, who delivers a monologue describing how he will not skimp on repairs to any Phoenician ship. The shifts in both time and symbolism typical of *The Anathemata* are in evidence in this seemingly slight section: the late Victorian Bradshaw becomes a contemporary of the Phoenician sailors; the wood of the mainmast is subtly transfigured into the wood of the cross.

The monologue is developed in grand fashion in part 5 ("The Lady of the Pool"), where the central "character" is a mythic female who appears as a lavender seller in the streets of late medieval London while also having about her suggestions of a number of goddess-muse figures. She gives to the Phoenician captain a wandering mythical history of the City of London based upon her insight that "What's under works up" (p. 164). Taking up themes already broached in earlier sections, the Lady tells how pagan cultures underlie the Christianity enacted in the churches of the city, just as a lost Roman city lies beneath the modern one and as the strata of geology underlies them all. But her approach to history is essentially an uncertain one, built on doubt and shifting sands rather than truth and solid rock:

> Though there's a deal of subsidence hereabouts
>   even so:
>   gravels, marls, alluviums
> here all's alluvial, cap'n, and as unstable as
>   these old annals
> that do gravel us all.
>
>   (p. 164)

Part 6 ("Keel, Ram, Stauros") develops and complicates some of the imagery from earlier in the work, finding in the symbol of wood the possibilities of ship's keel, battering ram, and religious idol, and transcending all the wood of the cross. The Phoenician ship is seen for the last time, its fabric now clearly a metaphor for the Church, its helmsman a kind of priest. In part 7 ("Mabinog's Liturgy") Jones returns to the Crucifixion as the basis for human, historical time. Like in "The Lady of the Pool," female characters dominate, especially Gwenhwyfar, wife of the Romano-British commander Arthur, and prototype of the Queen Guinevere of the later medieval romance tradition. The liturgical rituals of the Catholic Mass provide the central shape of the section, linking together ancient pre-Christian religion, the death of Christ and the Christmas Mass enacted in North Wales and in the City of Rome:

>   ...the Magian and the Apollinian word
> that shall make of the waiting creatures, in the
>   vessels on the board-
> cloths over the Stone, his body who said, DO THIS
>   for my Anamnesis.
>   By whom also this column was.
> He whose fore-type said, in the Two Lands
>   I AM BARLEY.
>   (pp. 204–205)

The eighth and final part ("Sherthursdaye and Venus Day") figures Christ, through the medium of his self-sacrifice (both of himself and to himself, the Son to God the Father), as the freer of waters: "VNVS HOMO NOBIS / (PER AQVAM) / RESTITVIS REM ['One man, by water, restores us to our state']" (*Anathemata*, p. 238). With the act of the Crucifixion represented

as potential regenerator of the wasteland of the modern "megalopolitan" culture, the Mass assumes its momentous place as the act literally and physically recalling that earlier sacrifice; in the last lines of the work divine and secular history, the past and the present, and the diverse geographies of the world meet:

> He does what is done in many places
> what he does other
>   he does after the mode
> of what has always been done.
> What did he do other
>   recumbent at the garnished supper?
> What did he do yet other
>   riding the Axile Tree?
>   (p. 243)

Using Jones's own imagery, a bald summary of a work as complex as *The Anathemata* can only map the surface features, little of the underlying geology. Nevertheless, the grand themes of the work are, in themselves, relatively clear and in many cases are developed out of ideas already present in *In Parenthesis*. For example, the importance of queens, mothers, and goddess figures in the later work grow out of the Queen of the Woods in the earlier. Equally, the attachment to a pan-British literary tradition, identified most closely by Jones with that of post-Roman and medieval Wales, continues and is developed. Jones's characteristic ideas about language are most fully worked out in the preface to *The Anathemata* and in the essay of 1955, "Art and Sacrament": that content and form must be fused as in postimpressionist art; that the making of signs, either in writing or in the Christian Mass, is a sacramental activity that make us truly human; that the poet must attempt to find the fullest possible significance for each individual word, despite modern alienation from the mythic deposits of the past and the poetic impoverishment of modern formulae such as H2O beside the traditional "water." Yet Jones had earlier sought a form of ritual or sacramental language, "a primitive creativeness, an apostolic actuality, a correspondence with the object, a flexibility" (*In Parenthesis*, p. 28), for his soldiers on the western front. Indeed, his theories on language, art, and the Christian sacraments had crystallized in the early 1920s, long before he even began writing. And while *In Parenthesis* is in part an act of remembrance for those who fought both in the First World War and in past wars real and imagined, *The Anathemata* takes remembrance as its central subject. Or as Jones termed it *anamnesis*, that is, the physical recalling in the present of things from the past, the foundational act of which is the Catholic Mass, effectively representing the Last Supper of Christ and the disciples.

One of the key images to unlock the meaning of the work occurs in the "Mabinog's Liturgy" section, where a Romano-British priest reads from the Bible at Christmas Mass. But his Gospel book is a palimpsest; it has older texts beneath it:

Just where, in a goodish light, you can figure-out the ghost- capitals of indelible eclogarii, rectilineal, dressed by the left, like veterani of the Second, come again to show us how, from far side shadowy Acheron and read
IAM REDIT . . VIRGO
...IAM REGNAT APOLLO

(p. 219)

The Latin quotation is from Virgil's fourth *Eclogue* ("Now returns the virgin / Now reigns Apollo"), a poem believed in the Middle Ages to prophesy the birth of Christ. In Jones's imagination human culture itself is a palimpsest, like the landscape and the book built up of layer upon layer of work, of belief, of society. Celtic, Roman, and Germanic cultures lie beneath the visible world of Britain, occasionally and unexpectedly forcing their way to the surface. Long genealogies of what Jones call sign-makers trail back into prehistory connecting modern day artists and poets with the Palaeolithic cave painters of Lascaux, with the primeval Briton found in 1822 in South Wales, buried with rites before the last Ice Age. And remembering his *Golden Bough* Christianity is foreshadowed for Jones by fertility cults, by dying gods since human history began. But, and it is the critical qualification to this great chain of existence, Christ's Crucifixion on Calvary is the event to which all previous history looks forward and all present times should look back. Unlike the Lady of the Pool's careful "you never know, captain / you never know, not with what you might call metaphysical certainty,

captain: out phenomenology is but limited, captain" (p. 164), the priest who reads the palimpsest can be sure that the Gospel "wonder-tale" is also a "true historia" (p. 220). The biblical text is written on top of and supersedes (while not completely erasing) Virgil. While celebrating diversity there is no place for true relativism in the scheme of *The Anathemata*: the multiplicities of time and place are ultimately reconciled and united under the divine light of Christian revelation.

THE SLEEPING LORD

AT the heart of *The Anathemata* lies a profound disillusionment with modern life, with what Jones called megalopolitan civilization, an homogenizing, utilitarian, and ultimately impoverishing state antipathetic to the world of art and the rooted and historic cultures celebrated in his work. Most of all this technocratic tendency, opposed to what Jones termed the world of signs, threatened the universality and centrality of the Christian liturgy by isolating and alienating the nonutilitarian maker (which can include both artist and priest) from the rest of society. This politics came to dominate both Jones's poetics and his critical writings from the 1940s to the end of his life. The poems gathered into *The Sleeping Lord* historicize this into an opposition between the Roman Empire, a state that embraces the utilitarian fact, the mass produced, the technical, a tedious universality, against the local, the differentiated, the rooted folk cultures identified with the Celtic peoples clustered at the edges of the classical world. And yet it is in the Cockney voices of the Roman legionaries doing sentry duty on the wall of Jerusalem that those British soldiers stationed in Palestine found themselves affectionately portrayed. David Jones hated what empire stood for in the abstract and what politicians gained from it in terms of worldly riches; "robbery is conterminous with empire" was his guiding principle, derived from St. Augustine of Hippo (*The Anathemata*, p. 85). But his own experiences on the western front made him identify throughout his life with the foot soldiers, the cannon (or javelin) fodder who are swept up by all great empires and turned into instruments of oppression.

Something of this ambiguity can be seen in two poems that Jones himself identified as companion pieces, "The Tribune's Visitation" and "The Tutelar of the Place." In the first of these an officer of the Roman army makes a surprise visit to his command stationed in Palestine sometime in the early first century A.D. Assuming something of the character of prophet, he tells them the unpalatable truths of empire:

> It's the world-bounds
> we're detailed to beat
>   to discipline the world-floor
> to a common level
>   till everything presuming difference
> and all the sweet remembered demarcations
>   wither
> to the touch of us
>   and know the fact of empire.
>
> (pp. 50–51)

But to achieve this world dominion the tribune recognizes that he and his men must begin by killing the love for origins, for memories of Italian localities inside themselves, must privilege the cold facts of the immediate over the poetical longings for tradition. A new kind of universal fraternity may grow out of a world empire, but it will be a sham, an empty masquerade of life, defined by the necessity of service to Caesar, to power. This will never replace the "remembered things of origin and streamhead, the things of the beginnings, of our own small beginnings," but these things have now been swallowed up by a world-state and must be killed if that state is to prosper (p. 51). It hardly needs to be pointed out that Jones is writing less of the historical realities of the Roman Empire than of late imperial Britain, with its bureaucracies, nationalized industries and institutions, and materialist ethics.

"The Tutelar of the Place" provides an answer of a sort to the lessons of "The Tribune's Visitation." Here Jones hymns the goddess who is both lover and mother of "place, time, demarcation, hearth, kin, enclosure, site, differentiated cult"

(p. 59), finding in the multiplicity of language and terminology a way towards worship:

> from tower'd *castra*
> paved *civitas*
> treble-ramped *caer*
> or wattled *tref*
>   stockaded *gorod* or
>   trenched *burh*
>
> from which ever child-crib within whatever enclosure
> demarked by a dynast or staked by consent
> wherever in which of the wide world-ridings
>   you must not call her but by that name
> which accords to the morphology of that place.
>
> (p. 61)

The poem then modulates into a long prayer to "Sweet Jill of the demarcations," invoking her as a defense against the "bland megalopolitan light" (p. 63).

Jones specifically calls on the goddess to protect the organic economies of Europe (and it is of Wales that he is thinking especially) in "all days of *Gleichschaltung*, in the days of the central economies" (p. 63). The specific use of the German term is of interest—it was used by the Nazis to describe the ordering of all aspects of cultural and political life through the institution of the party—and has been a major weapon in the hands of critics seeking to show that Jones's work is free of any taint of fascism. As with *In Parenthesis* the case remains open. Jones clearly lost whatever sympathy he had for Hitler and the Nazis after 1939 and the philosophy that underpins all of the later work is not one that can be aligned with the centralizing and technocratic regime of Nazi Germany. There is no doubt that Jones was appalled as news of the Holocaust seeped into British public consciousness as the war neared its end. However, he continued to espouse anticapitalist, antimodern visions after the war, the nativist and organic forms of community that undeniably attracted much right-wing support in the 1930s and which it was mistakenly believed Hitler would inaugurate. And if the central economies might be taken to refer to the Soviet Union, might it not also allude to the social democratic landscape of 1950s Britain as it appeared to a conservative Catholic, suspicious of even the slightest whiff of socialism? It is well documented that liberal parliamentary democracy was seen as the ultimate evil among the right-wing circles Jones involved himself with in the 1930s; their attitude to Britain's post-1945 Labour government was predictably suspicious. If David Jones abandoned Hitler as the savior of Europe, this does not mean that he abandoned the attitudes and opinions that had led him to a qualified respect for Nazism in the first place.

"The Tutelar of the Place" gains in complexity however because transcending the heterogeneity of the world stands that single goddess herself, many-in-one. The fault line dividing the tribune's vision and the prayer to Sweet Jill runs not between singularity and plurality but between a singularity that incorporates and dissolves difference and one which embraces and encourages it. And even in the midst of prayer for rooted and diverse cultures the tribune's statement that they are already moribund is accepted: "Though they shall not come again because of the requirements of the Ram with respect to the world plan, remember them where the dead forms multiply, where no stamen leans, where the carried pollen falls to the adamant surfaces, where is no crevice" (p. 63). Yet just as Dai Greatcoat disappeared, who knows where, from the slaughter in Mametz Wood, so the possibility is held out that a secret seed may survive deep underground from which regeneration can spring. Throughout his life Jones was drawn to the figure of the eternally Dying Gaul, embodied in the famous sculpture of the same name, who would never quite die. In the essay he wrote on the subject in 1959 it was to James Joyce that he looked for the seeds of vitality, finding in his writings "an art-form in which the Celtic demands with regard to place, site, identity, are a hundred-fold fulfilled" (*Dying Gaul*, p. 58). The war may have been lost long ago, but resistance of a sort still went on in the mountains.

But this "politics" (if it can be called such, in that it provides no possibility for individual action) achieves its fullest and finest expression in the poem that gives *The Sleeping Lord* its title. "The Sleeping Lord" itself is probably the finest expression of Jones's attraction to the culture of

medieval Wales, and a work that is identifiably of a part with some of the sections of *The Anathemata*. The themes are again geology and archaeology, the idea of strata of culture laid down like sediment that may be lost or may be mined, and the role of the Christian rite in recalling all that have gone before. But the dominant myth is a secular one, exemplified in the figure of the Sleeping Lord, a figure identified with the increasingly ruined land of Wales itself. The mining for coal in the valleys of South Wales has brought the technocratic values into the heart of the rooted economies, physically wounding the Lord himself. For Jones has rethought the question of whether the king is made for the kingdom or the kingdom made for the king by suggesting that the kingdom might actually be the king:

> Is the configuration of the land
>   the furrowed body of the lord
> are the scarred ridges
>   his dented greaves
> do the trickling gullies
>   yet drain his hog-wounds?
> Does the land wait the sleeping lord
>   or is the wasted land
> that very lord who sleeps?
>
>   (p. 96)

Wales is not the setting for myth as in some of Jones's most famous paintings, such as *Vexilla Regis* (1947) or *Annunciation in a Welsh Hill Setting* (1963); the land has become the myth. And it is from the Sleeping Lord who is also Wales that the last movements of a dying culture turn into the first stirrings of a new: "are the stunted oaks his gnarled guard / or are their knarred limbs / strong with his sap?" (*Sleeping Lord*, p. 96). As the mines dig deeper in their pollution and destruction of the land so they risk waking the Lord. As the English soldier stationed in the Welsh marches who hears a something on the night wind admits, echoing the Lady of the Pool, "you never know *what* may be / — not hereabouts" (p. 96). The mountains might literally be a place of resistance to the power of megalopolitan empire.

THE place of David Jones in the canon of British poetry remains an ambiguous one. His major books remain in print, at least a few pages of standard histories of the poetry of the twentieth century are devoted to him, and he has become an accepted presence in retrospective anthologies. But despite these very real achievements his work as a writer remains largely unread, even by those with real knowledge of the century's poetry. Students are unlikely to encounter him, even in courses that laud his contemporaries and admirers. A modest critical industry has flowered in the years after his death, but despite several distinguished contributions it has failed to make much impact on a wider literary community.

Among the reasons for this obscure fame Jones's self-conscious insularity and love of Celtic and Arthurian myth must rank highly. Poetic trends in post–Second World War Britain have not been kind to Jones's project. Certain high-profile poets of the 1950s, known to literary history as "the Movement," reacted strongly against what Philip Larkin called "a common myth-kitty," perceived to be a form of pretension and an insulation against fresh perception rather than a means toward it. The continuing presence of Larkin's suburban muse in British poetry has certainly rendered Jones's work unfashionable. Equally detrimental to his reputation has been a growing internationalism in British poetry, a looking toward the United States in particular, and a shying away from anything that hints of nationalism or an advocacy of roots and origins.

And yet, like the Dying Gaul or the Sleeping Lord, his books do maintain their precarious hold. The part his work played in the modernist movement attracts readers with a taste for the avant-garde and experimental, who find in him an international allegiance much stronger than the largely conservative forms preferred in mainstream poetry. And with the dominance of England within Britain now being effectively challenged both politically and culturally, his so-called insularity, his allegiance to the whole of the *insula* of Britain, begins to look like a great and prophetic strength. If, to adapt the words of Donald Davie, David Jones preferred *Y Gododdin* to Dante and recognized Welsh and the other Celtic languages as tongues of the island alongside English, then his work "is more notable for what it disconcertingly invites in than what it comfortably shuts out" (*With the Grain*, p. 233).

SELECTED BIBLIOGRAPHY

I. SEPARATE WORKS: POETRY. *In Parenthesis* (London, 1937; New York, 1961); *The Anathemata* (London, 1952; New York, 1963); *The Sleeping Lord and Other Fragments* (London, 1974 and New York, 1974); *The Roman Quarry and Other Sequences*, ed. by Harman Grisewood and René Hague (London and New York, 1981).

II. SELECTED WORKS. *Introducing David Jones: A Selection of His Writings*, ed. by John Matthias (London, 1980); *Selected Works of David Jones*, ed. John Matthias (Cardiff, Wales, 1992); *David Jones, A Fusilier at the Front: His Record of the Great War in Word and Image*, ed. by Anthony Hyne (Bridgend, Wales, 1995).

III. PROSE. *Epoch and Artist: Selected Writings*, ed. Harman Grisewood (London, 1959); *The Dying Gaul and Other Writings*, ed. by Harman Grisewood (London, 1978).

IV. LETTERS. *Letters to Vernon Watkins*, ed. by Ruth Pryor (Cardiff, Wales, 1976); *Ten Letters to Two Young Artists Working in Italy, Juliet Wood and Richard Shirley Smith*, ed. by Derek Shiel (London, 1976); *Letters to William Hayward*, ed. by Colin Wilcockson (London, 1979); *Letters to a Friend*, ed. by Aneirin Talfan Davies (Swansea, Wales, 1980); *Dai Greatcoat: A Self-Portrait of David Jones in His Letters*, ed. by René Hague (London, 1980); John Mathias, "Letters to Jim Ede," *PN Review* 22 (1981); *Inner Necessities: The Letters of David Jones to Desmond Chute*, ed. by Thomas Dilworth (Toronto, 1984).

V. COMMENTARIES AND STUDIES OF INDIVIDUAL WORKS.
René Hague, *A Commentary on the* Anathemata *of David Jones* (Wellingborough, 1977); Henry Summerfield, *An Introductory Guide to the* Anathemata *and the* Sleeping Lord *Sequence of David Jones* (Victoria, B.C., 1979); Neil Corcoran, *The Song of Deeds: A Study of the* Anathemata *of David Jones* (Cardiff, Wales, 1982); Douglas Lochhead, *Word Index of* In Parenthesis (Sackville, N.B., 1983); Christine Pagnoulle, *David Jones: A Commentary on Some Poetic Fragments* (Cardiff, Wales, 1987);

VI. BIOGRAPHICAL AND CRITICAL STUDIES. John H. Johnston, *English Poetry of the First World War* (Princeton, N.J., 1964); *Agenda*, David Jones special issues 5, nos. 1–3 (1967), 12, no. 1 (1974); David Blamires, *David Jones: Artist and Writer* (Manchester, 1971); Jon Silkin, *Out of Battle: The Poetry of the Great War* (Oxford, 1972); Kathleen Raine, *David Jones: Solitary Perfectionist* (Ipswich, 1974; enlarged edn., 1975); Paul Fussell, *The Great War and Modern Memory* (Oxford, 1975); René Hague, *David Jones* (Cardiff, 1975); Jeremy Hooker, *David Jones: An Exploratory Study of the Writings* (London, 1975); Roland Mathias (ed.), *David Jones: Eight Essays on His Work as Writer and Artist* (Llandysul, 1976); Samuel Rees, *David Jones* (Boston, Mass., 1978); Thomas Dilworth, *The Liturgical Parenthesis* of *David Jones* (Ipswich, 1979); Elizabeth Ward, *David Jones, Mythmaker* (Manchester, 1983); Thomas Dilworth, *The Shape of Meaning in the Poetry of David Jones* (Toronto, 1988); John Matthias, ed., David Jones: Man and Poet (Orono, Me., 1989); Jonathan Miles, *Backgrounds to David Jones: A Study in Sources and Drafts* (Cardiff, 1990); Jonathan Miles, *Eric Gill and David Jones at Capel-y-Ffin* (Bridgend, Wales, 1992); Kathleen A. Staudt, *At the Turn of a Civilization: David Jones and Modern Poetics* (Ann Arbor, Mich., 1994); Huw Ceiriog Jones, ed., *The Library of David Jones (1895–1974): A Catalogue* (Aberystwyth, 1995);

Jonathan Miles and Derek Shiel, *David Jones: The Maker Unmade* (Bridgend, Wales, 1995); Tony Conran, *Frontiers in Anglo-Welsh Poetry* (Cardiff, Wales, 1997); Paul Hills, *David Jones: Artist and Poet* (Aldershot, England, 1997); Donald Davie, *With the Grain: Essays on Thomas Hardy and Modern British Poetry*, ed. by Clive Wilmer (Manchester, 1998).

VII. BIBLIOGRAPHY. Samuel Rees, *David Jones: An Annotated Bibliography and Guide to Research* (New York, 1977).

PATRICK KAVANAGH

(1904–1967)

Robert Welch

"FAR AWAY": BACKGROUND AND EARLY WORK

> The Castleblaney besoms, the best that ever grew
> Were sold for two a penny on the Hill of
> Mullacrew.

THESE TWO LINES from an old ballad come into Kavanagh's head as he's on his way to the fair at Carrickmacross with a man who's going to meet his prospective son-in-law. His neighbor, Kavanagh tells us in the autobiographical *The Green Fool* (1938), is fidgety: negotiating the marriage of a daughter is a ticklish business. The old bachelors who are, more often than not, the objects of these financial allurements so they will take the jump into matrimony, often shy at the last fence. One of them walked out of the church where he was to be wed, leaving the young girl at the altar, because, like many of his kind, he was terrified of the commitment and the uncertainty that would follow giving up a solitary, if celibate, life. Capturing one of these cautious men calls for all kinds of diplomatic skills, as well as hard cash. The neighbor, Kavanagh tells us, showed him the roll of money he was carrying so he could clinch the deal: one hundred and fifty pounds, with the same amount to be paid after the wedding. This is money that the father had scraped together over the years to ensure a solid marriage for his girl, having started out with nothing. As he tells Kavanagh: "when I came home from Scotland I hadn't as much money as would put earnest in a besom" (p. 205). Which brings to Kavanagh's mind the couplet from the ballad, which also evokes poverty, economic depression, the misery of want.

Things are only worth what people will pay for them, and in a depressed economy they carry minimal value, no matter how fine they may be. It matters very little if whatever it is, is the best

that ever grew, if poverty controls the market. This grinding declension of value, where there is only the tiniest margin of surplus, is the world in which Patrick Kavanagh came to manhood.

He was born on 21 October 1904 in the townland of Mucker, outside Inniskeen, Monaghan, in Ireland. The Kavanagh family was dirt-poor. His father, James, was a country cobbler who made and repaired shoes in the main room of the house. He and his wife Bridget (Quinn) Kavanagh had nine children, and the family diet consisted mostly of potatoes and oatmeal porridge. The two most important things in domestic life were the saying of the rosary and the making of money, with the latter being given far greater importance than the former. The family home had three rooms, a kitchen, which also served as the workroom for the cobbling trade, and two others. However, the parents were, like many of their neighbors, industrious and careful folk, who put away every spare shilling. Even though they had, initially, no land they kept hens and sold eggs, and this, along with whatever extra could be set aside from the shoe trade, allowed them to build, when Kavanagh was around five, a new house with a slated roof and two storeys. Later on the family acquired some land and a farm, which the poet was to work and eventually to inherit.

The economic circumstances in which Kavanagh grew to manhood were harsh, though not unrelievedly so. There was a period of prosperity during the 1914–1918 war, when farm prices rose dramatically, and most people in his locality had spare money in their pockets: even the blackberries which grew wild in the woodlands and wild places fetched five shillings a stone. Writing of these times Kavanagh says: "We were barbarians just emerged from the Penal days... Money was pouring in every door and pouring out the back door" (p. 79)

However, the last phrase here gives pause, as does the mention of the penal days: this money, a product of boom time, is, he suggests, unstable. While he goes on to make the point that his family did all they could to stop the outflow, nevertheless Kavanagh is, very clearly, indicating that this period of plenty was entirely uncharacteristic in that long durance of survival and subsistence that extended from the 1840s and the Great Irish Famine well into the twentieth century. Indeed, it may be stated, with a fair degree of certainty, that this slow emergence from dependency, subservience, and necessitous penny-pinching to independence and economic autonomy, in the Irish state, did not conclude until the first waves of affluence that began in the 1960s, by which time Kavanagh's career as a poet was over. There is a sense, and it is one of the reasons why Kavanagh is a writer of profound significance in modern Ireland, that he, more than anyone else, is the laureate of the actualities of the formative phases of the modern Irish state. The struggles that beset him, as an artist and as a man trying to function economically in a society with very little margins for cultural surpluses, arise from the tensions generated between the need to be an imaginative and feeling creature, on the one hand, and on the other, a solid citizen/farmer with money in the bank. It is an aspect of Kavanagh's emotional strength, and his psychic honesty, that each of these tension-generating poles—that of financial probity and that of the creative imagination—exercised a profound magnetism over his impulses, so that they (and he was a deeply impulsive person) were profoundly divided and at variance with each other.

The economic buoyancy that animated rural Ireland (even remote, though fertile parts of it, such as Kavanagh's Monaghan) during World War I was deflated by the re-emergence in these years of militant Irish nationalism, eventually focusing on the at-first-aborted though subsequently seismic Easter Rebellion, led by Patrick Pearse in Dublin. Rebellion led to a fully fledged Anglo-Irish War, waged on the traditional republican principle that "England's difficulty is Ireland's opportunity." This war led to a troubled settlement, negotiated in the Treaty of 1921, which sanctioned partition, ensuring that six counties of the old province of Ulster remained within the United Kingdom and the empire; this agreement in turn issued in a division among Irish nationalists, some wanting to break the connection completely with Britain and secure all the territory of the island, while others, including Michael Collins, were ready for compromise. This division lies at the heart of the modern Irish state, and its effects are still active (and lethal) eighty years later; in 1921 it drove the country into civil war. The partition, the border, a line on a map symbolizing defeat (or victory snatched from the jaws of disgrace—it all depends on one's point of view) was drawn, with border posts no more than a few miles distant from where Kavanagh was born and grew up. From nearby his family's fields he could see Slieve Gullion across what became the border in Armagh. This was (and still to some degree is) given differences in tax regimes and currency values, what is known as "bandit country," where a degree of lawlessness permeated many aspects of life, in spite of an apparently rigorously enforced set of religious observances by the Catholic Church. It was one of the notable divisions of this society, which accommodated many contradictions, that a studious piety co-existed alongside ferocious greed and rampant sexual desire. And, once again, it is Kavanagh who, more than any other single writer of his period, bears witness to the moral and psychological arenas of trial that open up under the pressures of these antagonistic forces.

Between extremities
Man runs his course

W. B. Yeats declared, in his oracular fashion, in "Vacillation" written in 1932. Yeats's great strength as a poet was his capacity to absorb, emotionally, the huge torsions of his time, both in Ireland and globally, and to create a moving fabric of intense and subtly analyzed thought out of these forces, coloring his poetry with the complexions of his mind and personality. Yeats negotiates extremes of love and hate, self and soul, Ireland and England, mask and face, and so on, but the negotiation is conducted within the shaping precincts of a securely fashioned and even embattled fortification, the tower of his own multiple, but unified personality. Kavanagh was never the master of his extremities, he never "accomplished fate," to use a phrase of Yeats's from "Under Ben Bulben" (1938); it was more like fate accomplishing him. Whatever strength Kavanagh has, and he does have resources of resilience, flexibility, and openness, it lies in his capacity to allow his personality to be a receptor for a great many of the frequencies, messages, and signals the Ireland of his time transmitted to itself and to the world, but without (and here lies the profound difference between Yeats and himself) seeking to impose any preordained form on these transmissions as he sought to translate them into art. Like Yeats, Kavanagh's mind and emotions ran between "extremities"—of north and south, tradition and modernity, imagination and cash, Dublin and Inniskeen—but unlike Yeats, who exacted a fierce composure out of a racked personality, Kavanagh would allow one or another of these antinomies to let rip at any one time. His was a technique of exposure to maximum risk, and to a great extent he paid the price. He went into the formations of the political and economic weather of his time, without holding back; and he did this again and again. This was his technique; he threw himself into the material (emotional, financial, and cultural) of his world. It was a kind of abandon, a letting go. It was, in imaginative terms, exactly the same kind of impulse that, physiologically, made him an alcoholic. As such, he is not unlike some of the finest writers of the twentieth century who concentrated less on preserving the fortifications of the self, than on opening up the personality for it to become a laboratory for manifold, contradictory, and often tortured experience. Among those who share Kavanagh's technique of high-energy risk and abandon are John Berryman, John Ashbery, Robert Lowell, Sylvia Plath, and Dylan Thomas. Naming his fellow high-energy conductors it is evident that openness and receptivity are not necessarily a prelude to cacophony and disorder, formally and technically speaking, and it will be necessary to look at the

nature of the technique that Kavanagh developed to accommodate his reception and transmission of open frequencies. Each of the poets cited with him above developed special techniques for fashioning their own particular distress, such as to make it current for a readership who could become involved in its dynamics, instead of being estranged from a broken and uncoordinated misery.

Kavanagh's county was, and is, border country. Even before the fault line of partition was inscribed around the six counties that make up Northern Ireland, his territory, northeast of Dundalk and southwest of Armagh, was strange country. It was a place of mummers, these remnants of folk drama and pre-Christian ritual; of storytelling, wake amusements, rhyming, superstition, fairy lore (fairies were strongly believed in), the evil eye, ghosts, the banshee. This is not to say that Kavanagh's country was unique: there are, today, probably, places not unlike it in Albania or Georgia in the Urals, or in Siberia. And at the beginning of the twentieth century there would have been, in other parts of Ireland, areas not dissimilar in the survival of ancient and traditional habits of mind—in, say, Connemara, or West Cork, or Donegal. But these would have been Gaeltacht or Gaelic-speaking areas, where it would be expected that such survivals would persist. What was unusual about Kavanagh's locale was that although it was English speaking, and had been for thirty or forty years or more, its culture retained deep memory banks of Gaelic lore. So that his territory was a borderland linguistically as well as geographically and politically.

Kavanagh's father was a thrifty and resourceful man. Despite the fact that business was conducted in the main room of the house, he would sometimes have as many as four journeyman shoemakers working for him. These characters, in Kavanagh's narratives, come directly from the seventeenth century. They would work for Kavanagh's father for a month or more, then move on again, part itinerant worker, part tramp, part highly skilled craftsman, proud of their ability to find employment wherever they went. One of these was Jem Fagan, a great storyteller:

He used to tell stories in which he would lose himself. One time, with breakfast before him, he began a tale and completely forgot to eat. I looked at Jem as one looks at something that might belong to another world and time. I looked at him as Saint Patrick must have looked at Ossian when that great Fenian returned from Tirnanogue.

(The Green Fool, p. 74)

In other words, even though his stories were probably in English, Jem Fagan came out of the world of Gaelic lore and oral culture, one of the richest survivals in Europe of folk tradition and its often complex conventions of narrative, poetry, and proverb. One does not wish to make too much of this, but it is worth noticing what Kavanagh says about Fagan as a storyteller: he used to "lose himself." This is the kind of self-forgetting that the artist, the actor, or the writer can sometimes experience; but it also conveys the sense, again a feeling not unfamiliar to the poet or artist, of going astray, of going somewhere dangerous, enthralling, and mysterious.

The landscape itself, sited between the known and attested worlds of Dundalk, Belfast, and Enniskillen, was also a place for opening up, for abandonment, for relinquishing the irritable holds on logic and reason. When Kavanagh writes of Rocksavage, the big estate surrounded by the small farms owned by the likes of him, he evokes a place of wonder and danger. The Forth Hill, for example, has whins (or gorse) ten feet high, and among these bushes grows the foxglove: "The banshee's thimble was the wild foxglove. I once put the thimbles on my fingers and was told that the banshee would call for me before a year" (p. 81). And inside the hill itself was a door into another world, the "Otherworld" of Celtic myth, which led, he tells readers, "far away, far way" (p. 82).

Moving along the border northwestward into Tyrone, one comes to the area around Augher, Cloghar, and Fivemiletown associated with Kavanagh's predecessor and the writer with whom he has most in common: the nineteenth-century novelist William Carleton. Kavanagh is unique, in the twentieth century, in that he became an artist who was almost entirely representative of his people, and, as such, representa-

tive of a great many Irish men and women, irrespective of which part of the island they hail from. Carleton accomplished something very similar for his region (and therefore for the broad mass of Irish people) in the nineteenth century. When Yeats wrote in "Coole Park and Ballylee, 1931" that what he and John Synge and Lady Gregory sought was a literature that came out of "the book of the people," he was expressing an ideal that he was not at all sure had been realized in the literary movement he had inaugurated in Ireland in the 1890s. Carleton, Yeats knew, came out of "the book of the people," as did Kavanagh one hundred years later. Carleton's *Traits and Stories of the Irish Peasantry* (1830; 2d series, 1833) are what Kavanagh's *The Green Fool* and *Tarry Flynn* (1948) are modeled on. Carleton's stories, like these two autobiographical works of Kavanagh, are rooted in his native landscape and culture: the Tyrone trees, hills, fairy forts, shebeens, cottages, big houses, priests, pedants, misers, maniacs, secret societies, drink, talk, superstitions. What is remarkable is how much has survived, from the pre-famine Ireland in which Carleton was reared, into Kavanagh's twentieth-century Monaghan. Even more significant, however, than a similarity of content and material, is the relationship these two writers have with the texture of the life out of which they came. They retain a deep sense of *pietas* toward their people and their society. They are "parochial" writers, in Kavanagh's special sense of the word, in which he attributes immense, even universal, value to the parish and its networks of filiation and communion, setting it against the category defined by "provincial," where the latter is associated with narrowness, fear, inwardness, and suspicion, and insecurity. In 1952 he wrote, in *Kavanagh's Weekly*, a newspaper he set up with his brother Peter, and which ran from 12 April to 5 July in that year, "Parochialism and provincialism are opposites. The provincial has no mind of his own; he does not trust what his eyes see until he has heard what the metropolis—towards which his eyes are turned—has to say on any subject. All great civilizations are based on parochialism—Greek, Israelite, English" (*Collected Pruse*, p. 282). The parish is universal, and has epic dimensions, because it deals with the "fundamentals," to use Kavanagh's own word from the same essay. Carleton he admires when he does not allow his gaze to become preoccupied with what the metropolis dictates he should see; and Carleton, like Kavanagh, left his native parish and went astray in the distortions of Dublin, where he was instructed on to how he should view his own people, and ultimately himself. Appraising Carleton, and, needless to say, finding a pattern in that artistic life which corresponded with his own struggle to keep his eye clear of the dictates of other people's visions, he wrote: "he recorded the lives of his own people with a fidelity that preserves for us the culture of Pre-Famine Ireland" (*Irish Times*, 13 January 1945, p. 200). But, he says, when he adapted the judgemental and condescending attitudes of the evangelical Church of Ireland, to which he converted, he became a provincial, seeing his own people as exemplars of folly, vice, and disorder. This division, this contradiction, may very well have been the unresolvable dilemma that made Carleton a writer, while at the same time creating a tension of mutually antagonistic attraction and repulsion that would eventually prove intractable. A similar dilemma, with not unconnected origins, lies at the heart of Kavanagh's work, in that he too loved his own people, while at the same time remaining all too conscious of their meanness and spite, traits which he shared in as well, as he was prepared to admit. The difference between Carleton and Kavanagh is that the latter doesn't strive to adopt a superior tone toward the life which has made him, partly because he is all too aware that he is also that which he abhors: the contradiction is internalized, not without cost, but he doesn't allow one part of his mind, the cultivated, metropolitan, "provincial" side, to dominate his intimate, close, and parochial instincts. This is not to suggest that Kavanagh struck some kind of equable balance: rather does he create a method of knowing and realization whereby the shifts of temperament, its instability, are allowed. His attitude toward his own contradictions is like that of Montaigne, the French essayist of the sixteenth century, whose courage resides in embracing, without intervening moral-

ism or judgement, the shifts of his own temperament and the waywardness of feeling. Only George Moore, the novelist and autobiographer, achieved anything like Montaigne's risky openness in Irish writing before Kavanagh. This is Kavanagh's courage, his uniqueness, and his importance—a capacity to sing "inconsequently" and not give a damn:

Sitting on a wooden gate
He didn't care a damn.
Said whatever came into his head,
And inconsequently sang.
While his world withered away,
He had a cigarette to smoke and a pound to spend
On drink the next Saturday.
("The Great Hunger," Collected Poems, p. 43)

This Montaigne-like inconsequence depends for its lightness and brio on a fidelity to who he was, a refusal to deny even the vilest traits in those from whom he came. In *The Green Fool* he tells readers how pleased all his neighbors were when, as a child, he fell seriously ill from the fever. But then he says: "When anybody around fell sick it pleased us all" (p. 194). Open confession is good for the soul, while a false morality damages the imagination. There was no false morality in Kavanagh.

Although his aesthetic of the parish and its morality of acceptance were not consciously formulated until the 1950s, its basic premises underlay his writings from the 1930s onward. His first versings in the 1920s were, as the scholar Antoinette Quinn has shown, very much under the influence of Victorian models such as Alfred, Lord Tennyson and Algernon Charles Swinburne, with some admixture of an impetus from local ballad tradition. He then was attracted by the airy mysticism of the poet George Russell ("AE"), who edited the *Irish Statesman* and who published some early lyrics.

Ploughman and Other Poems (1936) was published by Macmillan in their inexpensive but prestigious series devoted to contemporary poets. Many of the poems here are artful attempts at luminous country sketches, which convey Kavanagh's desire to create a landscape which will be imbued with spiritual intimations.

in the green meadows
The maiden of Spring is with child
By the Holy Ghost.

("April," *Collected Poems*, p. 18)

There is one poem in this collection, however, that breaks free of this reverential provincialism into the parish of his own impulse, his own way of saying. The arrival of the real thing announces itself in the swift and nonchalant opening, the assurance of the language, the sense of a human voice speaking to us of its own world, known and accepted:

The bicycles go by in twos and threes—
There's a dance in Billy Brennan's bar to-night,
And there's the half-talk code of mysteries
And the wink-and-elbow language of delight.

("Inniskeen Road: July Evening," *Collected Poems*,
p. 19)

One is in the parish of Kavanagh's mind, but one is also at the heart of his dilemma: he both belongs and does not belong. After the flurry of all these people going to the dance, in their small units of communal association, the poet is alone; there is not a sound, not a "footfall tapping secrecies of stone." This is a sonnet, and after the eight opening lines, the octet, the concluding sextet turns to face into the ambiguity and sad tension out of which the poem arises. How may imagination connect with what it loves and yet retain its own integrity?

I have what every poet hates in spite
Of all the solemn talk of contemplation.

What he has is the plight of solitude, which may confer its own bliss, but not without sorrow. But this solitude is needed if the poetry is to become truly attentive to the community that gives it energy. The poet's plight is to be, he says, "king and government and nation," in the imagination, whereas the harsh reality is that he is king "Of banks and stones and every blooming thing."

Where "blooming" is a curse as well as implying that solitude is the condition by means of which a community blossoms into the articulacy that is the poem he is writing. This is a complex and a beautiful piece, that lives and thinks through an actual situation, and draws it into relationship with the way the imagination uncovers its own forms, distinct from yet profoundly engaged with what happens to the human creature in time and circumstance. He is of the parish, yet apart from it also.

When *Ploughman and Other Poems* appeared Kavanagh was thirty-two, and ambitious and insecure at once. He went to London, attempting to make the most of the limited success the volume had, and met Helen Waddell, the Belfast-born poet and novelist, and author of *The Wandering Scholars* (1927), a study of the medieval goliardic tradition of itinerant poets, satirists, and learned men. They took to each other, probably because there was something of the goliard in Kavanagh, and she suggested he write an account of his life in Monaghan, realizing that it was Kavanagh's fortune (or, as he might say, misfortune) to be brought up in a society that had, apart from the language change, altered very little in "fundamentals" in hundreds of years. Out of this urging came *The Green Fool*, originally to be published by Constable, for whom Helen Waddell was an editor and reader, then taken up by Michael Joseph. This volume, comic and self-deprecating in its approach, reveals, beneath the fun and games, the lawlessness, the devil-may-care attitude to the political violence of the civil war (during which Kavanagh was tangentially involved with the Irish Republican Army)—that ambiguity towards his background which gives his narrative edginess and surprise. His world starts into life not just because he retains a deep affection for it, but also because he is trying to understand its nature, and the quality of his own feelings about it.

DUBLIN *AND* THE GREAT HUNGER

IN 1939 he made what he came to think was the mistake of his life: he moved to Dublin, and walked straight into full encounter with what he later called the provincial mind set. When he got there he found that the "Irish literary affair" (*Collected Pruse*, p. 14), as patented by Yeats, Lady Gregory, and Synge, was still booming. Except, of course, that the real thing had run its course: Yeats died in 1939, and in any case his imaginative world had long developed its own integral daring and strange freedom; Lady Gregory was gone; the Abbey Theatre had entered its long phase of waiting for something to happen; and the Irish Free State and Catholic Church had formed a moral and civil alliance that quickly led to the development of a society which was watchful, inert, submissive, and profoundly distrustful of creative energy. The Irish Free State evolved, for all kinds of understandable reasons, given its imperial and colonial legacy, and its economic vulnerability, a deeply conservative, indeed provincial society, where authority always rested in the institution, whether the church or the civil service, never the individual. Responsibility was always somebody else's business: in such a mood subservience entered the soul. Given very high unemployment, the main preoccupation of most people was not integrity, or truth, or vision, but the getting (and holding on to) a job. The author Frank O'Connor once, in profound despair about how the Abbey Theatre in these years slid into lethargy and inactivity, blamed in part the importation into the theater of a civil service mentality, where people courted a job like they courted girls whom they hoped to marry: it was to be for life (*My Father's Son*, 1968, p. 194).

By Night Unstarred (1977), a posthumously published autobiographical novel put together from separate drafts by Kavanagh's brother, Peter, tells, in nervously horrified detail, how the writer humiliated himself in his quest for that Holy Grail of midcentury Irish life: a good job. Excruciatingly, and with a ferocious and un-self-forgiving honesty, Kavanagh narrates his adventures in the bohemian jungle of 1940s Dublin. He sketches in its shoddy beau monde of artistically minded solicitors; hangers-on in pubs, concurring with the whims of literary editors from whom they might get to do a review; and people with influence who are much sought after. But the interesting thing here is that the satire and the contempt are directed as much at himself as at others. He too wants a job; he too would sacrifice his integrity if only he could get that position as director of publicity in a new plastics firm:

because such security would allow him to marry the girl he loves, buy a house, settle down. For this reason he goes to the Bishop of Dublin (modeled on John Charles McQuaid, to whom Kavanagh did, in fact, have not infrequent recourse) to see if he can pull a few strings. He is told to pray to the Mother of God for intercession, and is given a few pounds, which he takes, gratefully, in spite of the burning shame of it. *By Night Unstarred* is a shapeless work and was never completed, but it gives a devastating account of the conflict between the imaginative world and the realities of power and bank balances; and it does this without renouncing the need for a person to survive, to be accepted in society and given a role, and not just that of poet and artist. This work, like so much else of Kavanagh, bears witness to the fact that he himself is well aware that he is not immune to the infection he so detests: that of provincialism, and its damaging tendency to undermine all autonomy, all self-respect, because ultimately it looks to an authority outside itself located in some citadel of power: whether the bishop's palace, the houses of parliament, the big house, or London.

Although the life he and his brother shared in Dublin flatland was poverty-stricken and bleak, nevertheless his removal there allowed him to witness firsthand the shallowness of much of what passed as "culture" in the city, while, at the same time, providing a necessary distance on the world of Inniskeen and Monaghan. The perspective so acquired allowed him to appraise his background, while not neglecting to praise it. "Stony Grey Soil" was published in the first number of *The Bell*, a journal founded by the critic and short-story writer Sean O'Faolain in October 1940. O'Faolain's aim, in *The Bell*, was to create a forum for critical dissent from the conservatism in Irish cultural life which irked him as much as it did Kavanagh. "Stony Grey Soil" was dedicated to O'Faolain, and attacks all the halts and obstacles a rural upbringing sets against the imagination. It is, in fact, a curiously callow poem, its exclamatory righteousness lacks conviction, expressing, as it does, a superior attitude to the life it evokes:

You flung a ditch in my vision
Of beauty, love and truth.
O stony grey soil of Monaghan
You burgled my bank of youth!

(*Collected Poems*, p. 82)

And yet this dismissal is a kind of strength, because it is the antidote to any tendency in Kavanagh to idealization; the antagonism between the two impulses of attraction and repulsion is precisely where his poetic and creative energy is founded; save that here the negative is overvalued and rhetoric supervenes.

Much more compelling, because much more complex and beautiful are two other poems he wrote about this time: "Spraying the Potatoes" (July 1940) and "Art McCooey" (April 1941). Unlike in "Stony Grey Soil," where, like Carleton in his false moments, he is outside the experience, adopting an attitude toward it, here he is inside it, and inside his own mind in the process of realizing the nature of the series of events that go to evoke a segment of life lived. The poetry is alive. In "Spraying the Potatoes" the heady heat of July is recreated, relived in the small space of the poem. The dandelions in the lines that follow are a completely successful evocation of the quality of openness that the poem moves into and through:

And over that potato-field
A lazy veil of woven sun.
Dandelions growing on headlands, showing
Their unloved hearts to everyone.

(*Collected Poems*, p. 78)

The poet, in Dublin, recalling the intensity and heat, the encounter with an old man and the blessing he gave to the work as they hunkered down in the shade of an orchard wall, is now outside all of this life. And yet, because he is out of it he can write about it, a dilemma and contradiction that enters into the last verse, and all but overwhelms the syntax:

And poet lost to potato-fields
Remembering the lime and copper smell

Of the spraying barrels he is not lost
Or till blossomed stalks cannot weave a spell.

(p. 78)

The poet is "lost" and "not lost" at once. Memory and language can go back in, but only because there is actual absence.

"Art McCooey" is named after Art Mac Cumhaigh, an eighteenth-century Gaelic poet from Armagh, and therefore someone, like Carleton, from Kavanagh's territory. The reference is, in fact, quite oblique, because there is no direct allusion to Mac Cumhaigh in the poem; rather does Kavanagh connect a memory of carrying dung to outlying land in Shancoduff to a celebrated incident preserved in folklore about the Gaelic poet, when he, lost in visionary trance, went back and forth four or five times between the field and the farmyard, forgetting to tip out a load of manure each time. The memory is powerful, an engine of feeling to set against the provincialism of official authority. His language strives to realize that parish of the senses, "far away":

The steam rising from the load is still
Warm enough to thaw my frosty fingers.
In Donnybrook in Dublin ten years later
I see that empire now and the empire builder.

(*Collected Poems*, p. 76)

This experience, "now," connecting with that experience then, ten years ago, which is itself connected to an experience of Mac Cumhaigh's two hundred years before, has its own laws and logic, and these must inhabit the new world of the poem, and they must be its impulse and energy. Washing out the dung cart at the end of the day becomes a ritual act, imbued with permanence in the live realization of the poem, over which "Jupiter" presides:

Wash out the cart with a bucket of water and a wangel
Of wheaten straw. Jupiter looks down.
Unlearnedly and unreasonably poetry is shaped
Awkwardly but alive in the unmeasured womb.

(p. 77)

In 1964, when he wrote an "Author's Note" for his *Collected Poems*, he declared his dislike for *The Great Hunger*, a long poem about the hardship and loneliness of country life, written in Dublin in 1942 and published that year. He came to disapprove of it because, he says, "*The Great Hunger* is tragedy and Tragedy is undeveloped Comedy, not fully born" (p. xiv). Whatever his own misgivings about this poem, there is no question but that *The Great Hunger* is one of the finest Irish longer poems of the twentieth century, to be set alongside Yeats's "The Tower," Anthony Cronin's "RMS Titanic," John Montague's "The Rough Field" or Seamus Heaney's "Station Island." Its theme is the sterile and loveless misery that is the life of the Monaghan farmer, Patrick Maguire, the central figure of the poem, and not too different from what Kavanagh feared he might have become had he not left Monaghan in 1939. On the other hand, the poem also refers to the famine of the affections and emotions that the conservative and narrow-minded alliance of church and state had brought about in postrevolutionary, archconservative Ireland. There is a deliberate allusion to the Great Famine of the 1840s and the influence that the new rulers of the Irish Free State had wrought an emotional starvation just as lethal, in its own way, as the physical one created by the laissez-faire indifference of the British Empire one hundred years before. So that Maguire's Monaghan isolation and his lonely masturbation in front of the embers of the dying fire, while his sister grunts in the bed upstairs, becomes an image for the desolation of the inner life in 1940s Dublin as much as Monaghan. It is a poem about psychological dereliction, as much as one about the isolation and sadness of country life in midcentury Ireland. The poem creates an image of human existence reduced to circumstance and exiguousness. It opens with an antigospel of materiality and function, presided over by money, and compelled by its unanswerable authority:

Clay is the word and clay is the flesh
Where the potato-gatherers like mechanised scarecrows move
Along the side-fall of the hill—Maguire and his men.
(*Collected Poems*, p. 34)

The poem opens out, in fourteen sections, to encompass an Ireland of oppression, impotence, frustrated impulse, fear, subservience, insecurity, hatred, resentment; a country and a people far from liberated from the empire, but subdued by their own failure of will. This is a life, all right, but one "broken-backed over the Book / Of Death"; the poem begins in a potato field which is a cemetery of the impulses, and concludes in another graveyard, an "actual" one in the world of the poem, where Maguire's mother is buried, and mourners cannot express grief because even sorrow has departed, so inauthentic has life become. This is an Ireland cut off from the mainstream of existence, and the mood of the poem has not a little to do with Ireland's neutrality in World War II, when the country, for understandable reasons maybe, given its colonial history, refused to support the Allies in their war against the evident brutality and bestiality of Nazi Germany and the Axis powers. Such a stance was to have its psychological consequences in the consciousness of Irish people, and the critic Terence Brown is accurate when he acclaims this poem of Kavanagh's as registering in its moods and turns of despair and remorse, a "sensitivity to the shifts" of community and national conscience (p. 187). The gloom of this work is formidable in its unrelenting sadness. Kavanagh declared the work tragic, setting it against the comic muse, which he claimed to be truer, because more disengaged, more carefree. But tragedy involves a kind of dignity, and the creatures of Kavanagh's poem do retain some element of nobility, in their persistence and tenacity if in little else. But no one ever made a poem out of sheer misery: dejection annihilates the vitality necessary to imaginative creation. And what drives this poem is not remorse or bitterness but pity, a pity contaminated with elements of self-pity, maybe, but Patrick Maguire and his plight do not end up the object of Kavanagh's contempt: instead they elicit compassion and fellow-feeling. And because Maguire is so implicated with the poet's own self-image, the imaginative creativity of the poem enacts a kind of self-forgiveness, so there is a sense of release, of "casting out remorse," in Yeats's phrase ("A Dialogue of Self and Soul," *Collected Poems*, p. 267). There is, even, a glimmer of the cloud of unknowing, of acceptance of what befalls in the process of being:

Maybe life is not for joking or for finding happiness in—
This tiny light in Oriental Darkness
Looking out chance windows of poetry or prayer.
one rare moment he heard the young people playing on the railway stile
And he wished them happiness and whatever they most desired from life.

(pp. 48–49)

The integrity of the poem resides in the shoots of pity and compassion that unsettle any fixed attitude of contempt or superiority. Kavanagh's poem deals honestly with his own people; his eyes are wide open to what they are, but there is no attitude bearing down upon them. For this reason the poem's form and technique is entirely adapted to its moral fluidity, which is also its humane probity. The poem's technique, of loosely rhyming strophes, with lines that stretch out to encounter a run of possibility or contract in to focus on a shocked impulse of realization, is a superbly adapted mechanism for tracking and measuring the variety of impressions of the swiftly changing coloratura of emotion. From this point onward Kavanagh can call upon a technical resource of great flexibility, one in which his language shapes can move and respond to the ways in which thought and feeling evolve. Later, he was to reject this technique of attentive and troubled responsiveness, as he strove for a more remote, detached, and comic perspective, a not caring; but there is no doubt that this poem is a harrowing, complex, and compassionate opening out to the Ireland of midcentury in which the technique is entirely integral to the qualities of the emotion:

The fields were bleached white,
The wooden tubs full of water
Were white in the winds

That blew through Brannigan's Gap on their way from Siberia

(p. 50)

The Siberia here recalls James Clarence Mangan's poem "Siberia," written in 1846 at the height of the Great Famine; but these winds are also blowing from Stalinist Russia that has been invaded by Hitler, as the German-Soviet Non-Aggression Pact broke down.

The companion piece to *The Great Hunger* is Kavanagh's other long poem *Lough Derg* (1978) based on two pilgrimages to this site of fasting and penance, famous in Catholic Europe from the late Middle Ages. He undertook the pilgrimage in deliberate imitation of his Tyrone predecessor, William Carleton, whose first published work was "A Pilgrimage to St. Patrick's Purgatory" for Caesar Otway's *Christian Examiner* in 1828. Carleton revealed, in this work, the conflict between attachment to his own people and their religion, and his desire and need to distance himself from both that was the driving force and the impediment in his creative life. Kavanagh's attitude was quite the contrary and, it is not unreasonable to assume, deliberately so. Instead of the "provincial" superiority Carleton evinces, and which is a torment to the affection he retains for the people from whom he's come, Kavanagh consciously extends his creative imagination to embrace, with as little admixture of judgment as possible, Catholic Ireland of the 1940s, in all its leaden anxiety and craven piety. The poem is a listening device to the "banal beggary" that God hears from the oppressed hearts of a defeated people. In Lough Derg Kavanagh seeks, he tells his readers, to put down all that happened and was said as clearly and faithfully as he could, using his technique to register the broad panorama of human love and need:

All happened on Lough Derg as it was written
In June nineteen-forty-two
When the Germans were fighting outside Rostov.

(pp. 23–24)

He wished his version of pilgrimage, unlike Carleton's, to be as "integral and completed as the emotion" men and women experience as they cover what they feel in the banal rags of "commonplace" exchanges. He too, he says, was one of them; he too, like them, tried to get away from his own vanity, but found that it remained there, waiting for him:

He too denied
The half of him that was his pride
Yet found it waiting, one the half untrue
Of this story is his pride's rhythm.

(p. 24)

Insincerity and superiority destroy authentic rhythm and pervert it to a rhetoric of unacceptance, unforgiveness. When the poetry truly runs, it accelerates into a profound and moving charity and love. An old man from Leitrim explains his servility:

When I stoop
It is my mother's mother mother's mother
Each one in turn being called in to spread—
"Wider with your legs" the master of the house said.
Domestic servants taken back and front.

That's why I'm servile.

(p. 16)

A SOUL FOR SALE, TARRY FLYNN, AND KAVANAGH'S WEEKLY

BY the time *The Great Hunger* was published in 1942 Kavanagh had begun to move, in sometimes erratic orbits, in the system of Dublin's literary life, an environment he despised and craved. He was a reviewer for the *Irish Times*, then under the benign editorship of R. M. Smyllie, who provided, in his review and features pages, the means of scratching much-needed income for Dublin's army of poets and writers, a standing army, Kavanagh once declared, which never fell below five thousand. The Palace Bar in Fleet Street was a place of resort for the Dublin literary set in the 1940s, after which their shoals removed to McDaids off Grafton Street. The English critic and memoirist Cyril Connolly described the atmosphere of the Palace Bar in the war years as being "as warm and friendly as an alligator tank" (Quinn, p. 259).

These environs, and the humiliations and expectations they created, form the background to Kavanagh's Alexander Pope–like satires on Dublin literary culture. Some of these were included in *A Soul for Sale: Poems* (1947) and others were collected in *Come Dance with Kitty*

Stobling and Other Poems (1960) having previously been issued in small magazines and literary journals. They include "A Wreath for Tom Moore's Statue," "The Paddiad" (an Irish version of Pope's *Dunciad* in which his contemporaries receive the kind of treatment Pope reserved for his enemies), and "Adventures in the Bohemian Jungle." These have a nasty and visceral energy, and are, as Anthony Cronin pointed out, the counterenergy to the innocence and openness which combine to create the distinctive impulse of his verse. In "defining the enemies of his vision through satire [he/] added a dimension to his personal epic" (pp. 190–191), which Cronin sees as an attempt (and a successful one at that) of writing the story of the discovery and development of his own character, a story in which integrity is retained, in spite of the odds. And the odds were: the gloom and lethargy of unthinking rural existence, dealt with in *The Great Hunger*; stupid rejection of devotion and belief, faced into in *Lough Derg*; and the banality and arrogance of provincialism, nowhere more in evidence than in the bohemian jungle of "The Paddiad":

In the corner of a Dublin pub
This party opens—blub-a-blub—
Paddy of the Celtic Mist,
Paddy Connemara West
Chestertonian Paddy Frog
Croaking nightly in the bog

(*Collected Poems*, 90)

The other side of this coin is expressed in "Pegasus," the piece from which the title *A Soul for Sale* comes. "My soul," he writes, "was an old horse" (*Collected Poems*, p. 59), which has been for sale in twenty fairs: to church, to the state, then to the tinkers, all of whom turn their back on this soul that's for sale. Again Kavanagh is scrupulously careful in implicating himself in the condemnation; after all, he has tried to sell his most precious possession, because it is "broken-winded" and "spavined" and looks as if it's worth nothing. So, at the end, he accepts what he cannot be rid of, in spite of his best efforts at self-betrayal:

"Soul,
I have hawked you through the world

Of Church and State and meanest trade.
But this evening, halter off,
Never again will it go on.
On the south side of the ditches
There is grazing of the sun "

As I said these words he grew
Wings upon his back

(p. 60)

Father Mat, in the poem of that name, is an embodiment of this spirit of responsibility, imagination, and creativity. He is a saintly figure but utterly undogmatic, unlike his young curate, who knows the uses of the will and of ambition, and who will force life to yield to him. Father Mat is unfitted for these brute engagements with circumstance, because he will

Stare through gaps at ancient Ireland sweeping
In again with all its unbaptized beauty:
The calm evening

(*Collected Poems*, p. 61)

He remains conscious always of "the undying difference in the corner of a field." He knows change, and knows that life changes. And here, again, one sees Kavanagh's technique of openness: he allows the poem to travel with its own gait as it reveals the purity of the mind of a truly good person, someone the antithesis of the "Chestertonian Paddy frog" in "The Paddiad." "God the Gay is not the Wise" is the voice that comes through the hedges to Father Mat.

In "A Christmas Childhood," another poem of wonder and blessing of this phase, Kavanagh goes back in imagination to his boyhood; the poem is the "stem of memory" on which the imagination blossoms. And there is a powerful flourishing of wonder and magic in this poem as, breathlessly, it evokes the sheer glory of being alive, of being loved, and of the world being a place charged with potential and goodness. Here is the little boy hiding in the doorway on Christmas Eve, listening to his father playing the melodeon, breathing in the cold, the starlight, and the wonder. He tells us that he

tightened the belt of my box-pleated coat.
I nicked six nicks on the door-post
With my penknife's big blade—

There was a little one for cutting tobacco.
And I was six Christmases of age.

My father played the melodeon,
My mother milked the cows,
And I had a prayer like a white rose pinned
On the Virgin Mary's blouse.

(*Collected Poems*, p. 72)

Tarry Flynn took Kavanagh a long time to write. A version of it was rejected by Methuen in 1942; extracts from the work in progress appeared in various places, until it was published, to almost total lack of interest, by the Pilot Press in London in 1948; it is the "Father Mat" systole to the diastole of *The Great Hunger* and "The Paddiad." In a sense it is a return, once more to William Carleton and the world of *The Green Fool*, but there is a profound difference between this work and its model and its predecessor earlier work. There is a lightness in *Tarry Flynn*, a brio; the community that Kavanagh evokes in the novel have their meannesses and barbaric narrowness, but somehow it doesn't matter. The people are seen in a light clarified of all desire to make them other. It is a profoundly rural narrative in that it, like the later fiction of George Moore (whom Kavanagh came greatly to admire), eschews all desire to judge or to approve. Things and people just are, in all their comedy, and dignity, and foolishness.

About two-thirds of the way through the novel there is an episode that illustrates this lightness of being, in the phrase of the Czech writer Milan Kundera. Tarry Flynn is deeply in love with Mary Reilly, someone who, he feels, is so much his better that he can hardly speak to her when he meets her. One day he is up in his room, his writing space, studying phrenology, thinking that the shape of his head is such that he will be nearly "as great a poet as Clark" (p. 165). This is Austin Clarke, one of those in the bohemian jungle of Dublin that drove Kavanagh up the wall. Next thing, he hears his mother talking to Mary Reilly. The shame of this! His mother embarrasses him profoundly. On this occasion she even blows her nose with her fingers. It turns out one of Mary's tires is flat, and his mother roars to Tarry to come down and pump it up. This throws Tarry into such a "swether" that he cannot decide whether he should change his trousers. But he has delayed long enough and goes down as he is. The horror of this, and the humor, lies in the repair work his mother has done on these working pants. He is so ashamed, he walks out sideways toward the girl, so that she won't see what is tormenting him: the big overcoat button in the fork of his trousers that his mother has stitched in to repair the crotch. Now he has to pump up her tire, hide his crotch, and at the same time endure the excruciating proximity of her lovely legs. The suffering is there of course, but somehow the writing has moved onto a comic level in which human folly and inadequacy are all to be forgiven or just discounted in the clarified light of the higher understanding comedy brings.

At the end of *Tarry Flynn*, Tarry is back up in his attic, on a level with the horizon:

> it was a level on which there was laughter. Looking down at his misfortunes he thought them funny now He was in his secret room in the heart now. Having entered he could be bold.
>
> (p. 241)

However the "secret room of the heart" (p. 241), while it may be realizable in moments of vision and though these moments can be tracked and measured in the higher forms of mental activity that are poetry and fiction, such a space is never a sacrosanct reservation for permanent refuge.

When he and his brother were running *Kavanagh's Weekly* in 1952 he made some formidable enemies. Nothing new in that of course. What was different about this situation was the fact that a vicious but very clever and even witty profile of Kavanagh appeared, anonymously, in *The Leader* on 11 October 1952. His voice was described by the writer of the profile (whom Antoinette Quinn revealed was the poet-diplomat Valentin Iremonger, a person equipped with powerful friends as well as a formidable intelligence) as "reminiscent of a load of gravel sliding down the side of a quarry"; while his mind was characterized as "labyrinthine" but also as being marked by "solid peasant cunning" (*Collected Pruse*, p. 165). These were insulting remarks, and Kavanagh took a libel case against *The Leader*, which he lost, after days of cruel

and very effective cross-examination by John A. Costello, a barrister who later became Taoiseach. Kavanagh was exhausted, demoralized, and very ill when the verdict came in, which went against him. Now alcoholism took hold and the cancer, which had been probably developing for years, became rampant in his weakened state. He was hospitalized in 1955 and underwent surgery for lung cancer, from which he was to recover. From 1955 onwards, for a few years, he experienced astonishing imaginative renewal and vitality.

THE COMIC MUSE: LATER POEMS AND WRITINGS

BEFORE his breakdown and illness he was already preparing himself for some kind of transformation. He concluded the run of *Kavanagh's Weekly* in 1952 with a poem which he later revised as "Having Confessed," where the openness and receptivity to experience that were to illumine the best of his later poems with an absolute and steady light is actually thought through. This is the kind of thinking that maybe only can be done in poetry, as instinct, intellect and vision combine in the self's articulation of itself. He goes back to the room in the heart with which *Tarry Flynn* concluded, warning himself not to close down what is going to happen, mentally or spiritually, by prediction, the conscious mind, striving:

> We must not anticipate
> Or awaken for a moment. God cannot catch us
> Unless we stay in the unconscious room
> Of our hearts. We must be nothing,
> Nothing that God may make us something...
> We have sinned, sinned like Lucifer
> By this anticipation.
>
> (*Collected Poems*, p. 149)

In another poem, first published in *The Bell* in October 1951, and later titled "Auditors In," he proceeds to give an account of the self as the location for the beginning of wisdom. The problem is to be both eloquent and sincere, because the actualities of situations, whether social, psychological, or aesthetic, are hard to get at, and require an art which is both open and complex, truthful and fluid, simple and difficult—a problem faced by all writers from Dante, Geoffrey Chaucer, and Sir Philip Sidney. "Fool," Sidney admonished himself, "look in thy heart and write," but that is a very tricky thing to do, and takes elaborate sonnet sequences to sound out of the labyrinth. But "Auditors In" shows Kavanagh displaying the necessary integrity without which no poetry can get written; he is taking stock of what he is:

And you must take yourself in hand
And dig and ditch your authentic land.
(*Collected Poems*, p. 124)

Digging drains makes the water run clear and sweetens the stagnant fen, but it is necessary, as you do this, to create some protective barriers. Again, how is it possible to be honest and deeply true and at the same time not be overrun by marauders and incursors? At the end Kavanagh's method was to open up and not to care. Towards the close of "Auditors In" he turns away from the "sour soil" of the town, where "all roots canker" to

where the Self reposes
The placeless Heaven that's under all our noses
Where we're shut off from all the barren anger
(*Collected Poems*, p. 126)

The lesson he is arduously instructing himself in here is that creativity only really functions when all self-regard and self-pity disappears. This is the "placeless Heaven," that is neither the sour soil of Dublin or of Monaghan, but the active connective energy that links all things in a plural universe. This is the God of openness, of placelessness; if this God is not worshipped he or she "withers to the Futile One," the words with which the poem concludes. Monomania, monotheism, monoliths, all end up in a futile monotony, when the world calls upon the self to remove to lightsome and spacious fluidity and placelessness. Seamus Heaney, in his essay "The Placeless Heaven: Another Look at Kavanagh," written at a crucial phase in Heaney's own development as he was writing the buoyant poems of weightless-

ness and airiness that went into *Seeing Things* (1991), described Kavanagh in this last phase as being "like a Chagall, afloat above his native domain, airborne in the midst of his own dream place rather than earthbound in a literal field" (p. 13). This "airborne" quality is hard won; the comic muse emerges from sadness tracked and measured and thought through. "Prelude," a poem Kavanagh dedicated as a Christmas present in 1954 to Costello, the barrister, now Taoiseach, who cross-examined him in 1952, puts it as follows:

all true poems laugh inwardly
Out of grief-born intensity.
(*Collected Poems*, p. 131)

In March 1955 he had his cancer operation, and, famously, convalesced on the banks of the Grand Canal in Dublin, with his sister in Longford, and in St. Stephen's Green. In a couple of essays he wrote about those days of release and reprieve as a time in which he rediscovered the reality of the creative spirit. The work had, of course, been going on all his life, and in particular during the worsening of his health he was preparing himself for some kind of a transformation, were he to receive the gift of realizing that possibility. He did. Life relented, and in the midst of his suffering and distress, new blessings awoke. In "From Monaghan to the Grand Canal," he describes a hegira, a journey, back to a fresh interinvolvement with the grace and beauty of life just happening:

I have been thinking of making my grove on the banks of the Grand Canal near Baggot Street Bridge where in recent days I rediscovered my roots. My hegira was to the Grand Canal bank where again I saw the beauty of water and green grass and the magic of light. Real roots lie in our capacity for love and its abandon. Lying at the heart of love we wander through its infinities.
(*Collected Pruse*, p. 223)

Real roots, he is almost saying, entwine themselves in the air of placelessness and of prayer. He reflects upon what "real technique" is: "a spiritual quality, a condition of mind a method of being sincere" (p. 229). It means being able to track a situation or an emotion according to its own nature and its corresponding coherence with the tracks and pathways of the human mind. Such a correspondence, when it is struck, is a concord, and its mood is comic. All true poetry, he goes so far as to say, "laughs inwardly," because "laughter is the most poetic thing in life" (p. 230). Why? Because when a work or a person is imbued with comedy, it (or he or she) is facing up to the way things are, rather than being seduced by the "claptrap" which is usually put up as morality by those who are living according to codes not their own, or reality's, but inauthentic constructs.

In *Self Portrait*, a television program broadcast in 1962 and published in 1964, he connected creativity, the comic spirit, and "the difficult art of not caring" (*Collected Pruse*, p. 18). This art is as complex and as simple as having the "courage and rectitude" of one's own feelings, of having the integrity not to convert them to the uses of officialdom and institutionalized morality. The real morality lay in attentiveness to the inward laugh of things, their energy, and technique is as simple and as complex as retaining access to the shifts and pulses of that energy. A poetry and a technique that is responsive in this way is a profound not-caring, a theology of pure openness: "A poet is a theologian" (*Collected Pruse*, p. 22). In "Canal Bank Walk," a sonnet (a form, incidentally, to which Kavanagh returned again and again throughout his life), the writing opens out to a theology of variousness and of multiple significances; while the form expresses correspondences between the elements in the plurality of experience, the integration between these, as they unfold, and the emotional onward impulse of the poem:

Leafy-with-love banks and the green waters of the canal
Pouring redemption for me, that I do
The will of God, wallow in the habitual, the banal,
Grow with nature again as before I grew.

Growing with nature in the form of the poem creates a writing which is as much prayer as it is art: the poet is here theologian. He goes on:

The bright stick trapped, the breeze adding a third
Party to the couple kissing on an old seat,

And a bird gathering materials for the nest for the Word
Eloquently new and abandoned to its delirious beat.

Materials multiply. The poem is the nest; the poet is a bird, airborne, as the form multiplies into complexity and the unity of the Word of God. The world is renewing in the formal "delirious beat":

O unworn world enrapture me, encapture me in a web
Of fabulous grass and eternal voices by a beech,
Feed the gaping need of my senses, give me ad lib
To pray unselfconsciously with overflowing speech

For this soul needs to be honored with a new dress woven
From green and blue things and arguments that cannot be proven

(*Collected Poems*, p. 150)

The banal now clothes the soul, no longer for sale, in a web of grass and of things various and normal, a gown of rapture that is also composed of arguments that hold good even though they evade logic. There is a multifarious openness of work in the process enacted here, a lightness of touch, a placelessness, in which all the materials are gathered, and then gone beyond into an "airborne-ness" of Zen-like stillness and rapture. The poetic is, to recall a term of the 1950s and 1960s "way out," a form that attains a transcendental calm through a movement through and in the material world itself. Another of these poems of comic and lightsome wonder is "The Hospital." Kavanagh remarked that the more energy a poem has the more comic it is. (*Collected Pruse*, p. 229.) The opening line is funny and accurate; and the rhyme between lines one and four (this is another sonnet, a Petrarchan) is pure genius with the surprise and lift of the actual:

A year ago I fell in love with the functional ward
Of a chest hospital: square cubicles in a row
Plain concrete, wash basins—an art lover's woe,
Not counting how the fellow in the next bed snored.

(*Collected Poems*, p. 153)

Form is used to remind us of the divine and comic conspiracy in which all things are connected, so that naming the variousness is "the love-act," the avoidance of "claptrap," a word which, in the sestet, rhymes brilliantly with the "suntrap" at the back of a shed in the grounds of the Rialto Hospital.

There are other such poems of tremulous composure from the late 1950s, among them "Lines Written on a Seat," "The One," "In Memory of My Mother"; but also, at this time, he began experimenting with philosophical doggerel to create a mood of abandonment of self and self-importance. These poems have a good deal of "humorosity," as he called it in *Self Portrait*, but they are often strained and self-conscious, ironically so when it is considered that they were meant to be exercises in self-negation:

The important thing is not To imagine one ought
Have something to say,
A raison d'être, a plot for the play.
The only true teaching
Subsists in watching
(Collected Poems, p. 154)

There is a good deal of this kind of material, entertaining enough but slackly organized, animated by high spirits rather than creative energy, which latter gathers to itself power of connection. He knew the problem himself very well. His system was to have no system; his care was not to care, a poetic practice that can work only if the lines of connection between the creative mind and actuality are kept clear, something hard to achieve if addiction tightens its grip, as it did on Kavanagh.

No System, No Plan,
Yeatsian invention
No all-over
Organisational prover.
(Collected Poems, p. 173)

One of the last poems he wrote, "Personal Problem," shows him wondering about this placeless and contentless aesthetic, asking himself whether he shouldn't, at last, turn to some framework, a myth or a saga, as an instrument:

To play upon without the person suffering
From the tiring years.

The void grows "more awful" by the hour. What is he to do? With the searing honesty he has made his method he confronts his own bleakness and dejection:

I grew
Uncultivated and now the soil turns sour,
Needs to be revived by a power not my own...

But this was always his strength, the faith in his own powers, trust in the soul that stubbornly clung to him. Now he hankers after

Heroes enormous who do astounding deeds—
Out of this world. Only thus can I attune
To despair an illness like winter alone in Leeds.
(in Quinn, p. 448)

The illness is too great to be attuned to poetry; in any case we know that a poetic attuning bodily decrepitude to sadness is not the way of him. This is the problem he faces. The story is over, but outlined in one of the great poems of dejection, to be set beside Samuel Taylor Coleridge's "Ode" and Yeats's "The Circus Animals' Desertion."

CONCLUSION

Kavanagh's achievement lies in bringing into the literature of modern Ireland the actuality of rural experience, as distinct from the mythologized versions of it devised for their own, and undeniably serious, purposes by Yeats, Synge, and Lady Gregory. In some respects, Kavanagh's own literary career was a wrestling off of their influences, a getting clear of them and their visions, so he could claim his own ground. In doing this he moved, strategically, back to the writer whom he claimed as his predecessor, and for whose *Autobiography* he wrote an introduction, William Carleton. The Irish literary revival, and the Gaelic revival (the latter inaugurated by Douglas Hyde in 1893 with the Gaelic League, and perpetuated by the Irish Free State propaganda machine after 1922) to some degree invented an Irish rural existence which idealized the Irish peasant. Kavanagh was the real thing, and more than that, took the trouble to track the cultural heritage of his people to its sources in their way of life, their language (even though in English), and their frequently unprepossessing habits of life. The strength of his affection for his own people finds expression in the autobiographical prose works, *The Green Fool* and *Tarry Flynn*; while his appraisal of their spiritless dereliction, and the causes (economic, sexual, and psychological) is worked through in that pained and painstaking poetic analysis *The Great Hunger*.

Pity and compassion animate his Carleton-like poetic evisceration of Catholicism in *Lough Derg*; while a new openness to actuality, evincing a spirituality based on experience that stands comparison with Montaigne's openness and acceptance, comes through in the postwar *A Soul for Sale*. In the 1950s his poetics of acceptance matures, and imaginative energy comes through in spite of a life-threatening cancer. Stillness and praise are rediscovered in an ecstasy that is both secular and spiritual at once. A Buddhism of process is uncovered in masterly poetry uncovering new techniques of attentiveness and sincerity. There is a final lapse into frank dejection, creatively speaking; although in his last years in Dublin he enjoyed the esteem and admiration of the young to whom he was kind and generous. He died on 30 November 1967.

His legacy has profoundly affected the practices of many poets, often at critical points in their own development. Among these are John Montague, Seamus Heaney, Derek Mahon, Paul Durcan, and Greg Delanty.

SELECTED BIBLIOGRAPHY

I Separate Works. *Ploughman and Other Poems* (London, 1936); *The Green Fool* (London, 1938; New York, 1939); *The Great Hunger* (Dublin, 1942); *A Soul for Sale: Poems* (London, 1947); *Tarry Flynn: A Novel* (Dublin, 1948; New York, 1949) *Recent Poems* (New York, 1958); *Come Dance with Kitty Stobling and Other Poems* (London, 1960; Philadelphia, Pa., 1964); *Self Portrait* (Dublin, 1964); *By Night Unstarred: An Autobiographical Novel*, ed. by Peter Kavanagh (Curragh, Ireland, 1977; New York, 1978); *Lough Derg* (London, 1978).

II Collected Works. *Patrick Kavanagh: Collected Poems* (London, 1964); *Collected Pruse* (London, 1967); *November Haggard: Uncollected Prose and Verse of Patrick Kavanagh*, ed. by Peter Kavanagh (New York, 1971); *Patrick Kavanagh: The Complete Poems*, ed. by Peter Kavanagh (New York, 1972).

III Critical, Biographical and Contextual Studies. Frank O'Connor, *My Father's Son* (London, 1968); Alan Warner, *Clay Is the Word: Patrick Kavanagh (1904–1967)* (Dublin, 1973); Brendan Kennelly, "Patrick Kavanagh" in Seán Lucy, ed., *Irish Poets in English* (Cork and Dublin, 1973); Darcy O'Brien, *Patrick Kavanagh* (Lewisburg, Pa., 1975); Anthony Cronin, *Dead as Doornails* (Dublin, 1976); Peter Kavanagh, *Sacred Keeper: A Biography of Patrick Kavanagh* (Curragh, Ireland, 1979); John Nemo, *Patrick Kavanagh* (Boston, Mass., 1979); Seamus Heaney, "From Monaghan to the Grand Canal: The Poetry of Patrick Kavanagh" in his *Preoccupations: Selected Prose, 1968–1978* (London and New York, 1980); Anthony Cronin, "Patrick Kavanagh: Alive and Well in Dublin" in *Heritage Now* (Dingle, 1982); Terence Brown, *Ireland: A Social and Cultural History* (Ithaca, N.Y., 1985); Peter Kavanagh, ed., *Patrick Kavanagh: Man and Poet* (Orono, Me., 1986); John Wilson Foster, *Fictions of the Literary Revival* (Syracuse, N.Y., 1987); Seamus Heaney, "The Placeless Heaven: Another Look at Kavanagh" in *The Government of the Tongue* (London, 1988); John Montague, "Patrick Kavanagh: A Speech from the Dock" in his *The Figure in the Cave and Other Essays* (Dublin and Syracuse, N.Y., 1989); Antoinette Quinn, *Patrick Kavanagh: Born-Again Romantic* (Dublin and New York, 1991).

IV Letters. *Lapped Furrows: Correspondence 1933–1967 between Patrick and Peter Kavanagh with Other Documents*, ed. by Peter Kavanagh (New York, 1969).

V Bibliographical Studies. *Garden of the Golden Apples: A Bibliography of Patrick Kavanagh*, ed. by Peter Kavanagh (New York, 1972).

VI Manuscripts. There is a Kavanagh Archive in the Library of University College, Dublin. Other manuscripts are preserved in the National Library of Ireland: Mss. 3213–3220; and Ms. 9599.

Anna Kavan

(1901–1968)

David Breithaupt

IT WOULD PERHAPS be easier to write of Anna Kavan's time or focus strictly on her books, as her life left few footholds for biographers to grasp. She destroyed all personal correspondence in her possession along with the vast majority of her diaries. Throughout her life she used several pseudonyms, including Helen Ferguson, Helen Edmonds, and, of course, Anna Kavan. Most of her books were published under the Kavan name (as they all are today). However a few of her early publications first saw light under the name Helen Ferguson. She was born on 10 April 1901 as Helen Emily Woods. Why the secrecy and deception? Why several false names instead of one? Even those close to Kavan seem at a loss for an answer. Her longtime friend and fellow writer Rhys Davies was thought by her agent, David Higham, to be a good choice for Kavan's biographer after her death. However, Davies refused. After an acquaintance with Kavan for thirty years, he declared he still did not know her well enough to pen such a personal work. The intimate details of Kavan's life remain a mystery to this day.

EARLY LIFE

THERE are some facts that are easy to document in the case of this writer's life. Kavan's parents were apparently wealthy enough to be of the leisure class, pursuing the lives of British expatriates in Cannes, France, when their daughter was born. Claude Charles Edward Woods came from a family that owned a large estate in England near Newcastle upon Tyne. In his mid-thirties Claude fell in love with a woman of no great economic means but of fine beauty, named Helen Eliza Bright. Both came from a background of some intellectual ability as several members of

Claude's family were in academia and Helen was a grand-daughter of Dr. Richard Bright who sometimes served as physician to Queen Victoria and who was also noted as the discoverer of Bright's disease. Such were the parents who brought forth one of the twentieth century's finest and most enigmatic writers. Kavan spent many of her childhood years under the care of various nurses. Shortly after her birth, she was sent away "to a place where there was nothing but snow and ice" (Callard, p. 16). In later years, Kavan developed the theory that the nurse did not like the cold climate they were sent to and that this dislike came out in the wet nurse's milk. This might also explain Kavan's fascination with colder climates which eventually led her to write one of the more well-known novels of her later years, *Ice* (1967).

Anna finally resettled in the first few months of her life back at the home of her mother and father in West London, in a house called Churchill Court. A wet nurse named Sammy was Anna's initial caregiver in her early years, watching over Anna even as her parents left her once again to visit the United States. Apparently, Anna's father was making financial investments in America as he was living off an inheritance that was becoming smaller as time went on. He eventually bought an orange grove in Rialto, California, and it was here to which he brought Anna and Sammy to live in a simple bungalow, isolated amidst the rows of ripening orange trees. Here she lived until the age of six when she was "betrayed" and sent off to a round of American boarding schools. She very seldom saw her parents during these years.

Her time at the American boarding schools was interrupted when, at the age of fourteen, she learned of her father's death. Biographers are still not clear as to what happened to Claude Woods. According to the testimony of a fellow shipmate, Claude jumped overboard while bound for South America. No one is quite sure as to the cause of this sudden departure from the living—biographers speculate his marriage, his handling of money, or simply a family tendency toward depression and melancholy. It remains a mystery to this day. What is more certain is the effect that Claude's death had on his daughter. "Now I feel myself alone against the whole world, more than I'd ever been ..." (Callard, p. 18).

Anna's mother promptly withdrew her from boarding school and eventually brought her back to England. At the peak of her adolescent years, a rough time on any child let alone one whose father had just committed suicide, she was entered into what was called at the time a "progressive" girls school, the Parsons Mead School in Ashtead, Surrey.

If one can believe any of the autobiographical material in her later stories and novels, one can conclude that these were not happy years for Kavan. Her short story, "Out and Away," from her book *Julia and the Bazooka and Other Stories* (1970), is about a young girl in a boarding school such as the ones Kavan attended. "That girl is maladjusted," said the schoolmates of the story's hero. "I simply detested the place, loathed everything about it ..." continues the narrator (*Julia and the Bazooka*, p. 77). Indeed, Kavan's time at the Parsons Mead School was not a success and she was later transferred to Malvern Girls College. She was only a slight bit happier at this school for it was here that she made her first real friend, one she would keep for life. The friend was Ann Ledbrook, and she came into Kavan's life at just the right time. These were bleak years, not just for Kavan who was still struggling with the meaning of her father's death, but for the world at large as World War I had been raging and now, in 1918, the Spanish influenza was taking a record number of lives.

Although Kavan did not have an idyllic childhood, hers was not unique for a child growing up in late Victorian and Edwardian eras. These years were differentiated by a culture which had so little to do with its children, more so than any before it or since. Young boys and girls were sent off into the care of wet nurses and nannies while parents carried on and nobody thought the worse for it.

Just what effect did this particular brand of child rearing have on its generation? That subject would be the topic of a whole other essay or book. However one may discuss how such an upbringing altered the outlook Anna Kavan had on the world, and how it may have contributed greatly to her sense of isolation and loneliness. Perhaps the pain of these early years was the muse which first called her to pick up her pen.

In 1919 Kavan left Malvern College and returned to her mother's home in Earley, near Reading, to a place called Manor House. Since the death of her father, she was now at the mercy of her mother, a relationship well chronicled in later novels and stories. In real life, it was a relationship which was always strained, though they were generally able to get along. Any independence she may have had financially while her father lived vanished when he died with the exception of a small trust fund. On Kavan's eighteenth birthday she was granted an allowance of six hundred pounds a year—a significant amount of money for the time but not enough to fund her dream of attending Oxford. The sudden death of her father left the family's finances in a shambles. She was now completely under her mother's control who did not have Oxford as a high priority for young Anna.

EARLY WORKS

KAVAN'S 1930 novel *Let Me Alone*, published originally under the name of Helen Ferguson, is possibly the best autobiographical source we have of her adolescent feelings at this time regarding the death of her father and the complete takeover of her life by her mother.

In this novel, Kavan recasts her mother as Aunt Lauretta in a far from flattering portrait. Kavan recasts herself as Anna Forrester (maybe a pun on her family name) who later becomes Anna Kavan when she marries, the name she finally legally adopts as her nom de plume in later years

ANNA KAVAN

(this novel represents the first appearance of the Kavan name).

Early in the novel, Aunt Lauretta assumes full control of Anna after her father dies. The book hints that Anna's mother died giving birth to her and brings the eventual death of the father by his own hand. Aunt Lauretta wastes little time making life miserable for Anna. When Anna finally makes a friend at school, a girl named Sydney, Aunt Lauretta is quick to forbid any further contact with the new acquaintance. As Anna is cut off from Sydney, she describes her feelings about her dear aunt in the novel:

> It was horrible to her (Anna) to see the slightly sagging face on which was a tormenting, ugly look. She hated to see the cruel smirk of triumph on the relaxed mouth. And the bright eyes watching her like a wicked, predatory bird, with a gleam of ferocity, sinister.
>
> (*Let Me Alone*, London, 1974, p. 92)

Thus begins a battle of wills between Anna and her aunt from which there seems no escape until the entrance of Matthew Kavan, a friend her uncle had met at the war office and then later began a correspondence. Presently on leave in England from his post in the Shan States, he is invited to stay in their house (called Blue Hills) for a brief time. Based on the real-life figure of Donald Ferguson, Kavan's first real-life husband whom she married in 1920, Matthew is literally forced on Anna and thus into marriage as Aunt Lauretta offers no other options. The dream of attending Oxford is long gone, extinguished by her aunt with a false complaint of financial hardship.

Anna finds her hand forced as her aunt and uncle begin to close up Blue Hills for the winter, her friendship with Sydney is long gone, and she is left only with a stubborn Matthew Kavan who is intent on having Anna as his bride. She finds she has no choice but to accept his proposal.

In real life, little is known of how Donald Ferguson entered into Anna Kavan's life. What is known is that Ferguson was born in Bovey Tracey in Devon and had a father wealthy enough to lend his son the title of "gentleman." During this time (1919–1920), Ferguson was working as an engineer on the railways set up in Burma by the Colonial Administration.

It is important to remember the time and place of Kavan's life and how it influenced her to enter into matrimony. Kavan was a young woman, fresh from high school in which she was kept almost completely in the company of women. Although she was young, she may have received her first inkling of mortality after living through the carnage of World War I and the almost equally brutal Spanish influenza. Those first postwar months provided the perfect opportunity for spreading a world wide epidemic. Soldiers were crossing borderlines, exiles were returning home and with them they carried the seeds of one of the worst outbreaks of deadly disease the world had seen since the bubonic plague. Surely Kavan was affected by the numerous deaths from war and disease that surrounded her like waves beating upon an island shore. Scholars also speculate that she may have decided to jump into life as she sensed the brevity of her time on this planet, and who better to do it with than someone who could afford to fund various explorations into the heart of her curiosities? D. A. Callard, in his biography of Anna Kavan, *The Case of Anna Kavan*, offers the interesting theory that Kavan may have entered into this seemingly strange marriage to replace the father figure she barely knew and lost early in life. Ferguson was thirty at the time of their marriage to Kavan's nineteen. The match was also strongly encouraged by her mother, just as with Aunt Lauretta in *Let Me Alone*.

Let Me Alone was the second novel published under the name of Helen Ferguson (with *A Charmed Circle* being the first, in 1929). The novel's hero, Anna Kavan, faces a continual series of setbacks equaled perhaps by Job or the characters in the novels of Charles Dickens. The suicide of her father lands her into the not-so-caring domain of her Aunt Lauretta thus, dashing her dreams of attending Oxford University, the rejection of her poetry manuscript by a publisher who teased her into believing it would be published, the forced isolation from being able to write her one true friend, Sydney, and, finally, the placement into a loveless and nightmarish marriage. Anna Kavan, the heroine, becomes a prototype version of a sort of feminist David Copperfield or Oliver Twist. She does not want the conventional life of marriage and domesticity: Kavan has talent, she wants to write her visions as well as paint them, she wants to read and study and create poetry that will be on the lips of generations to come. All of these desires come tumbling down as she is cornered by Aunt Lauretta into a dismal marriage with Matthew Kavan.

Let Me Alone adopts a conventional style influenced by the writers Kavan admired at the time, such as D. H. Lawrence. Although the atmosphere is oppressive in this novel, it is not quite so bleak as the reader would find in some of the previously mentioned novels of Dickens or even *Sons and Lovers* by Lawrence. It is, in fact, an updated version of both, depicting the helplessness of women imprisoned by the conventions of their time. Instead of coal mines and harsh orphanages, there is the social etiquette that has a predetermined role for all women on how to live out their lives. This is its own hell for any woman with visions and ambitions beyond child rearing and homemaking as Anna Kavan had in both real life and her books.

Critics have remarked on Kavan's debt to D. H. Lawrence, especially in her early novels and stories. In his 1974 essay, Stanley Reynolds wrote his thoughts on the subject:

Miss Kavan's style with its repetition with words resembles that of D. H. Lawrence. There are also certain passages which also could be mistaken for Lawrence ... The spirit is Lawrence's too. Anna, the hero, is disenchanted like Lady Chatterly ... she is sort of a reversed Constance Chatterly because she cannot stand to have her husband touch her. But the husband's British insensitivity is very Lawrence and the jungle that surrounds her in a Lawrention way and the natives are sensitive, delicately natural men and women. The echo of the great English novelist is not a bad thing. Even the repetition of words works fine and makes you wonder, as with Lawrence, why we have acquired the odd notion that to use the same word twice in a sentence is a sign of bad writing.

(*New Statesman*, 11 January 1974)

It is on points such as this that scholars wish they had more of Kavan's diaries to glean what writers she was reading at the time. Instead, scholars may simply draw their own conclusions from her work and rely on scraps of remembered conversations with Kavan that may have survived over the years.

Scholars know, however, that Kavan spent a large part of the next two years after her marriage in Burma where her husband worked. Details of these months are hazy and if scholars are to rely on her novels as indicators for how happy the newlyweds were, they may conclude that this was not a successful union. By 1922, the marriage had come to an end after only two years. However, 1922 also brought a beginning in addition to the end of the marriage: the birth of their son, Bryan Ferguson.

Kavan left Burma with Bryan to return to England, perhaps in part because she feared the lack of standard medical facilities in the country. If anything can be salvaged from these years besides the birth of her son and the stoic philosophy of learning from one's mistakes, it is that Kavan probably started writing at this time. Although nothing survives from these years, scholars might theorize that the heat and isolation helped begin her passion for the written word, which remained a constant to the end of her days.

Enter the Jazz Age. The 1920s held many reasons for being the flamboyant, jazzy, and experimental times that they were. The world was still recovering from a world war and finishing a period of mourning which, for some, would not end for many years to come. By the time of Kavan's marital dissolution in 1922, she, as well as the rest of the world, were ready for some uplifting times. These were the years of speakeasies, flappers, the Charleston, and fox-trotting. Gangsters such as Al Capone and John Dillinger were heroes as they made millions by bootlegging and robbing banks. It was indeed a strange era of postwar recovery. Everybody it seemed, was looking for some excitement. Jay Gatsby was on the rise.

1925 was a formative year for Kavan. In the winter of 1925–1926, she moved to Sainte Maxime, a village in the south of France. It was roughly around this time that Kavan is believed to have started using heroin, as well as other drugs such as cocaine and possibly opium. In later years, Kavan claimed to have been introduced to heroin by a tennis coach (an anecdote also referred to in one of her last short stories, "Julia and the Bazooka," from the book of the same name) with the purpose of improving her game. More likely, if there was any connection with tennis, it was used to help cope with a sore elbow or arm, as heroin would be a very unlikely aid in any player's tennis game. In any case, it seems that by 1926 she was addicted to the then-popular narcotic.

Referring once again to her short story, "Julia and the Bazooka" (bazooka being a slang word she invented for the syringe), the influence of heroin upon her life is mentioned. Julia is speaking of a doctor friend who may be based on Kavan's old acquaintance, Dr. Bluth:

In his opinion she is quite right to use the syringe, it is as essential to her as insulin is to a diabetic. Without it, she could not lead a normal existence, her life would be a shambles, but with its support she is conscientious and energetic, intelligent, friendly. She is most unlike the popular notion of a drug addict. Nobody could call her vicious.

(p. 153)

In addition to forming a relationship with this powerful narcotic (which lasted longer than any of Kavan's marriages), Kavan met and fell deeply in love with Stuart Edmonds, a well-to-do son of a department-store owner. A small portion of Kavan's diaries survives from this period from July 1926 to November 1927 when she first met Edmonds. Kavan told her friend Raymond Marriott that she kept these few diaries because it was "the only time I was ever in love" (Callard, p. 32). In these surviving pages, Kavan also recorded the fact that she had to take a walk to help curb her craving for drugs.

Her feelings for Edmonds, who later became her common-law husband, were almost at the complete opposite end of the spectrum from her feelings for Donald Ferguson. For every nerve with which she loathed Ferguson, she loved Edmonds, almost to the point of obsession. She wrote in her journals: "If S does not exist my life is intolerable and I shall kill myself" (p. 33).

All scholars know for sure about this time in Kavan's life is that she was writing in her diaries. There may have been some false starts in attempting to write fiction, although there is no mention of any such effort in these diaries or remembered by friends in conversations. Scholars do know that she was experiencing and storing a reserve of material in the life she was living for her future writing as seen in *Let Me Alone* and various short stories.

Stuart Edmonds was separated from his wife at the time of his romance with Kavan. This was complicated even further by Edmonds' Catholicism and his father's threat to cut off his allowance if he pursued his attentions to Kavan.

It was probably in the second half of the 1920s, from 1927 onward, that Kavan started doing some serious writing. By 1930, Jonathan Cape published three of her novels, all under the name of Helen Ferguson. In 1929 she published *A Charmed Circle*, which was followed by *Let Me Alone* and *The Dark Sisters* in 1930. In Cape, Kavan found the ideal editor and publisher, a man who believed wholeheartedly in her work. At this point in her career, Kavan could be described as an author who was critically but not commercially acclaimed. Still, Cape looked forward to seeing more of her work despite the fact that Kavan might not become one of his big moneymaking authors.

Despite the lack of commercial success, Kavan was at last getting her work before the public both at home and abroad and with a major publisher. In addition, she had also been working on her drawings and paintings, which she would later exhibit (in 1935) at the Wertheim Gallery in a show titled "Landscapes in Oil." It is hard to imagine how she found the time and energy to be so creative and successful while under the influence of a powerful narcotic and struggling with the termination of her marriage from Ferguson while she became entangled in her next liaison.

In tone and pace, *A Charmed Circle* resembles a sort of updated novel by Thomas Hardy. The action is sufficient to keep the reader interested although it lacks the cliffhanging drama at the end of each chapter as in the serialization days of Charles Dickens. The dialogue and manners of the characters are such that they almost belong to those in the late nineteenth century. *A Charmed Circle*, a title chosen perhaps for its irony, describes the Deane family of the village of Hannington, a once peaceful town now in the throes of industrialization. The Deanes, however, live on a plot completely shielded from the neighboring commercialization by gardens, trees, and shrubs, which further isolates them from others in their area. Almost every member of the Deane family is at odds with the other and visitors often sense "the cross-currents of tension" (p. 92) within the household. The novel continues to detail the lives of Beryl and Olive Deane, two sisters of late high school age, and their older brother Ronald, who is their mother's favorite and whom can do no wrong in her eye. Mrs. Deane is mired in the manners and beliefs of her generation and is mostly resistant to any changes taking place in society. She spends her days inviting guests over for tea and worrying about her children, especially Ronald. Mr. Deane, a retired doctor and practicing grouse, has little to do with the family and spends the bulk of his time with the books in his study. Olive and Beryl are more than anxious to leave their stifling home environment and seek the freedom of life in London. Both sisters are in fierce sibling competition with each other and both are jealous of Ronald as he has already made the leap to London and thus freedom. Ronald is vastly indifferent to all members of his family except when they are able to serve his needs. As for Mrs. Deane, her main concern is how her children make her look to her tea society associates. Finally, gruff Mr. Deane is equally contemptuous of all. Under these circumstances hardly any family member can make a move without some repercussion happening. When Ronald quits his job in London and returns home, he upsets Beryl who was planning on us-

ing her brother to gain her own foothold in London. To placate his disappointed sister, Ronald tricks a friend in London, a sculptor named Christofferson, into visiting their house in Hannington for a weekend. The hope is for the friend to be a help someday in getting work for Beryl in London. However, Ronald describes their home as being "out in the country" (p. 74), which is stretching the truth.

Initially, Christofferson is not disappointed when he discovers his weekend will not be the vacation he thought it would be. However, when Beryl confesses to the guest her brother's plan to have him help her in London, he begins to become a bit chagrined. Christofferson leaves after the weekend with a bad taste in his mouth, Ronald accepts a job with the theater which displeases his mother, Beryl, displeased with everyone, runs away to London, Olivia is left alone and bored, and Mrs. Deane is disgruntled with all of the above. Only Mr. Deane plods along in his usual aloof manner living in his own world, which admits no one but himself.

Although the characters in this novel may have drawn bits and pieces from those in real life that Kavan knew, the story line does not follow a strong autobiographical chronology as does *Let Me Alone*. In fact, Mrs. Deane is the only writer in this charmed circle. Kavan writes of her:

> She took up writing chiefly as a method of self-assertion. She thought that she was using it as a means of expressing her personality, repressed by her family's lack of sympathy. Really, it afforded her an excellent excuse for domestic tyranny.
>
> (p. 24)

Perhaps the most autobiographical element that Kavan used in this novel is the chaos her characters were feeling. Surely this was not written during a tranquil time in her life, especially as she had to deal with the ups and downs of heroin availability on the black market and her continuing entanglement with Edmonds. She was also trying to straighten out a set pattern of custody of her son Bryan.

Kavan finally ends *A Charmed Circle* with the two sisters back in Hannington after failed transplants in London. One wonders if the author felt his pessimistic prophecy applicable to her own life. In any case, Kavan created a very competent novel if somewhat conventional, what critics might call "promising."

The Dark Sisters is also, as the title suggests, a story of sisters. In post–World War I London are Emerald and Karen, sisters who want to live the modern and independent life. Emerald is the motivated sister, who finds success as a fashion model, while Karen prefers to live in a fantasy world, dreaming rather than working, Emerald tries to remedy this situation by matching her shiftless sister with a rich man, a match that comes to a bad end. Finally, Karen returns her sister back home to her life of dreaming, motivated more by guilt than love. At the novel's close, the sisters end up where they began, much the same as those in *A Charmed Circle*. Maybe Kavan felt she herself was spinning her wheels, getting nowhere, as she began to become as disillusioned with Stuart Edmonds as she was with Donald Ferguson.

With her third novel, *Let Me Alone*, Kavan at least begins to break out of her literary stalling. *Let Me Alone* begins to show some of the style and passion that she is known and admired for. With two published books to her credit and a lifetime of anxiety to fuel her muse, it is easier to understand why *Let Me Alone* was a departure for Kavan at least stylistically. Her previous two books were written in the more conventional styles of the accepted English writers of her time (such as Lawrence). The following passage from *Let Me Alone* contains the power of her prose that foreshadows the style of her later novels. Kavan uses her most powerful imagery to date for this description of a marshy swamp:

> The marsh itself had beauty. The great strange lake of swampy ground, mysterious with velvety patches of black ooze; the sinister, sudden gleams of iridescence, like glasses mirroring some magic sky; the succulent, emerald leaves, dangerous and poison-green; the piercing blueness of the small flowers. It had some half-evil glamour. But at night, when the darkness took it, it was a demon world.

Let Me Alone is a book for readers who admire the poetic quality of a book's prose rather than

seek escapism in a fairy-tale world where all ends well. The characters take the names of real-life personalities. As the book's character, Anna, follows her common-law husband, Stuart Edmonds, to Burma where he is assigned to work as an engineer on the railways, she returns to her former isolation and loneliness as casual social mingling with the Burmese is not permitted. She is allowed, however, to mingle with the established wives from England who frequent the local club for officers. This, of course, is not the type of crowd Kavan is anxious to associate with. She finds herself sinking deeper into despair as the rains amplify her loneliness. The crisis peaks when she discovers she is pregnant, a horror that forces her into a frenzy which makes her run into the heart of the monsoon rains. Soaking and half conscious, she loses her baby. The book ends with a scene that could have been painted by Pablo Picasso during his blue period, with Kavan, now fully estranged from her husband, waiting on a hard wooden bench for the arrival of a female friend from England who is en route to Burma to rescue her from this dour episode in her life. While not exactly a feel-good book, it is a significant one in terms of Kavan beginning to break away from local influences and finding her own voice.

The early 1930s found Anna living with Stuart Edmonds in the Chiltern village of Bledlow Cross. They were able to buy a large house in the village called The Elms which had room for a painting studio. Kavan and Edmonds both painted, with Anna being the more serious of the two while Edmonds was described as a weekend painter. It was not until 1935 that Kavan broke both her literary and fine arts silence by publishing *A Stranger Still* and exhibiting her paintings at the Wertheim Gallery.

While still drawing upon much of her own autobiography for this novel, Kavan expands her story line into the lives of other people she knew thus creating the most ambitious piece of writing she had created to date. Each chapter tells a separate episode, almost as though the book were a collection of short stories. As the tales continue, there is a slow overlap of one character appearing in a chapter later in the book. Eventually many of the people in the book begin to mesh and the work forms one tightly constructed, cohesive story.

A Stranger Still once again features Anna Kavan as the book's hero. Recently returned to London from Burma, Anna meets Martin Lewison, the son of a wealthy family overseen by the widower William Lewison who runs a fleet of stores across greater London. Readers find Martin very unhappy in his marriage, not to mention Anna, who has almost entirely estranged herself from husband Matthew, who still has hopes of a reunion.

Both Anna and Martin are at strange crossroads in their lives: Martin has caught his wife sleeping with his best friend while Anna has suddenly given up her fashion design shop just as it was starting to thrive, for no reason at all.

Anna and Martin have ample fuel to ponder the thorns of life, which they do, until they meet by chance, taking a walk by a cliff along a seashore. Martin unexpectedly grabs Anna by the arm as he fears she is looking too closely over the edge. This chance meeting allows them to introduce themselves; Martin confesses his career as a fine artist while Anna speaks of the borrowed money she wasted from her aunt by letting her boutique run into the ground.

A Stranger Still provides a variety of stages for the young couple as they enter into each other's world—the bohemia of Martin's artistic life and the waif-like existence of the orphaned Anna who was raised by her aunt after both her parents died. She wrote:

> She [Anna] had allowed chance external circumstances to control her life. She had relied vaguely for support on something in definable and non-existent, on something outside her life. there were, she knew, elaborate systems of thought, philosophies and religions specially designed to provide external support. But as far as she was concerned she knew they were useless, void.
>
> (p. 85)

The transformations Anna and Martin undergo by entering into each other's world, visiting places and people they would otherwise not have met

changed them in ways they never would have on their own.

According to D. A. Callard's biography of Kavan, *A Stranger Still* received lavish praise. The *Illustrated London News* commented: "Helen Ferguson, whose books are always good, has done nothing better than *A Stranger Still*. She sees people very clearly: she sees through their pretty skins and turns them inside out. *A Stranger Still* is a complete drama in which every actor is fitted out with a significant part" (pp. 57–58).

In the end, the book reflected one of the main autobiographical facets of Kavan's life, her penchant for failed relationships. Martin, who was most likely based on Stuart Edmonds, imitates life as the affair ends in failure. Martin commemorates their relationship with a portrait of Anna.

The year is now 1935 and Anna finds herself thirty-four-years old with a small reputation as a critical if not commercial success in the literary business. *A Stranger Still* will be her most acclaimed book for awhile as she begins to write her last two books under the name of Helen Ferguson: *Goose Cross* in 1936 and *Rich Get Rich* in 1937. Neither novel provokes much notice. *Goose Cross* is another departure in style for Anna. In this work she sets out to write a type of fantasy novel (which might foreshadow her later novel, *Ice*). The tale involves a small village which is cursed by the discovery of an ancient Roman skeleton. Meanwhile, a married couple in the village, Judith and Thomas Spender, are trying to save their marriage. Thomas is a jealous man, rapidly crossing the line into alcoholism (as were the real-life Edmondses). The curse disrupts the town's inhabitants but eventually lifts leaving the survivors stronger, especially in more spiritual ways than before. The *Times Literary Supplement* criticized it for lacking much of a plot. Elsewhere, the book received little attention.

For a woman so plagued by personal problems including drug addiction, failed marriages, and undependable income, Kavan was not lacking in a fairly prolific output for, in 1937, she wrote *Rich Get Rich*. In this novel readers follow the life of Swithin Chance, a man who has a purpose in life which he simply cannot determine, despite his trying a series of professions. Swithin works with the mentally ill, becomes a tutor, marries and divorces a rich woman, and finally drops out of society to live a simple Thoreaulike life. Swithin grows close to a woman whose brother runs a leftist bookshop and tries to enlist him in the cause. However our hero is interested only in writing his memoirs and remaining apolitical. Alas, Swithin dies in an accident with many of his ideals unrealized.

With such a promising life wasted in such a tragic and premature manner, it is no wonder that Kavan suffered one of her most severe nervous breakdowns after the publication of this book, which received faint notice from the press (although the notice was positive). In 1937, England had other matters on its mind such as Adolph Hitler's advancement through Europe. Who had times for novelsespecially those of a competent but obscure writer?

After emerging from the sanitarium in 1938, Kavan was ready to begin life anew, literally. This time she would leave Helen Ferguson behind and reemerge as the real-life Anna Kavan. During the autumn of 1938, Kavan recuperated in London. She took advantage of this time to renew her friendship with fellow writer Rhys Davies. Davies and Kavan met during the 1930s (the exact date is disputed) and remained close literary friends throughout their lives. Born in Rhondda, Davies came to London determined to become a writer. While renewing his acquaintance with Kavan, Davies was quick to see the deterioration of her marriage to Edmonds.

For reasons unknown, Anna was still using heroin from the black market rather than registering with a doctor and receiving a maintenance dose. Edmonds, in the meantime, was turning more and more to alcohol as a balm for the frustrations of his life.

Anna and Edmonds' drugs of choice took them in directions that alienated themselves from each other even more. Anna, with her daily intake of heroin, began to live in her own world, refusing to speak to family and friends. Readers might recall a scene from the early memoir of William S. Burroughs called *Junky*, in which he described the perfect happiness in performing simple acts

while high such as staring at his feet for twelve hours at a time. Edmonds, with his ever-present bottle, was a much more social creature.

This chemical dependency led the couple further away from each other as their habits became progressively worse. Their days as a couple were drawing rapidly to a close. Edmonds fueled his frustration with his lack of success with his fine arts career. As a student of Paul Cézanne (of which there were many in the 1930s and 1940s) he drew yawns from the journalists and critics. Anna, on the other hand, garnished critical praise from all around with both her writings and paintings but her critical success did not result in financial success.

By 1937, Anna was still riding the leftover waves of her success with *A Stranger Still*. Yet another rave about the book had just appeared in the *[London] Sunday Times*: "It lives from start to finish. ... the theme of the book is the essential solitude of the individual. It engages the mind uncompromisingly, and its style is well knit" (Callard, p. 58).

Once again, Kavan produced a mature and ambitious novel under such stress that readers can only imagine. However, readers might find a clue of her mental condition at the end of *A Stranger Still*. If readers believe some of the episodes to be autobiographical, then they might examine one encounter she had with a violinist whom she hoped could help her out of her depression:

The violinist listened with not unkind eyes and finally said: "Of course, your mental attitude is simply fatal to happiness: it damns you irrevocably from the start."
"Why?" she wanted to know.
"You cerebrate far too much," he answered.
"You're hopelessly intellectualized. You've thought all your emotions out of existence, and left nothing but a bleak mental consciousness of yourself. There you sit like a buddha, examining your intestines and gazing at your navel and seeing nothing of the real world."
"What must I do then?" she asked in a humble voice.
"Stop all this introspection," he said.

(pp. 253–254)

If anything, Anna was an introspective woman. Perhaps it was an introspection which always wasn't welcomed when it overstayed its visit while dwelling too deeply.

MIDDLE WORKS AND LITERARY SUCCESS

THE 1930s had been a productive decade for Kavan's literary career. Exhausted from marriages, divorces, a few more near marriages, not to mention her regime of regular drug abuse and the worst mental breakdown of her life, she can almost be pictured the poor woman crawling across the finish line on hands and knees, leaving her final hand and knee prints across the decade's floor as she drags herself ever so slowly into the decade of the 1940s, where she will survive another round of tumultuous events. If that was not enough to complete any writer's career, Kavan began to write some of her most advanced and original pieces such as *Asylum Piece and Other Stories* (1940). The 1940s would bring a very impressive list of literary accomplishments for the harried Anna Kavan.

World War II found the little-known son of Anna Kavan, Bryan Ferguson, joining the Royal Air Force. Bryan seemed to hardly know his mother as his father, Donald, was granted custody of the boy after the couple's divorce in 1927. However, in 1942, Bryan was reported missing in action after flying a bombing raid over Germany.

Kavan was in New Zealand when she heard the news, probably seeking some isolation for a heroin cure. The news of her son's disappearance made her try to return to London. It took her three attempts to make the trip successfully, due to wartime activity. Once she was safe in London, Kavan learned that her missing son was presumed dead. The news landed her in a psychiatric hospital after she attempted to take her own life. Despite the long absences and lack of attention to her son, Kavan obviously had some strong feelings for him.

It was at this psychiatric hospital that Kavan met the man who was assigned to treating her, Dr. Theodore Bluth. Bluth was a literary as well as medical man and claimed Bertolt Brecht and Martin Heidegger among his friends. Bluth was

the doctor who finally persuaded Kavan to register her heroin addiction with the home office. Until he died, Dr. Bluth was the source of all of Kavan's legally obtained heroin. According to D. A. Callard, Bluth and Kavan soon felt a "mystical connection" with each other. Bluth believed that heroin was the only antidote to Kavan's bleak depressions and hence never tried to detoxify her with the goal of abstinence but instead tried to regulate her habit. According to friends such as Raymond Marriott, Kavan would never detox with the goal of complete sobriety. Instead, she tried to tame a habit that had rolled out of control.

The relationship with Dr. Bluth gave Kavan some much-needed stability in her life, allowing her to write articles for the newly created *Horizon* magazine, edited by Cyril Connolly and backed with money by Peter Watson. Kavan was able to contribute fiction with pieces such as "I Am Lazarus" and "The Case of Bill Williams," as well as critical reviews of the current writers that caught her eye for whatever reasons. Virginia Wolfe, for example, was not a writer made for short stories. Kavan felt Wolfe concentrated too much intensity in her shorter pieces. Kavan also reviewed *Let Us Now Praise Famous Men* by James Agee and Walker Evans (the later she had met and been photographed by in New York). She praised the book for its ability to awaken readers to the fate of "damaged and helpless human beings" and the responsibility of those more fortunate to be aware of the human race as a whole, to become active and participate in helping "these undefended ones" (Callard, p. 83).

At times it seemed as if Kavan wanted to burn the world down and start from scratch. While still writing for *Horizon* toward the end of World War II she wrote "Blood transfusions are no good at all. What is needed is a new earth and a new man too inhabit the earth" (p. 85).

It would not be until 1945 that Kavan would try to live up to her words. She would place her stories in American magazines such as the *New Yorker* and *Harper's Bazaar*. Her second collection of stories entitled *I Am Lazarus: Short Stories* (1945) would be published by Jonathan Cape to an appreciative audience. The best news was that the critical acclaim her magazine publications would bring her in the United States would lead the American publisher, Doubleday, to bring out Kavan's *Asylum Piece* with *I Am Lazarus* in one volume in 1946. This edition also received critical acclaim. When the war was over and Kavan's two failed marriages faded into the past, she would at last find a stability, albeit a still fragile peace, to carry her into her next phase of writing.

It is fitting that *Asylum Piece* and *I Am Lazarus* were the pieces of writing that allowed Kavan to introduce her work to a broader public. They are both groundbreaking books for her, shedding even more the influences of Lawrence and Hardy for a more experimental and contemporary feeling. Both works were instead influenced by the times and focus on the fragility of the human mind. *Asylum Piece* both in style and content is a brilliant collection of related short stories which portray various states of mental conditions.

The recent death of Sigmund Freud and a resurgence in his popularity, Kavan's own experience in therapy for her trembling mental foundation, and the collective experience of those soldiers fortunate to return (many of which were suffering from shell shock), give *Asylum Piece* an authentic psychological edge which mirrored the splintered realities of those who "survived."

Desmond MacCarthy was an influential critic at this time. He had already been a consistent supporter of Kavan, writing his reviews for England's influential *New Statesman* about one kind of fiction he still admired and it was "that which deals with queer psychological experiences and describes the world in which people live who are mad, half mad or criminals ..." MacCarthy went on to add, "What is fascinating is to note as one reads both the difference and the resemblances between their experience and that of normal people; also the enormous significance to them of small details which stand out with uncanny vividness" (Callard, p. 88).

Once again Kavan drew on autobiographical material but this was a chronology of her mind, not the day-to-day tally of which marriage lasted and which didn't and what her spiteful mother was up to now. The result was a stunning new insight into the writer's mind.

One of the first critics to praise *Asylum Piece* was Edwin Muir, one of the earliest translators of Kafka, who called Kavan a writer of "unusual imaginative power" (Callard, p. 64). Other critics joined in to add their own praise for the book including, once again, Sir Desmond MacCarthy, who wrote in the *Sunday Times*: "There is a beauty about these stories which has nothing to do with their pathological interest, and is the result of art" (Callard, p. 64).

Though Kafka was not widely known in England (Kafka's first book translated into English was *The Castle* in 1930), Kavan must have read his work in the late 1930s. *Asylum Piece* contains the mysterious and surreal tones which are trademarks of the Czech writer's work. She also uses the Kafkian element of referring to some characters by simple initials. However Kavan uses enough of her own experiences from sanitariums, recovering from nervous breakdowns, and her study of psychology and association with Dr. Bluth that the book is distinctly her own, an original work by Kavan and not a Kafka clone. Interestingly enough, this was the first book to be published under the pseudonym of Anna Kavan. Any similarity between the names Kavan and Kafka (as some have suggested) is purely coincidental as Anna had used the name in her books long before she heard of Franz Kafka.

As usual, *Asylum Piece* was a critical but not commercial success when it was published in England. Money was not as important to Kavan as was her embarkation into her new self-redefinition. After the reviews were in, Kavan left England. It would be three years before she would return.

Before Kavan found a small haven of stability in the mid-1940s, she busied herself in literally traveling the globe. In January 1940, she was issued a United Kingdom passport at Los Angeles (by the British Consul). The passport read as follows: "Name of Bearer, Mrs. Helen Edmonds, Maiden Name, Woods; Professionally known as Anna Kavan" (Callard, p. 70).

Scholars really know little of what was passing through Anna's mind at this time. There are corresponding images in some of her novels and stories that reflect a few of the people she met and places she traveled to at the time. Scholars can only speculate and look at the few solid facts that remain.

It seems Kavan did some of her post *Asylum Piece* traveling with a young man she met while in New Zealand named Ian Hamilton. Scholars know that Ian was much younger than Anna. He may have been a student fresh out of college who was taking a European vacation before settling into his chosen career. After a few months of traveling together they eventually parted, with Ian returning to New Zealand while Anna sailed on to Surabaya, Indonesia. She stayed long enough to gain a transit visa in order to catch a ship to South Africa. Her plan was to visit her mother and the man her mother had just married.

It was a visit that fate stepped in and prevented. Anna met a wealthy and fairly young American by the name of Charles Fuller. Fuller was on his way to becoming a full-time alcoholic. He was either a very entertaining drunk or was very, very rich, as Kavan canceled her trip to South Africa and traveled with Fuller back to New York via Batavia. Fuller was heading back to New York to marry his fiancée even though he and Kavan had spent a drunken night sleeping together. Kavan was drinking heavily at this time which can sometimes be a symptom of heroin withdrawal. Scholars do not know if she carried a large supply of the narcotic with her and was trying to make it last by using alcohol to curb any sickness from withdrawal. When the two of them arrived in New York, Kavan was allowed a sixty-day stay. During this time she was introduced to Fuller's circle, which was very Bohemian and hip. They were mostly artists and jazz musicians who smoked marijuana and even flirted with narcotics. It was here in New York at this time when Walker Evans photographed a portrait of Kavan that was used on many of her original book jackets.

The most important event of this quick stay in New York was the connection Kavan made with George Davis, the fiction editor of *Harper's Bazaar*. Davis had a keen eye for great literature and published the best his day had to offer. Kavan introduced herself, giving Davis a copy of *Asylum Piece*, which impressed him very much. He decided to publish three chapters from it in their next issue. By the time the issue was at the press, Kavan was already sailing back to New Zealand to see Ian Hamilton. Kavan had no desire to complicate her life anymore with Fuller. The two did remain correspondents for a few years, with Fuller sending money when Kavan was low on cash.

By the time Kavan reached New York, she had crossed the North Sea, the Atlantic and Pacific Oceans, and the Celebes and Java Seas, along with part of the Indian Ocean, for a total of over twenty-five thousand miles. Scholars really can't say if her travel was due to loneliness or restlessness or simply because she was searching for material for her next book Kavan may have had what those in recovery from drug addiction call the "geographical cure," which is the deluded belief that by changing one's physical locations one may also change or leave life's problems behind. Due to the lack of journals and close friends who conversed with her at this time, scholars are once more forced into the category of the educated guess.

Late in 1941 Kavan finally settled for some twenty months in Auckland, New Zealand. Amidst all her hectic traveling, she had somehow completed a novel called *Change the Name*, which she sent to Jonathan Cape. The novel was published that year but the public response was quiet. There was a war going on after all.

It wasn't until 1945 that Kavan began to find some stability in both her work and state of mind. The American publication of *Asylum Piece* as well as the articles for *Horizon* were a tremendous help in building her audience. Doubleday had even taken a contractual option on her next book after they published *Asylum Piece*, and they indeed published it when Kavan delivered the manuscript in 1947.

The House of Sleep actually came out in the United States a year before the British edition. According to Callard Kavan had tried to develop a "night-time language" (p. 91) to tell the story of an unhappy child who is reluctant to grow into adulthood. It seems the language was too experimental for American readers and the book took a beating in the press. The lack of sales caused Doubleday to cancel their option on her next book. Sales were poor when the book was published in England. Kavan's rising star was starting to fall. For the first time in her life she even suffered from writer's block.

Kavan was still writing in the early 1950s but a little gun-shy from the negative reviews of *The House of Sleep*. To help fill in the economic gaps left by her declining literary output, she started a partnership with an architect to form Kavan Properties. Their goal was to buy older houses that needed repair, renovate them, and resell them. The result was a financial success and an operation that occupied her for the rest of her life.

Kavan's life was rather calm until 1955 when her mother died. Despite the lifelong tension in their life, Kavan had always been dependent on her mother for medical and travel expenses. She discovered that her stepfather inherited her mother's estate and although she received some money from the sale of the house in Earley, found herself basically disinherited.

The bitterness that followed this financial turn of events found its outlet in Kavan's first major work in years, a novel called *A Scarcity of Love* (1956). Kavan was able to portray her mother as a thinly disguised character which far from flattered her. It is the story of a young child who retreats into a world of fantasy as the result of growing up unwanted. After failing numerous times to conform to normal living situations, she drowns herself.

Since her silence in the literary world during the previous few years, Kavan was forced to publish the book with a vanity press. Even so, reviews were generally good. Unfortunately, the vanity press went bankrupt after only a few review copies were distributed and almost the entire edition was pulped.

LATER WORKS

WHO knows how far Kavan might have sunk into literary oblivion if not for her meeting with Peter Owen, who became her publisher for the rest of her life. They met through a mutual friend of Rhys Davies in 1956. Kavan gave Owen her latest manuscript, a novel titled *Eagles' Nest*, which Owen published in 1957. Thus far, *Eagles' Nest* constituted Kavan's most surreal novel, a work that twenty-first-century readers would call Kafkaesque. The book marks an evolutionary stage in the writer's style which is almost equal to the content of the story.

This novel tells the story of a frustrated advertising designer who works in a department store. He finds his works so demeaning that he quits to become a library assistant to the administrator of a distant and sizable estate. The landscape is always changing as if in a dream, sometimes tropical, sometimes barren and arid. The hero of the book (who is unnamed) soon finds his new job to be as petty as his previous position. As the administrator is mostly absent, the hero finds himself ridiculed by the workers and servants also employed at the estate. He is told he does not understand the ways of the Eagles' Nest. When the hero finally meets the administrator, he finds himself fired for having broken some unknown laws he never understood.

The dreamy atmosphere which is juxtaposed with a solid, objective landscape confused many readers. Critics found the book too enigmatic. The only clear concept that many could understand was the frustration of the book's hero in his attempt to find even the simplest fulfillment in life.

Some saw the book as a statement on nonconformity, others simply as a piece of literature influenced by the surrealist movement. Although in many ways a conventional work, the story is collaged with the strange and unimaginable. The hero is constantly confused by what "laws" he has supposedly been breaking. He tries hard and wants so little, yet always seems to fail. This could almost be the story of the mildly ambitious Everyman.

Kavan found her novel oddly out of place in terms of literary trends. What the British reading public looked for in a novel was a sociological episode, a tale of the Angry Young Man, preferably in academia. *Lucky Jim* by Kingsley Amis is the perfect example of the type of novel in demand. A surreal, psychological work like *Eagles' Nest* baffled even the most well read. Even so, Kavan was still riding the waves from the small but devoted following that had read *A Scarcity of Love*. In any case, Kavan's name was back in the literary limelight, for better or worse.

In 1962, the final decade of Kavan's life, a manuscript which Kavan felt good about called *Who Are You?* was delivered to Peter Owen. Here was a fictional recreation of her disastrous first marriage. In some ways it covered much of the same ground that *Let Me Alone* did, although readers found the prose more experimental and the atmosphere much darker. Owen thought the book was too short to make much money and wanted her to work on a full-length novel. The book was eventually picked up by a small house called Scorpion Press.

A fellow writer who admired Kavan's novella was Jean Rhys, the author of *Wide Sargasso Sea*. Another well-known writer in the United States also admired Kavan's book. It was none other than Anaïs Nin, whose admiration of Kavan went back to *Asylum Piece*. Nin went so far as to write Kavan a fan letter which cheered her considerably. It was a great satisfaction to her to have the support of peers whose work she especially admired.

The pleasure she took in these communications was darkened by the death of Dr. Bluth in 1964 after he suffered a fatal heart attack. Kavan was devastated and friends close to her say her last years were reclusive and antisocial. When she felt up to working, Kavan was putting together a collection of short stories called *Julia and the Bazooka and Other Stories*, which would not be published until after her death.

At least four of the stories in *Julia and the Bazooka* have a character based on Dr. Bluth. Friends of Kavan have suggested that maybe she wrote the stories as therapy. Whatever the case, she told Peter Owen shortly after Bluth died that she herself was only Awaiting for death (Callard, p. 128).

Kavan found the change in attitudes and culture in art and living in general in the 1960s much more fascinating than the 1950s. Heroin was a topic of literary interest brought to the public's attention by such writers as William S. Burroughs in his classic *Naked Lunch* and *Junky* and also Alexander Trocchi with his infamous work *Cain's Book*. However, Kavan didn't associate with such writers or have much to say about them. (Shortly before Burroughs died in 1997, I asked him if he was familiar with Kavan's work. "Oh yes, certainly," he replied. "I especially admire her descriptions of the lynx in her books." Burroughs had strong feelings for any member of the cat family.)

In 1965, Kavan had completed a draft of a manuscript called *The Cold World*, which she submitted to Weidenfeld and Nicolson. After a drawn out debate among the editors, the book was rejected. The marketability of the book was in question. In 1966 and 1967 the book went through many revisions, the working title changing from *The Ice World* to *The Ice Palace*. Peter Owen accepted the book but did not care for either title. In one final attempt, Kavan suggested the title *Ice* and Owen agreed.

With the publication of *Ice* in 1967, Kavan found a new source of fame with the English and American subcultures. The hallucinatory and postapocalyptic scenario appealed to fans of both science fiction and mainstream literature. The science fiction writer Brian Aldiss nominated *Ice* for the best sci-fi novel of 1967. Other admirers included J. G. Ballard. Kavan was especially pleased with the nomination by Aldiss, as she was an admirer of his work.

Ice is a difficult novel to describe. The narrator pursues the Ice Maiden he once loved but who turns out to be one of the bullying wardens who work at policing the frozen world which is run by a secret government with strange, unknown laws, much as in *Eagles' Nest*. The book ends with a high-speed car chase, running down pedestrians, driving through changing climates and strange battle scenes. It is interesting to remember Kavan's earlier, conventional novels and contrast the difference in styles between her first and last books.

Kavan was not able to enjoy her fame for very long. Her heroin habit had reached the point where she needed an injection every three hours and had to be hospitalized for an abscessed leg, the result of too many careless needle injections. Government policies were changing and it was now difficult to find doctors to prescribe heroin, as the new, favored treatment was to give patients methadone. Thus Kavan began to stockpile enough heroin to last her through a very long drought.

When Kavan was invited to a party on 5 December 1968, and did not show up, concerned friends had police break into her flat. They found her body lying peacefully, her head resting on the Chinese lacquered box in which she kept her heroin. Anna had been dead for almost twenty-four hours. The official cause of death was "fatty myocardial degeneration." Although she is often reported to have committed suicide, doctors believe simply that her heart finally gave out.

A long life, full of abuse, stress, and addiction, had come to an end after sixty-seven years, but not before leaving behind a substantial body of quality literature. Should Kavan had lived another twenty years, she may have been happy to see the growth of appreciation for her work as each generation interested in writing rediscovered her work.

The proceeds from Kavan's estate were not enough to keep the house she had lived in on Hillsleigh Road and it eventually had to be sold, but not before her ashes were spread in the backyard garden that she loved so much. The house is occupied by tenants ignorant of the location's amazing past and history while Kavan returns quietly to the earth from which she came.

SELECTED BIBLIOGRAPHY

I. SEPARATE WORKS. Published originally under the name of Helen Ferguson: *A Charmed Circle* (London, 1929); *The Dark Sisters* (London, 1930); *Let Me Alone* (London, 1930); *A Stranger Still* (London, 1935); *Goose Cross* (London, 1936); *Rich Get Rich* (London, 1937).
Published originally under the name of Anna Kavan: *Asylum Piece and Other Stories* (London, 1940; New York, 1946); *Change the Name* (London, 1941); *I Am Lazarus: Short Stories* (London, 1945), short stories; *Sleep Has His House* (London, 1948; published in the United States as *The House of Sleep*, New York, 1947); *The Horse's Tale* (with K. T. Bluth) (London, 1949); *A Scarcity of Love* (Southport, England, 1956; New York, 1974); *Eagles' Nest* (London, 1957); *A Bright Green Field and Other Stories* (London, 1958); *Who Are You?* (Lowestoft, Suffolk, 1963); *Ice* (London, 1967; New York, 1970); *Julia and the Bazooka and Other Stories* (London and New York, 1970); *My Soul in China: A Novella and Stories* (London, 1975). All works currently in print are published under the name of Anna Kavan.

II. BIOGRAPHICAL AND CRITICAL STUDIES. Anaïs Nin, *The Novel of the Future* (New York, 1968); Brian W. Aldiss with David Wingrove, *Trillion Year Spree* (London, 1986); D. A. Callard, *The Case of Anna Kavan: A Biography* (London, 1992).

III. ARTICLES. "Life of Unreality," in *The Scotsman* (25 August 1967); "Icy Heroin," in *New Statesman* (6 March 1970); "Anna Kavan," in *Books and Bookmen* (March 1971); "People Have Always Hated Me," in *New York Times Book Review* (2 June 1980); "The Great Depression of Anna Kavan," in *The Village Voice* (December 1981).

JAMAICA KINCAID

(1949–)

Erik Kongshaug

WHAT'S IN A NAME?

HALF HER LIFETIME ago, Elaine Cynthia Potter Richardson, a young, black Antiguan woman living in New York, reinvented herself as Jamaica Kincaid. She began writing magazine interviews beneath that byline in 1973. The result was a name she could use, not the middle-class British one that had been literally and figuratively imposed on her by the shadow of a mother she'd left in the Caribbean with her childhood. Jamaica Kincaid could face the world directly.

She was living hand-to-mouth in self-imposed exile—a literary flâneur in a metropolis that had long outgrown the British colonial society both she and her mother had been educated to serve. Somewhere in the blur of that existence, she discovered a double vision of motherhood. Her own mother's control of her heart was recapitulated in a "mother" country's control of her history. Jamaica Kincaid combined them, brought them into focus as a single subject—domination—and turned it into a question of her own domain. Through a rainbow of different lenses—intimacy, hatred, love, not love, coldness, anger, anything but friendship—she created an exceptional vision of unequal relationships. That vision has left few rules unprobed: neither the rule of colonialism nor that of nationality; not the tyranny or the powerlessness of motherhood; not racial, political or gendered identity; not even the wealthy fruits of an innocent New England garden; and least of all her own position within them. In the small place of Jamaica Kincaid, every space is considered: her ideas are most often communicated through negative grammatical constructions; she recapitulates the watershed moments of her life at every turn.

She's told the story of her name, for example, numerous times and in numerous ways—in fictions, memoirs, historical essays, gardening columns, and intimate but elusive responses to interviewers' pointed questions over the years. When taken together these varied tales leave a singular impression. Of a name almost carelessly plucked—metaphors usually are—from the tip of her mother tongue.

Whatever their autobiographical origins, those two words together—Jamaica Kincaid—have come to express the mirrored relationship and multiplicity of meaning between personal power and public powerlessness across the English language.

To date, she has published four major works of fiction—*At the Bottom of the River* (1984), *Annie John* (1985), *Lucy* (1990) and *Autobiography of My Mother* (1996)—and four of literary nonfiction—*A Small Place* (1988), *My Brother* (1997), *My Garden Book* (1999), and *Talk Stories* (2001). The list's brevity is misleading. Her works combine as worlds within worlds. Each published book comprises many pieces previously published in journals and magazines, each with an individual history incorporated into the whole. Other significant pieces—of fiction, memoir, historical essay, or something in between—never have been gathered into books. Even in her edited conversations published in various venues—interviewers who run the gamut from political engagement to literary gossip mongering—disarmingly frank and frankly personal responses further mirror and multiply, and in some cases even constitute the specific details of her larger work. "To speak to me is really to read my books," she said in a 1995 interview for the online magazine *Salon*. "I don't know why I write sometimes, because if you just sat down I would tell you everything in them" (p. 2).

Jamaica Kincaid's published work defies classification, as does its apparently transparent relation to her personal life. Originally created to communicate with the predominantly white, liberal upper-class American audience of the *New Yorker* magazine, on whose writing staff she served from 1976 to 1996 and again in 2001, Kincaid's spare parenthetical style functions in large degree as a withering political and aesthetic indictment of that audience's privilege to consume it. She has created an indisputable space for herself at the high literary table of contemporary writers; yet she still would prefer to stand.

Her concentrated philosophical critique of colonial and neocolonial domination in her own experience growing up in Antigua has deservedly made her the subject of numerous books, articles, and dissertations on postcolonial literary theory that are currently being written and consumed, in turn, by an international generation of academics. In its broadest terms, postcolonial theory attempts to describe the first world's continuing imposition of its own meanings and values onto the peoples it has formerly colonized. But Kincaid's ambiguous use of language also undermines many ideological assumptions associated with the postcolonial theoretical position. Whenever Kincaid presumes to speak for the "Other," some ironic expression of her ambivalence is never far behind.

She has been similarly held up as a feminist writer, an African American writer, an Antiguan nationalist writer, a leftist, a modernist, and an anti-Romantic. Kincaid's work has looked back to make the beholder similarly uncomfortable in every incarnation. For Kincaid, the subjugation of her personal reality to any collective idea is anathema. And her work privileges the classification of British writer as most uncomfortable of all.

In her essay "On Seeing England for the First Time" (1991), after observing that island as a personal reality for the first time in her mid-thirties, she writes:

If now as I speak of all this I give the impression of someone on the outside looking in, nose pressed up against a glass window, that is wrong. My nose was pressed up against a glass window all right, but there was an iron vise at the back of my neck forcing my head to stay in place. To avert my gaze was to fall back into something from which I had been rescued, a hole filled with nothing, and that was the word for everything about me, nothing.

(pp. 35–36)

Elaine Potter Richardson was born on the 108-square-mile eastern Caribbean island of Antigua on 25 May 1949. So long as she remained, her own special day would forever follow in the shadow of May 24: Antigua's official celebration of the long-dead Queen Victoria's birthday. Both Elaine and her mother, Annie Richardson Drew, who was born on the neighboring eastern Caribbean island of Dominica, were colonial subjects of the British Empire. So were the taxicab-driving father she met only later in the 1990s, Frederick Potter; and the carpenter David Drew, the man she would know and name her father. She grew up around the edges of want in a lower-middle-class household. Antigua is a drought-ridden island, deforested from sugar plantations. Its population, nearly all of whom are descendants of African slaves, is hardly greater than that of Scarsdale, New York, the affluent nearly all-white suburb to which Elaine would be sent, never to return, as a sixteen-year-old au pair. Two decades later, the same year she first visited England, she would revisit Antigua for the first time as well, but as Jamaica Kincaid.

When Elaine was ten, as the Cuban Revolution was rocking the Caribbean, her mother and David Drew had the first of three children belonging to both of them, all boys. Kincaid has often construed the birth of her half-brother Joseph—followed in rapid succession by Dalma and then the youngest, Devon—as the origin of her own tragic fall from the undivided paradise of her mother's love. By thirteen, Elaine was one of Antigua's top students in the British colonial school system when, because of her father's failing health and the economic hardship that it engendered, her parents abruptly ended her education. Shortly after her sixteenth birthday, by mutual consent and economic necessity, she was on her way to America.

After a few months and some classes at Westchester Community College, Elaine left

Scarsdale and answered an ad for another au pair position in the heart of Manhattan, caring for the four little children of the *New Yorker* writer Michael Arlen and his first wife, where she remained for three years. Although Jamaica Kincaid would have her real introduction to the *New Yorker* a few years later through a friendship not immediately connected with the Arlens, Elaine Richardson Potter must have first experienced the idea of its name—America's literary drawing room to many—as a series of domestic moments glimpsed through the maid's room door.

Her emotional response to this nebulous new economic and social place somewhere between nanny, adopted older child, and modern servant would become the canvas for *Lucy*, Kincaid's most concentrated and immediate connection between her life and her art. Not withstanding the race and class differences subtly ascertained at least by the fictional Lucy if not the factual Elaine, the au pair position was one that closely recapitulated psychological realities within the family she left behind—those of an older daughter made to help her mother raise the young children of a man not her father.

While at the Arlens' she earned her high school equivalency diploma and in 1969 left for Franconia College in New Hampshire with a full scholarship. As with those in Scarsdale, these experiences away from the heat of New York's metropolitan core were dispiriting. She soon returned to a tenuous life on her own. Taking her cue from *Tan*, the African American fashion magazine, she bleached her hair yellow and left "Elaine" behind. In later years she would recall the earliest photograph taken of her, standing at two years old in a yellow dress her mother had made from English fabric. By 1973 Jamaica Kincaid had succeeded at least in turning her colonial situation on its head.

Jamaica Kincaid began her writing career by pitching, selling, and producing an interview with feminist and *Ms.* magazine founder Gloria Steinem that asked what Steinem was like when she was the age of the average reader of the teen beauty magazine *Seventeen*. The relation of that age—Kincaid's own passage not only from childhood to womanhood, but from Antigua to America—to this one—her passage from Elaine Potter Richardson to Jamaica Kincaid—was fortuitous. Her "When I Was Seventeen" column became a regular feature for *Ingenue* magazine.

Through a chance meeting in the early 1970s, she was introduced to the *New Yorker* staff writer George W. S. Trow, who took her under his literary wing. In the hallmark first-person plural of that magazine's "Talk of the Town" section, he began referring to her as "our sassy black friend." This racially charged introduction of Jamaica Kincaid to her future audience reveals a linguistically embedded colonialism in the *New Yorker*'s relationship to her: Kincaid, together with other non-white writers and readers, was implicitly invited to consider herself a visitor to the real community of "New Yorkers." When asked to make that connection for a 1991 interview with Kay Bonetti, however, Kincaid was quick to eschew it: "I seemed to be sassy, I said these things that he thought were sassy, and I was black" (*Missouri Review*, 1992, p. 135). Her comment is characteristic, both of her refusal to assume the position of victim and of her unwillingness to fully identify with black subjectivity.

After quoting her Caribbean anecdotes more and more extensively in the *New Yorker*'s unsigned "Talk of the Town" section, Trow introduced her to the *New Yorker*'s then-editor William Shawn. By the time New York was celebrating America's bicentennial, Kincaid was ironically commenting in "Talk of the Town" columns, albeit still anonymously, as her own imperial "we."

In "Flowers of Evil" (1992), the first essay of her regular gardening column to appear in the *New Yorker*, Kincaid addresses the subject of naming directly:

This naming of things is so crucial to possession—a spiritual padlock with the key thrown irretrievably away—that it is a murder, an erasing, and it is not surprising that when people have felt themselves prey to it (conquest), among their first acts of liberation is to change their names (Rhodesia to Zimbabwe, LeRoi Jones to Amiri Baraka).

(p. 159)

But perhaps Kincaid's need to reinvent her own name is best expressed by the final words of Elaine's fictional counterpart, Lucy—whose name, short for Lucifer, she fancies as a curse from her mother, whose name in Latin means light; whose name is likewise allusive of the longed-for, absent woman in the famous "Lucy" poems of William Wordsworth. The novel concludes with Lucy discovering the impossibility of using her given, colonial name sincerely:

At the top of the page I wrote my full name: Lucy Josephine Potter. At the sight of it, many thoughts rushed through me, but I could write down only this: "I wish I could love someone so much that I could die from it." And then as I looked at this sentence a great wave of shame came over me and I wept and wept so much that the tears fell on the page and caused all the words to become one great big blur.

(pp. 163–164)

One February afternoon in 1978, Kincaid wrote her first piece of fiction, "Girl"—a single, virtually uninterrupted sentence in which the second-person-imperative voice of her mother tells her exactly what she must do. It is a literal and moral laundry list, in which her mother's prescriptions encompass and assume control of everything in the girl's life, from washing the white clothes on Monday to making a medicine for abortion, leaving the girl no space for her resistance to be construed as anything other than further evidence of her guilt.

In 1979, she married the composer Allen Shawn, William Shawn's son. She kept her own name.

DISCOVERING AMERICA

JAMAICA Kincaid's meteoric rise as a major literary figure would coincide with an historical moment in which the American public was undergoing a major shift in the way it consumed the Caribbean. For Kincaid, the early 1980s would

underscore the complexities of a West Indian identity that produced not just simple insurgency but ambivalence as it attempted to situate itself within the Americas.

In 1979, back in a Caribbean world that had little now to do with Kincaid's own daily life, two of her contemporaries, Maurice Bishop and Bernard Coard, led the leftist New Jewel movement to power on the island of Grenada. Their movement was opposed to the "one-man, High Priest politics," so called in local parlance, that had left their country—like the politically parallel Antigua just a handful of islands and a few hundred miles away—no better off, if not worse, than it had been under British colonialism. Like Kincaid, they had spent their student days in the first world, but unlike Kincaid they had become inspired to political instead of literary action by the black power and civil rights movements of the mid- to late-1960s.

On the island of Manhattan, however, "Jamaica" was the talk of the town. New York's literary scene and publishing circles had never read anything quite like her. Just a few days following the appearance of "Girl," *Rolling Stone* magazine came out with a piece by her that they had entitled "Antigua Crossings" (1978), which further explored the hatred and lyrical love of a daughter for her guilt-tripping mother. Kincaid's cryptic, dreamlike style seemed pregnant with mysterious colonial meanings that readers couldn't quite put their fingers on; but they were transfixed by it just the same.

The lion's share of the short fiction her first book would comprise followed in subsequent issues of the *New Yorker*: "In the Night," (1978) in which strange "night-soil men" come to take away the waste in the darkness, and "Wingless" (1979), in which colonial children read British primers, began to mix in the minds of her readers, always through the shimmering glimpses of a child's direct perceptions in an exotic, romantic place where mothers washed clothes on stone heaps and the lamps were really lit, not simply switched on. Suddenly in "Holidays" (1979), a young woman dreams, out of place in American surroundings familiar to most of her readers. In "At Last" (1979), a chore-weary girl is again back in the Caribbean watching the children at play. In "The Letter from Home" (1981) the long arm of her mother reaches out to squelch a young woman's freedom with self-identified guilt from her homeland. After "What I Have Been Doing Lately" (1981) appeared in the *Paris Review*, the title piece for the book contract she would sign with Farrar, Straus, Giroux, "At the Bottom of the River," appeared in the *New Yorker* on 3 May 1982. She would write one more piece, "Blackness," to complete the work and rework a central section of "Antigua Crossing" into the thematically quintessential, "My Mother," which begins: "Immediately on wishing my mother dead and seeing the pain it caused her, I was sorry and cried so many tears that all the earth around me was drenched" (p. 53).

On 25 October 1983, back on Antigua's fellow island, Grenada, Prime Minister Maurice Bishop was assassinated in an internal coup d'etat and Bernard Coard was assumed to be in control of the government. President Ronald Reagan called for the U.S. invasion. He said it was to preempt a Soviet-Cuban invasion of the eastern Caribbean and to "rescue" a small affluent white campus of American medical students from the predominately black island. There was little factual basis for either cause as has been subsequently shown and as was widely understood at the time. The press was strictly prohibited from the theater of operations. Such a prohibition was unheard of before that invasion, but it has become more common in the American military operations since.

When the island was deemed "secure" and the press blackout was finally lifted, Reagan held a press conference. By his side was Eugenie Charles, the prime minister of Dominica, the island Kincaid's mother is from, saying that she, as head of a heretofore unheard of association of eastern Caribbean states, had invited the United States to invade. Like Kincaid's mother, Charles projected a fiercely passionate, imperturbable presence and was a stern conveyor of middle-class bourgeois values. Her position as a single woman governing a poor island in a rich man's world was once again parallel to that of Kincaid's mother, whose husband had died and left her in

financial hard straits shortly after Kincaid's migration. Charles even outdid Reagan in the from-the-hip passion of her anticommunist cold war rhetoric, offering an indignant, never-substantiated tale of a Soviet-Cuban-backed foreign payoff to foment discontent on her island and foreign scholarships offered to her citizens for terrorist training.

From the Caribbean perspective, the U.S. invasion of Grenada is generally seen as the symbolic moment when the colonial power of Great Britain (who was not consulted about the affair) was fully replaced by the neocolonial influence of the United States. And Charles, along with the several other eastern Caribbean leaders who joined her, is generally seen as having played the role of a collaborator.

After the smoke cleared, the reaction to this Caribbean military maneuver in the perfunctorily liberal "Talk of the Town" section of the *New Yorker*, 6 November 1983, protested its righteous indignation and mourned the loss of America's freedom of the press. It is unlikely that Kincaid made any direct contributions to those unsigned columns and the irony of her shifting position, at a time she was being celebrated by America, could not have escaped her. Reflecting on her own growing identity as an American in "Alien Soil" (1993) ten years later, she comments on the duplicity of a dominant culture's right to criticize itself:

> We are divided about how we ought to behave in the world. Half of us believe in and support strongly a bad thing our government is doing, while the other half do not believe in and protest strongly against the bad thing. The bad thing succeeds, and everyone, protester and supporter alike, enjoys immensely the results of the bad thing.
>
> (p. 48)

Ironically, *At the Bottom of the River*—which gathered her short fiction into something larger than its parts—appeared in bookstores across the United States at an historical moment when, for the first time ever, a handful of newly independent, former British colonies in the eastern Caribbean Sea had a face for the rest of the world to see: the face of Eugenie Charles. That face, for Kincaid, was in many ways the face of her mother. Kincaid made indirect reference to that relationship in Bonetti's 1991 interview when asked about "the absolute matter of factness" with which she had just turned the male Miltonic images of God and Lucifer from *Paradise Lost* into women. Kincaid's almost parenthetical reply only makes sense in the light of an historical event that most Americans had already erased from their memories:

> I am writing about power and powerlessness, and I think that these things have no sex. They have only their nature. I have never met a man more impressive than my mother. When Ronald Reagan was announcing the invasion of Grenada, at his side was Eugenie Charles, the Prime Minister of Domini[ca]. If you were from Mars, you would think that she was the leader of the powerful country and he was the leader of the weak country. My mother is like that—grand and impressive. I've never met any man with that sort of personal power.
>
> (p. 139)

In the crisp northern fall of 1983, when *At the Bottom of the River* went into final production, Jamaica Kincaid was crossing her own line from having lived most of her life on British-controlled Antigua to having lived more of it in the United States. Although Antigua had finally gained its full political independence within the British Commonwealth in 1981 (giving it power over its own foreign affairs for the first time), she hadn't set foot on the island since 1965 and had no direct experience with its current reality. Therein was the source of her ambivalence. It was not from the Antigua of 1983, but from the colonial Antigua of her earliest childhood that Kincaid drew inspiration for her first fictions, which were about to carry her across the often diametrically opposed thresholds of international scholarly attention and popular literary success.

"Perhaps I stand on the brink of a great discovery," the voice of one character in "Wingless" would say, "and perhaps after I have made my great discovery I will be sent home in chains" (p. 21).

The girl's voice in "Wingless" continues: "That woman over there. Is she cruel? Does she love me? And if not, can I make her? I am not yet tall, beautiful, graceful, and able to impose my will. Now I swim in a shaft of light and can see myself clearly" (p. 22).

"Girl" would become the first section of *At the Bottom of the River*. Jointly dedicated to her mother and her father-in-law William Shawn, whom Kincaid credits for finding, allowing, and encouraging her own voice, the book brings together the fragmented voices of a disembodied daughter waging an unwinnable war against the singular voice of her mother. The voices and the careful, spare detail of the small place that surrounds them are Kincaid's first attempt to sound out the relation of power to its opposite.

Whereas Kincaid's subsequent book-length fictions have been generally understood as novels, *At the Bottom of the River* was treated as a collection of separate short stories when it came out. However, a powerfully unified albeit nonlinear progression between the stories is undeniable.

The "girl" in these stories, if indeed the voices reduce to a single personality at all, is nameless. And her search for a name is not in the reinvention of her existing name in the future, but a searching backward to a vision at the bottom of the river, to perceptions as they are before any name is given by the conscious mind.

At the Bottom of the River—and its stylistic counterpart, *Annie, Gwen, Lily, Pam, and Tulip*, published in a very limited edition—expresses, in large part, the fragmented identities a mother's love engenders; it concerns itself almost entirely with domination as an unconscious experience.

The final section ends with an act of naming that withdraws *within* the mother's embrace, never breaking from it. Still in her mother's shadow, the girl in "At the Bottom of the River" looks down in the water and claims what she thinks is a vision of a writerly Eden for herself: "In the light of the lamp, I see some books, I see a chair, I see a table, I see a pen... I claim these things then—mine—and now feel myself grow solid and complete, my name filling up my mouth" (p. 82).

Ultimately, *At the Bottom of the River* first created a place for Kincaid on the Western literary map because it was a postmodern reaction *within* the tradition of English Romanticism. Unlike

Kincaid's later work, it questioned Western literary authority on that authority's own terms— looking for freedom within the structures of domination, as the Romantics and modernists had done, rather than through the rejection of those structures. In a 1990 interview with Donna Perry, Kincaid, makes this claim herself:

> I can see that *At the Bottom of the River* was, for instance, a very unangry, decent, civilized book and it represents sort of this successful attempt by English people to make their version of a human being or their version of a person out of me YI might go back to it, but I'm not very interested in that sort of expression any more.
>
> (Gates, pp. 498499)

In Bonetti's 1991 interview she elaborates further: "A sort of desire for a perfect place, a perfect situation, comes from English Romantic poetry. It described a perfection which one longed for... These things were a big influence, and it was important for me to get rid of them. Then I could actually look at the place I'm from" (pp. 130–131).

In *At the Bottom of the River* the link between mother and "mother land" is still indirect. Kincaid was finding her first voice to criticize colonialism in colonialism's own self- critical voice—the tradition of English Romantic poetry descendant from John Milton—in the same way she was finding the voice to criticize her own mother: by mimicking and ironically subverting the voice of her mother without ever challenging it. And, as she discovers in both cases, the subversion is itself subverted. For—as the final lines of "Girl" so powerfully record—from the mother's point of view it is the irony as much as the direct prescriptions that she is working to impart:

> ...this is how to spit up in the air if you feel like it, and this is how to move quick so that it doesn't fall on you; this is how to make ends meet; always squeeze bread to make sure it's fresh; *but what if the baker won't let me feel the bread?*; you mean to say that after all you are really going to be the kind of woman who the baker won't let near the bread?
>
> (p. 5)

For Kincaid, "Blackness," the only piece in *At the Bottom of the River* not previously published,

points the way from her modernist dilemma to the style she will finally inhabit as a mature writer. In the other stories, the image of light predominates. Light is in many ways indicative of a European "Enlightenment," which is something the girl's voices, like moths, are always moving toward. "Blackness," on the other hand, expresses a dispossession within the cycle of domination—what has been dominated and can therefore no longer be transmitted. In this section, it is the mother, not the daughter, who is narrating and resisting; here it is the daughter and not the mother who is a *jablesse*—a seductive, siren-like spirit in Antigua's creole belief system, Obeah. In "Blackness" there is also a looking back, but not for a name; for something before a name; not for an English Romantic vision of Eden, but the unseen something before that Eden was ever imposed, something before paradise itself or the Judeo-Christian God. With persistent biblical reference, "Blackness" unwrites "In the beginning was the Word." For if God went forth into the void, it is the void that precedes God. And if, as Kincaid suggests in "On Seeing England for the First Time," the experience of Englishness construes her as "nothing," then it is as nothing, as a negative, that she will find her way of speaking:

> The silent voice enfolds me so completely that even in memory the blackness is erased. I live in silence. The silence is without boundaries. The pastures are unfenced, the lions roam the continents, the continents are not separated. Across the flat lands cuts the river, its flow undammed. ...Living in the silent voice, I am no longer "I."
>
> (p. 52)

QUESTIONING COLUMBUS

HER most recently published piece at the moment the United States invaded Grenada was "Columbus in Chains," just off the stands in the 10 October 1983, issue of the *New Yorker*. Following the precedent established with *At the Bottom of the River*, it would soon recapitulate itself at the structural, emotional, and thematic turning point of her second book, a novel whose more navigable plot line would further widen her audience, *Annie John*.

In a characteristic moment one can now only call "Kincaidian," she forges the first direct link between her personal history and the political history of colonialism as an anecdotal symbol in the mind of a young girl, with layers of meaning so various they become impossible to separate. Star colonial pupil and precocious contrariant, the young-girl narrator is miles ahead of the others in her history class, while the one white British student in the class, from a colonizing family, wears the dunce cap for not knowing the exact date Christopher Columbus discovered Dominica. She is looking ahead in her history book to a picture entitled "Columbus in Chains," in which that venerated founding father later in his life has been imprisoned and returned to Europe for squabbling with colonial authority. Recalling a conversation from home in which her mother revels in the physical humiliation age has wrought on her domineering grandfather, the schoolgirl reproduces her mother's words in Old English lettering beneath the history book picture: "The Great Man Can No Longer Just Get Up and Go." She is caught. As punishment she is forced to copy and memorize the first two books of Milton's *Paradise Lost*. At this critical juncture in the story, the girl is abandoned by her mother's love, in a moment that recapitulates Lucifer's fall in *Paradise Lost*. In an image that cuts both ways, like the anecdote itself, the girl in "Columbus in Chains" sees her mother as if for the first time: "When she laughed, her mouth opened to show off big, shiny, sharp white teeth. It was as if my mother had suddenly turned into a crocodile" (p. 84).

In *Annie John*, a single, transparently clear character emerges—fallen from the fragmenting identity of her mother's love into the self-identified body of a pubescent girl. Following the familiar Western canonical form of the bildungsroman, or "coming-of-age" novel, here was something her readers could understand.

The eight sections, or chapters of *Annie John* were each published separately as "pieces" in the *New Yorker*—between May 1983 and November 1984. Chronologically and psychologically it is as realistic and precise as *At the Bottom of the River* is lyrical and oblique. Each temporally discrete section loosely corresponds to a consecutive year in Annie Victoria John's development between the ages of ten and seventeen. The place is specifically Antigua in the late 1950s and early 1960s, when she, like Elaine Potter Richardson, was a colonial schoolgirl. Annie John does not dream inside her mother's and her "motherland's" domination, like the voices in Kincaid's earlier work; she observes; she is exclusively preoccupied with, if not obsessed by conscious experience.

In the final section of the novel, "A Walk to the Jetty" when the seventeen-year-old heroine is saying goodbye to her parents and departing never to return, she begins: "'My name is Annie John.' These were the first words that came into my mind as I woke up on the morning of the last day I spent in Antigua…" (p. 130); her name was also the last thing she saw on the night before, written over her trunk, her prizes and everything she owns. The novel ends with the sound of waves at the bottom of the ship figuratively unnaming her: "They made an unexpected sound, as if a vessel filled with liquid had been placed on its side and now was slowly emptying out" (p. 148).

Although Kincaid laments that critics construed *Annie John* as "charming," in her 1990 interview with Perry she identifies in its central section, "Columbus in Chains," the more directly transgressive trajectory that would characterize her mature work:

I think that's the first place I began to know how to express it. …It was amazing that I could notice the politics the way I did, because most of those [in Antigua] who took notice did so in some sort of world context, like the man who became prime minister. But I took notice of it in a personal way and I didn't place it with the context of political action. I almost made a style out of it.

(Gates, p. 497)

Although Kincaid's subsequent work casts them in a far different light, both *At the Bottom of the River* and *Annie John* were first praised as the literary triumph of a black, third-world, woman writer who nonetheless conveyed "universal" experiences.

While this judgment, even of her earliest work, illustrates the first-world–imposed dualisms that postcolonial theory criticizes, it is also indicative of the climate in which many of her deeper themes not only function but were in fact created. In the end, it has been the confounded expectations of that audience, loosely her *New Yorker* audience, and the frankness, equanimity, dignity, and respect with which she has approached its preconceptions that have directed her work toward a deeper river. At first glance, Kincaid's equanimity is easily mistaken for coldness. Hers is a voice that neither asks for sympathetic compensation, nor feels it incumbent on her to educate the blindness that the privileged position of her reader may necessarily entail.

At the end of 1983, Kincaid received the Morton Dauwen Zabel Award from the American Letters for *At the Bottom of the River*. It was also nominated for the PEN/Faulkner Award.

In 1984 Kincaid discovered she was pregnant. Her daughter, Annie, would share her first name with Kincaid's mother on the one hand and her forthcoming novel on the other.

In 1985, her husband accepted a teaching position at Bennington College and Kincaid moved to the rural state of Vermont to become a mother herself. *Annie John* appeared that same year. Reviewers praised it to the sky almost without exception and it was nominated as one among three finalists for the highly coveted International Ritz Paris Hemingway Award.

ANGER AS A BURNING BRIDGE

FOLLOWING Annie's birth in 1985, Jamaica Kincaid returned to see her mother in Antigua. It had been twenty years. Combined with her recent intra-American migration from Manhattan to Vermont and her first trip to "mother England" that same year, those twin events precipitated what amounted to an internal revolution. That revolution first found expression in *A Small Place*, her book-length essay on Antigua as it really was, and "Ovando" (1989), her abandoned

epic fragment of the European conquest of the Caribbean. In the latter, Fray Nicolás de Ovando—the first colonial governor of the "New World" who introduced the *encomeinda*, a form of Indian servitude in the early 1500s with conditions akin to slavery—"was a complete skeleton except for his brain, which remained, and was growing smaller by the millennium...." The allegorical story goes on in a Caribbean woman's voice to relate her first and continuing encounter with him: "He stank. Immediately I was struck by his innocence..." (p. 75).

In "On Seeing England for the First Time," while glowering at Dover's dirty white cliffs, she casts her sea change philosophically:

The space between the idea of something and its reality is always wide and deep and dark. The longer they are kept apart—the idea of thing, reality of thing—the wider the width, the deeper the depth, the thicker and darker the darkness.... The existence of the world as I came to know it was a result of this: idea of thing over here, reality of thing way, way over there.... And so when they meet and find that they are not compatible, the weaker of the two, idea or reality, dies.

(p. 37)

Whereas Kincaid's earlier work tries to poetically bridge the gulf between the oppressive idea of her mother and the half-remembered paradise of childhood, after 1985, the idea of Kincaid's mother meets with Kincaid's own real, liberating experience of motherhood. The poetic idea of her colonial childhood meets with the politically disturbing reality not only of England but of Antigua from her own increasingly first-world perspective as—in the words of "On Seeing England for the First Time"—"a person who resides in a powerful country that takes up more than its fair share of a continent, the owner of a house with many rooms ... with the desire and will (which I very much act upon) to take from the world more than I give back to it" (p. 37). The idea of any creative friendship between power and powerlessness, an idea she now understands she is powerless to oppose, makes her angry. That anger ultimately ignites the creative fire of her mature work.

With the support of a Guggenheim Fellowship, Kincaid wrote *A Small Place*. The work was originally intended as a book-length article to run, as her published fiction so far had, in a series for the *New Yorker*. William Shawn commissioned and bought the piece before standing down as editor. Composed as a literary dialectic to express her shifting position in relation to Antigua's contemporary political reality, *A Small Place* is a form of discovery all its own. It is told first from the perspective of one tourist to another, then from the perspective of an Antiguan to a tourist, then from the combination of the two that she, herself, has become. On the one hand, its blistering, muckraking prose forthrightly "outs" Antigua's dysfunctional postcolonial legacy and the criminally insatiable corruption of its own "one-man High Priest politics"—the regime of Prime Minister V. C. Bird and his two sons. On the other, its formal innovations in narrative point of view creatively link the economic, environmental and social devastation of postcolonial Antigua with the foreign investment of a tourist economy—an economy created to service the niche demographic epitomized by the average reader of the *New Yorker*.

Kincaid engages a latter-day literary recapitulation of Grenada's New Jewel movement in her own indomitably personal and politically unclassifiable terms. A Small Place has for its denouement a literary and historical accusation. She airs the widely shared Antiguan belief that the phony corruption charge that brought down the opposition leader, the rightful "George Washington" of Antiguan independence, George Walter, is attributable instead to Prime Minister Bird's own youth when he literally and figuratively burned accounting books that recorded his misdeeds. The rightful legacy of independence becomes instead the unrequited dream of the opposition, an opposition in which her own mother was at one time politically active. After comparing Bird's sons, the inheritors of his political dynasty, to the corrupt American-backed leaders of Haiti— "Papa Doc" and "Baby Doc" Duvalier— she at last casts her own American link in terms of the thwarted Grenadian dream of the Antiguan opposition's could-have-been:

And so then they imagine another event, the event of Maurice Bishop in Grenada, and they imagine that such a man will materialise in Antigua and he'll do Maurice Bishop-like things and come to a Maurice Bishop-like end—death, only this time at the hands of the Americans.

(pp. 73–74)

She concludes *A Small Place* with a small historical coda in which "idea of thing" and "reality of thing" finally meet, as they did when she first saw England; her observations now apply to Antiguans and the *New Yorker* readers equally:

Of course, the whole thing is, once you cease to be a master, once you throw off your master's yoke, you are no longer human rubbish, you are just a human being, and all the things that adds up to. So, too, with the slaves. Once they are no longer slaves, once they are free, they are no longer noble and exalted; they are just human beings.

(p. 81)

While Kincaid's discovery did not—as the early literary voice in "Wingless" once feared—send her home, like Columbus, in chains; it did make an exile out of her, while burning the bridge of her readership at both ends.

On the shores of Manhattan, the *New Yorker* under the new editorship of Robert Gottlieb simply refused to publish *A Small Place*. It was too angry, he said. Although she now had the reputation to publish it cold as a book—which she did at William Shawn's suggestion— Kincaid's work had challenged how the *New Yorker* and its audience chose to consume the Caribbean. Although it was never directly mentioned by Gottlieb, or by Kincaid, the expanding advertising package of the magazine was and remains noticeably geared toward the upscale Caribbean tourist market.

On the shores of Antigua, her book was met with a not-unrelated form of silence in the government-controlled media. Only one small muckraking paper, *Outlet*, the last dogged vestige of an Antiguan political opposition, published a review. The government informally banned Jamaica Kincaid from her country; the ban remained in effect for four years, after which her sentence, like that of Columbus, was apparently lifted.

JAMAICA KINCAID

A LITERARY CROSSING

HER self-described political awakening brought Kincaid back to her fiction. *Lucy* was composed all at once, in the thick of it. She started it early in 1989 when her second child, Harold, was just three months old and finished it when he was a year and a half. Arguably her greatest work, this novel recapitulating her autobiographical experience as an au pair in Manhattan makes a direct, artistic connection between the two poles of her personal world—her Antiguan mother and her American children—and the two poles of her collective world—colonial Britain and capitalist America. From its poetic crucible in the opening pages, which describe the "bright sun-yellow" of the Caribbean being replaced by the "pale-yellow sun" (p. 5) of New York's winter, *Lucy*'s double image of yellow travels forward between Kincaid's Antiguan past and her American future.

The tension between those worlds becomes the focus of Lucy's dreams whose conflicting meanings—from the literate psychoanalysis of her American hosts, the Judeo-Christian eschatology her own colonial memory, and her mother's creole spiritual practice of Obeah—can only be resolved in a displaced woman's blurring tears before naming herself an artist. Her tears recall a psychologically and culturally allusive abyss of art from the colonizers' canon: Lucifer after the fall in the Judeo-Christian Bible and *Paradise Lost*, with the poetry of William Wordsworth, the paintings of Paul Gauguin, and the 1960s Greenwich Village arts scene all caught up in the mix.

The *New Yorker* opened its doors to Kincaid again for *Lucy*, publishing its individual pieces in order from February 1989 to June 1990. Set in an upper-class white household, the full literary depths of the novel's political anger only emerges when the individual pieces are seen as a whole. Once the novel had revealed the full shape of its vision in book form, Kincaid was harshly criticized by the man to whom it was dedicated, George W. S. Trow—who had first introduced her to her readers as "our sassy black friend." He and other *New Yorker* loyalists criticized her for availing herself so freely of the personal details of fellow *New Yorker* writer Michael Arlen's divorce. It remained unspoken that Kincaid had

come too close, in any less literal way, to biting the hand that fed her.

In Bonetti's 1990 interview Jamaica Kincaid claimed a birth right—for the novel, for her character and for herself—to both worlds:

> I was taught to think of ambiguity as magic, a shadiness and an illegitimacy, not the real thing of Western civilization.... The thing that I am branded with and the thing that I am denounced for, I now claim as my own. I am illegitimate, I am ambiguous. In some way I actually claim the right to ambiguity and the right to clarity.
>
> (p. 129)

Like Kincaid, the title character of *Lucy* questions her personal, social, economic, and historical position, from her first cloven steps into the metropolis, New York, among the monuments of exile's foreign idols. She equates the maid's room she now inhabits with a box meant for cargo; "But I was not cargo," she declares (p. 7), drawing attention to both her legacy of slavery and her refusal to be categorized within it. In that maid's room, she then dreams of a nightgown with drawings of children playing on it and finds it is "made in Australia," connecting the idea of slavery to that of colonialism and ultimately nationality, recalling Australia's own colonial childhood as a prison for the British Empire and, indirectly recalling an awareness of America's own former colonial relation to Britain. The first person besides Lucy that the narrative introduces is the household's American maid whose race remains suggestively ambiguous. Any sense of solidarity Lucy could feel with her as a servant and as a woman is prevented by what amounts to a national dislike: Lucy "talks funny" and "spoke like a nun" (p. 11).

Only after these considerations of nation, race, and class are readers introduced to the husband, wife, and four children of the host family as Lucy first perceives them: "Their six yellow-haired heads of various size were bunched as if they were a bouquet of flowers tied together by an unseen string" (p. 12). The reference is to a famous Wordsworth poem about daffodils often cited—for its prominent place in the British colonial school curriculum—as a symbol of intellectual oppression. Lucy, herself, remembers the poem in the novel's following section when her employer/host mother, Mariah, mentions daffodils as her favorite flower. Lucy explains to Mariah that she has never even seen a daffodil in real life, but at ten years old had been forced to memorize and recite the poem. Even while reveling in the praise she received, Lucy had privately vowed as a schoolgirl to erase it line by line from her memory: "I was then at the height of my two-facedness," she recalls (p. 18).

In the real Wordsworth poem, "I wandered lonely as a cloud," the poet, lifting the experience of observing "A host of dancing Daffodils" in large part from his sister's journal, suggests that the *idea* of daffodils recalled in solitary contemplation is greater than their reality. Lucy—who may or may not share her name with the absent figure in Wordsworth's "Lucy" poems, a figure scholars sometimes identify with Wordsworth's sister—has unconsciously recapitulated Wordsworth's words by likewise subjugating her first real experience of her American "hosts" to the idea of daffodils.

Before their embarking on a train trip to the Great Lakes, the employer/host-mother, Mariah, blindfolds Lucy to surprise her with the real vision of a field of daffodils, despite the story Lucy has told. Only on the train, after Mariah's unconsciously violent act, does Lucy become conscious of the racial difference between them. She notices the old serving men in the dining car are her color and the other diners are the color of Mariah and her children. So begins the historical sedimentation of another endlessly recapitulated Kincaidian symbol: yellow, first presented in the light of Wordsworth's daffodils, literally suffuses the language of *Lucy* and much of Kincaid's other work as well. For Kincaid, the color of power is yellow, the middle of the spectrum; the color of powerlessness is the absence of light, black: Lucy's ideal American host mother on the one hand and her real Caribbean mother on the other. Kincaid continues to ask—as she would also ask of Ronald Reagan and Eugenie Charles—which one is truly powerful and which truly powerless. For Kincaid, the true point between them is permanently astigmatic, a double image for which one must either chose one side or the other as the true image, or else put up with one's own blurry vision.

Written, appropriately, at more or less the halfway point of her twenty-two-year literary career to date, the action of *Lucy* takes place at a watershed moment in the world history of civil rights—1967–1968. It was also the year Antigua was first granted protectorate status within the British Empire, which meant that, while its foreign affairs were still to be ruled by the Crown, its internal affairs were now up to itself. Increasingly its internal affairs were being shaped by the economic and geopolitical concerns of the United States.

Lucy is allegorically crafted to capture not only Kincaid's ambivalence toward racial identity but toward national identity as well. For example, in a memory she tells Mariah, Lucy recalls the birth of her first brother against a blue sky, her second brother in a white chemise, and her third brother attacked by red ants. Together they recall the colors of Britain's Union Jack flag. This is followed by the image of black and white jail clothes. This image is then confused with the red, white, and blue tricolors of the French flag and, finally, as Lucy attempts to put pen to paper in the novel's final scene, they blur together with the colors America: Mariah has given her a blank book with a "dyed blood red" cover and "white and smooth like milk" pages, and a pen "full of beautiful blue ink" that *Lucy*'s final gesture will erase in tears (pp. 162–163).

In 1990, following *Lucy*'s publication, a visit from Kincaid's mother to her Vermont home triggered an emotional response Kincaid has likened to a nervous breakdown. Afterward, Kincaid came down with chicken pox, a one-time disease she had already had in childhood. During that period in the early- to mid-1990s she continued to thread the symbol of yellow she'd established in *Lucy* through the apparently disparate elements of her nonfiction essays.

In 1991, "On Seeing England for the First Time" begins with Kincaid as a child in a classroom being introduced to England on a map: " ...its yellow form mysterious, because though it looked like a leg of mutton, it could not really look like anything so familiar as a leg of mutton because it was England..." (p. 32).

"Alien Soil" (1993), part of her *New Yorker* "In the Garden" series, revisits the Wordsworth incident as autobiographically linked to her own hatred of daffodils; she contrasts the English and the Americans through their historical gardeners. The English slave owner Thomas Warner dominated his gardens directly, whereas Americans "are not interested in influencing people directly" (p. 48). The American slave owner Thomas Jefferson expressed his disinterest in the direct form of control exemplified by an English garden and replaced it with the idea of manifest destiny by sending "botany thief Meriwether Lewis" and "botany thief William Clark" into the wilderness. Here, with the invocation of Jefferson, the Kincaidian image of yellow now also carries its historical connotation from the American South of an ambiguous racial mixture, of hybridity—simultaneous proximity to the power of whiteness and exclusion from it.

"Homemaking" (1995)—the last piece she published in the *New Yorker* before quitting—reports her decision to move out of the house she and her family have long inhabited. She notes, parenthetically: "(It was painted yellow—a yellow common to houses in Finland, not the yellow of the Caribbean, the place I am from. This was a deliberate choice on my part, and I was expressing something quite ordinary—that is, liking the thing you are not)" (pp. 62–64).

In "The Flowers of Empire" (1996), published in *Harper's* just after she had publicly broken off her relationship with the *New Yorker*, Kincaid is acutely aware of her own growing privilege. She finds all these resonances in the image of a beautiful yellow flower she doesn't recognize in London's Kew Gardens: it turns out to be cotton. "White cotton from its black seed. They were inextricably bound, seed to fruit, and they were hard to separate," she recalls from childhood experience. She concludes, in one of her more straight forward addresses of slavery, exploitation, and colonialism's power to appropriate, "I only mind the absence of this acknowledgment: that perhaps every good thing that stands be-

fore us comes at a great cost to someone else" (pp. 30–31).

WHAT CAN'T CROSS THE WATER

AFTER a period of several years spent minding her inner garden (the rich fruits of which have now been gathered in *My Garden Book*), Kincaid returned to her fiction. Her creative revolution, forged in historical anger and motherly love, rediscovers its origins in the passionately ambivalent *The Autobiography of My Mother*. This novel was received uneasily by many critics and surrounded by speculations concerning Kincaid's impending breakup with the *New Yorker*. If *Lucy* can be seen as Kincaid's literary consummation of light and idea, *The Autobiography of My Mother* expresses what is other than those in her vision. Its art expresses itself through the negative constructions of language and through the bodily realities of smell, taste, sex, and blood.

Tilling a soil first surveyed in one of her earliest pieces, "Blackness," the novel functions thematically as an *Annie John* in reverse, as an "uncoming-of-age" story, reconnecting Kincaid's mother with a motherland separated, through an act of will, from the legacy of colonial domination. The story is set on Dominica primarily during the seventeen or so years before Kincaid's own birth. The heart of the novel—the young heroine's coming of age, her assertion of identity—is expressed through her self-performed abortion that literally prevents the colonial child within her to continue. Autobiographically, that child would have corresponded to Kincaid herself.

With children of her own, Kincaid could finally see the mother responsible for her identity as having once been a daughter herself. Through her own reversal of perspective, Kincaid could now identify with a heroine as her mother *and* as herself.

The fictional result expresses itself as a negative freedom, but a freedom nonetheless between the heroine and her own mother. As with Kincaid's other fiction, *The Autobiography of My Mother* records the legacy of domination, even in its absence, through the history of the character's own name:

> My own name is her name, Xuela Claudette, and in the place of the Desvarieux is Richardson, which is my father's name. ... My mother was placed outside the gates of a convent ... wrapped in pieces of clean old cloth, and the name Xuela was written ... in an ink whose color was indigo, a dye rendered from a plant ... how the name Xuela survived I do not know.
>
> (pp. 79–80)

Xuela's mother has died giving birth to her. Her mother is therefore erased from the well-lit history of colonialism and has become instead just the dream of a memory of a woman who died in childbirth with her history-less indigenous name intact. Like Kincaid's real grandmother—who, unlike the character, survived the birth of Kincaid's mother—Xuela's mother is a Carib Amerindian. Her presence as an absent figure in death allows Kincaid, through Xuela, to rewrite her mother as having been conceived in love instead of domination. Xuela has the personal freedom Kincaid's own mother could not conceive of—the personal freedom not to conceive, to never give birth, and so end the cycle of domination with herself. The novel allows Kincaid to love her own mother as a character, albeit through the tangible absence of herself in the story.

As the colonial legacy is lifted from her mother's shoulders, it comes to rest more fully on the domination of a father figure, who married through power for love. In many ways the central figure of the novel is not Xuela's mother, but her father—the man who would autobiographically correspond to the "great man" who "can no longer get up and go" in *Annie John*. Xuela's father would have been considered "yellow" in the language from the American South contemporary to the period. Like Kincaid's grandfather, he is the child of an interracial union between a colonial Scot and the descendant of African slaves. Like Kincaid's grandfather, he is a policeman who both enforces and profits from the colonial system.

At the end of the novel, Xuela in the present day—sharing the seventy years of Kincaid's own

mother—has married and buried a personally harmless white Englishman "not for love" and, having remained true to her self in her decision never to have children, she has moved away from the sea to the interior, with a mountain view not unlike Kincaid's own in Vermont. Xuela has dominated her husband personally while he contented himself in exercising his historical legacy of British colonial conquest within the parameters of Kincaid's own passion: gardening.

Looking back on her life, Xuela—in what must have been a moment of intense identification for Kincaid, at least from the point of view of her art—wishes for a larger meaning to the unrelenting loneliness and political isolation of her position:

> I am not a people, I am not a nation. I only wish from time to time to make my actions be the actions of a people, to make my actions be the actions of a nation.
>
> (p. 216).

MEMORY RETURNED

IN 1996—a year marked by both the death of her mentor and father-in-law William Shawn, and the death of her youngest brother Devon, whom she knew less well—Kincaid wrote *My Brother*. This second work of literary nonfiction for which she received the PEN/Faulkner Award examines the legacy of domination within AIDS, from which her brother died in Antigua, with as much ambivalence as she conjured up over the issue of Antigua's political independence in *A Small Place*. As a formal consideration of factual history and autobiography, this later work precedes from prose she established in the earlier one and no doubt anticipates some of the formal intricacies at work in *My Garden Book*. Since Kincaid had now broken her creative friendship with the *New Yorker*, *My Brother* never appeared serially prior to its publication.

My Brother is her firsthand account of Devon's dying in Antigua, written both before and immediately after his death. It is also the story of his birth in Antigua, which she also witnessed firsthand, and that birth's place at the heart of the love/hate relationship between her mother and herself. It is also the story of the space in between Devon's birth and dying, which she did not witness; and the space of his actual death, which she did not witness either. During both she was safely at home in America. The work ends by mourning the loss of her father-in-law, whom she names as "the perfect reader" (p. 198). Once again she explores her own complicated position between Antigua and America, this time not as a tourist, but as a first world provider of HIV treatment drugs that are systemically unavailable in Antigua.

Like the highly allusive prose of her gardening essays, the images of Devon's birth and death are intertwined with vegetal imagery. Kincaid also returns to the image of book burning, on which *A Small Place* turns, as indicative of the structures of memory and denial, between her brother and her mother, her brother and herself and, as always, her mother and herself.

Her mother's disruptive visit to her Vermont home apparently triggered a suppressed memory, the relation of which occupies the physical center of *My Brother*. Shortly before she would leave for America, with her father's immanent death about to leave her mother destitute, Kincaid, then still Elaine, was charged by her mother with caring for her newest brother, a duty she neglected in favor of her reading. As she relates in *My Brother*, when her mother discovered the two-year-old Devon weighed down by a heavily soiled diaper:

> She found my books, the things that had come between me and the smooth flow of her life, her many children that she could not support, that she and her husband (the man not my own father) could not support, and in this fury, which she was conscious of then but cannot now remember, but which to her regret I can, she gathered all the books of mine she could find, and placing them on her stone heap (the one on which she bleached out the stains and smudges that had, in the ordinariness of life, appeared on our white clothes) she doused them with kerosene (oil from the kerosene lamp by the light of which I used to strain my eyes reading

some of the books that I was about to lose) and then set fire to them.

> (pp. 132–134)

Like the bond with her mother, the relationship between Kincaid's "idea of thing"—her books—and her "reality of thing"—her lived experience—is not always straightforward. No matter how transparent that relationship initially appears to her reader, the two become incompatible when kept too long at a distance. When they finally meet, as she concluded in "On Seeing England for the First Time," "the weaker of the two, idea or reality, dies" (p. 37).

Now that *My Garden Book* has been published to comprise her gardening columns and *Talk Stories* has been published to comprise her "Talk of the Town" columns, Jamaica Kincaid has resumed at least her formal relationship with the *New Yorker*. After a half-decade absence her familiar byline returned in the magazine's 22 January 2001 edition.

Jamaica Kincaid's formal relationship with books was interrupted at age thirteen. Today she has received several honorary degrees from U.S. universities and is currently a fellow at the prestigious Du Bois Institute of Harvard University, where she also serves on the faculty of the African American Studies Department, teaching literature and creative writing for one semester per year. No doubt she is also beginning to probe a new form of power—academic privilege—and the position she now holds within it.

SELECTED BIBLIOGRAPHY

I. WORKS OF FICTION. *At the Bottom of the River* (New York, 1984), quotations cited from Plume edition (New York, 1992); *Annie John* (New York, 1985), quotations cited from Noonday edition (New York, 1997); Eric Fischl, *Annie, Gwen, Lily, Pam and Tulip* (New York, 1989); *Lucy* (New York, 1990), quotations cited from Plume edition (New York, 1991); *The Autobiography of My Mother* (New York, 1996).

II. COLLECTED PIECES—*AT THE BOTTOM OF THE RIVER*.
Quotations cited from book: "Girl," in the *New Yorker* (26 June 1978); "In the Night," in the *New Yorker* (24 July 1978); "Wingless," in the *New Yorker* (29 January 1979); "Holidays," in the *New Yorker* (27 August 1979); "At Last," in the *New Yorker* (17 December 1979); "The Letter from Home," in the *New Yorker* (20 April 1981); "What I Have Been Doing Lately," in the *Paris Review* 23 (1981); "At the

Bottom of the River," in the *New Yorker* (3 May 1982); "My Mother," in Stewart Brown, ed., *Caribbean New Wave: Contemporary Short Stories* (London, 1990).

III. COLLECTED PIECES—*ANNIE JOHN*. Quotations cited from book: "Figures in the Distance," in the *New Yorker* (9 May 1983); "The Red Girl," in the *New Yorker* (8 August 1983); "Columbus in Chains," in the *New Yorker* (10 October 1983); "The Circling Hand," in the *New Yorker* (21 November 1983); "Gwen," in the *New Yorker* (16 April 1984); "Somewhere, Belgium," in the *New Yorker* (14 May 1984); "The Long Rain," in the *New Yorker* (30 July 1984); "A Walk to the Jetty," in the *New Yorker* (5 November 1984).

IV. COLLECTED PIECES—*LUCY*. Quotations cited from book: "Poor Visitor," in the *New Yorker* (27 February 1989); "Mariah," in the *New Yorker* (26 June 1989); "The Tongue," in the *New Yorker* (9 October 1989); "Cold Heart," in the *New Yorker* (25 June 1990); "Lucy," in the *New Yorker* (24 September 1990).

V. COLLECTED PIECES—*THE AUTOBIOGRAPHY OF MY MOTHER*. Quotations cited from book: "Song of Roland," in the *New Yorker* (12 April 1993); "Xuela," in the *New Yorker* (9 May 1994); "In Roseau," in the *New Yorker* (17 April 1995).

VI. UNCOLLECTED PIECES. "Antigua Crossings: A Deep and Blue Passage on the Caribbean Sea," in *Rolling Stone* (29 June 1978), a section was rewritten as part of "My Mother" in *At the Bottom of the River*; "Ovando," in *Conjunctions* 14 (1989).

VII. WORKS OF NONFICTION. "The Fourth," in the *New Yorker* (19 July 1976); "Jamaica Kincaid's New York," in *Rolling Stone* (6 October 1977); "Dates and Comment," in the *New Yorker* (17 October 1977); "The Apprentice," in the *New Yorker* (17 August 1981); "Notes and Comment," in the *New Yorker* (3 January 1983); *A Small Place* (New York, 1988); "The Ugly Tourist," in *Harper's* (September 1988), collected, quotations cited from book; "On Seeing England for the First Time," in *Transition*, no. 51 (1991); with Ellen Pall, "Out of Kenya," in the *New York Times* (16 September 1991); "Biography of a Dress," in *Grand Street* 11, no. 3 (1992); "Flowers of Evil," in the *New Yorker* (5 October 1992); "A Fire by Ice," in the *New Yorker* (22 February 1993); "Just Reading," in the *New Yorker* (29 March 1993); "Alien Soil," in the *New Yorker* (21 June 1993); "This Other Eden," in the *New Yorker* (23–30 August 1993); "The Season Past," in the *New Yorker* (7 March 1994); "Putting Myself Together," in the *New Yorker* (20 February 1995); "Plant Parenthood," in the *New Yorker* (19 June 1995); "Homemaking," in the *New Yorker* (16 October 1995); "Flowers of Empire," in *Harper's* (April 1996); *My Brother* (New York, 1997); *My Garden Book* (New York, 1999); *Talk Stories* (New York, 2001); "Sowers and Reapers," in the *New Yorker* (22 January 2001).

VIII. INTERVIEWS. Patricia T. O'Conner, "My Mother Wrote My Life," in the *New York Times Book Review* (7 April 1985); Selwyn R. Cudjoe, "Jamaica Kincaid and the Modernist Project: An Interview," in *Callaloo* 12, no. 2 (Spring 1988); Donna Perry, "An Interview with Jamaica Kincaid," in Henry Louis Gates, ed., *Reading Black, Reading Feminist* (New York, 1990); Allan Vorda, "An Interview

with Jamaica Kincaid," in *Mississippi Review* 20 (1991); Kay Bonetti, "An Interview with Jamaica Kincaid," in *The Missouri Review* 15, no. 2 (1992), transcribed from an April 1991 interview for the American Audio Prose Library; Allan Vorda, "I Come from a Place That's Very Unreal: An Interview with Jamaica Kincaid," in his *Face to Face: Interviews with Contemporary Novelists* Houston, Tex., 1993); Donna Perry, "Jamaica Kincaid," in her *Backtalk: Women Writers Speak Out.* New Brunswick, N.J., 1993); Moira Ferguson, "A Lot of Memory: An Interview with Jamaica Kincaid," in the *Kenyon Review* 16, no. 1 (Winter 1994); Pamela Buchman Muirhead, "An Interview with Jamaica Kincaid," in *Clockwatch Review* 9, no. 1–2 (1994–1995); Dwight Garner, "The *Salon* Interview: Jamaica Kincaid," in *Salon* online magazine, www.salon1999.com/05/features/kincaid.html (8 November 1995); Ivan Kreilkamp, "Jamaica Kincaid: Daring to Discomfort," in *Publishers Weekly* (1 January 1996); Sally Jacobs, "Don't Mess with Jamaica Kincaid," in *Boston Globe* (20 June 1996); Allan Vorda, *Caribbean Writing* (Hattiesburg, MS, 1996); Kay Bonetti, *Conversations with American Novelists: The Best Interviews from the Missouri Review and the American Audio Prose Library* (Columbia, Mo., 1997); Marilyn Snell, "Jamaica Kincaid Hates Happy Endings." in *Mother Jones (September–October 1997)*.

IX. CRITICAL, BIOGRAPHICAL, HISTORICAL STUDIES. Selwyn R. Cudjoe, *Resistance and Caribbean Literature* (Athens, Ohio, 1980); Gordon K. Lewis, *Grenada: The Jewel Despoiled* (Baltimore, 1987); William Wordsworth, *Wordsworth's Poems of 1807*, ed. by Alun R. Jones (London, 1987); Selwyn R. Cudjoe, ed., *Caribbean Women Writers: Essays from the First International Conference.* Wellesley: Calaloux, 1990; Robert Coram, *Caribbean Time Bomb: The United States' Complicity in the Corruption of Antigua* (New York, 1993); Alison Donell, "Dreaming of Daffodils: Cultural Resistance in the Narratives of Theory," in *Kunapipi* 14, no. 1 (1993); Margaret R. Higonnet,, ed., *Borderwork: Feminist Engagements with Comparative Literature* (Ithaca, N.Y., 1994); Moira Ferguson, *Colonialism and Gender Relations from Mary Wollstonecraft to Jamaica Kincaid: Eastern Caribbean Connections* (New York, 1994); Diane Ellis Simmons, *Jamaica Kincaid* (New York, 1994); Moira Ferguson, *Jamaica Kincaid: Where the Land Meets the Body* (Charlottesville, Va., 1994); Louis F. Caton, Louis F. "'Such Was the Paradise That I Lived': Multiculturalism, Romantic Theory, and the Contemporary American Novel (Don Delillo, Jamaica Kincaid, Leslie Marmon Silko)" (Ph.D. diss., University of Oregon, 1995); Leela Gandhi, *Postcolonial Theory: A Critical Introduction* (New York, 1998), a highly literate overview for those unfamiliar with the subject; Harold Bloom, ed., *Jamaica Kincaid* (Philadelphia, 1998), comprises an invaluable "best-of" collection selected from the numerous critical essays appearing in current academic journals; Lizabeth Paravisini-Gebert, *Jamaica Kincaid: A Critical Companion* (Westport, Conn., 1999), the most comprehensive work to date on biographical aspects of Kincaid's work; the bibliography is comprehensive, including numerous unpublished Ph.D. dissertations.

THOMAS MORE

(1477/8 –1535)

John M. Headley

DISTINGUISHED LAWYER, LEADING humanist, troubled Lord Chancellor, *defensor fidei* (defender of the faith), Thomas More stands at the intersection of the major currents of his age; his life engages and reflects the history of England and of Europe at the beginning of the sixteenth century. His extensive writings chart the course of that career.

He was born in February 1478(?), the son of a well-established London lawyer, John More, who placed young Thomas at the age of twelve as a page in the household of John Cardinal Morton, in keeping with the practice of exposing, if possible, one's young to the great, the politically powerful, and the experienced; he would learn about politics and acquire the finesse and love for improvisation that distinguish his thought and career. Although obviously slated for the law after two years at Oxford and then the Inns of Court, More felt drawn to the religious life and lived without vow for four years in or about the London Charterhouse and its members. During this period, he first encountered Erasmus (1499), lectured on Augustine's *City of God*, and began his study of Greek. Driven by natural passion and persuaded that the Christian life could be lived meaningfully outside the cloister, he married. The fateful year 1505 also saw what would become his first publication—the translation and reshaping of the Latin biography of the great Italian Platonist Pico della Mirandola into the *Life of Pico* for devotional purposes.

The demands of a family and of a rising political career beckoned. More had four children and a burgeoning household with an extended family, which he supported by his engagement with the law. Increasingly he was drawn into public service, first for the city of London, but then into the personal orbit of the new king, Henry VIII.

These years that saw his growth as a recognized humanist, Greek scholar and associate of Erasmus also witnessed his heavy involvement in political responsibilities, culminating with the publication of *Utopia* in 1516 and his entry into the King's Council by March 1518.

As a royal councillor More found his energies claimed to opposing the Lutheran menace, first foreign, but soon all too domestic, against the English reformer and martyr William Tyndale (1492?–1536) and his followers. In the deepening conflict More's position became progressively strained by the king's divorce and royal gravitation away from Rome, made increasingly awkward by More's succeeding Thomas Wolsey (1475?–1530) as Lord Chancellor in 1529 in the highest civil office. Both in polemics and in politics he found himself fighting a rearguard action for the old order. Frustrated in his ambiguous position, now thwarted, More resigned his high office on 15 May 1532, the day following Parliament's passage of the Act of Supremacy and the consequent Submission of the Clergy to royal authority over the church in England. Late in 1533 the Royal Council ordered More to stop publishing his polemical writings. Arrested in April 1534 for his refusal to sign the oath associated with the Act of Succession confirming all Henry's actions against the Catholic Church, he was convicted of "misprision of treason" under the Act of Supremacy and beheaded on Tower Hill the morning of 6 July 1535.

THE HUMANISTIC WRITINGS

THE writings of Thomas More fall fairly neatly into three stages in the development of his career. The first and apparently most fundamental stage conformed to his encounter with the new literary and intellectual currents of the Renaissance and was marked by humanism. At this stage More was acquiring the rhetorical and philological techniques that would equip him as a Christian in the world to perform effectively as a spokesman in a number of legal, diplomatic, and political forums, culminating after March 1518 with his role as a royal privy councillor. By the spring of 1521 this stage gave way to the new forces created by Luther's reform and the emerging Protestant Reformation, which serve to transform More into the champion of Catholic orthodoxy and increasingly the defender of the traditional order at home as Henry VIII's program began to emerge. This polemical/controversial focus to his writings continued through January 1534 and in turn was displaced by the devotional stage of his literary output, ushered in by his refusal to take the oath of succession and his commitment to the Tower. Yet the apparent clarity with which these three stages can be distinguished proves deceptive in two respects. First, the express evidence of the devotional bent in More's intellectual world had been manifest from the start in his first published English work, the *Life of Pico* (1510), and from attitudes expressed in his earliest English poems of this period bearing on death and the Abrytill welth" of this world (1:10/30)1. In the second period of polemics, we have his more explicit meditation on death in the *Four Last Things* of 1522. The devotional cast of More's mind remains fundamental throughout. Secondly, the vibrance and depth of the classical humanist are not absent from the later stages of the polemical and the devotional. The humanist, the polemical, and the devotional invade each other in all his works, if in varying degrees, mutually reinforcing and clarifying the political, confessional, and spiritual dimensions to his life and work.

By humanism we intend not a specific philosophy but, in keeping with the scholarship of Paul Kristeller, an educational and literary culture that finds rhetorical models and methods in the authors of classical antiquity. Hence language, forsaking its previous mold within medieval Scholasticism of the universities, becomes a legacy rather than a set of mental constructs. Yet access to the *fontes*, and their effective imitation and representation in the present depended upon an exact command not only of classical Latin but also of Greek. Since formal training in the Greek language was nonexistent and depended entirely upon personal application and effort there were no dictionaries or grammars until far in the future, More's learning of Greek becomes a significant accomplishment. The appearance in 1518 of his *Epigrammata*, a collection of translated epigrams from the Greek together with his own epigrams, accents the first two decades of the century as a training period making possible the well-known achievements represented by *Richard III* and the supreme instance of the *Utopia*. We need to go behind these works to appreciate the earlier and less well known humanistic products of the early years. More's exposure to Greek took two avenues, each highly revealing as to his own inner needs and temperament, reinforcing and clarifying those qualities and each affording the opportunity of sharing his enthusiasm with the preeminent representative of this new literary culture. Of the two avenues, the first presented itself in terms of the satirical writings of Lucian; the second in terms of no one classical author but of a genre, that of the epigram.

Who was Lucian, and what made his work so crucial, even decisive, for More especially, but also for the reform movement gaining strength at this time from access to the classical past? Why did More's contemporaries—Erasmus, Hutten, and Rabelais, among others—find Lucian to be instrumental for their own purposes? Just as Cicero proved to be the major classical author behind the early Italian Renaissance, so Lucian assumed this role for the reform movement —often referred to as the Northern or Christian Renaissance—gaining ground during these years in the more traditional, ecclesiastically bound parts of northern Europe.

Lucian of Samosata (ca. 125–190) was a professional *rhetor*, a Greek-speaking Syrian who thrived by writing speeches for clients and in publicly exhibiting his skills, leaving eighty-two compositions embracing dramatic dialogues, rhetorical discourses, literary and social criticism, satire, fiction, and moral philosophy. Skeptical, incisive, ironic, he identified himself as a hater of all pomposity, hypocrisy, deceit, vanity, and especially the frauds of popular religion. His works recommended themselves to his audiences by their wit and irony. Since deceit, pretense, and pomposity always exist in abundance and especially in this late medieval world, Lucian's rhetorical techniques provided the best butter for the awakened critical tastes of reforming spirits. During the first quarter of the fifteenth century Lucian had become available to Italian humanists, and by the end of the century there existed twenty-one editions of thirteen different dialogues of the Syrian satirist. After 1500 a veritable deluge of his works followed, and it seemed only natural that More's Utopians should specifically seek and welcome these texts. In that Lucian quickly became synonymous with "mocker," "skeptic," even "atheist," however, More would need to temper his early, ready recourse to these materials.

More had met Erasmus of Rotterdam, soon to become the preeminent European humanist, on his first visit to England in 1499. By the autumn of 1501, More was working at Greek, first learning it from William Grocin and Thomas Linacre in London, not at Oxford. Shortly afterward, he availed himself of an experienced Graecist, William Lily, in a partnership that would lead him down that second and longer avenue of practicing and emulating the epigrams in the *Greek Anthology*, a late Byzantine collection, which he began to quarry as early as 1503 or 1504 but whose influence would extend down to 1520. Thus in this broader context of his exposure to the intricacies and potentialities of classical Greek More entered upon the famous partnership with Erasmus during that scholar's second sojourn in England, 1505–1506. Both humanist reformers turned to a cooperative venture of translating from Lucian as a means of perfecting their Greek and honing their satirical skills for purposes of social criticism. They worked from the Aldine 1503 edition of Lucian. By June of 1506 they had completed their labors, and by November Badius Ascensius of Paris had published the results of their efforts. The volume contained eighteen brief dialogues and ten longer

ones translated by Erasmus and four by More from the Greek to Latin; in addition, there was an original declamation by each on the *Tyrannicida*, which itself constituted the fourth and last of the pieces that More had translated.

In any assessment of the significance of this slim volume for More's development and for the history of classical studies in sixteenth-century England it needs to be emphasized that More here appears as the first Englishman to translate Lucian into Latin, his versions being the first by an Englishman to be printed. With the exception of two letters, these translations, together with More's declamatory reply to the problem or, better, riddle posed by Lucian in the translated *Tyrannicida*, constituted More's earliest surviving Latin prose compositions. The name of the English author on the title page of the Paris publication coupled a complete unknown to Erasmus, a humanist with an emerging European reputation. European praise and recognition of More derived from this modest, slender beginning. He would see no other of his writings occasion such repeated reprintings: at least nine by his death in 1535, as compared with *Utopia* six times in Latin, one in German, and one in Italian by 1549. In emphasizing the *Utopia*, we ignore More's Lucianic efforts today, but the sixteenth century appears to have seen him in a different light (3/I:xxv).

Other than a prefatory letter to the Royal Secretary, Thomas Ruthall, More's one original effort here was his declamation in response to the *Tyrannicida*. Its significance was considerable but indirect. The *declamatio* is the stock in trade of the trained *rhetor* and of the rhetorical education and culture of the classical world: stock speeches on stock subjects to promote verbal dexterity and oratorical polish. Given his flair for the dramatic and his professional commitment to the law, More found appealing Lucian's claimant in the *Tyrannicida*; it afforded him the opportunity to draw legal distinctions as well as to evoke his persuasive rhetorical talents. More would have also been drawn to the subject itself of tyrannicide, as is evident at this time from his epigrammatic treatment of monarchy and the dangers of any excessive concentration of political power. Beyond such general implications it is futile to seek any explicit import from the position taken by More in his reply. For More and his generation the significance lay in the purely literary exercise itself so expressive of the rhetorical education and culture of antiquity now being imbibed by him and his friends. The pervasive, long-range import serves to heighten the ludic and fictive qualities of More's impending masterpiece.

Beyond the pleasure of exploiting the racy satirist and adopting his style and genres for the exposure of fraud, superstition, and hypocrisy, what most recommended Lucian to the Christian humanist was the exemplary exercise of irony, that elusive quality—of praising when one is blaming and vice versa, of understatement, of apparent, Socratic self-deprecation—conveying an entire cast of mind and stance toward the world that combined "an amused tolerance of human foibles, a pretended ignorance, and sometimes a cool rationalism" (3/I:l–li). To the earnest Christian who had forsaken the cloister for living in the world, it became the essential ingredient of that armor which allowed him to engage and endure that world. It afforded More a special sort of engagement together with detachment from the harsh realities of that world. It also provided the humanists of his generation with the attraction of combining instruction with pleasure, thereby engaging their readers and avoiding the pitfall of boring them with moral exhortation.

During the first decades of the sixteenth century More's second avenue toward his mastery of classical Greek led him not to the appropriation of a particular author but to the conquest of a particular genre, the epigram. It spoke very much to the personal nature of More himself as well as arming him for his literary, reforming, humanistic enterprises. A huge mine of classical epigrams had become available to scholarly Europe through a Byzantine collection known as *The Greek Anthology*, constituting several layers of Greek poems through the ages, in collections that culminated with the anthology produced by the monk Planudes around 1300 and published in 1494. Among much lumber of all sorts existed an abundance of epigrams, some of sparkling qual-ity in their trenchant, incisive nature. Of the seventy-nine epigrams that More translated into Latin in this period five can be dated before 1500, but the majority derive from the first decade, 1500 to 1510—years marked at first by close association with William Lily. In March 1518, More and Lily brought out the *Progymnasmata* (or warm-up exercises), along with some of their own original epigrams. The newly founded St. Paul's School promptly adopted these preparatory exercises. In December 1518 and December 1520 the more definitive editions of his epigrammatic efforts were published, adding to the number of his own original Latin epigrams beyond those translated *e graeco*. Only with the edition of 1520 does the *Epigrammata* of More and Lily stand free of other works and authors. All of these editions were published in Basel, on the upper Rhine; the 1518 work also contained a new edition of the *Utopia*.

In writing the prefatory letter that appears in all three, the young humanist Beatus Rhenanus noted a distinct and important difference between earlier humanist epigrams and those of More. The Italian humanists had seen the epigram as a short love poem or an opportunity for a mannered flattery, thereby often assuming the posturings of classical mythology and license. More's urbane colleague, Erasmus, hardly did better in using the epigram to float dull religious commonplaces. Breaking with both these patterns, More sees the epigram as a short poem, usually in elegiac couplets, trenchant, witty and satirical, affording opportunities for his keen eye in noting the absurd, the poignant, the humanly revealing. In short More brings the epigram out of the scholar's closet and into the world of merchants, lawyers, and courtiers (3/II:54–56, 72–77). By his official duties and growing experience More knew the sewers and back alleys of London; he possessed an earthiness, or what we might call today street smarts, which recommended these short, witty literary exercises to a growing readership and allowed him to impart this broad, pungent humor to his other writings in the years ahead.

In one respect Beatus Rhenanus overshot the mark in his otherwise perceptive assessment of

More's poetic accomplishment. Led astray by an apparent parallel in the work of Terence where the Roman playwright speaks of one being every inch pure wisdom, Beatus, in praising More's wit, speaks of More as being every inch pure jest (3/II:8). It is not that More was ever lacking in wit and jest; rather, humor became an essential ingredient to his writing and in his own personal stance to the world. But it was never unbridled and free from its serious implications. His *festivitas* is balanced and even informed by a *gravitas*; together they shape both his personal bearing and his writings.

Of the two hundred eighty-one epigrams in the *Yale Edition*, a few are worthy of note here for their range and variety: the ironic notion of his two wives and himself as an imaginary *ménage à trois* (No. 258), which will figure later in his epitaph; his wistful encounter with his boyhood sweetheart after twenty years (No. 263); his epigram on the rabbit and wanton human heartlessness (No. 37), so reminiscent of the similar experience and reaction of his great enemy Luther; the discussion of the best form of government (No. 198), wherein he early expresses his distrust of kingship and his preference for the more collective device of a senate; or on choosing a wife (No. 143) (cf. 3/II:57). Yet by such a selection pathos and the serious would seem to prevail at the expense of the comic, even slapstick. Here one may resort to several of More's epigrams deriding the vainglorious exaggerations of the French humanist Germain de Brie or Brixius to trumpet the bravery of the French commander, Hervé, against the English. More shrewdly notes that altogether Brixius unaccountably equipped Hervé with four different weapons, which he somehow manages to exercise to the discomfiture of the English. Which leads More to hazard that Hervé either has five hands or, in another epigram, that he is wearing his shield on his head (Nos. 190 and 191). Such a rejoinder would inevitably lead to further convolutions and recriminations within the fracturing front of humanism before the flood of the Reformation.

It is in the context of More's and his generation's appropriation of Greek literary culture that the two outstanding single works of this period become possible—*The History of King Richard III* and the *Utopia*. Yet there exists another context that one needs to keep in mind as operative especially during these years and probably more influential in the longer perspective: the practical, political one. If there is any validity to the present thesis that More's writings and life offer a uniquely revealing case of the uncloistered yet inwardly recloistered Christian in the world of the early sixteenth century, then the problem of the worst state and the best state of a commonwealth, considered at the very time that he entered into royal political service, assumes greater meaning.

Richard III, composed between 1513 and 1518, considers the worst state of a commonwealth, or what happens when monarchy becomes artfully corrupted by a tyrant. More skillfully draws upon the literary techniques of the leading Roman historians—Sallust, Suetonius, and above all Tacitus—especially for his portrait of the Emperor Tiberius in all his cunning dissimulation. These are incorporated in a way that evinces a creative appropriation of classical themes in the re-creation and advancement of historical reality. What gives unusual immediacy and force to More's presentation is that the embers of the political conflict—this world of blood and iron, this tale of monstrous tyranny, pride, and corruption—are still warm, and their reality perdures in more than just the memories of men. More was eight-years old when Richard fell at Bosworth Field, and many of the players—his own father, and Cardinal Morton—were still available and to be consulted. It is from such vibrant material provided by living witnesses that More shapes his account according to classical guidelines; the legacy of the classical past becomes meaningful through its effective incorporation into what has been so recently experienced. In this way Richard as evil incarnate escapes being a caricature, becoming painfully real. And among those still living and to be seen, if not consulted, was the extraordinarily favored concubine of Edward IV and others, the generous-spirited Jane Shore. More's study of her—insightful, sensitive, poignant—represents him at his best. In the midst of his sketch, having already reconstructed her former beauty in gazing upon the present ruins of her face, he catches himself at a moment that suggests the tragic is not limited to princes and those of heroic mold but extends to the commoner, the base, and the human—four centuries before the salesman Willy Loman.

> I doubt not some shal think this woman to sleight a thing, to be written of & set amonge the remembraunces of great matters: which thei shal specially think, yt happely shal esteme her only by yt thei now see her. But me semeth the chaunce so much the more worthy to be remembred, in how much she is now in the more beggerly condicion, vnfrended & worne out of acquaintance, after good substance, after as gret fauour wt the prince, after as gret sute & seking to wt al those yt those days had busynes to spede, as many other men were in their times, which be now famouse, only by yt infamy of their il dedes. Her doinges were not much lesse, albeit thei be muche lesse remembred, because thei were not so euil. For men vse if they haue an euil turne, to write it in marble: & whoso doth vs a good tourne, we write it in duste which is not worst proued by her: for at this daye shee beggeth of many at this daye liuing, yt at this day had begged if she had not bene.
>
> (2:56–57)

And the world's vast panoply and parade move on.

Despite his broad, eclectic appeal to classical authors for his drama, More will nevertheless resorted to his direct knowledge of Lucian's *Menippus* for human existence seen as a stage play in which each has for a time a part to play. But it is best for underlings not to intrude upon those stage plays in which great matters be "Kynges games . . . plaied upon scafoldes" (2:81/6 –7). The rhythm of horror unfolds, revealing the ongoing themes of the fragility of human life, the abrupt reversal of fortune, the relentless march of a masterful evil.

More's composition of two separate, parallel presentations of the narrative, one in Latin, probably for a more international audience, the other in English, without either being a translation, marked a unique event in English literature. As will be seen in the case of the earlier *Life of Pico*, some Latin words occur as doublets, two words in the English. Lacking the original draft of either

version, the recently recovered Paris manuscript of the Latin in the Bibliothèque Nationale represents the most advanced and thus commanding draft of More's history. The *Historia/History* remained unfinished, and no manuscript evidence exists that a final revision occurred (15:cxliii, cli). Its incomplete state, no part of which would be published in his lifetime, can best be understood in terms of More's increasingly being drawn into royal service during these years. On 26 March 1518 he entered the King's Council.

To continue to treat such politically sensitive materials became quite inappropriate, if not dangerous. The solution More seems to have devised was to treat the problems of governance and government service in less immediately dramatic, politically sensitive form—in a different register and genre entirely, inviting greater freedom and the play of imagination. During the same period 1514–1518, he explored the danger of tyranny, the preference for a senatorial, collective type of government, and the virtues of *populus consentiens* (No. 121) in more than a dozen Latin epigrams. His most analytical, explicit epigram, "Quis Optimus Reipvb. Status" ("What Is the Best Form of the Commonwealth?"; No. 198), bears the same title as the forthcoming utopian study that would give birth to a new genre of literature.

More took a period of enforced leisure during a lapse in the diplomatic negotiations held at Bruges, the late Medieval financial center and trade emporium, to write Utopia, addressing in a supremely artful way the political, moral, and immensely personal issues that now came together and pressed upon him. In *Utopia* he creates an imaginary society in order apparently to clarify his thoughts on the dilemma of the new politics, the human predicament, and his own entry into this precarious context. By way of introduction, More recounts an imaginary meeting in Antwerp between himself and a sunburned Portuguese mariner, Raphael Hythloday, with whom he enters into conversation and receives from this fictional world traveler and philosopher a blistering critique of the ills and injustices of contemporary Europe. The criticism takes the form of a reported dialogue, the Dialogue of

Counsel, constituting what becomes Book I of the published *Utopia*, although actually composed later after More's return from the Netherlands. But the truly utopian part, describing an imaginary society of communistic bleakness and simplicity, awaits, already present in the earlier written discourse of Hythloday, constituting Book II. More, or rather More's fictional persona "Morus," figures in Book I but leaves Hythloday to his uninterrupted discourse on the island society in Book II, only reappearing at the very end. Through his intense exposure to Greek literary culture and his recently acquired mastery of classical rhetorical forms of satire, the epigram, and irony, the aspiring privy councillor could direct his considerable intellectual apparatus to a problem both general to humanism in its reforming tendencies and immediate to his own predicament. How does the Christian engage the world? And how does one serve royal government? But less immediately what are readers to understand as the author's larger intention: a mere *jeu d'esprit*—or playful pastime; a blueprint for the perfect society, espousing a radical communism; an anti-Europe tract begetting reform; a plan for a parallel Christian society; a commentary on humanism itself; an ongoing dialogue on an unsolvable problem? That it can be all of these, yet none pushed to its extreme, speaks to the literary artistry of the work.

Insofar as it is a philosophical expression of More's own intense political dilemma at this time, yet something to be shared more largely with the community of Christian humanists constituting the Renaissance in northern Europe, the most persuasive specific reading of *Utopia*'s political import appears not in its immediate communism but in the moral virtues, regimentation, and order represented by the monastery. Utopian society presents us with a vast lay monastery of fifty-four cities, which More, the hair-shirted Londoner with the values of its Charterhouse, offers to an ailing Christendom of city-states caught between imperial structures and national contexts. In fact, Erasmus was inspired to assert, in 1518, "What else is a city but a great monastery?" What recommends the new religion of the Christian missionaries to the Utopians is "that they had

heard that His disciples' common way of life had been pleasing to Christ and that it is still in use among the truest societies of Christians" (4:218 –219). In such an apparent endorsement of the monastery, More reveals the contrast between the virtues of a non-Christian society and the vices of a nominally Christian one and the problem of infusing the one and reinfusing the other with Christian principles and practices. If he raises here the problem of Christianity and public service, of moral man and immoral, howsoever infant, State, the thread of his own personal dilemma and emerging adjustment to this terrible issue of the age never disappears. And in any interpreter's foolish pursuit of a single answer to the political import of *Utopia*, while the historian and the philosopher each has a place, neither can afford to be too serious, too professional, too heavy-handed in reading an artistic achievement that belongs properly to literature.

Utopia is first and foremost a literary work, however charged and sparkling with philosophical import. All too often the title *Utopia* has threatened to become limited to the discourse or monologue of the earlier composed Book II, marginalizing the Dialogue of Counsel in Book I; here John Cardinal Morton reappears with his political prudence and the fictive Hythloday, speaking with far greater vehemence than the level-toned Raphael of Book II, disagrees radically with the fictive—or only semi-fictive —More. To pin its meaning to any one political solution for Europe in 1515 or for the human community in general overly contextualizes the work. If we can shift the contextual lens and redirect it more to the personal situation of the author himself, the emphasis may properly fall upon the immensity of the literary achievement, which opens up what has purported to become a final solution into an enduring problem, part of the enigma of human existence. In keeping with its author's own personal bearing toward the world, the work proclaims by its title to be both *festivus* and *salutaris*, entertaining and beneficial; if a *jeu d'esprit*, then a serious playfulness. Irony serves to reinforce the multiple layers of ambiguity. Indeed in the work's closing statement regarding the Utopians' communal living as removing all nobility, magnificence, splendor, and majesty, scholars continue to debate its probably ironic intent.

More returned early in 1516 from his Netherlandish diplomatic service to London and to court. The apparent prominence of the festive, the ludic, the utopian, afforded previously by the leisure derived from the delays in negotiations, recede before the intensified immediacy of the political and the personal. The shift in time and place that brings into being the better part of Book I as the Dialogue of Counsel accents More's own problem of entry into the Royal Council, the efficacy of counsel, and the specific problems of English governance. Behind all the delightful glitter and marvelous artistry, the work provides for its author a scaffolding upon which he can play out the ultimately ambivalent arguments regarding what Plato had identified as the highest existence given to humans, namely the political, and for its present sixteenth-century form, the issue of good counsel which posits the good counselor and the best state of a commonwealth. Yes, a festive book but along with *festivitas*, a darkly pessimistic *gravitas* that makes of political community and political existence no clear solution, in fact no solution at all, but always a choice and identification of at best the less bad, a dilemma which three years earlier a Florentine contemporary, Machiavelli, had defined in less ideal terms. Through the multiple frames, the shifting perspectives, the layers of paradox, satire and irony an apparently less fictive More speaks to the reader at the end of Utopia itself when he observes that "there are many features of the Utopian commonwealth which it is easier for me to wish for in our countries than to have any hope of seeing realized" and with greater import that at the end of Book I, to "not abandon the ship in a storm because you cannot control the winds. . . . What you cannot turn to good you must make as little bad as you can" (4:247, 99). The next twenty years remaining to him would demonstrate that it is here Thomas More who speaks and not just the "Morus" of the dialogue.

The period 1515 to 1520 saw the presentation of several letters advancing of the humanist program for educational, moral, and religious reform throughout Christendom. The letter in More's time was a vehicle for the exposition of major current intellectual issues and for the nurturing of a community of learned persons, the emerging *Respublica litteraria*. A member of the humanist community of correspondents wrote with the expectation that his missive could receive publication. The probability of a more diverse, learned readership beyond that of the immediate recipient required a most deliberate and refined Latinity. Of the five letters written by More in this period for the defense of the humanist program, the first and the last, to Martin Dorp and to Germanus Brixius, proved the most substantive and crucial; although the former would have to wait until 1563 to be published in More's Basel *Lucubrationes*, the latter saw separate publication in 1520. *Letter to a Monk* and *Letter to Edward Lee* would appear in collections of the same year. That to the University of Oxford had to wait until 1633 for the *editio princeps*.

Considered by one scholar as possibly "the most grandly ironic of all More's writings," the *Letter to Dorp* was written to a backsliding humanistic professor at Louvain, who had in 1514 written his friend Erasmus, objecting to the satire in *The Praise of Folly*. More skillfully deploys his persuasive rhetoric to dissolve Dorp's lingering adherence to dialectic and his opposition to the study of Greek. The letter becomes More's most profound theoretical statement of the humanist program: humanist techniques and attitudes seek to displace dialectic from its hold upon theology and the entire life of the universities and to restore grammar and rhetoric that learning might be redirected less to the mind than to the heart and total being of the individual. More's attack upon the theology of the schools as being foreign to the common feelings of humanity (*communis sensus hominum*) proves fundamental and devastating; in its place he advances true theology in its Erasmian form, based on the classics, Scripture, and the Church Fathers. More's aggressive defense of the new humanist learning and its practices further expresses itself in his programmatic advocacy of

Greek in his *Letter to Oxford* and his argument that secular learning in classical letters trains the soul in virtue and better serves theology than the petty questions in current scholastic philosophy. And in the *Letter to Edward Lee*, the least rhetorical and most technical of the five, More enters into controversy with the annotated criticisms of this young theologian to Erasmus's New Testament.

More's *Letter to a Monk* carries further, but in a significantly different register, many of the themes developed in his letter to Dorp. In being addressed "to a certain Monk whose ignorance was equaled by his pride," the letter indicates a radical change of tone and literary manner that introduces the reader to an emphatically polemical, abusive, and often bitter mood. More upbraids the Monk, John Batmanson, for his ignorance and arrogance in daring to treat Erasmus as a heretic. Not without considerable indignation does More advance the humanist Erasmian preference for Greek over Latin and the authority of the Church Fathers. More's style is one of direct public persuasion conforming itself to the poor learning of his recipient; epistolary decorum dissolves into a polemical pamphlet (15:cxv).

In his defense of humanism, More's transition to an expressly pugnacious, polemical mood becomes evident in the *Letter to Brixius*. This last of the quintet occupies a unique position in More's oeuvre, for as a savage satire of rare rhetorical elegance and force it at once offers his *ars poetica* and provides the effective hinge between his humanistic and polemical writings. If Dorp had been for More a sort of lapsed humanist, Brixius becomes for him a false humanist given to purple patches, servile imitation, and classical posturing. The question raised by the dispute between the two humanists is whether poetic license permits one who has chosen a historical subject to indulge in fantastic exaggerations and distortions. In short, the issue is of rhetorical *fides* (trustworthiness), which inevitably draws with it the comparably fundamental issue of that *imitatio* (use) of classical authors appropriate to a humanist.

Brixius or Germain de Brie was by no means an undistinguished humanist; friend of Erasmus and of the premier French humanist Guillaume Budé, the French court poet commanded respect within humanist circles. Nevertheless, in his *Chordigerae navis conflagratio* (1513) Brixius extravagantly celebrated the bravery of the French captain and crew engaging an English vessel in which both ships had perished in flames. Brixius's impossible feats had served as the butt for ten of More's epigrams, which in 1518 incited Brixius to respond with his *Antimorus*. Despite the obvious issue of patriotic, nationalist emotions, More, after four additional epigrams, returned to the controversy with his literary sensibility principally offended. The event provided him the opportunity, similar to that earlier enjoyed by Horace in his *Art of Poetry*, to give his clumsy opponent a lesson in the proper way to write as well as to attack the reality of his account. Beyond his many poetic transgressions More claims their source to lie in Brixius's total disregard of historical truth. With suitable recourse to Lucian's liar in that satirist's treatise *Quomodo historia conscribenda sit* (*How History Is to Be Written*), More represents Brixius as believing that false history embellished with glittering phrases makes poetic truth. By seeking to adhere to historical truth, the responsible author will allow his good faith to accredit the rhetorical argument, just as the bad faith of the irresponsible author promptly discredits it. Likewise the recourse to classical phrases and images should be dictated by the matter at hand in order best to convey that subject rather than ransacked to display the cleverness of the author. More effectively captures the supreme inappropriateness of Brixius' *imitatio*: "following in the footsteps of the ancients, but assuredly, Brixius you follow a bit too relentlessly ... so closely in their footsteps that you knock off their shoes and then wear them yourself, though your feet hardly fill them" (3/II:612 –613).

The letter to Brixius is of considerable importance in understanding More's literary career. It manifests a vehemence, intensity, and abusiveness that had already emerged in his *Letter to a Monk*. More presses into service the heavy humor of the classical Roman comic playwright, Plautus. He depicts Brixius as a drunken wrestler, flailing about:

> And what if at last, when he has racked himself for a long time in vain, unable to throw his adversary, lest he seem to have sallied forth wholly in vain he then spits in his opponent's face and throws up all over him, heaving the toxic and distempered vomit from his drunken stomach, and what if then, swelling with pride as if he had given a splendid performance, he goes off to celebrate his extraordinary triumph in low dives and taverns? Does such a wrestler then merit a victory crown? Or does he deserve rather to have his shins and his ankles broken?
>
> (3/II:608–609)

The advent of Martin Luther and the abruption of his challenge to the traditional order would further educe and enhance the polemical aggressiveness already present in Thomas More, the humanist, lawyer, and privy councillor.

THE POLEMICAL WORKS

AFTER 1520, as the effects of Luther's reform became increasingly evident, the whole tone of Europe's intellectual life began to change. More registered the shift in a letter of June 1520 to Guillaume Budé: Prudence now dictates that he be given the opportunity to revise his letters before their proposed publication for fear that "in my remarks upon peace and war, upon morality, marriage, the clergy, the people, etc., perhaps what I have written has not always been so cautious and guarded that it would be wise to expose it to captious critics" (Rogers, *Selected Letters*, 144–145).

The apparently charmed moment of Erasmian reform by persuasion and sweet reasonableness was giving way to the mounting violence of rancorous language and soon that of fire and steel. The abrupt assertion of religious priorities, hitherto lost amid the wealth of Renaissance culture, would transform the readership from the select learned to the common man and from the medium of Latin, the international language of scholarship and thought, to the regional vernacu-

lars. Thus the increasing recourse to English raises the additional issue of More's contribution to the development of this new, outlandish language.

At first for More the new audience inevitably created by the Reformation was not immediately evident; discussion, debate, controversy still moved in the grooves afforded by international Latin. More had been introduced to the expanding Luther affair as early as the first part of 1521 when he served with other luminaries in the construction of King Henry's *Assertio septem sacramentorum*, which would net that monarch the ironically resounding title of "Defender of the Faith"; here More described himself as a sorter out and placer of the principal matters therein contained. But as the controversy deepened and Luther replied to the king's defense with his nasty, abusive *Contra Henricum regem Angliae*, several factors recommended More as the obvious mouthpiece of the royal council to enter the fray on the king's behalf against the German reformer. More's tough legal training and experience made him not only a hard, combative opponent but also a formidably unpleasant negotiator; the Hanseatic representatives depicted him at the time as "full of deceit and cunning" (5:799–800). His recent letters to Batmanson and to Brixius left no doubt as to his pugnacity. Yet the gravity occasioned by doctrinal dispute could certainly require the tonic of a natural festivity. Such qualities recommended More. Thus beginning in January 1523 and for the next decade, very much in keeping with his own temperament and beliefs, Thomas More entered the enervating currents of religious and legal controversy that would produce the bulk of his entire oeuvre—about two-thirds of his English works and nearly half his Latin.

More constructs his response to Luther through the medium of persona of a fictional creation, Baravellus, whom he soon replaces with a new imaginary person, Rosseus. That More should hesitate between first a Spanish fictional setting for Luther's opponent in the Baravellus version and then for an English setting in the second and final Rosseus version of the *Responsio ad Lutherum* seems almost expectable from the fanciful author of *Utopia*. Yet More's complex of fictional frames goes beyond the obvious desire of a rising, dignified English royal councillor to distance himself from the stench arising from Luther's hometown and university residence of Wittenberg. His very contriving serves to suggest an effective mobilization of communities of thinkers, writers, printers, and readers in opposition to Luther's folly and even suggests the identity of the artful author of *Utopia*.

More adopted a method of controversy that went beyond the traditional apologetic practice of the fathers, whereby the opponent's work is selectively cited in patches to focus upon the relevant topic. In dealing with the heretic, where heresy is considered to be all of one piece and thus every aspect has to be examined and confuted, the controversialist must pursue a continuous verbatim quotation of the opponent's work. Committed to such thoroughness in refuting the challenge to what was conceived as a total body of absolute truth, the practice had three glaring disadvantages: it confined the defense to its opponent's organization of the work; it served to publish the heretic's work; and the resulting exhaustive refutation surely guaranteed the exhaustion of the reader. With Brixius More had been able to cut through to a single illustrative issue and address it without treating each and every point successively (3/II:588). But heresy, in raising a doctrinal issue that communicated itself to the entire body of doctrine, did not allow such selective treatment. Only by later opening a seam in Book I, chapter ten, of what had been the Baravellus version and elaborating upon the papal primacy and the nature and identity of the church would More be able to free himself momentarily from this pattern in the second, Rosseus version of the *Responsio*. More here opposes a known, visible, consenting church of the common multitude to what he sees as Luther's hidden, inner, mathematical church, which he artfully equates with some Platonic idea possibly in utopia (5:763)! His vision of the church as something known, visible, and recognizable in its being distinguished by consensus is thus early defined and constitutes the major theme in all More's polemical writings.

If the *Responsio* introduces one to relatively perduring features of More's polemical writing, it effectively throws into relief the question of humanism's continuity. Although the shift in orientation and attention occurring in 1520 is clear enough, More's humanism does not evaporate but, in the *Responsio* more than in any other of his controversial works, manifests itself and plays an important role. That the polemic follows immediately from a long period of humanistic writing and preoccupations and that its Latin medium derives from the previous controversy between Henry VIII and Luther over church and sacraments and is directed toward an international audience—such arguments provide explanations of only superficial worth. Rather, humanistic rhetorical practices and the appropriation of classical authors become integral to the task of saving More's case from boring his reader to distraction and alienating his audience by the missiles of scatological crudities. In the traditional context of polemical dispute, shaped by a maximum of intransigence couched in the most violent abusiveness, the resort to Roman comedy offered necessary relief and the tonic of humor along with the ridicule. More appeals to Horace and Juvenal for satire and to Virgil for mock solemnity. He has even more frequent recourse to Plautus and to his great favorite, Terence, in order to convey bombast, pretense, and farce with which to traduce Luther. He uses effectively such pretentious braggarts as Phormio, Gnatho, and, above all, Thraso from Terence and places them in a Plautine context of crude farce. He creates a scene of Luther, clothed only in a net, yet confident that his nakedness is quite covered, disporting himself before an audience of Bohemian rustics (5:436). Although never enough to salvage this ultimately ugly polemical crusher as a literary work, More also adopts the stylistic devices of the Roman playwrights: pleonasm, diminutives, anaphora, triads, alliteration and assonance, superlatives, and etymological word play (5:813–821).

With William Tyndale, one of the great founders of the English Reformation, the controversy deepened for More. Tyndale's translation of the New Testament and a number of polemical works by him and others appeared from 1525 to 1527. In March 1528 More received from his bishop, Cuthbert Tunstal, the license to read and the commission to refute heretical books. The regime certainly seized the advantage of having a distinguished layman defend the priesthood and orthodoxy (9:xxvi–xxvii). The need to explicate the heresies of certain books in English for the common man (*simplicibus et ideotis hominibus*) raised most forcefully the question of the vernacular in biblical and religious discussion. Ever since the execution in 1417 of Sir John Oldcastle, the leading Lollard (follower of John Wycliffe), the new problem of religious dissent, pervasive among a popular audience, could not be addressed in Latin but must attend the vernacular. Furthermore, because the commissioned work was directed toward the English reading public and not to Latinate scholars, More felt impelled to address and defend the living forces of current popular piety (Rogers, *Correspondence*, 387; *Complete Works* 6:542, 749).

For the execution of his assignment More significantly avoids the traditional method of successive quotation and refutation. Instead he returns to the device of a dramatic fiction by entering into a dialogue concerning heresies with one who goes by the name of the Messenger, and who appears as one having a good memory, "wyse," even learned and possessing "a very mery wytte," something that he shares with More (6:447). Indeed at one point in the course of discussion we are reminded of that distinctive feature of More to amalgamate *festivitas* with *gravitas*, when the Messenger complains:

> But ye use (my mayster sayth) to loke so sadly when ye mene merely / yt many tymes men doubte whyther ye speke in sporte / whan ye mene good ernest
>
> (6:68–69).

Throughout the Messenger is purportedly not stating his own ideas but reporting what he has heard men say, for he seems from a somewhat dark apostolicity to be in communication with a wealth of heretics and their master. To have made him any less than intellectually competent and respectable would have vitiated More's purpose

of presenting in brief compass a compendium that persuasively treats all the essential issues through lively discussion with a bright, if partly errant, student. More appears in name as "Mayster chaunccellour." (In the book's first edition of 1529, the title referred only to the Duchy of Lancaster. In the second edition of 1531, it pertains to the Lord Chancellor of England.) Otherwise the drama of the Dialogue plays itself out between "quod I" (More) and "quod he" (the Messenger) (6:440–441, 479–481).

While postponing any consideration of More's contribution to the English language for the last section on his devotional writings, we need at least at this point to appreciate the immensity of More's venturing into the vernacular as suitable for theological discourse. What were the capabilities of the English language as an effective literary medium? The Reformation as a religious movement had brought to the fore in a way impossible for the Renaissance the necessity of addressing the common man in his own language. More the layman boldly accepts the challenge as opportunity. Proceeding on the sensible principle that no good thing should be suppressed simply on account of its possible misuse, More affirms, a half century before Montaigne, that if "oure tonge is called barbarouse" it is but "as every lerned man knoweth / every straunge langage to other." In their times, Greek, Hebrew, and Latin as the spoken, popular language conveyed holy scripture to the understanding of the common people. Why not English "bycause it is vulgare and comen to every englyshe man" (6:337–338)? Consequently one recognizes the importance of More's earlier disputing with Tyndale his use of key words: "senyours" instead of "prestes," "congregacyon" for "chyrche," "love" for "charyte," "knowledgynge" for "confessyon," "repentaunce" for "penaunce," and "troubled harte" for "contryte" (6:285–287, 290). The problem, More claims, is not in the reading and receiving of the English translation but in the "bysy chammyng [chewing] thereof" (6:333). Much of the Reformation's import emerges therefrom.

In the same year, 1529, that saw the first edition of *The Dialogue Concerning Heresies* More also published his *Supplication of Souls*, written to counter Simon Fish's *Supplication of Beggars*, a highly anti-clerical pamphlet urging the appropriation of church goods for temporal ends. Although Fish barely touched upon the issue of purgatory, More devotes the second half of his treatise to the defense of the doctrine. There followed in More's polemical program the *Confutation of Tyndale's Answer* (Books I–III) of 1532 and the subsequent Books IV–VIII of 1533 (the fragmentary Book IX only being published in 1557) that marked a return to the slugfest of continuous, successive response—the current polemical method—and best suggests the futility of such a strategy. Five times longer than the work confuted, More's *Confutation* only attends to the first quarter of Tyndale's response (8/III:1259). Enormous, cumbersome, unfinished, the work conveys the growing exhaustion of both author and reader. Between the two parts, More finished in early December 1532 his *Letter against Frith*, another growing brush fire that raised the question of the Real Presence—how Christ is present in the sacrament of the Eucharist. Here More opposed the emerging Zwinglian, symbolic interpretation of the Eucharist, which threatened to undermine the objective nature of the sacrament and the Church. John Frith's response would be associated with the anonymous *Souper of the Lorde*, probably by George Joy, which occasioned More's *Answer to a Poisoned Book*, in December 1533, the last of his works published in his lifetime (11:xvii).

Polemics took a new turn during this same fateful year of 1533 in England's history. With the distinguished common lawyer Christopher St. German's anonymously presented *Treatise concernyng the division betwene spiritualitie and temporaltie*, polemics had now moved from the theological and abstract to the more expressly political register in the defense of the clergy and the operation of its courts—specifically, the procedures adopted by the ecclesiastical courts in detecting heretics and in conducting their trials. Although the Submission of the Clergy had already occurred a year earlier, More, now feigning ignorance of its author and its identification with royal propaganda, daringly came to the defense of the stricken clergy and the traditional

order: he published his *Apology* in April, and to St. German's anonymous response his own *The Debellation of Salem and Bizance* on November 1 (10:xxii–xxviii). The embattled More refers to his supposedly unknown opponent as "The Pacifier" to mock his claim to be composing the dissension between laity and clergy, while replying shortly to the truly unknown author of the *The Souper of the Lorde* as Master Masker; he had suitably referred to More as Master Mock (9:xl; 10:lxxxi). Master of all the techniques for reducing an opponent by disparaging his competence and mocking his arguments, More increasingly showed weariness, lashing out in exasperation at his pullulating opponents (9:lxxxviii–lxxxix).

THE DEVOTIONAL WRITINGS

WHILE More's humanistic and polemical works can be nicely confined to distinct periods in his career, 1510 to 1520 and 1523 to 1533, respectively, his devotional writings are everywhere present throughout his life and mark both his very first and very last works. True, humanistic and polemical qualities remain characteristic to all his immense productivity. But the study of the devotional works affords the opportunity to draw nearer to the man in all his complexity, as one who constructed and lived his own life, despite all its intense engagement with the world, so that at the end the world could successfully be set at naught.

Through *The Answer to the Poisoned Book* and its close relation by eucharistic controversy to the forthcoming pre-Tower works of the *Treatise on the Passion* and that on the *Blessed Body*, we are led to the final, incredibly intense creative period of confinement, April 17, 1534, to July 6, 1535, marked by the two last supreme works that would seem to distinguish the devotional as a final and distinct stage—*The Dialogue of Comfort* and the *De tristitia Christi* (13:xxxvii–xli). But the devotional marked the beginning of this man, who had hesitated during four years before the cloistered piety of the monastery of the London Charterhouse of the Carthusians (1499–1503), finally choosing marriage and a special engagement with the world, uncloistered yet armored. As it was in the beginning so would it be in the end.

For the historian there is much that is momentous in More's first publication, *Lyfe of Johan Picus Erle of Myrandula* (1510): first, the encounter with the foremost thinker and representative of the new cultural movement stemming from Italy; secondly, the translation of that Latin life by Pico's nephew, Gianfrancesco, into a new, emerging vernacular, when translation can offer a multitude of opportunities for interpretation; thirdly, the chance to appropriate an outstanding example of the intelligent layman turned religious —a splendid measure of the reception of the Renaissance in the north. As a translator More reduced or omitted whole sections, particularly that dealing with Pico's humanism and intellectual accomplishments, all in the interests of presenting individual lay piety and spiritual biography in the form of a devotional/contemplative manual. He recast the hitherto uninterrupted work into twenty-nine sections, each with its heading. In one notable instance he explains Pico's pursuit of knowledge not according to the Latin "a se ipso vi ingenii & veritatis amore" [by the force of his own genius and love of the truth], but "only for ye love of god & profit of his chirch" (1:320/1–2; cf. 1:65/11). He subordinates the intellectual and philosophical to the pious and religious, driven most probably by the needs of his immediate reader, a nun named Joyce Leigh, and his own spiritual needs in 1504, as he moved from the life of the cloister to that of marriage. Among the supporting materials More quarried from the *Opera omnia* (Strassburg, 1504) to complete his task he includes his subject's commentary on Psalm 15, "Conserva me domine quoniam speravi in te" [Kepe me god lorde] (1:94). It would later serve him well *in extremis.* (1:xliv–xlviii, 239). English prose had hardly before this moment had occasion to imitate the rhetorical resources of Latin. Here More suffers from the experience of a pioneer in evincing both clumsiness and haste in overly Latinate renderings as well as the limitations of the English language at this time. As with the later *Richard III* he uses doublets in conveying the sense of a Latin word, and he expands the English language by introducing over eighty new Latin-based words. At times he achieves a satisfactory rendering of the Latin's balanced cadences, but at this stage he reveals a conservative and literal translation (1:xlix –liii). While readily transposing sentences and omitting material More observes a practice to translate as literally as possible (2:lvii).

On the eve of what would be the decade of polemical writings More returns to or, better, reaffirms the expressly devotional in his *Last Things*. Freed from any commitment to a specific Latin text, he responds to the influences of late medieval English as well as Latin continental, devotional writers, including Walter Hilton and Denis the Carthusian. Along with the late medieval turning from the theocentric to the Christocentric and the humanity of Christ, More's rendering of this traditional theme on the *novissima*—death, judgment, hell and heaven—of which he will only treat death, is not without its humanist influences; among them can be seen his reworking of Seneca's fatalistic Stoic theme, *cotidie morimur* (Daily we are dying). Nevertheless, the weight of the late medieval *Ars moriendi* predominates. Here, however, More will give a bitter accent to those attending the death bed event:

> wil it not be . . . a pleasant thing, to see before thine eyen, & heare at thine eare, a rable of fleshly frendes, or rather of flesh flies, skippying about thy bed & thy sicke body, like rauens aboute thy corps now almost carreyn, cryinge to thee on euery side, what shall I haue what shall I haue?
>
> (1:141)

Amid the repeated practice of "stuffing" by means of listed sins and sinful states, sometimes cadenced, often alliterative, More is capable of providing memorable portraits of fortune's abrupt reversal in the appallingly sudden fall of the Great Duke (of Buckingham?) or the pathos of the Newgate pickpocket, soon to be hanged, yet still cutting a purse before the bar because, he explained, "it didde his heart good, to be lorde of that purse, one nyght yet" (1:172). The terrible brittleness of this world with all roads leading to the same end is reinforced by the continuing images of the scaffold/stage upon which we are for a moment actors, but when the play is done, the proud joy of one wearing "a gay golden gown" evaporates, with rich and poor joining in the equality of death (1:156). Moving rapidly from this Lucianic image to Plato's cave, More reverts to the image of the prison of this world:

> . . . al the while we liue in this world, we be but prisoners, & be wtin a sure prison, out of which ther can no man escape. . . . The prison is large and many prisoners in it, but the gailor can lese none, he is so present in euery place, that we can crepe into no corner out of his sight. For as holy Dauid saith to this gailor whither shal I go fro thy spirit, & whither shal I fle fro thy face: as who saith no-whither.
>
> (1:156–157)

Apparently as early as 1522 More had identified the world's jailer as God Himself.

While capable of presenting poignant moments and defining themes that will become part of his future armor, *The Last Things* remains uneven: of the four Last Things—death, judgment, hell, and heaven—More manages to treat only the first. Certainly the work's coherence and effectiveness suffer from More's attempt to include a treatment of the seven deadly sins and the interruption of his efforts by having to turn to confront the Lutheran specter. Nevertheless, if it falls short as a formal treatment of the Last Things, it succeeds as a stylistic experiment and the first work to attempt to deal with the subject in English (1:lxxvi–cix).

Closely associated with some of the themes and even the wording of *The Last Things* is More's English masterpiece, *A Dialogue of Comfort against Tribulation* written in the final year of his life. More constructs his dialogue between Antony and Vincent, uncle and nephew in a contemporary Hungary being overwhelmed by the Turks—a setting that lends drama but above all serves as an extended metaphor enfolding England under its own Great Turk. The basic subject is the question, how should the Christian behave and remain true to his conscience and faith under the tests of mounting persecution? Mirth, irony, detachment, transcendence again serve More in achieving that spiritual comfort as

he enters upon his own Gethsemane. He reverts to the Platonic image of the world/cave as prison:

> So is it now Cosyn that god the chiefe gaylour (as I say) of this brode prison the world / ys neyther cruell nor covetous / And this prison is also so sure & so subtilly bildyd, that albeit that yt lyeth open on euery side without any wall in the world / yet wander we neuer so ferre about therin, the way to get out at / shall we neuer fynd . . . . Vppon our prison we bild our prison: we garnysh yt with gold & make yt gloriouse / In this prison they bye & sell / in this prison they brall and chide. . . .
>
> (12:272–273)

Christ becomes our enveloping shield (*pavis*) before the world, his endurance our comfort. And in addressing ever anew the sufferings of Christ and the comfort derived from such endurance and the hope of heaven's rewards, More calls his reader to a greater conformity to Christ; More's import through the dialogue goes beyond the Christocentric to achieve the Christomorphic.

Concurrently and closely aligned with the theme of spiritual comfort and the subject of securing the conscience, beset by temptation as well as by persecutors, figures the ostensible letter of Margaret Roper to Lady Alington. Therein More and his daughter Margaret apparently conspire to construct a searching dialogue, often compared to Plato's *Crito*, that reveals each true to self in the examination of More's scruples of conscience. Are you alone wise when so many "well-Learned" men have found no difficulty in taking the oath? What does it mean to be a fool, Aesopic or not, in the world? In assuming to her father the role of Mother Eve, daughter Margaret manages to reveal the full proportions and meaning of conscience, this inmost knowledge that recognizes a superior, conditioning framework for the moral self. As More demonstrated here and before his accusers following his own condemnation, Christ's will and spirit, expressed in "the general counsel of the whole body of Christendom," trumps the law of any particular land. Equipped with such clairvoyance and certainty, More arrives at the riddle he appropriates: for "a man may lese his head and have no harme" (Rogers, *Correspondence*, 530/589–590). At the end of his own trial Socrates had arrived at the same hard-won truth before his accusers two thousand years earlier that no evil can befall a good man.

Before venturing upon a consideration of More's last and most moving work, *De tristitia Christi*, we need to assess the quality of the spiritual armor he had been forging for himself and at the same time look back upon the terrain covered. While conspicuously Christomorphic in character, that armor had been from the beginning of peculiarly Platonic alloy. In a notable article on More, H. R. Trevor-Roper drew attention to a consistent, inhering Platonism, early evident in More's exposure to Pseudo-Dionysius and Augustine's *City of God*, carried further with Pico, and apparently culminating with Plato's *Republic* in the creation of *Utopia* as an effort to escape history or end it and transcend this world. But this intensely held, deeply appropriated inner vision, this Platonism needs further consideration and to be extended beyond 1520, for it would pervade More's being even to prison and to the scaffold. In seeking the quality of More's Platonism, we can dispense with the astrological and magical proclivities of Marsilio Ficino, the preeminent philosopher of Renaissance Platonism. Nor is it the soul's flight of the alone to the Alone, or Socratic irony and the relentless drive toward truth. Rather, it seems ultimately to be the firmly held confidence in a higher order of absolutes, a cosmos of supreme ideals, providing detachment and leverage upon what he had early recognized as the brittleness of the world and now at the end with his daughter he refers to as "the friendship of this wretched worlde so ficle" (Rogers, *Correspondence*, 524/363 –364). Part of the complexity and wonder of this late medieval Catholic, this Renaissance man, so evident in his writing, is that he can long perform as civic humanist in a meaningful, intense engagement with that world through having forged for himself the transperspectival, uncoupling devices of irony, wit, and legal equivocation. The gaze remains beyond.

With *De tristitia Christi* More's Gethsemane was upon him, and with it the Christomorphic experience. He did not seek to expound Christ's whole passion but only what pertained to "ante captionem eius" (before his capture): hence Christ's humanity as evinced by his emotional anguish ("tristitia tedio"), "pavore," the extent of fear appropriate to a martyr, and the fervent prayer "oratione" exemplified by Christ, all key words figuring in the title (14/II:740). The fearful anxiety More appropriates from Jesus' agony crystallizes that most humanly meaningful question regarding the fearful martyr, who, in contrast to the bold martyr's almost relishing a dreadful death, must fight down "not only his other enemies but also his own weariness, sadness, and fear" (14/II:249). As More draws nearer to his Lord in His own painfully mastered anguish, he willingly accepts the offer to take courage, to take hold of the hem of his Lord's garment as he himself walks along this fearful road (14/II:105). The Christomorphic process achieves its apparent apotheosis in the work's final sentence, which mirrors More's own experience in having his writing materials and books removed in preparation for his execution: "tum demum primum manus in Iesum" (14/I:625); and in his granddaughter Mary Bassett's translation of the work for the 1557 Rastell edition— "that then after al this, dyd they fyrst lay handes upon Iesus" (14/II:1165).

When one considers that More could have expected to be executed as a traitor not by simple beheading but by first being disemboweled, then strung up and quartered, the sustained coherence, insight, and beauty of this work prove even further astonishing. Indeed he covers new exegetical ground in plumbing the mystery of the young man mentioned only in Mark (14:51) who, in the flight of the disciples, threw off the linen cloth around him and fled naked. In pursuing this issue steadily over twenty-six leaves, More resolves the problem in a significantly Platonic way as an analogue of the soul's divesting itself of the body to emerge "shining and young" (14/I:565–617).

Is it possible that More had chosen to use Latin over English in this extraordinarily personal work as the best means for expressing his most intimate thoughts? In his *Prayer Book*, possibly the most intimate of documents and the veritable source for both Tower Works, posterity may read, in English, his "Godly Meditation," which begins:

Give me thy grace, good Lord
To set the world at naught ....

(Martz and Sylvester, 3)

SELECTED BIBLIOGRAPHY

I. BIBLIOGRAPHIES. R. W. Gibson and J. Max Patrick published *St. Thomas More: A Preliminary Bibliography of His Works and of Moreana to the Year 1750* (New Haven and London, 1961). This volume lists the libraries where copies of the various items are to be found, for addenda, see Constance Smith, *An Updating of R. W. Gibson's St. Thomas More: "Preliminary Bibliography"* (St. Louis, 1981), and Ralph Keen and Constance Smith, "Updating an Updating," in *Moreana* 25, no. 97 (1988), 137–140; on later references to More see Jackson Boswell, *Sir Thomas More in the English Renaissance: An Annotated Catalogue*, Medieval Texts and Studies 83 (Binghampton, N.Y., 1994).

II. NOTABLE EDITIONS OF INDIVIDUAL WORKS. Of *Utopia* the earliest English translation is by Ralph Robinson, originally published in 1551 and reprinted many times, perhaps most usefully as the translation in J. H. Lupton's Latin-English edition of *Utopia* (Oxford, 1895); the best critical edition of *Utopia* and translation is *More: Utopia. Latin Text and English Translation*, ed. by G. M. Logan, R. M. Adams, and C. H. Miller (Cambridge, 1995). Of the Latin poems see *The Latin Epigrams of Thomas More*, ed. by Leicester Bradner and Charles A. Lynch (Chicago, 1953). For *The Apology* see *The Apologye of Syr Thomas More. Knight*, ed. A. I. Taft, Early English Text Society, Original Series, 180 (London, 1930). A critical, facsimile edition of More's prayer book is provided by Louis L. Martz and Richard S. Sylvester, eds., *Thomas More's Prayer Book* (New Haven and London, 1969).

IIII. BIOGRAPHICAL STUDIES. The earliest biography of More is the engaging *Life of Sir Thomas More*, by his son-in-law William Roper; it is published in *Two Early Tudor Lives*, ed. by Richard S. Sylvester and Davis P. Harding (New Haven and London, 1962). The other notable sixteenth-century biographies are Nicholas Harpsfield, *The Life and Death of Sir Thomas Moore*, ed. by E. V. Hitchcock (1932), and Thomas Stapleton, *The Life and Illustrious Martyrdom of Sir Thomas More*, trans. Philip E. Hallett, ed. by E. E. Reynolds (London, 1966). By far the most influential modern biography during the mid-twentieth century was R. W. Chambers, *Thomas More* (London, 1935), to be replaced for some by Richard Marius, *Thomas More* (New York, 1984). Marius' tough, unhagiographical revisionism follows the lead of G. R. Elton, in such studies as "Thomas More, Councillor (1517–1529)," in *St. Thomas More: Action and Contemplation*, ed. by R. S. Sylvester (New Haven and London, 1972), and "The Real Thomas More?" in *Reformation Principle and Practice*, ed. by Peter N. Brooks (London, 1980). Louis L. Martz attempts to correct the revisionist view in *Thomas More: The Search for the Inner Man* (New Haven and London, 1990). More's professional life is traced by J. A. Guy, *The Public Career*

of Sir Thomas More (New Haven and London, 1980); most recently and quite successfully he wrote a complete biography, *Thomas More* (London, 2000). Alistair Fox also interprets More's works in the context of an exploration of his complex psychology, in *Thomas More: History and Providence* (New Haven and London, 1983).

IV. COLLECTED WORKS. Of his English works the first is the admirable edition by his nephew, William Rastell, *The Workes . . . in the Englyshe tonge* (London, 1557). On the continent two quite differently oriented editions of his Latin works appeared shortly thereafter: the Basel, 1563 edition *Lucubrationes*, which emphasizes his humanistic, Erasmian qualities; the Louvain, 1565 *Opera omnia* reinforces Rastell's image of More as an orthodox Catholic. The Frankfurt *Opera omnia*, 1689, brings together these strands of More's Latin literary work—the humanistic reforming Erasmian of Basel and the saintly, apologetic of Louvain. In the early twentieth century W. E. Campbell, G. W. Reed, R. W. Chambers, and W. A. G. Doyle-Davidson edited *The English Works of Thomas More* (London, 1931). Beginning in 1963 *The Yale Edition of the Complete Works of St. Thomas More*, to which all references in the text here are made, provided a definitive, critical presentation of both More's English and Latin writings. More's writings fall into four groups: (1) humanistic; (2) controversial/polemical; (3) devotional; (4) letters. The humanistic writings comprise: *Translations of Lucian* (Yale Edition, Vol. 3, Pt. 1, ed. by C. R. Thompson); *Latin Poems* (Yale Edition, Vol. 3, Pt. 2, ed. by C. H. Miller et al.); *Utopia* (Yale Edition, Vol. 4, ed. by E. Surtz and J. H. Hexter); *Historia Richardi Tertii and History of King Richard III* (Latin and English versions: Yale Edition, Vol. 2, ed. by R. S. Sylvester); *Letter to Martin Dorp, Letter to the University of Oxford, Letter to Edward Lee, Letter to a Monk* (Yale edition, Vol. 15, ed. by D. Kinney). The controversial works comprise: *Responsio ad Lutherum* (Yale Edition, Vol. 5, ed. by J. M. Headley); *Dialogue Concerning Heresies* (Yale Edition, Vol. 6, ed. by T. Lawler et al.); *Confutation of Tyndale's Answer* (Yale Edition, Vol. 8, ed. by L. A. Schuster et al.); *Apology* (Yale Edition, Vol. 9, ed. by J. B. Trapp); *Debellation of Salem and Bizance* (Yale Edition, Vol. 10, ed. by John Guy et al.); *Answer to a Poisoned Book* (Yale Edition, Vol. 11, ed. by S. M. Foley et al.). The devotional writings comprise: *English Poems, Life of Pico, Four Last Things* (Yale Edition, Vol. 1, ed. by C. H. Miller et al.); *Dialogue of Comfort against Tribulation* (Yale Edition, Vol. 12, ed. by L. L. Martz et al.); *Treatise on the Passion, Treatise on the Blessed Body, Instructions and Prayers* (Yale Edition, Vol. 13, ed. by G. E. Haupt); *De Tristitia Christi* (Yale Edition, Vol. 14, ed. by C. H. Miller). More's letters are published in *The Correspondence of Sir Thomas More*, ed. by E. F. Rogers (Princeton, 1947); *St. Thomas More: Selected Letters*, ed. by E. F. Rogers (New Haven, 1961); *Sir Thomas More: Neue Briefe* ed. by H. Schulte Herbrüggen (Münster, 1966); C. H. Miller, ed., "Thomas More's Letters to Frans van Cranevelt," in *Moreana* 31 (1994).

V. CRITICAL STUDIES There is no comprehensive, definitive analysis of More as a pioneer of the modern English language, but Joseph Delcourt, *Essai sur la langue de Sir Thomas More d'après ses oeuvres anglaises* (Paris, 1914), provides the groundwork pending a more complete knowledge of More's contemporaries as a means of control and judgment. Other notable studies on aspects of More's thought: Brian Gogan, *The Common Corps of Christendom: Ecclesiological Themes in the Writings of Thomas More* (Leiden, 1982); Germain Marc'hadour, *Thomas More et al Bible. La place des livres saints dans son apologetique et sa spiritualité* (Paris, 1969); and André Prévost, *Thomas More, 1477–1535, et la crise de la pensée européenne*. Of articles there are several collections, the most notable being *Essential Articles for the Study of Thomas More*, ed. by R. S. Sylvester and G. P. Marc'hadour (Hamden, Conn., 1977) and "Quincentennial Essays on Thomas More," in *Albion* 10 (1978). The following articles are of fundamental importance and proved valuable for the present essay: B. Bradshaw, "The Controversial Thomas More," in *Journal of Ecclesiastical History* 36 (1985); Marie Delcourt, "Recherches sur Thomas More, La tradition continentale et la tradition anglaise," in *Humanisme et Renaissance* 3 (1936); D. B. Fenlon, "England and Europe: Utopia and Its Aftermath," in *Transactions of the Royal Historical Society*, 5th Series, 25 (1975); D. B. Fenlon, "Thomas More and Tyranny," in *Journal of Ecclesiastical History* 32 (1981); S. E. Lehmberg, "Sir Thomas More's Life of Pico della Mirandola," in *Studies in the Renaissance* 3 (1956); R. Marius, "Thomas More and the Early Church Fathers," in *Traditio* 24 (1968); R. S. Sylvester, "Thomas More: Humanist in Action," in O.

B. Hardison Jr., ed., *Medieval and Renaissance Studies* (Chapel Hill, 1966); H. R. Trevor-Roper, "The Intellectual World of Sir Thomas More," in *American Scholar* 48 (1978–1979); T. I. White, "Aristotle and *Utopia*," in *Renaissance Quarterly* 29 (1976); T. I. White, "*Festivitas, Utilitas, et Opes*: The Concluding Irony and Philosophic Purpose of Thomas More's *Utopia*," in *Albion* 10 (1978); Douglas Trevor, "Thomas More's *Responsio ad Lutherum* and the Fictions of Humanist Polemic," in *Sixteenth Century Journal* (forthcoming).

1 With a few exceptions all references are to the *Yale Edition of the Complete Works of St. Thomas More*. The first number in parentheses refers to the volume, sometimes followed by a slash and its Roman-numeraled part; the number after the colon refers, when Roman, to the editorial introduction to the volume, and, when Arabic, to the text itself. Occasionally a further slash followed by numbers refers to the specific lines on a page, when it involves poetry or a densely edited text. Consult the Selected Bibliography, "IV. Collected Works," for the Rogers editions of More's correspondence, and the subsequent "V. Critical Studies," where general credit is given to notable secondary sources found useful in the present essay.

ANDREW MOTION

(1952–   )

Robert Potts

ANDREW MOTION IS, at the time of writing, poet laureate of Great Britain, having succeeded to the position after the death of Ted Hughes in 1998. Although, in the brief period since his appointment in May 1999, Motion has only written a handful of "official" laureate poems, the position has undeniably created much of the current interest in him as a poet. Previously, Motion's fame was arguably greater as a biographer. Even now, his earlier and non-laureate poetry has received very little in the way of critical attention beyond the review pages of journals and newspapers.

In many ways, the appointment seems highly appropriate; Motion has always been a peculiarly, even quintessentially, English poet, and the influence on his work of both Edward Thomas and Philip Larkin (both of whom were important inheritors and custodians of a traditional yet evolving English line in poetry) are significant. He is, however, a lyric poet, writing a highly personal and often autobiographical poetry, and the laureateship, historically, has required a public and rhetorical voice. The laureateship, though, like the British monarchy itself, and the constitution of the United Kingdom, has changed radically since Ted Hughes's appointment in 1984, and it is important to consider how Motion, politically and poetically, can situate himself in this new context.

LIFE

MOTION was born Andrew Peter Motion on 26 October 1952. His grandfather had been the owner of Taylor Walker, a brewery business, and Motion's father, Andrew Richard Motion, followed him into the profession, saw active service in the Second World War, and continued to work through Motion's childhood, as well as spending many weekends with the Territorial army (at one point commanding the Essex yeomanry). Motion and his younger brother were brought up by their mother, Catherine Gillian (Bakewell) Motion, in a large Victorian house on the Suffolk-Essex border, spending the winters hunting and the summers riding horses—they were a "landed" family. Theirs was a wealthy and privileged background, and is recognized as such in poems like "The Spoilt Child" and "Firing Practice."

Motion attended an English preparatory school as a boarder—which he seems to have hated, and where he was bullied—before moving on to Radley, a famous private school, in 1965. Already he had been writing creatively for some time, despite the fact that his family read few books and preferred country activities to cultural pursuits. He mentions this in the prose-poem "Skating":

> Nevertheless, during my last few holidays from prep school, I found myself writing stories ... They were giftless—melodramatic accounts of car accidents and Indian massacres—but I'd be pleased and surprised by them, and take them into my mother's bed in the morning to read them to her. 'Why are you so bloodthirsty?' she'd ask—and I'd never be sure if this implied praise or blame. I can see now that the stories were ways of imagining the worst: ways of trying to prolong the idyll of her company by dreaming up some radically appalling alternative.
>
> (*Dangerous Play*, p. 67)

The recollections of his childhood offered in Motion's poetry and prose cannot be taken as wholly accurate—discrepancies occur as the result of his imaginative transformations of his material, and much of his work deliberately disrupts and questions the reliability of any narrative—but evidence of his prolific youthful writing can be found in his literary papers, acquired by the British Library in 1999: thousands and thousands of manuscript pages, from his schooldays onward, demonstrating frenetic and almost pedantic revising and rewriting, and often typed up in their later versions; occasionally doodles, or even terse self-criticisms ("KRAP"), decorate the margins. They make Motion's later anecdote—that he told his careers advisor at Radley that he was "a poet"—perfectly plausible. (The careers advisor apparently replied, "Well, there's nothing to say to you then.") Few children produce quite so much creative writing as Motion seems to have done (and fewer still would have kept it for nearly forty years). Motion's subtitle for his biography of Philip Larkin—"A Writer's Life"—could easily be applied to his own.

The reference to "trying to prolong the idyll of [his mother's] company by dreaming up some radically appalling alternative," however, might well be a retrospective rationalization by Motion, albeit an understandable one. When he was sixteen, his mother had a riding accident; she was thrown from her horse, landing on her head, and a blood clot formed on her brain. The operation to remove the clot caused some brain damage; Motion's mother was "more or less comatose for the next three years" and died after ten, without ever leaving the hospital. The significance of this early trauma seems impossible to overemphasize; the incident is returned to in numerous poems, and Motion continues to write about it. Furthermore, it is linked in "Skating" to the fact that Motion was away from home at the time of the accident, on his first potentially sexual date, which was curtailed by the tragedy. This may explain some of the more neurotic moments in his poetry; a sense of potential loss and doomed love permeates a large number of his pieces.

After Radley, Motion attended University College at the University of Oxford, where he studied English from 1972 to 1975, and where he married his first wife, Joanna Jane Powell; they divorced in 1983. He went on to do postgraduate work on Edward Thomas under the poet and don John Fuller, gaining his M. Litt. in 1977 (his thesis became a book, *The Poetry of Edward Thomas*). He was a lecturer at the University of Hull between 1977 and 1981, where he met the poet Philip Larkin, who was librarian at the university. He and Larkin became friends, and after Larkin's death in 1985 (shortly after Larkin turned down the laureateship), Motion became one of Larkin's literary executors. He had already written a critical work on Larkin's poetry, and subsequently wrote his authorized biography, published in 1993.

Between 1981 and 1983, Motion edited *Poetry Review*, a popular and predominantly mainstream quarterly magazine. He became poetry editor at Chatto and Windus (his then-publisher) in 1983, and between 1983 and 1989 was an editorial director at the company. He has since been an editorial director at Faber and Faber (his publisher at the time of this writing), as well as holding a number of positions on the Arts Council. He has also been in charge of a master's course in creative writing at the University of East Anglia. In every sense, his is a life spent in the service of literature, but also at the heart of the English literary establishment; factors which, it has been suggested, may have been considered when awarding him the laureateship. As well as the poetry—nine volumes (including a *Selected Poems*) between 1978 and 1997—and the biographies (of the Lamberts, Larkin, John Keats, and the forger and poisoner Jeffrey Wainewright), Motion co-edited an anthology (*The Penguin Book of Contemporary British Poetry*, 1982), with the writer Blake Morrison, and wrote two novels (*The Pale Companion*, 1989, and *Famous for the Creatures*, 1991). In 1985, he married Janet Dalley, a literary editor, with whom he has three children. In the 1990s, he was diagnosed with a tumor on his spine; he has since made a full recovery. These literary and domestic details are the facts as far as the public domain is concerned; it is important to mention them because Motion's poems have become increasingly personal, and, while he transforms many of his memories and emotions in his poetry, they are recognizable as, at root, autobiographical pieces.

ANDREW MOTION

THE POETRY OF EDWARD THOMAS

MOTION's critical study, *The Poetry of Edward Thomas* (1980), was started in 1975; while he was writing it, his first major poetry collection, *The Pleasure Steamers* (1978), was published. Motion's interest in Thomas was, and has remained, more than academic; in 1999 he chose Thomas's "Old Man" as his favorite poem (notable for its Keatsian echo—"And yet I still am half in love with pain"—and its embrace of death as an end to disappointment). It is unsurprising that the influence of Thomas is evident not only in his early work, but throughout all his collections (with *The Price of Everything* containing some particularly overt homage). Motion's commentary on Thomas arguably serves as a useful indicator of Motion's own poetic strategies.

Motion praises "the way in which [Thomas] refers to a variety of objects with such quick clarity that orthodox pictorial and narrative techniques are replaced by ... 'disconnected impressions' "; his Wordsworthian intent to keep to ordinary diction and speech patterns in his poems; a suspicion of rhetoric and merely sonorous phrasing; the concentration, rhythmically, on the phrase rather than the metrical foot; the use of modifiers and conditionals to suggest the twists and turns of the poet's mind; and the way in which Thomas achieves "an equipoise in which idealistic and realistic forces are fleetingly weighed against each other" (p. 74).

Many of these techniques are observable in Motion's work. While he displays, where appropriate, a fluent handling of regular meter, the poems mostly pull away from consistent rhythm. The tone is frequently anecdotal or conversational, in a diction which is ostensibly unpoetic and unrhetorical. He writes few memorable individual lines, and often closes poems with a gesture outward rather than, say, the closure of a ringing couplet. This is not to say that the poetry lacks music or form; it is more that the effects are more subtle, and there is a preference for ambiguity and ellipsis, shadowy narrative, the power of suggestion; it is also the case that his use of English idiom, which lends a prosaic flavor to some lines, often conceals sly double meanings that a casual reading will overlook.

In Thomas, Motion seems to have found a poetic model that appealed to him; it is also the case that Motion seems to feel a kinship with the poet beyond an admiration for his technique. In "Toot Baldon," from *Love in a Life* (1991), when he writes "when first we were married / and I was Edward Thomas" (p. 48) there is an aspect of self-mockery, but also an awareness that marriage, and financial responsibility, hampered Thomas as a writer; his poetry was written in the last two years of his life, after years of deadening hack work had made him ill and unhappy. Motion's domestic poems often carry similar notes of exhaustion, anxiety, and unhappiness.

Motion's work on, and friendship with, Philip Larkin also influenced him, though less decisively; there are a number of echoes and possible allusions to Larkin throughout the poems, and a preoccupation with the inevitability of death. In his critical study *Philip Larkin* (1982), Motion does remark, "Much recent English poetry is characterized by such a synthesis of modernism and the 'English line' ... to combine familiar and time-honoured techniques of storytelling with a degree of literary self-awareness and self-irony which the modernists made part of their stock-in-trade" (pp. 20–21). Just as the Edward Thomas volume attempted to suggest that Thomas was less a Georgian than a protomodernist, the Larkin volume makes links between Larkin and the French symbolists, suggesting he was not merely the antimodernist and traditional writer he had claimed to be. Since Motion himself combines traditional English themes and styles alongside more modernist or postmodernist strategies, these constructions of the tradition to which he sees himself as belonging are significant.

THE PLEASURE STEAMERS

WHEN Motion was a lecturer at the University of Hull, *The Pleasure Steamers* was published. Philip Larkin said that he liked it, but that the poems were "a bit out of focus"; in a later letter, he mentioned that "the comment has affected [Motion's] work since, he says" (*The Times*, 19 May 1999). It is true that these poems show early signs of the elliptical approach that Motion developed more profitably in later books, but it is probable that Larkin was picking up on an uncertainty in the first few poems of the volume. Larkin's own poetry had re-established a mode of poetic address in which a specific incident or observation can be broadened out to a rhetorical generalization ("Life is first boredom, then fear," for example); Motion's poetry resolutely refuses, on most occasions, to offer such decisive public statements.

Larkin's observation is not entirely unhelpful, however. *The Pleasure Steamers* is most successful in its last two sections; the dramatic monologues and narrative of "Inland," and the first of his stark, moving poems about his mother's accident and eventual death. The poems that begin the collection struggle to define Motion's chosen territory, a pastoral England; while highly attentive to topographical description, showing the fruitful influence of Thomas, they seem uncertain as to what to make of that terrain. England, as is so often the case in any such poetry, becomes an uncertain composite of myth, symbol, and countryside, and "Letter to an Exile" quietly corrects the romanticized version ("Though it gave nothing, now England / renews its wide promises ..." [p. 11]), but is unsure what might replace it. The poems make reference to his father's military service during the Second World War, and there is a sense that Motion, growing up in peace time ("we have no sirens, / no wars" [p. 12]), feels both guilty and frustrated that there is no substantial crisis or cause against which to define himself. (This idea is evident in later work, notably "Firing Practice," in *Natural Causes*, and is partly resolved in "Lines of Desire" from The *Price of Everything*). "I've no danger / of dying, having no cause," Motion writes more explicitly in "The Pleasure Steamers" (p. 22).

Some years later, Motion's joint introduction to *The Penguin Book of Contemporary British Poetry* mentioned, almost enviously, "the relationship between the resurgence of Northern Irish writing and the Troubles. The poets have all experienced a sense of 'living in important places' ..." (p. 16). Motion's early work frets at the absence of such stimulus; his poem on

Northern Ireland, "Leaving Belfast," might therefore be viewed as opportunistic (and indeed was, by some critics), but is also a useful example of the inappropriate restraint of these first few poems; Belfast is seen receding, from the safe position of an airplane, and becomes a set of hazy abstractions ("their stern geographies / of punishment" [p. 20]) in which an agnostic humanism comes close to patronizing disengagement ("whether / voices there pronounce me an intruder, / traitor or friend, I leave them now"). It is worth comparing this piece with the markedly more complex and successful poem "Belfast" in Love in a Life. It should also be said that many of the lines in The Pleasure Steamers knowingly rehearse this very problem, and, at best, "Letter to an Exile" does reflect a scepticism about England's national myths; the closing image is a distinct echo of the last lines of Larkin's key poem "Deceptions" in The Less Deceived (being "less deceived" came to be seen as central to the Movement poetics represented by Larkin; a championing of a sceptical, emotionally wary point of view).

What is evident in all these pieces, however, is a precociously assured descriptive talent; the evocations of light, shadow, cities, and distance are both pictorially successful and emotionally resonant. Where they fail is in precisely the sense of disengaged distance that Motion more successfully employs with regard to his most important subject; his mother's death. In a number of personal lyrics which form the final section of the volume, he describes the absence of his mother, and his yearly visits to her; but "A Dying Race" is more a poem for his father, whose daily visits speak of a devotion that Motion cannot match, and which culminate in a not untypical expression of a difficulty in loving:

If I was still there,
watching your hand push back
the hair from her desperate face,
I might have discovered by now
the way love looks, its harrowing clarity.

(Dangerous Play, p. 82)

It is through others that Motion conveys feelings which he is, as yet, unable to express directly for himself.

In "Inland," for example, the central sequence in the book, Motion writes a compelling sequence of loss, discovering the politics that underlie pastoral (the poem describes the period of the Enclosures in England, where villagers could be dispossessed by unscrupulous landowners); but typically, Motion's concern is not simply to play out the larger political theme but to imaginatively inhabit the forgotten people's lives, to represent exactly what the loss might have meant to them as individuals. The same is true of his moving dramatic monologue "Independence," in which the loss of India by the British Empire is merely a backdrop for a more personal drama, a young man losing his wife in childbirth in newly independent Kamaria, and ultimately returning to a drab, grief-ridden English landscape. The couple are "married in Independence week," and Motion never makes any explicit allegory between the private marriage and the imperial divorce; he instead sets up a series of dramatic tensions between independence and interdependence that will resonate through the rest of his work.

In these monologues, Motion seems to discover that his own sense of loss can be mediated through others' narratives while, equally, it enables him to empathize with the losses of others; there is a reciprocity in this process, and it therefore cannot be said that Motion simply hijacks other stories as a vehicle for his own concerns.

SECRET NARRATIVES *AND* DANGEROUS PLAY

IN 1983 *Secret Narratives* was published, a year after Motion had co-edited *The Penguin Book of Contemporary British Poetry*. The anthology was controversial for a number of reasons, and continues to attract the occasional negative comment. It is not worth rehearsing the criticisms in any great detail, but Motion and Morrison were both beginning their literary careers at this point, and accusations of opportunism and careerism were attached to them. The anthology ostensibly attempted to update A. Alvarez's highly influential 1960s anthology *The New Poetry* (1962,

revised 1966), which sealed the canonical supremacy of the Movement poets (Philip Larkin and Thom Gunn in particular), as well as of Ted Hughes and Geoffrey Hill, and introduced Sylvia Plath and John Berryman to a British audience. The most important figure in *The Penguin Book of Contemporary British Poetry* is Seamus Heaney, although his inclusion in a British anthology showed some confusion about Heaney's affiliation to the Irish Republic, as Heaney himself was later to point out. The book also gave prominence to the working-class voices of Douglas Dunn and Tony Harrison, and a number of Northern Irish poets (Paul Muldoon, whose influence on contemporary British poetry cannot be overstated, and Tom Paulin, for example). Its main mistake in terms of selection (apart from, politically, the absence of black writers, and the perceived underrepresentation of female writers) was that it faddishly overestimated the importance of the so-called Martian poets (Craig Raine and Christopher Reid).

What is most interesting about the anthology, though, is its introduction, which, at one point, suggests that English poetry at the beginning of the 1980s, in rediscovering the art of narrative poetry, was also assimilating the lessons of the novel, introducing a postmodern emphasis on the unreliability of narrators and narratives. The editors wrote of poets who are "not inhabitants of their own lives so much as intrigued observers, not victims but onlookers, not poets working in confessional white heat but dramatists and storytellers" and who display "a renewed interest in narrative—that is, in describing the details and complexities of (often dramatic) incidents, as well as in registering the difficulties and strategies involved in retelling them" (p. 12).

This is a remarkably efficient statement of Motion's own poetics in Secret Narratives, which are evident from the first poem, "Open Secrets." Two stanzas sketch a vivid and compelling narrative of rural life, sex, guilt, and filial ambivalence, before the rug is pulled from under the reader's feet: "Just now, prolonging my journey home to you, I killed / an hour where my road lay over a moor and made this up." The lines are shocking, breaking an unspoken contract between reader and author; furthermore, they open up an entirely fresh narrative, with its own troubling questions. The addressee is clearly a loved one; but the fact that the narrator is "prolonging" his journey home suggests that there might be a problem in that relationship. The line break in "killed / an hour" raises a hint of menace only to domesticate it. Furthermore, the exploded narrative is continued in outline ("I made him imagine ..."), with its sadistic and disturbing images, before a warning about interpretation is presented that raises even more questions than it answers:

                              He was never
myself, this boy, but I know if I tell you his story
you'll think we are one and the same: both of us
  hiding
in fictions which say what we cannot admit to
  ourselves.

                              (*Dangerous Play*, p. 11)

Secret Narratives offers a number of similarly challenging stories, predominantly in the form of dramatic monologues, that in one way or another question the trust we place in stories and storytellers. "Writing," for example, is a faintly chilling account of a female writer whose new house was previously owned by a widower, now in an old people's home, whose senility has turned into a paranoid forgetfulness that his wife has died. The narrator describes her gradually overwhelming temptation to write fictional and consoling letters back to the man, and hints at her motivations and rationalizations;

Lazily spinning the phrases out, and finally
writing them, telling myself it was
kindness, and might even turn into love.

                              (p. 14)

"Telling myself" is a good example of the mileage that Motion can extract from even the more prosaic phrases in his work, extending the writer's story making into her own self-deception; the poem as a whole is elegantly unsettling, even before one speculates on what the piece might say about Motion's own fictionalizing impulse. This disquieting approach is also applied to the myth making inherent in journalism ("The Great Man").

Nearly all of the poems in *Secret Narratives* were reprinted in *Dangerous Play: Poems 1974–1984*, a selection of old and new poems, published in 1984. The prose poem "Skating," published earlier in a fuller version in *Poetry Magazine* (September 1983), is an account of Motion's childhood, structured around his memories of his mother and culminating in her accident; it is told without self-pity—told, in fact, with a disconcerting calmness—and is the more moving for that. The other new poems develop the suspect narratives which Motion had found so useful; "The Whole Truth" is based entirely on imagined scenes of love and anticipation, which confesses its fictions at the end:

And all of it lies, just as my pictures
of you at your kitchen table were lies—
one tender imaginary scene succeeding
another, but only to prove what is true.

                              (p. 53)

This is carefully ambiguous; "only to prove what is true" could imply that the fiction represents a tender emotional reality, or that, by implication, it shows the reality to be the opposite of the compensatory fictional account. The title is thus ironic; the poem offers two "truths."

Other poems touch on imperial adventures and betrayals; and on twins, both in the ghost story "Coming to Visit," or "Explaining France," picking up on certain qualities Motion discovered in Edward Thomas—the use of a double or doppelganger to explore facets of his divided self. Within these experiments, Motion conveys a state of emotional remoteness and isolation; the description, in "Coming to Visit," of a histrionic attempt to find his own twin by staring at his reflection in the water, is deliberately self-mocking, even as Motion uses it to anxiously foreground his individual integrity: *"Whoever loves best / loves best by remaining themselves"* (p. 59). These poems, taken together, suggest the need to look behind rhetoric, artifice and narrative to discover deeper motivations and different tales; they are often disguised psychological portraits. At their most extreme, the layering of self-deception and revelation can be dizzying, as seen in "A Lyrical Ballad":

still thinking if any of these things mattered at all

it was only because I would one day describe them
to you, although you had told me already you thought
you were too far away to care—which, I should say,
I understood at the time, and have known, come to
that, ever
since.

(p. 98)

NATURAL CAUSES

THE concerns developed furtively in *Secret Narratives* and *Dangerous Play*, and the images by which they are expressed, were to find their strongest expression in *Love in a Life*, as Motion turned away from the disguise of narrative to more direct lyrical address. In the interim, he published *Natural Causes* (1987), a slim volume of eight pieces. A suite of personal poems (about family, school, love, and parenthood) are enigmatically topped and tailed by a prologue ("The Dancing Hippo") and an epilogue ("This Is Your Subject Speaking," an elegy for Philip Larkin). The arrangement is puzzling, in that the relationship between the three sections is not immediately obvious, and resists an easy explanation. The volume marks a small departure for Motion; elliptical though his earlier narratives were, there was never an absence of overt or covert commentary on that secretiveness, nor the reasons for it. In *Natural Causes*, Motion has the confidence to leave his mysterious stories unannotated; and the confidence also to attempt a more directly autobiographical approach in places. Motion's divisions of poems into several sections, and his arrangement of those poems within discrete sections in his books, is not always easy to interpret. Indeed, his different arrangements of those same poems in his later selected volumes make new links between them, suggesting fresh emphases. Sometimes, one suspects that there is an arbitrariness to these juxtapositions, or at least an indecisiveness; the introduction to *The Penguin Book of Contemporary British Poetry* had said approvingly of some writers that "they have demonstrated that if a poem draws a line round an incident or area of experience, observations which fall within its circumference seek each other out and establish relationships" (p. 18). This cedes power to the reader, who is encouraged to discern those relationships without authorial prompting.

In *Natural Causes*, one might start by considering a possible link between "The Dancing Hippo" and the Larkin elegy. The title of Larkin's first mature volume *The Less Deceived*, became something of a manifesto slogan for "the movement." (Motion's allusion to it in "Letter to an Exile" is noted earlier.) "The Dancing Hippo" begins with an undeceived statement:

I think you can see from my lack of illusion,
I have some experience—so when I tell you
This story caused me distress, do not ignore me.

(p. 11)

The lines are faintly ironic; the speaker is a circus owner, and the dancing hippo of the title never truly dances, but it does enough to give the audience a pleasing illusion of dancing. The love felt by audience (and circus staff) for the hippo as a result of this illusion is genuine, and when the hippo is burned to death, the owner reports the trainer's grief:

I know it was useless, of course, her dancing.
I know. Like everything else we do. But God above
it was beautiful. God!—or something like that.

(p. 12)

Despite the concession to cynicism and nihilism, this is, in a sense, a riposte to those positions; an effective partner, therefore, to an elegy for the resolutely nihilistic yet still grudgingly celebratory Larkin. Its other resonances—a lack of illusion paired with genuine if futile emotion—cast a darker shadow over the suite of poems in between. Of this volume, Motion only chose "The Dancing Hippo" for his *Selected Poems 1976–1997* (1998), suggesting perhaps a dissatisfaction with the others. Although there is no doubt that the poems are difficult, almost deliberately withholding from the reader any certainty as to how to read them, they are emotionally powerful. "Natural Causes," for instance, creates a triptych; a description of his newborn son in the first section and, in the second, an anecdote

257

about a man with amnesia, whose past is, hellishly, erased every few minutes. Intriguingly, the third section, in which one might expect a synthesis of these elements, meets that expectation only to dismiss it, proposing a different triptych: the amnesiac man, waking daily into a painful semi-existence; the boy, scarily abandoned in a coracle (small boat) floating into a storm; and finally, the parents:

intelligent, petrified,
no way out of a cupboard of shiny steel with walls
which steadily squeeze together until we die.

(p. 39)

That is, instead of the ever-learning child counterbalancing the man with a vanishing past, the picture is complicated by the presence of the parents, doomed to watch their offspring grow into an always dangerous world, while their own world shrinks, traps and crushes them (compare Larkin's line in "Afternoons," when parents find that "something is pushing them / To the side of their own lives" [Collected Poems, ed. Anthony Thwaite, 1988, p.121]; Motion's image is far more terrifying and terrified).

Particularly striking in this volume is "Firing Practice," which restates Motion's guilt about living in peacetime, aware that his idols (his father; Edward Thomas) were able to live lives of significant action. "The Pleasure Steamers" was quite explicit about this—a Romantic yearning for immortality through death in combat—and "Firing Practice" begins, "You knew you were lucky / born all of a piece and born into peace time," but that pun on "piece" and "peace" is neurotically developed into a sense of fragmentation and dislocation that can be found, clearly stated, in a significant number of Motion's poems:

Nothing connected with anything,
even then—not thoughts

with things, or you to him
(so what did it mean
to be lucky?)
no matter how hard you tried.

(p. 42)

The poem concludes with a sense of fateful mortality, unredeemed by meaning or cause, and the desolate realization that however early one is "undeceived," it cannot prevent even the closest of relationships from being destroyed by death, accident or war; "there's no one to save you now, / nowhere to hide in, nothing but hope" (p. 45). This sense of despair and futility pervades Motion's next collection, which shows him, on the back of the experiments of Natural Causes, perfecting a style of writing that allows him, as he said of Edward Thomas, to create "an equipoise in which idealistic and realistic forces are fleetingly weighed against each other" (The Poetry of Edward Thomas, p. 74).

LOVE IN A LIFE

Love in a Life is a far more dramatic book than any of its predecessors. This can partly be attributed to the content, but Natural Causes, which also attended to personal themes, does not give such unfiltered emotional color to its subjects. It is more that Motion employs a far wider verbal range in Love in a Life; from his careful narratives and descriptions to direct statement and—sometimes—an address of such immediacy that the poems seem to be recording precise shifts of emotion and thought at the very instant they occur. The imagery is more fantastical, hysterical, even surreal. Motion apostrophizes more, and by addressing the reader directly (rather than recounting a shared incident or anecdote to an imagined "you") he offers an exhilarating sense of emotional access that previously his writing seemed determined to avoid: even if that avoidance was itself one of the subjects of the poetry.

Love in a Life is an obsessively unhappy volume. The poems are fraught with a fear of death and harm, and his anxiety about his wife and children's safety seems constantly to shade into a feeling of isolation from them. "Why do I feel that I've died / and am lingering here to haunt you?," as he writes in "One Who Disappeared" (p. 12), is a not untypical rhetorical question. The collection accentuates this sense of dislocation and unbelonging with fluent and rapid shifts from dream to metaphor to realist description, in a dizzying and disorienting—yet remorseless—series of progressions. "Run" (suggesting both sequence and flight) offers a particularly rich example of this new, and more modernistic, technique. It consists of four sections; the first a memory of Motion's feelings after his mother had died; the second a memory of a friend who died in a boating disaster on the Thames, when a dredger ran down a pleasure boat, *The Marchioness*, and drowned many of its occupants; a Gothic dream involving his wife's face; and, finally, a description of his children which is poised between dream and reality, metaphor and symbol.

The first section recalls a time when Motion thought that grief, like the grieved for, could be buried; a feeling that he would "put [it] in the ground like a body / to visit from time to time, and otherwise forget" (p. 11). It becomes swiftly apparent that this is far from being the case. In the second section he writes:

But take Ruth
who drowned last week.

I used to fancy her—
now all I think
is what water can do,
easing off shoes,
making light
of the dense net of her tights.

To hell with out of place!
That's the fucking Thames dribbling down your face!
(p. 18)

A lot is going on in these few short lines. They start as a simple example, of how the dead cannot easily be forgotten; a girl who was once the object of sexual interest to the speaker has died. The next lines blend her death with that residual eroticism, with deft and tasteless puns; "easing off shoes / making light / of the dense net of her tights" combines the stripping away of clothes by the rush of water (this phenomenon, and Ruth's drowning, are also referred to in "Fresh Water" in Salt Water) with the clichés of seductive undressing; "making light" means "without difficulty" but also suggests the light pouring through the rent material, but it also means "trivi-

alizing." A reader's reaction to this tastelessness is immediately anticipated by Motion, and responded to with swift venom. "To hell with out of place! / That's the fucking Thames dribbling down your face!" turns the metaphorical phrase "out of place" (not appropriate; bad manners) into something grimly literal; that Ruth and the Thames were not supposed to be, as it were, juxtaposed. The use of the expletives is also shocking; but it marks Motion's own turning, from the emotionally restrained and coldly rhetorical language preceding it to something like a howl of anger and grief. The economy with which various ideas, including a commentary on language, and emotions, including both lust and grief, have all been mediated, is remarkable.

The fourth section promises an end to these horrific and surreal visions; the speaker is awake, "sunk on the bed / of a parched lake / where sleep ran out" (p. 19), listening as his children come down the corridor to his door. But there is a nightmarish and hallucinatory quality even to this; the children "drizzle" like liquid, the journey "takes them years," the speaker has to "brace himself." They stand there, "their almost inaudible / blobs of mouths / oo-ing and ah-ing / like shouting fish" (p. 20); and this returns readers to the element of water in which Ruth drowned, with the poet stranded on that "parched lake" of dry ground. It is a surreal statement of the fact that "the time they arrive / is the time they go"— that the children will grow up and go before the speaker can free himself from grief and embrace the living:

We travelled for ever
to reach your door,
and in the end
we found it locked.
Wake up, damn you!
Wish us good luck!

(p. 20)

In *Love in a Life* Motion constantly shifts between different elements—earth, air, fire, and water—to create resonant images of irredeemable separation and dislocation. In "Look," the scanned image of his fetal twins is described like a photograph of astronauts, revolving above an earth "which will bring them to grief / or into their own"; this is juxtaposed with the image of his hospitalized mother, attached to oxygen as if "she might lift into space / and never return / to breathe our air" (p. 7). The final, synthesizing section poises the narrator between space and earth:

like a man lost in space
might howl for the earth,
or a dog for the moon
with no reason at all.

(p. 8)

That final line implies madness (the loss of reason) as much as motivelessness. At times, these poems seem to describe imminent nervous breakdown.

In both these exemplary poems, and many others in the collection, Motion perversely establishes a more insistent rhythm than he has previously allowed himself; he often employs short two- or three-stressed lines, creating a nursery-rhyme meter which, combined with surreal imagery reminiscent of Lewis Carroll, has a sinister rather than soothing effect. This new interest in regular metre is therefore as anti-poetic as the deliberate eschewal of rhetoric and merely musical rhythms that has preceded it. In "The Vision of that Ancient Man," Motion parodies Samuel Taylor Coleridge's "The Rime of the Ancient Mariner" (and, possibly, calls attention to his own initials, AM). Its portrayal of an obsessive narrator, wracked with the guilt of the survivor, might be seen as a sardonic self-criticism by Motion, and it culminates, after another series of horrific and bitter juxtapositions and allusions, with a song-like series of similes before breaking off tersely "Like ... Sod it; who cares?" It is as if he employs conventional forms only to establish a grotesque contrast with his subject matter; as if he is actively contemptuous of poetry's ostensible role as a healing art.

THE PRICE OF EVERYTHING

It is typical of Motion's painstaking balance of opposed impulses—whether formal or thematic—that *The Price of Everything* (1994), his most

experimental book, should hark back to his most traditional influences and his earliest poetic preoccupations; Edward Thomas, England's military past, the threatened realm of the domestic.

The book, as its acknowledgements make clear, is "about various kinds of conflict," with the First World War as the *point de depart* of both of the long poems within it, "Lines of Desire" and "Joe Soap." Motion's frequently restated anxieties as to his peacetime legacy, particularly in relation to his military father, are again manifest. His description of parting from his father after an evening of talking "in a language not exactly dead but not exactly loving" employs the now-familiar imagery of people floundering in mutually alien elements: "My father turns back to his house like someone walking under water" (p. 14). It is an implicit theme in much of Motion's writing that he finds it hard to live up to his father's military achievements. In the uncollected poem "Territorial" (*Poetry Review* 89, no. 2, 1999) he speaks of a feeling "somewhere between a thrill and a warning. / Live up to him. Think what he went through" (p. 8). There is a subtle parallel between a section in "The Bone Elephant" in Love in a Life, and "Lines of Desire" in the eponymous long poem; in the former, his father has to step on the drowning head of a fellow soldier to make his way safely on to the French coast, and in the latter, "it starts with a father / who climbs his son / and weighs him down / begging to live" (p. 26). When Motion writes of Edward Thomas, "I went to discover his grave. / This was not being brave" (p. 9), the self-mockery (emphasised by the untypical full rhyme) fails to conceal a certain bitterness.

The Price of Everything also returns to Motion's related preoccupation with fracture and disconnection. (In "Firing Practice," the poet observes that "nothing connected / with anything ever"; in "I Do, You Do," he feels "like a stranger to myself / and all the lives I've led"; in "Reading the Elephant" comes the realization that "never would one of the several worlds I was living among / connect with another, that soon I would just disappear.") In "Dedication," the opening poem in "Lines of Desire," a moment of random urban violence triggers Motion's panic: once his sense of personal integrity is violated (as it was by the death of his mother, and of friends or acquaintances), he loses faith in the integrity of everything: *"The lives I trusted, even my own / collapse, break off, or don't belong"* (p. 4).

The structure of this volume—several many-sectioned poems within two larger poems within one book; collages, cinematic or photographic descriptions, lyrical utterances, prose, rhyming verses, pastiches, letters, ballads—also exploits this sense of fragmentation. Furthermore, the sense of personal threat in "Lines of Desire" is paralleled with more global and historical dramas in "Joe Soap," where "there is no story left":

I put these words down carefully, side by side,
Like a child building a sentence—
Parents, woman, streets, parks—
They just lie there.
They never become a story.

Again, the anti-poetic impulse discernible in *Love in a Life*—the almost sarcastic use of conventional meter—reaches its apotheosis in *The Price of Everything*, where onomatopoeic and rhythmic effects are used initially to describe the building of civilization, but swiftly become sinister and debased, before being reduced to isolated units:

Dum dum de dum, de dum de dum de start
Clack clackety clack, clack clackety clack clack see
Diddle di da da, diddle de da da heart.

(p. 30)

Da da, or Dada, indeed; although narratives—financial, military, familial, evolutionary—are depicted within The Price of Everything, it is their fragility and vulnerability that is stressed time and time again. It seems that while Motion still finds value in relationships, he feels that war and violence can and do destroy those relationships irrevocably. The idea of continuity down the generations (first raised in "The Legacy," with its image of a hand signing on family property and "transcribing itself forever" [p. 58]) is constantly pitched against its opposite (like the punning "family tie" washed up after a drowning

in "The Vision of that Ancient Man" from *Love in a Life* [p. 23]).

The Price of Everything is also, untypically, overtly political in its tackling of large, indeed global, public themes, while simultaneously raising questions about the mediation of such topics. The images of Britain at war still display Motion's tendency to align his own sense of loss and grief with Britain's imperial decline, but in painting a broader cross-generational picture, a more sophisticated politics than mere nostalgia becomes possible. "Money Singing" begins with three pairs of stanzas linking luxury to the labor and raw materials that produce them, in a lyrical reversal of the way in which commodities (in Marxist terminology) normally efface all traces of the processes of their production. In another vignette, in the same poem, Motion looks out from his own backyard, a space of bourgeois safety, at the lights from the city of London, a financial centre that came to represent the unfettered free-market politics of the Thatcherite 1980s, and tries to "pretend they mean nothing to me" (p. 23).

The poem does not resolve the many tensions in the relationships it discusses. It does, however, suggest the complexity of questions of value and worth; and in its imaginative leaps and links, it pays tribute to the soldiers, including Motion's father, who fought to obtain the peace that Motion's generation inherited. Yet it also manages to display the stresses and difficulties of that inheritance, not least in relation to the next generation, Motion's children, and the invisible mechanics of capitalism that allow luxury and domesticity even as they generate so much work, anxiety, and violence.

The overt political themes of *The Price of Everything* do call attention to their absence in most of Motion's earlier work; it is notable that the 1980s were a decade of remarkable political change in Britain, engendering a decisive shift in political sensibility and economic conditions, and yet Motion's poetry contains almost no traces of those changes. In *Love in a Life*, the central section deals with political themes; two poems treating the end of the cold war in 1989 are placed on either side of a light poem Motion wrote on the

261

issue of the fouling of pavements by dogs. The banality of this concern, juxtaposed with the serious repressions and deprivations of Soviet-controlled Czechoslovakia, is hard to ignore, and can only be deliberate, though its final couplet displays a humanism that can, indeed, be applied either parochially or more seriously: "On the one hand, it's only shit; on the other, shit's shit, / and what we want in the world is less, not more of it" (p. 39).

"The Prague Milk Bottle" is deft at situating the personal and erotic in a broader depiction of totalitarianism, as well as dutifully recognizing the speaker's privilege as a visitor rather than victim; it ends with a typical Motion image of a silent scream. Its companion piece, "The Bone Elephant," parallels the liberation of Europe (in particular his father's part in it) with the fall of the Berlin Wall and Vaclav Havel's revolution in Czechoslovakia; a fishing image is used to suggest a continuity of liberation between the two events, as well as the unwitting contribution of the Second World War to the cold war that followed.

In *The Price of Everything*, the juxtaposing of the fall of the Berlin Wall to the father's memories is more troubling, asking what a united Germany might mean to the different generations; and though the failure of this dialogue is resonant ("'Yup,' was all he would say, 'Yup,' and kept on looking away"), the poem tactfully says no more than "It must make you wonder" (p. 12). Motion has frequently quoted, with approval, Keats's line that readers dislike poetry "with palpable designs on us," especially since becoming poet laureate. He prefers to offer a picture of appropriate complexity and allow the reader's political and emotional responses to reconcile, or not, the contradictions within. At the same time, this considerately undogmatic approach does leave Motion vulnerable to accusations that his politics are little more than middle-class humanist platitudes, and his background will inevitably lend weight to those reservations.

"Joe Soap" suggests that this would be an unfair approach to the later poems. Not only is it resolutely global and historical in its reach, it interrogates the poetic voice incessantly. As a disembodied Everyman, Joe Soap is, at one level, the imaginative voice of a poet seeking to write about worlds beyond his immediate experience, and the volume as a whole is scrupulous in inscribing into the text the means by which information about global concerns is brought to a comfortable and privileged audience by satellites and televisions. A particularly resonant section describes a satellite camera zooming in on the earth's trouble spots, before:

It sees a minuscule dot among high-rise rubble
which looks like a fire,
but might be the terrified, rolling-back, rearing
white of my eye.

(p. 77)

In another, Motion channel-hops across various televised scenes of war and dispossession until the blank screen reflects only the faces of the poet and his family. These are images that combine fear, impotence, distance, privilege, and witness, and make the text of the poems truly postmodern in their scope.

SALT WATER

Salt Water (1997) was Motion's last new book of poetry before he became laureate. It marks a consolidation of Motion's themes more than a fresh departure. A significant development, though, is the directness of emotional expression in some of the poems. "I love it. I love the river," he writes in "Fresh Water" (p. 9); "I hate—I really hate," in "On the Table" (p. 43). Motion's endeavor—to match the speaking voice to the line of poetry, the greatest lesson he took from Edward Thomas—culminates in an apparent desire for greater clarity: "I would like to make it clear" (p. 43), "You must know" (p. 35), "I shall tell you, then" (p. 25), "I won't say much about it now" (p. 10). There is a distinct contrast here with the secret narratives of the past, represented most comically in "Belfast" when Motion's driver says, *You don't mind plain-speaking / do you? You do? Right; let's go* (p. 56).

It would be wrong, though, to imagine that this clarity of speech and ostensible clarity of purpose mark an end to Motion's patiently achieved poetry of ambiguity. The volume was written during Motion's researches for his biography of Keats (1997), and, while nothing could be less Keatsian (in the sense of Romantic excess) than Motion's careful, empirical poems, Keats's notion of the "negative capability"—the retention of mystery and uncertainty, the refusal to reach for closure and settled fact—is part of Motion's own poetic impulse. Unsurprisingly, there is much in Motion's reading of Keats that can be applied to his own poetry; for example, the notion of the chameleon poet which, in Motion's words, "allows the lack of a fixed identity to become a means of entering the world" (p. 210).

"Fresh Water," the first poem in *Salt Water*, combines four sections to approach, by indirection, another elegy for Ruth Haddon. It is worth considering this poem in some detail, because, beneath its apparently rambling descriptive surface, Motion is covering a great deal of ground in a very subtle fashion.

The first section is a description of Motion and his brother searching for the source of the Thames. The incident has been described before, in "Bloodlines" from *Natural Causes*, but there are considerable differences between the two accounts. In the former, Motion and his brother are schoolchildren ("they'd told us to disappear"; "whisked off to school" [pp. 15–16]), in the latter, young adults (they are living separately, since "I am visiting my brother," "not yet twenty" but old enough to drive [pp. 3–4]). In the former, it is afternoon ("pewter afternoon light" [p. 15]) and in the latter, morning ("we leave early before the sun has / taken the frost off the fields" [p. 4]). Not even the season seems to be precisely the same. The lesson is clear; whatever the autobiographical origins of such stories, it is the way Motion treats them as symbols that is important. (The third section, likewise, is a reprise of a passage in "The Pleasure Steamers" where divers search a river for a corpse.)

The brothers are searching for the source of the Thames, and a statue of Old Father Thames. The statue is absent, but in this poem Motion does discover the source of the river. It is tempting to see Motion liberated by the absence of the

patriarchal figure, a stand-in for his own father, just as, in "Cleaned Out" from *Love in a Life*, the "vanload of pricks" (p. 24); note the Oedipal resonance of "pricks") who rob his father's home of "all the family things" engender a triumphant fantasy of freedom and creation ("brilliant, particular leaves come rioting out of my mouth" [p. 25]).

It is in the final section of the poem, after Motion's many memories of the river are concluded, that readers reach a destination: his drowned friend, Ruth, swimming upstream like a salmon, rewinding time as she does so, until she vanishes. One is reminded of Edward Thomas' "Over the Hills":

Recall
Was vain: no more could the restless brook
Ever turn back and climb the waterfall
To the lake...
(*The Collected Poems of Edward Thomas*. Oxford: OUP, 1978, p. 77)

It is as if, in refutation of Thomas, Motion's reconstruction of his memories of the water may indeed turn back what Motion sees as the inevitable direction of all lives towards death. It is a rare redemptive note in a poetry that has mostly dwelt on despair.

Motion, of course, continues to question such redemption. In "Reading the Elephant," a vision of perfection in a foreign landscape is rendered as "pure pattern, pure beauty, pure pleasure in living, pure sight" (p. 11) in an overt allusion to Larkin's "Essential Beauty" ("Proclaim pure crust, pure foam, / Pure coldness to our live imperfect eyes" [*Collected Poems*, p. 144] and it is therefore no surprise to find the realist in Motion reassert himself "I'm not quite a fool" [p. 11]). In "Does That Hurt?," Motion plays off the difference between appearance and reality, when the repeated question "Does that hurt?," apparently asked of his son, stung by a bee, is actually being asked of Motion, and his agony at seeing his child in pain: "Just look at me watching him go / and you'd say I felt nothing at all" (p. 23). Since this poem also contains another glimpse of his comatose mother (emblematic of pain, loss and grief "without redress"), it can be compared with the much earlier poem "Wooding," where the family, "still destitute of ways to show our grief," would, from a distance, have looked comical and happy (*Dangerous Play*, p. 84). This, in turn, makes the line in "Fresh Water" that "We are the picture of a family on an outing. I love it" (p. 9) rather less certain in its pleasure; the picture is not necessarily going to be the truth. "In Memory of Zoë Yalland" also undermines the redemptive image that closes "Fresh Water" when he writes of a friend, dying of cancer, "it seems you're living backwards, seems you might / be young again, and well, and free to live. Not true" (p. 26).

Yet the collection does contain other, broader emotional tones. "On The Table" is a tender and erotic lyric for his wife. "To Whom It May Concern" conjures up images of political violence precisely by its insistence that the poem is only "a poem about ice cream" (p. 33); it is reminiscent of the censor-wary East European poetry written in totalitarian states. "Salt Water" itself alternates between myth and modernity to paint pictures of xenophobia and torture, instructively linking modern military surveillance with the prejudice of twelfth-century islanders discovering a merman. The final section, a prose account of Motion's sea journey to Naples in the footsteps of Keats, offers some entertaining contrasts between romanticism and reality, often in an endearingly self-deprecatory fashion.

THE LAUREATESHIP

In contrast to the United States' poet laureate (or, more correctly, "poet laureate consultant in poetry," formerly "poetry consultant to the Library of Congress"), which is a yearly (potentially renewable) appointment, the British laureate was, until 1999, a life appointment. Furthermore, the appointment is technically made by the queen of England, as the constitutional head of state; in reality, the appointment is made by the prime minister, in consultation with civil servants, politicians, and figures from the literary world. The position was first held officially by John Dryden; in the early eighteenth century the

poet laureate became a member of the royal household, and a tradition of writing a New Year's ode and a birthday ode for the monarch was instated. The office fell into disrespect over this period, and has always been the target of satire and derision. The formal requirement was dropped during the tenure of Robert Southey. To this day, there are no compulsory duties to the role, though John Betjeman and Ted Hughes, the last two holders, did voluntarily write poems for royal and state occasions when the mood took them; Hughes, indeed, wrote surprisingly passionate pieces, locating the crown as the hub of the wheel of the nation, and evoking a primal sense of national identity and integrity.

The year 1997 had seen two events that would radically alter the constitution of Britain, one politically, the other symbolically. The landslide victory by Tony Blair's Labor Party in May 1997 marked the beginning of the most radical constitutional reform of the twentieth century. Power was devolved from Westminster; Scotland was granted its own parliament, Wales its own assembly, in moves that could only bring closer the possibility of independence for both. Peace talks began in Northern Ireland, and the prospect that its six counties might share power with the Republic of Ireland was raised. It is common for England to be treated as synonymous with Britain or the United Kingdom, since the latter's constituent parts had for so long been run from Westminster in London. These devolutionary moves made clearer the very great differences in law, culture, aspiration, and even language between the countries, provinces, and principalities of the kingdom.

The symbolic event was the death of Princess Diana in a car crash in Paris. In the wake of her death, there was an outpouring of grief and anger in Britain which was almost unique, and which took politicians, the media, and the monarchy by surprise. Britain's constitutional monarchy looked vulnerable, for the first time, to a popular mood of republican contempt. Although there seems little realistic prospect that Britain would exchange its constitutional monarchy for a republic in the foreseeable future, the Crown, plagued by divorces and scandals, has become more human and more vulnerable; it is no longer the focus of largely unquestioning and undemanding respect, and can no longer be said to unequivocally embody the values and desires of the nation.

In this atmosphere, the business of appointing a poet laureate, an obviously archaic and arguably anachronistic post, was fraught with difficulty and elements of farce. Poetry hardly enjoys a more positive profile in modern Britain than does the monarchy. When Andrew Motion was finally appointed in 1999, after a rancorous debate fueled by media speculation and professional feuding, he was faced immediately with the prospect of writing a poem for a royal wedding, Prince Edward's marriage to Sophie Rhys-Jones. Edward's three siblings had all seen their own marriages end in divorce. In a multicultural society in which monarchy, poetry and even marriage are more fragile institutions than they were, this was not going to be an easy task.

Motion's approach to his job is laid out in a published speech to the Arts Council called "Poetry in Public" (2000). It is something of a manifesto, and cleverly tackles the difficulties of the post while arguing that they are best met by precisely the sort of poetry that Motion already writes. It begins by mentioning Diana's death (for which Motion had written a poem at the time), and the number of mourners who had expressed themselves, however artlessly, in poetry; Motion suggests that "in their various kinds of distress," people found that poetry expressed their feelings "in a way that prose could not" (p. 3). Motion then turns to the idea of what "public poetry" might entail. "Public poetry is poetry about an event or a person (or people) of general interest," he says, but also involves "a largely sympathetic audience ... their apprehension of national values ... their sense of what is heroic and fine" (pp. 4–5), and instructively cites the example of Alfred, Lord Tennyson in poems like "The Charge of the Light Brigade." The possibility of a large public voice, consensual, confident, part of "a broadly-based public discourse"—Victorian public poetry—Motion sees as having been irrevocably destroyed by the First World War.

Here he turns again to two of his favorite poets and influences; Edward Thomas, whose war poetry rarely mentioned the war directly, and Keats, who Motion reads as undidactically political; again he cites Keats's dislike of "poetry with palpable designs on us" and his belief that "axioms in philosophy are not axioms unless they are proved on our pulses." Motion argues that Thomas' poetry offered a "layered approach" to public themes, rather than a "direct assault"; "wary individuals" rather than "heroic types"; and "highly personalised voices" rather than "ringingly centred language" (p. 13). It is no surprise that Motion endorses Thomas as "an exemplary figure"; these have all been aspects of Motion's own poetry from his earliest published work.

So when Motion tackles the difficulty in writing for a "national occasion" when "much of the delight we take in our contemporary society has to do with its diversity," he is able to stick to his guns: "I knew that I was a personal kind of poet, and I felt that I should therefore respond to occasions in a personal way. As a private citizen, putting my work into a public space without any illusions that I would necessarily echo universally-held thoughts and opinions" (p. 16). In practice, this has been, arguably, successful. It is reasonable to suggest that Motion's laureate poetry will never be his finest work, and he continues to write his own poetry; but already he has broadened and changed the role of the laureate.

At an administrative level, the post will no longer be held for life, but for a period of ten years; the salary has also finally been modernized, though the "butt of sack" (approximately 126 gallons of wine) has been retained. What Motion has brought to the post (as well as the intention to promote and fund poetry more widely and more imaginatively) is a determination to write "public poetry" about a range of events beyond British state occasions. In poems printed in most British newspapers, he has written about his experience of bullying in "The Game"; in support of the charity ChildLine (4 March 2000); the Paddington rail crash, in "Cost of Life" (12 October 1999); the Trade Union Congress in "A Perfect World" (8 September 1999); Nelson

Mandela's release from prison in "Mandela" (written in a House of Commons Tribute Book, 8 July 1999); and the millennium in "2000: Zero Gravity" (*Daily Mail*, 26 December 1999). Several of these poems, though, have been commissioned by newspapers or institutions, and it is not clear at the time of this writing which can be considered "laureate poems" and which are his own "public poems," written partly because of his position, but essentially remaining part of his personal work.

The Mandela poem, like his poem "Mythology" for Princess Diana, is a lapidary quatrain, with a grandeur of diction and imagery. His poem for the Paddington rail disaster is a more human piece, displaying imaginative empathy (or rather, with its repeated exhortations to "imagine," demanding it) with the unknowing victims. His poem for the Trade Union Congress conference, "A Perfect World," is a description of a walk along the Thames, with inoffensive images of freedom and diversity, making it obliquely affirmative but scarcely risk-taking.

The royal poems, to date, are "Epithalamium," for Prince Edward's wedding (all newspapers, 19 June 1999), and "Picture This" and "A Hundred Years," both for the hundredth birthday of the queen mother (19 July 2000). They offer an idea of what Motion, a self-confessed supporter of the Labour Party and hardly an uncritical monarchist, can offer the British public on these celebratory occasions. "Epithalamium" is a rare example of Motion employing a classically traditional form, the sonnet. Within it, he describes the church wedding in terms of the Creation, with faint echoes of the language of Ted Hughes ("a people-river floods those empty pews") in gentle tribute to his successor. He also offers wishes that might satisfactorily accompany any nuptials—for truth, hope, trust, and love—while delicately hinting at the divorces and media attention that the royal family have suffered. It is a masterpiece of tact, restraint, dignity, and convention, most notably in the fact it does not even name the royal couple.

Motion's hard-earned technique—of letting plain language and diction convey a complex variety of feelings and ideas—serves him especially well in the poems for the queen mother.

"Picture This" tells the story of her century through photographs of her; that is, he represents the representation of the queen mother, and tacitly suggests it is only through such representations that the public can be said to "know her." In sketching out her history, he also invokes the nation's history, especially the two world wars. It requires a poet with the subtlety of Dryden to achieve what Motion does here; which is to offer a poem that can be read by a monarchist or republican. He does this by emphasising the world of appearances ("no changes on the face of it") and a delicate punning, as when he describes the queen mother's walk in the East End of London during the Blitz, to improve morale:

and you as one of us—or like enough
to make a crowd of wind-frayed kids
and peering mums, the husbands jostling
with the press-men in their burly coats
all think you are. And thank their lucky stars.

The qualification in this poem ("or ... think you are") is finished off with a line of calculated ambiguity. "And thank their lucky stars" is an idiomatic phrase expressing gratitude for good fortune; but with the royal family essentially media celebrities in the twentieth century, they too are "stars," and the adjective "lucky" is not inappropriate; the royal family did not, of course, suffer as much deprivation during the Second World War as their subjects. So Motion's verse caters for those who believe that the queen mother did indeed boost morale in the war, and also for those who find it unpalatable that her subjects should have adored her when she was so protected and privileged during their hardships (especially since she had been a consistent advocate of appeasement with Adolph Hitler during the 1930s).

Motion's twin impulses, tradition and modernization, are well suited to the peculiar role of poet laureate in a contemporary Britain which is finding its own way between its cherished continuities and the demands of ever-changing modernity, globally, and locally. His continued insistence on a modern speaking voice to which the poetic line is subordinate comes into its own at a time when a grandiose public rhetoric is no longer feasible; his linking of the political to the personal is also very much in tune with a society where individual rights are being articulated against social and global responsibilities as ever before. His is a poetry of carefully balanced ambiguities and passionate ambivalences, as well as loss. While it is impossible to believe that a poet can speak for "the people," his public voice is as close to undivisive as is conceivable in a diverse nation. And while he is indeed the privately and Oxford-educated son of a landed family, with connections at the heart of the literary establishment—which some critics have found unpalatable in itself—his values are humanist and politically moderate; all of these are traditional British attributes for what is, essentially, a traditional British post.

SELECTED BIBLIOGRAPHY

I. POETRY. *The Pleasure Steamers* (Manchester, 1978); Independence (Edinburgh, 1981); *Secret Narratives* (Edinburgh, 1983); *Dangerous Play: Poems 1974–1984* (Edinburgh, 1984); *Natural Causes* (London, 1987); *Love in a Life* (London, 1991); *The Price of Everything* (London and Boston, 1994); *Salt Water* (London, 1997); *Selected Poems 1976–1997* (London, 1998).

II. BIOGRAPHY. *The Lamberts: George, Constant and Kit* (London, 1986; New York, 1987); *Philip Larkin: A Writer's Life* (London and New York, 1993); Keats (London, 1997; New York, 1998); *Wainewright the Poisoner: The Confessions of Thomas Griffiths Wainewright* (London, 1999; New York, 2000).

III. CRITICISM. *The Poetry of Edward Thomas* (London, 1980); *Philip Larkin* (London and New York, 1982).

IV. NOVELS. *The Pale Companion* (London and New York, 1989); *Famous for the Creatures* (London and New York, 1991).

V. ANTHOLOGIES. *The Penguin Book of Contemporary British Poetry* (London, 1982).

VI. LECTURES. *Poetry in Public* (London, 2000).

VII. LITERARY PAPERS. In 1999, the British Library acquired Motion's literary papers. At the time of writing, they have not been fully cataloged; the author of this essay would like to thank Dr. Christopher Fletcher for allowing access to them.

LES MURRAY

(1938–)

Gerry Cambridge

LES MURRAY IS the most imposing and contrary figure in contemporary Australian poetry. He is a poet of place, and of loyalty to place, in a largely rootless age; a physically large man who champions the unfashionable both in thought and in dress in an age of political correctness and svelte fashion, he is a practicing Catholic who since 1983 has dedicated all his books "to the glory of God," and aimed satire at an intelligentsia he sees as predominantly atheist. In a period dominated by the private lyric voice in poetry he aspires to "bardship," and speaking for a significant section of Australian people: namely, the white rural poor in his own area of New South Wales, while also being influenced significantly by the Aboriginal literary tradition.

Any new reader of Murray's poetry is likely to be startled and bewildered by its variety, bulk, and a certain inspired oddness. Like that of an Australian Whitman crossed with a Robert Frost, the work is a cornucopia of images and references, in free verse or traditional forms; slangy Australian speech rubs shoulders with elevated diction; and the poet, especially in the early work, displays an engaging humor and optimism. Murray has been called Australia's unofficial laureate, the bard of a nation of 18 million made up originally of convicts, their jailers, and the indigenous Aborigines, a nation that still, at least on paper, acknowledges the British queen as head of state. In some ways he is like the Scottish poet Hugh MacDiarmid, to whom he claims to be related; his presence casts a similarly long shadow over his country's literary world—he has been called, in this context, "a mastodon among gazelles"—and he shares something of his distant relative's talent for controversy and polemic. Even the publication of his recent biography by Peter F. Alexander was attended by dispute:

originally published in Australia, it was pulped before distribution when an individual featured in the book threatened legal action for libel. Dropped without explanation by his American publishers, the book was posted on the Internet in October 2000. It was finally published by OUP Australia in November 2000. Unlike MacDiarmid, however, who lived his life largely unacclaimed for his poetry, Murray has from the first been showered with awards, prizes, and grants. At sixty-two, he is considered one of the world's foremost English-language poets.

LIFE

THE early environments of some poets seem unimportant to their art. For Murray, a great poet of place, his was crucial. Leslie Allan Murray was born on 17 October 1938 in Nabiac, some fifteen miles from the family home in Bunyah, New South Wales, set in rich agricultural land. His mother, Miriam (Arnal) Murray, came from the nearby town of Newcastle, where she had been a nurse. His father Cecil Murray worked as a tenant on a farm for his father. The family ancestry was Scottish, and Murray would later claim, with some relish, his relation to Sir James Murray, the first editor of the Oxford English Dictionary, a fifth cousin.

Miriam Murray's labor was slow, and Murray had to be induced, in part to make way for another woman's labor expected to be more difficult. Murray's belief that his birth led to his mother's physical problems was later to have devastating effects on him psychologically.

The young Murray had no local school to attend, until Bulby Bush Primary opened when he was eight. Its children were often barefoot. Many

269

of them, having been up working since before dawn, would fall asleep during lessons. Murray's parents were more lenient with regards to his farm work.

At the age of twelve, the poet had just started secondary schooling when his mother died, suddenly. She was thirty-five This tragedy had a delayed effect on Murray. He would not write about it directly for almost thirty years, when in Scotland. He later recounted recalling on the morning of his mother's funeral, as her cortege passed by, an old Aborigine by the roadside, bowing his head in acknowledgment. This provided an early example for Murray's dismissal of divisive polarities. Murray has posited this day as his "natal day" as a poet.

A few years later, in adolescence, Murray found himself castigated and victimized for his size by his peers, though, again, these experiences would not be featured directly in his work until forty years later. His suffering at this time, however, helped develop his empathy with outcasts, outsiders, the unofficial, the marginalized. In his last year at secondary school three teachers introduced him to poetry. He discovered an early fondness for the work of Gerard Manley Hopkins that would influence some of his later writing.

In 1957, the poet began attending Sydney University. At the Fisher library, he resolved to read all of its 2 million volumes. He claims to have "got through a good many of them" (Verse, No. 5, p. 162). At the university, to all accounts, he cut a remarkable figure, discoursing with Johnsonian wit on almost any subject, and capable of reading numerous languages. (He would later be able to read over twenty.) His relationship with the Academy was already problematical. He has called its effects those of "a large relegation machine" (The Paperbark Tree, p. 8), inimical to most students' reception of poetry.

Following a bout of depression and poverty the poet had to discontinue his formal studies in 1960, though he continued intermittently to frequent the campus until 1962. In that same year, after a spell of wandering, sleeping rough, and writing poems, Murray married Valerie Morelli, a

Swiss teacher, whom he met when she was acting as a costume mistress for a production of Faust. In 1963, despite having no formal degree, he so impressed the translation department of Australian National University that they employed him to translate western European languages on a wide variety of subjects, a job he undertook intermittently for four years.

In 1965, under the recommendation of A. D. Hope, The Ilex Tree appeared. A joint publication with Geoffrey Lehmann, the book was awarded the Grace Leven Prize, and garnered an invitation to Cardiff for Murray. In all, with his wife and family (the poet now had a daughter and a son, Christina and Daniel), he spent fourteen months in Europe, including a spell in Scotland. By 1969, he was again in Sydney, where he completed his degree in German and linguistics. By 1971, following the publication of his first solo book, The Weatherboard Cathedral in 1969, Murray decided to become a professional writer. In 1972 he was awarded a three-year writer's fellowship by the Australian Literature Board, and his third book, Poems Against Economics, appeared.

By any standards, Murray's next five years were prolific: not only did he serve as editor of Poetry Australia, but he published two further books of poems, Lunch and Counter Lunch and Ethnic Radio in 1974 and 1978 respectively, a book of selected poems, The Vernacular Republic, in 1976, and a book of essays, The Peasant Mandarin: Prose Pieces, in 1978. In that year, too, he also served as a writer in residence at the University of New England (Australia); 1980 saw him in Fiji, the United States, and Canada; that same year his experimental verse novel, told as a sonnet sequence, The Boys Who Stole the Funeral: A Novel Sequence, appeared and won the Grace Leven prize.

The 1980s were a time of great external success for Murray. Not only did he publish several new acclaimed collections, including The People's Otherworld (1983) and The Daylight Moon and Other Poems (1987), which all won prizes, but his books were now being published by British and American imprints: Carcanet brought out his Selected Poems in Britain in

1984; Persea of New York published *The Daylight Moon* in 1988. He also traveled widely, and held a residency at Stirling University, in Scotland. However, 1988 also marked the beginning of an eight-year depression, triggered by a meeting with a former pupil at his secondary school, in which repressed memories of his adolescence returned. As the poet himself put it in an interview in 1997, "Externally I had all these things, it's just that the past was there and the past, if it's not dealt with, comes back and insists on being dealt with" (Billen).

His depression lasted until 1996 when the poet almost died from a liver abscess. On recovery, his depression was gone. His illness also showed him that he wasn't, as he suspected, "the pariah of Australian poetry" on account of his forthright political and aesthetic views. (The poet has been identified with the political right.) The first telephone call inquiring as to his condition was from the Australian expatriate celebrity Clive James. Cards and messages of goodwill flooded in.

Despite his depression, Murray received poetic accolades and awards for work done throughout the 1990s. In 1992 he had been made a vice president of the Poetry Society of Great Britain; Stirling University had awarded him an honorary degree; in 1991 his *Collected Poems* had been published in Britain and New York, updated in 1994, and republished in an expanded edition in 1998, to coincide with the poet's sixtieth birthday. This same year saw publication of Murray's massive verse novel, the ten-thousand-line *Fredy Neptune*, which won the Queen's Gold Medal for poetry. It was followed in 1999 by his collection, *Conscious and Verbal*, the declaration by the hospital on his awakening from his coma during his near-fatal illness; and in 2000 by *Learning Human: Selected Prose*, a re-issued selected poems. In 1996, his provocatively titled *Subhuman Redneck Poems* had thrown down the gauntlet to those believed to be critical of Murray's self-identification with the white rural poor in Australia. It won the T. S. Eliot Prize in Britain for that year.

Murray has also been active as an essayist. His books of essays were collected in volumes such as *The Peasant Mandarin* and *The Paperbark Tree: Selected Prose* (1992) and contain major statements on his practice of poetry. His essays are also critical of the academy and of modernism. He largely blames both for alienating a formerly sizeable audience for poetry.

THE ILEX TREE

THE Ilex Tree, which appeared when Murray was just twenty-four, was a joint publication with Geoffrey Lehmann, who had been Murray's friend and fellow poet since their days at Sydney University, and encouraged him to write directly out of his rural background. The book's title was significant, and particularly to Murray, for several reasons. It came from a quote from Virgil's *Eclogues*, about two young men competing to make verses underneath a tree; the *Eclogues* themselves Murray found full of resonance for him, being about country people, as he put it at the time, "gradually losing their hold on the land and being pushed out by other interests." Murray's most notable contributions to *The Ilex Tree* quickly establish a tension between a rural world and that of the world beyond, of modernity. Some of its significant poems are set in the present of a troubled narrator, caught between the distant urban and his sense of rural belonging: "Though I myself run to the cities, I will forever / be coming back here to walk, knee deep in ferns, / up and away from this metropolitan century, to remember my ancestors … " he writes (*Collected Poems*, p. 5). Technically, Murray's contributions to the book are unshowy but well made, being mainly in blank verse or anapests. Their subject matter too is mainly unshowy and documentary. He commemorates relatives who lived and worked in the wilderness. A piece such as "The Widower in the Country," which calls to mind Robert Frost's "An Old Man's Winter Night," and is based on Murray's father, takes the form of a monologue spoken by the widower. Almost nothing happens, yet the verse's gravitas and tone of "a man speaking to men" is quietly convincing. "Driving Through Sawmill Towns," sparely written in free verse, is a four-part sequence, each part a vignette, describing the

LES MURRAY

small towns and their people from the driver's perspective. A line such as "a light going out in a window here has meaning" (*Collected Poems*, p. 11) conveys both the positive value of close-knit community, concern for neighbors, with the negative, a sometimes claustrophobic intimacy. "The half-heard radio / sings its song of sidewalks" (*Collected Poems*, p. 11) and reminds the reader that American culture is being elaborated here: a pavement in Australia is called a "footpath" (noted by James, p. 31). The inhabitants have yet to come into a full possession of their own culture. Silence—the silence of wilderness—encircles the poem. Indeed, the poems are full of silence, which Murray, in "Noonday Axeman," a monologue again inspired by his father, calls "a challenge," which "seems to others / to be waiting here for something beyond imagining" (*Collected Poems*, p. 4).

One of the volume's exceptional poems, "Spring Hail," however, leaps free of the dualities present elsewhere. The poem is set in an idealized past. A boy and his pony are caught during a hailstorm and take shelter in a shed. When the storm and its "beaded violence" ceases, they become "uneasy at the silence" and come out. The after-squall brilliance, the Edenic calm of the sunlight, the way the clouds have been "whirled away" are beautifully evoked. The boy and the pony walk out into the sun, and the boy sits contemplating the worms deep in the earth and the life around. Finally, his pony approaches him, and the poem ends:

It was time, high time, the highest and only time
to stand in the stirrups and shout out, blind with wind
for the height and clatter of ridges to be topped
and the racing downward after through the lands
of floating green and bridges and flickering trees.
It was time, as never again it was time
to pull the bridle up, so the racketing hooves
fell silent as we ascended from the hill
above the farms, far up to where the hail
formed and hung weightless in the upper air,
charting the birdless winds with silver roads
for us to follow and be utterly gone.

This is for spring and hail, that you may remember
a boy and a pony long ago who could fly.
(Collected Poems, pp. 9–10)

The poem has an air both of triumph and plangency: triumph in that the narrator can conjure such a reality through art; and plangency in its elegiacally being "for a boy long ago," and a pony that could fly. The poem's clean diction and bouncing anapestic rhythms endow the language with a nimbleness that is especially apt for the poem's closure. The refrain also changes subtly. Repeated four times, minor changes in its punctuation and phrasing convey different effects, and contribute to the elegiac tone.

The Ilex Tree marked an auspicious beginning and was greeted respectfully by reviewers. The early emergence of some of Murray's main themes here, a fidelity to place and ancestry, and the visionary, would be consolidated in his next book.

THE WEATHERBOARD CATHEDRAL

MURRAY's first solo book, *The Weatherboard Cathedral*, wittily hints in its title at the poet's father's shack as an unexpected locus for spirituality, and the volume includes "Evening Alone at Bunyah," a five-part sequence about the poet's relationship with his father and with Bunyah, his local area. The poet's father, Cecil, goes off to a dance, leaving his son, who only dances "on bits of paper" (*Collected Poems*, p. 12) to ponder his own memories of the house, of his father, and of the loved, intimately known landscape. As he puts it: "This country is my mind" (*Collected Poems*, p. 15). Like Patrick Kavanagh, who wrote "I have lived in important places, times / when great events were decided" (*Selected Poems*, 1996, p. 202) and who made lasting art in celebration of his own local landscape of Monaghan in Ireland, Murray begins to map out his own bucolic reality of Bunyah. It is a way of taking psychological possession. The matter of Bunyah is to be a constant concern and preoccupation. A sense of uncertainty prevails in the sequence, as if the poet is still unsure of his attitude to "home," and it is mainly interesting for

272

its documentary detail, and witty understated depiction of the poet's relationship with his father.

Elsewhere, the notion of catharsis, of safety valves for dangerous human energies, is a frequent motif in these poems, even when the realities may be regarded as horrific. Murray's poem, "Blood," written in graceful quatrains unsettlingly at odds with the poem's brutal subject matter, deals with the slaughtering of a pig. It is interesting to compare the poem with a similar account by the Orkney poet Edwin Muir, whom Murray began reading in the early 1960s. Writing in his *An Autobiography* (Saint Paul, 1990, pp. 36–37), Muir spares no detail in his depiction of the horror of a pig with its throat cut. His account presents the event with eerie starkness, from a child's point of view, without justification or symbolic meaning but, as it were, in absolute terms of life and death. In Murray's poem the slaughter is recounted more matter-of-factly. Having had its throat cut:

... our beast
flees straight downfield, choked in his pumping gush
that feeds the earth, and drags him to his knees—
Bleed, Georgie, pump! And with a long-legged rush

my cousin is beside the thing he killed
and pommels it, and lifts it to the sun:
I should have knocked him out, poor little bloke.
It gets the blood out if you let them run.
                              (*Collected Poems*, pp. 20–21)

The pig, however, is emblematic of the necessary blood sacrifice which "frees / sun, fence and hill, each to its holy place." The farmer's knife is described as "priestly."

A related poem, "The Abomination," portrays the author out killing rabbits. He tosses one, suddenly, presumed to be dead, into a fire smoldering among tree roots:

Afterwards, I tramped the smoking crust
heavily in on fire, stench and beast
to seal them darkly under with my fear
and all the things my sacrifice might mean,
so hastily performed past all repair.
                              (*Collected Poems*, p. 22)

Again, there is the notion of sacrifice. People are inhabited by often- murderous energies that they may not understand or control. The poet, with considerable candor, risks telling things his audience may find distasteful. It is a measure of the seriousness of his purpose. In another piece, "The Incendiary Method," to "clean out the mind" the poem's narrator puts a match to a paperbark tree in the swamps, and watches it "howl up / a tower of flame" (*Collected Poems*, p. 28). Murray's wrestling with such fundamentals as the roots of violence, which prefigured later work, were not, however, to prevent him writing delicately when occasion presented. "Once in a Lifetime, Snow" is a marvelous evocation of an Australian snowfall; here, the landscape itself offers catharsis from without, and the poem is a graceful hymn of astonishment, lightfooted and nimble in its loosely rhymed quatrains.

In this volume too appeared a theme which would become important to Murray: the value of individuality over bureaucracy and imposed conformity, as people indulge their passions in what he calls "the groove" (*Paperbark Tree*, p. 352): any activity pursued irrespective of its relevance to fashion. In the "Canberra Remnant," he imagines, late at night:

only a few
souls still awake

to polish a bead,
to turn a page,
to label a fly
or a golden age,

in a thousand redeeming
projects they
keep safe from the Government
of the day.
                              (*Collected Poems*, p. 36)

It was a theme which would develop a strong satirical streak in the poet's later work.

POEMS AGAINST ECONOMICS

IN mid-1972, *Poems against Economics* appeared. The book takes its title partly from the difficulties Murray had been facing financially. In

LES MURRAY

1971 he had made the difficult decision to try and make a living full time from his writing. In the new volume, Murray made his first mention of Boeotia. Most of civilization, he has written in his essay "On Sitting Back and Thinking of Porter's Boeotia," exists as a dialectic between the ancient, nurturing, bucolic reality of the region of Boeotia, and the city state of Athens. Murray's essay refers to and was prompted by Peter Porter's poem "On First Looking into Chapman's Hesiod." Peter Porter is an Australian expatriate who moved to London in the 1960s and is well known for his urbane, witty verse. Hesiod, author of *Works and Days*, was a Boeotian poet, claims Murray, whose influence can be traced in poets as recent as William Wordsworth and Frost. Porter compares the rural world with his own preference, "The permanently upright city where / Speech is nature and plants conceive in pots" (*New Oxford Book of Australian Verse*, 1991, p. 262). The tension between an Athenian outlook and a Boeotian demonstrate, as Murray has indicated:

> ... two contrasting models of civilisation between which Western man has vacillated; he has now drawn the rest of mankind into the quarrel, and resolving this tension may be the most urgent task facing the world in modern times. In the past, Athens, the urbanizing, fashion-conscious principle removed from and usually insensitive to natural, cyclic views of the world, has won out time and again. ...
>
> (*Paperback Tree*, p. 57)

Murray proposes that Australian poetry, and certainly his own, is soundly Boeotian in outlook: celebratory, commemorative, family oriented, and profoundly rural. This outlook, albeit with complications, becomes more noticeable in the poet's work from this point on.

Boeotian values are richly celebrated in "Toward the Imminent Days," an epithalamium for Geoffrey and Sally Lehmann. Written primarily in loose-limbed free verse, the poet wittily celebrates:

Midmorning, September, and red tractors climb
on a landscape wide as all forgiveness. Clouds
in the west horizon, parrots twinkling down

on Leary's oats, on Stewarts' upturned field—
good friends are blood relations that you choose.
(*Collected Poems*, p. 37)

Readers in the Northern Hemisphere must recall that September, associated in a Western literary tradition with autumn, is spring in Australia. Parrots twinkle down, not pigeons, yet this touch of exoticism to a Western reader is brought up short by the Irish and Scottish surnames of the farmers who own the fields: a reminder of a Celtic diaspora which Murray often refers to and of which he is a part. Later in the poem, home is sanctuary:

In my aunt's house, the milk jug's beaded crochet cover
tickles the ear. We've eaten boiled things with butter.
Pie spiced like islands, dissolving in cream, is now
dissolving in us. We've reached the teapot of calm.

The table we sit at is fashioned of three immense
beech boards out of England. The minute width of the years
have been refined in the wood by daughters' daughters.
In the year of Nelson, I notice, the winter was mild.

But our talk is cattle and cricket. My quiet uncle
has spent the whole forenoon sailing a stump-ridden field
of blady-grass and Pleistocene clay never ploughed
since the world's beginning.
(*Collected Poems*, p. 39)

Murray's wit and close observation is here everyone on display, from the milk jug's cover tickling the ear as the aunt—presumably—pours the milk out, to the notion of the pie and teapot as destinations. There is hyperbole, too, though to make a point: the poet imagines he can see by the narrow grain of the table's wood the mild winter "the year of Nelson"—presumably 1805, that of the Battle of Trafalgar—but rapidly halts such flights of imagination in the face of talk of "cattle and cricket," before rapidly reminding readers that he is writing in a landscape "never ploughed / since the world's beginning."

The volume closes with Murray's major hymn to cows, "Walking to the Cattle Place." Numbered one to fifteen, it is subtitled "A MEDITATION"

LES MURRAY

and carries an epigraph from Rabindranath Tagore: "At once I came into a world wherein I recovered my full being" (*Collected Poems*, p. 55). Prompted by Murray's discovery that the oldest word in Indo-European languages is "cow" and that the cow is prominent in both the ancestral Indo-European and Bantu cultures, the poem, obscure in parts, takes place over a single day in which the poet considers the ancient relationship between cattle and humans. Murray claims his ambition is "to speak the names of all the humble"; the poem begins with Sanskrit names for cows, and proceeds to examine the cow in culture. Linguistically virtuosic, some of its liveliest moments occur, as often with Murray, when the material is anchored in his home soil. Sections 2 and 3 are rich with local anecdote, and the verse technique is flexible, allowing for a range of effects: in section 3, for instance, the poet "climbs through into [his] thought" and watches the cows. The verse is an effective shorthand for the description:

I go on being harmless
and some graze closer, gradually. It is like watching
an emergence. Persons.

(*Collected Poems*, p. 58)

The single word sentence "Persons" is like the sudden focusing of a lens, clarifying the cow's emergence into their individuality. In section 4, "The Artery," Murray contemplates the brutal slaughter of cattle as having been the practice, "beyond the great ice, that launched us"; this is also a reference to the Norse mythical cow Audhumla, said to have licked men and beasts as they stood frozen in primordial ice and brought them to life; the poet asks: "What silk will tie this artery of knowledge?" (*Collected Poems*, p. 61). The sequence, however, is many toned: "The Boeotian Count" confirms the way farmers have of knowing most of their cattle as individuals: the section is an exhilarating naming of a farm's cattle, individual by individual, many of them found in Murray's own father's herd or in that of his grandfather; aurally delightful, it confirms what Murray identifies as the Boeotian tendency to list and name.

LUNCH AND COUNTER LUNCH

MURRAY was, by now, firmly established as one of Australia's most significant young poets. At thirty-six, his age at the appearance of *Lunch and Counter Lunch*, he had been identified as conservative in both sensibility and literary technique, though his was a conservatism, as David Malouf pointed out, "very critical, complex, and flexible," and perhaps, in the increasingly liberal intellectual climate of Australia at that time, "the most way-out form of radicalism" (Malouf, pp. 70–72). Among the book's riches is "The Broad Bean Sermon," one of five poems recommended to readers new to Murray by Peter Porter. The poem's title is wittily subversive, for this is a sermon advising not restriction, but abundance. Murray is often at his best when praising. The poem begins:

Beanstalks, in any breeze, are a slack church parade
without belief, saying trespass against us, in unison ...

(*Collected Poems*, p. 112)

The reference is to the Catholic form of the Our Father: "forgive us our trespasses as we forgive those who trespass against us"; having amusingly humanised the stalks as a church parade, yet one without belief and therefore unconcerned about transgression against them, Murray continues the conceit:

Upright with water like men, square in stem-section
they grow to great lengths, drink rain, keel over all ways,
kink down and grow up afresh, with proffered new greenstuff.

(*Collected Poems*, p. 112)

The straggling verdancy of the stalks, with the pun on "go to great lengths" which would be effort on the part of men, but here is biological ease, and the implicit comedy of their drunken keeling "over all ways" is beautifully achieved; rather than the more predictable "foliage," "greenstuff," in its vernacular casualness, seems exactly right, the f sound repeating as it does that in "proffered" and "afresh," confirming them. The beans themselves are symbolic not just of ideas, they are "edible meanings," "templates for subtly broad grins," "unique caught expressions"; no sooner has the narrator picked them than more appear in their place.

Elsewhere in the volume Murray both exemplifies and extends the notion of plurality suggested in this poem. His vignette "Folklore," spoken by an unnamed narrator, is the remarkable account of how a cord attached to a skeleton in a bar to the undersprings in the bed of the honeymoon suite above, dances, quivers, or jiggles according to the activity of the newlyweds. Anecdotally vivid, the poem is interesting also for the way the poet notates the hesitations implicit in the speaker, who cuts off his own ponderings on whether a "larger cord" goes up similarly to the stars, with a curt: "but I doubt it / I mean / but then I'm no dancer. / Besides that, there's meatwork and mines" (*Collected Poems*, p. 80). A whole unspoken world is hinted at, brought abruptly to a halt by the flat closure.

This hint at a complexity where the conventionally minded would not expect it is taken further in a poem in "The Police: Seven Voices," a series of seven monologues spoken by the Law. Country people of Murray's background in Australia are traditionally suspicious of police. A number of the monologues deal in police brutality. One of the series' strongest poems, however, "The Breach," is spoken by Special Sergeant Harry Ware, the founder and first Officer-in-Charge of the New South Wales Police Cliff Rescue Squad (*Vernacular Republic*, 1982, p. 216). In the poem Ware is faced with a man who has run amok and injured three people. Psychologically acute, the policeman explicates a philosophy of law and order, while preparing to enter "that house opposite." The poem begins:

I am a policeman
it is easier to make me seem an oaf
than to handle the truth

(*Collected Poems*, p. 86)

The complexity of the truth, exemplified by his own resistance to the overly simple, is a recurring theme in Murray. He is the great resister of group opinion.

ETHNIC RADIO

DURING the writing of *Ethnic Radio*, Murray was able to buy back, as commemorated in the plangent little poem "Laconics: The Forty Acres," written in 1975, part of the farm from which his father had been evicted, paradoxically by Murray's cousin. Murray's father had been kept in subservience by his own father, who omitted to leave him the family farm; it was part of a cycle of ill feeling that may have stemmed from the death of one of Murray's uncles. The purchase was to have profound ramifications for the development of Murray's art. While he had always professed Bunyah as his spiritual home, having installed his father in a weatherboard house on the family's ancestral land, the area would become more significant in his writing, a spiritual base from which he examined contemporaneity. "If Bunyah is a fillet / this paddock is the eye," he wrote (*Collected Poems*, p. 128).

Murray's eye roved over numerous subjects in *Ethnic Radio*. His poem "Cowyard Gates" recounts his visiting the family's old house, now a ruin, and other pieces explicitly celebrate Murray's Scots-Gaelic ancestry. In "Sydney and the Bush," however, Murray examines the antipathy between Australia's largest city, with a population of some 3 million, and rural Australia. The poem is deftly written in ballad stanza, and contrasts the early amicable relationship with the present:

When Sydney and the bush meet now
there is antipathy
and fashionable suburbs float
at night, far out at sea.

(*Collected Poems*, p. 124)

The adjective "fashionable" and the cadence of that line deftly echoes Auden's "fashionable madmen," and the poem's central point is reinforced when the last stanza drops the rhyme prevalent in abcb pattern throughout; the resultant aural discord confirms that explicated in the poem.

The volume is also notable for containing "The Buladelah-Taree Song Cycle," Murray's most extensive borrowing from Aboriginal culture. The poet defended himself against charges of cultural appropriation as follows:

LES MURRAY

It will be a tragedy if the normal processes of artistic borrowing and influences, by which any culture makes part of its contribution to the conversation of mankind, are frozen in the Aboriginal case by what are really the manoeuverings of a battle for political power within the white society of our country, or by tactical use of Third World rhetoric by jealous artists trying to damage each other professionally.

(*Paperbark Tree*, p. 71)

Based upon the *Wonguri-Mandjikai Song Cycle of the Moon Bone* translated by Ronald M. Berndt, which, Murray has said, "may well be the greatest poem ever composed in Australia" (*Paperbark Tree*, p. 90), Murray's poem is set in thirteen sections, like its model, and tracks the annual return for holidays of people to their rural backgrounds, in a long free verse line reminiscent of Hopkins or Whitman: "It is the season of the Long Narrow City; it has crossed the Myall, it has entered the North Coast, / That big stunning snake ..." The "long narrow city" is a kenning for holiday traffic; Murray then wittily converts the twentieth-century cars into a natural symbol. The piece is an exhilarating mix of poetic catalogue and action. The Aboriginal model repeatedly refers to "The place of the Dugong" (*Paperbark Tree*, p. 91; the complete text of this poem may be found in *New Oxford Book of Australian Verse*, pp. 239–246); Murray writes of "the place of The Big Flood that Time." Similarly, the original is full of observations of other creatures, all viewed in a non-homocentric light, which Murray echoes, and which prefigure importantly some aspects of his later work. Section 8 of the original features observations concerning leeches; Murray's, observations on mosquitoes, and the delicacy of his attention is apparent where ibis "discover titbits kept for them under cowmanure lids, small slow things" (*Collected Poems*, p. 144); any country child will recall how grubs and worms congregate under cowpats. Murray's sequence finishes with a hymn to the constellations, watched by the people at their business below them: "The stars of the holiday step out all over the sky. / People look up at them, out of their caravan doors and their campsites" (*Collected Poems*, p. 146). Murray's poem transposes the stylistic techniques of its model, and something of its sensibility, in act of homage both to his own and to the older culture.

Another outstanding poem in this collection is "The Future." It begins at what can be a dangerous level for a poem, that of statement: "There is nothing about it. Much science fiction is set there / but is not about it" (*Collected Poems,* p. 154). In one of his favorite techniques, the poet takes a subject and examines it from numerous angles. The gravity of this poem's tone and the unexpectedness of its perceptions give it an air of awe which sets it apart from a good deal of Murray's other work. The poem's subject is the phenomenon of time. It is radiant with it, not hectoring; its quietness engages the reader in a mystery in which everyone is implicated; Murray imagines:

A day to which all our portraits,
ideals, revolutions, denim and deshabille
are quaintly heart rending. To see those people is impossible,
to greet them, mawkish. Nonetheless, I begin:
"When I was alive—"

and I am turned around
to find myself looking at a cheerful picnic party,
the women decently legless, in muslin and gloves,
the men in beards and weskits, with the long
cheroots and duck trousers of the better sort,
relaxing on a stone verandah. Ceylon, or Sydney.
And as I look, I know they are utterly gone,
each one on his day, with pillow, small bottles, mist,
with all the futures they dreamed or dealt in, going
down to that engulfment everything approaches;
with the man on the tree, they have vanished into the Future.

(*Collected Poems*, p. 155)

Contemplating the future, the poem's narrator is "turned around" to find himself contemplating people at a picnic party who had existed, but are gone: not, however, into the past, but as Christ himself, into "the Future." It is interesting to note that in Murray's Catholic cosmogony, everything is future.

THE PEOPLE'S OTHERWORLD

MURRAY had been baptized a Catholic, as his wife already was, in 1963. Twenty years later,

The People's Otherworld became the first of his commercial collections to be dedicated "To the glory of God." The book's title is taken from the closing line of the centerpiece of the volume, "Three Poems in Memory of My Mother, Miriam Murray née Arnall." The poet's mother died in tragic circumstances, of complications from a miscarriage, when he was twelve. There was doubt as to whether the doctor involved acted negligently in refusing to send an ambulance for the stricken woman. By the time she reached the hospital it was too late; after rallying briefly, she died. Murray's poem was written while he was in Scotland in 1981. Despite the sensitivity of its subject matter for the author, it is a tour de force, powerfully plain and spare. The poem is in three sections: "Weights" and "Midsummer Ice" are both memories of the poet's mother when alive; "The Steel," a 175-line poem, deals with the situation which caused her death, and its aftershock on the poet and his father. The "steel" of the poem's title is, variously, the instrument with which Murray believed he was induced, the long traditions of the Murray family, and what may be equated with determination or, perhaps, bitterness. Deeply autobiographical, with a narrative impetus, the poem is structured in three-, four-, and occasionally five-line stanzas in no particular pattern; irregular rhyme endows the verse with an aural cohesion. The poet soliloquizes, and addresses and questions his mother, the doctor, and his never-to-be born sibling. The verse is powerfully affecting, as the poet's questions are now unanswerable. The poem finally contrasts his mother's being just, in allowing his induction so as to make way for a presumed more difficult birth in a small hospital, with his father's desire for justice from his dead father, who omitted to leave him the family farm, and had him work as a hired hand. A mix of registers, from the vernacular to the elevated, the poem ends powerfully:

> The poor man's anger is a prayer
> for equities Time cannot hold

> and steel grows from our mother's grace.
> Justice is the people's otherworld.

> (*Collected Poems*, p. 191)

Justice, for "the people," is unattainable in this world. The "otherworld," which, in Murray's Catholic outlook, can be taken as afterlife, is the people's justice. This, however, does not serve to palliate the pain evident in the poem's closure; for many readers, indeed, the poem's closure may indicate that justice is unattainable absolutely.

Contrasting with this grievous poem are a number of pieces in which the expansive side of Murray's sensibility holds sway. One of these is "Quintets for Robert Morley," a paean to the fat. Murray was once mistaken for Morley, a well-known English actor of the 1950s and 1960s, at an airport. In "Quintets" Murray wittily credits the fat with inventing civilization, leisure, the self, fertility, some theology (divine feasting, and, with lovely irony, Unmoved Movers), and self-deprecation. Gracefully written in five-line stanzas, the poem has a relaxed expansiveness typical of Murray at his abundant best. It finishes:

> So much climbing, on a spherical world;
> had Newton not been a mere beginner at gravity
> he might have asked how the apple got up there
> in the first place. And so might have discerned
> an ampler physics.

> (*Collected Poems*, p. 177)

The little pun on "gravity" indicates the narrator's seriousness behind his light-hearted front; levity of tone, he implies, is not shallowness. The "ampler physics," as well as being a pun on body size, is also an acerbic reference to the Cartesian mindset which Newtonian physics helped usher in, with its attendant qualities of the veneration of logic and empiricism, among others. Murray implies its limitations as a paradigm. He is famously dismissive of the Enlightenment, which apotheosized such analytical qualities, endorsing Goya's observation that the sleep of reason produces monsters.

The expansive note continues in what might be Murray's *Ars Poetica*, "The Quality of Sprawl." Sprawl is the permanent stepper-over of boundaries, a good-humored, sometimes intransigent refusal of convention. It is not necessarily rebellion, but the fulfilling of its own nature. The poem defines the quality in a catalogue of witty statements, ending:

Sprawl leans on things. It is loose-limbed in its mind.
Reprimanded and dismissed
it listens with a grin and one boot up on the rail
of possibility. It may have to leave the Earth.
Being roughly Christian, it scratches the other cheek
and thinks it unlikely. Though people have been shot
 for sprawl.

(*Collected Poems*, p. 184)

There is a lovely ambiguity in the "roughly," which could mean either "approximately" or "coarsely," and the sudden seriousness of tone at the poem's closure is typical of Murray. It raises one of his fundamental themes, linking to early poems such as "The Canberra Remnant" and prefiguring later poems: the persistence, and likely fate, of individuality held in the face of group opinion.

THE DAYLIGHT MOON

ONE of the constants in Murray's work has been the importance to him of Bunyah, the locus of many of the values asserted in his poetry. Poetry does not appear in a vacuum; Murray felt that he had to begin living a life more closely connected to the roots of his art. On the last day of 1985 the poet with his family returned to the area of his birth, an event which bears rich fruit in *The Daylight Moon*, and would have future complications. The volume is generally a vigorous anecdotal celebration and commemoration of Murray's kinsfolk and landscape. Relaxed and intimate, the poems's subject matter is compelling, and applicable to rural communities in the West, not just in Australia. They illustrate what Wordsworth meant when he intimated that rural environments show people at their most fundamental. Many of the poems, too, are fascinating for narrative reasons. "Joker as Told" is a comic and touching story about a little horse with a liking for coming indoors. The poem contains lively incidentals:

He liked to get in the house.
Walk in, and you were liable
to find him in the kitchen
dribbling over the table
with a heap behind him

(*Collected Poems*, p. 270)

Gelded, "he couldn't grow up to be a / full horse, and he wouldn't be a slave one" (*Collected Poems*, p. 271). The narrator concludes that the little horse was looking for "his foalhood and ours, when we played. / He was looking for the Kingdom of God." The poem bears an interesting relationship to "Spring Hail" in Murray's first book, in which boy and pony achieve transcendence. "Joker as Told" instead takes its power from its lack of transcendence. While the closure courts sentimentality, it is made more convincing by the straightforward tone of the rest of the poem.

"Letters to the Winner," meanwhile, demonstrates Murray's mastery of vernacular speech. A neighbor wins "the special lottery" (*Collected Poems*, p. 243) equivalent to half a century of his earnings as a small farmer. Soon, he begins receiving begging letters in sackfuls. One rainy day, he finally reads them, and the poet expertly captures the tone of the letters in his quotes from them, a mix of pathos and bathos:

You sound like a lovely big boy we could have such
 times
her's my photoe Doll Im wearing my birthday swim-
 suit
with the right man I would share this infallible system.

(*Collected Poems*, p. 243)

A whole world of human misery and poverty is revealed, and finally the winner's

... head throbbed as if busting with a soundless shout
of immemorial sobbed invective *God-forsaken, God-*
 forsakin
as he stopped reading, and sat blackened in his riches.

(*Collected Poems*, p.244)

Individual good fortune is of dubious value in the small community. Unwittingly, the small farmer becomes a victim of sorts. Relative riches are shown to be an isolating poverty in this context.

LES MURRAY

Pieces such as "The Young Woman Visitor" and "The Grandmother's Story" show the poet consolidating his command of the dramatic monologue. Both are spoken by women, though men form their subject matter, and the pieces are acutely observed. "The Young Woman Visitor" is touching in its particulars. An old farmer boasts continuously of his achievements to the young women narrator of the poem. He appears to be unmarried for, though he claims to have been best at everything, and to have had the best of everything—dog, cattle, crops—a wife is conspicuously absent. In its delineation of a world of overcompensation for unfulfillment, the poem achieves a plangency all the more powerful for being understated. The imagination of the reader is engaged; the poet doesn't express opinion, or preach. A world is presented.

"The Grandmother's Story" is similarly striking. It is a monologue by the old woman, and from the same tradition as a poem such as Frost's "The Code," in its observation of country manners. As Murray had earlier written in "Walking to the Cattle Place," "there is no life more global than a village" (*Collected Poems*, p. 57). Human beings have a personal history there, with all that that implies about knowledge of their behavior. The poem begins:

Just a few times in your life, you speak
those strange words. Or they speak themselves
out of you, before you can bite your tongue.
They are there, like a dream. You're not sure you've
  spoken
but you see them hit the other person
like a stone into floodwater.
(Collected Poems, p. 272)

The male character, Ted Quarrie, pinches her at a show, so she hits him and, albeit improbably, knocks him out. When he curses her upon consciousness, she says "those strange words." Quarrie bears a grudge which lasts for years, and one night threatens her when she's sick in bed with a revolver. She recalls: "Poor thing. I nearly laughed. / Of course, I might have been shot for that." The gun, retrieved from the man by the woman's son, who forces him to hand it over in public, is dropped down inside the kitchen wall of her home; the poem ends: "It's still rusting

there, I fancy" (*Collected Poems*, p. 273). The suggestiveness of this image is far more powerful than any direct explication. The gun, which may symbolize masculine aggression, perhaps something necessary in a difficult environment, rusts away, an outdated mode, yet one which has a certain ambiguous protectiveness, having been dropped there in the kitchen walling by the woman's "boys" (*Collected Poems*, p. 273).

Such poems are the highlight of this collection. Murray's future work, however, would mark considerable advances in his range.

DOG FOX FIELD

MURRAY'S return to Bunyah, though it produced the various celebrations of *The Daylight Moon*, was not without its problems. The poems in *Dog Fox Field* are not those of a poet settling to write out of a rural idyll. Frequently satirical and combative in tone, they take their title from an epigraph from the Judgement at Nuremberg: "The test for feeblemindedness was they had to make up a sentence using the words dog, fox, and field" (*Collected Poems*, p. 332). The fourth of Murray's five children, Alexander, is autistic, and when Murray checked, the boy couldn't pass this test. Murray's own mental stress at the time, according to the poet's biographer, Peter F. Alexander, had drawn him closer to his autistic son. While it can be misleading to draw artistic conclusions from a poet's biographical details, the poet's stress had been caused by a clinical depression: the return to Bunyah had begun to release buried memories of the Murray's adolescence which would play a significant part in future work. A few of the poems, "The Past Ever Present" and "The Torturer's Apprenticeship," for example, make glancing reference to the more personal themes which would surface in his next but one collection. The poet is not yet prepared, or perhaps able, to couch these poems in the first person. In "The Past Ever Present" he writes:

If love is always an awarded thing
some have cursed the judging and screamed off down

LES MURRAY

old roads
and all that they killed were the song they couldn't
  sing.

(*Collected Poems*, p. 349)

The poem can reasonably be read as referring to Murray's own experiences; the phrase "old roads" may be taken not only literally but as meaning "the usual psychological safety valves," and the final line implies blocked impulse transferred to violence against others, in Murray's case, animals he shot with his rifle.

Additionally, Murray was, by now, the pre-eminent Australian poet, and any such figure has literary enemies. The response to his poem "The Fall of Aphrodite Street," which appeared first in the *London Review of Books* in 1987, shows how Murray's detractors misunderstood and misread his work. The poem charts the background to a generation blighted by AIDS:

For just one generation
the plateglass turned to air—
when you look for that generation
half of it isn't there.

(*Collected Poems*, p. 307)

Following the poem's appearance, in letters to the *LRB* Murray was castigated and denounced by another Australian poet for slandering homosexuals. A close reading of the poem, however, fails to support this accusation:

God help the millions that street killed
and those it sickened too,
when it was built past every house
and often bulldozed through.

(*Collected Poems*, p. 308)

Murray's target, in fact, is "an ugliness of spirit" which has been taught to see "everything outstanding" as "knobs on a skin machine." He castigates the beliefs, not the believers.

While, overall, the tone of the book can seem harsh and antagonistic, a handful of poems escape Murray's satirical compulsion. "The Emerald Dove" recounts how an emerald dove being chased by a sparrowhawk entered an open sash window of the poet's house. The sparrowhawk, on realizing it is indoors, escapes by the window

it entered by; the dove, however, is found "tracked down in a farther room, / clinging to a bedhead." Gorgeously described as "barefoot in silks / like a prince of Sukhothai," it is "modest-sized as a writing hand," "an emerald Levite." The comparison of a dove to "a writing hand" imbues it with an authorly significance and implications of peace-giving; as an "emerald Levite" it is an exemplar of holiness, its emerald emphasizing not just the freshness of green but a gemlike perdurability (*Collected Poems*, pp. 310–311). In his subsequent book, Murray, as if weary of his satirical themes, would turn to nature for refreshment.

TRANSLATIONS OF THE NATURAL WORLD

AFTER *Dog Fox Field*, Murray perhaps instinctively felt he needed another subject. Satire is an exhaustingly human activity. It also emotionally binds the satirist to his or her resented subject matter. And it makes one enemies. Perhaps, as Robert Frost once intimated, ultimately praise is best: "I should hate," he wrote in a notebook in 1935, "to spend the only life I was going to have here in being annoyed with the time I happened to live in" (*Robert Frost: A Life*, Jay Parini, London, p. 291).

In *Translations of the Natural World*, the creatures' otherworld provided Murray with a fresh subject. The poet had always written about animals, frequently domesticated ones: the pony in "Spring Hail" in his first book, for instance, and the pig being slaughtered in "Blood" in his second. "Walking to the Cattle Place," his great hymn to cows, implicitly emphasizes the interdependence between humankind and cows; human interests form the focus of such poems.

In *The Daylight Moon* Murray had published the poem "Bats' Ultrasound" (p. 36), which would prove a precursor for the sequence of forty poems which comprise Translations. (Indeed, Murray would add it to his sequence in his *Collected Poems*.) The poem finishes with a curiously convincing stanza in bat speech:

ah, eyrie-ire; aero hour, eh?
O'er our ur-area (our era aye

281

ere your raw row) we air our array,
err, yaw, row wry—aura our orrery,
our eerie ü our ray, our arrow.

A rare ear, our aery Yahweh.
                    (*Collected Poems*, p. 368)

Developed from two englynion—an englynion is
a Welsh stanza form—which Murray had come
across on a visit to Wales, the speech has a
strange colloquial appeal. The repetition of r
consonants and narrow and broad vowels
strangely mimics the imagined ultrasound of the
bats, as well as making a rudimentary sense: the
phrase "eyrie-ire," for instance, may be considered a shorthand for the bats' frustration at being
at roost, in the "eyrie," or nest; they quiz one
another with the interrogative "aero hour, eh?";
that is, time for flight. The "aye," is Scots for
"yes" or "always," for example. Here for the first
time Murray attempts to translate the otherness
of nature into a humanly comprehensible language. He adopts a tradition rising from Anglo-
Saxon riddles: the creatures themselves tend to
speak in these poems. However, their voice is far
from cozily human. These are indeed translations, risky ones, in that, first, they don't court
human self-interest and, second, they can seem
obscure, despite being undoubtedly impressive as
language. Translations' "Goose to Donkey," with
its waddling amiableness, represents the bestiary
at its most approachable:

My big friend, I bow help;
I bow Get up, big friend:
let me land-swim again beside your clicky feet,
don't sleep flat with dried wet in your holes.
                    (*Collected Poems*, p. 386)

This has a beguiling simplicity: the goose
converts walking into terms of motion it can
understand: "land-swim"; wet dung becomes
"dried wet"; the poem beautifully conveys the innocent incomprehension of the goose to the "big
friend's" supine state—perhaps the Donkey is ill,
or has died.

   One of *Translations'* other domestic poems,
"Pigs," and a poem later added, "The Cows on
Killing Day," also comprise the most accessible
of the sequence, almost as if their proximity to

humanity had "civilized" their otherness. Here
are the pigs:

Us all on sore cement was we.

               ...

We nosed up good rank in the tunnelled bush.
Us all fuckers then. And Big, huh? Tusked
the balls-biting dog and gutsed him wet.
                    (*Collected Poems*, p. 381)

This has a vivid earthiness; it is pure id, from the
comic vigor of "fuckers" to the colloquial interrogative "huh?" The garbled syntax of the first
line quoted lends the pigs' utterance an air of
confusion and pathos in keeping with their situation. The verbalization of nouns in "tusked" and
"gutsed," with their corresponding u vowels
emphasize the briskness of the pigs' actions.
There is no individual in this world; the collective, "we" and "us," is the individual. "The Cows
on Killing Day," originally from Dog Fox Field
but later added to this sequence, in part continues
this: "All me" is the collective for "cows." This
terrifying poem arguably marks a considerable
extension of sensibility on the poet's part since
his poem "Blood" in *The Weatherboard Cathedral*. It describes from the point of view of the
herd the slaughter of a cow "old and sore-boned,
little milk in that me now" (*Collected Poems*, p.
382); interestingly, the construction "that me,"
with its sense of identification with others, avoids
the same-species factionalism which may lead to
mobs and their victims in the human world. The
old cow is separated in the yard from the herd,
and shot. The narration continues:

All me come running. It's like the Hot Part of the sky
that's hard to look at, this that now happens behind
  wood
in the raw yard. A shining leaf, like off the bitter gum
  tree
is with the human. It works in the neck of me
and the terrible floods out, swamped and frothy. All
  me make the Roar,
some leaping stiff-kneed, trying to horn that worst
  horror.
The wolf-at-the-calves is the bull human. Horn the

bull human!

(*Collected Poems*, p. 382)

The sun becomes "the Hot Part of the sky"; the knife is "a shining leaf" which doesn't "cut" but, terrifyingly, "works"; blood is "the terrible." The poem is a charting of genuine horror, full of projected compassion.

Poetry frequently extends human perceptions. It either explicates what one already knows but hadn't realized one did, or introduces one to wholly new ways of being. Many of the poems in this remarkable sequence—which deals with grass, echidnas, cuttlefish, the snake's heat organ, among others—attempt the latter. Unexpected verbs and nouns, and dislocation of tenses and unusual syntax endeavor to jolt the reader out of habitual perceptions. "Eagle Pair" opens: "We shell down on the sleeping-branch. All night / the limitless Up digests its meats of light" (*Collected Poems*, p. 368). The perception of the birds is to translate everything into terms which they understand: they don't "land," but "shell down"; the sky is "the limitless Up," which is seen as a predator digesting day during the dark. "I am lived. I am died" (*Collected Poems*, p. 371), the cockspur bush announces, vaguely reminiscent of a child still learning the nature of tenses, yet the odd construction conveys the notion of the cyclical biology of the plant.

For all its predominant lack of anthropomorphism, the collection closed with a return to the human. The final poem, "Crankshaft," takes readers back again to, and comprises a catalogue of dwellings in Murray's area, and their related stories. It prepared the way for *Subhuman Redneck Poems*, rather unfairly considered one of Murray's most contentious books.

SUBHUMAN REDNECK POEMS

PROVOCATIVELY titled, when it was published in Australia the cover of this collection showed a photograph of the poet's father, Cecil, holding a fiddle. The book contains an elegy for his father, plainly written, entitled "The Last Hellos." It may be seen as a companion piece to the elegy for the poet's mother, and is similarly affecting,

charting as it does the old man's last days before his death from a brain tumor in 1995. It concludes:

Snobs mind us off religion
nowdays, if they can.
Fuck thém. I wish you God.

(*Collected Poems*, p. 450)

Murray's decision to make even an elegy, at some level, a response against perceived relegation, drew opprobrium. The volume's satires were generally not well received, and to some extent the book's reputation was overshadowed by them. One Australian academic dismissed at least one of the poems as "vile." A close reading, however, will diminish the importance of the satires in the volume as a whole, and Murray himself later appeared to disregard them.

Such satirical vehemence in the verse was a new development. Also new was Murray's attitude in regard to himself and his size. Previously, the poet had seldom written so personally. In "Quintets for Robert Morley," his size produced an attitude of liberal largesse, laced with wit and heavily breathing tolerance. Here, however, it's treated in a disparate trio of poems, full of pain, in which the poet recounts aspects of his adolescence. A fat teenager—he has said that, of the two categories of fatness, those born to it, and those who achieve it, he belongs to the first—he suffered greatly from the taunts of his contemporaries, especially girls, who perhaps sensed his sexual neurosis, which may have been linked to his suspicion that his birth may, at some level, have been responsible for his mother's death. This is detailed in "On Home Beaches" from "The Sand Coast Sonnets," "The Head Spider," and "Burning Want." The latter opens:

From just on puberty, I lived in funeral:
mother dead of miscarriage, father trying to be dead,
we'd boil sweat-brown cloth; cows repossessed the
  garden.
Lovemaking brought death, was the unuttered principle.

(*Collected Poems*, p. 446)

In the poem the poet befriends Marion "a tall blond girl," but is too damaged by "erocide:

destruction of sexual morale" to make anything of it. The girl, an outsider unsure of her origins, killed herself at nineteen and was therefore "spared from seeing what my school did to the world" (*Collected Poems*, p. 447). The poet extrapolates from the pattern of prejudice and brutality encountered by him as an adolescent to "the world": the pattern at his school is the same anywhere. In "The Head Spider," Murray envisages the damage caused him by "girls' derision-rites" as a spider, numbing him "to a crazed politeness" (*Collected Poems*, p. 446). If these are pivotal poems in the volume, *Subhuman Redneck Poems* becomes a defense of all those whom Murray sees as brutalized by prejudice, not least the *Subhuman Redneck* of the book's title. Murray reserves for himself the right not to belong. As the critic Elizabeth Lowry has written, "Murray's poetry, grounded as it is in the assertion of the private claims of the individual against public pressures, might just conceivably be liberal in the original sense of the word" (Alexander, p. 278, Internet edition). He is the great non-joiner, as he makes explicit in "Demo," his justification for joining no cause:

Nothing a mob does is clean,

not at first, not when slowed to a media,
not when police. The first demos I saw,
before placards, were against me,
alone, for two years, with chants, ...

(*Collected Poems*, p. 461)

Murray is too accomplished a writer to ever forget the art of the poem; one can indicate in the movement of the stanza quoted, for example, the way the rhythm and the poet's placement of commas is mimetic of the chanting of a mob, in particular in the last two lines. Yet the presence of the poet as a suffering character in his own work introduces elements other than artistic ones. These complicate the reader's responses to some more directly personal poems, even while those poems mark a development in the poet's range. At this stage, the poet has reached the point of being "subject matter": autobiographical revelation carries a weight it would not have at an earlier stage of his development. Personal poems that escape the possibility of being interpreted as

self-pity, however, such as "The Devil," show Murray's gift for vivid recollection. The poem amusingly recounts his being threatened by his "splintery." Scottish Presbyterian church with the devil's punishment for swearing, and he a member of "a clan of operatic swearers" (*Collected Poems*, p. 457). The child's terror is expertly recalled:

Bats flitted, the moon shone in.
Will the old Devil get me?
I quavered, four years old, through the wall,
Will he get me? The agile long-boned man
of pure horror, clinging to the outside
weatherboards like the spur-shouldered
hoatzin bird in my mother's
encyclopedia books ...

(*Collected Poems*, p. 458)

Murray expertly splits nouns from their adjectives at line ends here: this introduces a lineal tension into the verse, in which the reader experiences a little moment of uncertainty and suspense at each line break, in keeping with the poem's content.

Where Murray is not so directly implicated himself he achieves outstanding poems: "Cotton Flannelette" is a story based upon one of his aunts, badly burnt in a hearth fire, and "It Allows a Portrait in Line Scan at Age Fifteen" is an affecting portrait of the poet's autistic son, Alexander. The "it" is the condition of autism.

Some of the themes of *Subhuman Redneck Poems* would refigure in Murray's massive verse novel *Fredy Neptune*. Indeed, occasional phrases found in *Subhuman Redneck Poems* are repeated in the bigger book. In it, in the figure of Fredy, Murray found an objective correlative for his own pain; through him, some of his themes received their fullest treatment.

THE VERSE NOVELS: THE BOYS WHO STOLE THE FUNERAL *AND* FREDY NEPTUNE

MURRAY has always been, at some level, a narrative poet. This penchant for storytelling took the form of *The Boys Who Stole the Funeral*, a vigorous sequence of 140 nominal sonnets which used filmic techniques to tell the story of Kevin Forbutt and Cameron Reeby, who steal the corpse of Forbutt's great-uncle from a city funeral parlor and return it to his country home for proper burial. The sonnet novel drew considerable attention, not least for its portrayal of Noeline Kampff, which caused anger in feminist circles. The sequence may be considered, at the least, a fascinating experiment. It prepared, however, for a much more substantial work, *Fredy Neptune* with a striking cover in the book's Australian edition showing a bare-torsoed man lifting an ocean liner above his head out of the sea.

The reader of the verse novel is first struck by the poem's bulk: ten-thousand-lines long, in loose hexameters, occasionally rhymed, of eight-line stanzas. The poem is the first-person account of Friedrich Boettcher—the Fredy Neptune of the book's title, a name given to him when working as a circus strongman—who is German-Australian. Fredy's tale is Murray's lightning tour through the horrors of the twentieth century. The story is told in five books. Book 1 finds Fredy caught up, as a young merchant seaman, in the First World War. In book 2, he returns to Australia to find his German-born father dead, his mother untraceable (though he later finds her), and antipathy against Germans prevalent. He marries and becomes a father. Book 3 finds him in America, where he has been sent by government forces to track down and bring back an Australian "Mr. Big," Basil Thoroblood, a eugenicist fascinated by strongmen and the concept of the Nietzschean superman. While there, the stock market crashes, and Fredy has numerous adventures: befriended by Marlene Dietrich he acts a part in *All Quiet on the Western Front*, and becomes, among other things, a hobo. By book 4, his double nationality has enabled him to find work on a zeppelin in the run up to nazism; he rescues a retarded German boy due for castration by the Nazis. They return to Australia. The final book shows him drafted as a merchant seaman in the Second World War, sailing to China and elsewhere, before returning home safely, like Ulysses in the Odyssey, one of his literary forebears, to his wife Laura and family in Australia.

That is the story in outline. Fredy, however, is remarkable for at least two things: after witnessing the burning alive of Armenian women in the first few pages of the novel, he becomes bodily numb in a guilt reaction; he also develops tremendous strength, and the ability to heal his own wounds rapidly. One critic compared him to the Incredible Hulk, and the comparison has a certain aptness.

The novel moves rapidly, adopting filmic techniques like its briefer forebear, and is full of conflict and color: a panther escapes and is restrained by Fredy; he lifts horses for bets; he is forever rescuing people in moments of crisis, irrespective of their color or creed or nationality (so, in book 3, he sides with a black man being baited by white men in a railway truck, and, in book 4, saves a German from certain death); as he is frequently picked on for fights, which he invariably wins, his difference, his strange otherness, is recognized, and he has to move on. He carries his secret like a heavy gift: his numbness removes his ability to feel physical pain, but also pleasure, including sexual pleasure. In book 3 he survives a knife to the heart, and simply faints. Fredy, the reader feels, is almost invincible: consequently, while one is interested in his plight, one never feels worried for his safety. The way his numbness, both the source of his power and his plight, returns and vanishes, forms a recurring tension in the poem. He learns after a trip to Jerusalem in book 1 that if he can ever pray "with a whole heart," he will be cured, as he is during the poem's last few pages when, in a curious twist, he forgives the victims of all the atrocities weighing on his conscience, and an implicated God.

The main subject of the novel is ideological violence, which involves the simplification of the "Other" into an object. Fredy, however, is both German and Australian. He therefore cannot adopt simplified polarities of feeling; he discriminates only between the powerful and the weak, in the weak's favor, against a backdrop of mass discrimination and its attendant violence upon what Murray called "the unarmed victims of ideologies, tribalisms" (Alexander, p. 289, Internet edition): blacks, Jews, and the different, such as Fredy himself, who are victimized by the "normal." Despite his strength, Fredy quickly learns to feign pain; not even he could survive the uncomprehending violence of a mob, frightened by his abilities.

The poem contains interesting echoes of Murray's biography. "There's a lot of me," he has commented, "in Fredy" (Alexander, p. 293, Internet edition). Murray's strength, as a young man, for instance, was such that he could lift the ends of cars single-handedly; Fredy's numbness, which Murray identified as macular anesthesia, is similar to what may be suffered by autists who may bang their heads off objects in an attempt to feel something, and may be related both to Murray's son and to his own psychological numbness. Whereas Fredy's plight is caused by the death of the Armenian women, Murray's as it appears in his poetry was caused by the early death of his mother, for which he thought himself to blame.

The poem's language, as the author has indicated, was an attempt at something unliterary; in effect it's the vernacular of his home area of Bunyah. Not only is it supple enough to describe fights and conflicts convincingly; it also shows how deft Murray can be in handling more commonplace situations. Especially lucid sections occur in book 2, when Fredy returns to Australia, the breakup of his family, and the sudden aggression against his German origin. Dealing with a known landscape and situation, Murray writes with lucent documentary grace. In this stanza, newly returned to Australia after World War One, Fredy is warned by an old schoolfriend:

> Freddy? Fred Beitcher? It was a schoolmate of mine half-whispering through his rag like a conspirator. You back? How are you? I shook hands. It made him nervous. He kept his voice down like that and I didn't know why. How've you been, Arthur—I started, and he cut in: Watch out. The Pages, they lost two boys in the war. The Pages from Main Creek. They never said a cross word to me in all the years. But I realise, now, that I've been braced for one.
>
> (*Fredy Neptune*, p. 49)

Such writing is nearly transparent. It doesn't draw attention to itself as a made object, but presents, as it were, the scene itself. Later episodes, which deal with the courtship between Fredy and Laura, show how delicately Murray can write on human relationships when occasion requires; in such episodes, sheer narrative interest holds the reader's attention, and the work is not devoid of humor: Fredy, eager to reconcile with Laura on discovering he's fathered her child, approaches her hostile family: " 'Are you the bastard?' " screams her father. / Er, no, I'm the father,' I answered him" (*Fredy Neptune*, p. 83).

Murray uses poetic techniques, however, when necessary, and the poem is full of striking one-liners. Fredy recounts, for instance, when a hobo in the America: "I rode under stars like the glints on a surgeon's cutlery" (*Fredy Neptune*, p. 147). The image, unelaborated on, is left to ramify and unfold its resonance in the reader's mind. The image is of the universe being like a vast surgery: but who, or what, is the surgeon? A surgery has the intent of making a patient better, of curing disease, but there are also, in the context of Fredy's story, hints of medical experimentation. The image has a complex resonance.

CONSCIOUS AND VERBAL

FREDY Neptune, for which the poet received the Queen's Gold Medal for poetry in Britain, marked the end of a highly significant stage of the poet's work. His last published collection as of the time of this writing, *Conscious and Verbal*, has the air of the work of a poet in transition. The volume contains a number of occasional poems, and elsewhere Murray continues along expected lines. In "A Deployment of Fashion," for example, he further satirizes the contemporary media: the poem can fairly be read as a defense of Helen Demidenko, author of a prize-winning novel, *The Hand That Signed the Paper*, who was discovered not to be the daughter of Ukrainian immigrants, as she had claimed, but English, and her real name Helen Darville. Exposed, she was subjected to intense personal abuse. In a sense, it is almost—if not quite—irrelevant what she stands for: isolated, she is exemplary of that individuality Murray defends customarily; his

LES MURRAY

response is not so much against the rightness or wrongness of her attitude as against consensus against her, and consensus, to Murray, often converts to the mob, and, by extension, to his own brutalized adolescence.

One of the volume's key poems, "The Disorderly," is in parts a touching reminiscence of Murray's rural childhood. It begins with the children in the poem wondering out loud how old they will be in the year 2000, and sets them jogging, complete with a "day-blind glider possum" (*Conscious and Verbal*, p. 41) found on the way, on their journey to school. It is no truism to say that country youngsters, and especially those of the era Murray grew up in, unused to the acerbities of an urban environment, have an unguarded quality:

> Only later
>
> At the shoe-wearing edge of our world
> did we meet kids who thought everything
> ridiculous. They found us incredible.
>
> Cream-handed men in their towns
> never screamed Christ-to-Jesus! at the hills
> with diabetes breath, nor talked fight
>
> or Scotch poetry in scared timber rooms.
> Such fighters had lost, we realised
> but we had them to love
>
> or else we'd be mongrels.
> This saved our souls later on,
> sometimes, crossing the cousinless
>
> detective levels of the world
> to the fat-free denim culture,
> that country of the Attitudes.
>
> (*Conscious and Verbal*, p. 41)

The "cream-handed men" to whom Murray refers, perhaps derisively, in the towns of such children are markedly less colorful as characters than the bawling, diabetic-prone, reciters of poetry of Murray's rural childhood, "fighters" who have lost, but whom, loved nonetheless on pain of being considered "a mongrel," help save the children's souls, "sometimes," when they enter "that country of the Attitudes," which may be broadly equated with urban life and intellectual fashions. This plainly autobiographical poem is almost a microcosm of Murray's art to date. "That country of the Attitudes" is one his poetry has reacted against with distinction since the beginning of his vocation. It could be argued of course that such reaction is itself one more attitude in "that country." In general, Murray's best work is not found in his satires. It is his distinction to have turned the matter of Bunyah and his own family, and the insight from that perspective, into lasting art. Australian in provenance it may be, but the best of it is for a world readership. He is a poet of locality whose finest work is of wide relevance, at once intimate, humane, "loose-limbed in its mind," and celebratory. His Bunyah has also been, for his many readers, to some extent, the world.

SELECTED BIBLIOGRAPHY

I. COLLECTED WORKS. *Selected Poems: The Vernacular Republic* (Sydney and London, 1976; Edinburgh 1982; New York, 1982; rev. ed. Sydney, 1988); *The Peasant Mandarin: Prose Pieces* (Queensland, 1978); *Persistence in Folly* (Sydney, 1984); *The Australian Year: The Chronicle of Our Seasons and Celebrations* (Sydney, 1985); *Blocks and Tackles: Articles and Essays 1982–1990* (Sydney, 1990); *Collected Poems* (Manchester, 1991), repub. as *The Rabbiter's Bounty: Collected Poems* (New York, 1991); *The Paperbark Tree: Selected Prose* (Manchester, 1992); updated *Collected Poems* (Port Melbourne, 1994; Manchester, 1998); *A Working Forest* (Sydney, 1997); *Learning Human: Selected Poems* (Sydney, 1998; New York, 2000).

II. SEPARATE WORKS. *The Ilex Tree*, with Geoffrey Lehmann (Canberra, 1965); *The Weatherboard Cathedral* (Sydney, 1969); *Poems Against Economics* (Sydney, 1972); *Lunch and Counter Lunch* (Sydney, 1974); *Ethnic Radio* (Sydney, 1978); *The Boys Who Stole the Funeral: A Novel Sequence* (Sydney, 1980; New York, 1991); *Equanimities* (Copenhagen, 1982); *The People's Otherworld* (Sydney, 1983); *The Daylight Moon and Other Poems* (Sydney, 1987; Manchester and New York, 1988); *The Idyll Wheel: Cycle of a Year at Bunyah, New South Wales, April 1986–April 1987* (Canberra, 1989); *Dog Fox Field* (Sydney, 1990; New York, 1992); *Translations from the Natural World* (Sydney, 1992, New York, 1994); *Subhuman Redneck Poems* (Sydney, 1996; New York, 1997); *Fredy Neptune* (Sydney, Manchester, and New York, 1998); *Conscious and Verbal* (Sydney, Manchester, and New York, 1999).

III. EDITED WORKS. *The New Oxford Book of Australian Verse* (Melbourne and New York, 1986; expanded ed., Oxford and New York, 1991); *Anthology of Australian Religious Poetry* (Blackburn, Victoria, 1986); *Five Fathers: Five Australian Poets of the Pre-Academic Era* (Manchester, 1994).

LES MURRAY

IV. INTERVIEWS AND PROFILES. Bruce Beaver, "Murray, Les(lie) A(llan)," in *Contemporary Poets* (London and Chicago, 1975); Ron Blair, "Les Murray Talks," in *24 Hours* 1, no. 10 (Nov. 1976); Robert Gray, "An Interview with Les Murray," in *Quadrant* 113 (Dec. 1976); Helen Frizell, "Les Murray Takes Off" in *Sydney Morning Herald* (23 Feb. 1980); Graham Kinross Smith: " ... 'The Frequent Image of Farms'—a profile of Les Murray," in *Westerly* no. 3 (Sept. 1980); Sandra McGrath, "An Otherworld of Dreaming in Poetry," in *Weekend Australian* 56 (Nov. 1983); Paul Kavanagh and Peter Kuch, "An Interview with Les Murray," in *Southerly* 44, no. 4 (1984); Judith Rodriguez, "Murray, Les(lie) A(llan)," in James Vinson and K. L. Kirkpatrick, eds., *Contemporary Poets* (London and Chicago, 1985); Lawrence Bourke, "Les Murray Interviewed," in *Journal of Commonwealth Literature* 21, no. 1 (1986); Deborah Hope, "Murray Goes Back to the Bush to Retrieve Australian Poetry," in *Bulletin* (11 Mar. 1986); Carole Oles, "Les Murray: An Interview by Carole Oles," in *American Poetry Review* 15, no. 2 (Mar./Apr. 1986); Robert Crawford, "Les A. Murray Talking with Robert Crawford," in *Verse* no.5 (1986); Candida Baker, in *Yacker* 2 (1987); Alan Gould and Geoff Page, "A Wild and Holy Calling: A Conversation with Les A. Murray on Religion and Poetry," in *Eremos Newsletter* 19 (1987); Susan Chenery, "The Bard of Bunyah," in *Australian* (4 May 1991); Noel Peacock, "Embracing the Vernacular: An Interview with Les A. Murray," in *Australian and New Zealand Studies in Canada* 7 (1992); William Scammell, "In Conversation with Les Murray," in *PN Review* no. 110 (JulyAug. 1996); Rosslyn Beeby, "Gold Is a Giggle for Poet Les," in *Age* 28 (Aug. 1984); Andrew Billen, "Les Miserable: The *Observer* Interview," in *Observer Life* 22 (June 1997).

V. CRITICAL STUDIES. Dianne Ailwood, "The Poetry of Les A. Murray," in *Southerly* 31 (1971); David Malouf, "Subjects Found and Taken Up," in *Poetry Australia*, no. 57 (1975); Penelope Nelson, "Listening to Lives: Les A. Murray's Vernacular Republic," in *Poetry Australia* 64 (1977); Penelope Nelson, *Notes on the Poetry of Les A. Murray* (Sydney, 1978); Peter Porter, "Country Poetry and Town Poetry: A Debate with Les Murray," in *Australian Literary Studies* 9 (May 1979); Christopher Pollnitz, "The Bardic Pose: A Survey of Les A. Murray's Poetry," in *Southerly*: part 1 in 40, no. 4 (Dec. 1980); part 2 in 41, no.1 (Mar. 1981); part 3 in 41, no. 2 (June 1981); Clive James, "His Brilliant Career," in *New York Review of Books* (14 Apr. 1983); John Barnie, "The Poetry of Les Murray," in *Australian Literary Studies* 12 (1985); Lawrence Bourke, "The Rapture of Place: From Immanence to Transcendence in the Poetry of Les A. Murray," in *Westerly* 33 (1988); Kevin Hart, " 'Interest' in Les A. Murray," in *Australian Literary Studies* 14, no. 2 (Oct. 1989); Lawrence Bourke, *A Vivid Steady State: Les Murray and Australian Poetry* (Kensington, NSW, 1992); Robert Crawford, *Identifying Poets: Self and Territory in Twentieth-Century Poetry* (Edinburgh, 1993); Bert Almon, "Fullness of Being in Les Murray's 'Presence: Translations from the Natural World,' " in *Antipodes* 8, no. 2 (Dec. 1994); Nicholas Birns, "Religions Are Poems: Spirituality in the Poetry of Les A. Murray," in J. S. Scott, ed., *And the Birds Began to Sing: Religion and Literature in Post-Colonial Cultures* (Amsterdam, 1996); John Bayley, "Slightly Sacred Poet," in *New York Review of Books* (9 Oct. 1997), http://www.nybooks.com/nyrev/WWWarchdisplay.cgi?19971009045R; Carmel Gaffney, ed., *Counterbalancing Light: Essays on the Poetry of Les Murray* (Armidale, NSW, 1997); Peter F. Alexander, *Les Murray: A Life in Progress* (Melbourne, 2000), http://www.aussiepoet.com/[chapter number/].htm; Adam Kirsch, "Robes, Tat, Rig, and Scunge," in *The New Republic* (June 2000), http://www.tnr.com/061200/kirsch061200.html.

JOHN HENRY NEWMAN

(1801–1890)

Laurie Dennett

JOHN HENRY NEWMAN is revered as one of the towering figures of nineteenth-century letters, but he was first and foremost a Christian apologist: for almost half his life as an Anglican, and subsequently as a Roman Catholic. His religious genius injected new vigor into the moribund Church of England, establishing a strain of Anglicanism that is still the most expressive of that communion's rich heritage. As a Roman Catholic, Newman did more than any other prominent member of the Catholic Church to bridge the chasm of misunderstanding that had for centuries divided it from the English mainstream. As a theologian and philosopher of religion, the scale of what he attempted defies comparison. So does the stylistic and characteristic fusion of order and feeling that ensures that his prose will be read as long as the English language, even though much of his subject matter has lost the attentive audience it once had. However secular the twenty-first century, one must not forget that Newman was before all else a priest, whose intellectual and spiritual quest for religious truth and personal holiness was the wellspring from which all else flowed.

EARLY LIFE AND EDUCATION

JOHN Henry Newman, the first child and oldest son of John Newman, a partner in a London banking firm, and Jemima Foudrinier Newman, the daughter of a papermaker of Huguenot descent, was born at 80 Old Broad Street in the City of London on 21 February 1801. He and his five brothers and sisters were brought up in the Church of England, but it was his grandmother and aunt who instilled in him a love of reading the Bible.

From May 1808 until December 1816 Newman attended a private boarding school run by a Dr. Nicholas at Ealing, who later claimed that "no boy had run through the school, from the bottom to the top, so rapidly as John Newman" (*Autobiographical Writings,* p. 29). In his last year at school the failure of his father's bank brought on a nervous crisis that resulted in the deepening of his piety. So far the timid and sensitive boy had been "without religiousconvictions," happy merely to study and play his violin, but now, on reading Evangelical and Calvinist authors, he found himself "under the influences of a definite Creed, and received into my intellect impressions of dogma ..." (*Apologia,* Ker, ed., p. 25), which reinforced childhood beliefs in a truer, higher reality behind the appearances of the material world. During his recovery Newman also came to believe that it was God's will that he should lead a celibate life, so as to be completely available for the "missionary work among the heathen" to which he believed himself called (*Apologia,* p. 28).

At sixteen—three years younger than most students—he was accepted at Trinity College, in Oxford and in May 1818 won the college's Open Scholarship, worth 60 pounds a year for nine years. Oxford became the center of his life. With his close friend, John Bowden, that year he wrote a verse drama entitled *St Bartholomew's Eve: A Tale of the Sixteenth Century in Two Cantos* and began a short-lived periodical, *The Undergraduate.* Every indication suggested that Newman would do well in his final examinations in November 1820, but overwork and nerves led to a poor performance and a bachelor's degree "below the line" (an unqualified grade below the rank of lower second class). Newman spent a year tutoring private pupils to pay for the Oxford education of his brother Francis (later a professor of classics at King's College, London) following their father's bankruptcy early in 1821.

Determined to reverse his academic fortunes, Newman mustered his shaken confidence to take the examinations for one of the prestigious Oriel College Open Fellowships in April 1822. He achieved brilliant results and was duly elected a fellow of Oriel on 12 April—a date which he thereafter held to be the turning point of his life.

AN OXFORD PERSONAGE

AT the time Newman entered it, the Oriel Common Room was the gathering place of the best minds in Oxford. The extrovert logician Richard Whately (subsequently the archbishop of Dublin, whom Newman later claimed "opened my mind, and taught me to think and use my reason") (*Apologia*, p. 31) enlisted Newman's help in the preliminary drafts of his own *Elements of Logic*, and in writing articles (one on Cicero, then two more, on miracles and Apollonius of Tyanaesa) for the *Encyclopaedia Metropolitana*. His influence led Newman to see "the idea of the Christian Church as a divine appointment, and as a substantive body, independent of the State, and endowed with rights, prerogatives, and powers of its own" (*Autobiographical Writings, ed Tristram*, p. 69). This anti-Erastian view later became one of the most prominent features of the Oxford Movement. (*Apologia*, p. 28). Another influential friendship was formed with Edward Bouverie Pusey, later a professor of Hebrew and a high church figure.

Newman became curate of the Oxford working-class parish of St. Clement's Church in May 1824; he was ordained deacon in June, and priest in May 1825. Parish work brought him into contact with Edward Hawkins, the vicar of the University Church of St. Mary, whose influence eroded Newman's Evangelicalism. Belief in justification by faith gradually ceded to an acceptance of baptismal regeneration. From another Oriel fellow Newman learned the doctrine of the apostolic succession. The writings of the early church fathers established the third and fourth

centuries in his mind as the period when Christianity was most pure and vigorous, and led him to an appreciation of tradition, in addition to Scripture, as the cornerstone of doctrine. All of this ran counter to the prevailing tendencies in the Anglican Church, which were latitudinarian and Evangelical, and to the liberal and rational spirit of the age.

His father's death in 1824 left Newman responsible for his mother and sisters, to whom he remained devoted all his life. Following his appointment as a tutor of Oriel in March 1826, his complex personality and sensitive nature found support in the friendship of Hurrell Froude, elected a fellow at the same time. Froude's love of the Middle Ages and hatred of the Protestant Reformation opened new perspectives for Newman, who still viewed Rome with only slightly less suspicion than liberalism. He and Froude were united, however, in their regard for tradition, and once Newman came to reject Evangelicalism as symptomatic of the liberalism he abhorred, it was Froude who fostered his friendship with the high church Oriel fellow John Keble.

Keble's book of devotional verses *The Christian Year* was published in 1827, and "... struck an original note and woke up in the hearts of thousands a new music ...," and a longing for real devotion (*Apologia,* p. 36). Two of Keble's ideas impressed Newman. The first was that of the "sacramental system," or the idea that material phenomena are both the prefigurations and the instruments of real things unseen; and the second the doctrine of "probability" ("likelihood" or "disposition" perhaps best approximates this term), by which people may be persuaded through faith and love to assent to beliefs that are probable but not in themselves logically provable.

Newman, increasingly attracted to the pure apostolicity of the primitive Anglican Church, found common ground with Keble and Froude in a contempt for liberalism, the desire to strengthen the Anglican episcopate and to resurrect the faded glory of the liturgy. The zealous opposition of the three to any threat to the predominance of the Established Church became a matter of principle.

(The Catholic Emancipation Act in 1829 and the 1832 Reform Bill were each be resisted on such grounds, regardless of the civil injustice implied, as was the admission of Dissenters to Oxford University some years later.)

Newman became vicar of the University Church of St. Mary and the parish of Littlemore, outside Oxford, on the election of Edward Hawkins as provost of Oriel in January 1828. This position made him became better known in Oxford; similarly his opinions on church affairs began to involve him in controversy. In 1829 his opposition to the re-election of Sir Robert Peel (a supporter of the Catholic Emancipation) as member of Parliament for Oxford University led to estrangement from Whately and Hawkins, who had supported Peel. Newman and others disagreed with Hawkins over reforms to the Oriel tutorial system, resigning their tutorships in the summer of 1830, and ceasing to teach soon after.

He could now dedicate himself to writing. In March 1831 he took on a history of the Anglican Church Councils for editor Hugh James Rose, the high church rector of Hadleigh in Suffolk. Newman's fascination with one aspect of his subject led to his first book, completed in July 1832 and published as *The Arians of the Fourth Century* in 1833. It is not a major work; indeed, he always considered it "very imperfect," although its preparation confirmed his view that the doctrinal foundations of the Church of England were to be found in antiquity. Admiration for the teachings of Athanasius, "the champion of truth" against the Arian heretics, and for those of Clement and Origen, reinforced the influence of *The Christian Year* regarding the ways God reveals Himself through time—the "Economies or Dispensations of the Eternal":

I understood them to mean that the exterior world, physical and historical, was but the outward manifestation of realities greater than itself: Nature was a parable, Scripture was an allegory; pagan literature, philosophy, and mythology, properly understood, were but a preparation for the Gospel. ... Holy Church in her sacraments and her hierarchical appointments will remain even unto the end of the world, only a symbol of those heavenly facts which fill eternity. Her mysteries are but the expressions

in human language of truths to which the human mind is unequal.

(*Apologia*, pp. 43–44)

Between 8 December 1832 and 8 July 1833 Newman accompanied the Froudes, father and son, to the Mediterranean, taking in North Africa, Malta, Corfu, Sicily, and Rome. Despite his reservations about Roman Catholicism, Rome itself exceeded all expectations. Returning to Sicily alone, Newman fell seriously ill with a fever and nearly died. The voyage home, while still recovering, elicited some religious verses intended for Rose's *British Magazine*. One was the famous "Pillar of the Cloud," better known as "Lead, Kindly Light," whose lines, "Keep Thou my feet, I do not ask to see / The distant scene; one step enough for me" (*The Book of Common Praise*, 1962, p. 368), succinctly express their author's belief, born of countless hours of solitary prayer, that the understanding to discern the divine will is imparted only gradually, sufficient for the dependent and trusting soul to advance one step at a time and no farther. It was a conviction that would be mirrored in the course of his own life, and in the organic way his own thought, reflected in his writings, would evolve.

While ill, the thought that God had work for him to do in England had strengthened Newman. Only days after his arrival there, in response to the proposed suppression of ten Irish bishoprics under the Irish Church Temporalities Bill due to become law on 14 August, John Keble preached the Assize Sermon in the University Church on the subject of "National Apostasy." Newman thereafter considered this date, 14 July 1833, as the beginning of the "Oxford Movement" to revive the Church of England.

TRACTS FOR THE TIMES *AND OTHER WRITINGS*

THE meeting called by Hugh Rose at Hadleigh rectory in late July 1833 reached no workable conclusions about what should or could be done to turn the liberal tide. Though Newman had not attended, the idea of the *Tracts for the Times* (1833–1841) was his, and he wrote the first three (*Thoughts on the Ministerial Commission, The*

Catholic Church, and *On Alterations in the Liturgy*) and later many more. Their purpose was "to bestir the clergy, teach the Apostolic Succession, and defend the Liturgy" (*Letters* I, p. 449). The tracts were to be anonymous and independent in outlook. Bowden, Keble, Froude, and Pusey were among the authors of the twenty tracts published before the end of 1833.

Reactions to the tracts varied from Evangelical suspicion—including that of Evangelical bishops whose office the Tractarians defended, and that of Thomas Arnold, who thundered against "The Oxford Malignants" in the *Edinburgh Review*—to gratitude from Anglican clerics around the country. Their support soon coalesced into a movement with Newman as its somewhat unwilling head. Attendance at the University Church was swelled by the curious, and his slight figure pointed out to visitors in the Oxford streets.

The tracts themselves are little read in the twenty-first century, but not so the other work relevant to the Tractarian cause, the two volumes of Newman's *Parochial and Plain Sermons,* preached between 1825 and 1833 and published in 1834 and 1835 (six additional volumes would follow). These, as their title suggests, were aimed at parishioners rather than members of the university and alone of Newman's writings as an Anglican have become spiritual classics, still read for their insights into the workings of the human heart as well as for their expression of the most elevated spiritual realities in lyrical but simple prose. The sermons address such topics as sanctification, good works, grace, and the sacraments; they contain a discussion of "nominal" and "real" Christianity that would be echoed in many future works, and the often quoted description of the indwelling of the Holy Spirit. There are also multiple instances where Newman's understanding of human nature mercilessly exposes the spiritual temptations along the path to holiness. One comforting message that emerges from the body of solid doctrine imparted by these sermons is that God is one with the believer who struggles to be one with Him; for although the gifts of grace are a mystery, the perfection for which Christians must strive is attainable, through consistent and loving attention to the small tasks,

events and setbacks of every day. As Ian Ker has written in his 1988 biography of Newman, it was his ability to bring the Christ of the Gospels alive that made his four o'clock Sunday sermons at St. Mary's "the most potent spiritual force of the Oxford Movement" (p. 100).

To the doctrinal revival of the Church of England Newman brought not only his scholarship, spiritual insights, and natural eloquence, but an extraordinary gift for preaching that made an indelible impression upon all who heard him. Matthew Arnold, in his essay "Emerson," captured the charisma of "... that spiritual apparition, gliding in the dim afternoon light through the aisles of St. Mary's, rising into the pulpit, and then, in the most entrancing of voices, breaking the silence with words and thoughts that were a religious music." (*The Complete Prose Works of Matthew Arnold*, vol. 10, R. H. Soper, ed., 1960–1977, p. 175) Not only Newman's "thrilling" and musical voice, but his style of delivery, was part of the fascination he exerted, with its impression of "... a rush of thoughts and feelings" which "... poured themselves out in a torrent of eloquence all the more impetuous from having been so long repressed. The effect of these outbursts was irresistible, and carried his hearers beyond themselves at once" (Church, *The Oxford Movement*, 1891, p. 125). James Anthony Froude, Hurrell's younger brother, compared the effect to "an electric stroke" passing through the church, yet Newman engaged in no gestures or histrionics, and it is doubtful whether he consciously sought to move his listeners in this way, any more than he consciously wrote for literary effect. His singularly expressive voice and mode of delivery, like his prose style (modelled on that of Cicero), were mere instruments with which to communicate the truths of religion as simply as possible. Newman did not write to live, nor was his writing driven by his imagination, powers of observation, or human affinities; he neither frequented literary circles nor read much outside the fields of theology and history. His genius was employed in the cause of discovering and defending religious truth. Even as an editor (of the *British Critic* from 1838 to 1841) and poet (his verses appeared with Froude's in *Lyra Apostolica* in

1836) this was the case. From the publication of the first three *Tracts for the Times* in September 1833 until 1839, Newman's dominant theme was that of the Anglican Church as the *via media* (or the middle way) between Roman Catholicism and Protestantism. The promotion of this idea demanded the lucid exposition of complex theological or philosophical matter and the making of fine distinctions. A firm, organically evolving structure and a subtle analysis came to characterize Newman's writing. These qualities, coupled with the depth of his erudition and his love of realistic imagery, made the task of composition a painstaking one:

> I write—I write again—I write a third time, in the course of six months—then I take the third—I literally fill the paper with corrections so that another person could not read it—I then write it out fair for the printer—I put it by—I take it up—I begin to correct again—it will not do—alterations multiply—pages are rewritten—little lines sneak in and crawl about—the whole page is disfigured—I write again. I cannot count how many times this process goes on.
>
> (*Letters*, vol. 6, p. vi. 193)

Yet despite his perfectionism, Newman produced a flood of writings during these years, beginning with two articles published in the *British Magazine* in 1834 and 1836 entitled "Home Thoughts Abroad." (The second one was later included in his *Collected Works* as "How to Accomplish It"). The aim of these pieces was to forestall Evangelical criticism that the Tractarians were advocating "popery." They are cast in the form of dialogues—a form that Newman would later use in works as disparate as his novel *Loss and Gain* (1848), and the poem *The Dream of Gerontius* (1865)—between two friends visiting Rome, the narrator being Newman, and his interlocutor, Froude. The discussion centers on the Anglican Church's prospects for survival, distinguishing between the Roman claim to be the authentic *church*, and the Anglican claim to adhere to authentic *faith and doctrine,* as propounded by the church fathers. The true Anglican position is found in the writings of Archbishop William Laud and other divines such as Lancelot Andrewes, Thomas Ken, and Joseph Butler,

although the "friends" acknowledge that this had never been put into practice.

Newman believed that the best defense against accusations of "popery" (which he classed as a system, self-serving and full of error, while Anglicanism was the histoic and universal Catholic Church in the British Islands) lay in the clear presentation of the *via media*. This was the aim of the *Lectures on the Prophetical Office of the Church Viewed Relatively to Romanism and Popular Protestantism*, published in March 1837, which grew out of a correspondence with a French theologian, the Abbé Jean-Nicholas Jager, in the Paris daily *L'Univers*. At the outset Newman asks what is demanded by the theory of the *via media*, and challenges the sceptical objection that because it has not been tried, it cannot be true. While Anglo-Catholicism had much in common with Romanism, it also exhibited notable differences from it. Even greater were its differences from Protestantism, whose emphasis on Scripture as the only source of doctrine is shown to lead to subjectivism. The Anglo-Catholic *via media,* like the Roman Church, acknowledged Scripture to be unique while relying also on tradition, but whereas Anglicanism took this to mean antiquity, the Roman Church was held to have performed a sleight of hand in substituting the authority of the church itself for that of the church fathers. The main part of the book centers on a definition of two kinds of tradition: the "Episcopal," deriving from apostolic teaching, and the "Prophetical," which consists of interpretations of points of doctrine not fundamental to faith, generally accepted by the Anglican Church and recorded according to the dispositions of Providence. The first kind is that which informed the primitive church of the early centuries and was a faithful reflection of Scripture; the second that which has been elaborated according to historical circumstances and possibly become corrupted. Newman identified the first kind of tradition as the foundation of the *via media*, while the Roman Catholic Church was shown to demand obedience to the second:

> They hold that Faith depends on the Church; we say that the Church is based upon Faith. By the Catholic Church we understand the universal

Church, descended from the Apostles; they only recognise as such those branches that are in communion with Rome. ... They teach that Faith is what the Church declares to be so through time; we say that Faith is what was declared from the beginning. ... We maintain that the Church possesses a gift of fidelity. They speak of a grace of discernment. The Roman Creed is subject to alteration. Ours has been established for once and for all.

(*Letters on the Prophetical Office of the Church,*
p. 212)

The confident distinction between the Anglo-Catholic and Roman positions was restated in Newman's *Lectures on Justification*, preached at St Mary's between 13 April and 1 June 1837 and published in 1838 (later published as *Lectures on the Doctrine of Justification*). Here Newman sets the Lutheran doctrine of justification by faith alone against the Roman Catholic belief in justification through obedience. But the latter, to Newman, is "real" in a way that the Protestant view is not, since it involves the will in a struggle to manifest love in deeds. Faith may lead to good works, but need not necessarily do so; it may, quite literally, be fruitless. Newman then suggests that both doctrines are inadequate, and that even prior to having faith, a soul must possess the divine grace which impels and leads it to faith. The problem of justification can be transcended if, as the New Testament makes clear, grace is equated with the presence, or "indwelling" of the Holy Spirit, the presence of Christ in the soul of the believer, which leads him to an ever-closer approximation to Christ in action and way of life. This path between the rival positions shows that salvation and sanctity are indissolubly united: "...the one cannot be separated from the other except in idea, unless the sun's rays can be separated from the sun, or the power of purifying from fire or water" (*Justification*, p. 154).

These lectures cost Newman much revision, but show the agility in argument and masterly prose style that he had by this time attained, especially in the attack on Protestant error that forms the last lecture, "On Preaching the Gospel." A comparison of this piece with an article entitled "The State of Religious Parties" written for the *British Critic* of April 1838, which he would one day claim as "the last words which I ever spoke as an Anglican" (*Apologia*, pp. 91–92), reveals how far he had come in his frankness. Here he traces the origins of the spirit underlying the movement—of "the character of mind and feeling of which Catholic doctrines are the just expression"—to which the romanticism of the novels of Sir Walter Scott and the cold rationalism of the eighteenth century had each contributed, the one by bestirring feeling, the other by repressing it. His tone, in these and other writings of about the same time, is uncompromising, the imagery betraying his frustration with the Established Church, which considered comprehensiveness a virtue:

In the present day mistiness is the mother of wisdom. A man who can set down half a dozen general propositions, which escape from destroying one another only by being diluted into truisms, who can hold the balance between opposites so skilfully as to do without fulcrum or beam, who never enunciates a truth without guarding himself from being supposed to exclude the contrary, who holds that Scripture is the only authority, yet that the Church is to be deferred to, that faith only justifies, yet that it does not justify without works, that grace does not depend on sacraments, yet is not given without them, that bishops are a divine ordinance, yet those who have them not are in the same religious condition as those who have,—this is your safe man and the hope of the Church; this is what the Church is said to want, not party men, but sensible, temperate, sober, well-judging persons, to guide it through the channel of No-meaning, between the Scylla and Charybdis of Aye and No.

(*Apologia*, p. 104)

The derisive tone of this piece was a foretaste of the gift for satire that Newman would display a few years later in his "Catholicus" letters to *The Times* in February 1841, published later that year as *The Tamworth Reading Room*. In them Sir Robert Peel appears as the epitome of liberalism, crassly proposing to separate knowledge from faith, and deluded into thinking that the study of the "new" sciences can lead to religion. As Newman would write years later in *The Idea of a University* (1873), science is not denied a place in the curriculum of the educated man, but Newman notes that belief in an Unseen Being is the only known principle for onquering moral evil and bringing order out of chaos in human society.

Newman's influence in the intellectual and religious life of Oxford was at its height in 1837 and early 1838. Hurrell Froude had died in 1836, and his private journals, left virtually unexpurgated by Newman and Keble, were published as *Remains* in February 1838. The descriptions of the fasts and physical mortifications which had accompanied Froude's struggle for holiness scandalized the Evangelicals and roused the anti-Catholicism that was never very far under the surface of public life. In the university, the tolerance accorded to the Oxford Movement now hardened into denunciation of its "Romanising" tendencies. By the end of 1838 some friends on whom Newman relied as writers of the tracts favored ceasing them; while others, such as William Ward, were more extreme and viewed the *via media* as a mere halt on the road to Rome.

A DIFFICULT TRANSITION: TRACT 90 AND AFTER

NEWMAN himself had no misgivings about the Anglican cause until the summer of 1839. Some of the most moving passages of the *Apologia pro Vita Sua* (1864) describe the uneasy stages by which his patristic studies brought him to the realization that the theory of the *via media* was fatally flawed: his sudden awful insight that if the Monophysite heretics of the fifth century were separated from Rome, so too was the Anglican Church of the nineteenth; Nicholas Wiseman's *Dublin Review* article, quoting the fateful judgment of St. Augustine upon the schismatic Donatists—"Securus judicat orbis terrarum," "The verdict of Christendom will be conclusive"—that left Newman's intellectual ideal "pulverised." His response was to retreat to Littlemore in March 1840 to formulate a defense of the Anglican Church's Catholicity that would at once vindicate the claims of the movement and pre-empt defections to Rome:

Anglicanism claimed to hold, that the Church of England was nothing else than a continuation in this country ... of that one Church of which in old times Athanasius and Augustine were members. But, if so, the doctrine must be the same: the doctrine of the Old Church must live and speak in Anglican formularies, in the 39 Articles. Did it? Yes, it did ... it did in substance, in a true sense. Man had done his worst to disfigure, to mutilate, the old Catholic Truth; but there it was, in spite of them, in the Articles still. It was there,—but this must be shown. It was a matter of life and death to us to show it.

(*Apologia*, p. 126)

Tract 90 was issued on 27 February 1841. It was entitled *Remarks on Certain Passages of the 39 Articles*, and consisted of an introduction, twelve sections in which specific articles were examined, and a conclusion. Newman purported to show that "while our Prayer Book is acknowledged on all hands to be of Catholic origin, our Articles also, the offspring of an uncatholic age, are, through God's good providence, to say the least, not uncatholic, and may be subscribed to by those who aim at being catholic in heart and doctrine" (*Via Media*, vol. 2, p. 272). The scrutiny of the meaning of individual Articles revealed, as Newman termed it, that they rejected the "popular corruptions" of Roman Catholicism, while admitting Catholic doctrines; they condemned certain teachings, but not the solemn principles upon which these were based. Neither, he contested, were the articles directed against the decrees of the Council of Trent, and therefore intentionally anti-Catholic, since they had in fact been drawn up before it.

Tract 90 was not meant as a step toward reconciliation with Rome, but as an impassioned demonstration that secession from the Anglican Church was not necessary. This was not, however, how his motive or the document itself were widely perceived. Amidst a furor of newspaper protest, Tract 90 was denounced in the House of Commons as proof of disloyalty toward the Church of England, while in Oxford University it was condemned by the vice-chancellor and heads of houses as contrary to the statutes demanding adherence to the articles in their "true" or Protestant sense. Tract 90's somewhat clinical tone is at odds with Newman's purpose, and is best read together with the letters defending his position, such as the dignified reply to the bishop of Oxford, which brought *Tracts for the Times* to an end to avoid further polarizing the Anglican Church. The furor over Tract 90 caused Newman to resign as editor of the *British Critic* in the summer of 1841. Littlemore offered Newman a retreat from controversy while he pondered his future relationship with a Church and a university which he believed had misunderstood and rejected him.

THE PATH TO ROME

NEWMAN'S long intellectual and spiritual journey had now reached a critical stage. The course of it, which covered the next four years, is partially recorded in the *Apologia*; but the many *Letters* to his sisters and friends offer better insights. The process was marked by deepening disillusion with the Anglican Church; there was now a groundswell of opposition to Tractarianism and distrust of Newman himself which he felt helpless to combat. The affair of the Jerusalem bishopric highlighted the ease with which the Established Church could be manipulated for political ends. Acting upon him like a magnet drawing him Rome-ward was the return of the dread suspicion that had struck him in 1839: that—like the Arians whom he was once again studying—the Anglican Church was in schism.

Life at Littlemore was dominated by prayer, study, and writing; Newman set the small group of men who had gathered around him in a monastic-style community to work on *Lives of the English Saints* (1844). Alongside the stream of sermons, articles, and letters that he continued to produce, he began to draw together the strands of the treatise on doctrinal development that would be his greatest single contribution to theology.

An important publication during this time was the volume of Oxford University Sermons preached between 1826 and 1843 (*Sermons, Chiefly on the Theory of Religious Belief, Preached Before the University of Oxford*, 1843), which contain concepts that he had aired in earlier works (such as that of "antecedent prob-

abilities"—the pre-existing principles or conditions which may dispose the individual soul to faith) and ideas and arguments that would appear in more developed form in later books. The last six sermons form a sustained exploration of the nature of faith and reason, and the relationship of one to the other, that reveals the brilliance of Newman's analysis of the workings of the human mind, and the refinement of his own interior life. Newman suggests that the idea that faith and reason are opposed derives from one's habit of applying each in the wrong way: faith is no more intended for the determination of "physical" questions than reason is the "judge of those truths which are subjected to another part of our nature, the moral sense" (*University Sermons*, 1843, p. 59). He then proceeds to define and test the idea of each, showing that faith is in fact a higher form of reasoning, rather as genius is, acting upon probabilities without demanding immediate evidence; indeed, as Newman is at pains to emphasize, if one demands absolute certainty before one is prepared to venture anything, one will remain immobile! What distinguishes faith from superstition and other errors, and protects it from them also, is shown to be the very love which has engendered it. It is this love which enlightens the mind, and gives it a power of discernment that is superior to reason alone. The last two sermons, on the nature of wisdom, and on the theory of doctrinal development, consider the organic growth of knowledge and understanding, and contain in essence the highly original ideas which would be treated more amply in *The Idea of a University* and *An Essay on the Development of Christian Doctrine* (1845).

This writing of the last-named work spanned Newman's time at Littlemore. Like almost all his writings, it grew out of the circumstances surrounding him, and was an attempt to display to his own satisfaction, but also for the benefit of others in the same religious quandry as himself, the unequivocal descent of the Roman Catholic Church from the primitive apostolic foundation of the early centuries. It is his most powerful book in terms of scope, reasoning, and exposition. There is a tangible sense of a great intellect and imagination drawing order and form from the vast panorama presented by eighteen hundred years of Christianity. In both philosophical and literary terms the *Essay* is a masterpiece, its beauty of expression, like all Newman's prose, marrying a classical dignity with realistic imagery, giving the reader an immediate grasp of the matter being illustrated.

It is impossible to do justice to such a work in few words, for quite apart from its size, the *Essay* was the hinge upon which Newman's thought—and life—turned. He first sets out the elements of his argument: "ideas," the "aspects" of which they are composed, and the difference between "real" and "living" ideas; then how a "living idea" grows into a body of thought, and as such, "develops," by using human communities as instruments. Ideas modify and are modified through time and circumstance. Christianity is shown to be a "living idea," and to have developed according to an "antecedent probability," which suggests provision in the divine plan for having endowed this development with authority.

There can be only one such divinely ordained authority, which, surveying the rival claimants, Newman affirms to be the Church of Rome, as the clearest descendant of the primitive apostolic church. His previously held view that the Roman Church had advanced by doctrinal "corruptions" is now examined according to seven characteristics or proofs, which Newman called "Notes" and identified as true of genuine development. The doctrinal development of the Roman Church is then evaluated according to these criteria— unity of type, dogmatism, power of assimilation, logical sequence, anticipation of tendencies, antecedent development, and chronic vigor—and found to be consistent with them. In the course of these evaluations Newman logically demolished such aberrations as heresy and liberalism, and showed that the universality of the Roman Church, according to the early church fathers, rested not upon her descent from the Apostles, but on the fact that Christ had proclaimed one kingdom only.

At the end of the book Newman addressed his readers, urging them not to put aside the conclusion to which he had led them, for "Time is short,

eternity is long" (*Essay*, p. 445). He had himself resolved to enter the Roman Catholic Church on finishing the book if his convictions remained unchanged. As the many explicit references to this possibility in his *Letters* reveal, one by one he had been cutting the links that held him to the Anglican communion. On 18 September 1843 he had resigned as Vicar of St Mary's, preaching his moving "Parting of Friends" sermon a week later. Finally, after two years more of deliberation and the writing of all but the conclusion of the *Essay*, he resigned his fellowship of Oriel and membership of Oxford University on 3 October 1845. On 9 October, he was received into the Catholic Church by Father Dominic Barberi.

THE "ONE TRUE FOLD OF THE REDEEMER"

NEWMAN'S *Letters and Diaries* reveal his pained awareness of the consternation that his abandonment of the Anglican Church had caused his friends, and his sensitivity to the distrust it aroused in Oxford. He departed for Rome with a companion, Ambrose St. John. After eighteen months and ordination as a Catholic priest, he returned to England in May 1847 as supervisor of the English Oratory of St. Philip Neri to be established at Birmingham. His first literary venture thereafter was the novel *Loss and Gain*, published in 1848, the story of a young man's conversion to Roman Catholicism. While not strictly speaking an attempt at persuasion, this slight but frequently humorous work nonetheless uses the ideas of "unreality" and "reality" and much catechetical dialogue to produce a stirring impression of the Catholic Church. The novel also contains some satirically funny minor characters. Newman did not actually put his name to it until 1874, his first acknowledged book as a Catholic being a set of sermons entitled *Discourses Addressed to Mixed Congregations*, published in 1849. But the idea of "reality" recurs in his *Lectures on Certain Difficulties Felt by Anglicans in Submitting to the Catholic Church* (1850), written in the wake of the Gorham Judgment which had prompted many conversions. Rather than being an apologetic for Catholicism, these lectures were directed to Newman's former co-religionists in the high church camp, with the aim of demonstrating to them the hollowness of Anglican claims. If the overall theme was the falseness of the Anglican position, the means Newman used to display this ranged widely in tone and treatment, from autobiographical references that anticipate the *Apologia* to the demolition by logic of a sequence of Anglican errors and pretensions. What is new is the sense that hitherto guarded aspects of Newman's personality have finally been given full rein. He addressed his audience on a variety of levels, and employed irony, wit, satire, merciless metaphor, and rhetorical device as the tools of persuasion. It is as if the gloves had finally been cast aside in the battle for souls.

In 1850 a Roman Catholic hierarchy was reestablished in England; Nicholas Wiseman, now a cardinal, issued his pastoral letter "From out the Flaminian Gate" and thereby touched off a wave of anti-Catholic feeling against "Papal Aggression." In a sermon for the installation of Bishop Ullathorne of Birmingham entitled "Christ upon the Waters," Newman delivered a scathingly satirical attack on the English spiritual philistinism that underlay the national suspicion of Catholics. His *Lectures on the Present Position of Catholics in England*, delivered during the summer of 1851, continued even more vigorously in the same vein. Here Newman sought to lay bare the roots of English anti-Catholicism, pillorying it as a tradition nurtured on scandal, complacency and ignorance. The "Prejudiced Protestant" knows no Catholics, yet his dread of them is boundless; Catholic doctrine is a closed book to him, yet, like the caricature of the Russian count who imagines himself an expert on the British Constitution, he prefers to believe "... a crude farrago of ideas, words and instances, a little truth, a deal of falsehood, a deal of misrepresentation, a deal of nonsense, a deal of invention" (*Lectures on the Present Position*, p. 26) than ask some simple questions. The cutting humor which dissects the hypocrisies of Protestantism is probably the most extreme of any Newman ever employed; his imagery too is untrammeled by proprieties. Protestantism may be "at best but a fine piece of wax-work, which does

not look dead, only because it is not confronted by that Church which really breathes and lives" (p. 9); yet it is "unreal," and full of inconsistencies. Protestants are blind to these, and continue to wrap themselves in the same web of falsehoods down the centuries, for prejudice "is superior to all facts, and lives in a world of its own" (p. 199). An unfortunate postscript to these lively lectures was the famous Achilli libel case. Newman's costs were covered by Catholic donations, in an expression of regard that vindicated his frankness.

A CATHOLIC UNIVERSITY

IN 1851 Newman eagerly accepted the invitation of the Irish bishops to become rector of a new Roman Catholic university in Dublin. In doing so he entered a minefield of competing interests, but the project, which occupied him for the next seven years, gave him the opportunity to pursue his interest in education and to write what is probably his most influential book, popularly known as *The Idea of a University*. In an educational panorama that has altered out of all recognition it is debatable whether Newman's ideas can be practically applied in the twenty-first century, but this does not render the book less appealing.

Its early discourses are basically persuasive, for the case for the new university had yet to be made to the Dublin Catholics whose sons would attend it. Newman first defines the nature of a university as a place where universal knowledge is taught, and outlines the need for a specifically Catholic education. (Hitherto the education available to Irish Catholics was limited, and most facilities in any case avoided religious instruction). No institution that omits theology, however, can be considered a university, for "whereas it is the very profession of a University to teach all the sciences, on this account it cannot exclude Theology without being untrue to its profession" (*Idea of a University*, Turner, ed., p. 75). Nor does the Catholic Church fear any branch of knowledge, since all knowledge reflects the Creator. Knowledge and religion, then, are not opposed. Newman is at pains to point out that the Catholic understanding of what is meant by God differs profoundly from what others may hold, and that this perspective, which takes eternity as its measure, is a fundamental condition of general knowledge.

Newman's most memorable discourses are those that posit an education in the liberal arts, rather than professional training, as proper to a univerity. Here he draws to some extent upon his own Oxford experience and acquaintances, yet advances much farther. Knowledge for its own sake, considered as inward development, is contrasted with instruction for utilitarian ends. The ideal product of such a liberal education is the "gentleman," whose mind has acquired a philosophical outlook capable of "viewing things in relation to each other and to the whole," and whose capacity to discern and judge enables him to assume a responsible role in society.

Yet—and this is Newman's essential point—the acquisition of the cultivated mind through intellectual development is not and must not be an end in itself. Such a mind can become more sensitive to social niceties than to the promptings of conscience, and so fall into a kind of idolatrous self-awareness like that which Newman had attributed to the Evangelicals in the *Parochial Sermons*. Estimable as the liberal education is, it is not the highest good, for it does not teach moral virtue. Only theology as taught in the Catholic university can counterbalance the tendency to evil inherent in intellectual equiry, especially scientific inquiry, undertaken without a supernatural outlook.

Four lectures on "University Subjects" form the second part of the book. In exploring the best areas of study through which to develop the intellect, Newman raises such themes as the nature of civilization, the differences between science and theology, and freedom of investigation. The book closes with an evocation of the philosophical or "imperial" intellect, a fitting finale for a treatise so magisterial in concept and the ordering of ideas.

The Idea of a University also marked the end of a particularly fecund period for Newman. The university itself was finally established in 1854, but Newman, disillusioned by delays and competing interests, resigned as rector when his term of office expired. Problems connected with the Oratory, the founding of its school, and the reception of his ideas on education by the Catholic hierarchy conspired to depress him further, and for some years he published little, apart from his second novel, *Callista: A Tale of the Third Century* (1856). Set in Roman Africa, this concerns the conversion and martyrdom of a young Greek girl and is far superior to *Loss and Gain*, especially in descriptive writing. Newman also edited two numbers of the Catholic journal the *Rambler* in May and July 1859, and from the Birmingham Oratory kept up a vast correspondence, but by the early 1860's he believed himself forgotten, and the years since his conversion largely unfulfilled.

THE APOLOGIA *AND AFTER*

In the January 1864 issue of *Macmillans Magazine*, the novelist and historian Charles Kingsley alleged that the Catholic clergy, and Newman in particular, employed cunning as a matter of course and were unconcerned with the virtue of truthfulness. In the interchange of letters and pamphlets that followed, Newman found himself once again, through no desire of his own, at the centre of controversy. Lacking redress or apology—and aware that his Tractarianism and conversion had rendered him incomprehensible to much of the Protestant reading public—he resolved to write the true account of his religious opinions. Speed of composition was of the essence: six weekly parts, published separately beginning on 21 April, were written at a rate of some sixteen hours a day, and then reissued, together with the pamphlets written by himself and Kingsley, as the book best known by its short title of the *Apologia pro Vita Sua*.

Newman's overriding concern was to vindicate his honesty, especially, for the sake of all those associated with him in the Oxford Movement, during the time he was an Anglican. The *Apologia* is not, strictly speaking, an autobiography, but an account in five sections of the development of

Newman's beliefs, beginning in childhood and ending with a lengthy section covering the period since leaving the Anglican communion. It cost him intense pain to write, largely because reliving the Tractarian years revived the losses and misunderstandings he had suffered en route to his conversion. But after the literary battering he had taken, he was convinced that a less forthright effort would simply be dismissed.

It is surely paradoxical that while the *Apologia* is the book for which Newman is best remembered, it shares almost none of the characteristics of his other work except perhaps the brilliant sarcasm of the early 1850s sermons, which flashes out in the rejoinder to Kingsley's insult that forms the *Apologia*'s first section. The personal narrative that follows is direct, factual, and wholly engaging, and it was this part of the book that won for it the acclaim that it has never lost. Newman reveals himself in the pages of the *Apologia* as nowhere else in his writings: readers see him as an Oxford scholar and priest, invigorated with a sense of purpose, desolate at the loss of friends, filled with misgivings as his certainties evaporate, and trustingly following the Light where it led him, leaving all else behind. It is a courageous portrait of a courageous life.

The final section covers the years since 1845, and addresses the issue so fundamental to the Catholic Church and so often a stumbling block to those outside it: that of authority and infallibility. It was, of course, the issue that underlay some of the problems Newman himself had experienced since becoming a Catholic, and he quickly scotches the rumors of his discontent. Catholic doctrine presented no problems of belief once he had come to believe that "the Roman Catholic Church was the oracle of God" (*Apologia*, p. 215); and "the being of a God," as he goes on to declare in one of the most stirring passages in all his writings, "is as certain to me as the certainty of my own existence" (p. 216). The knowledge of God, or religious truth, is the ultimate end of rational enquiry, yet reason unguided by religion tends to scepticism, and so to abuse of its own powers. The Catholic Church's authority, as Newman saw it, was part of the divine economy, ordained "to preserve religion in the world, and

to restrain that freedom of thought, which of course in itself is one of the greatest of our natural gifts, and to rescue it from its own suicidal excesses" (p. 219). To those who complain that authority destroys freedom of thought, Newman proposes the idea that truth in fact emerges from the collisions between authority and private judgment. The authentic vigor of each depends on conflict with the other, just as in the state advances come about not out of the monopoly of authority but out of the rivalries of its constituent parts.

Newman's most subtle use of language and argument are reserved for his long exposition of the reasons for authority and the need for submission that occupy the last two dozen pages of his *Apologia*. Newman hints obliquely at his own longstanding difficulties with the extreme traditionalists here, but resists the temptation to go farther; rather, he reemphasizes the universality of the Catholic Church, reminding his readers at the same time that it was Pius IX who by giving English Catholics a church of their own, "... prepared the way for our own habits of mind, our own manner of reasoning, our own taste, and our own virtues, finding a place, and thereby a sanctification, in the Catholic Church" (p. 241). The moving dedication which brings the book to an end enfolds in Newman's gratitude all those, living and dead, who had faithfully assisted his spiritual progression.

The *Apologia* not only routed Kingsley; it repositioned Newman in the eyes of the reading public. He was from now on acknowledged as one of the foremost writers of the century, although even as such he would not be immune from the intrigues of the ultramontane Catholic establishment. He was now sixty-three years old, and increasingly recorded in his private writings the awareness of things unaccomplished. Not unnaturally, his thoughts turned to death and judgment. Out of such considerations emerged the greatest of his poems, not only in length but in subject matter: *The Dream of Gerontius*, which appeared in the Jesuit review the *Month* in May and June 1865. Once again Newman employs the catechetical form of the dialogue. The soul of Gerontius, who has just died, is on its way to purgatory, accompanied by the angel who had been his guardian in life. The action is envisaged as lasting but a fraction of time, during which the soul's separation from the body and the purifying experiences that await it are described. Newman's vision of eternity is a merciful one: the soul is afforded a glimpse of the Beatific Vision and assured that it will eventually once again see God. Were it not for Edward Elgar's magnificent oratorio, the poem would not be as well known as it is; similarly, the words of the hymn "Praise to the Holiest in the Heights" are far better known than the poem from which they come.

LATE PROJECTS

THE train of thought that had found its outlet in the *Dream of Gerontius* now revived an idea that Newman had entertained since the *Oxford University Sermons*: that of enlarging his perspective on the subject of faith and reason to produce a justification for religious belief. It was his most ambitious work, which he feared would encounter criticism since it did not conform to the received tradition of scholastic philosophy. When after four years' labor *An Essay in Aid of a Grammar of Assent* was published on 15 March 1870, the edition sold out on the same day and two more editions within the year.

Newman considered it one of five works of lasting value that he had written—the others being *Lectures on the Prophetical Office, Lectures on Justification, An Essay on the Development of Christian Doctrine,* and the Oxford University Sermons. Overall, the aim of the *Grammar of Assent* is to inquire into the psychology of belief: to analyse the process by which beliefs, in particular, religious beliefs, come to be held, and to affirm the validity of believing with certitude even though demonstrable evidence may be lacking. It is impossible to do more than allude to the main themes of so subtly reasoned a book; it is a philosophical study of the first order and demands patient and attentive reading. In the first of its two parts, terms such as "assent," "apprehension," "inference," and "certitude" are defined, and their interrelationships set out. The famous

distinction between "notional" (roughly speaking, "intellectual") and "real" (or "imaginative") assents is thoroughly elaborated before Newman applies it to the truths and dogmas of Catholicism.

The second part considers certitude as a unique state of mind, how one attains it and is justified in holding it. Newman suggests that certitude is gained through probabilities—small dispositions or "likelihoods"—which individually may be weak, but which, united to many others of the same kind, produce unshakable belief. Certitude is "an active recognition of propositions as true" when presented with evidence (although this need not mean evidence in the scientific sense), the guide in such situations being a virtue which he called the "illative sense," or right judgment in ratiocination (*Grammar*, Ker, ed., p. 222). In applying these conclusions to Christianity, Newman employs a favorite argument, that of first principles, to prove the truth of divine revelation "in the same informal way in which I can prove for certain that I have been born" (p. 264). One's' ability to accept the arguments put forward in favor of Christianity depends on one's acceptance of basic premises at the more general level of natural religion. The section concludes with a historical survey showing Chrisitanity as the culmination of God's covenants with the Jews, then as the unstoppable force that converted the Roman Empire. Throughout it, the many allusions drawn from other disciplines to support Newman's arguments enliven his analysis. Similarly, Newman's inclusion of what later would be known as the subconscious can be seen as much in advance of its time. But overall the *Grammar of Assent* is not an easy book to read, any more than it had been easy to write.

A few years' peaceful interlude was broken by the controversy occasioned by a pamphlet published in 1874 by W. E. Gladstone, lately the prime minister and still the leader of the Liberal Party. Entitled *The Vatican Decrees in Their Bearing on Civil Allegiance: A Political Expostulation*, it was an attack upon what he saw as the pretensions of the Roman Catholic Church, in response to the Vatican Council's recent decree on Papal Infallibility. The suggestion that English

Catholics had renounced their personal freedom and effectively transferred their allegiance to a foreign power was particularly offensive to Newman, who had never considered himself as other than a loyal Englishman. His *Letter Addresses to His Grace the Duke of Norfolk* (1875) was not only a reasoned explanation, for the benefit of Catholics and Anglicans alike, of the meaning of the Vatican Council's decree; it was a definition and an impassioned defence of conscience. It was a subject he had often addressed, but in this context he was intent on clarifying the position of individual conscience in relation to the authority of the Catholic Church. "Conscience" was the law of God as grasped by the individual genuinely seeking to understand such law; not, as in the secular definition that prevailed in civil society, the right to do as one likes without reference to God. In a conflict with legitimate church authority, the individual was in principle bound to submit, unless—and it was a firm "unless"—his conviction to the contrary resulted from sincerely pondering the matter in the presence of God. In such a case, conscience reigns supreme.

In the 1870s Newman began to revise some earlier works, including *Lectures on the Prophetical Office*, in the light of his Catholic experience. The essay that formed the preface to the third edition, published as volume 1 of *The Via Media* in August 1877, was his last important work: an attempt to present "the conflicting interests, and therefore difficulties of the Catholic Church, because she is at once, first a devotion, secondly a philosophy, thirdly a polity" (*Letters*, vol. 27, p. 70). Newman suffered greatly on the death of his friend Ambrose St. John, the headmaster of the Oratory School, in 1875. In contrast to this, the invitation to become the first honorary fellow of his old Oxford college, Trinity, in December 1877 meant a highly emotional return to the town he had loved after a thirty-two-year absence. Re-editing his translation of Athanasius to complete the edition of his *Collected Works*, begun in 1868, was the task upon which he was working when—following overtures from the duke of Norfolk to the newly elected Pope Leo XIII—he received the pope's offer to make him a cardinal, in recognition of his great service to the Catholic Church in England. He traveled to Rome to receive the honor in April 1879, taking his title from the church of St. George in Velabro and as the motto for his coat of arms the saying of St. Francis de Sales, *Cor ad cor loquitur*, "Heart speaks to heart." As a rare privilege Pope Leo permitted him to remain at his beloved Birmingham Oratory; his mental faculties remained unimpaired and he continued to work until his death on 11 August 1890.

SELECTED BIBLIOGRAPHY

I. COLLECTIONS, FIRST AND SUBSEQUENT EDITIONS. *Collected Works*, 36 vols. ("uniform" edition of works first published by Rivingtons, Burns & Oates, Pickering, and Longmans, Green and Co., London, 1868–1881), 37 vols. (1870–1877), 40 vols. (1874–1921, with index by Joseph Rickaby), 38 vols. (1890–1897), 34 vols. (1898), 41 vols. (1908–1918), 38 vols. (1917) (post-1886 all Longmans, Green and Co.); *Selected Works*, ed. by Charles Frederick Harrold, 9 vols. (New York, 1947–1949).

II. SELECTIONS. William Samuel Lilly, ed., *A Newman Anthology. Characteristics from the Writings: Being Selections, Personal, Historical, Philosophical and Religious, from His Various Works* (London, 1875); William John Copeland, ed., *Selection Adapted to the Seasons of the Ecclesiatical Year from the Parochial and Plain Sermons* (London, 1878); *Sayings of Cardinal Newman* (London, 1890); Wilfred Meynell, ed., *Cardinal Newman* (London, 1907); Cyril C. Martindale, ed., *The Spirit of Cardinal Newman* (London, 1914); George O'Neill, ed., *Readings from Newman* (London, 1923); Erich Przywara, ed., *A Newman Synthesis* (London, 1930), repub. as *The Heart of Newman* (London, 1963); Joseph J. Reilly, ed., *The Fine Gold of Newman* (New York, 1931); Aloysius Ambruzzi, ed., *The Newman Book of Religion* (1937); Daniel M. O'Connell, ed., *Favorite Newman Sermons* (New York, 1940); Charles Frederick Harrold, ed., *A Newman Treasury: Selections from the Prose Works of John Henry Cardinal Newman* (London and New York, 1943); Roger J. McHugh, ed., *Newman on University Education* (Dublin, 1944); Charles Frederick Harrold, ed., *Essays and Sketches*, 3 vols. (New York, 1948); Henry Tristram, ed., *The Living Thoughts of Cardinal Newman* (London, 1948); Charles Frederick Harrold, ed., *Sermons and Discourses*, 2 vols., 1825–39 (New York, 1940), 1839–57 (New York, 1949); Henry Tristram, ed., *The Idea of a Liberal Education: A Selection from the Works* (London, 1952); Geoffrey Tillotson, ed., *Newman: Prose and Poetry* (London and Cambridge, Mass., 1957); Vincent Ferrer Blehl, ed., *Realizations: Newman's Selection of His Parochial and Plain Sermons* (London, 1964); Ian Ker, ed., *The Genius of John Henry Newman* (London, 1989).

III. FIRST EDITIONS OF INDIVIDUAL WORKS. *St Bartholomew's Eve: A Tale of the Sixteenth Century in Two Cantos*, anon., with John W. Bowden (Oxford, 1818); *Memorials of the Past* (Oxford, 1832); *The Life of Apollonius Tyanaeus; with a Comparison between the Miracles of Scrip-*

JOHN HENRY NEWMAN

tures and Those Elsewhere Related, as Regards Their Respective Object, Nature and Evidence, in *Encyclopaedia Metropolitana* (London, 1824, 1853 and 1825, 1853), repr. in *Historical Sketches,* vol. 1 (London, 1872) and *The Miracles of Scriptures* in two essays on Scripture miracles and Ecclesiastical miracles (London, 1870); *Suggestions Respectfully Offered to Certain Resident Clergymen of the University in Behalf of the Church Missionary Society, by a Master of Arts* (Oxford, 1830); *The Arians of the Fourth Century: Their Doctrine, Temper and Conduct, Chiefly as Exhibited in the Councils of the Church, between AD 325 and AD 381* (London, 1833; New York, 1882);

Tracts for the Times, by Members of the University of Oxford, ed. by Newman, 6 vols. (Oxford, 1833–1841) [Of the 90 *Tracts* issued anonymously between 9 September 1833 and 27 February 1841, Newman wrote the following: vol. 1, nos. 1–3, 6–7, 8, with R. H. Froude; 10–11, 15, with Sir W. Palmer; 19–21, 31, 33–34, 38, 41, 45; vol. 2, no. 47; vol. 3, nos. 71, 73, 74, with B. Harrison; 75–76; vol. 4, nos. 79, 82; vol. 5, nos. 83, 85, 88; vol. 6, no. 90. List of tracts appears in Henry Parry Liddon, *Life of Pusey,* vol. 3 (London, 1897)];

The Restoration of Suffragan Bishops Recommended, as a Means of Effecting a More Equal Distribution of Episcopal Duties, as Contemplated by His Majesty's Recent Ecclesiastical Commission (1833), *Parochial Sermons,* 3 vols. (1834–1836), 6 vols. (1834–1842), 6 vols. (1837–1842, 1838–1844); 8 vols. repub. as *Parochial and Plain Sermons,* ed. by W. J. Copeland (1868); *Elucidations of Dr. Hampden's Theological Statements* (Oxford, 1836); *Make Ventures for Christ's Sake: A Sermon* (Oxford, 1836); *Lectures on the Prophetical Office of the Church, Viewed Rlatively to Romanism and Popular Protestantism* (London, 1837); *A Letter to the Rev Godfrey Faussett D.D., Margaret Professor of Divinity, on Certain Points of Faith and Practice* (Oxford, 1838); *Lectures on Justification* (London, 1838), repub. as *Lectures on the Doctrine of Justification* (London, 1885); *The Church of the Fathers,* anon. (London, 1840); *The Tamworth Reading Room: Letters on an Address Delivered by Sir Robert Peel Bart M.P. on the Establishment of a Reading Room at Tamworth, by Catholicus, Originally Published in The* Times, *and Since Revised and Corrected by the Author* (London, 1841); *A Letter Addressed to the Rev. R. W. Jelf D.D., Canon of Christ Church, in Explanation of No Go in the Series called the Tracts for the Times, by the Author* (Oxford, 1841); *A Letter to the Right Reverend Father in God, Richard [Bagot], Lord Bishop of Oxford, on Occasion of No. 90 in the Series Called the Tracts for the Times* (Oxford, 1841); *An Essay on the Miracles Recorded in the Ecclesiastical History of the Early Ages* (Oxford, 1843); *Sermons, Bearing on Subjects of the Day* (London, 1843; New York, 1844); *Sermons, Chiefly on the Theory of Religious Belief, Preached Before the University of Oxford* (London, 1843); *Plain Sermons by Contributors to the Tracts for the Times,* vol. 5, anon. (London, 1843); *The Cistercian Saints of England; An Essay on the Development of Christian Doctrine* (London, 1845); *Dissertatiunculae quaedam critico-theologicae (ex nupera Oxoniensi Biblioteca Patrum maxima ex parte desumpta; Latine autem liberius reddita etc)* (Rome, 1847; London, 1874); *Loss and Gain,* anon. (London, 1848), repub. as *Loss and Gain; or The Story of a Convert* (Boston, 1854); *Discourses Addressed to Mixed Congregations* (London, 1849; Boston,

1853); *Lectures on Certain Difficulties Felt by Anglicans in Submitting to the Catholic Church,* 12 pts. (London, 1850, as 1 vol.; New York, 1851); *Christ upon the Waters: A Sermon Preached on Occasion of the Establishment of the Catholic Hierarchy in This Country* (Birmingham, 1850); *Lectures on the Present Position of Catholics in England, Addressed to the Brothers of the Oratory* (London, 1851), repub. as *Lectures on Catholicism in England* (Birmingham, 1851); *Discourses on the Scope and Nature of University Education, Addressed to the Catholics of Dublin,* 11 pts. (Dublin, 1852), rev. and repub. with *Lectures and Essays on University Subjects* (London, 1859) as *The Idea of a University Defined and Illustrated* (London, 1873), repr., ed. by Frank M. Turner (New Haven, 1996), in-text references and pg. numbers refer to Turner edition; *The Second Spring: A Sermon Preached in the Synod of Oscott, on Tuesday July 13th 1852* (London, 1852), repr. in his *Sermons Preached on Various Occasions,* ed. by F. P. Donnolly (New York, 1911); *Verses on Religious Subjects,* anon. (Dublin, 1853); *Lectures on the History of the Turks in Its Relation to Christianity, by the Author of Loss and Gain,* anon. (Dublin, 1854); *Callista: A Sketch of the Third Century,* anon. (London and New York, 1856); *The Office and Work of Universities* (articles repr. from *Catholic University Gazette,* London, 1856); *Sermons Preached on Various Occasions* (London, 1857; New York, 1887); *Lectures and Essays on University Subjects* (London, 1859); *The Tree Beside the Waters: A Sermon Preached in the Chapel of St Mary's College Oscott on Friday November 11 1859, at the Funeral of the Right Rev. Henry Weedall D.D.* (1859); *Mr. Kingsley and Dr. Newman: A Correspondence on the Question Whether Dr. Newman Teaches That Truth Is No Virtue?* (London, 1864); *Apologia pro Vita Sua: Being a Reply to a Pamphlet [by Charles Kingsley] Entitled "What, Then, Does Dr. Newman Mean?"* 7 pts. (London, 1864, as 1 vol.; New York, 1865), rev. as *History of My Religious Opinions* (London, 1865), repr. as *Apologia Pro Vita Sua,* ed. by Ian Ker (London, 1994), in-text references and pg. numbers refer to this edition; *The Dream of Gerontius* (London, 1865; New York, 1885); *A Letter to the Rev. E. B. Pusey D.D. on His Recent Eirenicon* (London, 1866); *The Pope and the Revolution: A Sermon Preached in the Oratory Church Birmingham on Sunday October 7 1866* (London, 1866); *Verses on Various Occasions* (London and Boston, 1868); *An Essay in Aid of a Grammar of Assent* (London and New York, 1870), repr. ed. by I. T. Ker (Oxford, 1985), text references are to this edition; *Two Essays on Scripture Miracles and on Ecclesiastical Miracles* (London, 1870); *Essays Critical and Historical,* 2 vols. (London, 1871); *Historical Sketches,* 3 vols. (London, 1872–1873); *Discussions and Arguments on Various Subjects* (London, 1872); *Orate pro anima Jacobi Roberti Hope Scott* [a sermon] (1873), repub. as *In the World but Not of the World,* in *Sermons on Various Occasions,* 5th ed. (London, 1881); *The Idea of a University* (1873), repr. in his *Discourses on the Scope and Nature of University Education; Tracts Theological and Ecclesiastical* (London, 1874); *A Letter Addressed to His Grace the Duke of Norfolk on Occasion of Mr. Gladstone's Recent Expostulations* (London and New York, 1875); *The Via Media of the Anglican Church, Illustrated in Lectures, Letters, and Tracts Written Between 1830 and 1841; with a Preface and Notes,* 2 vols. (London, 1877); *Two Sermons Preached in the Church of St. Aloysius, Oxford* on *Trinity Sunday 1880* (Oxford, 1880); *Prologue to the Andria of Terence* (written 1820), ptd. for priv. circ. 1882; *What Is of Obligation for a Catholic to Believe Concerning the Inspiration of the Canonical Scriptures: Being a Postscript to an Article in the February No. of the Nineteenth Century Review in Answer to Professor Healy* (1884), repub. as *Further Illustrations*, in his *Stray Essays on Controversial Points Variously Illustrated* (Birmingham, 1890); *Stray Essays on Controversial Points Variously Illustrated* (Birmingham, 1890); *Poetry, with Reference to Aristotle's Poetics* (Boston, 1891); *The Mission of St. Philip Neri: An Instruction Delivered in Substance in the Birmingham Oratory, January 1850, and at Subsequent Times* (Rome, 1901); *The Mission of the Benedictine Order* (London, 1908), repr. in his *Historical Sketches; Sermon Notes 1849–1878*, ed. by Fathers of the Birmingham Oratory (London, 1913); *John Henry Newman: Autobiographical Writing*, ed. by Henry Tristram (London, 1956); *Faith and Prejudice and Other Unpublished Sermons*, ed. by the Birmingham Oratory (New York, 1956; London, 1957); *On Consulting the Faithful in Matters of Doctrine*, ed. by J. Coulson (1961), orig. pub. in *Rambler* (July 1859), repr. with addns. and amends. as appendix to 3d ed. of *The Arians of the Fourth Century* (London, 1871).

IV. SELECTED WORKS EDITED OR WITH CONTRIBUTIONS BY NEWMAN. Newman edited or contributed to the following publications: *British Critic* (July 1838–July 1841), *Rambler* (May and July 1859), *London Review, British Magazine,* Dublin *Review, Catholic University Gazette* (Dublin), *Atlantis, Month, Nineteenth Century, Conservative* (see Jan.-Feb. 1843 for retraction of anti- Catholic views); E. Smedley, Hugh J. Rose, and Henry J. Rose, eds., *Encyclopaedia Metropolitana*, 29 vols. (London, 1817–1845), 40 vols. (London, 1848–1858); R. Whately, *Elements of Logic* (London, 1826), *Tracts for the Times, by Members of the University of Oxford,* 6 vols. (1833–1841); *Lyra Apostolica* (London, 1838), which includes, as No. 25, the poem "The Pillar of the Cloud" (better known as "Lead, Kindly Light"), orig. pub. anon. as "Faith" in *British Magazine* (1 February 1834). See listed Bibliographies, in particular *The New Cambridge Bibliography of English Literature*, for complete listing of Newman's editing and contributions, and for works translated by him.

V. LETTERS. *Letters and Correspondence of Newman During His Life in the English Church; with a Brief Autobiography*, ed. by Anne Mozley, 2 vols. (London, 1891); *Correspondence of Newman with John Keble and Others 1839–45*, ed. by the Fathers of the Birmingham Oratory (London and New York, 1917); Gordon Huntingdon Harper, ed., *Cardinal Newman and William Froude FRS: A Correspondence* (Baltimore, 1933); *The Letters and Diaries of John Henry Newman*, ed. by Charles Stephen Dessain, Ian Ker, and Thomas Gornal, vols. 1–6 (Oxford, 1978–1984), vols. 11–22 (London, 1961–1972), vols. 23–31 (Oxford, 1973–1977); *Newman Family Letters*, ed. by Dorothea Mozley (London, 1962).

VI. BIBLIOGRAPHIES. Joseph Gillow, *A Literary and Biographical History, or Bibliographical Dictionary of the English Catholics*, vol. 5 (New York, 1902); Joseph Rickaby, *Index to the Works of John Henry Newman* (London and New York, 1914); Clarence E. Sloane, *Newman: An Illustrated Brochure of His First Editions* (Worcester, Mass., 1953); George Watson, ed., *The New Cambridge Bibliography of English Literature,* vol. 3 (1800–1900) (Cambridge,

England, 1969); John R. Griffin, *Newman: A Bibliography of Secondary Studies* (Fort Royal, Va., 1980).

VII. SECONDARY WORKS. Hugo M. de Acheval and J. Derek Holmes, *The Theological Papers of John Henry Newman on Faith and Certainty* (Oxford, 1976); *Achilli v. Newman: A Full and Authentic Report of the Prosecution for Libel Tried before Lord Campbell and a Special Jury, June 1852; with Introductory Remarks by the Editor of the Confessional Unmasked* (London, 1852); Louis Allen, ed. *John Henry Newman and the Abbé Jager: A Controversy on Scripture and Tradition (1834–1836)* (New York, 1975); Josef Lewis Altholtz, *The Liberal Catholic Movement in England: The Rambler and Its Contributors 1848–64* (London, 1962); Gaius Glen Atkins, *The Life of Cardinal Newman* (New York, 1931); Joseph Ellis Baker, *The Novel and the Oxford Movement* (Princeton, N.J., 1932); James E. Bastable, ed., *Newman and Gladstone. Centennial Essays* (Dublin, 1978); Edward Bellasis, *Cardinal Newman as a Musician* (1892); Adrian J. Boekraad, *The Personal Conquest of Truth According to Newman* (Louvain, 1955); Adrian J. Boekraad and Henry Tristram, *The Argument from Conscience to the Existence of God According to Newman* (Louvain, 1961); Piers Brendan, *Hurrell Froude and the Oxford Movement* (London, 1974); Oliver J. Brose, *Church and Parliament: The Reshaping of the Church of England 1828–1860* (Stanford, Calif., 1959); Owen Chadwick, *From Bossuet to Newman: The Idea of Doctrinal Development* (Cambridge, England, 1957); Owen Chadwick, *The Mind of the Oxford Movement* (London and Stanford, Calif., 1960); Owen Chadwick, *The Victorian Church*, 2 vols. (London and New York, 1966–1970); Richard William Church, *The Oxford Movement: Twelve Years 1833–1845* (London and New York, 1891), ed. by G. Best (Chicago and London, 1970), in-text references and pg. numbers refer to 1891 edition; John Coulson and A. M. Allchin, eds., *The Rediscovery of Newman: An Oxford Symposium* (London, 1967); John Coulson, *Newman and the Common Tradition* (Oxford, 1970); B. J. Lawrence Cross, ed., *John Henry Newman, Theologian and Cardinal. Symposium 9–12 October 1979* (Rome, 1981); A. Dwight Culler, *The Imperial Intellect: A Study of Newman's Educational Ideal* (New Haven, Conn., 1955); Christopher Dawson, *The Spirit of the Oxford Movement* (New York, 1933); David DeLaura, "O Unforgotten Voice: The Memory of Newman in the Nineteenth Century," in *Sources for Reinterpretation: The Use of Nineteenth Century Literary Documents. Essays in Honour of C. L. Cline* (Austin, Texas, 1975); Charles S. Dessain, *John Henry Newman* (London, 1966); George J. Donahue, *John Henry, Cardinal Newman* (Boston, 1927); Gertrude Donald, *Men Who Left the Movement* (London, 1933); Augustus Blair Donaldson, *Five Great Oxford Leaders: Keble, Newman, Pussy, Liddon and Church* (London, 1900); Leonard E. Elliott-Binns, *English Thought 1860–1900: The Theological Aspect* (1956); Geoffrey C. Faber, *Oxford Apostles: A Character Study of the Oxford Movement* (London, 1933); William R. Fay, OFM, *Faith and Doubt. The Unfolding of Newman's Thought on Certainty*, with a preface by Charles S Dessain (Shepherdstown, W.V., 1976); Joseph M. Flood, *Cardinal Newman and Oxford* (London, 1933); Francis J. Friedel, *The Mariology of Cardinal Newman* (New York, 1928); Richard Hurrell Froude, *Remains of the Rev R. Hurrell Froude*, ed. by Newman and J. Keble. 2 pts. (London, 1838–1839); Sheridan Gilley, *Newman and His Age*

(London, 1990); Hilda C. Graef, *God and Myself: The Spirituality of John Henry Newman* (London, 1967); Charles Frederick Harrold, *Newman: An Expository and Critical Study of His Mind, Thought and Art* (New York, 1945); J. Derek Holmes and R Murray, S.J., eds., *On the Inspiration of Scripture: John Henry Newman* (London, 1967); J. Derek Holmes, ed., *The Theological Papers of John Henry Newman on Biblical Inspiration and on Infallibility* (Oxford and New York, 1979); Walter Edwards Houghton, *The Art of Newman's Apologia* (New Haven, Conn., 1945); Joseph W. Houppart, ed., *John Henry Newman* (St. Louis, 1968); Henry James Jennings, *Cardinal Newman: The Story of His Life* (Birmingham, England 1882); Humphrey John Thewlis Johnson, *Anglicanism in Transition* (London and New York, 1938); Terence Kenny, *The Political Thought of John Henry Newman* (London and New York, 1957); Ian T. Ker, *The Achievement of John Henry Newman* (London, 1990); Ian T. Ker, *John Henry Newman. A Biography* (Oxford, 1988); Mary Aloysi Kiener, *Newman the Romantic, the Friend, the Leader*, with an intro. by G. K. Chesterton (Boston, 1933); Nicholas Lash, *Newman on Development. The Search for an Explanation in History* (London, 1975); Gary Lease, *Witness to the Faith. Cardinal Newman on the Teaching Authority of the Church* (Shannon, Ireland, 1971); Shane Leslie, *Studies to Sublime Failure* (London, 1932); Shane Leslie, *The Oxford Movement 1833 to 1933* (London, 1933); William Lockhart, *Cardinal Newman: Reminiscences of Fifty Years Since* (London, 1891); James W. Lyons, *Newman's Dialogues on Certitude* (Rome, 1978); Hugh A. MacDougall, *The Acton-Newman Relations: The Dilemma of Christian Liberalism* (New York, 1962); Brian Martin, *John Henry Newman. Life and Work* (London, 1982); J. Lewis May, *Cardinal Newman* (London, 1929); Fergal McGrath, *Newman's University Idea and Reality* (Dublin, 1951); Fergal McGrath, *The Consecration of Learning: Lectures on Newman's Idea of a University* (Dublin, 1962); Robert Dudley Middleton, *Newman and Bloxam: An Oxford Friendship* (Oxford, 1947); Robert Dudley Middleton, *Newman at Oxford: His Religious Development* (Oxford, 1950); John Moody, *John Henry Newman* (New York, 1945); Thomas Mozley, *Reminiscences Chiefly of Oriel College and the Oxford Movement*, 2 vols. (London, 1882); Francis W. Newman, *Phases of Faith: Or Passages from the History of My Creed* (London, 1850); Francis W. Newman, *Contributions Chiefly to the Early History of Cardinal Newman*, 2nd ed. (London, 1891); David Newsome, *The Convert Cardinals. John Henry Newman and Henry Manning* (London, 1975); David Newsome, "Newman and Manning: Spirituality and Personal Conflict," in Peter Brooks, ed. *Essays in Honour of Gordon Rupp* (London, 1975); David Newsome, *The Parting of Friends* (London, 1966); Edmund Sheridan Purcell, *Life of Cardinal Manning*, 2 vols. (London and New York, 1895–1896); John Joseph Reilly, *Newman as a Man of Letters* (New York, 1925); Ernest Edwin Reynolds, *Three Cardinals: Newman, Wiseman, Manning* (London, 1958); Joseph Rickaby, *Newman Memorial Sermons* (New York, 1910); Luke Rivington, *The Conversion of Cardinal Newman* (London, 1896); Eleanor Ruggles, *Journey into Faith: The Anglican Life of John Henry Newman* (New York, 1948); Charles Sarolea, *Cardinal Newman and His Influence on Religious Life and Thought* (Edinburgh, 1908); Robin C. Selby, *The Principle of Reserve in the Writings of John Henry Cardinal Newman* (London and New York, 1975); Robert Sencourt, *The Life of Newman* (London, 1948); George Nauman Shuster, *The Catholic Spirit in Modern English Literature* (New York, 1922); George Nauman Shuster, *John Henry Newman: Prose and Poetry* (Chicago, 1925); Edward Sillem, ed., *The Philosophical Notebook of John Henry Newman*, 2 vols. (Louvain, Belgium, 1970); Basil A. Smith, *Dean Church: The Anglican Response to Newman* (London and New York, 1958); Roderick Strange, *Newman and the Gospel of Christ* (Oxford and New York, 1981); M. K. Strolz, ed., *John Henry Newman. Commemorative Essays on the Occasion of His Cardinalate 1879–May 1979* (Rome, 1979); Geoffrey Tillotson, "Newman's Essay on Poetry: An Exposition and Comment," in H. T. Levin, ed., *Perspectives of Criticism* (Cambridge, Mass., 1950); Meriol Trevor, *Newman. A Biography*, 2 vols. (London, 1962); Henry Tristram, *Cardinal Newman and the Function of Education* (Oxford, 1928); Frank M. Turner, ed., *The Idea of a University* (New Haven, Conn., 1996); Bernard Ward, *The Sequel to Catholic Emancipation*, 2 vols. (London and New York, 1915); Maisie Ward, *Young Mr Newman*. (London, 1948); William G. Ward, *A Few More Words in Support of No. 90 of the Tracts for the Times* (London, 1841) Wilfrid Philip Ward, "The Genius of Cardinal Newman," in *Last Lectures* (London, 1914); Wilfrid Philip Ward, *The Life of John Henry Cardinal Newman*, 2 vols. (London and New York, 1912); Alba H. Warren, "Poetry with Reference to Aristotle's Poetics, 1829," in *English Poetic Theory 1825–1865* (Princeton, N.J., 1950); Harold L. Weatherby, *Cardinal Newman in His Age. His Place in English Theology and Literature* (Nashville, Tenn., 1973); Clement Charles Julian Webb, *Religious Thought in the Oxford Movement* (London and New York, 1928); Clement Charles Julian Webb, *What Then Did Dr Newman Do? Being an Inquiry into His Share in the Catholic Revival* (Oxford, 1892); Basil Willey, *Nineteenth Century Studies. Coleridge to Matthew Arnold* (London and New York, 1949); V. R. Yanitelli, ed., *A Newman Symposium: Report on the Tenth Annual Meeting of the Catholic Renascence Society at the College of the Holy Cross, Worcester Mass. 1952* (New York, 1953); Fr. Zeno, OFM Cap. *Newman, Our Way to Certitude: An Introduction to Newman's Psychological Discovery, the Illative Sense, and His Grammar of Assent* (Leyden, Netherlands, 1957).

TERENCE RATTIGAN

(1911–1977)

John A. Bertolini

FROM THE LATE 1930s to the mid-1950s, Terence Rattigan's plays succeeded popularly on the British stage more than those of any other playwright with the possible exception of Rattigan's only commercial rival, Noel Coward. Although Rattigan's reputation with academics and theater critics was not high, he was respected as a skilled craftsman in the construction of effective dramas for the stage. And, as most of his plays were made into prominent films, he retained both fame and success with the general public. All that would change in the middle of the 1950s with the two-pronged revolution in British drama effected by the premiere in 1956 of John Osborne's socially class-conscious *Look Back in Anger*, which, through a careful and aggressive critical campaign, spearheaded by Rattigan's nemesis, the drama critic Kenneth Tynan, linked the good manners of Rattigan's characters to the skilled manner of his play construction in order to make both seem supportive of the political and social status quo. The other was the appearance of Samuel Beckett's universalist tragi-comedy, *Waiting for Godot* (written 1948–1949 but premiered in 1955 in London).

From Osborne's side came a play that voiced (vaguely but passionately) a discontent among the lower middle class and working class and their complaint against what they considered the smug complacency and bigotry of the upper middle class and the aristocracy, groups which, in the person of individual characters, Rattigan treated respectfully and compassionately in his plays. From Beckett's side came a style of writing plays influenced by the aesthetic avant-garde, especially the modernist writing of James Joyce, ostentatiously not accessible to middle-class audiences, and consequently very unlike Rattigan's plays which had traditional narrative structures,

recognizable character types, and carefully crafted dramatic moments of emotional power. In other words, the very aspects of Rattigan's plays that had made them successful with audiences and critics alike, came to seem, in the world of Osborne and Beckett, old-fashioned, suspect, even somehow corrupt.

But until the downgrading of Rattigan's reputation in the late 1950s and from the beginning of his playwriting career in the late 1930s, Rattigan had a spectacular reign as the most consistently successful and esteemed British playwright of his generation, with only Noel Coward as a serious rival. And since his death in 1977, as Osborne's star has declined, Rattigan's reputation has steadily risen as is shown by the number of major productions his best plays have received in Britain, and by the film remakes of two of his most famous plays, *The Browning Version* (1994), and *The Winslow Boy* (1999), the latter being especially significant because it was made by an American avant-garde playwright, David Mamet, who, in the foreword to his published screenplay adaptation of the play unashamedly proclaims his admiration for the play and his regard for Rattigan as a powerful playwright. Vestiges of the old view of Rattigan—that he is an apologist for class distinctions, or that his manner of constructing a play is musty—resurface occasionally, as in *The New Yorker*'s review of *The Winslow Boy* film, or in the *New York Times*'s reaction to Blythe Danner's revival of *The Deep Blue Sea*, but these are minority reports and mainly American.

Rattigan entered upon his career of play writing in a most traditional way—at least according to literary convention—by means of a bargain with his parents that if he did not succeed as a playwright in a specified period of time, he would have to take up his father's profession, the diplomatic corps, or some other suitable and respectable way of earning a living. Rattigan was born Terence Mervyn on 9 June 1911 to William Frank Rattigan and Vera Houston in London. His family was Protestant Irish by descent, which makes Rattigan—often referred to as the most English of English playwrights because his characters are so given to understatement—part of the long line of Anglo-Irish playwrights, stretching from William Congreve to Bernard Shaw. His grandfather, having emigrated from Ireland to England in the 1840s, subsequently attained a high reputation as a jurist in British India. Rattigan's father was a diplomat and, with his wife, lived in various foreign cities: Tangier, Cairo, Berlin. Terence, the younger of two boys born to Frank by Vera, attended the prestigious private school, Harrow, having already been separated for long periods from his parents, while they lived abroad and he and his brother, Brian, lived with their paternal grandmother in London.

Young Terence had long been a surreptitious playgoer, but at Harrow, along with studying and playing cricket, he also wrote several plays, privately. Also while at Harrow, Rattigan had his first long-term homosexual affair. At this time and for most of Rattigan's adult life, homosexual acts in England were illegal and punishable by fine and imprisonment; the prevailing psychiatric view at the time—and one that Rattigan shared—was that homosexuality was a developmental disorder. Although he never presented an overtly homosexual character directly in any of the produced versions of his plays (in some cases first drafts did, only to be revised before production), he often presented characters who have committed some transgressive act for which they have been, are being, or will be, punished, but for whom Rattigan solicits only tolerance and compassion. His own sexuality, therefore, probably accounts for this major characteristic of his plays. But something else about him emerged while he was at Harrow: his talent for being able to write dramatic scenes that hold an audience by engaging its attention and emotions. In an oft-repeated anecdote, Rattigan tells how, after he wrote an assigned one-page playlet for his French master, the completed assignment came back with

the concise judgment, "French execrable. Theatre sense first class." This was prophetic because what the French master had noticed is what anyone reading or seeing a Rattigan play senses: this is a real play and the playwright knows how it should go, he knows what he is doing.

FRENCH WITHOUT TEARS

FROM Harrow Rattigan won a scholarship to Trinity College, Oxford, but he would never graduate. For, while at Oxford, he wrote a play about a love quadrangle set among Oxford students, *First Episode*, with Philip Heimann, which, though it was not much of a success when it was performed, first in London (1933) and then New York (1934), was yet successful enough, given that the author was only twenty-two and had a play running in the West End, a play moreover that had garnered decent reviews. It was at this point that Rattigan struck the bargain with his father to try playwriting for two years, the consequence of failure being the dreaded diplomatic. At John Gielgud's invitation, Rattigan first tried adapting a novel to the stage, *A Tale of Two Cities*, but then Gielgud dropped the idea of producing it in deference to an older actor, the venerable Sir John Martin-Harvey, who made his living performing his own version of the Charles Dickens novel *The Only Way*.

Meanwhile, to mitigate Rattigan's disappointment, Gielgud's producer and associate, Bronson Alberry, agreed to read any other Rattigan plays that the playwright cared to send him. Rattigan sent him the manuscript of *French Without Tears*, its title then being *Gone Away*. Since Rattigan needed money at this point, he took a job working on film scripts for Warner Bros. Studios in Britain. But after some false starts, *French Without Tears* finally opened 6 November 1936, and was a hit with both the audience and (most of) the critics (James Agate being the dissenter). The youthful cast were all rising stars who would rise farther: Rex Harrison and Kay Hammond played the battling main couple, Alan and Diana, while Jessica Tandy and Robert Flemyng played the secondary couple, with Roland Culver providing additional comic touches.

TERENCE RATTIGAN

Terence Rattigan was only twenty-five years old when *French Without Tears* brought him fame and a small fortune. But more importantly, the play demonstrated his characteristic skills as a dramatic artist, revealed the key features of his style of writing plays, and thoroughly expressed his individual personality and identity. It also showed Rattigan's coming to terms with the literary presence of Bernard Shaw, the dramatist who bestrode the world of contemporary play writing like a colossus. Rattigan had always maintained that in the argument over whether plays should be about character or ideas, he was on the side of the former with Arthur Wing Pinero and Henry Arthur Jones rather than of the latter with Henrik Ibsen and Shaw. As early as his days at Harrow, Rattigan declared his allegiance to drama that had box-office appeal and saw himself carrying on in the tradition of Somerset Maugham, Coward, and Benn Levy. Nevertheless, *French Without Tears*, for all of its being a light comedy with great box-office appeal, shows distinct marks of Shaw's influence, particularly the Shaw of *Man and Superman*. Like that play, *French Without Tears* centers around a reversed love chase with a reluctant male chased by a determined female until he finally realizes that he loves her in return. Rattigan ends his play the same way Shaw ended his second act with the hero running away from marriage to the heroine, who undaunted pursues her man. Likewise, just as Shaw fills his play with allusions to animals in order to show humankind's obligatory assent to evolutionary purpose, Rattigan fills his similarly to show the spirit's domination by the body and its needs.

The original title of the play in manuscript and during much of the rehearsal period, *Gone Away*, a term from fox hunting signifying that the hounds have been loosed and the chase underway, suggested both Rattigan's view of sexual love as manifesting humankind's animal nature and alludes to Shaw's metaphoric depiction of sexual love as a hunt of male prey by female predator. The more particular perspectives that Rattigan adds derive from two aspects of his own identity: one political and the other personal. At the time Rattigan wrote the play, he (and many of his generation), having lived childhood through the

First World War, and being aware of the massive (and often pointless) slaughter entailed, was a pacifist—a view Rattigan would change after Adolph Hitler's evil became apparent. And thus he made his protagonist, Alan, the author of a novel about the futility of war. The pacifist theme is not emphasized, but it is present.

Likewise Rattigan's homosexuality does not make itself felt in any ponderous way, but is nevertheless a subtext. At the same time, the play has a central scene in which two of the male characters who were in love with the heroine, Diana, upon finding that she has deceived them both, declare her a "bitch," and express their preference for male solidarity over relations with treacherous females. While they do so, one of them is wearing the skirt of a Greek Euzone (that is, traditional garb for Greek policemen) because he is going to a costume party, to which the two men repair at the end of the second act, taking along with them Alan, the protagonist, who joins them in rejecting the heroine. The play does not end with the traditional comic uniting (or reuniting) of male and female but rather with an image of eternal male flight from the female huntress, as Alan is about to leave by train for London, while Diana runs to pack her bags to follow him. Underlying the entire play is the myth of Diana, the huntress, and Actaeon who, after he had seen the forbidden sight of Diana bathing nude with her exclusively female society, is turned into a stag by the goddess so that he may be pursued and devoured by his own hounds. The underlying myth suggests at the least an anxious attitude toward male-female sexual relations, an attitude that will develop much over the course of the playwright's career. This would not be the last time Rattigan would use his classical education from Harrow and Oxford. Several years later he would use the myth of Echo and Narcissus to underpin *The Deep Blue Sea* (1952).

Though the main battling couple, Alan and Diana, like Beatrice and Benedick before them, account for the comic success of the play, the true Rattiganesque note in the play is struck by the secondary couple, Kit and Jacqueline. The latter character, particularly, in her painful experience of loving and not being loved in return, in the humiliations she suffers for love, authentically embodies Rattigan's view that life is mainly a series of romantic and sexual misalliances.

One example from the play illustrates Rattigan's dramatic gift for understating the suffering involved in love. Jacqueline loves Kit who loves Diana who loves Alan. Near the end of act 1, in an effort to attract Kit's notice, Jacqueline enters with a new hairdo which copies that of the more beautiful and attractive Diana. Alan warns "Jack," as Jacqueline is called by the other characters (an echo of Marcel Proust's habit of giving his female protagonists feminized versions of men's names, as Gilberte, Albertine), that she should change her hairdo at once. She refuses and bets Alan five francs that Kit will notice her new hairdo. Kit enters in search of Diana and barely pays attention to Jack, until he finally does notice the change in her hairstyle. But then he is dismayed to learn that Diana may be interested in one of the other male characters, and while he is thus preoccupied, Jack keeps importuning him to notice her new hairdo further. He becomes impatient, telling her she's being a bore about her hair, and that yes she should keep it that way, and just before he exits, "It'll get a laugh anyway," whereupon Rattigan indicates a pause before Jacqueline goes to Alan and says, "Five francs please" (p. 30), and the curtain comes down.[1]

What makes this a Rattiganesque moment is the painful humiliation Jack experiences publicly and, most importantly, the feebleness and failure of her attempt to cover it over by pretending to have won the bet. Which she has, of course, literally, but as always in Rattigan, the smallest victories come at a cost that makes them feel more like defeats.

AFTER THE DANCE

WITH the popular success of *French Without Tears*, the prospect of a New York production in view, as well as a film version in the offing, Rattigan was enjoying his success, especially the

substantial addition to his income. But he also desired not to be limited, as Coward was, to the métier of light-comedy writing. Toward the end of establishing himself as a writer of serious drama, he worked on two plays which he himself would omit later from his collected plays: *After the Dance* and *Follow My Leader*. The latter, written jointly with a school friend, Anthony Goldschmidt (writing under the pen name of Anthony Maurice), was a send-up of Hitler and his associates, somewhere between Charlie Chaplin's *The Great Dictator* and Shaw's *Geneva* (where Hitler is renamed Battler). Rattigan calls his Hitler, Hans Zedesi, and turns the Nazi salute into Up Zedesi. Since Britain was not yet at war with Germany, the Lord Chamberlain, after consulting the Foreign Office, refused to license the play for public performance. After the war started and there was no diplomatic reason to prevent the play's production, it was duly licensed and opened (and closed) in January of 1940; with the war an actuality and German invasion a possibility, lampoon did not seem either an adequate or appropriate mode for dealing with Hitler and his gang of thugs.

After the Dance turned firmly away from comedy toward drama with a suicide at its center. The play concerns two different generations; David and Joan Scott-Fowler represent the people who came of age during the First World War and became the bright young things of the 1920s but then declined into idleness, failure and superficiality in the 1930s. Helen Banner embodies the next generation, serious and seriously interested in politics and writing. Joan has partnered her husband in conducting his life as a perpetual round of parties and pleasure, with alcohol as the soporific of choice, because she thinks this is what he truly desires and because her love takes the form of trying to please him. Helen sets herself the task of rescuing David from his stalled life and in the process of carrying out her project causes him to fall in love with her. Joan, being one of Rattigan's weak and defeated characters, looks on helplessly as her happiness is destroyed, and she kills herself by jumping from the balcony of their apartment.

---

1. Page references to Rattigan's plays discussed in this article are drawn from the volumes of the *Collected Plays* as cited in the bibliography, with the exception of those from *After the Dance* which are taken from Dan Rebellato, ed. (London, 1995).

Just before Joan kills herself, Rattigan creates an exquisitely painful moment where he reveals how Joan and her husband have completely misunderstood one another. She had thought he was bored by serious people, that he wanted to go on drinking. And he thought that she would have been bored by dealing with his drinking problem. She observes, with Rattigan's best economy and elegance of expression, "It's silly, isn't it? I wouldn't have been bored at all." The subtextual desperation of her understated utterance is punctuated by a burst of "*raucous*" (p. 62) laughter from the other room. The harshness of that mirthless sound accentuates her suffering, and within moments she has silently leapt from the balcony to her death. Rattigan is an equal-opportunity dispenser of despair and the play concludes with David's breaking of his engagement to Helen and his return to the bottle, which he has been told will surely kill him.

This will be the last time Rattigan will resort to such a melodramatic device as having a character commit suicide by leaping off a balcony. In most of his subsequent dramas, he will leave his characters to accept defeat, to live without happiness. Though he is not often seen as similar to Samuel Beckett, Beckett's epitomizing of life in the paradox, "I can't go on, I'll go on" (from *The Unnamable*), might be spoken by most of the protagonists in Rattigan's dramas.

After the Dance opened in London on 21 June 1939, garnered mostly laudatory reviews, and found enthusiastic audiences, but after a state of war was declared to exist between Germany and England in September, the audiences gradually disappeared. Since it had not been a hit, Rattigan did not include the play in his first volume of *Collected Plays*, published in 1953, but the play was revived in a 1992 British Broadcasting Company television adaptation that was immensely successful, and then republished in a series of new editions of Rattigan's plays in 1995.

FLARE PATH

DURING the early 1940s Rattigan continued writing screenplays, mostly adaptations of other people's novels or plays: *Quiet Wedding* (released 1941); two war films, *The Day Will Dawn* and *Uncensored* (both 1942); and an original comedy, *English Without Tears* (1944). All of these films, except *Uncensored*, were collaborations with the producer-writer, Anatole de Grunwald, and directed either by Anthony Asquith, who had directed the first film adaptation of a Rattigan play, *French Without Tears*, or Harold French, who had directed the first stage production of that same play. But Rattigan's next play, *Flare Path*, would be his first bonafide hit since *French Without Tears*, and one of his masterpieces. It was generated from Rattigan's own experiences as an air gunner and wireless operator in the Royal Air Force, which Rattigan joined in April 1940, at the suggestion of his psychoanalyst Keith Newman (née Kurt Neumann), an Austrian refugee. Rattigan had been consulting Newman, a mesmeric figure, to resolve his attitudes toward his father's many extramarital affairs, and toward his own homosexuality, among other issues. Newman prescribed the RAF because he felt Rattigan needed discipline and order in his life. The play that resulted from his service experiences brought Rattigan his biggest success since *French Without Tears*.

The pessimism that had made *After the Dance* so powerful seemed inappropriate to an England under siege by the *Luftwaffe*. Consequently, *Flare Path* offered its beleaguered audience some cause for optimism in its depiction of the camaraderie, courage, and good cheer exhibited by a community of RAF flyers and their wives, staying at a residential hotel near an air field where the flare path guides the flyers' returns from bombing raids. The central conflict in the play involves a wife, Patricia, who must choose between her lover, the handsome film actor Peter Kyle, whose looks are just beginning to go from aging, and her dull but decent, brave, and devoted husband Teddy Graham, a flyer.

Kyle is the most Rattiganesque character in the play, not so much because he is rejected and defeated in the end, but rather because he is so anxious about his sexual attractiveness, is so terrified of his body's decline, of the loss of his good looks, of losing the woman he needs. But like Shaw's Candida (in the Shaw play of the same name that Rattigan admired most), Patricia chooses the weaker of the two men who love her, or rather the one who needs her more. The transition occurs when Teddy finally shows his fear of being shot down to his wife and explains that only his knowledge of her love enables him to overcome that fear long enough to carry out his duty as a flight lieutenant. Where in *After the Dance*, the wife loses her husband to the other woman, here the husband regains the wife's love and the wife's lover is excluded. Only in the context of war where marital unity and group solidarity seem to be values necessary to survival does Rattigan present such a consolation to his audience. The context demands that the apparently narcissistic concern of Peter Kyle with his own physical attractiveness must be subordinated to the needs of the flyer risking his life for the group. But the kind of weak and needy figure Peter Kyle represents will be brought back by Rattigan for a new hearing in several later plays.

Flare Path opened in London in August 1942 and was such a success that it ran for a year and a half, and had many distinguished visitors in its audience, among them, Winston Churchill, who made a shrewd observation about the style of the play: "It is a masterpiece of understatement. But we are rather good at that, aren't we?" (Wansell, p. 126). By noting that the style of understatement is the English national style, Churchill implies that Rattigan is a very English playwright. And by noticing that a key feature of Rattigan's way of having his characters speak was to have them convey powerful emotions by saying little or nothing, he was anticipating Rattigan's own explanation of his essential style. In the preface to volume one of his *Collected Plays*, Rattigan identifies the following skill as the most important to the art of play writing: knowing "what *not* to have your actors say, and how best to have them *not* say it" (pp. xx–xxi). In Rattigan, there is no rhetoric of the passions except for a word, a phrase left incomplete, a pause, an interjection like "you see" that delays the expression of a painful thought, or even silence. Whenever the emotions are powerful in Rattigan, his instinct is to understate, to have his characters be reticent to speak.

In *Flare Path* there is a strong moment of emotion that belongs entirely to Rattigan's kind of theater. One of the secondary characters in the play is a Pole, Count Skriczevinsky, whose wife and child were killed by the Nazis. He is now flying missions with the RAF. He has married a barmaid, Doris, who was kind to him when he first arrived in England. Because she is overweight and lower in social class than he, she thinks he has married her as a convenience and that once the war is over, he will leave her (a typical Rattigan sexual insecurity), whereas the truth is he loves her deeply, partly because of her warmth and kindness, but mainly because she has rekindled in him the will to live and the capacity for human emotions that he felt he had lost when his wife and son were murdered. In the last act of the play, the audience has been led to believe that there is little chance of the Count's returning from a night bombing raid. Most of the main characters are gathered in the hotel lounge conversing, and Rattigan creates a reversal of the audience's expectations wholly in keeping with his principle of understatement, of knowing "what *not* to have your actors say, and how best to have them *not* say it." In the stage directions, Rattigan indicates that while the conversation is going on, the front door should open "quietly" (p. 163) and the Count should enter and take off his jacket. The Count then waits for a lull in the talking before making his presence known.

This is Rattigan's art of understatement at its best. The Count's being alive is a big emotional satisfaction to the audience, but his return is not a bursting into the room, or a shouting that he is alive. The door opens "*quietly*" and he himself stands there in silence while the audience's heart rejoices in his return, all the more so because Rattigan has known not to have him say anything self-regarding or exuberant, and has known that now is the moment for him not to say anything. The feeling of triumph, having been understated, is thus transferred to the audience where it belongs and where it will have the maximum impact because it has proceeded from an apparent minimum of effort.

TERENCE RATTIGAN

WARTIME PLAYS AND FILMS

HAVING proven himself capable of writing a successful serious play with *Flare Path*, Rattigan could afford to present the public a more relaxed work, especially since in 1943 the British audience needed distraction from the death and destruction that surrounded them. The first of the two plays he furnished was *While the Sun Shines* (1943), a light comedy in which three servicemen—an English aristocrat, a Frenchman, and an American—vie for the affections of an English girl, Lady Elizabeth Randall, engaged to the Englishman. A second young woman, Mabel Crumm, allows for various comic trajectories in the plot, as does Elizabeth's roguish father. In one way, the play is a good-natured allegory of the friendly rivalry among the Allies fighting the Nazis; in another way, it is a highly traditional comedy that depends on spiraling complications based on compounded misunderstandings. It was a hit that pleased everyone, including the critics. James Agate compared its playfulness favorably to Wilde's.

The second play was *Love in Idleness* (retitled *O Mistress Mine* for America), and it was written openly as a vehicle for Gertrude Lawrence, though when she rejected it, Rattigan soon proposed it to the American star couple, Alfred Lunt and Lynn Fontanne, who gladly took it. The play premiered in London in December 1944, to a jointly favorable decision by the public and the critics. The play itself centers on a widow, Olivia Brown, who has been living for the past few years with a prosperous cabinet minister (and a married man), Sir John Fletcher, when her son, Michael, who is a socialist, returns home from Canada; thereupon, the son and the lover begin a serious competition for the mother's regard and attention. Featuring prominently in the play is the conflict between generations over socialism. Rattigan allows both Sir John and Michael to state their case, but by the end of the play, as is traditional in comedy, the conflicts are resolved through the triumph of love: when Michael falls in love, Sir John helps him plan how to impress his new girlfriend, and all are reconciled. In both of these comedies, which are about nothing in particular, Rattigan was tilting with Noel Coward

on his own ground, showing that Rattigan could also hold an audience with charming characters, good-natured humor, wit and comical situations.

During this period, Rattigan also wrote a screenplay for his film associate, Anatole de Grunwald, called *The Way to the Stars* (1945; released in America as *Johnny in the Clouds* in 1946). The film was conceived as a tribute to the alliance between British and American flyers during the war, their heroism and self-sacrifice, while it also depicted in a friendly way their differences in temperament, social conduct, manners, and language. As he did for *Flare Path*, Rattigan drew on his experiences in the RAF. The film succeeded highly on both sides of the Atlantic, but it has a special significance for Rattigan's playwriting career in that it is the only one of his films from which he took a character relationship and reused it in one of his plays. In the film, there is a domineering older woman (an aunt played by Joyce Carey) who tyrannizes over a meek young female relation (here her niece, played by Renee Asherson) by forbidding her to socialize with the soldiers, and one of the film's climaxes is an audience-gratifying scene where the niece publicly defies her aunt, telling her off explicitly and at length, thus breaking the aunt's rule over her and acquiring her independence. Nine years later Rattigan would recreate the structure of this situation in the play *Separate Tables: Table by the Window and Table Number Seven* (1954), between Mrs. Railton-Bell and her sexually repressed daughter Sibyl, but with even greater dramatic skill and to more powerful effect.

THE WINSLOW BOY

RATTIGAN'S next project turned out to be probably his most famous play. Based on the famous Archer-Shee court case of the Edwardian era, which came to Rattigan's attention through an essay on the subject by the American critic Alexander Woolcott, *The Winslow Boy* concerns a young naval cadet, Ronnie Winslow, who is wrongly accused of stealing a five-shilling postal order and expelled from school after a summary proceeding. The boy's father, Arthur, a retired banker of modest means, believes his son's protestations of innocence, and begins an effort to clear his name. Since the naval academy from which Ronnie is expelled is the Royal Naval Academy, and therefore equivalent to the king of England, Arthur Winslow has no right under law to sue for review of the case unless a Petition of Right is granted by the king. Such a petition suspends the king's right not to be sued for the sake of the principle, "Let Right Be Done," which words the attorney general writes on the petition to show that the king has endorsed it.

The idea for the legal strategy of Petition by Right comes from Sir Robert Morton, the barrister Arthur hires to represent his son. In real life the Archer-Shee boy was represented by Sir Edward Carson, who less than a decade before had defended the Marquis of Queensberry when Oscar Wilde brought an action against him for libel because the Marquis had left a public note for Wilde implying that he was homosexual. In court, Carson was able to prove that Wilde indeed had committed homosexual acts and that therefore the Marquis of Queensberry could not be guilty of libel. That Rattigan, being homosexual himself, should have chosen to write a play which glorified the legal skills and moral steadfastness of a character based on the man who had exposed Wilde to the threat of imprisonment seems extraordinary. But, it would seem that Rattigan's instincts about good material for drama trumped whatever scruples he had about acknowledging Carson's brilliant role in the Archer-Shee case. He does, however, perhaps strike a blow for Wilde by describing Sir Robert Morton explicitly as a "fop" (p. 398), and by making him into a dandyish figure who always wears a mask to hide his inner feelings, thus turning Carson into a Wildean protagonist.

The Winslow Boy as a piece of dramatic writing is so technically brilliant that it is easy to be distracted from the intense emotion of the play. Rattigan set himself the task of writing a play about a famous trial that has not one single scene in a courtroom. This is but another version of Rattigan's gift for understatement. All the important legal turns in the case occur offstage and are reported to the main characters. By this means Rattigan takes the focus off the plot as information and shifts it to the plot as a series of developments that affect the chief characters. The audience then lives the action through the emotional reactions of the Winslow family.

The one taste of the courtroom Rattigan provides comes as the climax of the second act when Sir Robert comes to the Winslow home to interrogate Ronnie toward the end of deciding whether to represent the boy or not. Rattigan builds the whole interrogation to mislead the audience into thinking that Sir Robert will not accept the case because of the harshness with which he questions the boy, ending with his demand that Ronnie admit to all present that he is "a forger, liar, and a thief!" (p. 408). While the boy breaks down and weeps at his mother's breast, Sir Robert nonchalantly requests that all the papers relating to the case be sent to his office the next day. His request provokes skepticism about whether he needs the materials, considering his conduct of the interrogation, to which Sir Robert replies, "Oh, yes. The boy is plainly innocent. I accept the brief." He then *"walks languidly to the door"* (p. 409) and leaves, as the curtain falls. Sir Robert's simple declaration, which stuns and pleases audiences in equal measures, makes its emotional impact elegantly by means of its casualness and brevity.

The Winslow Boy does not, however, merely exhibit Rattigan's fabled sense of theater; it also bears the marks of it author's psyche. In *Flare Path*, Peter Kyle displayed a basic male insecurity about his physical attractiveness, a terror of its loss. As Rattigan's career progresses his male characters begin regularly to display evidence of physical decline, an illness, debility, or a wound —all indications of some kind of emasculation. In *Flare Path*, one of the minor characters, Squadron-Leader Swanson refers to himself as the "old wingless wonder" (p. 127) and his nickname is Gloria. In *The Winslow Boy*, no less than three of the main male characters are debilitated in some way. Arthur Winslow's health declines in each act with the result that he loses more and more his mobility until in the last act he is confined to a wheelchair. Likewise, Sir

Robert Morton, though his legal prowess is mighty, is far from a well man, and at various points throughout the play he must take a seat, or rest, or excuse himself because he feels ill. It is part of Rattigan's acute sense of individual psychology that he has Arthur's daughter, Catherine, who has during the whole of the play shown the closest emotional attachment to her father, fall in love with Sir Robert, a man who resembles her father in his physical weakness.

Even one of Catherine's suitors, the aging ex-cricket hero Desmond Curry, falls into this pattern by being well past his physical prime, and being aware of it. His proposal to her in the fourth act illustrates both his weakness and Rattigan's skill at representing it in the style of his speech. He has just told her he knows that she only feels "a warm friendliness" (p. 440) toward him, and he continues:

> Of course, the thing is that even if I proved the most devoted and adoring husband that ever lived—which, I may say—if you give me the chance, I intend to be—your feelings for me would never—could never—amount to more than that. When I was young it might, perhaps, have been a different story. When I played cricket for England—*He notices the faintest expression of pity that has crossed* Catherine's *face.*
>
> (*Apologetically.*) And, of course, perhaps, even that would not have made such a difference. Perhaps you feel I cling too much to my past athletic prowess. I feel it myself sometimes—but the truth is I have not much else to cling to save that and my love for you. The athletic prowess is fading, I'm afraid, with the years and the stiffening of the muscles—but my love for you will never fade.
>
> (p. 440)

Desmond's constant interjection of qualifiers, words, and phrases ("of course," "perhaps"), his frequent demurs ("could never"), his use of the conditional ("if," "might")—all contribute to the sense of a man trying to protect himself from further pain, to the sense that these verbal gestures are all delaying tactics to prevent the arrival of her inevitable refusal. The whole speech builds to the moment of greatest humiliation, the turn inward when he says, "I feel it myself sometimes." It is only "sometimes" because the

pain of seeing himself as he is would be unbearable if he always felt it. There is hardly another dramatist capable of depicting the quiet pain of humiliation while allowing his characters to retain their dignity and to attain audience sympathy.

THE BROWNING VERSION

RATTIGAN was at the height of his dramatic powers during this period, for of the plays that followed over the next few years two of them are generally regarded as his best work along with *The Winslow Boy*: *The Browning Version* (1948) and *The Deep Blue Sea*. The truth though is that while these plays may have extra distinction in their capacity to move audiences, Rattigan's plays rarely fall below a high level of structure, writing, characterization, and emotional power. There will be two odd missteps, *Variations on a Theme* (1958) and *Before Dawn* (1973), but otherwise Rattigan will maintain a remarkably consistent level of play writing.

Before writing *The Browning Version* in November 1946, Rattigan completed two screenplays to order, the first to be directed by Anthony Asquith (but later turned over to John Boulting), an adaptation of Graham Greene's novel (or "entertainment" as the author called it) *Brighton Rock*, and for the producer Anatole de Grunwald, *Bond Street* (both released in 1947), a film which consisted of interlocking anecdotes, each involving a different element from a bride's trousseau. Rattigan did this work essentially as a writer for hire, though he did put his mark on the first screenplay by emphasizing the small-time criminal, Pinkie's symbolic role as the devil.

The Browning Version was originally written as part of a trilogy of one-act plays, the other two being *Harlequinade* (originally titled *Perdita*) and *High Summer*. All were written in the hope that John Gielgud would play the leads. The last play was deemed unsuitable for production, and Gielgud turned down the offer, much to Rattigan's annoyance. Finally, Eric Portman agreed to play the male leads in each of the two surviving plays, while Mary Ellis took the female leads. *Harle-*

quinade takes a benevolent view of the self-absorption of actors through its comical portrait of a married couple (clearly based on the Lunts) who head an acting troupe putting on a production of *Romeo and Juliet.* Most of the best gags revolve around the actors' use of world-shattering historical events as aides-memoire to establishing when they were in this or that play, with the former events clearly of lesser moment to them than the latter.

The *Browning Version*'s title alludes to the translation Robert Browning made of Aeschylus' *Agamemnon,* a secondhand copy of which figures in the play as a gift—one of several gifts that structure the play. It is given by a student with the evocative name Taplow to the play's central character, the student's classics master Andrew Crocker-Harris. Taplow is moved to make this gift because he perceives that beneath Crocker-Harris' precise diction, fastidious manners, and cold-hearted treatment of his students lies a feeling creature who has "been about as badly hurt as a human being can be" (p. 40). And, when Crocker-Harris finally understands that he has been given a gift out of authentic human kindness and fellow feeling, he breaks down utterly, in a scene that is intensely moving exactly because the audience has only seen Crocker-Harris' seemingly sadistic manner with the students. His precise verbal formulations seem, at first, like an act of aggression against the world; they are, rather, a verbal wall he builds to defend himself from all feeling and, as the audience sees later, from the cruelty of his wife's bitter hostility toward him.

In the course of the play the audience learns that Andrew and his wife Millie are a sexual misalliance, as Crocker-Harris explains: "Both of us needing from the other something that would make life supportable for us, and neither of us able to give it" (p. 44). Though this sexual incompatibility may have originated in Rattigan's imagination as between a homosexual husband and a heterosexual wife, in the play itself it is left undefined—what hints there are point vaguely to different levels of sexual appetite or male impotence—and arguably is more powerful therefore, because most people experience some

form of sexual incompatibility at some time. At the end of the play, Rattigan allows his character some small measure of hope, in that he and his wife do not expect to go on living together, which as his wife's lover tells him is his only chance to go on living at all. Andrew also manages a small act of defiance against the headmaster who has asked him to speak first at his retirement ceremony rather than last, as would be his privilege.

One example will illustrate Rattigan's technique of getting the maximum effect from the simplest of means. Because his ill health is forcing him to retire, Crocker-Harris has to meet his younger successor, who inadvertently reveals to Crocker-Harris that his students and colleagues refer to him as "the Himmler of the lower fifth" (p. 30). This knowledge makes him aware that he is not merely disliked by the students but actually feared; it is an awareness he has avoided. Rattigan makes the audience understand the pain this causes Crocker-Harris by having him reiterate the phrase to himself four times during the remainder of his conversation with the new master who must replace him. Each time he does so, the repeated phrase has for him and for the audience a lacerating effect, until the last time, he imagines himself, like Prufrock, formulated in the phrase: "The Himmler of the lower fifth! I suppose that will become my epitaph" (p. 32).

ADVENTURE STORY

RATTIGAN had long wanted to write a play about Alexander the Great, and though it would be his first history play—not his last, however—it would present Rattigan's particular sense of life with uncommon clarity. This play about a world conqueror begins with him on his death bier, bidding farewell to his soldiers, barely able to move or speak, asking himself, "Where did it first go wrong?" (p. 107). So many of Rattigan's protagonists are always already defeated; Alexander is one of those. Whatever adventure one undertakes will end badly, in defeat, or in a victory so small or insignificant that it feels more like a defeat. When Alexander's generals urge him to pick a successor, he whispers the question, "Who shall I condemn to death?" (p. 106) as if the only thing one could succeed to is death.

Rattigan's growing sense that life has only different kinds of failure to offer is illustrated not just by Alexander's fate in the play, but also by that of his antagonist, Darius. In one of Rattigan's best scenes, the royal Persian family is relaxing at home in the palace garden; Darius reads them a dispatch about the upstart invader who has just cut the Gordian knot. Darius is amused by Alexander's audacity, but not afraid. The Queen Mother is also casually dismissive of any threat Alexander might pose, and she declares with confidence that Alexander will not be able to get through the Cilician Gates whatever happens. Then Rattigan distracts the audience from thinking about Alexander while the royals discuss a number of amusing domestic issues; another dispatch is brought to Darius, and while he continues taking part in the conversation, he reads it over; suddenly he breaks off speaking, and his mother asks him what the matter is. Rattigan indicates a long pause, and then Darius replies that Alexander "has broken through the Cilician Gates" (p. 123). Another pause allows the enormity of this news to have its impact. In other words, Darius is already defeated, for even before he knew it, Alexander had already penetrated a supposedly impregnable barrier.

Adventure Story starred Paul Scofield, and in spite of favorable audience response and good notices from the critics, it only ran for 107 performances in 1949. This was Rattigan's first play in several years not to be an outright success with audiences, and perhaps partly for that reason he named it as his favorite among his own plays. This succès d'estime would be followed soon by a play much more popular with audiences and even more highly praised by critics.

In terms of commercial success, Rattigan stumbled again after *Adventure Story*, when he wrote *Who Is Sylvia?* (1950), a comedy about a married man, who is always unfaithful to his tolerant wife with women who are all the same physical type, with red hair. Rattigan meant it as an indulgent portrait of his parents' marriage. As a light comedy, it has moments of charm and wit, and even emotion—for example, when the

wife explains why she turned a blind eye to her husband's infidelities—but the play did nothing to enhance his reputation with the critics, and was not a commercial success. Notwithstanding its lack of success, it was later turned into a film under the title *The Man Who Loved Redheads* (1954) with several members from the original cast, including the leading actor, Robert Flemyng. Moira Shearer played all the red-headed young women.

At this point in Rattigan's career he made a mistake that was the first breach in the wall of his reputation as a serious writer of drama. He dashed off an article declaring his allegiance to the play of character and situation as against the play of ideas and published it in *The New Statesman*. The battle Shaw had fought and won to have plays like those of Ibsen respected as literature above the conventional comedies and melodramas of his time was too recent a victory for its supporters to give up on it. Rattigan's article provoked a series of ripostes from: James Bridie, Benn Levy, Peter Ustinov, Sean O'Casey, and others, and finally from Shaw himself (then age ninety-four, the last year of his life). Several of them took Rattigan to task for setting up a false and simplistic dichotomy, but insisted that the theater must have room for thought. Rattigan was given the last word, and though he declared himself honored by the stature of his attackers, he also said he remained convinced that his view was right. It was a stance that was to cost him dearly during the next decade.

THE DEEP BLUE SEA

THE idea for *The Deep Blue Sea*, a play about a respectable upper-middle-class married woman who gives up her comfort and status to pursue her sexual passion for a younger man, handsome and heroic but totally self-absorbed, only to attempt suicide when she discovers that he will not stay with her, originated in the suicide of one of Rattigan's lovers, the young actor Kenneth Morgan in 1950. The play itself would be produced in 1952 after going though three successive drafts. When finally produced with Peggy

Ashcroft as the protagonist, Hester Collyer, it was well received by critics, with the exception of Kenneth Tynan, who objected to Rattigan's not letting Hester succeed in her suicide attempt. What Tynan failed to see was that Rattigan was getting at a worse fate for his heroine. He had already used suicide in *After the Dance* as a way of allowing his heroine to escape unhappiness and despair. In his subsequent plays, he does not let his characters kill themselves (except for *Man and Boy* (1963) where suicide is implied but not enacted and his last play, *Cause Célèbre* (1977), where he was being true to the facts of the real case the play was based on). Hester Collyer must learn to live without hope; it is a living death to which she resigns herself.

The power of the play derives from the way Hester devotes sincere love and obsessive sexual passion toward an individual who is simply incapable of feeling a commensurate emotion in return. Hester's lover, Freddie Page, is not unworthy, or even cruel. Although he drinks too much, he has been an RAF pilot in the Second World War, is a decent person, and does have feeling for her. But, he is completely self-absorbed. The play begins with Hester's attempting suicide because Freddie has forgotten to come home for her birthday dinner. In the last scene of the play, just before Freddie tells Hester he is leaving her, Rattigan has him look in the mirror to adjust his tie. This is Rattigan's way of showing Freddie's casual narcissism.

In many ways, the myth of Echo and Narcissus underlies the play. In Ovid's version, the nymph, Echo, because of her love for the beautiful young Narcissus who fell in love with his own reflection, pined away so much that her power of speech declined to the point where she could only repeat the last few words of what was spoken to her. Rattigan makes ingenious use of this motif by having Hester frequently repeat Freddie's words to her. For example, from the end of the first act, when Freddie returns, not knowing that the other tenants have saved Hester's life:

FREDDIE. I haven't done anything have I?
HESTER. No, Freddie. You haven't done anything
. . . .
FREDDIE. I've said I'm sorry. I can't say more, can I?

HESTER. No. You can't say more.
. . . .
FREDDIE. This is me, Freddie Page. Remember?
HESTER. I remember.
. . . .
FREDDIE. Still love me?
HESTER. I still love you.

(pp. 319–320)

The subtext of each of her resigned and laconic repetitions of his words is her realization of his shallowness and self-absorption coupled with her equal realization that she still cannot help loving him.

While he was working on *The Deep Blue Sea*, Rattigan also completed a screenplay for Alexander Korda, *The Sound Barrier*. The film, directed brilliantly by David Lean and released in 1952, was about an aircraft manufacturer who is obsessed with breaking the sound barrier and loses a son in the pursuit of that dream; it was an enormous success.

SEPARATE TABLES

RATTIGAN's next play, *The Sleeping Prince*, would be another light comedy and a play written for a public occasion, the coronation of Queen Elizabeth in 1953. It starred Laurence Olivier and his wife Vivien Leigh. It was a send-up of Ruritanian romance with the Acting Ruler being a lecherous predator who is humanized by the efforts of a wily showgirl. (In the film version which appeared in 1957, retitled *The Prince and the Showgirl*, Marilyn Monroe replaced Vivien Leigh as the Showgirl.) The critics dismissed the play, but the public rushed to see it, drawn no doubt by the twin allures of its being a play connected with a popular public event, and the star power of the Oliviers.

In 1953, Rattigan published the first two volumes of his *Collected Plays*. They included prefaces which, like the debate on the play of ideas in *The New Statesman*, damaged Rattigan's reputation as a serious playwright. For the second volume, as part of his defense of plays that deal with situation and character rather than ideas, Rattigan invented a figure, who for him embodied his middle-class audience, Aunt Edna. Rattigan claimed that he made his plays in such a way that they would please her middlebrow tastes: there would be nothing to offend her sensibilities, no ideas to hurl at her, not because she is incapable of understanding them but because in the theatre she cannot respond. The critics were aghast at Rattigan's seeming rejection of modernism, the avant-garde, of anything not acceptable to middlebrow tastes. So blinded were they by Rattigan's apparent rejection of innovation, that they neglected to notice that he had enunciated profound and perceptive ideas about the art of playwriting itself, particularly his own approach based on understatement and implication, knowing "what *not* to have your actors say, and how best to have them *not* say it." He had turned over another shovel full of dirt in the grave of his artistic reputation—without realizing it.

Nevertheless, Rattigan's skill as a playwright had not been lost, and the play that followed the light comedy *The Sleeping Prince* would be one of his masterpieces, *Separate Tables* (1954). Set at a residential hotel, *Separate Tables* tells two stories about its residents. The first story, *Table by the Window*, centers on one of Rattigan's obsessive themes, that of sexual incompatibility, this time between a left-wing journalist and his beautiful wife, who had separated because she did not want to have children, for fear that doing so would make her lose her looks and face the prospect of growing old. What each discovers by the end of their play is that they stand a better chance together of bearing their fears than they do apart.

The second story, *Table Number Seven*, is what allows *Separate Tables* its claim to greatness. It originally involved the discovery by residents at the hotel that one of their number, Major Pollock (his rank turns out to be fraudulent) has been charged with a homosexual offense, but because of possible censorship problems, Rattigan had to change the offense to molestation of women in a public place. Mrs. Railton-Bell, the self-appointed guardian of propriety at the hotel, bullies a majority of the other residents into voting to demand that the Major be asked to leave the hotel. But, in one of Rattigan's quietly inspiring scenes, when the moment comes to act, and the Major bravely decides to face the opprobrium by

taking his usual table for dinner among the other residents, they go against Mrs. Railton-Bell's will and one by one compassionately make small talk with the Major to show that they have changed their minds about shunning him. Not only do the other residents defy her, but her own daughter, Sibyl, a shy, sexually repressed and maternally oppressed young woman, finally exercises her own will against her mother's express command that she leave the dining room with her. The relationship between Sibyl and her mother is an expansion and finer treatment of the relationship Rattigan had invented for the film *The Way to the Stars* in which a niece publicly reproaches and breaks off relations with the tyrannical aunt who had been curtailing her freedom. But whereas in the earlier film the defiance consists of a long vehemently delivered speech denouncing the aunt, in *Separate Tables* Sibyl's rebellion is accomplished with two words, "No, Mummy" (p. 194). The defiance is more satisfying and moving for being so understated. The principle of less is more is the essence of Rattigan's dramatic art.

RATTIGAN'S DOWNFALL

BETWEEN *Separate Tables* (1954) and Rattigan's next play, *Variation on a Theme* (1958), Rattigan suffered a degradation in his stature that is unparalleled in the history of British drama. In 1955, Beckett's *Waiting for Godot* had its London premiere. Its difficulty of comprehension made Rattigan's accessibility seem meretricious, its new style made his realism seem suddenly old-fashioned. In 1956, another blow befell Rattigan: John Osborne's *Look Back in Anger* premiered. Suddenly here was a play that seemed dissatisfied not with the human condition, but with society, and it said so loudly, which made Rattigan's understatement seem somehow cowardly. In Kenneth Tynan's review of *Look Back in Anger*, he nominated it a play for people under thirty. Rattigan's plays now seemed only meant for people over thirty.

When *Variation on a Theme* (the theme being that of the Lady of the Camellias) opened, it was to mostly negative reviews. It was much publicized at the time that Shelagh Delaney, who had seen the play while it was on tour, declared that she could write a better play, and proceeded to write *A Taste of Honey* which was produced in due time by Joan Littlewood and became a success. For the next decade, Rattigan's plays would be received with a modicum of respect—for Rattigan still had an admiring public, even if only Aunt Ednas— and a large dose of condescension—for Rattigan still had the critics.

Ross (1960) was a play that resulted from Rattigan's failure to secure a producer for his original screenplay on the life of Lawrence of Arabia, which he had worked at sporadically throughout the 1950s. When David Lean's competing version was set for production, Rattigan's screenplay was no longer bankable, so he turned it into a play. It is easy to see why T. E. Lawrence (who used the alias "Ross" when he enlisted in the RAF after his participation in the Arab revolt) suited Rattigan as a protagonist. He was a man suffering from spiritual exhaustion, one who bore psychological wounds, partly as a result of the violence he participated in during the Arabs' war against the Turkish Empire, but also due to the violence he suffered when he was raped and beaten by a Turkish general. In this "Ross" is kin to Rattigan's other wounded or debilitated characters. The keynote of the play is struck by the line, "God will give you peace," which recurs several times. The self-knowledge "Ross" gained during the war only makes him long to be oblivious of self.

Though the reviews for *Ross* were generally favorable, those for a musical version of *French Without Tears* called *Joie de Vivre* (1960) were uniformly unfavorable. They were probably the worst notices any Rattigan work had ever received. It would be three years before Rattigan had another play produced in London. (In the interim, he wrote a teleplay for the BBC, called *Heart to Heart* [1962], about a political scandal revealed on a television program, which forces a cabinet minister to resign.) In 1963, *Man and Boy*, starring Charles Boyer, opened to mixed reviews. The main character was an international financier, Gregor Antonescu; he is in the last stage of a fight to keep himself from going to

prison for fraud. In one way, this is a suspense play: Will Antonescu save himself at the last moment yet again? In another way, it is a play about a strong father and a weak son, and the power that the weak wield over the strong.

RATTIGAN'S FINAL PLAYS

AFTER the partial success of *Man and Boy*, which to Rattigan felt like failure, for the next seven years he worked at various film and television projects but did not have a play produced until 1970, when *A Bequest to the Nation*, his play about Lord Nelson's *amour fou* for Emma Hamilton, was put on with Zoe Caldwell and Ian Holm. (Among the film projects was *The V.I.P.s* [1963], a star vehicle for Richard Burton and Elizabeth Taylor, which became MGM's highest grossing film of the year, and consequently made Rattigan the highest paid screenwriter of the time.)

In dramatizing the love triangle of Lord Nelson, his abandoned wife (who still loves him), and his mistress, Emma Hamilton, Rattigan returned to one of his favorite themes, sexual misalliance. Lord Nelson turns away from his wife because he cannot have with her the sensual relationship he has with Emma. Emma though is a social embarrassment to Nelson because of her excessive drinking and vulgar behavior. All three are doomed to perpetual dissatisfaction. The play's great coup de théâtre comes when Nelson reveals that he cannot bear to have his wife discussed, not because he hates her, but because she does not hate him for leaving her. The means whereby Rattigan shows this to the audience involves a letter she has written to her husband which he has seemed to refuse reading. In fact, not only has he read the letter but the letter's kindness and the forgiveness it expresses toward him are so unbearable a torment that the words have imprinted themselves on his brain: he recites the letter from memory at a climactic moment in the play. Thereby the audience comes to a sudden and compassionate revaluation of the love triangle.

Rattigan's next—and next to last—play, *In Praise of Love* (1973), has the strangest genesis of any of his plays. In 1957, Rattigan spent six weeks living with his old friend, Rex Harrison, and the woman he was about to marry, Kay Kendall, who was dying of leukemia, the knowledge of which Harrison had decided to conceal from her. The play that was performed sixteen years later involves a playwright who comes to stay with an old friend, a critic, named Sebastian Cruttwell, whose wife is dying of an incurable disease, the knowledge of which her husband decides to conceal from her. In London, Donald Sinden played Sebastian, but when the play opened a year later in New York, Rex Harrison played the character, based loosely on himself. In the play, the wife actually does know that she is dying, and plays along with her husband's ploy. Both husband and wife then play roles designed to spare one another's feelings, and the whole play is structured to lead to the moving revelation of the reality behind the role playing. *In Praise of Love* is one of Rattigan's most hopeful plays because it opposes the force of such love against the annihilating power of death.

Rattigan's last play, *Cause Célèbre*, based on the infamous Alma Rattenbury case, is certainly among his greatest plays but decidedly much darker than its predecessor. It tells the story of a vivacious, sexually vital woman married to an older man who is physically debilitated by illness and impotent (another of Rattigan's wounded males, another sexual misalliance). She begins an affair with a brutish, barely articulate handyman, George Wood, who eventually murders her husband in a savage manner. Since Alma blames herself for not having prevented the murder, she refuses to exculpate herself by giving evidence against her lover. When she is released for lack of evidence against her, and because she believes her lover will be executed, she commits suicide. Just before she does so with her son's boy scout knife, she says, "Thank God for peace at last" (p. 437). As in *Ross*, death is felt both as a horror and as a longed-for relief from the torment of love and life.

When Rattigan attended the premiere of his last play, he went as Sir Terence Rattigan, having been knighted in 1971, but he also went as a very sick man, having been diagnosed with leukemia in 1972. Terence Rattigan died of his illness in bed at his home in Bermuda, 30 November 1977. At the time he died, his diminished reputation as a playwright had begun to revive and has continued growing ever since. There will always be those determined to see him as a tacit apologist for class divisions and privileges, but for those who look at his plays with unprejudiced eyes they will find rather the most naturally gifted playwright of the midcentury, with a capacity to move audiences through the power of understatement, implication, and subtext rather than by rhetoric, or spectacle, or volume, a playwright able to represent the acutest pains of humiliation and heartbreak without a trace of the maudlin, a playwright whose characters communicate their deepest feelings to an audience more by what they do *not* say than by what they do say, and more by *how* they do not say it than by how they do.

SELECTED BIBLIOGRAPHY

I. PLAY COLLECTIONS. *Collected Plays of Terence Rattigan*, vol. I (London, 1953) (contains *French Without Tears, Flare Path, While the Sun Shines, Love in Idleness,* and *The Winslow Boy*), vol. II (London, 1953) (contains *The Browning Version, Harlequinade, Adventure Story, Who Is Sylvia?,* and *The Deep Blue Sea*), vol. III (London, 1964) (contains *The Sleeping Prince, Separate Tables, Variation on a Theme, Ross,* and *Heart to Heart*), vol. IV (London, 1978) (contains *Man and Boy, A Bequest to the Nation, In Praise of Love,* and *Cause Célèbre*); *Plays: One* (London, 1981), intro. by Anthony Curtis (contains *French Without Tears, The Winslow Boy, The Browning Version,* and *Harlequinade*); *Plays: Two* (London, 1985), intro. by Anthony Curtis (contains *The Deep Blue Sea, Separate Tables,* and *In Praise of Love*).

II. SINGLE PLAY EDITIONS. *After the Dance* (London, 1934); *French Without Tears* (London, 1937; New York, 1938); *Flare Path* (London, 1942); *Love in Idleness* (London, 1945); *The Winslow Boy* (London, 1946); *The Browning Version* (London, 1949); *The Browning Version* (London, 1949); *Harlequinade* (London, 1949); *Adventure Story* (London, 1950); *The Deep Blue Sea* (London and New York, 1952); *The Deep Blue Sea* (London, 1952; New York, 1955); *The Sleeping Prince* (London and New York, 1954); *Separate Tables: Two Plays* (London and New York, 1955); *Separate Tables* (London and New York, 1955); *Ross* (London, 1960; New York, 1962); *Man and Boy* (New York, 1963; London, 1964); *In Praise of Love* (London, 1973); *Cause Célèbre* (London, 1978). Nick Hern Books, London, has published the following plays, all edited and with extensive critical introductions by Dan Rebellato: *The Winslow Boy* (1994); *The Browning Version and Harlequinade* (1994); *French Without Tears* (1995); *After the Dance* (1995); *The Deep Blue Sea* (1999); *Separate Tables* (1999).

III. SCREENPLAYS (UNPUBLISHED). *French Without Tears,* with Anatole de Grunwald and Ian Dalrymple (1939); *Quiet Wedding,* with de Grunwald (1941); *The Day Will Dawn,* with de Grunwald (1942); *Uncensore*d, with Rodney Ackland (1942); *English Without Tears,* with de Grunwald (1944); *Journey Together* (1945); *The Way to the Stars* (1945); *Brighton Rock,* with Graham Greene (1947); *Bond Street,* with de Grunwald and Ackland (1947); *The Winslow Boy,* with de Grunwald (1950); *While the Sun Shines,* with de Grunwald (1950); *The Browning Version* (1952); *The Sound Barrier* (1952); *The Final Test* (1954); *The Man Who Loved Redheads* (1955); *The Deep Blue Sea* (1955); *The Prince and the Showgirl* (1957); *Separate Tables,* with John Gay (1958); *The V. I. P.s* (1963); *The Yellow Rolls Royce* (1965); *Goodbye, Mr. Chips* (1969); *Bequest to the Nation* (1973).

IV. INTERVIEWS. John Simon, "Rattigan Talks to John Simon," in *Theatre Arts* 46 (April 1962); Sheridan Morley, "Terence Rattigan at 65," in *Times* (9 May 1977).

V. BIOGRAPHICAL STUDIES. Michael Darlow and Gillian Hodson, *Terence Rattigan, The Man and His Work* (London and New York, 1979), rev. ed. (London, 2000); Geoffrey Wansell, *Terence Rattigan* (New York, 1997).

VI. CRITICAL STUDIES. Holly Hill, "A Critical Analysis of the Plays of Terence Rattigan," Ph. D. diss., City University of New York, 1977; Susan Rusinko, *Terence Rattigan* (Boston, 1983); B. A. Young, *The Rattigan Version: Sir Terence Rattigan and the Theatre of Character* (London, 1986).

VI. CRITICAL ESSAYS. T. C. Worsley, "Rattigan and His Critics," *London Magazine* (September 1964); Richard Foulkes, "Terence Rattigan's Variation on a Theme," *Modern Drama* 22, no. 4 (1979); Murray M. Carlin, "Lenin, Hitler and the House of Commons in Three Plays by Terence Rattigan: A Case for the Author of *French Without Tears,*" in *University of Cape Town Studies in English* 12 (1982); Holly Hill, "Rattigan's Renaissance," in *Contemporary Review* 240, no. 1392 (January 1982); Susan Rusinko, "Rattigan versus Shaw: The Drama of Ideas Debate," in *SHAW: The Annual of Bernard Shaw Studies,* vol. 2 (University Park, Pa., 1982); Robert F. Gross, "'Coming Down in the World': Motifs of Benign Descent in Three Plays by Terence Rattigan," in *Modern Drama* 33, no. 3 (1990); Christopher Innes, "Terence Rattigan: Updating the Well-Made Play," in *Modern British Drama 1890–1990* (Cambridge, England, and New York, 1992); John A. Bertolini, "Finding Something New to Say: Rattigan Eludes Shaw," in *SHAW: The Annual of Bernard Shaw Studies,* vol. 13 (University Park, Pa., 1993); Richard Foulkes, "Sir Terence Rattigan," in *British Dramatists,* ed. by K. A. Berney (Farmington Hills, Mich., 1994).

ALASTAIR REID

(1926–)

Jay Parini

ALASTAIR REID—THE Scottish poet, essayist, and translator of Spanish literature—has, over many decades, been associated with *The New Yorker*, which first published him in the early 1950s. His intensely lyrical and whimsical poems, which brood on the subjects of dislocation and grace, have been widely anthologized, and his essays (travel pieces, personal meditations, criticism and reportage) have attracted a devoted following on both sides of the Atlantic. His well-known translations from the Spanish of Pablo Neruda and Jorge Luis Borges have played an important role in fueling the so-called boom in Latin American literature.

Living abroad for most of his adult life, on several continents, Reid has been the quintessential foreigner, a condition as much metaphysical as physical in his formulation, as seen in his engaging essay "Notes on Being a Foreigner," where he writes: "Foreigners are, if you like, curable romantics. The illusion they retain, perhaps left over from their mysterious childhood epiphanies, is that there might somewhere be a place—and a self—instantly recognizable, into which they will be able to sink with a single, timeless, contented sigh. In the curious region *between* that illusion and the faint terror of being utterly nowhere and anonymous, foreigners live. From there, if they are lucky, they smuggle back occasional undaunted notes, like messages in a bottle, or glimmers from the other side of the mirror" (*Whereabouts*, pp. 18–19).

Reid has explored the condition of being a foreigner from endless angles, and his writing shares a sense of extraterritoriality with other literary exiles of twentieth-century literature, such as Vladimir Nabokov and Samuel Beckett, although Reid is not a "difficult" writer in the modernist sense. Rather, he has cultivated a quiet, clear-eyed voice and a highly accessible manner. The logic of his poems is neither strained nor disjunctive. Almost against the modernist vein, he has cultivated, as he writes in "Weathering," a crucial poem in his canon, "an equilibrium / which breasts the cresting seasons but still stays calm / and keeps warm" (*Weathering*, p. 69).

EARLY AND PERSONAL LIFE

BORN on 22 March 1926 in Whithorn on the west coast of Scotland, Reid spent the formative years of his childhood on the island of Arran, where his father, William Arnold Reid, was a minister of the Church of Scotland and his mother, Marian (Wilson) Reid, a physician. In a family of three children, he was the only son. As a child he was pulled between his mother's surgery at one end of the house, and his father's study at the other. These represented the practical and the more spiritual sides of existence, and he hovered between them. In his life, the practical side has been occupied with gardening and cooking, maintaining a household, and making a living. The spiritual side has, largely, been claimed by his writing and reading.

Reid was educated in local schools and at the University of St. Andrews—Scotland's oldest university—on the East Neuk of Fife. There he studied classics and English literature. His education, however, was interrupted by the Second World War, in which he served in the Royal Navy in the Indian and Pacific Oceans. It was during this time that he learned to travel with as little baggage as possible, since one had to carry one's possessions from ship to ship. Extra possessions, as he notes in a recent essay, "usually got lost or stolen." Thus he learned the virtues of having few tangible goods. (He says here that if he had a family motto, it would be: *omnia mea mecum porto* [all that is mine I carry with me].

After the war, he returned to St. Andrews to finish his degree, then migrated to the United States, where for several years he taught at Sarah Lawrence College. He never intended to pursue a career in teaching, however, and soon abandoned that profession to take up a career in letters. *The New Yorker* proved an ideal outlet for his work, and he has made a living for many decades by writing pieces for that and other magazines, by translating, and by taking occasional short-term jobs of teaching at institutions as various as Columbia, Antioch, Dartmouth, Colorado College, Yale, and Middlebury. He was thus able to live a peripatetic life, moving from country to country, never having to punch a clock.

An ideal guide to his self-conception is found in a statement he provided for the dust jacket of his first essay collection, *Passwords: Places, Poems, Preoccupations* (1963). He says: "I first saw the light in Scotland, and the sharp contrasts, rough and gentle, of its landscape and climate still haunt me strongly enough to keep me from returning. I left Scotland first during the war, when a spell at sea in the East gave me my first taste of strangeness and anonymity. Afterwards, following an irrelevant education, I crossed to the United States out of curiosity, and lived there off and on until the same curiosity propelled me back to Europe, to Spain in particular, which I discovered to be a cranky incarnation of the whole human paradox, joyful, harsh, loving and violent, all at once. I have lived peripherally in France, in Morocco, in Switzerland; the list I hope is not complete—a kind of wistful dissatisfaction keeps me on the move. I have been in and out of trouble; have taken great pleasure in games of all kinds, in friends, in children, in languages, in talking, in running water; and have tried above all to keep a clear eye. Although I am in love with the English language, I have no noticeable accent left. My passport says I am a writer, which has proved a useful cloak for my curiosity. Poems are for me the consequences of the odd epiphanies which from time to time miraculously happen; prose I keep for a calmer,

more reflective everyday attention to the world. I think I have always been a foreigner."

Since writing that Reid has lived in many countries, as he predicted, keeping New York City (and *The New Yorker*) as a base. Although he was twice married, neither marriage lasted for long. He raised a son, Jasper, by himself, moving from country to country during the 1960s and 1970s with his son in tow. For a while he and Jasper occupied a houseboat on the Thames, in London. They returned on two occasions to St. Andrews for a year. They maintained for over two decades a farm in Majorca, where Reid had once gone to work with the poet Robert Graves, his mentor and friend. After Jasper left home, Reid bought a small property in the Dominican Republic, where for nearly fifteen years he lived in the winters on a remote peninsula. Like Robinson Crusoe, Reid lived in a self-sufficient manner, growing his own food and relying on local products to sustain himself. He gathered water to drink in a cistern, and he lived without the usual amenities of modern life: telephones, electric lights, indoor plumbing.

Since that time, Reid has mostly lived in Greenwich Village, an old haunt from the early 1950s. He has, of course, continued to travel—to Mexico, the Caribbean, Chile, Colombia, and other Latin American countries, to Britain, Spain, and France. His curiosity has attracted him to various cultures and landscapes. While he has written relatively little poetry in the past decades, he has continued to produce steady quantities of prose—much of it related to his travels—and to translate both poetry and fiction. In everything he does, he seems to cultivate what he once called "the sense of oddness, of surprise, of amazement."

EARLY WORKS

REID's primary accomplishment lies in the field of lyric poetry. His aesthetic as a poet is made explicit in "A Lesson in Music," where the poet-narrator speaks to a young child at the piano. The advice given to the student pianist is, in a sense, the poet's advice to himself as he writes a poem. The poem's refrain line is: "Play the tune again." The poet explains that it's important to keep from watching your fingers, "letting flow / the sound till it surround you." The child is told to pretend that "the pace / of the sound were your heart beating." Music is regarded as "an arrangement of silence." Reid's poems do, magically, seem to arrange the silence around them; they flow naturally, without a hint of affectation. Their formalities are hidden, too: the rhymes oblique, the music internal, the rhythms subtle and varied. They move with a steady, mellifluous sound, like water running in a brook, making its way around stones, following the course of the bank.

Although Reid gathered a number of poems in a pamphlet while still a student at the University of St. Andrews, his first collection was *To Lighten My House*, published in 1953. The book is clearly an apprentice volume, where Reid attempts (with various degrees of success) to disentangle himself from his dominant influences: Gerard Manley Hopkins, William Butler Yeats, and Dylan Thomas. One hears a Celtic lilt in the poems, a rise and fall that arrests the ear almost too violently at times. Almost always, Reid keeps some formal element in play as a way of structuring the poem.

One hears Dylan Thomas too fiercely in "Poem for My Father," which Thomas himself might have written, with its heavily alliterative sprawl. It begins:

When my father first made me in a Scottish summer
he heard various voices. There was trouble in the
    island;
but the act of love was an evening matter, a heart-beat
that ran wild in the blood and swelled and burst and
    was
silence.

The Thomas mannerisms are also present in "Lay for New Lovers," as where he writes:

In the crux of the dark O under a lemon moon
    lying below the lap of the barn
being lovers we were born being warm and lovers
and sick with a secret O and the ogling owls
fell sideways out of the thinning dark

and our limbs were liquid and longed to tell
    under the lap of the barn
    in the cup of the dark

Somehow, even here, the mannered style fails to drown the distinctive voice of this singular poet, who writes about boyhood and village life in Scotland with astonishing lucidity and concreteness, as in "The Village," where he conjures an idealized town:

This village, like a child's deliberate vision,
shimmers in sunshine. Cottages bloom like flowers
and blink across the gardens thick with silence.

That last image is typical of Reid, especially as he personifies the cottages so that they can "blink." The notion of a garden "thick with silence" arrests the eye as well as the ear. Reid was busy at this time making poems that drew heavily on his own childhood circumstances.

Like all young poets, he was eager to investigate the sources and nature of his own poetic gift. His brief poem "Autobiography" is a memorable lyric composed of eight lines of stately iambic pentameter. One sees that, from early in his career, his instincts as a poet were highly formal, and his talent remains most visible in highly conventional forms, where his craftsmanship is on display:

A boy, I was content to cling to silence.
The first years found me unprepared for spring.
April spoke quickly with a quick excitement.
My sudden voice was too surprised to sing.

Year followed year, the faithful falling seasons.
My voice was never confident for long.
Now autumn haunts me with the fear of losing
anticipation, and the power of song.

Here Reid struggles free from his influences, dodging the mannerisms in the Hopkins-Thomas vein that could seem overwhelming when not quite in control, as in "Not Now for My Sins' Sake," which opens in an unpromising way:

Not now for my sins' sake,
not for Adam or anyone
a memory might wake
do I take this breaking day to grieve,
not for today's Eve

perpetually weeping in the nibbled apples,
and not for all the lost or two alone.

The problem here lies with the convoluted syntax, which makes it difficult to follow the sense of the narrative. One enters the poem at an odd angle, and the ear is too aggressively engaged; the sound of the poem outdistances the sense.

Nonetheless, Reid was gifted with an amazing ear, and he was going to play that talent for all it was worth, as in the opening line of "Song for Four Seasons": "Held and spelled in a golden fold, / I wished to find a windfall in the orchard." Whatever can the word "spelled" mean here? Caught in a spell? Probably. But clearly the sound was dictating that way the line unfolded, and "spelled" followed naturally from "held." Like Thomas Campion, the late Renaissance English poet who defined poetry as "a system of linked sounds," Reid occupied himself in these early poems with forging connections between vowels and consonants, depending on assonance and consonance as ways of yoking sounds.

In the early 1950s, Dylan Thomas was a vivid presence on American college campuses, giving oratorical and highly dramatic readings from his poems. Having grown up in rural Wales, he embodied the wild-eyed, Celtic bard, and his popular style became highly influential among younger poets. Reid met Thomas at this time, falling under his spell. His own gifts as a writer seemed to marry well with those of Thomas. Yet other interesting influences converged on Reid at this time, as in "The Question in the Cobweb," which seems to depend more on W. H. Auden than Thomas or Hopkins. Auden, who was a generation older than Reid, had come to the United States in 1939. He settled in New York, where he soon became the most influential voice among American poets, who admired his clever use of traditional verse forms and his far-reaching intellectuality.

Auden often combined a strongly cadenced iambic tetrameter with slant rhymes, and Reid adapted this form to his own purposes here:

The frog beneath the juniper
warns us where the terrors are,

crouched below a creaking root
grunts of water underfoot.

Auden's mannerisms, which include the use of multiple odd adjectives and disjunctive locutions, roar to the front in the second stanza:

Draped on a branch above, the crow
croaks a crude judicial No,
forbidding with a beady eye
any wayward wish to fly.

Auden was admired by critics for his almost devilish control of his craft, so this was a natural direction for Reid to follow, given his unusual facility for versification. Auden and Reid soon became friends, and one sees a continuous fascination with the older poet's work in Reid.

Auden admired the simple but exact language of nursery rhymes, and so did Reid, who in this first volume incorporated many childlike cadences into his verse. This is most obvious in "Nursery Songs," a sequence of two lyrics, where he shows an interest in legend and wordplay that would serve him well when, later, he would try his hand at writing for a younger audience, eventually publishing half a dozen books for children, including *Ounce, Dice, Trice*—a "word book," which he published in 1958 with drawings by the artist Ben Shahn. In a memorable line that concludes the poem "New Hampshire," Reid cautions himself against using words in a prodigal way: "Words, like the water, must be used with care." He seems always determined to husband his energies, to speak sparingly, to make each word and line carry as much freight as it will bear. The range of his diction, enhanced by his study of foreign languages (Latin, Greek, French, Spanish), is astonishing, as he reaches time and again for the exact word.

One of the most unforgettable poems in this volume is "The Waterglass," a portrait of a seaside town not unlike St. Andrews or his boyhood village on the island of Arran. "A church tower crowned the town," he writes, describing a village where the houses were "anchored" in air and water. "A sun burned in the bay," he tells us, painting what at first seems like an idyllic scene, until the narrator looks into the sea and observes his death "in the underworld of water." An ominous note invades the poem—a note that would become more commonplace in Reid's later work—as what at first seems familiar becomes frightening. He becomes the pursuer of "oddments, inklings, omens, moments," as he would later write.

To Lighten My House moves toward conclusion with a long poem in five parts called "Directions for a Map." The title and general conception seems to owe something to Robert Frost's "Directive," at least in the notion that a poet must study a landscape for inner direction. A poem becomes a kind of map, a visual field that is not the thing itself but its representation, a mirror into which the poet looks to find more than himself reflected back. "A globe-eyed child finds first a map for wonder," Reid says, but that isn't all a map is for. One must move through wonder to wisdom, from innocence to experience, and this poem explores "the plot of the land" in search of a larger plot, a human narrative that the poet can find sustaining. He looks for "the island in the mind" that lies, perhaps beyond the world of actuality, far away. This island, doubtless having much in common with the Arran of Reid's boyhood, seems to call through the mist, to invite the poet toward a condition where grace (as wisdom or experience) may find him.

The collection ends with evocations of the Maine coast, where the islands are all "anchored deep dark down," and the island of Arran, concluding on a fiercely independent note with the title poem, where Reid takes a rueful glance backward to Scotland and childhood. He once again turns his eyes toward the sea, which has played such a crucial role in his life—the sea that "moves and is patient, / bearing all bottled wishes, faithful to all its fables, / promising islands that will ask me back / to take my luck." Reid ends the poem in "the nowhere of the moment," a place of dislocation where all foreigners must dwell, having put his childhood behind him. He quite naturally assumes that a sense of being displaced defines the human condition generally. This poem offers little in the way of consolation except a desire "to love the world," however strange or isolated that world may be.

In 1959, Reid published a collection of poems called *Oddments Inklings Omens Moments*. This varied and rich collection stands up well over time. The mannerisms that marred the earlier work have largely been shed, and Reid steps into the sunlight realm of his major poetry, which is charming, lucid, whimsical, and life-embracing. The first poem is typical of the collection. Called "Was, Is, Will Be," it is organized along the obvious lines of the title, moving from past to present to future tense. "It was to have been / an enchanted spring," Reid says, with "the house friendly, the neighbors kindly, / the mornings misted," and so forth. But the present is "ill-at-ease," we learn in the second stanza, a place where "a plague of crows" gathers overhead and work seems "unlikely." The poet ponders the future in the third and final stanza, wondering if he himself "engendered / the spring's condition." While there is nothing intellectually challenging about the poem, the simple sentiments are neatly framed and beautifully embodied in two-beat lines full of attractive and unusual slant rhymes (friendly/kindly; easy/lazy; jumpy/skimpy; later/letter). There is a general aura of sophisticated malaise.

The next poem, "A Game of Glass," shows the poet being indecisive, unsure of his cognitive ground as he stares into a mirror: "What am I meant to do? / Which side is the mirror on?" As often in this volume, Reid asks more questions than he answers, looking for a place to stand, wanting certainty and solidity but aware of, even needing, ghosts and phantoms, as in the next poem, "Ghosts," where he addresses the "Ghost by my desk," begging for answers.

"Once at Piertarvit" comes next, a compelling narrative drama with characters: "Avril and Ann / and Ian and I / walked in the wind / along the headland." Ian throws an apple that hits a bird—a gull flying overhead. They all imagine disaster: "the thin ribs breaking, / blood, and the bird / hurtling downward." But it never happens. A miracle occurs, as it were, and the bird glides on as the apple falls "in the sea at Piertarvit." Gravity asserts itself, and the world comes right in the end, and it seems to happen without the active agency of any human being. The poem is haunting, an exploration of youth and the impulse to violence, a celebration of the way nature settles its own scores, often by simply avoiding human error. But the poem reaches beyond this to consider the power of an anecdote, a moment in youth that comes to stand for something. Years later, the four characters in the poem say with a sense of awe: "Ian hit a bird / with an apple, in April, once at Piertarvit." Life, for Reid, seems full of these ominous instances.

Some of the poems in this collection evoke landscapes, such as "The Rain in Spain," but these landscapes are almost always read as moods, as equivalents of a state of mind. One of the Spanish poems is a tribute to Robert Graves, "Poet with Sea Horse." Reid celebrates the older poet as a kind of hippocamp, known for its uncanny ability to remain "upright / in spite of wild waters and turgid seas." He generalizes from the condition of Graves to that of all human beings, noting how certain traits remain "unerringly our own," such as our laughs, our fascinations, certain essential features.

A number of the poems in the collection look at animals as mirrors of human traits. Reid adamantly prefers cats to dogs. In "Cat-Faith," for example, he praises the cat's instinct for landing on its feet in a fall. Gliding with the analogy, he writes: "so do we let ourselves fall morning-ward / through shelves of dream." The libertine character of the cat, who has no loyalty or allegiance to the past, seems deeply attractive to this poet of travel, this celebrant of fresh worlds and new languages, who feels a constant need to redefine himself in a new setting, where promises exist and where the past stiffens into old letters left in a box, unopened.

Among the most appealing poems in this volume is "An Instance," where Reid explores the creative act itself, as in the writing of a poem, where "a word / in that instant of realizing catches fire, / ignites another, and soon, the page is ablaze / with a wildfire of writing." In this instance, it was the "accident of a bird / crossing the green window," that set the poem in motion. When the bird has long disappeared, and many of the words that were initially summoned have been crossed out, the poem remains, a testament

to this rare but lovely accident that led the mind in a certain direction. Reid's view of creativity, of course, is deeply Romantic: a poem is an expression of sudden feeling, a shudder of self-expression, not the product of long and conscious deliberation.

A sister poem to "An Instance" comes next, "Growing, Flying, Happening," where Reid continues his examination of the poetic act itself. In the first stanza, he meditates on the difference between a name of a bird, *columba palumbus*, and the bird itself. What is the real bird? What does the poem have to do with the bird "straking the harbour water" and diving for a herring? Reid seems ill content with the situation, where words and things seem permanently cut off from each other. What he seeks, here as elsewhere, is "grace / beyond recognition," which entails a vision of "growing, flying, happening." At the end, he reaches for a wider meaning:

> Manifold, the world
> dawns on unrecognizing, realizing eyes.
> Amazement is the thing.
> Not love, but the astonishment of loving.

In other words, the act of seeing itself outdistances the reality of what is seen. "Not love, but the astonishment of loving" is a somewhat enigmatic formulation suggesting there is more to love than love itself, and that this involves the perception of loving, encoded in the word "astonishment," a favorite notion in this poet's work. The job of the poet involves looking, using the eyes and ears, catching and registering reality.

The astonishment of loving obsesses Reid through the middle poems of *Oddments*. "At First Sight" is about loving "recklessly, / hazarding certainty, / losing identity." "Calenture" is about the madness of lovers, as registered by the lovesick sailor who leaps from his ship and tries to walk across the water toward home, only to sink beneath the waves while "the others watch him drown." This magnificent poem ends with the poet confessing to his own self-sacrificial madness in the face of his beloved: "I walked toward her on the flowering water." "In Such a Poise Is Love" offers a meditation on the dilemma faced by lovers caught "between win fears, of losing and of having." "For Ring-Givers" meditates cunningly on the ring as a metaphor: "Given the gift of a ring, / what circle does it close?" Wittily, Reid plays off the notion of circularity. "Are you, in turn, expecting / love or the ring returned?" the poet asks, almost to challenge the reader.

Reid is mesmerized by impermanence, by the fact that love passes and nothing stays put in time. The title poem, which comes later in the book, rejoices in those small but passing fancies, glimmers, moments of grace, as when "a hand's touch / speaks past speech" or when "two sympathies / lighten each other, / and love occurs / like song, like weather." As ever, Reid pushes beyond the cliché, which would have love occurring merely like song. That love should occur also "like weather" adds a complex note here. Weather is not permanent. It shifts and sidles, challenges, tantalizes, delights, disappoints. And Reid is the poet of these shifting moods, asking rhetorically in "Two Weathers" the obvious question: "Why should they run so counter, / outer and inner weather?" (The poem seems to echo, however distantly, Robert Frost's "Tree at My Window," where the subject of inner and outer weather is addressed.)

Among the fine later poems in the collection is "Casa d'Amunt," where Reid contemplates "a tenant's station." As a celebrant of all that passes, Reid would seem to prefer his status as a renter to that of a landlord. "The garden is not ours"—a line full of lovely ambiguities—becomes a refrain in this poem where the renters of the villa, presumably the house of the title, offer "serious mute oblation / and a respectful word" to the natural setting. Like the garden of Eden, there is an apple tree here; but the speaker is aware of having himself put "the worm within the fruit." That is, one carries one's own innate capacities for evil wherever one goes; one may rent the garden, but will foul it; responsibilities cannot be avoided. In the end, it is time, not some archangel with a flaming sword (as seen at the end of John Milton's *Paradise Lost*) who will drive Adam and Eve from the garden into the fallen world.

This wry meditation on the fall of man leads directly into "Living in Time," a poem where the poet again occupies what seems like a rented house in a foreign climate. The poet climbs an escarpment to watch swallows, who are "larruping through the trees" rather pointlessly. He laments on his "slow way home" that he feels the "dark selves from the study / fall into step" beside him. This darkness and self-absorption are cast out, however, by the beloved, who appears in the doorway "so beautifully / occupying her body." Her presence drives away the darkness. "The moment is her home," he declares, perhaps in self-delusion.

A whimsical note recurs in "Pigeons," a set piece that seems to owe something to the manner of John Crowe Ransom, the American poet whose formal elegance inspired a generation of poets in the middle decades of the twentieth century. The poem describes the pigeons in their urban settings as they settle on statuary with great clarity and poise: "Stone becomes them," Reid says, "they, in their turn, become it." The poem ends with a grandly rolling celebration of these commonplace city birds:

All praise to them who nightly in the parks
keep peace for us; who, cosmopolitan,
patrol and people all cathedraled places,
and easily, lazily haunt and inhabit
St. Paul's, St. Peter's, or the Madeleine,
the paved courts of the past, pompous as keepers—
a sober race of messengers and custodians,
neat in their international uniforms,
alighting with a word perhaps from Rome.
Permanence is their business, space and time
their special preservations; and wherever
the great stone men we save from death are stationed,
appropriately on the head of each is perched,
as though for ever, his appointed pigeon.

In all, *Oddments* must be considered Reid's primary achievement in poetry, a volume of enchanting, highly musical, cosmopolitan poems that employ a variety of forms with easy virtuosity. Reid had by now fully absorbed his influences, although the poems clearly nod in the direction of Auden, Robert Graves, and (less frequently) Thomas.

Four years later, in 1963, Reid published a miscellaneous collection of essays and poems called *Passwords: Places, Poems, Preoccupations*. This volume brings together many of his pieces from *The New Yorker* with a dozen new poems, several of them among the best he has written. "The Figures on the Frieze" was among them, a poem in seven meticulous quatrains of elegant iambic pentameter. The poem is, as often in Reid, about a couple in difficulty. It begins:

Darkness wears off, and, dawning into light,
they find themselves unmagically together.
He sees the stains of morning in her face.
She shivers, distant in his bitter weather.

(p. 140)

The familiar tropes of weather and light are employed. The couple are seen in a double "frieze"—like figures in a plaster frieze, trapped in the work of art, and also like people in a deep freeze, rigid with dissatisfaction. One can see the influence of Graves here: his obsession with women as goddess figures, his sense that each individual is acting out various legends and myths. The poem ends powerfully:

When night falls, out of a despair of daylight,
they strike the lying attitudes of love,
and through the perturbations of their bodies,
each feels the amazing, murderous legends move.

(p. 141)

Reid clearly enjoys the playful doubleness of words like "attitudes" and "legends" here, each having a literal and figurative meaning—attitude, for example, meaning a particular disposition of the body as well as a mental tone.

Other fine poems in *Passwords* are "Outlook, Uncertain," a wistful poem about the failure of constancy in love, "Speaking a Foreign Language," where he meditates on the miracle of entering another language, and "The Syntax of Seasons," where the grammatical shape of a sentence is transformed into an anatomy of seasons. As ever, the poems in this collection are charming, and they display the poet's virtuosity with forms. One of the most vivid of these poems is "Curiosity," perhaps the most widely anthologized of Reid's verses. In it, the poet reflects on the difference between cats and dogs, siding (of course) with cats. "To distrust / what is always

said," is the cat's way in life, "to ask odd questions, interfere in dreams, / smell rats, leave home, have hunches." Dogs, on the other hands, prefer "well-smelt baskets, suitable wives, good lunches." He believes that "dead dogs are those who never know / that dying is what, to live, each has to do." (Reid has fiddled with the last lines in various editions; this excerpt is from the version in *Weathering*, pp. 53–54.) Like his imaginary cat, the poet wants to be "nine-lived and contradictory," and Reid seems to have managed that well. In poem after poem, he sides with change, with adventure, with the libertine who prowls the corridors of night.

"The Spiral" is the concluding poem in *Passwords*, a remarkable poem that reflects on moving from house to house, from life to life. The poet considers the present "a devious wind / obliterating days and promises." He maintains boldly and beautifully, as much to convince himself as the reader: "change, change is where I live" (p. 237). The poem ends magisterially with a buildup of associations as the stanzas dwindle (imitating a spiral) in their number of lines to a single-line statement:

Across the spiral distance,
through time and turbulence,
the rooted self in me
maps out its true country.

And, as my father found
his own small weathered island,
so will I come to ground

where that small man, my son,
can put his years on.

For him, too, time will turn.

(p. 238)

The metaphorical spiral narrows from past to present to future, from grandfather through father to son.

Reid has only published one more collection of poems, *Weathering* (1978). It opens with a fierce preface, where the poet claims: "I look on this book as something of a farewell on my part to formal poetry, which seems to me now something of an artificial gesture, like wearing a tie. I am more interested in the essential act of putting-well-into-words, good writing; and I feel that the fine attention one gives to words in poems can also be applied to prose" (p. i). Most of the these poems were to be found in the earlier collections, although a few miscellaneous gems were introduced here, including "Scotland," "The Color of Herring," "Weathering," "The Academy," "Daedalus," and "What Gets Lost."

Among these, "Daedalus" must be considered a masterpiece of sorts, beginning and ending with the refrain: "My son has birds in his head." The conceit is followed with great care and inventiveness, written from a father's viewpoint:

I know them now. I catch
the pitch of their calls, their shrill
cacophonies, their chitterings, their coos.

(p. 60)

The poet knows that, eventually, he must choose his self: "wren, hawk, / swallow or owl." He also knows that "Age, like a cage, will enclose him." Yet he celebrates his "morning twitterings" and "the *croomb* of his becoming" (p. 62). (*Croomb* is a made-up word for a sound birds make, or could make.)

The poem derives its title from the Greek myth of Icarus and Daedalus—a myth that also proved useful to James Joyce in *The Portrait of an Artist as a Young Man*. At the core of the myth, of course, is flying: in the myth escape, of testing one's wings, of risk. Seeing his son test the limits of experience, Reid wonders: "Am I to call him down, to give him / a grounding, teach him gravity?" Yes is the answer, but "Gently, gently." In a brilliant phrase Reid writes: "Time tells us what we weight, / and soon enough / his feet will reach the ground."

The poem gains a lot from Reid's wonderful ear, and the music of the poem is exquisite. It moves gently, easily, through its turns. There is lots of interior music, with Reid depending (as always) on the device of internal rhyme to create aural effects. His love of odd words plays into a line like: "Tomtit, birdwit," which is vaguely nonsensical and gives the poem a nursery rhyme

aspect that contributes to the overall effect. The clever rhyming at the ends of lines (air/terror/tower) works to stitch the poem into a unified whole.

"What Gets Lost / *Lo Que Se Pierde*" plays off the remark of Robert Frost that poetry is what gets lost in translation. The poem moves back and forth between English and Spanish—an obvious but rarely seen innovation. Reid explores the no-man's-land between languages, wondering about what is lost in the transition. He conceives of translators as "ghosts who live / in a limbo between two worlds." The question of what gets lost in translation, he notes, finally comes down to what gets lost "in language itself." What he suggests, by implication, is that anyone who enters a language—native or not—confronts the terrible separation that pertains between word and thing. Language is a chimera, a system of echoes, a difficult and deceptive mirror that never quite reflects what is held against it. There is a huge distance to cross, as Reid says, "between the happening of love or pain ... / and their coming into words" (p. 93)

MIDDLE YEARS

REID'S interest in translation was sparked by his journeys to Spain in the late 1950s. He bought a small farm in Majorca, where Robert Graves still lived, and settled there with his small son. He lived mostly by writing "pieces" for *The New Yorker*—travel essays, personal meditations, reportage, even sports writing (he covered European soccer). Perhaps inevitably, given his attraction to Spanish and to language in general, he tried his hand at translation. What began as an occasional task soon grew, and Reid quickly became a major translator of Latin American writers, who were just gaining worldwide attention for the first time. He traveled to Chile and Argentina, and there he met both Pablo Neruda and Jorge Luis Borges. He began to translate their work. He met other Latin American writers as well, including Gabrial García Márquez and Mario Vargos Llosa.

Reid's translations of Neruda became the gold standard for the translation of contemporary Latin

American poetry. His finest achievement in this regard was *Extravagaria*, which appeared in Reid's version in 1972. That collection, originally published in Spanish in 1958, was the great Chilean poet's most personal collection, and the modalities of that volume seemed ideally suited to Reid's aesthetic. It was written at a point in Neruda's career when, after a good deal of travel and wandering, he returned to Isla Negra, a small settlement on the Pacific coast of Chile that became his permanent home. The poems in this volume celebrate his coming to rest in a place where he felt at ease in his own being. The poems are lucidly rendered by Reid into sensuous English poetry.

Consider a poem such as "Forget about me," which celebrates the life of the sea, its plenitude and tangibility. Neruda catalogues the "things the sea throws up," such as "little skulls of dead fish, / smooth syllables of wood, / small countries of mother- of-pearl." Reid seems at home in this recital of the world's many wonders. His natural whimsy marries well with Neruda's as the Chilean poet searches for "secret things / somewhere in the world." This universe is hermetic: a sequence of signs and signifiers that the poet must, like the occult philosopher, disentangle. In many ways, these translations seem a natural extension of the work begun by Reid in his own poetry.

Reid had always been interested in food and cooking, and he shared this passion with Neruda. This parallel energy enhances a poem like "The great tablecloth," one of Neruda's finest poems of this period, where he writes about "the blue hour of eating," a time when the poet "abandons his lyre" and takes up "his knife and fork." The poem becomes elaborately metaphorical, a conceit, as the act of eating is equated with a sense of justice. "Let us sit down soon to eat / with all those who haven't eaten," Neruda declaims. He was, in fact, a member of the Chilean Communist Party, and he once even ran for the presidency of Chile. So it seems fitting that he should ask for "the justice of eating," wishing to spread the great tablecloth of the world for everyone.

Three years later, in 1975, Reid published a translation of *Fully Empowered*, another classic by Neruda. The original was called *Plenos Poderes* (1962), and it emerged from one of the most fruitful periods in Neruda's life—an anthology that showed the vast range of this poet's abilities. The book was published posthumously, and it appealed to Reid in particular because so many of the poems explored the contradictions and paradoxes of the poet's life, celebrating the diversity of his selfhood. It also attracted Reid because it examined the role of the poet in compelling ways. "I take the word and pass it through my senses," Neruda writes in "The Word." Reid had, of course, contemplated the relationship between word and world many times in his own poetic career, so it was a natural subject for him to address in the role of translator.

Reid's interest in Jorge Luis Borges was aroused in the 1960s, and he was among the first to translate the great Argentine writer for a broad English-speaking audience. With Emir Rodriguez Monegal, a scholar from Yale, he edited and partly translated *Borges: A Reader* (1981), a highly influential anthology of the writer's poetry, fiction, and criticism. In 1999, he contributed substantially (with Mark Strand, W. S. Merwin, and Robert Fitzgerald, among others) to an important new English version of Borges' *Selected Poems*. Here, too, his brilliance as a translator is everywhere apparent.

Great poetry is often motivated by a writer's sense of that terrible dislocation between the mind and the world; the poem itself rises between that gap, intrusive, begging for consideration, helpless and hopeless, trying to patch over the silence that is always (in theory) beyond improvement yet somehow unsatisfactory. Borges (in Reid's version) addresses this subject directly in "The Other Tiger." Here, Borges compares the "real" tiger, who exists "on the fringes of the Ganges" (p. 281), and the tiger created by the poet with his pen:

Evening spreads in my spirit and I keep thinking
that the tiger I am calling up in my poem
is a tiger made of symbols and of shadows,

a set of literary images,
scraps remembered from encyclopedias,
and not the deadly tiger, the fateful jewel
that in the sun or the deceptive moonlight
follows its paths, in Bengal or Sumatra,
of love, of indolence, of dying.

In the end, the poet seeks a "third tiger." "This one," he says:

will be a form in my dream like all the others,
a system and arrangement of human language,
and not the flesh-and-bone tiger
that, out of reach of all mythologies,
paces the earth

(p. 282)

As ever in Borges, as in Reid, the fictive tiger is more real, more satisfying, than the tiger who paws the earth or curls, sleeping, in the folds of the cerebrum. The fiction flares, takes on memorable life, between the unspoken world and the unspoken mind.

If anything, Reid seems to improve upon the Spanish of Borges. In the above passage, for instance, Borges writes about the third tiger becoming "*un sistema de palabras / Humanas*" or "a system of human words." Reid's phrase, an "arrangement of human language," interprets and extends what Borges has written in thrilling ways, faithful to the text yet substituting for the easy, more literal, translation an equivalent that possesses a life itself *as poetry in English*.

Reid has, indeed, been a pioneer in thinking about translation as an art. He has felt free to extend and modify the poem under translation, while remaining faithful to the poet's intention. There is no such thing as a direct version; there is only equivalence. The goal of the translator, in Reid's view, is to produce a genuine poem in English, one that pays homage to the original, that somehow recreates the achievement of the poem. A translation, in his view, is an attempt to recover, however partially, what gets lost—not only between language and language, but between word and thing. Few modern translators have been as successful as Reid in finding what has been lost, in bridging the gap between experience and utterance.

LATE WORKS

IN his collection of prose and poetry called *Oases* (1997), Reid comments: "Much of what I have written, in poetry and in prose, has had to do with place—with the interactions between places and the people who live in them, with what geographers call land-life relations." Reid has had plenty of these, traveling the world, rarely staying put for long. One can follow his travels by noticing what has attracted his attention, as subjects, for essays. He has written reports from Spain, Switzerland, South America, and the Caribbean. He has studied the fishing industry in Scotland, discussed the politics of the Dominican Republic, observed World Cup soccer in Mexico. He has written about Gypsies (called Tinkers in Britain), and explored the nature of life in a small Spanish town in a series of essays called "Notes from a Spanish Village." He has discussed the mysteries of the palindrome (a sentence that reads the same in both directions, as in "A man, a plan, a canal: Panama") and written recollections and appreciations of Borges, Neruda, and Robert Graves. He has even written some fiction, as in the short story "In Memoriam, Amada."

In the 1980s, Reid moved to the Dominican Republic, dividing his time between a small property on the Samaná peninsula and New York City, where he continued his affiliation with *The New Yorker*. Samaná was a unique environment, as Reid notes in an essay called "Waiting for Columbus": "As a place, Samaná is one of those geographical oddities which seem to invite a correspondingly eccentric history: it feels itself only marginally connected to the rest of the country; on early maps, it is sometimes shown as an island. A broad expanse of marsh—the estuary of the River Yuna, which flows into Samaná Bay— joins it to the mainland" (*An Alastair Reid Reader*, p. 58). This paradise became, of course, a kind of hell as Columbus and his fellow conquerors proceeded to decimate the population of local Taino Indians.

The current inhabitants, as Reid says, are commonly illiterate. They are, however, "passionate, dedicated talkers, often eloquent. Their mode, their natural wavelength, is to put themselves in story form" (p. 61). He observes, "for them, once a problem has been put right in words, it can be forgotten. The reality is another matter altogether" (p. 62). This approach to reality attracts Reid, as a storyteller himself, in poetry and prose. He spent his years on that island moving "from teller to teller," listening close, enjoying "the fictive cast of mind." His own work seems to have gained strength from contact with these native storytellers.

With the help of his Dominican neighbors, Reid constructed a house in a grove of coconut trees that overlooked a stretch of sea not far from the beach where Christopher Columbus landed in the New World. It was an idyllic spot, and Reid found it highly congenial for his purposes. For over a dozen years, until the late 1990s, Reid gardened, cooked, and wrote throughout the winter months in this isolated retreat. He continues to travel to the island frequently, although he now lives in New York.

In "Waiting for Columbus," Reid discusses the 1992 quincentennial, celebrating (or mourning) the anniversary of the arrival of Europeans in the New World. He notes that "ever since the quincentenary loomed ... there arose a countercry, close to an outcry, over the global fiesta, and it mostly came, understandably, from the countries of Spanish America—the discoverees, as it were, which were of course given no choice about being discovered." For most of Latin America, the "discovery" of their world led only to disaster: economic and political oppression, even genocide. The voyage by Columbus, as Reid explains, soon became legendary, and he sorts through the myths and separates them from the known facts. "About the wrongs of the past we can do nothing," he says, "but we can at least look at them squarely." He does so here, moving adroitly between the past history of Hispaniola and the contemporary political squabbles in the Dominican Republic. In brief space, he presents volumes of information and opinion—displaying a remarkable gift for elucidation.

In the 1980s, Reid published four long essays in *The New Yorker* under the general title of "Notes from a Spanish Village." These charming evocations of a place and a people, based on his

many years as a resident of Majorca, attracted a wide following. They also generated a bizarre controversy. Reid happened to address a journalism class at Yale University at this time, and he mentioned that it was his practice to use composite figures. That is, he might well interview several taxi drivers in a town, then combine their remarks into a single taxi driver. This is standard operating procedure for journalists, although rarely do they reveal their methods. Nevertheless, a woman in Reid's class decided to write an article for the *Wall Street Journal* that attacked Reid for his position as a "fictionist" in the world of nonfiction.

The article in the *Journal* prompted other articles, and a minor scandal erupted. Defending their territory, journalists rushed to attack Reid for applying methods associated with fiction to nonfiction. He seemed to be taking liberties that were commonly reserved only for those who put their work into the category of fiction. There was, in fact, a certain gloating on the part of these journalists. *The New Yorker* was famous for its fact-checking, and it seemed—on the surface, at least—that Reid had slipped through the cracks. He of course admitted freely to making things up, arguing that journalists have always relied on the technique of creating composite characters. This incident was troubling for Reid, and it prompted him to examine carefully his notions of fact and fiction.

As a student of Borges, he already possessed a deep understanding of the nature of fiction, and he went back to Borges to help him think through this matter. "I found at once with Borges a coincidence of mind," Reid recalls, "not simply an enthusiasm for his writings." Borges referred to all of his writing—stories, essays, criticism, memoirs—as fiction. Fiction is not something that is "untrue." On the contrary, it should be considered a technique for uncovering truth. The word itself derives from a Latin word (*fictio*) meaning "to shape." A writer must shape the material at hand, otherwise it would be unmanageable. In a suggestive series of jotting called "Fictions," published in *Oases*, Reid explains that "A fiction is any construct of language ... that gives a certain shape to reality." He also observes that reality functions by indecipherable laws, and that to give a sense of form to reality, any good writer must resort to making fictions.

Language, for Reid, is a slippery and treacherous element that "can glibly stray from the reality it is meant to deal with." Reid is quite radically skeptical about the ability of language to convey truth. On the other hand, he does not seem to worry excessively over this problem; rather, he accepts that language does present "a" truth, not "the" truth, and that the work of the writer is to shape the raw elements of reality, to make at least a version of reality visible. "Perhaps our fictions," he concludes, "if they find their way appropriately into words, ironically, are the most durable thing about us."

"Notes from a Spanish Village" remains at the center of Reid's accomplishment as an essayist. The linked essays, which were published in book form in *Whereabouts: Notes on Being a Foreigner* in 1987, contain a whole world in miniature. One senses from the outset that this village is as much a place in the imagination as anywhere that could really be found on a map of Spain. Reid purposefully never identifies the village, and the nature that surrounds it has a certain Mediterranean sameness: one might find a similar village in Portugal, Italy, France, or even North Africa. The dynamics of village life, furthermore, hold for most rural villages in the world, especially if the village at hand has not been overrun by modern life.

What Reid adores about village life are the "rituals and hierarchies" that govern activity. Coming back to the village again after a period of absence, he goes down the path in the morning to enact the rituals of arrival—shaking the gnarled hands, embracing old friends, exchanging gossip. He delights in falling into the rhythms of the place, assuming its assumptions, playing its games, taking on its coloration. He listens a lot at first—learning who has died, who has been married, what terrible and joyful things have occurred to the villagers while he was elsewhere. Communications in such a place are a matter of oral tradition, and they depend necessarily on memory—at best a fragile human organ. Thus, Eugenio the gardener comes every year to prune

the almond trees and cut back the terraces, but he also "tells me the wistful history of the village every year." Only these insistent repetitions make history possible.

Upon one arrival, he learns that the mayor, Don Anselmo, has died; his absence is "almost as tangible as his presence." He carried the "annals of the place in his head," and this loss is felt palpably by everyone; it becomes, for him, "a deprivation." But death is vividly real to the villagers; among the old ones "its inevitability sits like an attendant bird, like imminent nightfall." As usual, Reid resorts to metaphors, and he does so concretely and memorably here. One senses how much he learns from the ancient and ritualistic way of life that controls this village. Their sense of time is deeply human, and it includes a sharp awareness of what is past, or passing.

While Reid's village has much in common with similar villages around the world, it would be an error to regard it as generic. It's a Spanish village, and Reid is entranced by Spain itself, with its peculiar inflections. This country—perhaps the slowest in Europe to accede to modernity—became an indispensable place for this native of Scotland, who first went there as a young man seeking to escape from his past. The contrast was doubtless stark: a small, cold, and Calvinist country that seemed in vast contrast to this bright, Mediterranean, and Catholic country. He found himself instructed by everything he saw, and he proved a willing student of its ways and means. (The Dominican Republic would later provide instruction of a similar kind.)

Reid considered the Franco regime and its repressive tactics distasteful, but nevertheless he felt drawn to the people—especially those who made their homes in rural villages like the one he describes in such luminous detail in these "Notes." The world of Franco's regime seems far away from this almost medieval site, where the agricultural round dominates life—in Reid's village the basic work of the local population centered on making charcoal and cutting wood. The elemental activities of eating and community intercourse take precedence over anything like "politics" in a more global sense, while government itself resides in the hands of Don Anselmo, who seems to have nothing to do with the Generalissimo, although he hangs the photographs of Franco that arrive every year in a musty back corridor of the town hall—a memento of the aging process.

Reid has not been an especially prolific essayist, but every piece he has written has been distinctive and memorable. Unusually, he has liked to gather poems and essays in single volumes, showing the range of his voice: a model for shaping a book that began with *Passwords*. He has continued to use this form with successive volumes: *An Alastair Reid Reader: Selected Poetry and Prose* appeared in 1984, drawing on the best of his work in several genres. *Whereabouts*, a volume of essays on travel—mostly in Spanish-speaking countries—contains elaborate readings of the work of Borges and Neruda as well as Gabrial García Márquez. A decade later *Oases: Poems and Prose* appeared in 1997.

Oases begins with "Digging Up Scotland," a long and deeply autobiographical piece about the literal and figurative attempt to reclaim the past. Reid recalls his boyhood in Scotland, meditating on his need to live his life in self-imposed exile. The occasion of the essay was his return, after a ten-year hiatus, to St. Andrews, where he had lived with his son Jasper in 1970. Having just spend a year as visiting writer at Antioch College in Ohio, Reid arrived in St. Andrews with the notion that he might reclaim something of his former life in a place that had meant a good deal to him during a crucial period. (He also wanted his son to experience Scotland.) He had not been back, except briefly to visit relatives and friends, since he graduated from the university.

St. Andrews is located in a small town in Fife. Known as the "home of golf," it is famous for its Royal and Ancient Clubhouse—the emotional home of all serious golfers—and four windswept courses that periodically host the British Open. Reid was able to rent a house on the sea near the famous Old Course itself. It was called Pilmour Cottage, and Reid and his son liked it a great deal: "Of all the houses we rented, borrowed, occupied, Pilmour Cottage remains ... the warmest, most ample." The house was situated in a grove of elms, sycamores, oaks. The trees also formed

a rookery, fills with black-winged, loud-voiced rooks—the perfect home for a poet.

Reid and his son, with a couple of friends, planted a time capsule that year. It contained odd things that might seem interesting in ten years: a copy of the local newspaper, various personal artifacts and documents. The group agreed, somewhat arbitrarily, to dig up the box that contained these items on Jasper's twenty-first birthday—9 August 1980. This was just the sort of subject for Reid, who wrote this essay soon after returning. Not surprisingly, the digging became metaphorical—everything does in the hands of a poet—and he found himself digging into his Scottish past. He also found himself, perhaps for the first time, moving toward a sense of rapprochement with that past.

The final essay in *Oases* is "Other People's Houses," and it describes an itinerant life. Here Reid confesses to a certain hesitancy in admitting that his life has been such. He grew up in Scotland, where people tend to go "from the stark stone house where they first see the light to another such fortress, where they sink roots and prepare dutifully for death, their possession encrusted around them like barnacles." Reid has kept few possessions, making a credo of traveling light. He has been a house sitter, a renter, and rarely a landlord, having first tasted the itinerant life during the war, at sea, where he wandered all over the Indian Ocean in "small, cramped ships." Always, he has preferred small houses—a cottage in Scotland, a tiny farmhouse in Spain, a miniature apartment in Greenwich Village, a houseboat on the Thames, a minimal enclosure in the Dominican Republic.

The enchantment of other people's houses, of course, is that you get to take on their lives for a while, to read their books and try their cooking utensils. You become aware of the light that filters into their bedroom in the morning. You lounge in their bathtubs. Their world becomes yours. Reid, as a writer, finds this sort of engagement with another life irresistible, and—as a natural chameleon—he has been able to take on other lives with imaginative sympathy.

This sympathy, indeed, illumines his work from first to last. He has been, at home or abroad, a perpetual foreigner, observing the life around him with a bemused detachment, taking notes, occasionally entering into the bustle himself. His poems record places of particular enchantment or disappointment, and they might be considered a record of his attachments and disavowals. His essays, too, chronicle his movement among countries and languages, among friends and foreign peoples. He occupies other people's houses. He speaks their languages. He plays at fitting into their lives, describing the contours of their realities with precision and beauty. He translates their monumental works of poetry or prose. He delights their children with versions of Mother Goose. He plays the trickster, appearing and disappearing.

One cannot pin down Alastair Reid, as a man or a writer. He slips from genre to genre easily, taking on the role of poet or children's writer, translator, fictionist, wordsmith, reporter, travel writer, commentator. He appears to inhabit different skins as skillfully as he inhabits different countries and cultural identities. What remains consistent—the core of his verbal universe—is the warmth, the sympathy, and the delight in whatever he finds—the oddments and inklings that arouse him, the omens that frighten him, the moments when, however briefly, he feels the call of another human being and signals, precariously, across the barrier of silence.

SELECTED BIBLIOGRAPHY

I. POETRY. *To Lighten My House* (Scarsdale, N.Y., 1953); *Oddments Inklings Omen Moments* (Boston, 1959); *Weathering: Poems and Translations* (New York, 1978).

II. POETRY AND PROSE. *Passwords: Places, Poems, Preoccupations* (Boston, 1963); *An Alastair Reid Reader: Selected Poetry and Prose* (Hanover, N.H., 1994); *Oases: Poems and Prose* (Edinburgh, 1997).

III. PROSE. *Whereabouts: Notes on Being a Foreigner* (San Francisco, 1987).

IV. SELECTED TRANSLATIONS. Pablo Neruda, *Extravagaria* (London, 1972; New York, 1974); Pablo Neruda, *Fully Empowered* (New York, 1975); Jorge Luis Borges, *Borges: A Reader*, ed. by Emir Rodriguez Monegal and Alastair Reid (New York, 1981); Fernando Savater, *Amador* (New York, 1994); Jorge Luis Borges, *Selected Poems*, ed. by Alexander Coleman (New York, 1999).

V. CHILDREN'S BOOKS. *I Will Tell You of a Town* (Boston, 1956); *Fairwater* (Boston, 1957); *Allth* (Boston, 1958); *Ounce, Dice, Trice* (Boston, 1958); *Supposing* (Boston, 1960); *To Be Alive* (New York, 1966).

VI. CRITICAL STUDIES. Jay Parini, *Some Necessary Angels* (New York, 1998).

SYDNEY SMITH

(1771–1845)

Alan Bell

THE REVEREND SYDNEY Smith was one of the leading wits and essayists of the nineteenth century. He was famous for his verbal humor, of which many examples—"a square peg in a round hole," "my idea of heaven is eating patés de foie to the sound of trumpets," or "fate cannot harm me, I have dined today"—have found their way from contemporary anthologies into common usage. Much of his literary output consisted of review essays, originally anonymous, on political or religious subjects of the day, published in the *Edinburgh Review*, the quarterly magazine which he had helped to found. His political pamphleteering is remembered for its hard-hitting, witty argumentation and for its flights of fancy which transcend the details of the historical events that prompted it. His letters were cherished by their recipients and selections from them were first published in 1855 as an appendix to a family biography. They rapidly acquired a dedicated readership and have been much augmented since then, placing him high among the letter writers of his day. This mixture of literary activity in liberal good causes, together with his fame as a humorous correspondent on paper and as a maker of bon mots in society, is best seen in the light of his biography.

Sydney Smith, who was to become known to many of his contemporaries merely as Sydney, was born at Woodford, Essex, on 3 June 1771, the son of Robert Smith, a fairly prosperous London merchant with interests in the East Indies trade, and his wife Maria, who came from a refugee Huguenot family, the Oliers. Sydney was the second of five children, of whom his elder brother Robert Percy Smith (always known as Bobus) became distinguished in the Indian legal administration and also enjoyed some reputation as a wit. Sydney himself ascribed his humor to his partly French blood, but none of it came from his father, an unpleasant commercial figure with whom he was on bad terms in later life.

He was educated as a scholar at Winchester College, an ancient school linked by foundation to New College, Oxford, where he became a fellow after graduating. The exclusively classical curriculum was a matter on which he was to write with force and wit when he became a periodical journalist. The obvious career for a young Oxford scholar of the period lay in the Church of England, and he was ordained deacon in 1794, though without any apparent deep commitment to the theological tenets of his church. He was, however, to prove himself, in spite of his often humorous approach, a conscientious pastor and—in due course—an able and inventive country clergyman intent on his parish duties in Yorkshire and Somerset. Before then, however, his career as a clergyman in the church took a different turn.

He began, conventionally enough, in a curacy on Salisbury Plain, in remote countryside in the west of England. The local landowner, Mr. Hicks Beach of Netheravon House, had two sons whose usual gentlemen's education should have included a grand tour of the European continent. The French Revolution made other plans necessary and Smith was engaged as their tutor, destined for Edinburgh rather than Paris or Vienna. The Scottish capital provided a standard liberal education for the young gentlemen; for the young clergyman, only a decade or so older, the years 1798 to 1803 which he spent in Scotland were to be intellectually formative. Sydney Smith soon found himself among a group of liberal-minded Scots lawyers generally opposed to the Tory ruling party dominant in Scotland at the time. Among this lively group of advocates were Henry

Brougham (later Lord Brougham and Vaux, Lord Chancellor) and Francis Jeffrey (later a Scots judge as Lord Jeffrey). It was to be long before these accomplices achieved national fame in Whig politics but they were at a lively stage of their legal careers and of their involvement in Whig politics.

Edinburgh, where the intellectual ferment of the Scottish enlightenment had produced a highly cultivated metropolitan environment, was at the time a major intellectual center. Its publishers were lively and prosperous, and one of them, Archibald Constable, responded cautiously to suggestions by the group of bright young Whigs that they should undertake a quarterly review, with sprightly but anonymous contributions that would avoid (so Smith wrote when writing to a London friend) "religion, politics, excessive severity and irritable Scotchmen." It was hoped that whatever the result of this speculative venture, "it will at least have the effect of imparting some degree of animation to this metaphysical monastery" (1980, p. 3). Sydney Smith himself appears to have made the proposal to his Whig lawyer collaborators, and they engaged Constable as publisher. Smith much later recalled the foundation of the *Review*, in the preface to his own *Collected Works* (1839), volumes which included most of his own anonymous contributions to the periodical he had helped to set up, with a lively group of young Whig associates:[1]

> Among the first persons with whom I became acquainted were Lord Jeffrey, Lord Murray (late Lord Advocate for Scotland), and Lord Brougham; all of them maintaining opinions upon political subjects a little too liberal for the dynasty of Dundas, then exercising supreme power over the northern division of the island.
>
> One day we happened to meet in the eighth or ninth storey or flat in Buccleuch-place, the elevated residence of the then Mr. Jeffrey. I proposed that we should set up a Review; this was acceded to with acclamation. I was appointed Editor, and remained long enough in Edinburgh to edit the first number of the Edinburgh Review. The motto I proposed for the Review was

1. All quotations from Sydney Smith's writings can be found in Alan Bell, *Sydney Smith*, cited as (1980) or in Bell, ed., The Sayings of Sydney Smith, cited as (1993)

> "Tenui musam meditamur avena"
>
> ("We cultivate literature upon a little oatmeal")
>
> But this was too near the truth to be admitted, and so we took our present grave motto ["Judex damnatur cum nocens absolvitur"—"The judge stands condemned when the guilty is acquitted"] from Publius Syrus, of who none of us had, I am sure, ever read a single line; and so began what has since turned out to be a very important and able journal.
> (1980, pp. 34–35)

The speculation succeeded beyond anything they could have expected: the *Edinburgh Review* set an intellectual standard and a pattern of publication for much of the serious journalism of the following century. Its articles were anonymous, but their authorship was often known, or even notorious, and it did not avoid politics or religion, or "excessive severity." Sydney Smith was involved editorially only in its earliest issues, but was a regular contributor for many years. His humorous manner, developing with an increasingly well-practiced elaboration, was there from the start, not least when attacking pompous fellow clergymen.

The *Edinburgh Review*, launched almost conspiratorially in October 1802, was a success from its outset. It fulfilled Smith's intention that it should be "able, intrepid and independent," and in the editorial hands of Francis Jeffrey and the commercial management of the publisher Constable it became a major force in British intellectual journalism. The right-wing *Quarterly Review* started in 1809, goaded into existence by Tory reactions to the increasingly political tone of the by then well-established *Edinburgh*.

During his time in Edinburgh, where he preached occasionally and himself took some university courses in addition to performing his duties as a private tutor, Smith had married an Englishwoman, Catharine Pybus, in a match that received no support from his miserly father. He was obliged to support himself, and on moving to London after his tutorship came to an end, his *Edinburgh Review* contributions became a significant source of income. He also, with a view to professional advancement, produced two volumes of sermons, with a characteristic preface:

A clergyman clings to his velvet cushion with either hand, keeps his eye riveted upon his book, speaks of the ecstasies of joy, and fear, with a voice and a face which indicate neither, and pinions his body and soul into the same attitude of limb, and thought, for fear of being called theatrical and affected. ... Is it wonder, then, that every semi-delirious secretary who pours forth his animated nonsense, with the genuine look and voice of passion, should gesticulate away the congregation of the most profound and learned divine of the established church, and in two Sundays preach him bare to the very sexton? Why are we natural everywhere but in the pulpit?

(1980, p. 29)

His contributions to the *Edinburgh* were from the start hard-hitting, sharp and humorous. They were fearless too, taking on prominent figures in the ecclesiastical world. "When, in lieu of novelty and ornament, we can discover nothing but trite imbecility," he wrote judicially of a political sermon, "the law must take its course, and the delinquent suffer that mortification from which vanity can rarely be expected to escape, when it chooses dullness for the minister of its gratification." Even Jeffrey was alarmed by the tone, but Smith defended his article:

... grant that the man is a proper object of punishment, and in these literary executions I do not care for justice or injustice a fig. My business is to make the archdeacon as ridiculous as possible.

(1980, p. 39)

The Smiths left Scotland ("that knuckle-end of England, that land of oatcakes and sulphur") at the end of the tutorship with many regrets. Smith could tease his friends about their dour humor:

It requires a surgical operation to get a joke well into a Scotch understanding. Their only idea of wit, or rather that inferior variety of the electric talent which prevails occasionally in the North, and which, under the name of WUT, is so infinitely distressing to people of good taste, is laughing immoderately at stated intervals.

(1980, p. 19)

Edinburgh sanitation had also been a source of much anxiety:

No smells were ever equal to Scotch smells. It is the School of Physic; walk the streets, and you would imagine that every medical man had been administering cathartics to every man, woman and child in the town. Yet the place (Edinburgh) is uncommonly beautiful, and I am in a constant balance between admiration and trepidation: Taste guides my eye, where e'er new beauties spread, While prudence whispers, "Look before you tread."

(1980, p. 15)

Scottish hygiene provoked many sallies. "It is customary to fumigate Scotch tutors," Smith remarked: "They are excellent men but require this little preliminary caution." He did however appreciate their disputatiousness. "I take the liberty to send you two brace of grouse," he wrote to a friend in 1808, "curious, because killed by a Scotch metaphysician. In other and better language, they are mere ideas, shot by other ideas, out of a pure intellectual notion called a gun." Edinburgh provided Smith not only with a literary project that was to make him famous, but with some of his closest friendships and a good deal of nostalgia. "Never shall I forget the happy days passed there," he wrote later in life, "amidst odious smells, barbarous sounds, bad suppers, excellent hearts, and most enlightened and cultivated understandings."

Sydney Smith arrived in London in 1803, settling in the legal quarter, with a ready-made circle of acquaintances, mainly among bright young barristers. He kept closely in touch with his Edinburgh associates, especially Francis Jeffrey who was now making such a success of the *Review*. To friends such as Jeffrey he could offer trenchant but affectionate personal advice:

I ... protest against your increasing and unprofitable scepticism. I exhort you to restrain the violent tendency of your nature for analysis, and to cultivate synthetical propensities. What's the use of virtue? What's the use of wealth? What's the use of honour? What's a guinea but a damned yellow circle? What's a chamber-pot but an infernal hollow sphere? The whole effort of your mind is to destroy. Because others build slightly and eagerly, you employ yourself in kicking down their houses, and contract a sort of aversion for the more honourable, useful and difficult task of building well yourself.

(1980, p. 46)

Even more important to him than his lawyer friends was the smart and intellectual Whig salon at Holland House, in the then suburban Kensington, where a benign Lord Holland and his imperious wife presided over a political circle of great prominence. Smith started there as a shy guest but rapidly grew in confidence and favor. Clever conversation was much prized there, and he excelled at it, able to cast aside some of the decorousness even then expected of a clergyman. He had to be somewhat on his guard, however, against seeming to embrace the declared atheism of his friend John Allen, the Hollands' resident companion. The resolutely secular tone of the salon was one that a clergyman would ignore at his peril. Holland House was to provide a London base for him after he became a country clergyman. "Some of the best and happiest days of my life I have spent under your roof," he wrote to Lady Holland as early as 1810, "and though there may be in some houses, particularly those of our eminent prelates, a stronger disposition to pious exercises and as it were devout lucubrations, I do not believe all Europe can produce as much knowledge, wit and worth as passes in and out of your door under the nose of Thomas the porter." Lady Holland was notorious for her high-handedness, which left Smith determined not to be overawed by her manner. "Sydney, ring the bell!" she once demanded; "Oh yes!" was his reply, "and shall I sweep the room?" This warning shot did not go unheeded, and they settled into a bantering and affectionate relationship, which lasted for the rest of their lives.

Smith gained a reputation as a vigorous occasional preacher, without however being offered a pulpit of his own, and he attracted large congregations while attached to the Foundling Hospital, the famous London orphanage. He had an even greater success with a course of lectures at the Royal Institution, founded for scientific education, where each week he addressed a huge audience on "Elementary Sketches of Moral Philosophy." His discourses were not deep or original metaphysical treatises (Smith himself called them "the most successful swindle of the season") but they suited his audience well. Sometimes rather parsonical in tone (he had always to be on guard against charges of atheism), they were full of common sense and homely analogies. The notion of the square peg in the round hole, elaborated in a lecture "On the Conduct of the Understanding" became a classic:

> If you choose to represent the various parts in life by holes upon a table, of different shapes,—some circular, some triangular, some square, some oblong,—and the persons acting these parts by bits of wood of similar shapes, we shall generally find that the triangular person has got into the square hole, the oblong into the triangular, and a square person has squeezed himself into the round hole. The officer and the office, the doer and the thing done, seldom fit so exactly, that we can say they were almost made for each other.
>
> (1980, p. 58)

Less publicly, because his articles were unsigned, he continued intermittent work for the *Edinburgh Review*, mocking the extremes of Methodist evangelicalism, or of a vigilante body called the Society for the Suppression of Vice. Wickedly well-chosen quotations, arguments deftly reversed, points well driven home, a combative tone which did not need anonymity to bolster it, and above all a commonsensical humor, give such magazine contributions, each usually several thousand words long, an enduring interest.

In 1806, during a brief spell when some of his friends were in government, he accepted a minor ecclesiastical appointment, Foston-le-Clay in rural Yorkshire between York and Malton, "twelve miles," as he puts it, "from a lemon." At the time the rectory was nonresident (indeed there *was* no suitable residence) and there was the possibility of exchanging it for something nearer London. A hired curate performed the basic duties, and Smith drew the small income while continuing to live in London. There he became active in the cause of Catholic Emancipation, which sought to remove restrictions on civil appointments then closed to Roman Catholics. There was much confused, chauvinistic protestant opposition to any measure of relief, and thus an opportunity for a clear-headed advocate to make his mark. Smith, who had recently published a lively sermon on toleration, was well equipped to take on the role.

SYDNEY SMITH

Letters on the Subject of the Catholics, to my brother Abraham, who lives in the Country, ascribed to one Peter Plymley, began to appear (there were eventually to be ten of them) in summer 1807. There was much mystery made of their origin, and their author cannily disavowed them until late in his life, but they were widely believed to be the work of Sydney Smith. "Peter Plymley" writes to his country clergyman brother, who is "a bit of a goose" and who believes almost that a papal invasion is imminent. Abraham's conventional wisdom needs correcting. "When I hear any man talk of an unalterable law," Peter tells him, "the only effect it produces upon me is to convince me that he is an unalterable fool." Peter Plymley's arguments in favor of the Catholics are not based on their religious practices: "As for the enormous wax candles, and superstitious mummeries, and painted jackets of the catholic priests, I fear them not."

The Catholic problem, especially when the nation was faced with the possibility of a Napoleonic invasion, was seen in secular terms. At a time of national peril, Peter Plymley asked, "Are we to stand examining our generals and armies as a bishop examines a candidate for holy orders? And to suffer no one to bleed for England, who does not agree with you about the second of Timothy?" Were Spencer Perceval, the low-church chancellor of the exchequer, a ship's captain, he would catechize all his crew before setting them on deck against the enemy, "and positively forbid every one to sponge or ram who has not taken the sacrament according to the Church of England."

Ireland, with its large, repressed Roman Catholic population was seen as especially important, and some concessions were urgently needed there. "Peter Plymley's" broad and tolerant view of the Catholic question in Ireland was to secure the popularity of the *Letters* throughout the Victorian period. At the time of publication, however, the tracts were much appreciated but did nothing to secure any professional recognition or advancement for their pseudonymous author.

Regulations about the nonresidence of clergy in their parishes were beginning to take effect, and Smith resignedly accepted the obligation to move to Yorkshire. "I have bought a book about drilling beans, and a greyhound puppy for the Malton meeting," he wrote to Lady Holland at the end of 1808: "It is thought that I shall be an eminent rural character." And so, very unexpectedly, it was to prove. The parsonage was uninhabitable, so the family rented a house within riding distance until a simply designed but spacious, light and comfortable Georgian rectory was built: "a snug parsonage," he called it. Local society lacked any of the allure of the cultivated metropolitan circles Smith and his family had enjoyed in London, but the Smiths augmented their household with visitors from Edinburgh and London. When Lady Holland came to stay in 1810, Sydney wrote to her: "We have now another bed in which a maid or a philosopher, or a maid with a philosopher, may be put. God grant in this latter event that they may both merit their respective appellations the ensuing morning."

The visitors included people like the chemist Sir Humphry Davy and his bluestocking wife, and the young Thomas Babington Macaulay, then a barrister appearing at the York assizes but already a fellow contributor to the *Edinburgh Review*. "He is like a book in breeches," Smith remarked of this talkative new friend, "but now he has occasional flashes of silence, that make his conversation perfectly delightful." The local clergy offered few congenial friendships, not least because few of them shared Smith's bookish interests or his liberal political opinions: "A joke goes a great way in the Country," he said. "I have known one last pretty well for seven years." Even the annual York music festival, a high point of civic life, failed to amuse one with little taste for oratorios. "The festival seems to be at a discount," Smith wrote in 1828, "its organizer is said to have written to Catalani to know if her voice was *really* as good as it used to be. No answer, perhaps no Catalani. Two or three of their other female singers are (it is said) in the family way, and expect to be confined about the musical week; nevertheless they will come, though their medical advisers are rather apprehensive of the effects of grand choruses, but I hope all will go off quietly."

Meanwhile he was extending his friendships among the northern Whig aristocracy. He cemented his friendship with the future prime minister, Earl Grey, at Howick in Northumberland, and stayed with the immensely rich coal proprietor, John George Lambton, Earl of Durham, at Lambton Castle, reporting to another north-country aristocrat:

> From thence to Lambton. And here I ask, what use of wealth so luxurious and delightful as to light your house with gas? What folly, to have a diamond necklace or a Correggio, and not to light your house with gas! The splendour and glory of Lambton Hall make all other houses mean. How pitiful to submit to a farthing-candle existence, when science puts such intense gratification within your reach! Dear Lady, spend all your fortune in gas-apparatus. Better to eat dry bread by the splendour of gas than to dine on wild beef with wax candles.
>
> (1980, pp. 100–101)

Visits like these were an agreeable exception to the standard routine of country living in a remote parish. He was fully occupied as a diligent country clergyman and as well as educating his family he became "village parson, village doctor, village comforter, village magistrate and Edinburgh Reviewer," otherwise explaining his functions as "doctor, justice, road-maker, pacifier, preacher, farmer, neighbour and diner-out." For those who in his own lifetime as well as later were admirers of his social gifts as a metropolitan diner-out, it is a surprise to discover just how conscientious a country clergyman he was.

He attended to services in his tiny parish church, and fulfilled his obligations in the diocese by taking his turn at official services in York. He showed himself judiciously tolerant of the Dissenters who were so prominent in the area, even striking up a friendship with a Unitarian minister whose sect was suffering from various civil disabilities. He wrote to this pastor that:

> Your Unitarian preachers have stolen away four of my congregation who had withstood Ranters and Methodists. I shall make reprisals and open a chapel near the College, but it shall be generous and polite warfare, such as is the duty, not the disgrace, of Christian divines.
>
> (1980, p. 104)

York was, then as now, a Quaker center, and the Society of Friends impressed him by their simple piety and good works. Elizabeth Fry, with whom he had visited Newgate Prison, once caused him to remark, "She is very unpopular with the clergy: examples of living, active virtue disturb our repose, and give birth to distressing comparisons; we long to burn her alive." But the Friends were not to be taken altogether seriously. "A Quaker baby?" he once remarked, "Impossible! There is no such thing; there never was; they are always born broad-brimmed and in full quake."

The role of village doctor (and that of village comforter) devolved on the country parson, and he trained a favorite maidservant to act as assistant apothecary in making up simple remedies. As he wrote in one of his infrequent pieces of occasional verse:

> I know all drugs, all simples and all pills;
> I cure diseases, and I send no bills.
> The poor old women now no lameness know;
> Rheumatics leave their hand, the gout their toe.
> Fell atrophy has fled from Foston's vale,
> And health, and peace, and joy and love prevail.
>
> (1980, p. 107)

Garden allotments, savings bank schemes, advice on improved diets, and better schooling were some of the other benefits that this debonair metropolitan wit and periodical journalist brought to his backward area of Yorkshire, in a way that must have surprised his London friends. He also did duty as a local magistrate, trying lesser criminal cases and taking part in the administration of local turnpike roads and regional prisons. These were subjects in which his local experience proved to be of much value to his role as an *Edinburgh* reviewer. Articles on subjects like alehouse licensing policy deserved an airing in a national journal, and he became something of an expert on prison administration, knowing from experience on the bench the corrupting influence of contemporary jails if the old and young offenders, and particularly the sentenced and the merely accused, were not separated. He was not in favor of lighter punishments, and saw banishment to the Australian penal settlements as something of a luxury. He wrote about such matters in the *Edinburgh Review*; and even lobbied Sir Robert Peel about them:

A sentence of transportation to Botany Bay translated into common sense is this: "Because you have committed this offence, the sentence of the court is that you shall no longer be burthened with the support of your wife and family; you shall be immediately removed from a very bad climate, and a country overburthened with people, to one of the finest regions of the earth, where the demand for human labour is every hour increasing, and where is it highly probable you may ultimately regain your character, and improve your fortune. The court has been induced to pass this sentence upon you in consequence of the many aggravating circumstances of your life, and they hope your fate will be a warning to others."

(1980, p. 110)

Peel admitted that he saw the point of this argument and said that he hoped to be able to make transportation appear a salutary deterrent.

Part of the revenues of the parish of Foston derived from its farmland and Smith, "fresh from London and not knowing a turnip from a carrot," had to become a practical farmer, supervising his laborers closely and taking a keen interest in their work. "A wet harvest here," he remarked in 1821, "but I have saved all my corn by injecting great quantities of fermented liquors into the workmen, and making them work all night." Lord Holland commissioned him to find "Scotch sheep," presumably for their strong-flavored mutton, and turned to Sydney as an expert. When their poor quality was complained of, Sydney retorted, "When an human creature is lean, long and logical we know him to be a Scotchman, but how does this apply to sheep? The meaning of Scotch mutton is old, small mutton fed on poor pastures—these requirements attended to, the register of birth is idle."

Other country pursuits were if possible avoided. He had made it a rule not to take up game shooting:

for if I fed the poor, and comforted the sick, and instructed the ignorant, yet should I do nothing worth, if I smote the partridge. If anything ever endangers the Church, it will be the strong propensity to shooting for which the clergy are remarkable. Ten thousand good shots dispersed over the country do more harm to the cause of religion than the arguments of Voltaire and Rousseau.

(1980, p. 118)

His Yorkshire years saw the final stages of the Catholic Emancipation campaign, during which he became involved not so much as a journalist than as a practical political agitator, addressing self-important conservative meetings of local clergy and finding himself in a tiny minority. On one of these occasions a curate of his had asked permission to vote on the other side. "I assured him," Sydney told his audience, "nothing would give me more pain than to think I had prevented, in any man, the free assertion of honest opinions." There was further pamphleteering, much of it going over old ground for local circulation, but the tide of opinion was at last turning in favor of repeal of the ancient disabilities imposed on the Catholic laity.

Smith had listed *Edinburgh* reviewing as one of his functions as a country parson, and rightly so. He wrote for the review on the narrow curriculum of the public school system, and on the viciousness of using small boys to climb up chimney stacks to sweep down the soot. The local Quakers' skill in running lunatic asylums, the reform of the game laws, and the licensing of ale Bhouses were all subjects on which he used his local knowledge for a national audience. Naturally enough, the final and more political stages of the Catholic Emancipation campaign had also occupied him in the *Review*, but his days as one of the principal *Edinburgh* reviewers were coming to an end. But he could still (in 1823) send his friend Jeffrey an invoice for work done: "To an attack upon a Bishop in No. 74, said Bishop being a bigot and a tyrant, and for making said Bishop look ridiculous and so improving him. All executed in the best manner—good language, witty and clear of Scotticisms, and very provoking according to order."

Just as Holland House had provided a social and intellectual focus for the Smiths' life in

London, so Castle Howard, the palatial seat of the Howards, earls of Carlisle, only a few miles from Foston, became for them from about 1815 onward a welcome oasis in their remote, provincial existence. The Howard family took him up, but they did not take him over, for (as with the Hollands) Smith was considerate rather than deferential to its head, and always ready to speak his own mind as frankly as the occasion demanded. Lord Carlisle had ventured in 1824 to protest to Smith about the strident tone of some of his *Edinburgh* contributions, but received in reply some well-considered broadsides on the use of the gifts of wit and ridicule he had been favored with. "My opinions, and the free expression of them," Smith concluded, "I will surrender to no man alive—nor will I hold myself to any man for the exercise of the right." Such disputatiousness shows itself only rarely in Smith's correspondence, and it shows him well aware of the dangers of becoming merely the creature of aristocratic patronage, or indeed of being seen as such. More generally, he could write of this Lord Carlisle, who died in 1825, that "the old Earl is young, athletic, beautiful and merry. ... He is fond of quizzing me, but I give him as good as he brings, so all goes on well."

The next earl, previously Viscount Morpeth, was a near-contemporary of Smith's, and he was on close terms with him His wife, Lady Georgiana, appreciated Sydney's cheerful advice, and he once wrote to her, "I like in you very much that you are a religious woman, because, though I have an infinite hatred and contempt for the nonsense which often passes under and disgraces the name of religion, I am very much pleased when I see anybody religious for hope and comfort, not for insolence and interest." Soon after this, in spring 1820, probably when she was recovering from postnatal depression, he sent her his well-known "Advice on Low Spirits." His own experience of "low spirits," briefly alluded to here, seems to have been that of one who suffered from occasional melancholy, despite his general buoyancy of disposition:

Nobody has suffered more from low spirits than I have done, so I feel for you. 1. Live as well and drink as much wine as you dare. 2. Go in to the shower-bath with a small quantity of water at a temperature low enough to give you a *slight* sensation of cold—75 or 80°. 3. Amusing books. 4. Short views of human life not farther than dinner or tea. 5. Be as busy as you can. 6. See as much as you can of those friends who respect and like you; 7. and of those acquaintance who amuse you. 8. Make no secret of low spirits to your friends but talk of them fully: they are always the worse for dignified concealment. 9. Attend to the effects tea and coffee produce on you. 10. Compare your lot with that of other people. 11. Don't expect too much of human life, a sorry business at best. 12. Avoid poetry, dramatic representations (except comedy), music, serious novels, melancholy sentimental people, and everything likely to excite feeling or emotion not ending in active benevolence. 13. Do good and endeavour to please everybody of every degree. 14. Be as much as you can in the open air without fatigue. 15. Make the room where you commonly sit gay and pleasant. 16. Struggle little by little against idleness. 17. Don't be too severe upon yourself, but do yourself justice. 18. Keep good, blazing fires. 19. Be firm and constant in the exercise of rational religion. 20. Believe me dear Lady Georgiana very truly yours, SYDNEY SMITH.

(1980, pp. 137–138; 1993, p. 64)

Not long afterwards, and varying his tone considerably, Sydney ventured to give some counsel to Lady Georgiana's husband: "As I am an adviser by trade," he wrote, "allow me to recommend moderation in pursuing the pleasures of the chase. The fox was given to mankind not for business, but for amusement." That is very much the mood in which he had addressed the previous earl, writing to him in reply to some quizzical comments on a *Edinburgh* article on game law reform:

Your attack upon me is a very fair one. It never occurred to me in indicating the rights of humanity that my neighbours might be so literal as not to send me game. What a rash man I have been! Had I not better publish an advertisement stating that I never meant to push matters to such a disagreeable extremity, that I was only theorising and never intended to proceed to practical abstinence from such delicacies? As for you, my dear Lord, I never had the slightest belief that you put bullets in your

SYDNEY SMITH

guns. ... Thank you for the game, at whatever expenditure of human life obtained.

(1980, p. 136)

It was the Carlisle family who secured for Sydney Smith the temporary presentation to the prosperous parish of Londesborough, in East Yorkshire, to be caretaker until a relation of the Duke of Devonshire took over the parish. He preached there from time to time, but it was in the hands of a competent curate. The additional income was useful, although some family inheritances, including some small properties in the Ccity of London from an aunt, had eased his financial circumstances considerably. It remained for him to secure some permanent and well-paid advancement in his profession, which it was likely would take him away from Yorkshire, where he was by now well established.

His long, though mainly anonymous, services to the Whig cause had by the late 1820s led to the reasonable expectation of appropriate reward through government patronage within the Church of England. Recompense there was, but it was not to be at an episcopal level. Many years before, King George III had spoken appreciatively of Sydney's reviews in the *Edinburgh*. The king is said to have remarked that "He was a very clever fellow, but that he would never be a bishop." Smith was philosophical about the lack of promotion. "I have put myself so forward about the Catholic question that they will be very reluctant to promote me," he wrote in 1827. Lesser reward did come, however, first with a canonry at Bristol Cathedral, which necessitated a move from Yorkshire, which he left with great regret, to a well-appointed rectory near Taunton in Somerset.

The canon's stall at Bristol came unexpectedly at the nomination of the Tory Lord Lyndhurst. Smith relished his first brief exposure to life as a cathedral dignitary, "preceded by a silver rod, the very type of dignified gravity—they say I am a severe solemn-looking man." And in 1828 he much enjoyed preaching a Gunpowder Day sermon—on toleration—to a notoriously Tory and protestant civic corporation, letting off "no ordinary collection of squibs, crackers and *Roman* candles." The sermon, "On Toleration," was

an old one, carefully spiced up for the occasion. It was no wonder that the aldermen and councillors were, as he expressed it, scarcely able to keep the festive turtle on their stomachs.

He moved permanently to the southwest in 1829, sorry to leave his Yorkshire friends but reminding them that they would find "a better sort of Foston at Combe Florey." His new parish was more conveniently placed for getting to London. The possibility of rail travel to Bristol and then to Taunton tempted many visitors to stay at the large rectory house, and he continued to enjoy dining with those who appreciated his company even more than his politics. "I have never given way to that puritanical feeling of the Whigs against dining with Tories" he wrote in 1834:

Tory and Whig in turn shall be my host,
I taste no politics in boiled and roast.

(1993, p. 29)

It had been a matter of great satisfaction to him, when the final and inevitable stages of Catholic Emancipation were gone through. He had fought long and hard, in the transparent pseudonymity of *Peter Plymley's Letters*, in a series of pungent articles in the *Edinburgh Review*, and by courageous personal appearances on the minority side at country gatherings in Yorkshire. In 1830 a Roman Catholic was elected member of parliament for Carlisle, and Smith wrote to congratulate his father, Henry Howard of Corby: "It is a pure pleasure to me to see honourable men of an ancient family restored to their birthright. I rejoice in the temple that has been reared to Toleration; and I am proud that I worked as a bricklayer's labourer at it—without pay, and with the enmity and abuse of those who were unfavourable to its construction."

The major issue that the Whigs had to deal with as their fortunes at last revived, an even greater cause than the Catholic issue, was that of parliamentary reform. His friend Lord Grey became prime minister on a reform ticket, but Tory opposition to the Reform Bill continued among rural diehards in the provinces. At one of the last-ditch public meetings (in October 1831), Smith delivered the most famous of his political speeches at Taunton:

As for the possibility of the House of Lords preventing ere long a reform of Parliament, I hold it to be the most absurd notion that ever entered into human imagination. I do not mean to be disrespectful, but the attempt of the Lords to stop the progress of reform reminds me very forcibly of the great storm of Sidmouth, and of the conduct of the excellent Mrs. Partington on that occasion. In the winter of 1824, there set in a great flood upon that town—the tide rose to an incredible height—the waves rushed in upon the houses, and every thing was threatened with destruction. In the midst of this sublime and terrible storm, Dame Partington, who lived upon the beach, was seen at the door of her house with mop and pattens, trundling her mop, squeezing out the sea-water, and vigorously pushing away the Atlantic Ocean. The Atlantic was roused. Mrs. Partington's spirit was up; but I need not tell you that the contest was unequal. The Atlantic Ocean beat Mrs. Partington. She was excellent with a slop or a puddle, but she should not have meddled with a tempest. Gentlemen, be at your ease—be quiet and steady. You will beat Mrs. Partington.

(1980, pp. 158–159)

This contained just the right mixture of local allusion, common sense and boisterous good humor to carry his Somersetshire audience. The fame of the simile spread, and the speech was soon reported in the London press, and with Mrs. Partington represented by the Duke of Wellington it made one of the best-known political caricatures of its day. Smith saw his speeches as like the tootings of "a penny trumpet" in "a little market town" but through his humorous allusion he had helped achieve a victory for common sense. The Reform Act eventually became law in June 1832, a major step forward in the democratiszation of British parliamentary representation which would need much further development in the rest of the nineteenth century.

Reward within his profession, beyond his minor preferment at Bristol, became a more practical proposition now that his political associates were in office. Smith himself had reservations about accepting a bishopric—"to live with foolish people, do foolish and formal things all day, to hold my tongue or to twist it onto conversation unnatural to me"—and it was perhaps fortunate that his patrons saw that promotion should lie elsewhere. In 1831 Lord Grey, who had been anxious to do something for him, found for him the lucrative London dignity of a canonry at St. Paul's Cathedral—"a snug thing, let me tell you, being worth full 2000 per annum." Three months of official residence were required, the rest of his time being available for work in Somerset.

He proved to be a conscientious administrator of Wren's great building, which needed a firm hand, and showed himself before his London congregation as being a good, plain—and brief—preacher. Though he had some lingering regrets about having not been made a bishop, he was well pleased there, and proved a conscientious administrator of the cathedral. Heating and cleaning it were preoccupations. He wrote for advice to a canon of Westminster Abbey:

Pray tell me the sort of person you employ for cleaning the monuments. Is it the curate, or a statuary, or is it a mere mason's labourer? Or does it (as in the case of a Scotchman caught and washed for the first time) require acid? I propose to establish a cleaning fund and to compel every dead hero to pay something towards keeping himself clean.

(1980, p. 171)

Minor patronage fell in his way, not least in small matters like providing tickets for grand occasions. He once cautioned a friend for whom he obtained a good seat: "The Virgers have the strictest orders not to accept money just as the footmen have in all serious families not to kiss the maids. That these orders are equally well carried out neither you nor I have the smallest doubt." And he had a strong sense of the dignity of his office. When a livery company administrator offered to assist with the seating plan for a state visit by saying, "Too many cooks, you know, spoil the broth," Smith retorted: "Very true, Sir, ... but let me set you right in one particular: here there is but one cook—myself; you are only scullion, and will be good enough to take your directions from me."

Sydney Smith's position in the establishment in one of the greatest of English cathedrals conferred on him a more generally public position as spokesman in defense of such institutions when their endowments and privileges came under attack in a further phase of the reform

SYDNEY SMITH

movement. The government set up a permanent Ecclesiastical Commission in 1836 for the better management of cathedral establishments. Smith admitted the necessity of some degree of reform, but his defencse of cathedral revenues and patronage revealed his own limits as a reformer. His own view, however, was that the finances of cathedrals were under threat whereas the even more substantial endowments of bishoprics were left untouched, and that a strong defense was called for. Even if the Commission's recommendations protected existing rights, the future administration of St. Paul's was under threat, not least from the energetic Charles James Blomfield, the leading spirit of the Ecclesiastical Commission and, as bishop of London, Smith's own diocesan. It took a simple request for advice, made by a north-country clergyman, Thomas Singleton, to stir Smith into action and three *Letters to Archdeacon Singleton* (1837–1839) showed that the now senior dignitary of the church had lost none of his pungent manner.

Much rather technical ecclesiastical argumentation was essential, but Smith was prepared to view unequalized clerical incomes as part of the great professional lottery: abolishing the prizes and enforcing averages would reduce and coarsen the life of all, instead of only some, clergymen. As for the bishops, they were themselves often men of humble origin who had succeeded by tutoring noblemen's sons, attracting patronage and ending up "dressed in a magnificent dress, decorated with a title, flattered by Chaplains, and surrounded by little people looking up for the things which he has to give away." Not all bishops could be described thus, and Blomfield was a special case:

The Bishop of London is passionately fond of labour, and has certainly no aversion to power, is of quick temper, great ability, thoroughly versant in ecclesiastical law, and always in London. He will become the Commission, and when the Church of England is mentioned, it will only mean Charles James, of London, who will enjoy a greater power than has ever been possessed by any Churchman

since the days of Laud, and will become the Church of England here upon earth.

(1980, p. 180)

This, with its detailed ecclesiastical arguments, was written from a Whig point of view, but despite Smith's plausible declarations of ancient and continuing allegiance it failed to convince the Whig ministers, among them his old ally Lord John Russell:.

You say you are not convinced by my pamphlet. I am afraid that I am a very arrogant person. But I do assure you that, in the fondest moments of self-conceit, the idea of convincing a Russell that he was wrong never entered my mind. Euclid (dear John) would have had a bad chance with you if you had happened to form an opinion that the interior angles of a triangle were not equal to two right angles, the more Euclid demonstrated, the more you would not have been convinced. I shall have great pleasure in dining with you on Sunday. I thought you had known me better than to imagine I really took such things to heart. I will fight you to the last drop of my ink; dine with you to the last drop of your claret; and entertain for you, bibendo et scribendo, sincere affection and respect.

(1980, p. 181)

Sydney proceeded to a second *Letter*, in which he emphasized his previous arguments, for example on the unequal distribution of incomes. Of the offspring of an ambitious London baker hoping for the social advancement of his clever little lad:

Young Crumpet is sent to school—takes to his books—spends the best years of his life, as all eminent Englishmen do, in making Latin verses—knows that the *crum* in crumpet is long, and the *pet* short—goes to the University—gets a prize for an essay on the Dispersion of the Jews—takes orders—becomes a Bishop's chaplain—has a young nobleman for his pupil—publishes a useless classic, and a serious call to the unconverted—and then goes through the Elysian transitions of prebendary, Dean, Prelate, and the long train of purple, profit, and power.

(1980, pp. 182–183)

Some friends felt that in mentioning his friend Lord John Russell so frequently, Smith was going too far, but he was unrepentant. His two tracts, published under his own name, generated in that great age of controversial pamphleteering, a further salvo. The bishop of Gloucester, James Henry Monk, had attacked him for having been made a canon of St. Paul's not for piety and learning but as a reward for scoffing and jesting. "Is not this rather strong for a Bishop," Smith asked Archdeacon Singleton, "and does it not appear to you ... as rather too close an imitation of that language which is used in the apostolic occupation of trafficking in fish?" He reviewed some of the repressive tenets of contemporary ecclesiastical conservatism, and added, "If piety consisted in the defence of any of these—if it was impious to struggle for their abrogation, I have indeed led an ungodly life."

Smith remained courteous in tone to his own bishop, Blomfield, with whom he debated the Ecclesiastical Commission's concerns in detailed correspondence. He was, however, not prepared to yield. "I hope there was not incivility in my last letter," he had written to Blomfield in 1837: "I certainly did not mean that there should be any; your situation in life perhaps accustoms you to a tone of submission and inferiority from your correspondents, which neither you nor any man living, shall ever experience from me."

Blomfield was undeterred by Sydney's attacks, however courteously they were conducted toward his person rather than his office; the Ecclesiastical Commission was established with only minor amendments to its terms of reference. Later on, in 1840, Blomfield made in a House of Lords speech some remarks on Smith's facetiousness, which called forth a reply in a letter to the *Times*:

> You call me in the speech your facetious friend, and I hasten with gratitude in this letter to denominate you my solemn friend; but you and I must not run into commonplace errors; you must not think me necessarily foolish because I am facetious, nor will I consider you necessarily wise because you are grave: but whether foolish or facetious, or what not, I admire and respect you too much not to deplore this passage in your speech; and, in spite of all your horror of being counselled by one of your own canons, I advise you manfully to publish another edition of your speech, and to expunge with the most ample apology this indecent aggression

upon the venerable instructors of mankind.

(1980, p. 186)

This public dispute with the bishop of London was carried forward while Sydney Smith, already well known in upper Whig social circles, was establishing himself, at least during his long periods of ecclesiastical residence, as a leading figure in London society. He took a house in Mayfair, and gave as well as attended smart dinner parties, evening "routs," and the disputatious and well-fed breakfast parties that were fashionable at the time. "I have a breakfast of philosophers tomorrow, at ten punctually," he invited the poet Thomas More, "muffins and metaphysics, crumpets and contradiction. Will you come?"

The final decade of Smith's life is the period when he is best recorded as a table-talker and party wit, though with advancing years his ability to perform consistently to match the high expectations of his audience sometimes failed him. His lively social personality shines through the sometimes somberly recorded anecdotes. Hearing a neighbor refuse the gravy he declared, "Madam, I have been looking for a person who disliked gravy all my life; let us swear eternal friendship"; and so, on the basis of a lively introduction at table, it came to pass. Macaulay, known since the Smiths' time in Yorkshire, as "a book in breeches," continued as a friend, Smith relishing the historian's "waterspouts of talk." Charles Dickens, suddenly the talk of the town, was carefully assessed, but "he has conquered me"; the feeling was mutual, and they became good friends. The rising politician Richard Monckton Milnes was another of the younger generation, and Smith counseled the debonair newcomer against urging on too swiftly a social presence that soon enlivened the salons of the metropolis.

Sydney Smith's style of dinner-table repartee, based partly on the informalities of tavern wit of a previous generation, was becoming rather dated. As the etiquette of dining settled into a Victorian pattern, Sydney's bantering conversational style began to seem a little *passé*, and in his later years he often generated merely by his very presence a social expectation that was not always fulfilled. Nevertheless, enough of his actual sayings were recorded by diarists to convey his tone of voice, but the quizzical eyebrow, the anticipatory smile, and the chuckling laugh have to be provided from other descriptions. His correspondence, even in brief social acknowledgements, preserves something of the spontaneous tone of his humor, and his letters survive plentifully from the last decade of his life.

He enjoyed a less demanding life at Combe Florey, where he and his wife continued to entertain London visitors as he did in Yorkshire, but without the stimulus of family life surrounding him. One son, Douglas, had died in 1829, much mourned by his father. Another, Wyndham, had to be virtually banished from his family; in spite of the good fortunes of patronage he settled to no career beyond gambling and was a cause of much regret. The two daughters, Saba (named from the Old Testament, to give her a name more distinctive than "Smith") and Emily, did much better for themselves than their surviving brother. Both married happily, Saba to the eminent physician Sir Henry Holland; Lady Holland became her father's biographer. The two sisters provided several grandchildren to enliven long summers in the west of England.

The Devon parish and its elegant Georgian rectory were supported by a secure professional income and further family inheritances; his estranged brother Cecil, who had served in India, died intestate in 1843, "just in time to gild the nails of my coffin," as Sydney put it. It was a prosperous old age that made up for the straitened circumstances of his early life. The rapidly increasing range of the railway service put Taunton within easy reach of London, and visitors continued to come to Combe Florey as they had to Foston, relieving the tedium—as Smith himself saw it—of rural isolation. Country living he came to see as "a sort of healthy grave," lacking as it did the metropolitan stimulation of London.

It was rail travel that provoked Smith into one of his few late literary efforts. He conducted a short but effective press campaign against the insistence of the railway proprietors on locking up all the passengers inside the carriages. On political matters he had gradually become virtu-

ally silent. In late 1832 he had written to a friend, "I have taken no part in the county election, and am behaving quite like a dignitary of the Church; that is, I am confining myself to digestion." Nevertheless in 1839 he was sufficiently aroused by contemporary discussion to write a pamphlet on the secret ballot question, putting forward (with his nose for a fallacy as keen as ever) some of the continuing case against secret voting. It was a contribution that amused rather than convinced. The *Ballot* pamphlet was included in the third volume of his *Works* (1839), which gathered most of his writings, including those of Peter Plymley and the anonymous *Edinburgh Review* contributions. The collection, added to in 1840 and by some later and posthumous writings, makes up the bulk of his literary work, to which his correspondence would in due course add a substantial new element.

Among his later writings were some dealing with America. He had written in the *Edinburgh Review* of 1820, "The Americans are a brave, industrious, and acute people; but they have hitherto given no indications of genius, and made no approaches to the heroic, either in their morality or character." He went on to ask: "In the four quarters of the globe, who reads an American book? Or goes to an American play? Or looks at an American picture or statue?" He was at that time too early to catch a much-admired country at a high period of literary and artistic revival, but he made many American friends, among them Charles Sumner, Edward Everett, George Ticknor, and Daniel Webster whom he famously described as being "much like a steam-engine in trousers." Sydney regarded himself as being very much a "philoyankeeist."

In spite of his admiration for the new republic, however, he was stung by the repudiation by some states, at a time of general recession, of the debts incurred on bonds issued to finance public works schemes. Sydney had suffered through Pennsylvania's defaulting on his investment of about 1000 pounds worth of bonds. His "Humble Petition to Congress," which appeared in a London newspaper in May 1843, was widely reprinted, provoking transatlantic retorts about "bombast and impertinence." Sydney developed the argument: "In every grammar-school of the old world *ad Graecas Calendas* is translated, the American dividends." He admitted to feeling an urge, when meeting a Pennsylvanian at dinner in London, to seize his coat and beaver hat, his watch and chain, in order to give the proceeds to needy English widows and orphans. A modest increase in local taxation would have paid off the repudiated debt, he felt. But he soon tired of the argument. His final published letter on the subject declared that he had sold out at 40 percent discount and would therefore "sulkily retire" from the topic. He would no longer lend money to "free and enlightened republics," he wrote, but would employ it more usefully "in buying up Abyssinian bonds, and purchasing into the Turkish fours, or the Tunis three-and-a-half per cent funds." He continued to be much abused in America, but he had friends there too, and enjoyed the gifts of apples and cheeses sent to him by transatlantic admirers.

This was to prove his last public effort in spirited controversy. He had long been a sufferer from the gout, which he had kept under control by careful dieting. Now this accomplished trencherman was reduced to a strict medical regime. "If you hear any tidings of 17 or 18 pounds of human flesh, they belong to me," he told a friend; "I look as if a curate had been taken out of me." His health declined rapidly as he approached his mid-seventies, and he died peacefully in London on 22 February 1845.

As with any accredited wit, Sydney Smith's reputation depended on reported sayings as well as published writings, and he was fortunate that many of his contemporaries treasured his letters and that some of them systematically recorded his conversation. The result of this was that after his death there was soon established a core of authentic biographical information which that has been much developed since. His widow gathered many documents, and his daughter Saba (Lady Holland) shaped them into a memoir first published in 1855, complemented by a twin volume (edited by Mrs. Sarah Austin), providing a discreetly edited selection from letters that had been treasured by their recipients. These, together with a continual stream of reprints of his col-

lected works, in various forms, have kept his memory green among an appreciative Victorian (and later) following. They have relished his literary and polemical skills, his sincere if (for some later generations) understated Anglican piety, his lively humor, and his sharply focused wit.

SELECTED BIBLIOGRAPHY

I. INDIVIDUAL WORKS. *Six Sermons* (Edinburgh, 1800, en. as *Sermons*, 2 vols. (London, 1801); *Two Letters [of "Peter Plymley"] on the Subject of the Catholics, to my Brother Abraham, who lives in the Country* (London, 1807–1808, 1809); *Two Volumes of Sermons*, 2 vols. (London, 1809); *A Letter to Archdeacon Singleton, on the Ecclesiastical Commission* (London, 1837), with *Second Letter* (London, 1838) and *Third Letter* (London, 1839); *Ballot* (London, 1839); *Elementary Sketches of Moral Philosophy, delivered at the Royal Institution in the years 1804, 1805 and 1806* (London, 1850); for miscellaneous letters and speeches, see collected *Works* below.

II. COLLECTIONS. *The Works of the Rev. Sydney Smith,* 4 vols. (London, 1839–1840; 3 vols., Philadelphia (1844); *Wit and Wisdom of the Rev. Sydney Smith*, ed. by Evert A. Duyckinck (New York, 1856); *The Wit and Wisdom of the Rev. Sydney Smith: a selection of the most remarkable passages in his writings and conversation* (London, 1860); *Bon-Mots of Sydney Smith and Richard Brinsley Sheridan*, ed. by Walter Jerrold, illust. by Aubrey Beardsley (London, 1893); *The Letters of Peter Plymley Y with selected writings*, ed. by G. C. Heseltine (London and New York, 1929); *Sydney Smith, a Biography and a Selection*, ed. Gerald Bullett (London, 1951); *Selected Writings of Sydney Smith*, ed. by W. H. Auden (New York, 1956; London, 1957); *The Sayings of Sydney Smith*, ed. by Alan Bell (London, 1993); *Twelve Miles from a Lemon: Selected Writings of Sydney Smith*, ed. by Norman Taylor and Alan Hankinson (Cambridge, 1996).

III. LETTERS. *The Letters of Sydney Smith*, 2 vols., ed. by Nowell C. Smith (Oxford, 1953); *Selected Letters of Sydney Smith*, ed. by Nowell C. Smith (Oxford, 1956; repub., intro. by Auberon Waugh (Oxford, 1981).

IV. BIOGRAPHY AND CRITICISM. Saba Smith Holland, Lady Holland, *A Memoir of the Rev. Sydney Smith, by his daughter Lady Holland, with a selection from his letters, edited by Mrs [Sarah] Austin*, 2 vols. (London, 1855); Stuart J. Reid, *A Sketch of the Life and Times of the Rev. Sydney Smith* (London, 1884; New York, 1885); 4th ed., "with additional letters" (London, 1896); André Chevrillon, *Sydney Smith et la Renaissance des Idées libérales en Angleterre au XIXe siècle* (Paris, 1894); George W. E. Russell, *Sydney Smith* (London and New York, 1905); Osbert Burdett, *The Rev. Sydney Smith* (London, 1934); Hesketh Pearson, *The Smith of Smiths: Being the Life, Wit and Humour of Sydney Smith* (London and New York, 1934), repub., intro. by Richard Ingrams (London, 1984); John Clive, *Scotch Reviewers: The "Edinburgh Review," 1802–1815* (London and Cambridge, Mass., 1957); Sheldon Halpern, *Sydney Smith* (Boston, 1967); Alan Bell, *Sydney Smith, Rector of Foston 1806–1829* (York, 1972); Alan Bell, *Sydney Smith* (Oxford, 1980); Peter Virgin, *Sydney Smith* (London, 1994).

BARRY UNSWORTH

(1930–   )

Peter Kemp

EARLY WORK

BARRY (FORSTER) UNSWORTH started life a long way from the subject matter out of which he would create his finest fiction. Gaining acclaim in the 1980s and 1990s as a novelist who vividly evoked settings such as the gaudy twilight of the Ottoman Empire, the resplendent prime and velvety decadence of the Venetian republic, and the feverish turbulence of Africa's Guinea Coast at the height of the slave trade, he was born on 10 August 1930 into a mining community, the village of Wingate, in the industrially depressed northeast of England. His parents, Michael and Elsie (Forster) Unsworth, were both from that region. Working down the pits had long been a tradition for men in the Unsworth family. Unsworth's father—who was sent down the mine at the age of thirteen—broke away from this pattern and sailed steerage to the United States in search of work. When he later returned to his native County Durham, he found employment as an insurance agent. Barry Unsworth, the first man in the family for generations not to go down the mines, benefited from this tentative step toward middle-class life by attending grammar school at Stockton-on-Tees and then going on to the University of Manchester where he read English.

Neither of these moves took him into particularly exotic locales. In the 1940s Stockton-on-Tees was a town so dour and drab that "if you carried an umbrella people stared at you with suspicion," he recalled in a 1992 interview for the London *Sunday Times* (Books, p. 6). Throughout his English degree course at Manchester from 1948 to 1951, the austere spirit of the literary critic F. R. Leavis hung dampeningly in the air. Like other young men of his era, Unsworth had to undertake two years of national service (he spent it with the army's Royal Corps of Signals) but this carried him no further afield than Aldershot in southeast England.

Though Unsworth spent his early years in what could seem cramped and unpropitious circumstances, one way of rising above the ruck had suggested itself to him even when he was a child at school. "I was good at writing essays —compositions, as they were called in those days —and used to see my work on the wall with a gold star on it," he has said. "On parents' days, people stopped and looked. And I think I perhaps saw at that early stage that the way to attract attention was to get your work on the wall somehow" (Books, p. 6).

In 1992, Unsworth got his work very noticeably up on the wall when his novel *Sacred Hunger* was a joint winner of Britain's most prestigious fiction award, the Booker Prize (his fellow victor was Michael Ondaatje with *The English Patient*). But it took considerable time and a number of false starts before he set himself on course for achievement of this kind. After finishing his national service, he drifted desultorily in and out of a motley assortment of odd jobs—assistant in a French boarding school, deliverer of bags of coal, factory shift worker, even an attendant on a fairground rifle range at the seaside resort of Blackpool. Later in the 1950s, after his parents died, he moved to Cornwall. Renting a cheap cottage (no running water or electricity) there with money from the sale of the family house, he spent eighteen months writing short stories, none of which he managed to get into print. This was partly, he came to feel, because of their awkward attempt to imitate authors from America's Deep South—William Faulkner, Carson McCullers, Eudora Welty—for whom he had an especial admiration at that time. "I think it was the Gothic element that appealed

353

to me, the underlying hysteria," he remarked in a 1999 interview with the London *Times* (p. 43). "But I was still a lad from Stockton and there was a provincial Englishness about what I was writing. It was an uneasy mixture of Mississippi and Stockton-on-Tees. And it didn't work, judging by the rejection slips." Unsworth's breakthrough into getting his work published came after he was advised to abandon the short story form and try his hand at writing a novel. The result was *The Partnership* (1966). Like the other four novels Unsworth published during the first decade of his literary career—*The Greeks have a word for it* (1967), *The Hide* (1970), *Mooncranker's Gift* (1973), and *The Big Day* (1976)— it is set in the present. It wasn't until ten years after he began writing novels that Unsworth found his way to his real métier: narratives located in the past or overshadowed by it. However, although his first five books, with their present-day settings, can look very different from his later historical novels, they broach themes and introduce motifs that prove of continuing stimulus to his imagination. Chief among these are betrayal, obsession, and the callous abuse of power.

The Partnership sardonically surveys a bohemian enclave such as Unsworth had known in Cornwall. "For someone from the northeast, who was still pretty provincial, Cornwall was quite a revelation," he has amusedly remembered. "It was full of people in flight from various metropolitan entanglements. They were a kind of people that I hadn't met much before—easier in manner, more interesting, more cosmopolitan" (London *Sunday Times*, Books, p. 6). A scattering of such people, arty and sophisticated incomers to a picturesque corner of southwest England, provides the background to Unsworth's study of a lopsided relationship between two men: Ronald Foley and Michael Moss. Foley, a good-looking charmer who has previously worked as a photographer's model in London, lives by capitalizing on his personal appeal. In the passive way that is his wont, he has slid into a business partnership with Moss, turning out plaster statuettes of "lucky pixies" for the Cornish tourist trade. But, as the novel progresses, it

transpires that the gauchely conventional, almost comically staid Moss is a long-repressed but now increasingly emotional homosexual who wants the partnership to become more intimate.

Out of the heterosexual Foley's embarrassed endeavors to disengage himself from a more and more discomfiting situation Unsworth derives suave comedy. This is also to the fore in his satirical sketches of the inhabitants of the tourist village of Lanruan. Consumed with loathing of the Cornish, a painter—who resembles a malign version of the Cookham artist Stanley Spencer —toils at a panoramic canvas entitled "Crack of Doom at Lanruan" (to be followed by "The Inhabitants of Lanruan in Hell") on which brutishly caricatured portraits of local figures are seen in terrified disarray as apocalypse convulses their village. Two visiting metropolitan sirens are quizzically observed: dreamily affected Gwendoline and predatory, coolly cynical Barbara who finally takes Foley over, undoing the buttons of his shirt with "thin, hard fingers" (p. 221) in the novel's closing sentence. And there is sharp social comedy—very similar to that in Angus Wilson's gay milieu novel *Hemlock and After* (1952)—in scenes that revolve round a shrilly camp old thespian, Max, who is seized upon by Moss to fill the gap in his life after Foley defects.

An accomplished and witty debut, *The Partnership* is prevailingly ironic in tone. But, beneath this, something fiercer and rawer keeps making itself felt (a continuation, it seems, of "the underlying hysteria" Unsworth was aware of in his short stories). The uncomfortable relationship between the two men is depicted with an honesty that lets real panic and pain agitate the poised comedy. And pushing to the surface with intermittent insistence is something that will later pervade Unsworth's historical fiction: a concern with exploitation. Benefiting from his doting business partner's greater financial resources, hard work, and eager, almost spouse-like provision of domestic comforts, Foley has obviously exploited Moss's unspoken infatuation with him. He could be seen as merely a feckless and self-centered parasite. But Unsworth complicates things by disclosing depths of morbid, almost masochistic possessiveness in Moss. His desire to have a man dependent on him finally achieves fulfilment in a creepily ambivalent way when the ailing, alcoholic Max, cast off by his former protector, falls into the care of Moss, whose behavior toward him seems as suggestive of a jailer as of a nurse.

Foley's shifty betrayal of Moss is matched by Moss's savage betrayal of him. The scene in which Foley horrifiedly discovers the form that this has taken makes use of something that features significantly in almost every novel Unsworth has written: statuary. In his later books, this usually assumes grander forms, such as an archaic Greek bronze in *Pascali's Island* (1980, republished in the United States as *The Idol Hunter*) or a fifteenth-century Gothic Madonna in *Stone Virgin* (1985). In *The Partnership*, it is introduced on a small scale in mocking descriptions of the plaster pixies Moss and Foley manufacture, then takes on another aspect when readers learn that Foley takes pride in making copies of antique Cupids, cherubim and other angels with "suavely rippling limbs, clad in gilt" (p. 218). Smashed to fragments by the bitter, vengeful Moss, these artifacts which Foley lovingly crafted to boost his artistic and personal self-respect turn out to be "stuffed with dust only, lacking fibre and grain" (p. 218). Lack of fiber is, of course, also revealed in Foley. The symbolism is emphatically explicit in a manner Unsworth moves away from in his later fiction. But his imaginative fascination with statuary remains steadfast.

By the time Unsworth completed *The Partnership*, he had left Cornwall and was living abroad. In 1959, he had married. He and his wife Valerie spent their honeymoon in Greece, then decided to remain in the country as English teachers. The milieu of expatriates, academic bureaucrats, and assorted Athenians this opened up to Unsworth is caught with satiric zest in his second novel, *The Greeks have a word for it*. True to what would become a continuing propensity for putting a place into fiction only after he had moved on from it, the book was written in Turkey, to which his nomadic teaching career had by then taken him.

Although its characters are considerably more polyglot and cosmopolitan than those in

Unsworth's first novel, *The Greeks have a word for it* has marked affinities with *The Partnership*. Its central character is again a not unlikeable but distinctly untrustworthy sponger: Bryan Kennedy, a youngish man living on his wits as a language teacher in Athens. The story opens with his arrival in the city and ends, some months later, with his violent death just as he was planning to leave it. In between these two points, his ruses in pursuit of money have taken him into a world of private conversation classes and foreign language schools that Unsworth entertainingly portrays. Kennedy's sharp practices are perpetrated amid high- spirited scenes of ludicrous academic feuding and farcically tetchy staff-room power struggles.

As with *The Partnership*, though, darker elements fester behind the sparkle of Unsworth's comedy. The novel's ending is unexpectedly and uncompromisingly bitter. While drunk from celebrating the completion of his most profitable scam, Kennedy blunders into getting himself stabbed to death. Intensifying the sourness of this ending, a Greek girl who has been going around with him also comes to grief. Aghast that Kennedy has died before he was able to hand over money he had promised her, she plucks his wallet from his corpse and hurries away. The novel's closing line reveals that the banknotes she craves were actually tucked into Kennedy's hip pocket where they are now soaking up blood welling from his fatal knife wound.

The man who inflicted this wound, Stavros Mitsos, is the first intimation of a significant shift in Unsworth's fiction, as is the book's Athenian setting. For the first time in his writing, the past clusters around the present, and history exerts a pull on his imagination. There are, in fact, two historical hinterlands surrounding contemporary events in *The Greeks have a word for it*. Athens' monumental glories and its ancient myths of nemesis and the Furies throw the petty vendettas and peevish skirmishes among the language teachers into ignominious comic relief. A more recent past—the aftermath of the Second World War in Greece—casts a different kind of shadow. Mitsos, an early example of the dangerous obsessive, a type that will recur through Unsworth's fiction, has been traumatized by the ugly repercussions of the war. When he was a boy of twelve, vengeful partisans hunted down and murdered his father, a right-wing army officer who had collaborated with the Germans. One of the assassins then raped Mitsos' mother. Continuing the chain reaction of retaliation, Mitsos now stalks that man. Risible efforts to wreak revenge for slighted *amour propre* among staff in the language school are counterpointed by his tragically misdirected bid to exact revenge for the atrocities afflicted on his parents. Like *The Partnership*, *The Greeks have a word for it* juxtaposes humane, civilized comedy with savagery and vengeance.

Unsworth's next book, *The Hide* (perhaps his most suffocatingly grim novel) returns to an English setting. Its events occur in and around a large house and are watched from two contrasting viewpoints. Josh, a young fairground employee (recalling Unsworth's early experiences, he is first seen on a rifle range) finds a job as a gardener tending the sprawling grounds around the home of a middle-aged widow, Audrey. His naïvely blurted-out accounts of what then happens alternate with the more prim-lipped narrative of Audrey's brother, Simon, a voyeur who spends his days sexually snooping upon people from hiding places in the grounds.

Unsworth's first outstanding novel, *Pascali's Island*, takes a spy as its subject, as does its successor, *The Rage of the Vulture* (1982). The idea of making a career out of covert observation of fellow human beings is something Unsworth clearly relates to his own profession as a novelist. In *The Hide* apprehensions that there may be something unhealthily exciting and self-gratifying about this are released into the portrayal of Simon's surreptitious peerings and pryings. A contrasting surrogate for authorial activity—one which will receive its most elaborate treatment in *Stone Virgin*—is apparent in Josh's skill at carving likenesses of animals. Finely exhibited in a wooden model of a horse that he presents to Audrey, this talent displays the creatively appealing result of intense, sympathetic observation.

In *The Hide*, intense, unsympathetic observation is more usually in evidence. Its characters watch one another in a predatory way, and its author watches them unsparingly. At the center of it all is a far more ferocious version of the Moss-Foley imbroglio in *The Partnership*. Painfully simpleminded and easily led, Josh is under the sinister sway of Mortimer, an older man who is sadistically manipulative and driven by an urge to defile and destroy things from which others derive pleasure. His pathological jealousy and battened-down homosexuality are given vicious vent when he horribly ruins Josh's love affair with a young woman employed as a servant by Audrey. Deception, betrayal, domination, rape —already familiar presences in Unsworth's pages —tangle together into a particularly harsh and sickening conclusion.

"Something more sombre came into the way I felt," Unsworth has said with considerable justification of *The Hide* (London *Sunday Times*, Books, p. 6). This sombreness is also perceptible in *Mooncranker's Gift*. But it is here accompanied by a renewed attempt to incorporate comedy and (even more than in *The Greeks have a word for it*) a historical dimension. After uprooting themselves from Greece, Unsworth, his wife, and their three daughters, Madeleine, Tania, and Thomasina, moved to Turkey, where he taught in Smyrna and at the University of Istanbul. *Mooncranker's Gift* is at its most interesting when registering his first response to the places and culture this presented him with. Opening in Istanbul where a British Council employee, James Farnaby, reencounters Mooncranker—once a celebrated radio and television personality, now an alcoholic wreck—the novel soon shifts to Pamukkale, the hot-springs spa in western Turkey. Here, Unsworth sets up another of his juxtapositions of black comedy and rawer material. Steamy erotic entanglements in the baths are sardonically surveyed, and sometimes teasingly imbued with mythological resonances (talk of the cult of the goddess Cybele and her frenzied female worshippers intersperses scenes of hectic goings-on by 1970s women). But more serious turmoil is explored too. A decade earlier, when he was a morbidly sensitive thirteen-year-old racked by sexual and religious scruples, Farnaby was deeply upset by a practical joke

BARRY UNSWORTH

Mooncranker, a family friend, played on him. In a gruesome variant on Unsworth's customary fascination with statuary, this took the form of the gift of a small figure of Christ on the cross. Swathed immaculately in white, this figure was moulded, however, from sausage meat. Soon, before the boy's appalled gaze, maggots wriggled out of it. In Mooncranker's nasty prank, Unsworth's habitual concern with underlying rottenness finds horribly literal expression.

What is most striking about *Mooncranker's Gift*, though, and what makes sections of it a foreshadowing of Unsworth's mature fiction, is its alertness to what he has called "landscape and atmosphere redolent of the past, living a contemporary life within the setting of the past" (Books, p. 7). Pamukkale's antique hinterland of ruins keeps this in Unsworth's mind's eye throughout his novel's present-day scenes. In later books —*Stone Virgin, Sugar and Rum* (1988), and, most of all, *After Hannibal* (1996)—it would be put to powerful effect.

Before taking his decisive step into writing fiction which would be either historical or include history as a crucial component, Unsworth reverted for a final time to blackly comic portrayal of the world of language teaching, with his most stylized and least successful novel, *The Big Day*. Its setting is the Regional College of Further Studies, founded and run by its principal, Donald Cuthbertson, in an unspecified part of England. A spectacularly fraudulent organization whose activities make Kennedy's swindles in *The Greeks have a word for it* look decidedly unenterprising, Cuthbertson's college peddles bogus academic qualifications (twelve-week Honors degrees and the like) to gullible wealthy foreigners.

Cuthbertson, it soon becomes clear, is declining rapidly into lunacy. The members of his staff and his nymphomaniac wife (whose adventures are narrated in an outrageously black comic manner reminiscent of Joe Orton's sexual farces) are also at some level removed from reality. Throughout the novel, they remain weirdly oblivious to bulletins of social breakdown recurrently emitted by the radio. Finally, in another of the acrid endings Unsworth favors in these early novels, his

book's two aspects of anarchy collide: a terrorist bomb devastates the college during a zanily rampant masked ball.

The Big Day has some relishable moments and is of significance in containing Unsworth's first attack on mercantile values (the target of his longest and best-known novel, *Sacred Hunger*). But there is a sense of strain in its brittle, semi-surreal satire and its farcically caricatured characters. After it, Unsworth published nothing for four years. When he returned to print, it was as a noticeably different kind of novelist and with one of his finest works, *Pascali's Island*.

PASCALI'S ISLAND *AND* THE RAGE OF THE VULTURE

WHAT attracted Barry Unsworth to Istanbul, he told the London *Sunday Times*, was that "It's like Vienna or Madrid, one of those cities where you really feel the decline and the peculiar melancholy of imperial trappings that all the life has gone out of" (Books, p. 7). Imperial disillusion and dissolution were to be dominant themes in British fiction throughout the last three decades or so of the twentieth century. Two novelists most established this interest: Paul Scott with his five novels about the Raj and its aftermath (*The Jewel in the Crown*, 1966; *The Day of the Scorpion*, 1968; *The Towers of Silence*, 1971; *A Division of the Spoils*, 1975; *Staying On*, 1977) and J. G. Farrell with his trilogy highlighting episodes of British imperial crisis or discomfiture (*Troubles*, 1970; *The Siege of Krishnapur*, 1973; *The Singapore Grip*, 1978). With *Pascali's Island*, Unsworth joined them and moved into fictional territory that he increasingly made his own. The scenarios of betrayal, exploitation and callous bids for mastery that his fiction previously saw acted out in personal or private spheres now extend into a political arena. The glamours and rapacities of empire become his great subject. By the middle of the 1980s and into the 1990s, his attention would move to the Venetian and British Empires. But he began his sequence of novels about imperial cruelties and imperial collapse with depictions of the last days of the Ottoman

Empire, whose remains he had been living among in Istanbul and Smyrna.

Pascali's Island observes the finale of that empire from a vantage point on its outermost limit: an Aegean island in 1908. Here, as the rotten jigsaw of the Ottoman empire falls jaggedly apart, a man whose own time is running out contemplates a panorama of disintegration. Basil Pascali is a paid informer who for twenty years has been sending reports (more than a million words, he calculates) to Constantinople. No one has ever suffered as a result of these bulletins, which have been unacknowledged and apparently unread. Now, though, Pascali fears the local Greeks have discovered what he does. As he waits for them to kill him, he writes his last report, packing it with symptoms of approaching doom. Grim symbolic felicities emphasize his plight. The Moslem Sacrifice Festival is in progress: all over the island, the green flag of the Prophet flutters over sharpened knives; ritually decorated sheep—horns gilded, fleece hennaed—are being pointed toward Mecca and butchered. In the Greek church, a shattering portent occurs, the scared Pascali thinks, when the venerated effigy of Saint Alexei overbalances and breaks.

Politically, ugly cracks are gaping ever wider. In the garrisons, disaffected Turkish troops barely obey orders; in the hills, Greek freedom fighters become every day more venturesome. Nor are things merely crumbling at the empire's edge: the center, it seems, cannot hold either. Clogged with corruption, the administrative channels have seized up. Rumors seep out from Constantinople—where there are said to be more spies than police—of a paranoid Sultan virtually self-imprisoned in his Yildiz Palace.

Everything is fragmenting and, as Pascali pithily notes, "Fragments mean pickings" (p. 175).1 Eager to snap these up, international adventurers are on the scene, scavenging for booty, from bauxite concessions to Greek statuary. The latter, as might be expected, proves of especial interest to Unsworth. Central to his novel's narrative is a plan secretly to excavate and smuggle away from the island a life-sized Greek bronze of a young man (leaving a hideous rubberized modern doll in its place to mock the local Pasha who also

covets the treasure trove). The statue, Unsworth spells out, isn't merely high-grade loot but an artefact endowed with emblematic significance. "Greek sculpture," claims Bowles, the English opportunist who is scheming to possess the bronze not just for mercenary but also for aesthetic reasons, "provides us with a sort of universal paradigm, a model for all human affairs" (p. 173). He elucidates this by outlining the progress of the Greek sculptural tradition from early unindividualized images to statues where there is "an awakening to personality" and "perfect balance of form and spirit," then on to figures with "more differentiation, more insistence on naturalistic detail" but which are "not so secure, not so self-contained," and finally down through the Hellenistic period into mere "drama and decoration" (pp. 173–174). Bowles's thesis, "The whole art becomes decadent, and so does the society," finds a receptive audience in Pascali who goes on to remark that this trajectory "from a collective idea of man, to a very brief period of perfect balance, then to increasing anguish and disunity, finally to breakdown and fragmentation" took almost five hundred years. This is, he points out "for the sake of the parallel," "roughly the duration" of the Ottoman Empire too (p. 175).1

"Your Empire," Pascali has earlier written to his remote master, the Sultan in Istanbul, "is the most cosmopolitan the world has ever seen, a multiplicity of races, creeds and tongues, united in the Ottoman state. A perfect equivalent, in political terms, of that unity in diversity which has exercised philosophers ever since Thales" (pp. 49–50). Now, this unity is fatally fracturing. Unsworth's novel counterpoints this breaking apart of the massive, variegated Ottoman Empire with the rising stridency of jingo nationalism. English and Irish, French and Germans ominously grate against each other in his story. As the sound of distant Balkan animosities also becomes audible as well, the reader catches the warning sounds of the caving in of European order.

A polyglot Levantine of mixed descent, bisexual, cosmopolitan, easily familiar with both Christian and Moslem observances, Pascali throws all this divisiveness into relief. He is, in

1. Page references are from the U.S. edition, *The Idol Hunter* (1980).

addition, a fusion of two character types that have hitherto co-existed unconnectedly in Unsworth's fiction: the sponger and the surrogate novelist. In his perceptive but parasitic reactions to others, Pascali constitutes a more humanly complex version of figures such as Foley or Kennedy. As with them, charm goes along with self-aware seediness, but his wheedling and chicanery are given more urgency by the fact that if they don't succeed he may starve. The dispatches to Constantinople for which Pascali receives a meager stipend of piastres link him to another kind of character in Unsworth's fiction: the authorial alter ego. Twenty years as an informer have honed his powers of observation and communication and turned him into something very like a novelist. He takes an author's pride in his writings (to the extent of hoping to be able to go to Constantinople and extract them from the state archives). He knows the dread of "the blank, tyrannical pages there before me, still waiting to be filled" (p. 99). He experiences moments of rebellious wretchedness similar to those of a frustrated novelist: "Why should I sit here, hatching other people's motives and purposes?" (p. 94). He is, like many fiction writers, fascinated by symbols, patterns, and parallels. His reports are blends of reality and illusion. He is dextrous at describing place: "the white houses with their shallow roofs and ramshackle storks' nests; the whole town enmeshed in the green of its terraces; the minarets of the mosques and the broken towers of the Frankish castle sticking up through the net, brown falcons loitering in the sky above" (p. 13). He turns people around him into characters who suit his literary purposes. Sympathetic consonance between author and narrator is a crucial strength in this graceful, elegiac, and ironic novel with its striking knowledgeability about Asia Minor at the start of the twentieth century.

The Rage of the Vulture—which travels into the imploding core of the Ottoman Empire, the chaotic Constantinople of 1908—shows Unsworth's interest in observers continuing. Surveillance lurks in every quarter of this novel. Where Pascali was an informer frightenedly conscious of being under hostile scrutiny, the hero of *The Rage of the Vulture*, Robert Markham,

is a political agent aware that he is stationed in a city riddled with spies (the most bizarre of whom is the Sultan, Abdul Hamid II himself, peering out across Constantinople through telescopes sited in an observatory on the roof of his palace).

Almost at the end of the novel, Markham and the Abdul Hamid fleetingly meet in one of the imperial torture chambers (situated near the palace zoo so that any screams will be attributed to animals). Before this, Unsworth memorably captures the ghastly futility as well as the brutal monstrousness of the Sultan's autocratic regime. A prisoner of his fears despite his panoply of power, Abdul Hamid timorously skulks at the center of a labyrinth of secret passages, concealed doors, blind alleys, corridors designed to mislead and thwart would-be assassins. Seventy-eight pistols with which to protect himself in case of attack are disposed around the palace. Attendants are deaf and mute. Courtiers perform their duties with exaggerated slowness lest a too-rapid movement panic the scared Sultan into killing them.

While paranoia paralyzes Abdul Hamid in his palace, Markham is numbed by guilt. Memories keep surfacing of his engagement party twelve years earlier that was nightmarishly transformed when Turkish fanatics broke in and raped and killed his Armenian fiancée, Miriam. This horrific incident partly recalls the rape and murder Mitsos witnessed in *The Greeks have a word for it*. But, more than that, it opens up the issue of the late-nineteenth-century Armenian massacres in Turkey (in which over 50,000 people were slaughtered, Markham reminds himself), and initiates a habit that will recur through Unsworth's later fiction of inserting actual historical atrocities into his narratives. What makes the outrage addedly agonizing to Markham is his shamed feeling that he betrayed Miriam by terrifiedly asserting his English nationality to save his own life. Just as much as their shared status as spies, this instinct for self-preservation links him with Pascali. Superficially very different—the shabby obese Levantine and the smart lean British officer—the central figures in these two novels of Unsworth's have distinct affinities.

BARRY UNSWORTH

Pascali's Island and *The Rage of the Vulture* are also similar in that each constitutes a masterly feat of fictional archaeology, exhuming historical scenes with crisp immediacy and in teeming detail. Both testify to a prodigious amount of research. Like some of his characters, Unsworth is a sedulous keeper of journals and scrapbooks ("wodges and wodges of them," he said in his interview in the London *Sunday Times*). Before starting work on a novel, he amasses a plethora of data—"material that will strengthen the illusion you're trying to create"—then uses, he reckons, "about 20%" of it (Books, p. 7). Nowhere is this shown to greater effect than in his next novel, *Stone Virgin*.

STONE VIRGIN

LIKE *The Rage of the Vulture,* Unsworth's Venetian novel, *Stone Virgin*, displays a forte for atmospherically recreating beautifully moldering cities. This partly comes from his receptive roamings around them, taking copious notes. But history as well as topography contributes to the novels' substance. *Stone Virgin* is indebted to months Unsworth spent in Venice but also to his family's move back to England for the sake of his daughters' education. They settled in Cambridge, about which he had mixed feelings. But one thing that did make that city a congenial stopping point was its libraries. *Stone Virgin*, with its wealth of fifteenth- and eighteenth-century detail, is evidence of his purposeful ransacking of them. It also brings compellingly together his fascination with imperial moribundity and his keen response to statuary.

With *Stone Virgin*, Unsworth constructs a three-tier book dominated by a masterpiece of Venetian Gothic—a sculpted limestone Madonna that casts its shadow over a trinity of stories: one set in the fifteenth century, one in the eighteenth, and one in the 1970s. As with *Pascali's Island* and *The Rage of the Vulture*, much of the novel aims to restore the past with paint-fresh vividness. Fifteenth-century Venice leaps to life in letters a sculptor condemned to death for an alleged murder pleadingly writes to his patron. Three centuries on, glimpsed through the swaggering, pornographic memoirs of a now decrepit debauchee, a very different city appears. The medieval world of faith and earthiness, resounding to the oaths and clatter of stonecutters working on new churches, has given way to a silky milieu of masks, adulterous assignations, and machinations. Now, when the Angelus bell sends its vibrations through the flushed dusk of Venice, it's not to summon the pious to their devotions but to signal the advent of pleasure.

Decadence has always excited Unsworth's attention. In *Stone Virgin*, alongside moral and social specimens of it, there is a tangible instance of corruption at the heart of the narrative: a disfiguring crust of chemical filth that is eating into the limestone Madonna on a church façade. Attempting to remove this cancerous coating is Simon Raikes, a restorer working for the Rescue Venice organization. With enthralling informativeness, Unsworth charts every stage of his conservation exercise, as an air-abrasion instrument delicately blasts away the corrosion. Matching the expertise with which this process is recorded is the elegance with which it is used to symbolize what the novel itself is doing: stripping away accretions of time and decay to reveal an underlying shape.

As shared motifs and symmetries of behavior gradually come to light, Unsworth's trio of stories emerge as intricately connected. All three are tableaux—part-horrific, part-ironic—illustrating the tensions between love and lust, creation and destruction, fertility and sterility. Only in the final panel of this triptych, the 1970s story where Raikes is involved with a present-day Venetian sculptor and his wife, is an equilibrium reached. But, even here, ambiguities and paradoxes linger—appropriately in a book whose central image is an ambivalent Madonna: a Virgin carved in the likeness of an artist's prostitute mistress.

Stone Virgin contrives to be both robustly concrete and subtly cerebral. Ideas animate it everywhere, from aesthetic theories to theological doctrines and speculations on art and sexuality. At the same time, it reconstructs phases of Venice's history with sensuous solidity. Unsworth steers his readers down medieval canals ringing to the din of bells and hammers, or into candlelit eighteenth-century gaming rooms frequented by seedy revellers in chalky, bird-beaked masks. His depiction of contemporary Venice, with its menaced, melancholy glamour, is a tour de force of informed, atmospheric writing. Whether climbing scaffolding with Raikes to inspect the recent ravages of industrial pollution or surveying the remoter reaches of the Lagoon where gulls dip and scream over drowned islands, he seems in his element. Venice's gorgeous past and precarious present have rarely been so engrossingly chronicled.

SUGAR AND RUM *AND* SACRED HUNGER

IN 1985, the year that saw the publication of *Stone Virgin*, Barry Unsworth moved to Liverpool as writer-in-residence at the city's university. Ironically, the busy flow of literary productivity that he had maintained throughout his years as a peripatetic English teacher in the Eastern Mediterranean immediately dried up. As a writer-in-residence, he ran into the only writer's block of his career. Coinciding with the breakdown of his first marriage, this traumatic experience was caused, he said in a 1996 interview with the British newspaper the *Independent*, by the consternation Liverpool provoked in him: "I'd come from Cambridge, and I was shocked at first by how dilapidated and deprived the city was. And then there was the highly politicized nature of the university, which was rather a new thing for me. And one way or another I got so involved that I didn't write anything for a year, and then I couldn't. It was awful. For fifteen months I was blocked, the first time I'd ever had that" (Winder, *Independent*, Weekend Review, p. 3).

In the long run, Unsworth's time in Liverpool proved advantageous to his writing. Among other things, it gave him the subject for his longest novel, the Booker Prize–winning *Sacred Hunger*. In his mind, this port in the northwest of England had affinities with the two cities his fiction had been contemplating most recently: "Liverpool, Venice, Istanbul—all to me have similar qualities, imperial connections," he affirmed in the

London *Sunday Times* (Books, p. 7). But there was a significant difference. Where the remnants of former imperial prosperity in Istanbul and Venice took picturesque and exotic forms, in Liverpool there was merely squalid dereliction. "Going to Liverpool was a revelation," Unsworth declared. "It was so awful. It was so devastated at the time. It was urban decay in a way I'd never seen it, and I was pitched right in the middle of it" (Books, p. 7). He was "stricken by the sight of so much stricken around me" (Sutcliffe, *Independent on Sunday*).

What compounded the shock was that this immersion in depressed industrialism stirred memories not only of Liverpool's past but of Unsworth's own. "It chimed in," he considered, "with the feeling that I've always had that I should be writing about my own past —that is mining and the northeast. I should have been doing that rather than writing about exotic places and faraway things" (London *Sunday Times*, Books, p. 7/[18/]). It wasn't Liverpool alone that accentuated Unsworth's guilt about not using his fiction directly to confront social and economic inequities such as he had known among the deprived colliery villages of his youth. The period when he was there, the 1980s, also had an impact on him. During that decade, when Britain was experiencing the full force of the monetary policies of its prime minister Margaret Thatcher, Unsworth was appalled by what he saw as an increasing divide between the privileged and the unprivileged. "I found the triumphalism and full-blown entrepreneurial spirit of the 1980s crass and distasteful," he said (Books, p. 7). As gaps widened between the affluent and the unemployed in 1980s Britain, his mind went back to the world riven by gulfs of wealth and opportunity into which he had been born and from which his writing had more and more distanced him. Gradually, though, his qualms about having retreated into literary escapism subsided into something more purposeful. He perceived how he could reconcile writing historical fiction with doing justice to his own past. In a 1999 interview in the London *Times* he spelled this out: "For many years I felt a certain kind of guilt that I wasn't dealing with my roots, that I was turning away from reality. I don't feel that any longer. I feel there is a radiance, an essential reality in the things I write about. And I don't feel they are dated or belong to the past. I think they are as true in terms of human behavior and human nature as they ever were. The scenes have shifted, but the voices and the feelings are very much the same" (p. 43).

In Unsworth's historical fiction, almost subliminal-seeming analogies with the colliery world of his formative years can sometimes be discerned. The sculptor in *Stone Virgin* who earns his livelihood by chipping away at rock isn't entirely dissimilar to the coal miners in Unsworth's family. The black slaves clanking with ironmongery in the dark depths of the ship in *Sacred Hunger* are like monstrously more victimized versions of the miners with coal dust-blackened faces confined amid the clank of metal in the dark depths of the pit. Set in Unsworth's home territory, although back in the fourteenth century, *Morality Play* (1995) unrolls a scenario of the exploitation of the weak by the strong. So, of course, does *Sacred Hunger*, which occasionally sends parallels forking out from its eighteenth-century story to the 1980s. "As I wrote," Unsworth told *Independent on Sunday*, "I began to see more strongly that there were inescapable analogies. You couldn't really live through the Eighties without feeling how crass and distasteful some of the economic doctrines were. The slave trade is a perfect model for that kind of total devotion to the profit motive without reckoning the human consequences" (p. 23). *Sacred Hunger* shows him confidently evoking a distant historical era and simultaneously airing apprehensions about his own. *Sugar and Rum*, one of Unsworth's most personally revealing novels, traces the psychological and literary maneuverings by which he attained this equilibrium.

With characteristic tenacity, Unsworth overcame his writer's block by writing a novel about a novelist with a writer's block. Clive Benson, the author of a historical novel set in Venice, is in Liverpool struggling—unsuccessfully—to complete a novel about the city's involvement in the eighteenth-century African slave trade. Paralyzed with despondency at the unemploy-

ment and deprivation he sees everywhere around him, he ekes out a living by providing tuition in creative writing to a mixed bunch of solitaries and misfits. This partly allows Unsworth to return to the vein of sardonic comedy about the absurdities and embarrassments of adult education that he had tapped to entertaining effect in his early fiction. *Sugar and Rum* is profuse in often very funny pastiche of the literary endeavors of Benson's students. Historical fiction of the most stagily escapist kind ("Nay then, an you list, let us ride into the coverts. I will not gainsay you. 'Twould be impolite in a hostess," p. 10) is an especially favored target. But Unsworth also tellingly relates the type of fiction each student produces to his or her own frustrated predicament.

It is Benson's frustrated predicament to which *Sugar and Rum* devotes most attention, though. Resembling Unsworth in that he is a historical novelist who is "a great note-taker and researcher ... an inveterate scrapbook man" (p. 17), Benson has spent two years reading about the Liverpool slave trade. But the novel for which this is intended as preparation stubbornly refuses to get underway. Supposedly helping his students to overcome impediments to writing, he is unable to overcome impediments of his own. From the stark divides of eighteenth-century Liverpool (on the one hand, the elegant mansions of the merchants; on the other, the fetid slave ships) his mind keeps flickering over to the stark divides in the present-day city (especially as exemplified by the run-down tenements of down-and-outs and the gracious Georgian house of a Tory merchant banker, Slater, whose enmity Benson has aroused). It is Slater who voices a belief that Unsworth's novel is set up to refute: "We hear a lot about division these days from the gloom and doom merchants. The North-South divide, all this stuff about two nations. England is one nation ... can't help but be, considering our history" (p. 180). The reference to "two nations" points the book back toward nineteenth-century "Condition of England" novels—works such as Elizabeth Gaskell's *North and South* (1855) and Charles Dickens' *Hard Times* (1854)—which portrayed the Britain of their time as deplorably split

BARRY UNSWORTH

between rich and poor (a split often associated with the geographical divide between the north and south of England). Benjamin Disraeli's *Sybil or The Two Nations* (1845), the novel that put the phrase "two nations" into accusatory circulation, provided the model for a 1980s novel, David Caute's *Veronica; or The Two Nations* (1989), which proclaimed the same message in present-day terms. David Lodge's *Nice Work* (1988) likewise drew explicit parallels between the social gulfs perceived by Victorian novelists and those apparent in 1980s Britain. Using Liverpool, a city once aggrandized by imperial trade, now pauperized by its loss, as a basis from which to survey past vistas of empire and present social prospects, *Sugar and Rum* aligns itself with this development in 1980s British fiction.

At one point in *Sugar and Rum*, Benson is seen in a library familiarizing himself with the details of a 1782 court case concerning the slave ship *Zong*. Unsworth lays out the appalling actualities of what happened on that ship at some length:

> The *Zong*, sailing out of Liverpool with Luke Collingwood as master, had left Sao Thomé on September 6, 1781, with 440 slaves and a crew of 17. The Middle Passage had been difficult—they were delayed by bad weather, mortality among the negroes was very high. On November 29, with land in the West Indies already sighted, the captain called his officers together. There were only 200 gallons of fresh water left in the tanks, not enough to last out the voyage. If the remaining slaves died of thirst or illness the loss would fall upon the owners of the vessel, but if they were thrown into the sea they could be regarded as legal jettison, covered by insurance. Following this conference, 132 slaves were thrown overboard in three batches. Back in England the owners claimed £30 insurance money for each of the jettisoned slaves. The underwriters refused to pay. The owners duly appealed. The appeal was heard at the Court of Exchequer, presided over by Lord Mansfield. After admitting that the law was with the owners, Lord Mansfield said, "A higher law applies to this very shocking case," and he found for the underwriters—the first case in which an English court ruled that a cargo slaves could not be treated simply as merchandise.
>
> (pp. 152–153)

Unsworth's reason for spotlighting this incident becomes evident in *Sacred Hunger* (a novel he wrote in Helsinki where he had moved with his second wife, Aira, a Finnish translator). In this book—the novel, as it were, that Benson tried and failed to write in *Sugar and Rum*—an episode closely resembling the atrocity on the *Zong* provides the climactic turning point in the story and stands as an instance of the almost literally dehumanizing results of the lust for profit.

Where *Sugar and Rum* was constructed around contrasts in eighteenth-century and 1980s Liverpool, *Sacred Hunger* is built around the opposition between two cousins: Erasmus Kemp, a ferociously mercantile Liverpool entrepreneur, and Matthew Paris, a freethinking and progressive physician who embarks as ship's doctor on Kemp's trading vessel, the *Liverpool Merchant*. Where Paris embodies humane rationality, Kemp personifies heedless appetite for gain. Occasionally, analogies are highlighted between Kemp's ethos and that prevailing in 1980s Britain. But, for the most part, *Sacred Hunger* remains a robustly traditional historical novel, epic in scope and length. Physical immediacy is one of its great strengths. You can almost smell the canvas, tar, and hemp as the *Liverpool Merchant* with its figurehead of the Duchess of Devonshire as the Spirit of Commerce (Unsworth's taste for satirical statuary surfacing again) launches out down the river Mersey. Later, the reek of scorched flesh from the slavers' branding irons and the stench of terrified captives in the ship's feculent hold wafts sickeningly from the pages. Even the novel's most audacious section—portraying a would-be utopian community in the wilds of Florida where Paris and a group of runaway slaves and sailors have fled after mutinying against the captain's attempt to throw shackled Africans overboard as jetsam—is solid with local detail. The abundant research into the "Triangular Trade" (the immensely profitable maritime shuttling between Liverpool, West Africa, and the West Indies), which Unsworth undertook to give credibility to Benson's work in *Sugar and Rum*, was complemented by a further three years of immersion in the archives of eighteenth-century naval and commercial history. The wealth of material this equipped him with is imaginatively transformed in *Sacred Hunger* into a vast grim parable about the physical shackling of blacks and the ideological fettering of whites.

MORALITY PLAY

SACRED *Hunger* and its successor *Morality Play* are both "moral tales, moral fables," Unsworth told the *San Francisco Review of Books* in 1996 (p. 19). But, where *Sacred Hunger* is expansive and slow moving, *Morality Play* is clenched and swift. Returning Unsworth to his native northeast England, it travels back in time to a fourteenth century of plague and famine, destitution and lawlessness, where fields lie untilled and starving soldiers who have straggled home from the wars in France desperately resort to brigandry.

Unsworth's observer of this harsh world, where many believe that the last days are imminent, is Nicholas Barber, a young cleric who has run away from Lincoln Cathedral where he was a subdeacon. The first thing he sees as the book gets underway is six shabbily but gaudily attired figures clustered in the dying light of a bitter December day around an expiring man. This tableau, which reminds Nicholas of "that scene in the *Morality Play* when the besieged soul flies free at last" (p. 9), is one of many moments in this novel that suggest it could as well have been called *Mortality Play*. Death and deathliness pervade this book. Burial mounds of the unfortunates who perished of the plague during the sultry summer bulge in graveyards. Two corpses are the motivating agents of the novel's plot. On Saint Lazarus's Day, a feast commemorating the raising of someone from the tomb, a ghastly secret begins to be unearthed.

The six mourners whom Nicholas sights are, it transpires, a troupe of traveling actors journeying to Durham for the Christmas festivities. The death of one of their number puts them in a quandary as to how to find the money to pay for his Christian burial. They will earn it, they eventually decide, by performing some of their morality plays, with Nicholas standing in for the deceased man, at a small town they will pass through on their route.

As they travel toward this destination, the reek of mortality from the cadaver in their cart becomes more and more unignorable. On entering the little community huddled around the castle of a northern nobleman, Sir Richard de Guise, the players are plunged into an even more tainted atmosphere. A climactic scene shows Nicholas being escorted past a doorway out of which emanates "a stench of decay ... not the smell of death but of disease, of poisoned tissue and corrupted blood, the rot of the living body" (p. 170). This sickening stink is only the most open manifestation of the noxiousness shrouding the town. Always displaying a keen nose for decay and the polluted in his books, Unsworth here closes in on a particularly rank instance of corrupt power.

Soon after their arrival, the players learn that a local woman awaits execution for killing a twelve-year-old boy. When the townsfolk prove indifferent to such venerable theatrical fare as the Play of Adam—preferring to watch a rival troupe of rope walkers—the leader of the actors conceives the bold plan of attracting an audience by a dramatization of this murder.

The audacity of this notion is something Unsworth emphasizes by his vivid reconstruction of the theater world these people have always been accustomed to. For them, he demonstrates, drama is a means of exhibiting God's designs, not man's depravities. The vigorous, inventive stagecraft by which the performers act out their biblical parables is enthrallingly recreated. Out of the property basket come such essential items as Eve's flaxen wig and glass beads, the red-painted paper apple to be plucked from the pasteboard tree, the devil's fork, the wings worn by Lucifer before his fall, and God's six-inch stilts and long robe. A mime repertoire of hand movements —from the palm-out silencing gesture to the sinuous indication of tempting female allure —is engrossingly demonstrated. And, also rendering credible the players' need to turn to something new, Unsworth has them glumly aware of the ruinous competition now mounted by the rich guilds who stage lavish cycles of mystery plays boasting costly special effects: realistic-looking beheadings of the Baptist, spectacular Resurrections with the help of elaborate machinery.

The players' bid to retrieve their fortunes, though, pitches them into mortal danger. As they reenact their scenario of the strangled boy, his supposed murderess, and the monk who claimed to have witnessed the crime, improbabilities and inconsistencies increasingly deflect their improvisations in a new and ever more menacing direction. Following this to its conclusion, *Morality Play* adds the pace, suspense, and twisty unexpectedness of a gripping detective tale to its other accomplishments.

The torchlit makeshift stage in the inn yard isn't, it becomes apparent, the only arena in which role playing, masks, and feigning hold sway. Nor does the chill this novel strikes come simply from the glacial wintriness of its scenes: claddings of frost on cobblestones, a swirling blizzard through which knights on horseback dramatically break into view. Silhouetted against a cheerless background of mass graves, of the death throes of feudalism and the demise of liturgical drama, the novel takes Unsworth's continuing concern with the brutal exploitation of the vulnerable to bleak lengths. In *Stone Virgin*, Girolamo, a powerless sculptor, was destroyed by incurring the displeasure of one of the dominant Fornarini family, a man of "arrogant and implacable vindictiveness" (p. 67). In *Morality Play*, the implacable arrogance of another high-caste family, the de Guises, cruelly manifests itself. Unsworth's next novel, *After Hannibal*, also looks at barbarities inflicted on the weak by powerful medieval clans (in this case, the Baglioni and the Oddi of Perugia). It does so, however, not through the terrified eyes of their hapless contemporaries, as in *Stone Virgin* and *Morality Play*, but from a modern viewpoint.

AFTER HANNIBAL *AND* LOSING NELSON

Morality Play took Unsworth's imagination as far back into the past as it had yet traveled. As if in reaction to this, his next two novels are set in the present, though very much a present lived within the context of the past. The title of each

novel—*After Hannibal, Losing Nelson* (1999)—features the name of a hero. Each counterpoints his prowess with less glamorous but usually less bloody happenings in the 1990s.

After Hannibal jumps from the deathly cold medieval Northumbria of *Morality Play* to a radiant summer in present-day Umbria (where Unsworth and his wife Aira live). Instead of a troupe of half-starved traveling players, the roving characters here surveyed are affluent in-comers settling into renovated properties in rural Italy. This doesn't, however, mean that Unsworth's imagination is taking a holiday from the concern with rapacious power and brutal oppression of the vulnerable that always pulses through his best fiction.

Much of *After Hannibal* is poised comedy; some of its episodes relax into broad farce. But also packed into the novel's mosaic-like structure are sections that are darker, ferocious, edged with sharp pain. As the storyline winds through the picturesque Umbrian countryside, the region's harsh history is kept to the fore. Close to the scatter of converted dwellings whose new inhabitants Unsworth observes lies Lake Trasimeno where, in 217 B.C., the Roman army suffered at the hands of Hannibal's Carthaginian forces what was perhaps its worst defeat, a massacre so wholesale that the lake turned crimson as its marshy reed beds became sumps of carnage. Twenty-two centuries later, local place names —Sanguineto, Ossaia, Sepoltaglia—still reek of blood, bones, and the sepulchre.

One recent arrival in the area, Professor Monti from Turin, an academic historian of the central Italian states, has an especially acute awareness of the horrors strewing the locality's past —in particular, the welter of slaughter among feuding families in fifteenth-and sixteenth-century Perugia. Twentieth-century atrocity is unearthed by a German expatriate trying to come to terms with the guilty legacy of his father's collusion as a military intelligence officer in killings in wartime Italy: as he clears undergrowth surrounding the house he has bought, reminders of Nazi murders come to light.

Nothing comparable in scale to all this bygone butchery occurs in Unsworth's novel. Its main skirmish—over problems arising from the neighborhood road that the newcomers share with a fearsomely quarrelsome peasant family—is fought with words and writs. But, although weapons of war in Umbria have become less lethal and lawyers have taken the place of soldiers, persisting patterns of cruelty and betrayal are as apparent in the squabbles of the present, Unsworth stresses, as they were in the bloodbaths of the past.

Domestic clashes especially rage among his characters. Monti's wife has dealt him a devastating blow by deserting him. A disaffected gay couple fight bitter court battles over the house they once shared. The Chapmans, a vulgarly competitive property speculator and his daintier-souled wife, find that uprooting themselves to Umbria brings out into the open their warring incompatibilities.

It isn't only sexual partners who perpetrate betrayal in this book. Business partners prove perfidious too, especially when it comes to refurbishing buildings. Unsworth's exasperation over his own unfortunate experiences when acquiring and renovating a farmhouse in Umbria is vented in his cautionary tale of the Greens, a trustful pair of retired art teachers from Michigan who, after becoming the delighted owners of an old farmhouse in need of conversion, fall into the grasping hands of a ruinous "project manager."

At the same time, warm responsiveness to the region where he has chosen to make his home mellowly suffuses Unsworth's novel. Appreciation of Umbria's natural splendors refreshes even his most bitter scenes. Admiration for its handsome artistic heritage gleams among his vignettes of meanspiritedness and greedy aggression. In keeping with this blend of disenchantment and enchantment in *After Hannibal*, the figure linking its various plots is a lawyer, Mancini, who combines disillusioned irony with openness to life's wider aesthetic and moral horizons. Part amused, part melancholy, humane, sophisticated, suavely resourceful, he encapsulates the spirit of this appealing book with its highly civilized look at savagery.

Where savagery was the subject of *After Hannibal*, *Losing Nelson* takes heroism as its subject —and suggests that, in some ways, the two are not very far apart. The story is narrated by Charles Cleasby, a man well into middle age. Like several of Unsworth's earlier characters, he is an obsessed loner. And like Benson in *Sugar and Rum*, he is a would-be author faced with writer's block: he has "run into a difficult patch" (p. 8) with a biography of Nelson, *The Making of a Hero*, which he is trying to write. What has caused this impasse is his problem in reconciling his adulatory attitude to Nelson with his hero's seemingly ignominious behavior in Naples in June 1799 (where, after promising a safe conduct to France to republican rebels who had risen against the corrupt tyranny of the Bourbon monarch, he perfidiously handed them over to torture and execution).

Cleasby's resolutely idealized image of Nelson is further shaken when he engages a secretary, Miss Lily, to help with his book. Much of the novel turns into a beautifully rendered comedy of contrasting viewpoints as her deflatingly commonsensical but shrewd observations—"If you look at it one way, he was a sort of serial killer" (p. 254), "There is more to life than shooting broadsides at the French, that's all I'm saying" —collide with Cleasby's romanticized veneration. Under Miss Lily's barrage of embarrassing questions and disconcerting comments, Nelson's charisma starts to disperse; the hero is shown to be a kind of victim, someone shaped ("As I see it, they took him away at twelve and sort of processed him," p. 253), into an implement of imperialism.

Concurrently, Cleasby's hero worship is exposed as a desperate survival mechanism. When an undergraduate, readers learn, he had a nervous breakdown in which he came to dread other people's eyes. This stemmed from a miserable childhood spent under the sarcastic surveillance of his father ("a watcher. Not, I think now ... a very kind one," p. 63). Cleasby's fear of hostile observation (something which lurks in most of Unsworth's novels) plunges him into pathological paranoia. In an increasingly vain attempt to combat this, he struggles to keep his attention fixed on Nelson, a man who lived boldly in the public eye.

Losing Nelson contains a self-portrait of Uns–worth. A disastrous lecture Cleasby gives is attended by "a writer who has just published a long novel about the eighteenth-century African slave trade." He has "a voice that contained traces of north-east England" and "a slightly crooked smile and large grey eyes behind thin-rimmed glasses. The eyes were mournful in spite of the smile" (pp. 180 –181]). More than in this teasing walk-on part, though, *Losing Nelson* displays Unsworth's distinctive lineaments as a novelist. The past is scrutinized to moral purpose and for its relevance to the present. Betrayal is a central issue. The turmoil under Cleasby's clipped exterior harks back to the Gothic undertow which authors such as Faulkner, Welty, and McCullers first inspired Unsworth to introduce into his work. The nineteenth-century maritime world this novel is so informed about (the book is, in fact, Unsworth's inventive response to a publisher's proposal that he write a biography of Nelson) bears out his affirmation that Joseph Conrad and William Golding are "great influences on his mature work" (London *Times*, p. 43). Imperial swagger is again subjected to withering inspection. Exploitation (this time of a more subtle kind: the transforming of a lonely young boy into an instrument of empire) is once more on display. So is one of Unsworth's favorite fictional properties: statuary. Cleasby's collection of Nelson memorabilia boasts as a prized item a papier-maché bust of the hero. Solitary destructive obsession again leads to catastrophe. Elegantly funny comedy shades through black irony into bleak tragedy.

CONCLUSION

THE last three decades of the twentieth century saw a remarkable fascination with the past among British novelists. Historical fiction enjoyed a greater vogue than it had ever previously done. Heritage became a widespread concern. By the year 2000, Barry Unsworth—an author whose career was slow to start but which blossomed in the 1980s and 1990s—had established himself as a major contributor to this development. No late-twentieth-century British novelist has written of history more variously, more thought-provokingly, more engrossingly, and with more humane commitment.

SELECTED BIBLIOGRAPHY

I. NOVELS. *The Partnership* (London, 1966); *The Greeks have a word for it* (London, 1967); *The Hide* (London, 1970; New York, 1996); *Mooncranker's Gift* (London, 1973; Boston, 1974); *The Big Day* (London, 1976; New York, 1977); *Pascali's Island* (London, 1980), repub. as *The Idol Hunter* (New York, 1980); *The Rage of the Vulture* (London, 1982; Boston, 1983); *Stone Virgin* (London, 1985; Boston, 1986); *Sugar and Rum* (London and New York, 1988); *Sacred Hunger* (London and New York, 1992); *Morality Play* (London and New York, 1995); *After Hannibal* (London, 1996; New York, 1997); *Losing Nelson* (London and New York, 1999).

II. INTERVIEWS. Tom Sutcliffe, "Unchained Maladies in the Age of Greed," in the *Independent on Sunday* (23 February 1992); Peter Kemp, "Trading Places," in the London *Sunday Times* (23 February 1992): Books section; Susannah Hunnewell, "Utopia Then and Now," in *New York Times Book Review* (19 July 1992); Matthew Humphrey, "Foul Play," in the *San Francisco Review of Books* (January/February 1996); Robert Winder, "Unsworth Before and After Hannibal," in the *Independent* (7 September 1996): Weekend Review; James Eve, "Digging for Truths in the Past," in the [London] *Times* (29 July 1999); Charles Nicholl, "Grey Skies and Blue Seas," in the *Independent* (31 July 1999): Weekend Review.

SYLVIA TOWNSEND WARNER

(1893–1978)

Claire Harman

THE CRITIC JAN Montefiore lamented in 1987 the "near total silence in literary histories about the poet and novelist Sylvia Townsend Warner" (*Feminism and Poetry*, p. 24). Montefiore pointed out that despite the critical attention lavished on other writers of the 1930s—a decade during which Warner was particularly active—she remained "invisible or, if noticed, ludicrous." "Ludicrous" refers specifically to Stephen Spender's caustic portrait of Warner as "the English Lady Communist" in his 1951 memoir World Within World, but "invisible" is more widely applicable. Warner was gifted, original, and prolific. Why, apart from a certain niche market opening up in gender studies, has she escaped the close attention of literary critics and the academic establishment?

Misogyny and the critical double standards applied to male and female writers have certainly contributed to Warner's neglect, but there are several other factors, too. Her very name, her inexpungable Englishness. and her privileged middle-class background seem to bury her in a particular time, class and style: she sounds like that thing she despised, the genteel "lady novelist." The titles of her books can also seem offputting, with their misleading impression of quaintness: *The Cat's Cradle Book* and *Kingdoms of Elfin* are not fairy stories but satires. Warner was one of the most mordantly witty writers of her generation, with a scrupulous, searching, acid mind. She never courted publicity or popularity; she was not in the least interested in developing a presence as a novelist or story writer; in fact, she expressed impatience with the idea. The individual work was what absorbed her, and there is remarkably little similarity—except in a powerful prevailing intelligence—between one of her works and the next; the inconsistency is particu-larly marked in her novels. Such diversity is on the whole indigestible by canon-mongers.

Warner often worked against the grain of fashion. Her poetry remained immune to the modernist revolution going on around it and she began writing novels with historical backgrounds and complex structures—nineteenth-century novels, in some respects—while the idea of the twentieth-century literary novel was coming into vogue. Serious critics of the modern novel have tended to overlook works with historical settings, but Warner, a committed Communist, chose to set her most ambitious novels in the past for the very reason that she could tackle political issues more openly there and offer precedents and examples from outside the present.

Warner was clear about her priorities, as she explained in a 1975 interview, in which she spoke about "the importance of the narrative, the interest one has in the narrative. That's why Defoe is such a master, because he's *really* interested in the story" (*PN Review* 23, vol. 8, no. 3). Her short stories, for which Warner was probably best known, exhibit a remarkable knowledge of human nature and range of technical expertise. At the time when they were written, between the 1930s and the 1970s, the English short story was in its heyday; the falling off of interest in the form and its dramatically reduced importance in contemporary literary culture have undoubtedly also contributed to Warner's neglect.

LIFE

SYLVIA Townsend Warner was born on 6 December 1893 at Harrow-on-the-Hill, Middlesex, the only child of George Townsend Warner, a senior history teacher at Harrow School for boys, and his wife, Nora. She attended a kindergarten for one term before being removed for disruptive behavior—an early indication of her lifelong outspoken individualism—and was subsequently educated at home by her parents. In her teens, she studied privately with some of the masters at the school, including the distinguished musician Percy Buck, and acquired informally the sort of high-powered classical education that was only available to upper-middle-class boys at that date.

Warner was a talented pianist and by the age of seventeen was composing music regularly. In 1914 she had been preparing to study composition in Vienna with Arnold Schoenberg, but the outbreak of the First World War prevented it. During the war she worked in the Vickers munitions factory at Erith and in the relief effort for Belgian refugees. In her studies she concentrated increasingly on the history of music, particularly of the fifteenth and sixteenth centuries, and in 1917 she was elected to the editorial board of *Tudor Church Music*, a long-term research project funded by the Carnegie Trust to collect, edit, and publish the manuscript church music of the Elizabethan age. Warner was the youngest member of this distinguished scholarly committee and the only female.

The *Tudor Church Music* project lasted twelve years and resulted in ten volumes of music published between 1923 and 1929. During this period, Warner began her career as a writer, first of poetry, then fiction. In 1922 she had met the reclusive T. F. Powys, a then unpublished novelist, and was instrumental in getting his works into print. Her contact with Powys's new publisher, Charles Prentice of Chatto & Windus, encouraged Warner to show him her own poems, which she had been writing steadily since her teens. In 1925 her first collection, *The Espalier*, appeared, and the following year Chatto & Windus (her main British publisher for life) published her novel, *Lolly Willowes*. The critical and popular success of the novel on both sides of the Atlantic encouraged Warner to keep on writing, and by the time *Tudor Church Music* was completed in 1929, she had published two more novels, *Mr. Fortune's Maggot* (1927) and *The True Heart* (1929), and a second collection of

poems, Time *Importuned* (1928). Warner decided to give up professional music scholarship and write full time. Money was a deciding factor. Warner's inheritance from her father was entailed on her mother's estate until 1950 and she was self-dependent all the rest of her adult life.

Warner's early novels brought her fame and a reputation for eccentricity that she was happy to indulge, especially the suggestion that she, like her heroine Lolly Willowes, was a witch. She remained an outsider from literary cliques all her life, too individualistic and too satirical for the Bloomsbury group, though she was the friend separately of David Garnett and of Duncan Grant. Warner's admiration for T. F. Powys (1875–1953), whose biography she attempted to write, but abandoned, was partly in reaction to the insularity of London literary life: many of her poems and short stories from the 1920s dealt, as did Powys, with pastoral grotesque and are set in a remote countryside very like the part of Dorset where Powys lived.

On her frequent visits to Powys' home in the village of East Chaldon, Warner met and fell in love with a young poet named Valentine Ackland who was in retreat from a failed marriage. The two women set up home together in 1930 and their passionate relationship (which lasted thirty-nine years, until Ackland's death in 1969) was celebrated in their joint collection of poems, *Whether a Dove or Seagull* (1933) and in hundreds of love letters, published posthumously as *I'll Stand by You* (1998). With the exception of a brief residence in Norfolk, the couple spent the rest of their lives in Dorset, moving in 1937 to a small riverside house in Maiden Newton. The relationship was intense but troubled: Valentine's attractiveness to other women led to many affairs, and her failure to win recognition as a poet was an obvious cause of jealousy in a household almost entirely run on the proceeds of Warner's work.

Ackland's increasing concern about the ascendancy of right-wing regimes in Europe during the early 1930s led both women to join the Communist Party in 1935 and become involved in politics at local and international levels. During the Spanish Civil War in 1936 Warner and Ackland went to Barcelona to do voluntary work for the Red Cross, and in 1937 they were delegates at the 2nd International Writers Conference in Madrid. Though Ackland eventually renounced Communism (and converted to Roman Catholicism, much to the dismay of her partner), Warner's political sympathies remained strongly left-wing, and she was for some years a member of the executive committee of the Association of Writers for Intellectual Liberty and a regular contributor to the left-wing press.

Warner wrote poetry all her life, but little of it was published after the joint collection with Ackland in 1933. She became best known for her novels, four more of which, on historical themes, were published between 1936 and 1954, and for her short stories, which she continued to write till her death in 1978. From the mid-1930s onward, Warner found a lucrative and rewarding market for her stories at *The New Yorker*, becoming one of the magazine's most frequently published writers in the 1950s and 1960s and a recognized master of the form. She published ten collections of stories in her lifetime, and two more have appeared posthumously.

Ackland's death from breast cancer in 1969 clouded Warner's last years. She continued to write, but in a bleaker vein, producing one of her most remarkable books, *Kingdoms of Elfin*, a collection of satires, during this period. The 1970s saw a resurgence of interest in her work with the rediscovery and republication of feminist works from the early century, and by the time of her death in 1978, at the age of eighty-four, several of her novels were back in print and there were plans to published her *Collected Poems*.

POETRY

WARNER's development as a poet was pivotal to her art, however much it dropped from public view after the publication of *Whether a Dove or Seagull* in 1933. Poetry formed a bridge between her formerly intense musical life (which did get left behind) and every branch of her literary composition. Her style, whether in prose or verse, is alert to cadence, form and tempo, and she cre-

ated successful musical effects in her work without sacrificing sense. In turn her works have appealed to musicians; several of her poems have been set to music by John Ireland, Alan Bold, Paul Nordoff, and John Cracken.

Warner's first collection, *The Espalier* (1925), was an idiosyncratic book, resembling at first glance the kind of pastoral lyric verse associated with the popular Georgian poets, but in fact differing violently from them in tone and intention. The influence of Walter de la Mare, Thomas Hardy and A. E. Housman can be sensed rather than seen; Warner is as unlike these admired poets as she is like them. Some of the poems exploit familiar forms, such as the ballad or jog-trot quatrain, to subvert a wide range of poetic stereotypes and situations while others lie entirely *within* the convention (the ballads "Nelly Trim" and "The Image," for example). Warner used monologue and dialogue (most of these early poems are written in the first person) to dramatize a wide range of experience, from the contemplative ("Quiet Neighbours") to the menacing ("Common Entry"), and ranged from high to low style promiscuously. The poem "Blue Eyes," for example, is ostentatiously vulgar and included in the collection, one imagines, primarily to *épater les bourgeois*, as, in their different ways, do the poems "The Lenten Offering" and "I Bring Her a Flower," the latter a tribute to the Marxist revolutionary Rosa Luxemburg.

Warner's second collection, *Time Importuned*, showed a continuing interest in a Powysian style of blackly comic pastoral ("Country Measures," "The Rival," "Epitaphs") and a playful vein of literary imitation in poems strongly reminiscent of, or parodying, Blake and Marvell ("Triumphs of Sensibility"), Housman ("The Tree Unleaved"), and Hardy ("The House Grown Silent," "The Record"). The period during which Warner composed this book was one in which she claimed, "I want to read and write nothing but poetry" (this despite the recent success of her first two novels), and there is a sense of ease and facility about the verse that is sometimes giddying. Warner's storytelling impulse is evident in her ballads, ghost stories and a rhapsodic *liebestod* about the death of a phoenix called "The

Loudest Lay." This poem displays both Warner's virtuosity and some of her syntactic oddities (archaic long before 1928): "Swift he wrought, as though within / His breast he felt the implicit flame / Quicken" (*Collected Poems*, p. 170–171). It is ironic that Warner's frequent use of inversion sounds clumsy to modern ears but was very probably chosen by the poet for its musicality.

Warner's homage to the English poet George Crabbe (1754–1832), a novella in rhyming couplets called *Opus 7* (1931), stands midway between the short story and full-blown satirical verse and tells the story of a woman, Rebecca Random, who in the lean postwar years can only pay for her addiction to gin by growing and selling flowers. The shortcomings of the plot are lost in the eloquence and vivacity of the verse, full as it is of extravagantly rhetorical writing, such as this aside about the Great War:

I knew a time when Europe feasted well:
bodies were munched in thousands, vintage blood
so blithely flowed that even the dull mud
grew greedy, and ate men; and lest the gust
should flag, quick flesh no daintier taste than dust,
spirit was ransacked for whatever might
sharpen a sauce to drive on appetite.

(Collected Poems, p. 198)

The subject and setting of *Opus 7*, the immediate aftermath of the Great War, were original and challenging; perhaps for this reason the poem marks an epoch in the decline of the pastoral convention in English verse.

From 1930 onward, Warner's style was undoubtedly affected by her relationship with Valentine Ackland, whose poetic ambitions became for some years centrally important in the lives of both women. The ebullience of Warner's verse mellowed in sympathy with Ackland's more reflective, lyrical free-verse style. In 1933 they published their joint collection of poems, *Whether a Dove or Seagull*, dedicated to Robert Frost, which was ostensibly "an experiment in the presentation of poetry" (according to a jointly authored note), "a protest against the frame of mind which judges a poem by looking to see who wrote it." The gesture toward an ideal of impersonality was flawed on several counts. Although the poems of the two writers are mixed

and unattributed in the text, there is a key at the end (in the British edition) that identifies them. This was presumably demanded by the publisher, who may have been less concerned with the "protest" than with the salability of Ackland's work, of which *Whether a Dove or Seagull* was the first and only mainstream example.

The book, which has never been reprinted, contains many extremely interesting poems by both writers, including Warner's "Though you should sorrow as only the young can sorrow" and "I watch the mirror's grace." But the collection is remarkable for its lesbian love poems, many of which were so sexually explicit as to pass contemporary reviewers without comment:

For long meeting of our lips
Shall be breaking of ships,
For breath drawn quicker men drowned
And trees downed.
Throe shall fell roof-tree, pulse's knock
Undermine rock,
A cry hurl seas against the land,
A raiding hand,
Scattering lightning along thighs
Lightning from skies
Wrench, and fierce sudden snows clamp deep
On earth our sleep.

("Since the first toss of gale ..., "
Whether a Dove or Seagull, p. 116)

Whether a Dove or Seagull also showed the beginnings of a declamatory style that was to become dominant in Warner's political poems of the 1930s and 1940s, which were published in some of the many little magazines of the time, including Edgell Rickword's *Left Review,* the *New Republic, The London Mercury, Our Time,* and *The Countryman.* Warner and Ackland's admission into the Communist Party in 1935 and their increasing involvement in the Spanish Civil War produced many ideologically motivated poems. Warner's "Red Front" was read as a declamation in Battersea in 1935 and in Whitechapel the following year. It looks back again at the Great War and takes an overview of the intervening period, using an extended image of "the saddest wine that ever was pressed in France" for the war's legacy: "Who would have thought the blood of our friends would taste so thin? / Would so soon lose body[?]" On the whole, Warner's propaganda poems do not resolve the problem of how to express her message forcefully without become strident; she is "out to shock us, one way or another," as the critic A. K. Weatherhead has said (*Stephen Spender and the Thirties*, p. 61). Warner's poems about her journeys to Spain in 1936 and 1937, though still noticeably rhetorical, are much more evocative of the anxieties and anticipations of war and of the realities of life in the war zone. "Benicasim" ends as follows:

But narrow is this place, narrow is this space
of garlanded sun and leisure and colour, of return
to life and release from living. Turn
(Turn not!) sight inland:
There, rigid as death and unforgiving, stand
the mountains—and close at hand.
(Collected Poems, pp. 35–36)

Inversion and contraction sound peculiarly out of place in this topical poem of 1937–1938, especially in the context of the prevailing fashion for pared-down Audenesque verse. Warner's continued use of such devices in many poems cut her off from the mainstream pretty effectively.

After the war poems of the 1930s and a handful of striking poems about the home front in the Second World War, Warner published very little verse during the rest of her lifetime, except one privately printed pamphlet in 1968, "King Duffus." The unpublished verse of fifty years, appearing posthumously in her *Collected Poems* (1982), displays a wide range of form, tone, and language: "A Woman out of a Dream," "The Absence," "Wish in Spring," "Woman's Song," "Seven Conjectural Readings," "The birds are muted." They are remarkable not just for their wit, humanity and technical accomplishment but for intellectual substance, as in Warner's love poem "Drawing you, heavy with sleep":

And as the careless water its mirroring sanction
Grants to him at the river's brim long stationed,
Long drowned in thought, that yet he lives
Since in that mirroring tide he moves,

Your body lying by mine to mine responded:
Your hair stirred on my mouth, my image was dandled

Deep in your sleep that flowed unstained
On from the image entertained.
(Collected Poems, p. 29)

EARLY NOVELS

WARNER'S first novel, *Lolly Willowes*, was written, so she claimed, to entertain herself in the evenings when she lived alone as a young musicologist in London. Like many first novels, it contains an element of pent-up autobiography (notably in Lolly's adoration of her father and her distress at his death); it also reflects something of the somber postwar mood, "the insistent *malaise* of this generation," that A. C. Ward (writing in 1930) thought underlay the 1920s vogue for fantasy (*The Nineteen Twenties*, p. 135).

The degree to which *Lolly Willowes* can be called a fantasy or even an allegory is debatable. In a lecture on mystery and fantasy in 1929, Warner made a claim that bears on each of her first three novels: "The nature of the events which he describes obliges the fantasist to adopt a sober and ungarnished method of narration. ... Since his main thesis surprises by itself, he must deny himself further surprises. ... by asking for one vast initial credit [he] must do on that credit to the end" (quoted in Ward, *The Nineteen Twenties*, p. 132). The "main thesis" of *Lolly Willowes* certainly surprises by itself: the novel tells the story of a disregarded spinster who becomes a witch. But the rest of the tale is carefully rationalized to the extent that it is hard not to read it as purely realist fiction, within which the supernatural is depicted as perfectly commonplace and easily accessible.

The book is now, inevitably, read as a feminist text of self-empowerment. Until she is almost fifty, Lolly lives as a mild maiden aunt dependent on her brothers and their wives, "a middle-aging lady, light-footed upon stairs, and indispensable for Christmas Eve and birthday preparations." Moved by an irrepressible and seemingly unaccountable melancholy, she decides at last to break away and live by herself in the country, despite the discovery that her inheritance, mismanaged by her brother, has lost much of its value (she insists that it is reinvested in something like a

War Loan, which "will pay a proper dividend"). To the profound disapproval of her family, she takes a room in a small Bedfordshire village, Great Mop, and in the company of her landlady and a local poultry farmer, Mr. Saunter, she leads a happily aimless life only slightly disturbed by intimations that there is a secret in herself she has yet to discover.

The arrival in the village of Lolly's self-important nephew, Titus, puts an end to her peace, and Lolly realizes that the only escape route left is into witchcraft, and that she has had a vocation for it all along. A vicious and ugly kitten appears, her familiar, as confirmation of her pact with the Devil, and Lolly begins to understand that most of the villagers, including the parson, are witches too. With her landlady as chaperone, she attends her first Sabbath but is bitterly disappointed; it is just as constraining as any other social occasion. Concluding that witchcraft, too, may prove inadequate, Lolly wanders off alone, only to discover Satan in the guise of a kindly gamekeeper. Her faith in the devil is restored. Her irritating nephew (also present at the Sabbath) is subsequently bedeviled by a series of plagues that drive him out of the village. Lolly, meeting Satan again, is able to come to an understanding of his character and her own, which leaves her free to live undisturbed, "a hind couched in the Devil's coverts."

The story presents a thesis similar to that of Virginia Woolf's in *A Room of One's Own* (published three years after *Lolly Willowes*), but with an important difference. Woolf's formula of "a room of one's own [in which to write fiction] and five hundred a year" is almost absurdly exclusive, whereas Warner's feminism, as expressed in Lolly's desire for "a life of one's own, not an existence doled out to you by others," addresses the lot of the common woman:

When I think of witches, I seem to see all over England, all over Europe, women living and growing old, as common as blackberries, and as unregarded. I see them, wives and sisters of respectable men, chapel members, and blacksmiths, and small farmers, and Puritans ... child-rearing, housekeeping, hanging washing from currant bushes; and for diversion each other's silly conversation, and listening to men talking together in the way that men talk and women listen. ... If they could be passive and unnoticed, it wouldn't matter, But they must be active, and still not noticed.

(pp. 239–240)

To struggle for privacy rather than power is not a widely held feminist ideal, and the retiring, apologetic nature of the heroine may have persuaded some readers that it was not a serious one, either. But Lolly's ordinariness and inarticulateness (the speech quoted above is a marked exception to the rule) is central to the purpose of the book: Warner is able to depict a simple person's concerns without sentimentalizing or glamorizing her. Lolly's witchcraft, especially, is not sensationalized, but shown as potentially banal, and though the book is fanciful, it is ultimately far more interesting and substantial than the other popular "fantasy" books of the 1920s (such as David Garnett's *Lady Into Fox*, John Collier's *His Monkey's Wife*, and T. F. Powys's *Mr. Weston's Good Wine*) with which it was quickly associated. The novelty of *Lolly Willowes* may have led to its message being largely ignored, but Warner's sardonic observations about the oppression of women in the years following the Great War were evidence of a lifelong concern for social justice that found far more explicitly political expression later.

The success of *Lolly Willowes* on both sides of the Atlantic (it was the first ever Book of the Month Club choice in America and nominated for the Prix Femina) established a wide market for Warner's later books. Her second novel (set just before the Great War) had as protagonist another unglamorous middle-aged English failure, the bank clerk Timothy Fortune. *Mr. Fortune's Maggot* (1927) tells the story of how this Prufrockian character becomes a missionary and goes to live on a Polynesian island with the idea of converting its inhabitants. The "maggot" of the title (defined as "a whimsical or perverse fancy") refers initially to Mr. Fortune's expectations of success among the carefree pagans of Fanua, but as the story progresses from a light-hearted satire on western Christian values to a love story with tragic overtones, it becomes clear that the hero's maggot is of another sort, a symbol of corruption and of newly hatched, consuming remorse. The missionary's efforts produce only one convert, a boy named Lueli, a pubescent Man Friday whose devotion to the minister is much stronger than his devotion to (or understanding of) his new faith. Mr. Fortune's distress as he perceives this leads to him losing his own faith, and by the time he leaves the island at the end of the story, he is in a state of profound disillusionment:

> For man's will is a demon that will not let him be. It leads him to the edge of a clear pool; and while he sits admiring it, with his soul suspended over it like a green branch and dwelling in its own reflection, will stretches out his hand and closes his fingers upon a stone—a stone to throw into it.
>
> (p. 193)

Mr. Fortune loses his faith during a volcanic eruption on Fanua, but Lueli's loyalty to his own pagan god persists even when the idol representing it is destroyed. The boy begins to pine and in despair attempts to drown himself, leading Mr. Fortune to conclude that the best chance of saving Lueli is to go away: "That was the only stratagem by which love could outwit its own inherent treachery. ... Death had vouchsafed him a beam of darkness to see clearly by."

In a letter to David Garnett while the novel was in progress, Warner described Mr. Fortune as "fatally sodomitic" (*Sylvia and David*, p. 31), but in the finished book she was careful to define the hero's extraordinarily intense relationship with Lueli as a spiritual love, not "what is accounted a criminal love" (p. 192). However, it is evident from the fact that Warner returned to the character and situation of Mr. Fortune in "The Salutation" that she felt there was a certain amount of unfinished business here in her treatment of homoerotic attraction and the extremes of guilt it could generate.

The True Heart, Warner's third novel, published in 1929, retold the story of Cupid and Psyche in a late Victorian setting. Sukey Bond, a young girl from the Warburton Memorial Female Orphanage, has just gone into service with a farmer's family in the Essex marshes when she meets and falls in love with Eric Seaborn. Eric is a well-bred simpleton and a victim of fits, who, being a

social impediment, has been sent away by his parents, a rector and his beautiful, haughty wife. Mrs. Seaborn (Venus in the myth) does all she can to thwart the match between Sukey (Psyche) and her son, but Sukey's true heart triumphs, after a long separation and adventures that include an interview with the madam of a brothel (Juno) and an audience with Queen Victoria (Persephone).

The difficulties of dealing with simple, even simpleminded, main characters in this novel were immense (and many would say ultimately unrewarding). Eric's silence and passivity do nothing to enhance the reader's interest in Sukey's quest: "he would sit there like one in a dream, like one in another world, vaguely smiling or staring at the roses on the milk-jug; if by chance their eyes met, he would meet her glance without a sign of recognition or remembrance." The later stages of the story develop a vein of whimsy—talking dogs, gracious queens, Mrs. Seaborn running mad—that is hard to swallow. The novel is valued for its atmospheric descriptions of the Essex saltings and marshes (reminiscent of the beginning of Dickens' *Great Expectations*), a landscape Warner had been intensely excited by when she discovered it for herself on a solitary visit in the early 1920s.

> Next morning a sea-fog covered the marsh. Looking from her window, [Sukey] could see nothing but the tops of the farm buildings emerging from the vapour, their mouse-coloured thatch flushed in the sunrise. There was no wind, yet the vapour was stirred with innumerable small eddies that circled and dissolved in strange soundlessness.
>
> (*The True Heart*, p. 14)

The name of the farm where Sukey lives, surrounded by creeks and muddy flats, is Derryman's Island. It links *The True Heart* with the two earlier novels as fables of individualism under attack. The real island of *Mr. Fortune's Maggot*, Lolly Willowes' isolated country village, and the remote landscape of the marshes where Eric has been "put out of the way" emphasize the oppressive social values from which the characters are in retreat. Society's intolerance of the meek, the flawed, the individualist, the *other*, is a recurrent theme in Warner's work, returned to symbolically in each of the novels. The barricades in *Summer Will Show*, the besieged castle in *After the Death of Don Juan*, the convent on the former island of Oby in *The Corner That Held Them* and the chill fortifications around Anchor House in *The Flint Anchor* are all symbolic of the self under siege.

THE LATER NOVELS

WRITTEN between 1932 and 1936, *Summer Will Show*, marked a change in Sylvia Townsend Warner's approach to novel writing from the short and lyrical early books to much more ambitious works, taking in large numbers of characters, complex action, and convincing historical backgrounds. Summer Will Show is set in 1848, the year of revolution, and tells the story of a young Englishwoman, Sophia Willoughby, who on the deaths of her children from smallpox is faced with an unsought and unwanted freedom. Searching for her feckless estranged husband Frederick, Sophia travels to Paris and meets his mistress, an aging demimondaine, Minna Lemuel, whose charismatic personality has an immediate hold over her. The events of the two very different Parisian revolutions of that year unfold as the women's intimacy grows and as Sophia becomes increasingly involved in the revolutionary cause, of which Minna is a vociferous exponent.

The novel is remarkable for its understated but unequivocally lesbian love story and its realistic depiction of the chaotic nature of concerted action. No two people on the same "side" have identical goals or perceptions; the communist Ingelbrecht is alone in his ideas, "seeming to trot on some intent personal errand"; Minna's followers seem not entirely sure whether they support a cause or a personality; Sophia is made uncomfortably aware of being snubbed by the working-class revolutionaries. "With what desolation of the spirit one beholds the dream made flesh," Minna says as she watches the barricades go up: a difficult admission, surely, for a novelist who was herself involved in political action at the time of writing. Perhaps the only real concession

to 1936 Party feeling is the ending of the book, when Sophia picks up one of the smuggled pamphlets and begins to read the Communist Manifesto. The heroine's gradual absorption in it strikes a rather false note in relation to the book's otherwise bleak and sardonic view of "the human delusion."

The erotic charge of the relationship between Minna and Sophia in the novel is indisputable, but lesbianism is not a theme dealt with explicitly in this or any other of Warner's works (even the poems of *Whether a Dove or Seagull* can be read "straight," and there is plenty to suggest that Warner and Ackland enjoyed the ambiguity). Nevertheless, it has been called "an exemplary 'lesbian fiction'": it "clearly, indeed almost schematically, figures [the relationship between the two women] as a breakup of the supposedly 'canonical' male-female-male erotic triangle" (Terry Castle, *Textual Practice* 4, no. 2, pp. 218, 219).

Warner demonstrated the ordinariness of historical events, even revolutions, in *Summer Will Show*, her identification with the period going far beyond the usual scope of the "historical novel." It is also a novel with a strong undertow of imagery, and much of its force is poetic rather than dramatic. The chestnut trees at Sophia's Dorset home that have lost their flowers and are "brooding, given over to their concern of ripening their burden of fruit" are at first a symbol of maternal pride to the heroine, later an omen which she failed to recognize. The portrait of Sophia's grandfather, too, provides some ironically flexible interpretations: "with his gun and supple wet-nosed retriever he seemed to be watching through the endless bronze dusk of an autumnal evening, paused on the brink of his spinney and listening with contemplative pleasure to the steps of the poacher within." The poacher seems at first to Sophia to be her good-for- nothing husband Frederick, but in the long term the person threatening the existing order of the estate / state is Sophia herself.

Warner's next novel, which she later believed was "swamped in the circumstances of the time" (1938–1939), returned less obliquely to the issues raised in the 1930s struggle against fascism.

After the Death of Don Juan (1938) is an ebullient satire set in eighteenth-century Spain and takes up the *Don Giovanni* story of Da Ponte's libretto where the opera leaves off, with the libertine's death and descent into hell. In Warner's realist sequel, Don Juan is not dead and the opera's dire climax is recast as another of his servant Leporello's tall tales. The divide between the gullible characters who have trouble accepting this and the cynics who understand human nature sets up a comic dialectic to underpin the political one played out between exploiters and the exploitable.

Most of the action takes place in an arid provincial backwater, Tenorio Viejo, where Don Juan's father resides. With its chronic irrigation problems and discontented villagers, Tenorio is socially and materially unrewarding ground. Don Juan's father, Don Saturno, has been a relatively philanthropic landowner with a long-standing plan to irrigate the valley, but there is never enough money to do this because of the profligate Don Juan's debts and demands. Don Saturno sincerely wishes to educate and empower his tenants (within reason), but his combination of broad-mindedness and passivity eventually proves disastrous. One of the book's many ironies is that at the end it appears that the estate will get its water, but only because Don Juan intends to reclaim the tenants' land, virtually useless until now, and put them to work for him. The story ends fatalistically midway through the violent suppression of the villagers' protest by Don Juan: an allegory of "the political chemistry of the Spanish War," as Warner said in 1945 (*Letters*, p. 51). The suggestion is not only that the Spanish Civil War was doomed to failure but that third parties have no place in the revolutionary process, that their intervention (represented in the novel by Don Saturno's well-meant plans) is troublesome. Warner's own part in the Spanish war is only just spared the same damning criticism of middle-class intellectual meddling.

The style of the novel veers dramatically from an (appropriately) operatic, slightly farcical beginning set in Seville through the exposition of the situation in Tenorio Viejo to the development of the plot's crisis, in which Warner shifts atten-

tion on to the doomed, embattled villagers. Warner displays a sort of Marxism in her method of composition; there is no protagonist in *After the Death of Don Juan*, and the effect of individual action going on independent of the plot is even more marked than in *Summer Will Show*.

Warner's sixth novel was highly praised when it first appeared, in 1948, and stayed in print longer than any of her other works during her lifetime. *The Corner That Held Them* combined complex and highly entertaining narrative with technical innovation to brilliant effect. The action centers around a Fenland convent in the fourteenth century. As in *After the Death of Don Juan*, there is no protagonist: five prioresses and four bishops come and go, novices arrive, grow up, die, and what story there is (strands of it are often abandoned without warning) takes place within a very small area. The movement of the novel is like that of the Waxle Stream which flows from the convent to the sea, "a muddy, reluctant stream, full of loops and turnings, and constantly revising its course." Warner wrote to a friend when she was composing the book (at intervals throughout the years of the Second World War) that she was tempted to call it *People Growing Old*; "It has no conversations and no pictures, it has no plot, and the characters are innumerable and insignificant" (*Letters*, p. 91). By not providing the conventional novel properties, Warner was able to create a powerful illusion of historical actuality.

In the chronicle of small things happening or half-happening, certain characters and episodes stand out: the clerk Henry Yellowlees hearing the new polyphonic music for the first time, the fake priest Ralph Kello's humanist sermons (discounted because of his supposed madness), Prioress Alicia among the laity at a christening and the young nun Dame Isabel, possibly the most sympathetic character in the book, who dies young, regretting to exchange "the ambiguity of this world for the certitude of the next."

The novel is noticeably free from what Warner once called "the arthritis of antiquarianism"; historical detail is kept to a minimum and is limited generally to what the fourteenth-century characters themselves might have found noteworthy. Thereby, the wars with France affect life at Oby as another set of taxes and the Peasant's Revolt only reaches them as a night of fairly mild copycat vandalism in a year of rumors and fears. The Black Death, on the other hand, is described in vivid terms:

The short dusky daylight and the miry roads and the swollen rivers were no impediment to it, as to other travellers. All across Europe it had come, and now it would traverse England, and nothing could stop it, wherever there were men living it would seek them out, and turn back, as a wolf does, to snap at the man it had passed by.

(pp. 13–14)

In her last novel, *The Flint Anchor* (1954), Warner used historical settings to explore timeless human dilemmas and provided a further sophistication of the idea of the historical novel. Set in the town of Loseby in the first half of the nineteenth century, the book begins with a description of the protagonist's elaborate memorial in the local church and ends with his dying wish not to be memorialized. It therefore becomes an object lesson in the unreliability of sources—all written and spoken reminiscences in the story are undermined. The narrative itself demonstrates how history gets made, how reputations derive from hearsay and misinterpreted facts, how rarely facts themselves can be pinned down or verified.

The story centers around John Barnard, a melancholic merchant and paterfamilias, contemplative by nature but forced by sense of duty to lead a life deeply uncongenial to him. His wife, Julia, worn out by childbearing and boredom, takes to the bottle and semi-invalidism early in the novel and becomes the first of Barnard's many shameful family burdens. In the fishing town where they live, Barnard is a man of influence and status, but fatally lacks the common touch and is as effectively cut off from his fellow man as his home, Anchor House, is cut off from the rest of the town by the spiked wall that surrounds it. Barnard's stern morality blights the lives of his children: five die young, two run away, and the remaining son refuses to continue the family business. The one child whom Bar-nard loves unreservedly, his pretty middle daughter, Mary, is the least worthy object of affection. His partiality makes him mistake her superficiality for candor and her literal-mindedness for truthfulness; Barnard in fact encourages in her the selfishness and heartlessness that torment him and finally break his spirit.

Barnard's over-fine conscience is seen ultimately as a form of moral vanity. He cannot imagine the scope of other people's motives, which is what the novel is at pains to expose. In a story with a large number of characters where everything proceeds, to some extent, through misinterpretation, irony is built into the very method, dramatizing the difference between private motives and public actions. No character can be trusted to remain peripheral; the dying child Julius, who enters the story for a few pages only, comes to life as soon as he observes his sister from his sickbed "with listless malice"; the poor relation Mutty, seemingly an irredeemable fool, suddenly shows by her intuition that she is not wanted at Anchor House more sensitivity than one has been led to expect possible; and the interfering neighbor Madame Bon, who could easily have slipped into a caricature once her main part in the action is over, still seeps character and potential malignity whenever she appears.

The sea is a powerful presence in this novel, as in many of Warner's works. Thomas Kettle's night spent on board his father-in-law John Barnard's fishing boat, the *Mary Lucinda*, is evoked with lyrical intensity and links symbolically with another night when he lies in bed with the real Mary Lucinda (Barnard), his wife. He smells the sea in her hair and thinks about the child she is carrying, itself like a mariner, or like the fish he saw hoisted into the wrong element, "choking on air." These moments of perception connect with each other, allowing the author to leave as much as possible unstated. The idea of being in the wrong element, for instance, is enforced by the episode of Thomas and Mary's residence with the eccentric Miss Basham, where Thomas is employed sorting a shell collection. This in turn feeds into the ambiguity of what happens to Thomas when he runs away from Loseby, having been accused of homosexuality. When he leaves, the accusation is not true, but a declaration of love by a fisherman, Crusoe Bullen, strikes Thomas as morally authentic: "so rang the long harsh sighs of the waves embracing the shore, an elemental voice, alien and indisputable." When his death abroad from a "wound" is reported, there is a suggestion that the evidence has been faked and that Thomas may at last have found an element he feels comfortable in, and wishes to enjoy it untrameled.

SHORT STORIES

WARNER wrote short stories for more than fifty years and published ten collections in her lifetime (two more have followed her death). At first a rather marginal part of her oeuvre, the short story became, in the last two decades of her life, virtually her only writing, her main source of income and an artistic preoccupation. She achieved an extremely wide range within the form, and her work stands comparison with the best English short story writers of the mid-century, Elizabeth Bowen and V. S. Pritchett. Her unpredictable choice of subject matter in her stories once prompted the novelist John Updike to remark that Warner had "the spiritual digestion of a goat."

Warner's first collection of short fiction, *The Salutation* (1932), was a crossover book; it included two novellas, one fragment ("Early One Morning," which had started life as a sketch for a novel), and the contents of four previous small press editions. Three stories that had appeared together in 1930 as *A Moral Ending and Other Stories* were heavily derivative of T. F. Powys' style, "Elinor Barley" was derived from a ballad narrative ("The Brisk Young Widow"), and the whimsical "Perdita"—a story about a lost cat, which even the author called "silly"—sat rather uncomfortably alongside Warner's powerful and ambitious title story.

"The Salutation" is one of Warner's best stories, almost certainly begun in the expectation that it would grow into a full-length novel. It is a

sequel, or extended coda, to her 1927 novel, *Mr. Fortune's Maggot*. Late in her life Warner said that she had experienced "a feeling of compunction, almost guilt, towards this guiltless man [Mr. Fortune] I had created and left in such a fix," and on rereading the book three years after its publication, she was moved to continue his story. It is not, strictly speaking, a sequel, for the reader doesn't need to know of the connection with the novel; in fact, Warner seems to have been at pains to play it down: the protagonist is never named, and his former vocation is not specified. The only important fact about the stranger who turns up at Mrs. Bailey's house in the middle of the Brazilian pampas is that he was once happy and is unlikely to be so again.

The man's anonymity and the uncertain cause of his great sadness make him an interesting if unlikely hero. The people Mrs. Bailey's home, The House of the Salutation, and whose lives he subtly disrupts, are aware solely of his physical distress from long traveling. He does not strike them as a romantic figure and excites only his hostess's solicitude and her grandson Alfonso's contempt. The latter is made clear in a scene on the pampas in which the stranger identifies himself with a shabby rhea. When Alfonso shoots the bird dead, for no other reason than that it is ungainly, the stranger's first impulse of anger and pity is quelled by his recognition of a force of nature at work:

> The bird was dead, the slayer justified by that complete absence of justification. I, I am of the rhea's party, he thought, standing beside the bird like a mourner, like a chief mourner and blood relation; and rousing in his flesh, the independent soul exclaimed, Oh it should have been me, been me! But instead the bird had fallen, and he, alive, must carry on, willy-nilly, the warfare pledged between the ungainly and the dexterous, the harmless and the destroying.
>
> (The Salutation, p. 81)

Alfonso, "slender, fiercely erect, racked with youth and pride," is a vengeful counterpart of Lueli, the Fanuan boy with whom Mr. Fortune had fallen guiltily in love. Alfonso is also a sort of nightmare (as becomes half-clear at the end of the story, when the protagonist may or may not be dreaming); he is a projection of Mr. Fortune's bad conscience and the summary execution of the rhea is symbolic punishment for all the former priest's shambling, morally confused behavior.

The acceptance of one of Warner's stories, "My Mother Won the War," by *The New Yorker* in 1936 and the magazine's subsequent establishment of a "first reading" agreement with her (meaning that she was paid a basic fee regardless of whether or not the story was taken) was of undoubted significance, and not merely financially. For the first time, Warner had a potentially large, sophisticated, cosmopolitan audience. There were pitfalls—Warner was valued by the magazine for her wit and her Englishness, both of which could lead her astray—she had always, for instance, had a certain difficulty inventing proper names that didn't draw attention to their fictitiousness—but her "take" on contemporary life also became more deliberately analytical, the challenge to interpret it more pressing.

In stories written during and just after the Second World War, the difficulties and pettiness of life in provincial wartime England are revealed with caustic clarity (see "Poor Mary," "English Climate," and "The Cold," all from *The Museum of Cheats*, 1947; and "Setteragic On," a story about the effects of rationing, "The Level-Crossing," about a young recruit's horror of possible mutilation, and "Apprentice," all from *A Garland of Straw*, 1943). Warner found the ironic possibilities presented by life on the home front almost endless, and astutely identified the way in which social and class war were accelerated by war conditions. Life's winners and losers became instantly recognizable and, as usual, Warner sided firmly with the underdog.

Warner's stories often have arresting beginnings: "She planted a high Spanish comb in her pubic hair and resumed her horn-rimmed spectacles" ("The Foregone Conclusion"); "Private charity still exists in England though mostly it is practised in the disorderly, hole-in-corner style recommended by Jesus" ("A Work of Art"); "Like a stone into water, death drops a weight into the ground, and the ripples spread" ("Over the Hill"). The stories' symbolic patterning remains embedded, casually significant; in "A View of Exmoor," a family named Finch chase a bird (formerly caged) across the moor and are interrupted by a holidaying walker (usually caged in his town job) whose legs are described as "bare, ruined," recalling the "choirs where late the sweet birds sang" of Shakespeare's sonnet. Neither forced nor "literary," the overall effect is subtly powerful. Ambiguous endings seem to move away from the action rather than conclude it, such as in the splendid "Heathy Landscape with Dormouse" (*A Stranger with a Bag*, 1966), "On Living for Others" (*A Spirit Rises*, 1962), and "Swans on an Autumn River" (*A Stranger with a Bag*). As John Updike has written, "her stories tend to convince us in process and baffle us in conclusion; they are not rounded with meaning but lift jaggedly toward new, unseen developments" (*New Republic*, 5 March 1966).

Warner's consecutive collections Winter in the Air, A Spirit Rises, and *A Stranger with a Bag* showed her gift in its prime. The title story of the first is a delicate study of the misery of a discarded wife: set beside "An Act of Reparation" from *A Stranger with a Bag*, a story dealing with an ostensibly identical situation, one can see the extraordinary fertility of Warner's imagination. The one story is tragic, the other slyly comic (the wife in question secretly relieved to have been discarded). A similar mirroring of theme prevails in "Their Quiet Lives" and "In a Shaken House" and in Warner's many stories about returning to a significant place ("Hee-Haw," "Idenborough," "A Second Visit"). Warner presents situations rapidly, with spare, sure strokes, and she moves seamlessly between one point of view and another (notably in "Absalom, My Son" and "Heathy Landscape with Dormouse"), affecting the reader's sympathies almost before the reader is aware of being worked on. Probably Warner's most vivid statement about illicit love is found in one of her best-known stories, "A Love Match" (from *A Stranger with a Bag*), which won the Katherine Mansfield prize in 1968. This tale of brother-sister incest and the response it meets with in a provincial English village between the wars clearly draws partly on Warner's own experience of social ostracism as a lesbian, a rare foray into an autobiographical theme.

The Innocent and the Guilty, published in 1971, was Warner's last book of stories with a contemporary setting, and bore the marks of a fruitful restlessness with the conventions of the form. The most striking (and longest) story is "But at the Stroke of Midnight," an ambitious study of schizophrenia (composed, appropriately enough, in shifting time scales and points of view) in which a middle-aged, middle-class wife, Lucy Ridpath, leaves home without warning or apparent reason. She adopts the name and characteristics of a dead "cousin Aurelia," presumably (though this is not made clear) an invention by Lucy to cover periodic absences from home over a number of years. Lucy's husband, Aston, sympathetically portrayed despite his chronic insensitivity, hasn't noticed anything happening to his wife; the shortcomings of their marriage are cleverly suggested rather than stated.

Freed by irrationality, Lucy (now Aurelia) inspires awe in those she meets as she wanders around London. She is "a nova," "seen where no star was and ... seen as a portent, a promise of what is variously desired." She sleeps with an art publisher she meets at the Tate Gallery, who is captivated by her: "she was middle-aged, plain, badly kept, untravelled—and she had the aplomb of a *poule de luxe*." She then impresses a clergyman as "so innocently frank, it was as if she had come down from the west front of Chartres." Retreating to the provinces for cheapness, Aurelia befriends a broken-down tomcat whom she perversely names Lucy, and it is the gruesome death of this animal that unhinges her back into her former self and propels her almost instantly to suicide by drowning, in a vividly imagined climax:

> The hollow booming hung in the air. Below it was an incessant hissing and seething. the ground rose under her feet; the level of water had fallen to her knees. Tricked and impatient, she waded faster, took longer strides.
>
> (*The Innocent and the Guilty*, p. 77)

The story has many oblique parallels to *Lolly Willowes*: the invisibility of meek middle-aged women ("She was thoughtful about [domestic] matters—which was one reason why her conversation was so seldom arresting"), the sudden turning of the worm, the strong preference for poverty above dependence. The otherworldliness of the heroines is similar (Lolly makes a pact with the Devil, Lucy / Aurelia loses her mind), the rough tomcat Lucy is as demanding a familiar as Lolly Willowes', the disruption of their solitary lives is as devastating. It was as if Warner was returning to the earlier story and deliberately making it darker, suggesting the themes had become even more significant to her as the years went by.

Warner's social observations in *The Innocent and the Guilty* are as sharp as ever (she was in her seventies when the stories were written). The "villagers" trapped overnight in the hotel by the sea in "Truth in the Cup" are the inhabitants of holiday cottages and retirement homes, "villagers only in a xenophobic determination to keep out caravans and coach parties." They represent a wide range of petty vices, are all very drunk, and condemn everyone else's behavior, especially that of the young (their horror of the incipient drug culture is acutely observed: the story was written in 1968). Their morals and their vices are virtually interchangeable, as one fleeting remark neatly indicates: "old Bilby's shrill voice reiterated a demand for a good old-fashioned whacking. Janey brisked up and called across the room, 'Now, Bibbles, you'd better be careful. we all know the sort of books you read'."

"Bruno," a tragi-comic story about an aging Scottish landowner and the nineteen-year-old toyboy he has picked up abroad, was one of two stories in *The Innocent and the Guilty* not to appear in *The New Yorker*, presumably because of its homosexual theme. The magazine faced a stronger challenge with the stories Warner began to write in 1970, a year after Valentine Ackland's death; they were eventually published as *Kingdoms of Elfin* (1977). It wasn't Warner's first foray into systematized fantasy; in 1940 she had published a collection of animal fables, *The Cat's Cradle Book*, in which political allegory hid behind whimsical anthropomorphism. The anarchic amoral potential of fairy stories appealed to her strongly and suited the dark, detached mood of her bereavement; she used the elfin legends, unsentimental and ruthlessly rational, as a parallel to (rather than a satire on) the human world; in fact the author affects to be too *uninterested* in human dealings to aim at them with any care. Her fairy kingdoms are idiosyncratic, drawing on her knowledge of Scottish border ballads, fairy lore, and ancien régime court life (derived in part from Saint-Simon's memoirs of Louis XIV). The narrative style she adopted for these stories was detached, spare and deliberately heartless:

So the poor wretch was not a fairy; and the bedding would have to be paid for. But if the body could be got to the anatomists in Edinburgh, thought Adam, taking heart again, I shall break about even.

(p. 14)

These stories "celebrate the singular without declining into singularity," as the critic Glen Cavaliero has said (*PN Review* 23, vol. 8, no. 3). As with much of Warner's best work, there is an air of genteel bloodymindedness about it. "I hope some of it will annoy people," she said, in an interview in *The Guardian* in 1977 when the book was published (she was eighty-two years old), "because that is the surest way of being attended to."

CONCLUSION

LATE in her life, Sylvia Townsend Warner wrote to her publisher, "if I ever hear the word style about myself again I shall burst and die." But it was her fate to be thought of as a stylist. The critic Donald Davie has written admiringly of the "specifically *verbal* intelligence" displayed in her poetry (*Under Briggflatts*, p. 60) and the observation is true of all her work. Plain diction in Warner certainly does not always convey plain meaning. She had a highly developed sense of the history of words, their multivalent meanings and literary precedents; as a result, her prose is both densely textured and extremely clear.

Much of the charge of Warner's books comes from the fact that they are emotional and yet firmly controlled by intellect. The freshness of

her style, though, is very largely due to the construction of her similes and metaphors. In them she chooses apparent incongruities to illuminate a real relation, often juxtaposing two or more different sense impressions to discover possibilities in description outside the expected. To take three examples from thousands, she has likened a chamber pot draped in a white cloth to "a coquettish confirmation candidate" (*Diaries*, p. 178), described a dead heron in the river as "extraordinarily flat in its rigid pattern: like a squashed iris" (*Diaries*, p. 284), and compared the sound of singing coming suddenly from a chapel to "the gush of juice when one cuts open a rhubarb tart" (*Somerset*, p. 50). All of these comparisons take the reader several steps further than expected; often there is a moral comparison involved as well as a startlingly original sensual one.

Warner was a perceptive critic and editor, producing a short study of Jane Austen (1951), a selection from Gilbert White's journals and letters (1946) and a highly praised life of the novelist T. H. White (1967) as well as translations from the French of Proust's *Contre Sainte-Beuve* (1958) and Jean-Rene Huguenin's *La Côte Sauvage* (1963). A generation or two later, when middle-class intellectual women would as naturally gravitate toward the academy as they previously avoided it, Warner might have made a formidable don. But in many ways her literary achievements all derived from staying firmly independent of any artistic or intellectual establishment. In conversation with the writer and editor Arnold Rattenbury in the 1970s, Warner referred to her position as that of a sniper: "You can pick odd enemies off, you know, by aiming a short story well" (*PN Review* 23, vol. 8, no. 3, p. 47).

Warner's originality and independence have tended toward an undervaluing of her achievement as a whole, but posterity may well regard her as one of the great belles-lettrists of the twentieth century. Since her death, her occasional writing, especially her *Letters* (1982), *Diaries* (1994) and love letters to and from Valentine Ackland (*I'll Stand By You*, 1998), have impressed readers with their intelligence, humor and precision. Though she has escaped the attention of a wide reading public, as an English prose stylist, a student of character, and an anatomist of hypocrisy she has few rivals.

SELECTED BIBLIOGRAPHY

I. POETRY. *The Espalier* (London and New York, 1925); *Time Importuned* (London and New York, 1928); *Opus 7* (London and New York, 1931); (with Valentine Ackland) *Whether a Dove or Seagull* (New York, 1933; London, 1934); *Boxwood* (London, 1957); *Twelve Poems (London, 1980); Collected Poems* (Manchester and New York, 1982); *Selected Poems* (Manchester and New York, 1985).

II. NOVELS. *Lolly Willowes* (London and New York, 1926); *Mr. Fortune's Maggot* (London and New York, 1927); *The True Heart* (London and New York, 1929); *Summer Will Show* (London and New York, 1936); *After the Death of Don Juan* (London, 1938; New York, 1939); *The Corner That Held Them* (London and New York, 1948); *The Flint Anchor* (London and New York, 1954).

III. SHORT FICTION. *Some World Far from Ours* (London, 1929); *Elinor Barley* (London, 1930); *A Moral Ending and Other Stories* (London, 1931); *The Salutation* (London and New York, 1932); More Joy in Heaven (London, 1935); *The Cat's Cradle Book* (New York, 1940; London, 1960); *A Garland of Straw* (London and New York, 1943). *The Museum of Cheats* (London and New York, 1947); *Winter in the Air* (London, 1955; New York, 1956); *A Spirit Rises* (London and New York, 1962); *A Stranger with a Bag* (London, 1966), repub. as *Swans on an Autumn River* (New York, 1966); *The Innocent and the Guilty* (London and New York, 1971); *Kingdoms of Elfin* (London and New York, 1977); *Scenes of Childhood and Other Stories* (London and New York, 1981); *One Thing Leading to Another* (London and New York, 1984); *Selected Stories* (London and New York, 1988).

IV. NONFICTION. *Somerset* (London, 1949); *Jane Austen* (London, 1951); (trans.) Marcel Proust, *By Way of Sainte-Beuve* (London, 1958); (trans.) Jean-Ren, Huguenin, *A Place of Shipwreck* (London, 1963); *T. H. White: A Biography* (London, 1967; New York, 1968).

V. LETTERS AND DIARIES. *Letters* (London and New York, 1982); *The Diaries of Sylvia Townsend Warner* (London, 1994); *Sylvia and David: The Townsend Warner/Garnett Letters* (London, 1994); *I'll Stand by You: The Letters of Sylvia Townsend Warner and Valentine Ackland (London, 1998).*

VI. CRITICAL AND BIOGRAPHICAL STUDIES. Valentine Ackland, *For Sylvia: An Honest Account* (London, 1985; New York, 1986); Walter Allen, *The Short Story in English* (Oxford, U.K., 1981); Terry Castle, "Sylvia Townsend Warner and the Counterplot of Lesbian Fiction," in *Textual Practice* 4, no. 2 (Summer 1990); Glen Cavaliero, "Sylvia Townsend Warner: An Appreciation," in *Powys Review* 5 (Summer 1979); Valentine Cunningham, *British Writers of the Thirties* (Oxford, U.K., 1988); Donald Davie, *Under Briggflatts: A History of Poetry in Great Britain 1960–1988* (Manchester, U.K., 1989); Claire Harman, ed., "Sylvia Townsend Warner: A Celebration," in *PN Review* 8, no. 3 (1981); Claire Harman, *Sylvia Townsend Warner, A Biography* (London, 1989); Jan Montefiore, *Feminism and Poetry: Language, Experience, Identity in Women's Writing* (London and New York, 1987); Wendy Mulford, *This Narrow Place: Sylvia Townsend Warner and Valentine Ackland; Life, Letters and Politics 1930–1951* (London, 1988); Bonnie Kime Scott, ed., *The Gender of Modernism: A Critical Anthology* (Bloomington and Indianapolis, 1990); Gillian Spraggs, "Exiled to Home: The Poetry of Sylvia Townsend Warner and Valentine Ackland," in *Lesbian and Gay Writing: An Anthology of Critical Essays*, ed. by Mark Lilly (London, 1990). W. J. Strachan, " Sylvia Townsend Warner; A Memoir," in *London Magazine* (November 1979); A. C. Ward, *The Nineteen-Twenties: Literature and Ideas in the Post-War Decade* (London, 1930).

MASTER INDEX

The following index covers the entire British Writers series through Supplement VII. All references include volume numbers in boldface Roman numerals followed by page numbers within that volume. Subjects of articles are indicated by boldface type.

"Another September" (Kinsella), **Supp. V:** 260

"Ansell" (Forster), **VI:** 398

Anstey, Christopher, **III:** 155

"Answer, The" (Wycherley), **II:** 322

"Answer to a Paper Called 'A Memorial of true Poor Inhabitants'" (Swift), **III:** 35

Answer to a Poisoned Book (More), **Supp. VII:** 245

Answer to a Question That No Body Thinks of, An (Defoe), **III:** 13

"Answer to Davenant" (Hobbes), **II:** 256n

"Answers" (Jennings), **Supp. V:** 206

"Ant, The" (Lovelace), **II:** 231

Ant and the Nightingale or Father Hubburd's Tales, The (Middleton), **II:** 3

"Ant-Lion, The" (Pritchett), **Supp. III:** 105–106

Antal, Frederick, **Supp. IV:** 80

Antechinus: Poems 1975–1980 (Hope), **Supp. VII:** 159

"Antheap, The" (Lessing), **Supp. I:** 242

"Anthem for Doomed Youth" (Owen), **VI:** 443, 447, 448, 452; **Supp. IV:** 58

"Anthem of Earth, An" (Thompson), **V:** 448

Anthology of War Poetry, An (ed. Nichols), **VI:** 419

Anthony Trollope: A Critical Study (Cockshut), **V:** 98, 103

Antic Hay (Huxley), **VII:** 198, 201–202

"Anti–Christ; or, The Reunion of Christendom" (Chesterton), **VI:** 340–341

Anticipations of the Reaction of Mechanical and Scientific Progress upon Human Life and Thought (Wells), **VI:** 227, 240

Anti–Coningsby (Disraeli), **IV:** 308

Anti–Death League, The (Amis), **Supp. II:** 14–15

Antigua, Penny, Puce (Graves), **VII:** 259

"Antigua Crossings" (Kincaid), **Supp. VII:** 220, 221

Antiquarian Prejudice (Betjeman), **VII:** 358, 359

Antiquary, The (Scott), **IV:** xvii 28, 32–33, 37, 39

Anti–Thelyphthora (Cowper), **III:** 220

Antonina; or, The Fall of Rome (Collins), **Supp. VI:** 92, 95

Antonio and Mellida (Marston), **II:** 27–28, 40

Antonioni, Michelangelo, **Supp. IV:** 434

Antonio's Revenge (Marston), **II:** 27–29, 36, 40

Antony and Cleopatra (Sedley), **II:** 263, 271

Antony and Cleopatra (Shakespeare), **I:** 318, 319–320; **II:** 70; **III:** 22; **Supp. IV:** 263

Antony and Octavus. Scenes for the Study (Landor), **IV:** 100

Ants, The (Churchill), **Supp. IV:** 180–181

"Antwerp" (Ford), **VI:** 323, 416

"Anxious in Dreamland" (Menand), **Supp. IV:** 305

"Any Saint" (Thompson), **V: 444**

Anything for a Quiet Life (Middleton and Webster), **II:** 21, 69, 83, 85

Apartheid and the Archbishop: The Life and Times of Geoffrey Clayton, Archbishop of Cape Town (Paton), **Supp. II:** 343, 356, 357–358

"Apartheid in Its Death Throes" (Paton), **Supp. II:** 342

"Ape, The" (Pritchett), **Supp. III:** 325

Apes of God, The (Lewis), **VII:** xv, 35, 71, 73, 74, 77, 79

Aphorisms on Man (Lavater), **III:** 298

Aphrodite in Aulis (Moore), **VI:** 88, 95, 99

Apocalypse (Lawrence), **VII:** 91

"Apollo and the Fates" (Browning), **IV:** 366

"Apollo in Picardy" (Pater), **V:** 355, 356

"Apollonius of Tyre" (Gower), **I:** 53

"Apologia pro Poemate Meo" (Owen), **VI:** 452

Apologia pro Vita Sua (Newman), **Supp. VII:** 289, 290, 291, 294, 295, 296, 298, 299–300

Apologie for Poetry (Sidney), *see Defence of Poesie, The Apologie for the Royal Party, An . . . By a Lover of Peace and of His Country* (Evelyn), **II:** 287

Apology Against a Pamphlet Call'd A Modest Confutation of the Animadversions upon the Remonstrant Against Smectymnuus, An (Milton), **II:** 175

"Apology for Plainspeaking, An" (Stephen), **V:** 284

Apology for the Bible (Watson), **III:** 301

Apology for the Life of Mrs. Shamela Andrews, An (Fielding), *see Shamela*

"Apology for the Revival of Christian Architecture in England, A" (Hill), **Supp. V:** 189, 191–192

Apology for the Voyage to Guiana (Ralegh), **I:** 153

Apophthegms (Bacon), **I:** 264, 273

"Apostasy, The" (Traherne), **II:** 191

Apostles, The (Moore), **VI:** 88, 96, 99

Apostes, The (Cambridge Society), **IV:** 331; **V:** 278; **VI:** 399

"Apotheosis of Tins, The" (Mahon), **Supp. VI:** 172

"Apparition of His Mistresse Calling Him to Elizium, The" (Herrick), **II:** 113

Appeal from the New to the Old Whigs, An (Burke), **III:** 205

Appeal to England, An (Swinburne), **V:** 332

Appeal to Honour and Justice, An (Defoe), **III:** 4, 13

Appeal to the Clergy of the Church of Scotland, An (Stevenson), **V:** 395

"Appius and Virginia" (Gower), **I:** 55

Appius and Virginia (R. B.), **I:** 216

Appius and Virginia (Webster), **II:** 68, 83, 85

Apple Broadcast, The (Redgrove), **Supp. VI:** 235

Apple Cart, The: A Political Extravaganza (Shaw), **VI:** 118, 120, 125–126, 127, 129

"Apple Tragedy" (Hughes), **Supp. I:** 351, 353

"Apple Tree, The" (du Maurier), **Supp. III:** 138

"Apple Tree, The" (Galsworthy), **VI:** 276

"Apple Tree, The" (Mansfield), **VII:** 173

Applebee, John, **III:** 7

Appley Dapply's Nursery Rhymes (Potter), **Supp. III:** 291

"Appraisal, An" (Compton–Burnett), **VII:** 59

Appreciations (Pater), **V:** 338, 339, 341, 351–352, 353–356

"Apprentice" (Warner), **Supp. VII:** 380

"April" (Kavanagh), **Supp. VII:** 188

"April Epithalamium, An" (Stevenson), **Supp. VI:** 263

April Love (Hughes), **V:** 294

"Apron of Flowers, The" (Herrick), **II:** 110

Apropos of Dolores (Wells), **VI:** 240

"Arab Love Song" (Thompson), **V:** 442, 445, 449

"Arabella" (Thackeray), **V:** 24

Arabian Nights, The, **III:** 327, 335, 336; **Supp. IV:** 434

Aragon, Louis, **Supp. IV:** 466

"Aramantha" (Lovelace), **II:** 230, 231

Aran Islands, The (Synge), **VI:** 308–309

Ararat (Thomas), **Supp. IV:** 484

Aratra Pentelici (Ruskin), **V:** 184

Arbuthnot, John, **III:** 19, 34, 60

"Arcades" (Milton), **II:** 159

Arcadia (Sidney), **I:** 161, 163–169, 173, 317; **II:** 48, 53–54; **III:** 95

Arcadian Rhetorike (Fraunce), **I:** 164

Archeology of Love, The (Murphy), **Supp. V:** 317

Archer, William, **II:** 79, 358, 363, 364; **V:** 103, 104, 113

Architectural Review (periodical), **VII:** 356, 358

Architecture in Britain: 1530–1830 (Reynolds), **II:** 336

Architecture, Industry and Wealth (Morris), **V:** 306

"Arctic Summer" (Forster), **VI:** 406

Arden of Feversham (Kyd), **I:** 212, 213, 218–219

Arden, John, **Supp. II:** 21–42

"Ardour and Memory" (Rossetti), **V:** 243

Ardours and Endurances (Nichols), **VI:** 423

"Are You Lonely in the Restaurant" (O'Nolan), **Supp. II:** 323

Area of Darkness, An (Naipaul), **Supp.I,** 383, 384, 387, 389, 390, 391–392, 394, 395, 399, 402

Arendt, Hannah, **Supp. IV:** 306

Areopagitica (Milton), **II:** 163, 164, 169, 174, 175; **IV:** 279

Aretina (Mackenzie), **III:** 95

"Argonauts of the Air, The" (Wells), **VI:** 244

Argonauts of the Pacific (Malinowski), **Supp. III:** 186

Argufying (Empson), **Supp. II:** 180, 181

Argument . . . that the Abolishing of Christianity . . . May . . . be Attended with some Inconveniences, An (Swift), **III:** 26, 35

Aylott & Jones (publishers), **V:** 131

"*B*aa, Baa Black Sheep" (Kipling), **VI:** 166

Babees Book, The (*Early English Poems and Treatises on Manners and Meals in Olden Time*) (ed. Furnival), **I:** 22, 26

Babel Tower (Byatt), **Supp. IV:** 139, 141, 149–151

Babes in the Darkling Wood (Wells), **VI:** 228

"Baby's cradle with no baby in it, A" (Rossetti), **V:** 255

Babylon Hotel (Bennett), *see Grand Babylon Hotel, The*

Bachelors, The (Spark), **Supp. I:** 203, 204

Back (Green), **Supp. II:** 254, 258–260

"Back of Affluence" (Davie), **Supp. VI:** 110

"Back to Cambo" (Hartley), **Supp. VII:** 124

Back to Methuselah (Shaw), **VI: 121– 122,** 124

"Background Material" (Harrison), **Supp. V:** 155

Background to Danger (Ambler), **Supp. IV:** 7–8

Backward Place, A (Jhabvala), **Supp. V:** 229

Backward Son, The (Spender), **Supp. II:** 484, 489

Bacon, Francis, **I: 257–274; II:** 149, 196; **III:** 39; **IV:** 138, 278, 279; annotated list of works, **I:** 271–273; **Supp. III:** 361

Bad Boy (McEwan), **Supp. IV:** 400

"Bad Five Minutes in the Alps, A" (Stephen), **V:** 283

Bagehot, Walter, **IV:** 289, 291; **V:** xxiii, 156, 165, 170, 205, 212

"Baggot Street Deserta" (Kinsella), **Supp. V:** 259–260

Bagman, The; or, The Impromptu of Muswell Hill (Arden), **Supp. II:** 31, 32, 35

"Bagpipe Music" (MacNeice), **VII:** 413

Bailey, Benjamin, **IV:** 224, 229, 230, 232–233

Bailey, Paul, **Supp. IV:** 304

Baillie, Alexander, **V:** 368, 374, 375, 379

Bainbridge, Beryl, **Supp. VI: 17–27**

Baines, Jocelyn, **VI:** 133–134

Baird, Julian, **V:** 316, 317, 318, 335

"Baite, The" (Donne), **IV:** 327

Bakerman, Jane S., **Supp. IV:** 336

"Baker's Dozen, The" (Saki), **Supp. VI:** 243

Bakhtin, Mikhail, **Supp. IV:** 114

"Balakhana" (McGuckian), **Supp. V:** 284

"Balance, The" (Waugh), **Supp. VI:** 271

Balance of Terror (Shaffer), **Supp. I:** 314

Balaustion's Adventure (Browning), **IV:** 358, 374

"Balder Dead" (Arnold), **V:** 209, 216

Baldwin, Stanley, **VI:** 353, 355

Bale, John, **I:** 1, 3

Balfour, Arthur, **VI:** 226, 241, 353

Balfour, Graham, **V:** 393, 397

Balin; or, The Knight with Two Swords (Malory), **I:** 79

Ball and the Cross, The (Chesterton), **VI:** 338

Ballad at Dead Men's Bay, The (Swinburne), **V:** 332

"Ballad of Bouillabaisse" (Thackeray), **V:** 19

"Ballad of Death, A" (Swinburne), **V:** 316, 317–318

Ballad of Jan Van Hunks, The (Rossetti), **V:** 238, 244, 245

"Ballad of Life, A" (Swinburne), **V:** 317, 318

Ballad of Peckham Rye, The (Spark), **Supp. I:** 201, 203–204

Ballad of Reading Gaol, The (Wilde), **V:** xxvi, 417–418, 419

"Ballad of the Investiture 1969, A" (Betjeman), **VII:** 372

"Ballad of the Long–legged Bait" (Thomas), **Supp. I:** 177

"Ballad of the Three Spectres" (Gurney), **VI:** 426

"Ballad of the White Horse, The" (Chesterton), **VI:** 338–339, 341

"Ballad of Villon and Fat Madge, The" (tr. Swinburne), **V:** 327

"Ballad upon a Wedding, A" (Suckling), **II:** 228–229

Ballade du temps jadis (Villon), **VI:** 254

Ballade of Truthful Charles, The, and Other Poems (Swinburne), **V:** 333

Ballade on an Ale–Seller (Lydgate), **I:** 92

Ballads (Stevenson), **V:** 396

Ballads (Thackeray), **V:** 38

Ballads and Lyrical Pieces (Scott), **IV:** 38

Ballads and Other Poems (Tennyson), **IV:** 338

Ballads and Poems of Tragic Life (Meredith), **V:** 224, 234

Ballads and Sonnets (Rossetti), **V:** xxiv, 238, 244, 245

Ballads of the English Border (Swinburne), **V:** 333

Ballard, J. G., **III:** 341; **Supp. V: 19–34**

Ballast to the White Sea (Lowry), **Supp. III:** 273, 279

Balliols, The (Waugh), **Supp. VI:** 273

Ballot (Smith), **Supp. VII:** 351

"Ballroom of Romance, The" (Trevor), **Supp. IV:** 503

"Bally *Power Play*" (Gunn), **Supp. IV:** 272

Ballygombeen Bequest, The (Arden and D'Arcy), **Supp. II:** 32, 35

Balthazar (Durrell), **Supp. I:** 104–105, 106, 107

Balzac, Honoré de, **III:** 334, 339, 345; **IV:** 153n; **V:** xvi, xviii, xix–xxi, 17, 429; **Supp. IV:** 123, 136, 238, 459

Bancroft, John, **II:** 305

"Bangor Requiem" (Mahon), **Supp. VI:** 177

"Banim Creek" (Harris), **Supp. V:** 132

Banks, John, **II:** 305

"Barbara of the House of Grebe" (Hardy), **VI:** 22

Barbara, pseud. of Arnold Bennett

Barbauld, Anna Laetitia, **III:** 88, 93

"Barber Cox and the Cutting of His Comb" (Thackeray), **V:** 21, 37

Barcellona; or, The Spanish Expedition under . . . Charles, Earl of Peterborough (Farquhar), **II:** 353, 355, 364

Barchester Towers (Trollope), **V:** xxii, 93, 101

"Bard, The" (Gray), **III:** 140–141

Bardic Tales (O'Grady), **Supp. V:** 36

"Bards of Passion . . ." (Keats), **IV:** 221

Barker, Granville, *see* Granville Barker, Harley

Barker, Sir Ernest, **III:** 196

Barker, Pat, **Supp. IV: 45–63**

Barker, Thomas, **II:** 131

Barker's Delight (Barker), *see Art of Angling, The*

Barksted, William, **II:** 31

"Barley" (Hughes), **Supp. I:** 358–359

Barnaby Rudge (Dickens), **V:** 42, 54, 55, 66, 71

Barnes, William, **VI:** 2

Barnes, Julian, **Supp. IV: 65–76,** 445, 542

"Barney Game, The" (Friel), **Supp. V:** 113

"Barnfloor and Winepress" (Hopkins), **V:** 381

"Barnsley Cricket Club" (Davie), **Supp. VI:** 109

Barrack–Room Ballads (Kipling), **VI:** 203, 204

Barreca, Regina, **Supp. IV:** 531

Barren Fig Tree, The; or, The Doom . . . of the Fruitless Professor (Bunyan), **II:** 253

Barrett, Eaton Stannard, **III:** 335

Barrie, James M., **V:** 388, 392; **VI:** 265, 273, 280; **Supp. III: 1–17,** 138, 142

Barry Lyndon (Thackeray), **V:** 24, 28, 32, 38

Barrytown Trilogy, The (Doyle), **Supp. V:** 78, 80–87, 88, 89

Barsetshire novels (Trollope), **V:** 92–96, 98, 101

Bartas, Guillaume du, **II:** 138

Bartered Bride, The (Harrison), **Supp. V:** 150

Barth, John, **Supp. IV:** 116

Barthes, Roland, **Supp. IV:** 45, 115

Bartholomew Fair (Jonson), **I:** 228, 243, 324, 340, 342–343; **II:** 3

Bartlett, Phyllis, **V:** x, xxvii

Barton, Bernard, **IV:** 341, 342, 343, 350

Barton, Eustace, **Supp. III:** 342

"Base Details" (Sassoon), **VI:** 430

Basement, The (Pinter), **Supp. I:** 371, 373, 374

"Basement Room, The" (Greene), **Supp. I:** 2

Basic Rules of Reason (Richards), **Supp. II:** 422

Basil: A Story of Modern Life (Collins), **Supp. VI:** 92, 95

Basil Seal Rides Again (Waugh), **VII:** 290

"Basking Shark" (MacCaig), **Supp. VI:** 192

Bateman, Colin, **Supp. V:** 88

Bateson, F. W., **IV:** 217, 323n, 339

Bath (Sitwell), **VII:** 127

Bath Chronicle (periodical), **III:** 262

"Bath House, The" (Gunn), **Supp. IV:** 268–269

Bathurst, Lord, **III:** 33

"Bats' Ultrasound" (Murray), **Supp. VII:** 281

Batsford Book of Light Verse for Children (Ewart), **Supp. VII:** 47

Batsford Book of Verse for Children (Ewart), **Supp. VII:** 47

Battenhouse, Roy, **I:** 282

"Batter my heart, three person'd God" (Donne), **I:** 367–368; **II:** 122

Battiscombe, Georgina, **V:** xii, xxvii, 260

"Battle Hill Revisited" (Murphy), **Supp. V:** 323

Battle of Alcazar, The (Peele), **I:** 205, 206

Battle of Aughrim, The (Murphy), **Supp. V:** 321–324

"Battle of Aughrim, The" (Murphy), **Supp. V:** 317, 321–322

"Battle of Blenheim, The" (Southey), **IV:** 58, 67–68

Battle of Life, The (Dickens), **V:** 71

Battle of Marathon, The (Browning), **IV:** 310, 321

Battle of Shrivings, The (Shaffer), **Supp. I:** 323–324

Battle of the Books, The (Swift), **III:** 17, 23, 35

Baucis and Philemon (Swift), **III:** 35

Baudelaire, Charles **III:** 337, 338; **IV:** 153; **V:** xiii, xviii, xxii–xxiii, 310–318, 327, 329, 404, 405, 409, 411; **Supp. IV:** 163

Baum, L. Frank, **Supp. IV:** 450

Baumann, Paul, **Supp. IV:** 360

Baumgartner's Bombay (Desai), **Supp. V:** 53, 55, 66, 71–72

Bay (Lawrence), **VII:** 118

Bay at Nice, The (Hare), **Supp. IV:** 282, 293

Bayley, John, **Supp. I:** 222

Bayly, Lewis, **II:** 241

"Baymount" (Murphy), **Supp. V:** 328

"Be It Cosiness" (Beerbohm), **Supp. II:** 46

Be my Guest! (Ewart), **Supp. VII:** 41

"Be still, my soul" (Housman), **VI:** 162

Beach, J. W., **V:** 221n, 234

"Beach of Fales, The" (Stevenson), **V:** 396

Beachcroft, T. O., **VII:** xxii

Beaconsfield, Lord, *see* Disraeli, Benjamin

Beardsley, Aubrey, **V:** 318n, 412, 413

"Beast in the Jungle, The" (James), **VI:** 55, 64, 69

Beasts and Super–Beasts (Saki), **Supp. VI:** 245, 251

Beasts' Confession to the Priest, The (Swift), **III:** 36

Beatrice (Haggard), **Supp. III:** 213

Beattie, James, **IV:** 198

Beatty, David, **VI:** 351

Beau Austin (Stevenson), **V:** 396

Beauchamp's Career (Meredith), **V:** xxiv, 225, 228–230, 231, 234

Beaumont, Francis, **II: 42–67,** 79, 82, 87

Beaumont, Joseph, **II:** 180

Beaumont, Sir George, **IV:** 3, 12, 21, 22

Beauties and Furies, The (Stead), **Supp. IV:** 463–464

Beauties of English Poesy, The (ed. Goldsmith), **III:** 191

"Beautiful Lofty Things" (Yeats), **VI:** 216

"Beautiful Young Nymph Going to Bed, A" (Swift), **III:** 32, 36; **VI:** 256

"Beauty" (Thomas), **Supp. III:** 401–402

Beauty and the Beast (Hughes), **Supp. I:** 347

Beauty in a Trance, **II:** 100

Beauvoir, Simone de, **Supp. IV:** 232

Beaux' Stratagem, The (Farquhar), **II:** 334, 353, 359–360, 362, 364

"Because of the Dollars" (Conrad), **VI:** 148

"Because the pleasure–bird whistles" (Thomas), **Supp. I:** 176

Becket (Tennyson), **IV:** 328, 338

Beckett, Samuel, **Supp. I: 43–64; Supp. IV:** 99, 106, 116, 180, 281, 284, 412, 429

Beckford, William, **III:** 327–329, 345; **IV:** xv, 230

"Bedbug, The" (Harrison), **Supp. V:** 151

Beddoes, Thomas, **V:** 330

Bedford–Row Conspiracy, The (Thackeray), **V:** 21, 37

"Bedroom Eyes of Mrs. Vansittart, The" (Trevor), **Supp. IV:** 500

Bedroom Farce (Ayckbourn), **Supp. V:** 3, 12, 13, 14

Bedtime Story (O'Casey), **VII:** 12

"Bedtime Story for my Son" (Redgrove), **Supp. VI: 227–228,** 236

Bee (periodical), **III:** 40, 179

"Bee Orchid at Hodbarrow" (Nicholson), **Supp. VI:** 218

"Beechen Vigil" (Day Lewis), **Supp. III:** 121

Beechen Vigil and Other Poems (Day Lewis), **Supp. III:** 117, 120–121

"Beehive Cell" (Murphy), **Supp. V:** 329

Beekeepers, The (Redgrove), **Supp. VI:** 231

Beerbohm, Max, **V:** 252, 390; **VI:** 365, 366; **Supp. II: 43–59,** 156

"Before Action" (Hodgson), **VI:** 422

Before Dawn (Rattigan), **Supp. VII:** 315

"Before Her Portrait in Youth" (Thompson), **V:** 442

"Before I knocked" (Thomas), **Supp. I:** 175

Before She Met Me (Barnes), **Supp. IV:** 65, 67–68

"Before Sleep" (Kinsella), **Supp. V:** 263

"Before the Mirror" (Swinburne), **V:** 320

"Before the Party" (Maugham), **VI:** 370

Beggar's Bush (Beaumont, Fletcher, Massinger), **II:** 66

Beggar's Opera, The (Gay), **III:** 54, 55, **61–64,** 65–67; **Supp. III:** 195

"Beggar's Soliloquy, The" (Meredith), **V:** 220

Begin Here: A War–Time Essay (Sayers), **Supp. III:** 336

"Beginning, The" (Brooke), **Supp. III:** 52

Beginning of Spring, The (Fitzgerald), **Supp. V:** 98, 106

Behan, Brendan, **Supp. II: 61–76**

Behind the Green Curtains (O'Casey), **VII:** 11

Behn, Aphra, **Supp. III: 19–33**

"Behold, Love, thy power how she despiseth" (Wyatt), **I:** 109

"Being Stolen From" (Trevor), **Supp. IV:** 504

"Being Treated, to Ellinda" (Lovelace), **II:** 231–232

"Beldonald Holbein, The" (James), **VI:** 69

"Belfast vs. Dublin" (Boland), **Supp. V:** 36

Belief and Creativity (Golding), **Supp. I:** 88

Belief in Immortality and Worship of the Dead, The (Frazer), **Supp. III:** 176

Belin, Mrs., **II:** 305

Belinda (Edgeworth), **Supp. III: 157–158,** 162

Belinda, An April Folly (Milne), **Supp. V:** 298–299

Bell, Acton, pseud. of Anne Brontë

Bell, Clive, **V:** 345

Bell, Currer, pseud. of Charlotte Brontë

Bell, Ellis, pseud. of Emily Brontë

Bell, Julian, **Supp. III:** 120

Bell, Quentin, **VII:** 35

Bell, Robert, **I:** 98

Bell, Vanessa, **VI:** 118

Bell, The (Murdoch), **Supp. I:** 222, 223–224, 226, 228–229

"Bell of Aragon, The" (Collins), **III:** 163

"Bell Ringer, The" (Jennings), **Supp. V:** 218

Bellamira; or, The Mistress (Sedley), **II:** 263

"Belle Heaulmière" (tr. Swinburne), **V:** 327

"Belle of the Ball–Room" (Praed), **V:** 14

Belloc, Hilaire, **VI:** 246, 320, 335, 337, 340, 447; **VII:** xiii; **Supp. IV:** 201

Belloc, Mrs. Lowndes, **Supp. II:** 135

Bellow, Saul, **Supp. IV:** 26, 27, 42, 234

Bells and Pomegranates (Browning), **IV:** 356, 373–374

Belmonte, Thomas, **Supp. IV:** 15

Belsey, Catherine, **Supp. IV:** 164

Belton Estate, The (Trollope), **V:** 100, 101

"Bench of Desolation, The" (James), **VI:** 69

Bend in the River, A (Naipaul), **Supp. I:** 393, **397–399,** 401

Bender, T. K., **V:** 364–365, 382

Bending of the Bough, The (Moore), **VI:** 87, 95–96, 98

Benedict, Ruth, **Supp. III:** 186

Benjamin, Walter, **Supp. IV:** 82, 87, 88, 91

Benlowes, Edward, **II:** 123

Benn, Gotfried, **Supp. IV:** 411

Bradley, A. C., **IV:** 106, 123, 216, 235, 236

Bradley, F. H., **V:** xxi, 212, 217

Bradley, Henry, **VI:** 76

Brady, F., **III:** 249

Braine, John, **Supp. IV:** 238

Brand (Hill), **Supp. V:** 199, 200–201

Brander, Laurence, **IV:** xxiv; **VII:** xxii

Brantley, Ben, **Supp. IV:** 197–198

Branwell Brontë (Gerin), **V:** 153

Branwell's Blackwood's (periodical), **V:** 109, 123

Branwell's Young Men's (periodical), *see Branwell's Blackwood's*

Brass Butterfly, The (Golding), **Supp. I:** 65, 75

Brassneck (Hare and Brenton), **Supp. IV:** 281, 282, 283, 284–285, 289

Brave New World (Huxley), **III:** 341; **VII:** xviii, 200, 204

Brave New World Revisited (Huxley), **VII:** 207

"Bravest Boat, The" (Lowry), **Supp. III:** 281

Brawne, Fanny, **IV:** 211, 216–220, 222, 226, 234

Bray, Charles, **V:** 188

Bray, William, **II:** 275, 276, 286

Brazil (Gilliam), **Supp. IV:** 442, 455

"Breach, The" (Murray), **Supp. VII:** 276

"Bréagh San Réilg, La" (Behan), **Supp. II:** 73

"Break My Heart" (Golding), **Supp. I:** 79

"Break of Day in the Trenches" (Rosenberg), **VI:** 433, 434

"Breaking Ground" (Gunn), **Supp. IV:** 271

"Breaking the Blue" (McGuckian), **Supp. V:** 287

Breath (Beckett), **Supp. I:** 60

Brecht, Bertolt, **II:** 359; **IV:** 183; **VI:** 109, 123; **Supp. II:** 23, 25, 28; **Supp. IV:** 82, 87, 180, 194, 198, 281, 298

"Bredon Hill" (Housman), **VI:** 158

Brendan (O'Connor), **Supp. II:** 63, 76

Brendan Behan's Island (Behan), **Supp. II:** 64, 66, 71, 73, 75

Brendan Behan's New York (Behan), **Supp. II:** 75

Brennoralt (Suckling), *see Discontented Colonel, The*

Brenton, Howard, **Supp. IV:** 281, 283, 284, 285

Brethren, The (Haggard), **Supp. III:** 214

"Breton Walks" (Mahon), **Supp. VI:** 168, 172

Brett, Raymond Laurence, **IV:** x, xi, xxiv, 57

Brickfield, The (Hartley), **Supp. VII:** 131–132

Bricks to Babel (Koestler), **Supp. I:** 37

Bridal of Triermain, The (Scott), **IV:** 38

"Bride and Groom" (Hughes), **Supp. I:** 356

Bride of Abydos, The (Byron), **IV:** xvii, 172, 174–175, 192

Bride of Frankenstein (film), **III:** 342

Bride of Lammermoor, The (Scott), **IV:** xviii, 30, 36, 39

Brides of Reason (Davie), **Supp. VI:** 106–107

"Brides, The" (Hope), **Supp. VII:** 154

"Bride's Prelude, The" (Rossetti), **V:** 239, 240

Brideshead Revisited (Waugh), **VII:** xx–xxi, 290, 299–300; **Supp. IV:** 285

"Bridge, The" (Thomas), **Supp. III:** 401

"Bridge for the Living" (Larkin), **Supp. I:** 284

"Bridge of Sighs, The" (Hood), **IV:** 252, 261, 264–265

Bridges, Robert, **II:** 160; **V:** xx, 205, 362–368, 370–372, 374, 376–381; **VI:** xv, **71–83**, 203

Brief History of Moscovia . . . , A (Milton), **II:** 176

Brief Lives (Aubrey), **I:** 260

Brief Lives (Brookner), **Supp. IV:** 131–133

Brief Notes upon a Late Sermon . . . (Milton), **II:** 176

Briefing for a Descent into Hell (Lessing), **Supp. I:** 248–249

Briggflatts (Bunting), **Supp. VII:** 1, 2, 5, 7, 9–13

Bright, A. H., **I:** 3

"Bright Building, The" (Graham), **Supp. VII:** 109, 110–111

"Bright–Cut Irish Silver" (Boland), **Supp. V:** 49–50

Bright Day (Priestley), **VII:** 209, 218–219

"Bright Star!" (Keats), **IV:** 221

Brighton Rock (Greene), **Supp. I:** 2, 3, **7–9**, 11, 19

"Brilliance" (Davie), **Supp. VI:** 113

Bring Larks and Heroes (Keneally), **Supp. IV:** 345, 347, 348–350

"Bringing to Light" (Gunn), **Supp. IV:** 269–270

Brink, Andre, **Supp. VI: 45–59**

Brinkmanship of Galahad Threepwood, The (Wodehouse), *see Galahad at Blandings*

Brissenden, R. F., **III:** 86n

Bristow Merchant, The (Dekker and Ford), **II:** 89, 100

Britain and West Africa (Cary), **VII:** 186

Britannia (periodical), **V:** 144

Britannia (Thomson), **Supp. III:** 409, 411, 420

Britannia Rediviva: A Poem on the Birth of the Prince (Dryden), **II:** 304

"Britannia Victrix" (Bridges), **VI:** 81

"British Church, The" (Herbert), **I:** 189

British Dramatists (Greene), **Supp. I:** 6, 11

"British Guiana" (Ewart), **Supp. VII:** 38

British History in the Nineteenth Century (Trevelyan), **VI:** 390

British Magazine (periodical), **III:** 149, 179, 188

British Museum Is Falling Down, The (Lodge), **Supp. IV:** 363, 365, 367, 369–370, 371

British Women Go to War (Priestley), **VII:** 212

Briton (Smollett), **III:** 149

Brittain, Vera, **II:** 246

Britten, Benjamin, **Supp. IV:** 424

"Broad Bean Sermon, The" (Murray), **Supp. VII:** 275

"Broad Church, The" (Stephen), **V:** 283

Broadbent, J. B., **II:** 102, 116

Broadcast Talks (Lewis), **Supp. III:** 248

"Brodgar Poems" (Brown), **Supp. VI:** 71

Broken Chariot, The (Sillitoe), **Supp. V:** 411, 421

Broken Cistern, The (Dobrée), **V:** 221, 234

Broken Heart, The (Ford), **II:** 89, 92, 93–98, 99, 100

"Broken Wings, The" (James), **VI:** 69

Brome, Richard, **II:** 87

Brontë, Anne, **IV:** 30; **V:** xviii, xx, xxi, 105, 106, 108, 110, 112–119, 122, 126, **128–130**, 131, 132, **134–135, 140–141, 145, 150, 153; Supp. III:** 195; **Supp. IV:** 239

Brontë, Branwell, **V:** xvii, 13, 105, 106, 108–112, 117–119, 121–124, 126, 130, 131, 135, 141, 145, 150, 153

Brontë, Charlotte, **III:** 338, 344, 345; **IV:** 30, 106, 120; **V:** xvii, xx–xxii, 3, 13–14, 20, 68, 105–107, **108–112,** 113–118, **119–126,** 127, 129, 130–140, 144, 145–150, 152, 286; **Supp. III:** 144, 146; **Supp. IV:** 146, 471

Brontë, Emily, **III:** 333, 338, 344, 345; **IV:** ix, xvii, xx–xxi, 13, 14, 105, 106, 108, 110, **112–117,** 118, 122, 130, 131, **132–135, 141–145,** 147, 150, 152–153, 254; **Supp. III:** 144; **Supp. IV:** 462, 513

Brontë, Patrick, **V:** 105–108, 109, 122, 146, 151

Brontë Poems (ed. Benson), **V:** 133, 151

Brontë Story, The: A Reconsideration of Mrs. Gaskell's "Life of Charlotte Brontë" (Lane), **V:** 13n, 16

Brontës, The, Their Lives, Friendships and Correspondence (ed. Wise and Symington), **V:** 117, 118, 151

Brontës of Haworth, The (Fry), **Supp. III:** 195

Brontës' Web of Childhood, The (Ratchford), **V:** 151

"Bronze Head, The" (Yeats), **VI:** 217

Bronze Horseman: Selected Poems of Alexander Pushkin (tr. Thomas), **Supp. IV:** 495

Brooke, Arthur, **I:** 305

Brooke, Jocelyn, **VII:** xviii, xxxvii; **Supp. II:** 202, 203

Brooke, Rupert, **VI:** xvi, 416, **419–420,** 439; **VII:** 35; **Supp. II:** 310; **Supp. III:** 45–61

Brooke Kerith, The. A Syrian Story (Moore), **VI:** xii, 88, 89, **93–94,** 99

Brooke–Rose, Christine, **Supp. IV: 97–118**

Brookner, Anita, **Supp. IV: 119–137**

Brooks, C., **IV:** 323n, 339

"Brooksmith" (James), **VI:** 48, 69

Brophy, Brigid, **IV:** 101

"Brother Fire" (MacNeice), **VII:** 414

Brotherly Love: A Sermon (Swift), **III:** 36

"Brothers" (Hopkins), **V:** 368–369

Clark, Sir George, **IV:** 290

Clarke, Charles Cowden, **IV:** 214, 215

Clarke, Herbert E., **V:** 318*n*

Clarke, Samuel, **II:** 251

Clarkson, Catherine, **IV:** 49

Classic Irish Drama (Armstrong), **VII:** 14

Classical Tradition, The: Greek and Roman Influence on Western Literature (Highet), **II:** 199*n*

Classics and Commercials (Wilson), **Supp. II:** 57

Claude Lorrain's House on the Tiber (Lear), **V:** 77

Claudius novels (Graves), **VII:** xviii, 259

Claudius the God and His Wife Messalina (Graves), **VII:** 259

"Claud's Dog" (Dahl), **Supp. IV:** 214

Claverings, The (Trollope), **V:** 99–100, 101

Clayhanger (Bennett), **VI:** 248, 250, 251, 257–258

Clayhanger series (Bennett), **VI:** xiii, 247, 248, 250, 251, 257–258

Clea (Durrell), **Supp. I:** 103, 104, 106, 107

"Clean Bill, A" (Redgrove), **Supp. VI:** 234

"Cleaned Out" (Motion), **Supp. VII:** 263

"Cleaning Out the Workhouse" (McGuckian), **Supp. V:** 291

Cleanness (*Gawain*–Poet), **Supp. VII:** 83, 84, 98–99

Clear Light of Day (Desai), **Supp. V:** 53, 55, 62, 65–67, 68, 73

Clear State of the Case of Elizabeth Canning, A (Fielding), **III:** 105

"Clearances" (Heaney), **Supp. II:** 279–280

"Cleator Moor" (Nicholson), **Supp. VI:** 214

"Cleggan Disaster, The" (Murphy), **Supp. V:** 313, 319–320

Cleomenes, The Spartan Hero (Dryden), **II:** 296, 305

"Cleon" (Browning), **IV:** 357, 360, 363

Cleopatra (Daniel), **I:** 162

Cleopatra (Haggard), **Supp. III:** 213, 222

"Cleopatra" (Swinburne), **V:** 332

"Clergy, The" (Wilson), **Supp. VI:** 305

Clergyman's Daughter, A (Orwell), **VII:** 274, 278

"Clergyman's Doubts, A" (Butler), **Supp. II:** 117

Clergymen of the Church of England (Trollope), **V:** 101

"Cleric, The" (Heaney), **Supp. II:** 279

Clerk, N. W., *see* Lewis, C. S.

Clerk's Prologue, The (Chaucer), **I:** 29

Clerk's Tale, The (Chaucer), **I:** 34; **Supp. IV:** 190

Cleveland, John, **II:** 123

"Clicking of Cuthbert, The" (Wodehouse), **Supp. III:** 462

Clifford, J. L., **III:** 244*n*

Clifford, W. K., **V:** 409*n*

"Clinical World of P. D. James, The" (Benstock), **Supp. IV:** 320

Clio: A Muse (Trevelyan), **VI:** 383–384

Clishbotham, Jedidiah, pseud. of Sir Walter Scott

"Clive" (Browning), **IV:** 367

"Clock Ticks at Christmas, A" (Highsmith), **Supp. V:** 180

"Clocks, The" (Christie), **Supp. II:** 135

Clockwork Orange, A (Burgess), **Supp. I:** 190–191

Clockwork Testament, The; or, Enderby's End (Burgess), **Supp. I:** 189

Clodd, Edward, **V:** 429

Cloning of Joanna May, The (Weldon), **Supp. IV:** 535, 536

"Clopton Hall" (Gaskell), **V:** 3

"Clorinda and Damon" (Marvell), **II:** 210, 211

Closed Eye, A (Brookner), **Supp. IV:** 120, 133

Closing the Ring (Churchill), **VI:** 361

"Cloud, The" (Fowles), **Supp. I:** 304

"Cloud, The" (Shelley), **IV:** 196, 204

Cloud Nine (Churchill), **Supp. IV:** 179, 180, 188–189, 198

"Clouds" (Brooke), **VI:** 420

Clouds (Frayn), **Supp. VII:** 61

"Cloud–Sculptors of Coral–D, The" (Ballard), **Supp. V:** 26

Clouds of Witness (Sayers), **Supp. III:** 338, 339

"Cloud's Swan Song, The" (Thompson), **V:** 443

Clough, Arthur Hugh, **IV:** 371; **V:** ix, xi, xviii, xxii, 7, **155–171,** 207, 208*n*, 209, 211, 212

"Club in an Uproar, A" (Thackeray), **V:** 25

Clune, Frank, **Supp. IV:** 350

Coakley, Thomas P., **Supp. IV:** 350

"Coast, The" (Fuller), **VII:** 431

"Coat of Many Colors, A" (Desai), **Supp. V:** 53

Cobbett, William, **VI:** 337

Cobra Verde (film), **Supp. IV:** 168

Coburn, Kathleen, **IV:** 52, 55–57

Cocaine Nights (Ballard), **Supp. V:** 31–32, 34

"Cock: A Novelette" (Self), **Supp. V:** 404–405

Cock and Bull (Self), **Supp. V:** 404–406

Cock and the Fox, The (Henryson), **Supp. VII:** 136, 137–138, 147

Cock and the Jasp, The (Henryson), **Supp. VII:** 136, 137

Cock–a–Doodle Dandy (O'Casey), **VII:** xviii, 9–10

Cockatoos, The (White), **Supp. I:** 132, 147

Cockburn, Alexander, **Supp. IV:** 449

"Cockcrow" (Herrick), **II:** 114

"Cock–crowing" (Vaughan), **II:** 185

Cockrill, Maurice, **Supp. IV:** 231

Cockshut, A. O. J., **V:** 98, 100–101, 103

Cocktail Party, The (Eliot), **VII:** 158, 159, 160–161

"Coda" (Kinsella), **Supp. V:** 271

Code of the Woosters, The (Wodehouse), **Supp. III:** 459–460

"Codham, Cockridden, and Childerditch" (Thomas), **Supp. III:** 401

Coelum Britannicum . . . (Carew), **II:** 222

Coetzee, J(ohn) M(ichael), **Supp. VI: 75–90**

Coffin for Dimitrios, A (Ambler), **Supp. IV:** 9–11, 12

Coggan, Donald, archbishop of Canterbury, **I:** vi

Cohen, Francis, **IV:** 190

Colasterion: A Reply to a Nameless Answer Against the Doctrine and Discipline of Divorce (Milton), **II:** 175

Colburn, Henry, **IV:** 254, 293; **V:** 135

"Cold, The" (Warner), **Supp. VII:** 380

"Cold, clear, and blue, The morning heaven" (Brontë), **V:** 115

Cold Coming, A (Harrison), **Supp. V:** 150

"Cold Coming, A" (Harrison), **Supp. V:** 161–163

"Cold in the earth" (Brontë), **V:** 114, 133, 134

Colenso, Bishop John William, **V:** 283

Coleridge, Derwent, **IV:** 48–49, 52

Coleridge, Hartley, **IV:** 44; **V:** 105, 125

Coleridge, Samuel Taylor, **III:** 338; **IV:** viii–xii, **41–57,** 59, 75–78, 82, 84, 115, 204, 253, 257, 281; **V:** 244; and De Quincey, **IV:** 143, 144, 150; and Hazlitt, **IV:** 125–130, 133–134, 137, 138; and Peacock, **IV:** 161–162, 167; and Wordsworth, **IV:** 3–4, 6, 15, 128; at Christ's Hospital, **IV:** 75–78, 82; critical works, **II:** 42, 119*n*, 155, 179, 249–250, 298; **III:** 174, 281, 286; **IV:** 4, 6, 18, 96, 253, 257; literary style, **II:** 154; **III:** 336, 338; **IV:** viii, xi, 18, 180; **V:** 62, 361, 447; Pater's essay in *"ppreciations,* **V:** 244, 340–341; **Supp. IV:** 425, 426–427

"Coleridge" (Mill), **IV:** 50, 56

"Coleridge" (Pater), **V:** 338, 340–341, 403

Coleridge on Imagination (Richards), **Supp. II:** 422–423, 429

Coleridge's Miscellaneous Criticism (ed. Raysor), **IV:** 46

Coleridge's Shakespearean Criticism (ed. Raysor), **IV:** 51, 52, 56

Colette, **Supp. III:** 86; **Supp. IV:** 136

"Coleum; or, The Origin of Things" (Bacon), **I:** 267

Colin Clout (Skelton), **I:** 84, 86, 87, 91–92

Colin Clout's Come Home Again (Spenser), **I:** 124, 127–128, 146–147

"Collaboration" (James), **VI:** 48, 69

"Collar, The" (Herbert), **II:** 120–121, 216

Collected Essays (Greene), **Supp. I:** 9

Collected Essays, Papers, etc. (Bridges), **VI:** 83

Collected Ewart 1933–1980, The (Ewart), **VII:** 423, **Supp. VII:** 35, 36, 37, 38, 41, 43

Collected Impressions (Bowen), **Supp. II:** 78, 82

Collected Letters (Cowen), **VI:** 448

Collected Papers on Analytical Psychology (Jung), **Supp. IV:** 3, 4

Collected Plays (Maugham), **VI:** 367

Collected Plays (Rattigan), **Supp. VII:** 311, 312, 318

Collected Poems (Amis), **Supp. II:** 15

Day of Creation, The (Ballard), **Supp. V:** 29

"Day of the Ox" (Brown), **Supp. VI:** 69

Dark Tower, The (MacNeice), **VII:** 407, 408

"Darkling Thrush, The" (Hardy), **VI:** 16

Darkness at Noon (Koestler), **V:** 49; **Supp. I:** 22, 24, 27, 28, 29–30, 32, 33; **Supp IV:** 74

Darkness Visible (Golding), **Supp. I: 83–86**

Darwin, Charles, **Supp. II:** 98, 100, 105–107, 119; **Supp. IV:** 6, 11, 460; **Supp. VII: 17–31**

Darwin, Erasmus, **Supp. II:** 106, 107; **Supp. III:** 360

"Darwin Among the Machines" (Butler), **Supp. II:** 98, 99

Darwin and Butler: Two Versions of Evolution (Willey), **Supp. II:** 103

"Darwin and Divinity" (Stephen), **V:** 284

Das Leben Jesu (tr. Eliot), **V:** 189, 200

Daughter of the East (Bhutto), **Supp. IV:** 455

Daughter-in-Law, The (Lawrence), **VII:** 119, 121

Daughters and Sons (Compton–Burnett), **VII:** 60, 63, 64–65

"Daughters of the Late Colonel, The" (Mansfield), **VII:** 175, 177, 178

"Daughters of the Vicar" (Lawrence), **VII:** 114

"Daughters of War" (Rosenberg), **VI:** 434

Davenant, Charles, **II:** 305

Davenant, Sir William, **I:** 327; **II:** 87, 185, 196, 259

Davenport, Arnold, **IV:** 227

David, Jacques–Louis, **Supp. IV:** 122

David and Bethsabe (Peele), **I:** 198, 206–207

"David Balfour" (Stevenson), *see Catriona*

David Copperfield (Dickens), **V:** xxi, 7, 41, 42, 44, 59–62, 63, 67, 71

David Lodge (Bergonzi), **Supp. IV:** 364

Davideis (Cowley), **II:** 195, 198, 202

Davidson, John, **V:** 318n

Davie, Donald, **VI:** 220; **Supp. IV:** 256; **Supp. VI: 105–118**

Davies, W. H., **Supp. III:** 398

Davis, Clyde Brion, **V:** 394

Davis, H., **III:** 15n, 35

Davy, Sir Humphry, **IV:** 200; **Supp. III:** 359–360

Dawkins, R. M., **VI:** 295, 303–304

"Dawn" (Brooke), **Supp. III:** 53

Dawn (Haggard), **Supp. III:** 213, 222

"Dawn at St. Patrick" (Mahon), **Supp. VI:** 174

"Dawn on the Somme" (Nichols), **VI:** 419

Dawson, Christopher, **III:** 227

Dawson, W. J., **IV:** 289, 291

"Day Dream, A" (Brontë), **V:** 142

Day Lewis, Cecil, **V:** 220, 234; **VI:** x, xxxiii, 454, **VII:** 382, 410; **Supp. III: 115–132**

Day of Creation, The (Ballard), **Supp. V:** 29

"Day of Days, At" (James), **VI:** 69

"Day of Forever, The" (Ballard), **Supp. V:** 26

Day of the Scorpion, The (Scott), **Supp. I:** 260, 267

"Day They Burned the Books, The" (Rhys), **Supp. II:** 401

"Day We Got Drunk on Cake, The" (Trevor), **Supp. IV:** 500

Day Will Dawn, The (Rattigan), **Supp. VII:** 311

Daydreamer, The (McEwan), **Supp. IV:** 390, 406–407

Daylight Moon and Other Poems, The (Murray), **Supp. VII:** 270, 271, 279–280, 281

Daylight on Saturday (Priestley), **VII:** 212, 217–218

Day's Work, The (Kipling), **VI:** 204

De arte graphica (tr. Dryden), **II:** 305

De augmentis scientiarium (Bacon), **I:** 260–261, 264; *see also Advancement of Learning, The*

de Beer, E. S., **II:** 276n, 287

De casibus virorum illustrium (Boccaccio), **I:** 57, 214

De doctrina christiana (Milton), **II:** 176

De genealogia deorum (Boccaccio), **I:** 266

"De Grey: A Romance" (James), **VI:** 25–26, 69

De Guiana Carmen Epicum (Chapman), **I:** 234

"De Gustibus—'" (Browning), **IV:** 356–357

De inventione (Cicero), **I:** 38–39

"De Jure Belli ac Pacis" (Hill), **Supp. V:** 192

de la Mare, Walter, **III:** 340, 345; **V:** 268, 274; **VII:** xiii; **Supp. III:** 398, 406

de Man, Paul, **Supp. IV:** 114, 115

De Profundis (Wilde), **V:** 416–417, 418, 419

De Quincey, Thomas, **III:** 338; **IV:** ix, xi–xii, xv, xviii, xxii, 49, 51, 137, **141–156,** 260, 261, 278; **V:** 353

De Quincey Memorials (ed. Japp), **IV:** 144, 155

"De Quincey on 'The Knocking at the Gate'" (Carnall), **IV:** 156

De rerum natura (tr. Evelyn), **II:** 275, 287

De sapientia veterum (Bacon), **I:** 235, 266–267, 272

de Selincourt, E., **IV:** 25

De tranquillitate animi (tr. Wyatt), **I:** 99

De tristitia Christi (More), **Supp. VII:** 245, 248

"De Wets Come to Kloof Grange, The" (Lessing), **Supp. I:** 240–241

Deacon Brodie (Stevenson), **V:** 396

"Dead, The" (Brooke), **VI:** 420; **Supp. III:** 57–58, 59

"Dead, The" (Joyce), **VII:** xiv, 44–45; **Supp. II:** 88; **Supp. IV:** 395, 396

"Dead and Alive" (Gissing), **V:** 437

Dead Babies (Amis), **Supp. IV:** 26, 29–31

"Dead Bride, The" (Hill), **Supp. V:** 189

"Dead Love" (Swinburne), **V:** 325, 331, 332

Dead Man Leading (Pritchett), **Supp. III:** 311, 312, 313, 314

"Dead Man's Dump" (Rosenberg), **VI:** 432, 434

"Dead on Arrival" (Kinsella), **Supp. V:** 261

Dead Secret, The (Collins), **Supp. VI:** 92, 95

"Dead–Beat, The" (Owen), **VI:** 451, 452

"Deadlock in Darwinism, The" (Butler), **Supp. II:** 108

Dealings with the Firm of Dombey and Son . . . (Dickens), *see Dombey and Son*

Dean, L. F., **I:** 269

"Dean Swift Watches Some Cows" (Ewart), **Supp. VII:** 40

Deane, Seamus, **Supp. IV:** 424

Dear Brutus (Barrie), **Supp. III:** 5, 6, 8, 9, **11–14,** 138

"Dear Bryan Wynter" (Graham), **Supp. VII:** 115

Dear Deceit, The (Brooke–Rose), **Supp. IV:** 98, 99, 102–103

Dearest Emmie (Hardy), **VI:** 20

"Death and Doctor Hornbook" (Burns), **III:** 319

"Death and Dying Words of Poor Mailie, The" (Burns), **IV:** 314, 315

"Death and the Professor" (Kinsella), **Supp. V:** 260

"Death Bed" (Kinsella), **Supp. V:** 267

"Death by Water" (Eliot), **VII:** 144–145

"Death Clock, The" (Gissing), **V:** 437

Death Comes as the End (Christie), **Supp. II:** 132–133

"Death in Bangor" (Mahon), **Supp. VI:** 177

"Death in Ilium" (Kinsella), **Supp. V:** 263

Death in the Clouds (Christie; U.S. title, *Death in the Air*), **Supp. II:** 131

"Death in the Desert, A" (Browning), **IV:** 358, 364, 367, 372

Death in Venice (Mann), **Supp. IV:** 397

Death of a Naturalist (Heaney), **Supp. II:** 268, **269–270,** 271; **Supp. IV:** 412

Death of a Salesman (Miller), **VI:** 286

"Death of a Scientific Humanist, The" (Friel), **Supp. V:** 114

"Death of a Tsotsi" (Paton), **Supp. II:** 345

"Death of a Tyrant" (Kinsella), **Supp. V:** 261

Death of an Expert Witness (James), **Supp. IV:** 319, 328–330

"Death of an Old Lady" (MacNeice), **VII:** 401

"Death of an Old Old Man" (Dahl), **Supp. IV:** 210

"Death of Bernard Barton" (FitzGerald), **IV:** 353

Death of Christopher Marlowe, The (Hotson), **I:** 275

Death of Cuchulain, The (Yeats), **VI:** 215, 222

"Death of King George, The" (Betjeman), **VII:** 367

Death of Oenone, The, Akbar's Dream, and Other Poems (Tennyson), **IV:** 338

Dorian Gray (Wilde), *see Picture of Dorian Gray, The*

"Dorinda's sparkling Wit, and Eyes" (Dorset), **II:** 262

Dorothy Wordsworth (Selincourt), **IV:** 143

Dorset, earl of (Charles Sackville), **II:** 255, **261–263**, 266, 268, 270–271

Dorset Farm Laborer Past and Present, The, (Hardy), **VI:** 20

Dostoyevsky, Fyodor, **Supp. IV:** 1, 139

Dostoevsky: The Making of a Novelist (Simmons), **V:** 46

Doting (Green), **Supp. II:** 263, 264

Double Falsehood, The (Theobald), **II:** 66, 87

"Double Life" (MacCaig), **Supp. VI:** 186

"Double Looking Glass, The" (Hope), **Supp. VII:** 159

Double Marriage, The (Fletcher and Massinger), **II:** 66

"Double Rock, The" (King), **Supp. VI:** 151

"Double Vision of Michael Robartes, The" (Yeats), **VI:** 217

Double–Dealer, The (Congreve), **II:** 338, 341–342, 350

Doublets: A Word–Puzzle (Carroll), **V:** 273

Doubtful Paradise (Friel), **Supp. V:** 115

Doughty, Charles, **Supp. II:** 294–295

Doughty, Oswald, **V:** xi, xxvii, 246, 297n, 307

Douglas, Gavin, **I:** 116–118; **III:** 311

Douglas, Keith, **VII:** xxii, 422, **440–444**

Douglas, Lord Alfred, **V:** 411, 416–417, 420

Douglas, Norman, **VI: 293–305**

Douglas Cause, The (Boswell), **III:** 247

Douglas Jerrold's Weekly (periodical), **V:** 144

"Dovecote" (McGuckian), **Supp. V:** 280

"Dover" (Auden), **VII:** 379

Dover Road, The (Milne), **Supp. V:** 299

"Down" (Graves), **VII:** 264

Down Among the Women (Weldon), **Supp. IV:** 524–525

Down and Out in Paris and London (Orwell), **VII:** xx, 275, 277; **Supp. IV:** 17

"Down at the Dump" (White), **Supp. I:** 143

Down by the River (O'Brien), **Supp. V:** 344–345

"Down by the Sally–Garden" (Yeats), **VII:** 368

Down from the Hill (Sillitoe), **Supp. V:** 411

"Down Kaunda Street" (Fuller), **Supp. VII:** 80

Down There on a Visit (Isherwood), **VII:** 315–316

Downfall and Death of King Oedipus, The (FitzGerald), **IV:** 353

Downs, Brian, **III:** 84, 93

"Downs, The" (Bridges), **VI:** 78

Downstairs (Churchill), **Supp. IV:** 180

Downstream (Kinsella), **Supp. V:** 259, 260, 261–262

"Downstream" (Kinsella), **Supp. V:** 262

Dowson, Ernest, **V:** 441; **VI:** 210

Doyle, Arthur Conan, **III:** 341, 345; **Supp. II:** 126, 127, **159–176**

Doyle, Roddy, **Supp. V: 77–93**

Dr. Goldsmith's Roman History Abridged by Himself . . . (Goldsmith), **III:** 191

Dr. Jekyll and Mr. Hyde (Stevenson), *see Strange Case of Dr. Jekyll and Mr. Hyde, The*

"Dr. Woolacott" (Forster), **VI:** 406

Dr. Wortle's School (Trollope), **V:** 100, 102

Drabble, Antonia, *see Byatt, A. S.*

Drabble, Margaret, **VI:** 247, 253, 268; **Supp. IV:** 141, **229–254**

Dracula (Stoker), **III:** 334, 342, 345; **Supp. III: 375–377,** 381, 382, 383, **386–390**

Dracula (films), **III:** 342; **Supp. III:** 375–377

"Dracula's Guest" (Stoker), **Supp. III:** 383, 385

Drafts and Fragments of Verse (Collins), **II:** 323n

Dragon of the Apocalypse (Carter), **VII:** 114

Drake, Nathan, **III:** 51

Drama in Muslin, A (Moore), **VI:** 86, 89, **90–91,** 98

"Drama of Exile, A" (Browning), **IV:** 313

Dramatic Character in the English Romantic Age (Donohue), **III:** 268n

Dramatic Idyls (Browning), **IV:** xxiii, 358, 374; **V:** xxiv

Dramatic Lyrics (Browning), **IV:** xx, 374

Dramatic Romances and Lyrics (Browning), **IV:** 374

Dramatic Works of Richard Brinsley Sheridan, The (ed. Price), **III:** 258

Dramatis Personae (Browning), **IV:** xxii, 358, 364, 374

Dramatis Personae (Yeats), **VI:** 317

Drapier's Letters, The (Swift), **III:** 20n 28, 31, 35

"Drawing you, heavy with sleep" (Warner), **Supp. VII:** 373

Drayton, Michael, **I:** 196, 278; **II:** 68 134, 138

"Dread of Height, The" (Thompson), **V: 444**

Dreadful Pleasures (Twitchell), **Supp. III:** 383

"Dream" (Heaney), **Supp. II:** 271

"Dream" (Kinsella), **Supp. V:** 273

"Dream, The" (Galsworthy), **VI:** 280

"Dream, The" (MacCaig), **Supp. VI:** 185

"Dream, The. A Song" (Behn), **Supp. III:** 37–38

Dream and Thing (Muir), **Supp. VI:** 208

Dream Children (Wilson), **Supp. VI: 308–309**

"Dream in Three Colours, A" (McGuckian), **Supp. V:** 285

Dream of Destiny, A (Bennett), **VI:** 262

"Dream of Eugene Aram, The Murderer, The" (Hood), **IV:** 256, 261–262, 264, 267; **Supp. III:** 378

Dream of Gerontius, The (Newman), **Supp. VII:** 293, 300, 301

Dream of John Ball, A (Morris), **V:** 301, 302–303, 305, 306

"Dream of Nourishment" (Smith), **Supp. II:** 466

"Dream of Private Clitus, The" (Jones), **Supp. VII:** 175

Dream of Scipio, The (Cicero), **IV:** 189

Dream of the Rood, The, **I:** 11

"Dream Play" (Mahon), **Supp. VI:** 178

"Dream Work" (Hope), **Supp. VII:** 155

"Dream–Fugue" (De Quincey), **IV:** 153–154

"Dream–Language of Fergus, The" (McGuckian), **Supp. V:** 285–286

Dreaming in Bronze (Thomas), **Supp. IV:** 490

"Dreaming Spires" (Campbell), **VII:** 430

"Dreams" (Spenser), **I:** 123

Dreams of Leaving (Hare), **Supp. IV:** 282, 289

"Dreams Old and Nascent" (Lawrence), **VII:** 118

"Dream–Tryst" (Thompson), **V:** 444

Drebbel, Cornelius, **I:** 268

Dressed as for a Tarot Pack (Redgrove), **Supp. VI:** 236

"Dressing" (Vaughan), **II:** 186

Dressing Up—Transvestism and Drag: The History of an Obsession (Ackroyd), **Supp. VI:** 3–4, 12

Dressmaker, The (Bainbridge), **Supp. VI:** 19–20, 24

Drew, Philip, **IV:** xiii, xxiv, 375

"Drink to Me Only with Thine Eyes" (Jonson), **I:** 346; **VI:** 16

Drinkers of Infinity (Koestler), **Supp. I:** 34, 34n

"Drinking" (Cowley), **II:** 198

Driver's Seat, The (Spark), **Supp. I:** 200, 209–210, 218n

"Driving Through Sawmill Towns" (Murray), **Supp. VII:** 271

Droe wit seisoen, 'n (Brink), **Supp. VI:** 50–51

"Droit de Seigneur: 1820" (Murphy), **Supp. V:** 321

Drought, The (Ballard), **Supp. V:** 24–25, 34

"Drowned Giant, The" (Ballard), **Supp. V:** 23

Drowned World, The (Ballard), **Supp. V:** 22–23, 24, 34

"Drummer Hodge" (Housman), **VI:** 161

Drummond of Hawthornden, William, **I:** 328, 349

Drums of Father Ned, The (O'Casey), **VII:** 10–11

Drums under the Windows (O'Casey), **VII:** 9, 12

"Dunciad Minimus" (Hope), **Supp. VII:** 161

Dunciad Minor: A Heroick Poem (Hope), **Supp. VII:** 161–163

Drunken Sailor, The (Cary), **VII:** 186, 191

"Dry Point" (Larkin), **Supp. I:** 277

Dry Salvages, The (Eliot), **V:** 241; **VII:** 143, 144, 152, 154, 155

Dry, White Season, A (Brink), **Supp. VI: 50–51**

215, 310, 367; **VI:** 207, 226; **VII:** 162–165; style, **II:** 173; **IV:** 323, 329; in drama, **VII:** 157–162; in poetry, **VII:** 144–157; **Supp. I:** 122–123; **Supp. II:** 151, 181, 420, 428, 487; **Supp. III:** 122; **Supp. IV:** 58, 100, 139, 142, 180, 249, 260, 330, 377, 558

"Elixir" (Murphy), **Supp. V:** 326

"Ella Wheeler Wilcox Woo, The" (Ewart), **Supp. VII:** 41

"Elvers, The" (Nicholson), **Supp. VI:** 214

"Ely Place" (Kinsella), **Supp. V:** 267

Elizabeth Alone (Trevor), **Supp. IV:** 509–510

Elizabeth and Essex (Strachey), **Supp. II:** 514–517

Elizabeth and Her German Garden (Forster), **VI:** 406

Elizabeth Cooper (Moore), **VI:** 96, 99

Elizabeth I, Queen of England, **Supp. IV:** 146

Elizabethan Drama and Shakespeare's Early Plays (Talbert), **I:** 224

"Elizas, The" (Gurney), **VI:** 425

"Ellen Orford" (Crabbe), **III:** 281

Ellen Terry and Bernard Shaw, a Correspondence (ed. St. John), **VI:** 130

Ellis, Annie Raine, **Supp. III:** 63, 65

Ellis, Havelock, **I:** 281

Ellis–Fermor, U. M., **I:** 284, 292

"Elm Tree, The" (Hood), **IV:** 261–262, 264

"Eloisa to Abelard" (Pope), **III:** 70, 75–76, 77; **V:** 319, 321

Elopement into Exile (Pritchett), *see Shirley Sanz*

Eloquence of the British Senate, The (Hazlitt), **IV:** 130, 139

Elton, Oliver, **III:** 51

Emancipated, The (Gissing), **V:** 437

"Embankment, The" (Hulme), **Supp. VI:** 134, 136

Embarrassments (James), **VI:** 49, 67

Embers (Beckett), **Supp. I:** 58

Emblem Hurlstone (Hall), **Supp. VI:** 129–130

"Emerald Dove, The" (Murray), **Supp. VII:** 281

Emerson, Ralph Waldo, **IV:** xx, 54, 81, 240; **V:** xxv

Emigrants, The (Lamming), **Supp. IV:** 445

Emilia in England (Meredith), *see Sandra Belloni*

Emilie de Coulanges (Edgeworth), **Supp. III:** 158

Emily Brontë: A Biography (Gérin), **V:** 153

Eminent Victorians (Wilson), **Supp. VI:** 305

Eminent Victorians (Strachey), **V:** 13, 157, 170; **Supp. II:** 498, 499, 503–511

Emma (Austen), **IV:** xvii, 108, 109, 111, 112, 113, 114, 115, 117, 119, 120, 122; **VI:** 106; **Supp. IV:** 154, 236

Empedocles on Etna (Arnold), **IV:** 231; **V:** xxi, 206, 207, 209, 210, 211, 216

"Emperor Alexander and Capo d'Istria" (Landor), **IV:** 92

"Emperor and the Little Girl, The" (Shaw), **VI:** 120

Emperor Constantine, The (Sayers), **Supp. III:** 336, 350

"Emperor's Tomb Found in China" (Fuller), **Supp. VII:** 80

Empire of the Sun (Ballard), **Supp. V:** 19, 29–30, 31, 35

Empire State (Bateman), **Supp. V:** 88

Empson, William, **I:** 282; **II:** 124, 130; **V:** 367, 381; **Supp. II:** 179–197

"Empty Birdhouse, The" (Highsmith), **Supp. V:** 180

Empty Purse, The (Meredith), **V:** 223, 234

"Enallos and Cymodameia" (Landor), **IV:** 96

Enchafèd Flood, The (Auden), **VII:** 380, 394

Enchanted Isle, The (Dryden), **I:** 327

"Enchantment of Islands" (Brown), **Supp. VI:** 61

Enchantress, The, and Other Poems (Browning), **IV:** 321

Encounter, **Supp. II:** 491

Encounters (Bowen), **Supp. II:** 79, 81

Encyclopaedia Britannica, **Supp. III:** 171

"End, The" (Beckett), **Supp. I:** 50

"End, The" (Milne), **Supp. V:** 303

"End, The" (Owen), **VI:** 449

"End of a Journey" (Hope), **Supp. VII:** 156–157

End of a War, The (Read), **VI:** 436, 437

End of the Affair, The (Greene), **Supp. I:** 2, 8, 12–13, 14

End of the Beginning, The (O'Casey), **VII:** 12

End of the Chapter (Galsworthy), **VI:** 275, 282

"End of the City" (Fuller), **Supp. VII:** 69

"End of the Relationship, The" (Self), **Supp. V:** 403

"End of the Tether, The" (Conrad), **VI:** 148

Enderby Outside (Burgess), **Supp. I:** 189, 194–195

Enderby's Dark Lady; or, No End to Enderby (Burgess), **Supp. I:** 189

Endgame (Beckett), **Supp. I:** 49, 51, 52, 53, 56–57, 62

Ending in Earnest (West), **Supp. III:** 438

Ending Up (Amis), **Supp. II:** 18

Endimion (Lyly), **I:** 202

Endless Night (Christie), **Supp. II:** 125, 130, 132, 135

Ends and Means (Huxley), **VII:** xvii 205

Endymion (Disraeli), **IV:** xxiii, 294, 295, 296, 306, 307, 308; **V:** xxiv

"Endymion" (Keats), **III:** 174, 338; **IV:** x, xvii, 205, 211, 214, 216–217, 218, 222–224, 227, 229, 230, 233, 235

"Enemies, The" (Jennings), **Supp. V:** 211

Enemies of Promise (Connolly), **VI:** 363; **Supp. III:** 95, 96, 97, 98, 100–102

"Enemy, The" (Naipaul), **Supp. I:** 386n

"Enemy Dead, The" (Gutteridge), **VII:** 433

Enemy in the Blanket, The (Burgess), **Supp. I:** 187–188

"Enemy Interlude" (Lewis), **VII:** 71

Enemy of the People, An (Ibsen), **VI:** ix

Enemy of the Stars, The (Lewis), **VII:** 72, 73, 74–75

Enemy Within, The (Friel), **Supp. V:** 115–116

Enemy's Country, The: Word, Contexture, and Other Circumstances of Language (Hill), **Supp. V:** 196, 201

England (Davie), **Supp. VI:** 111–112

"England" (Stevenson), **Supp. VI:** 255–256, 264

"England" (Thomas), **Supp. III:** 404

England and the Italian Question (Arnold), **V:** 216

England in the Age of Wycliffe (Trevelyan), **VI:** 385–386

England Made Me (Greene; U.S. title, *The Shipwrecked*), **Supp. I:** 6, 7

"England, My England" (Lawrence) **VII:** xv, 114

England, My England, and Other Stories (Lawrence), **VII:** 114

England Under Queen Anne (Trevelyan), **VI:** 391–393

England Under the Stuarts (Trevelyan), **VI:** 386

England Your England (Orwell), **VII:** 282

"England's Answer" (Kipling), **VI:** 192

England's Helicon, **I:** 291

"England's Ireland" (Hare), **Supp. IV:** 281

England's Pleasant Land (Forster), **VI:** 411

"English and the Afrikaans Writer" (Brink), **Supp. VI:** 48–49

English, David, **Supp. IV:** 348

English Bards and Scotch Reviewers (Byron), **IV:** x, xvi, 129, 171, 192

English Bible, **I:** 370–388; list of versions, **I:** 387

"English Climate" (Warner), **Supp. VII:** 380

English Comic Characters, The (Priestley), **VII:** 211

English Eccentrics, The (Sitwell), **VII:** 127

English Folk–Songs (ed. Barrett), **V:** 263n

English Historical Review, **VI:** 387

English Hours (James), **VI:** 46, 67

English Humour (Priestley), **VII:** 213

English Humourists of the Eighteenth Century, The (Thackeray), **III:** 124, 146n; **V:** 20, 31, 38

English Journey (Bainbridge), **Supp. VI:** 22–23

English Journey (Priestley), **VII:** 212, 213–214

English Literature: A Survey for Students (Burgess), **Supp. I:** 189

English Literature and Society in the Eighteenth Century (Stephen), **III:** 41; **V:** 290

"English Literature and the Small Coterie" (Kelman), **Supp. V:** 257

English Literature, 1815–1832 (ed. Jack), **IV:** 40, 140

English Literature in Our Time and the University (Leavis), **VII:** 169, 235, 236–237, 253

English Literature in the Sixteenth Century, Excluding Drama (Lewis), **Supp. III:** 249, 264

"English Mail–Coach, The" (De Quincey), **IV:** 149, 153, 155

English Mirror, The (Whetstone), **I:** 282

English Music (Ackroyd), **Supp. VI:** 9–10, 11, 12

English Novel, The (Ford), **VI:** 322, 332

English Novel, The: A Short Critical History (Allen), **V:** 219

English Novelists (Bowen), **Supp. II:** 91–92

English Pastoral Poetry (Empson), *see Some Versions of Pastoral*

English People, The (Orwell), **VII:** 282

English Poems (Blunden), **VI:** 429

"English Poet, An" (Pater), **V:** 356, 357

English Poetry (Bateson), **IV:** 217, 323n, 339

English Poetry and the English Language (Leavis), **VII:** 234

English Poetry of the First World War (Owen), **VI:** 453

English Poets (Browning), **IV:** 321

English Prisons under Local Government (Webb), **VI:** 129

English Protestant's Plea, The (King), **Supp. VI:** 152

"English Renaissance of Art, The" (Wilde), **V:** 403–404

English Review (periodical), **VI:** xi–xii, 294, 323–324; **VII:** 89

English Revolution, 1688–1689 (Trevelyan), **VI:** 391

"English School, An" (Kipling), **VI:** 201

English Seamen (Southey and Bell), **IV:** 71

English Social History: A Survey of Six Centuries (Trevelyan), **VI:** xv, 393–394

English Songs of Italian Freedom (Trevelyan), **V:** 227

English South African's View of the Situation, An (Schreiner), **Supp. II:** 453

English Through Pictures (Richards), **Supp. II:** 425, 430

English Town in the Last Hundred Years (Betjeman), **VII:** 360

English Traits (Emerson), **IV:** 54

English Utilitarians, The (Stephen), **V:** 279, 288–289

"English Wife, The" (Ewart), **Supp. VII:** 36

English Without Tears (Rattigan), **Supp. VII:** 311

Englishman (periodical), **III:** 7, 50, 53

"Englishman in Italy, The" (Browning), **IV:** 368

Englishman in Patagonia, An (Pilkington), **Supp. IV:** 164

Englishman Looks at the World, An (Wells), **VI:** 244

Englishman's Home, An (du Maurier), **Supp. III:** 147, 148

"Englishmen and Italians" (Trevelyan), **V:** 227; **VI:** 388n

Englishness of English Literature, The (Ackroyd), **Supp. VI:** 12

"Enigma, The" (Fowles), **Supp. I:** 303–304

Ennui (Edgeworth), **Supp. III:** 154, 156, **158–160**

Enoch Arden (Tennyson), **IV:** xxii, 388; **V:** 6n

"Enoch Soames" (Beerbohm), **Supp. II:** 56

Enormous Crocodile, The (Dahl), **Supp. IV:** 207

"Enormous Space, The" (Ballard), **Supp. V:** 33

Enough Is as Good as a Feast (Wager), **I:** 213

Enough of Green, (Stevenson), **Supp. VI:** 260

Enquiry Concerning Human Understanding, An (Hume), **Supp. III:** 231, 238, 243–244

Enquiry Concerning Political Justice, An (Godwin), **IV:** xv, 181; **Supp. III:** 370

Enquiry Concerning the Principles of Morals, An (Hume), **Supp. III:** 231, 238, 244

Enquiry into the Causes of the Late Increase of Robbers (Fielding), **III:** 104

Enquiry into the Occasional Conformity of Dissenters . . . . An (Defoe), **III:** 12

Enquiry into the Present State of Polite Learning in Europe, An (Goldsmith), **III:** 179, 191

Enright, D. J., **Supp. IV:** 256, 354

"Enter a Cloud" (Graham), **Supp. VII:** 103

"Enter a Dragoon" (Hardy), **VI:** 22

Enter a Free Man (Stoppard), **Supp. I:** 437, 439–440, 445

"Enter One in Sumptuous Armour" (Lowry), **Supp. III:** 285

Entertainer, The (Osborne), **Supp. I:** 332–333, 336–337, 339

Entertaining Mr. Sloane (Orton), **Supp. V:** 364, 367, 370–371, 372, 373–374

Entertainment (Middleton), **II:** 3

"Entertainment for David Wright on His Being Sixty, An" (Graham), **Supp. VII:** 116

"Entire Fabric, The" (Kinsella), **Supp. V:** 268

"Entrance" (Kinsella), **Supp. V:** 271

"Entreating of Sorrow" (Ralegh), **I:** 147–148

"Envoy Extraordinary" (Golding), **Supp. I:** 75, 82, 83

"Eolian Harp, The" (Coleridge), **IV:** 46

Epicoene (Johnson), **I:** 339, 341

"Epicure, The" (Cowley), **II:** 198

"Epicurus, Leontion and Ternissa" (Landor), **IV:** 94, 96–97

Epigram CXX (Jonson), **I:** 347

Epigrammata (More), **Supp. VII:** 234, 236–237

Epigrammatum sacrorum liber (Crashaw), **II:** 179, 201

Epilogue (Graves), **VII:** 261

Epilogue to the Satires (Pope), **III:** 74, 78

"Epipsychidion" (Shelley), **IV:** xviii, 204, 208; **VI:** 401

"Epistle, An: Edward Sackville to Venetia Digby" (Hope), **Supp. VII:** 159

"Epistle from Holofernes, An" (Hope), **Supp. VII:** 157

Epistle to a Canary (Browning), **IV:** 321

Epistle to a Lady . . . , An (Swift), **III:** 36

Epistle to Augustus (Pope), **II:** 196

Epistle to Cobham, An (Pope), *see Moral Essays*

"Epistle to Davie" (Burns), **III:** 316

Epistle to Dr. Arbuthnot (Pope), **III:** 71, 74–75, 78

"Epistle to Henry Reynolds" (Drayton), **I:** 196

Epistle to Her Grace Henrietta . . . , An (Gay), **III:** 67

"Epistle to John Hamilton Reynolds" (Keats), **IV:** 221

Epistle to . . . Lord Carteret, An (Swift), **III:** 35

"Epistle to Mr. Dryden, An, . . ." (Wycherley), **II:** 322

Epistle to the . . . Earl of Burlington, An (Pope), *see Moral Essays*

Epistle upon an Epistle, An (Swift), **III:** 35

Epistles to the King and Duke (Wycherley), **II:** 321

Epistola adversus Jovinianum (St. Jerome), **I:** 35

Epitaph For A Spy (Ambler), **Supp. IV:** 8

"Epitaph for Anton Schmidt" (Gunn), **Supp. IV:** 264

Epitaph for George Dillon (Osborne), **Supp. I:** 329–330, 333

"Epitaph on a Fir–Tree" (Murphy), **Supp. V:** 317–318

"Epitaph on a Jacobite" (Macaulay), **IV:** 283

"Epitaph on an Army of Mercenaries" (Housman), **VI:** 161, 415–416

Epitaph on George Moore (Morgan), **VI:** 86

"Epitaph on the Admirable Dramaticke Poet, W. Shakespeare, An" (Milton), **II:** 175

"Epitaph on the Lady Mary Villers" (Carew), **II:** 224

"Epitaphs" (Warner), **Supp. VII:** 371

Epitaphs and Occasions (Fuller), **Supp. VII:** 72

"Epitaphs for Soldiers" (Fuller), **Supp. VII:** 72

Epitaphium Damonis (Milton), **II:** 175

"Epithalamion" (Hopkins), **V:** 376, 377

Epithalamion (Spenser), **I:** 130–131; *see also Amoretti and Epithalamion*

"Epithalamion for Gloucester" (Lydgate), **I:** 58

"Epithalamion Thamesis" (Spenser), **I:** 123

"Epithalamium" (Motion), **Supp. VII:** 266

Epoch and Artist (Jones), **Supp. VII:** 168, 170, 171

Epping Hunt, The (Hood), **IV:** 256, 257, 267

Farina (Meredith), **V:** 225, 234

Farm, The (Storey), **Supp. I:** 408, 411, 412, 414

Farmer Giles of Ham (Tolkien), **Supp. II:** 521

"Farmer's Ingle, The" (Fergusson), **III:** 318

Farmer's Year, A (Haggard), **Supp. III:** 214

Farnham, William, **I:** 214

Farquhar, George, **II:** 334–335, 351–365

Farrell, Barry, **Supp. IV:** 223

Farther Adventures of Robinson Crusoe, The (Defoe), **III:** 13

Farthing Hall (Walpole and Priestley), **VII:** 211

Fascinating Foundling, The (Shaw), **VI:** 129

"Fashionable Authoress, The" (Thackeray), **V:** 22, 37

Fashionable Lover, The (Cumberland), **III:** 257

Fasti (Ovid), **II:** 110n

"Fat Contributor Papers, The" (Thackeray), **V:** 25, 38

Fat Woman's Joke, The (Weldon), **Supp. IV:** 521, 522–524, 525

"Fatal Boots, The" (Thackeray), **V:** 21, 37

Fatal Gift, The (Waugh), **Supp. VI:** 276

"Fatal Sisters, The" (Gray), **III:** 141

Fate of Homo Sapiens, The (Wells), **VI:** 228

"Fates, The" (Owen), **VI:** 449

Father and His Fate, A (Compton–Burnett), **VII:** 61, 63

"Father and Lover" (Rossetti), **V:** 260

"Father and Son" (Butler), **Supp. II:** 97

Father Brown stories (Chesterton), **VI:** 338

Father Damien (Stevenson), **V:** 383, 390, 396

"Father Mat" (Kavanagh), **Supp. VII:** 194

Fathers and Sons (tr. Friel), **Supp. V:** 124

Father's Comedy, The (Fuller), **Supp. VII:** 74, 75–76, 77, 81

"Fathers, Sons and Lovers" (Thomas), **Supp. IV:** 493

Fathers, The; or, The Good–Natur'd Man (Fielding), **III:** 98, 105

"Fatigue, The" (Jones), **Supp. VII:** 175

Faulkner, Charles, **VI:** 167

Faust (Goethe), **III:** 344; **IV:** xvi, xix, 179

"Faustine" (Swinburne), **V:** 320

Faustus and the Censor (Empson), **Supp. II:** 180, 196–197

Faustus Kelly (O'Nolan), **Supp. II:** 323, 335–337

Fawkes, F., **III:** 170n

Fawn, The (Marston), **II:** 30, 40

Fay Weldon's Wicked Fictions (Weldon), **Supp. IV:** 522, 531

"Fear" (Collins), **III:** 166, 171, 336

"Fear, A" (Jennings), **Supp. V:** 214

Fear, The (Keneally), **Supp. IV:** 345

Fears in Solitude . . . (Coleridge), **IV:** 55

Feast of Bacchus, The (Bridges), **VI:** 83

"Feast of Famine, The" (Stevenson), **V:** 396

"Feastday of Peace, The" (McGuckian), **Supp. V:** 291

"February" (Hughes), **Supp. I:** 342

"Feeding Ducks" (MacCaig), **Supp. VI:** 187

Feeding the Mind (Carroll), **V:** 274

"Feeling into Words" (Heaney), **Supp. II:** 272, 273

Felicia's Journey (Trevor), **Supp. IV:** 505, 517

"Félise" (Swinburne), **V:** 321

Felix Holt, The Radical (Eliot), **V:** xxiii, 195–196, 199, 200

"Felix Randal" (Hopkins), **V:** 368–369, 371

"Fellow–Townsmen" (Hardy), **VI:** 22

Fellowship of the Ring (Tolkien), **Supp. II:** 519

Female Friends (Weldon), **Supp. IV:** 534–535

Female God, The (Rosenberg), **VI:** 432

"Female Vagrant, The" (Wordsworth), **IV:** 5

"Feminine Christs, The" (McGuckian), **Supp. V:** 290

Feminine Mystique, The (Freidan), **Supp. IV:** 232

Fen (Churchill), **Supp. IV:** 179, 188, 191–192, 198

Fénelon, François, **III:** 95, 99

Fenton, James, **Supp. IV:** 450

Fenwick, Isabella, **IV:** 2

Ferdinand Count Fathom (Smollett), **III:** 153, 158

Ferguson, Helen, *see* Kavan, Anna

Fergusson, Robert, **III:** 312–313, 316, 317, 318

Ferishtah's Fancies (Browning), **IV:** 359, 374

Fermor, Patrick Leigh, **Supp. IV:** 160

"Fern Hill" (Thomas), **Supp. I:** 177, 178, 179

Fernandez, Ramon, **V:** 225–226

Ferrex and Porrex (Norton and Sackville), *see* Gorboduc

Festival at Farbridge (Priestley), **VII:** 219–210

"Festubert: The Old German Line" (Blunden), **VI:** 428

"Fetching Cows" (MacCaig), **Supp. VI:** 188

"Fetish" (Harris), **Supp. V:** 138

Feuerbach, Ludwig, **IV:** 364

"Feuille d'Album" (Mansfield), **VII:** 364

"Few Crusted Characters, A" (Hardy), **VI:** 20, 22

Few Green Leaves, A (Pym), **Supp. II:** 370, 382–384

Few Late Chrysanthemums, A (Betjeman), **VII:** 369–371

Few Sighs from Hell, A (Bunyan), **II:** 253

Fichte, Johann Gottlieb, **V:** 348

Ficino (philosopher), **I:** 237

Fiction and the Reading Public (Leavis), **VII:** 233, 234

Fiction–Makers, The (Stevenson), **Supp. VI:** 262–263

"Fiction: The House Party" (Ewart), **Supp. VII:** 42

"Fictions" (Reid), **Supp. VII:** 334

"Fiddler of the Reels, The" (Hardy), **VI:** 22

Field, Isobel, **V:** 393, 397

Field, Nathaniel, **II:** 45, 66, 67

Field of Waterloo, The (Scott), **IV:** 38

Field Work (Heaney), **Supp. II:** 268, 275–277

Fielding, Henry, **II:** 273; **III:** 62, 84, 94–106, 148, 150; **IV:** 106, 189; **V:** 52, 287; **Supp. II:** 57, 194, 195; **Supp. IV:** 244

Fielding, K. J., **V:** 43, 72

Fifer, C. N., **III:** 249

Fifine at the Fair (Browning), **IV:** 358, 367, 374

Fifteen Dead (Kinsella), **Supp. V:** 267

"Fifth Philosopher's Song" (Huxley), **VII:** 199

Fifth, Queen, The (Ford), **VI:** 324

Fifth Queen Crowned, The (Ford), **VI:** 325, 326

"Fifties, The" (Fuller), **Supp. VII:** 73

"Fifty Faggots" (Thomas), **Supp. III:** 403

Fifty Years of English Literature, 1900–1950 (Scott-James), **VI:** 21

"Fight, The" (Thomas), **Supp. I:** 181

Fight for Barbara, The (Lawrence), **VII:** 120

"Fight to a Finish" (Sassoon), **VI:** 430

Fighting Terms (Gunn), **Supp. IV:** 256, 257–259

"Figure in the Carpet, The" (James), **VI:** 69

"Figures on the Freize" (Reid), **Supp. VII:** 330

File on a Diplomat (Brink), **Supp. VI:** 46

Filibusters in Barbary (Lewis), **VII:** 83

Fille du Policeman (Swinburne), **V:** 325, 333

Film (Beckett), **Supp. I:** 51, 59, 60

Filostrato (Boccaccio), **I:** 30

Filthy Lucre (Bainbridge), **Supp. VI:** 23

Final Passage, The (Phillips), **Supp. V:** 380–383

"Final Problem, The" (Doyle), **Supp. II:** 160, 172–173

Finden's Byron Beauties (Finden), **V:** 111

Findlater, Richard, **VII:** 8

Finer Grain, The (James), **VI:** 67

Finished (Haggard), **Supp. III:** 214

"Finistére" (Kinsella), **Supp. V:** 268

Finnegans Wake (Joyce), **VII:** 42, 46, 52–54; critical studies, **VII:** 58; **Supp. III:** 108

Firbank, Ronald, **VII:** 132, 200; **Supp. II:** 199–223

"Fire and Ice" (Kinsella), **Supp. V:** 261

Fire and the Sun, The: Why Plato Banished the Artists (Murdoch), **Supp. I:** 230, 232

"Fire and the Tide" (Stevenson), **Supp. VI:** 260

Fire of the Lord, The (Nicholson), **Supp. VI:** 219

Fire on the Mountain (Desai), **Supp. V:** 53, 55, 64–65, 73

Greene, Robert, **I**: 165, 220, 275, 286, 296, 322; **II**: 3

Greenlees, Ian Gordon, **VI**: xxxiii

"Greenshank" (MacCaig), **Supp. VI**: 192

Greenvoe (Brown), **Supp. VI**: 64, **65–66**

"Greenwich—Whitebait" (Thackeray), **V**: 38

Greenwood, Edward Baker, **VII**: xix, xxxvii

Greenwood, Frederick, **V**: 1

Greer, Germaine, **Supp. IV**: 436

Greg, W. R., **V**: 5, 7, 15

Greg, W. W., **I**: 279

Gregory, Lady Augusta, **VI**: 210, 218, **307–312, 314–316,** 317–318; **VII**: 1, 3, 42

Gregory, Sir Richard, **VI**: 233

Greiffenhagen, Maurice, **VI**: 91

Gremlins, The (Dahl), **Supp. IV**: 202, 211–212

"Grenadier" (Housman), **VI**: 160

Grenfell, Julian, **VI**: xvi, 417–418, 420

"Gretchen" (Gissing), **V**: 437

"Gretna Green" (Behan), **Supp. II**: 64

Greuze, Jean-Baptiste, **Supp. IV**: 122

Greuze: The Rise and Fall of an Eighteenth Century Phenomenon (Brookner), **Supp. IV**: 122

Greville, Fulke, **I**: 160, 164; **Supp. IV**: 256

Grey Area (Self), **Supp. V**: 402–404

Grey Eminence (Huxley), **VII**: 205

Grey of Fallodon (Trevelyan), **VI**: 383, 391

"Grey Woman, The" (Gaskell), **V**: 15

Greybeards at Play (Chesterton), **VI**: 336

Greyhound for Breakfast (Kelman), **Supp. V**: 242, 249–250

"Greyhound for Breakfast" (Kelman), **Supp. V**: 250

"Grief" (Browning), **IV**: 313, 318

Grief Observed, A (Lewis), **Supp. III**: 249

"Grief on the Death of Prince Henry, A" (Tourneur), **II**: 37, 41

Grierson, Herbert J. C., **II**: 121, 130, 196, 200, 202, 258

Grigson, Geoffrey, **IV**: 47; **VII**: xvi

Grim Smile of the Five Towns, The (Bennett), **VI**: 250, 253–254

Grimus (Rushdie), **Supp. IV**: 435, 438–439, 443, 450

Gris, Juan, **Supp. IV**: 81

Groatsworth of Wit, A (Greene), **I**: 275, 276

Grosskurth, Phyllis, **V**: xxvii

Grote, George, **IV**: 289

Group of Noble Dames, A (Hardy), **VI**: 20, 22

"Grove, The" (Muir), **Supp. VI**: 206

"Growing, Flying, Happening" (Reid), **Supp. VII**: 328

"Growing Old" (Arnold), **V**: 203

Growing Pains: The Shaping of a Writer (du Maurier), **Supp. III**: 135, 142, 144

Growing Points (Jennings), **Supp. V**: 217

Growing Rich (Weldon), **Supp. IV**: 531, 533

Growth of Love, The (Bridges), **VI**: 81, 83

Growth of Plato's Ideal Theory, The (Frazer), **Supp. III**: 170–171

Grünewald, Mathias, **Supp. IV**: 85

Gryffydh, Jane, **IV**: 159

Gryll Grange (Peacock), **IV**: xxii, 166–167, 170

Grylls, R. Glynn, **V**: 247, 260; **VII**: xvii, xxxviii

Guardian (periodical), **III**: 46, 49, 50

Guardian, The (Cowley), **II**: 194, 202

Guarini, Guarino, **II**: 49–50

Guerrillas (Naipaul), **Supp. I**: 396–397

Guest of Honour, A (Gordimer), **Supp. II**: 229–230, 231

Guide Through the District of the Lakes in the North of England, A (Wordsworth), **IV**: 25

Guide to Kulchur (Pound), **VI**: 333

Guido della Colonna, **I**: 57

Guild of St. George, The, **V**: 182

Guillaume de Deguilleville, **I**: 57

Guillaume de Lorris, **I**: 71

"Guilt and Sorrow" (Wordsworth), **IV**: 5, 45

"Guinevere" (Tennyson), **IV**: 336–337, 338

Guise, The (Marlowe), *see Massacre at Paris, The*

Guise, The (Webster), **II**: 68, 85

Gulliver's Travels (Swift), **II**: 261; **III**: 11, 20, **23–26,** 28, 35; **VI**: 121–122; **Supp. IV**: 502

Gun for Sale, A (Greene; U.S. title, *This Gun for Hire*), **Supp. I**: 3, 6–7, 10

Gunn, Ander, **Supp. IV**: 265

Gunn, Thom, **Supp. IV**: **255–279**

Guns of Navarone, The (film, Ambler), **Supp. IV**: 3

Gurdjieff, Georges I., **Supp. IV**: 1, 5

Gurney, Ivor, **VI**: 416, **425–427**

Gutch, J. M., **IV**: 78, 81

Gutteridge, Bernard, **VII**: 422, 432–433

Guy Domville (James), **VI**: 39

Guy Mannering (Scott), **IV**: xvii, 31–32, 38

Guy of Warwick (Lydgate), **I**: 58

Guy Renton (Waugh), **Supp. VI**: 274–275

Guyana Quartet (Harris), **Supp. V**: 132, 133, 135

Guzman Go Home and Other Stories (Sillitoe), **Supp. V**: 410

"Gym" (Murphy), **Supp. V**: 328

Gypsies Metamorphos'd (Jonson), **II**: 111n

"Gyrtt in my giltetesse gowne" (Surrey), **I**: 115

"Healthy Landscape with Dormouse" (Warner), **Supp. VII**: 380

"Hee–Haw" (Warner), **Supp. VII**: 380

"House Grown Silent, The" (Warner), **Supp. VII**: 371

H.G. Wells and His Critics (Raknem), **VI**: 228, 245, 246

H. G. Wells: His Turbulent Life and Times (Dickson), **VI**: 246

H. G. Wells: The Critical Heritage (ed. Parrinder), **VI**: 246

Ha! Ha! Among the Trumpets (Lewis), **VII**: 447, 448

Habermas, Jürgen, **Supp. IV**: 112

Habington, William, **II**: 222, 237, 238

Habit of Loving, The (Lessing), **Supp. I**: 244

"Habit of Perfection, The" (Hopkins), **V**: 362, 381

Hadjinicolaou, Nicos, **Supp. IV**: 90

"Hag, The" (Herrick), **II**: 111

Haggard, H. Rider, **Supp. III**: **211–228; Supp. IV**: 201, 484

Haight, Gordon, **V**: 199, 200, 201

Hail and Farewell (Moore), **VI**: xii, 85, 88, 97, 99

"Hailstones" (Heaney), **Supp. II**: 280

Hakluyt, Richard, **I**: 150, 267; **III**: 7

Hale, Kathleen, **Supp. IV**: 231

"Half-a-Crown's Worth of Cheap Knowledge" (Thackeray), **V**: 22, 37

Halidon Hill (Scott), **IV**: 39

Halifax, marquess of, **III**: 38, 39, 40, 46

Hall, Donald, **Supp. IV**: 256

Hall, Edward, **II**: 43

Hall, Joseph, **II**: 25–26, 81; **IV**: 286

Hall, Radclyffe, **VI**: 411; **Supp. VI**: **119–132**

Hall, Samuel (pseud., O'Nolan), **Supp. II**: 322

Hall of Healing (O'Casey), **VII**: 11–12

Hall of the Saurians (Redgrove), **Supp. VI**: 236

Hallam, Arthur, **IV**: 234, 235, 328–336, 338

Hallam, Henry, **IV**: 283

Haller, Albrecht von, **III**: 88

Halloran's Little Boat (Keneally), **Supp. IV**: 348

"Hallowe'en" (Burns), **III**: 315

Hallowe'en Party (Christie), **Supp. II**: 125, 134

Ham Funeral, The (White), **Supp. I**: 131, 134, 149, 150

"Hamadryad, The" (Landor), **IV**: 96

Hamburger, Michael, **Supp. V**: 199

Hamilton, Sir George Rostrevor, **IV**: xxiv

Hamlet (early version), **I**: 212, 221, 315

Hamlet (Shakespeare), **I**: 188, 280, 313, 315–316; **II**: 29, 36, 71, 75, 84; **III**: 170, 234; **V**: 328; **Supp. IV**: 63, 149, 283, 295

"Hamlet, Princess of Denmark" (Beerbohm), **Supp. II**: 55

Hammerton, Sir John, **V**: 393, 397

Hammett, Dashiell, **Supp. II**: 130, 132

Hampden, John, **V**: 393, 395

"Hampstead: the Horse Chestnut Trees" (Gunn), **Supp. IV**: 270–271

Hampton, Christopher, **Supp. IV**: 281

"Hand, The" (Highsmith), **Supp. V**: 179–180

"Hand and Soul" (Rossetti), **V**: 236, 320

Hand of Ethelberta, The: A Comedy in Chapters (Hardy), **VI**: 4, 6, 20

"Hand of Solo, A" (Kinsella), **Supp. V**: 267, 274

"Hand that signed the paper, The" (Thomas), **Supp. I**: 174

Heart and Science (Collins), **Supp. VI:** 102–103

"Heart, II, The" (Thompson), **V:** 443

"Heart Knoweth Its Own Bitterness, The" (Rossetti), **V:** 253–254

Heart of Darkness (Conrad), **VI:** 135, **136–139,** 172; **Supp. IV:** 189, 250, 403

"Heart of John Middleton, The" (Gaskell), **V:** 15

Heart of Mid–Lothian, The (Scott), **IV:** xvii, 30, 31, 33–34, 35, 36, 39; **V:** 5

Heart of the Country, The (Weldon), **Supp. IV:** 526–528

Heart of the Matter, The (Greene), **Supp. I:** 2, 8, 11–12, 13

Heart to Heart (Rattigan), **Supp. VII:** 320

Heartbreak House (Shaw), **V:** 423; **VI:** viii, xv, 118, **120–121,** 127, 129

Heartland (Harris), **Supp. V:** 135, 136

Hearts and Lives of Men, The (Weldon), **Supp. IV:** 536

"Heart's Chill Between" (Rossetti), **V:** 249, 252

Heat and Dust (Jhabvala), **Supp. V:** 224, 230, 231–232, 238

Heat of the Day, The (Bowen), **Supp. II:** 77, 78, 79, 93, 95

"Heather Ale" (Stevenson), **V:** 396

Heather Field, The (Martyn), **IV:** 87, 95

"Heaven" (Brooke), **Supp. III:** 56, 60

Heaven and Earth (Byron), **IV:** 178, 193

Heavenly Foot–man, The (Bunyan), **II:** 246, 253

"Heber" (Smith), **Supp. II:** 466

Hebert, Ann Marie, **Supp. IV:** 523

Hebrew Melodies, Ancient and Modern . . . (Byron), **IV:** 192

Hecatommitthi (Cinthio), **I:** 316

Hedda Gabler (Ibsen), **Supp. IV:** 163, 286

"Hedgehog" (Muldoon), **Supp. IV:** 414

"Hee–Haw" (Warner), **Supp. VII:** 380

Heel of Achilles, The (Koestler), **Supp. I:** 36

Hegel, Georg Wilhelm Friedrich, **Supp. II:** 22

"Height–ho on a Winter Afternoon" (Davie), **Supp. VI:** 107–108

Heilbrun, Carolyn G., **Supp. IV:** 336

Heine, Heinrich, **IV:** xviii, 296

Heinemann, William, **VII:** 91

"Heiress, The" (McGuckian), **Supp. V:** 282

Heit, S. Mark, **Supp. IV:** 339

"Hélas" (Wilde), **V:** 401

Helen (Scott), **Supp. III:** 151, **165–166**

Helena (Waugh), **VII:** 292, 293–294, 301

Hélène Fourment in a Fur Coat (Rubens), **Supp. IV:** 89

Hellas (Shelley), **IV:** xviii, 206, 208

Hellenics, The (Landor), **IV:** 96, 100

Héloise and Abélard (Moore), **VI:** xii, 88, 89, **94–95,** 99

Hemans, Felicia, **IV:** 311

Hemingway, Ernest, **Supp. III:** 105; **Supp. IV:** 163, 209, 500

Hemlock and After (Wilson), **Supp. I:** 155–156, 157, 158–159, 160, 161, 164

Hello, America (Ballard), **Supp. V:** 29

"Hen Woman" (Kinsella), **Supp. V:** 266–267

Henceforward (Ayckbourn), **Supp. V:** 3, 10, 11, 13

"Hendecasyllabics" (Swinburne), **V:** 321

"Hendecasyllabics" (Tennyson), **IV:** 327–328

Henderson, Hamish, **VII:** 422, 425–426

Henderson, Hubert, **VII:** 35

Henderson, Philip, **V:** xii, xviii, 335

Henderson, T. F., **IV:** 290n

Hengist, King of Kent; or, The Mayor of Quinborough (Middleton), **II:** 3, 21

Henley, William Ernest, **V:** 386, 389, 391–392; **VI:** 159

Henn, T. R., **VI:** 220

"Henrietta Marr" (Moore), **VI:** 87

Henrietta Temple (Disraeli), **IV:** xix, 293, 298–299, 307, 308

"Henrik Ibsen" (James), **VI:** 49

Henry Esmond (Thackeray), *see History of Henry Esmond, Esq. . . ., The*

Henry for Hugh (Ford), **VI:** 331

Henry James (ed. Tanner), **VI:** 68

Henry James (West), **Supp. III:** 437

"Henry James: The Religious Aspect" (Greene), **Supp. I:** 8

"Henry Purcell" (Hopkins), **V:** 370–371

Henry II (Bancroft), **II:** 305

Henry IV (Shakespeare), **I:** 308–309, 320

Henry V (Shakespeare), **I:** 309; **V:** 383; **Supp. IV:** 258

Henry VI trilogy (Shakespeare), **I:** 286, 299–300, 309

Henry VI's Triumphal Entry into London (Lydgate), **I:** 58

Henry VIII (Shakespeare), **I:** 324; **II:** 43, 66, 87; **V:** 328

"Henry VIII and Ann Boleyn" (Landor), **IV:** 92

Henry Vaughan: Experience and the Tradition (Garner), **II:** 186n

Henry's Past (Churchill), **Supp. IV:** 181

Henryson, Robert, **Supp. VII:** **135–149**

Henslowe, Philip, **I:** 228, 235, 284; **II:** 3 25, 68

Henty, G. A., **Supp. IV:** 201

Her Triumph (Johnson), **I:** 347

Her Vertical Smile (Kinsella), **Supp. V:** 270–271

Her Victory (Sillitoe), **Supp. V:** 411, 415, 422, 425

Herakles (Euripides), **IV:** 358

Herbert, Edward, pseud. of John Hamilton Reynolds

Herbert, Edward, *see* Herbert of Cherbury, Lord

Herbert, George, **II:** 113, **117–130,** 133, 134, 137, 138, 140–142, 184, 187, 216, 221

Herbert of Cherbury, Lord, **II:** 117–118, 222, 237, 238

Hercule Poirot's Last Case (Christie), **Supp. II:** 125

"Hercules and Antaeus" (Heaney), **Supp. II:** 274–275

Hercules Oetaeus (Seneca), **I:** 248

"Here" (Larkin), **Supp. I:** 279, 285

Here Comes Everybody: An Introduction to James Joyce for the Ordinary Reader (Burgess), **Supp. I:** 194, 196–197

Here Lies: An Autobiography (Ambler), **Supp. IV:** 1, 2, 3, 4

"Heredity" (Harrison), **Supp. V:** 152

Heretics (Chesterton), **VI:** 204, 336–337

Hering, Carl Ewald, **Supp. II:** 107–108

Heritage and Its History, A (Compton–Burnett), **VII:** 60, 61, 65

Hermaphrodite Album, The (Redgrove), **Supp. VI:** 230

"Hermaphroditus" (Swinburne), **V:** 320

Hermetical Physick . . . Englished (tr. Vaughan), **II:** 185, 201

Hermit of Marlow, The, pseud. of Percy Bysshe Shelley

"Hero" (Rossetti), **V:** 260

"Hero and Leander" (Hood), **IV:** 255–256, 267

Hero and Leander (Marlowe), **I:** 234, 237–240, 276, 278, 280, 288, **290–291,** 292

Hero and Leander, in Burlesque (Wycherley), **II:** 321

"Hero as King, The" (Carlyle), **IV:** 245, 246

Hero Rises Up, The (Arden and D'Arcy), **Supp. II:** 31

"Heroine, The" (Highsmith), **Supp. V:** 180

Herodotus, **Supp. IV:** 110

Heroes and Hero–Worship (Carlyle), **IV:** xx, 240, 244–246, 249, 250, 341

Heroes and Villains (Carter), **Supp. III:** 81, 84

Heroic Idylls, with Additional Poems (Landor), **IV:** 100

"Heroic Stanzas" (Dryden), **II:** 292

Heroine, The; or, The Adventures of Cherubina (Barrett), **III:** 335

Herrick, Robert, **II:** **102–116,** 121

Herself Surprised (Cary), **VII:** 186, 188, 191–192

"Hertha" (Swinburne), **V:** 325

"Hervé Riel" (Browning), **IV:** 367

Herzog, Werner, **IV:** 180

"Hesperia" (Swinburne), **V:** 320, 321

Hesperides, The (Herrick), **II:** 102, 103, 104, 106, 110, 112, 115, 116

Heyday of Sir Walter Scott, The (Davie), **Supp. VI:** 114–115

Heylyn, Peter, **I:** 169

Heywood, Jasper, **I:** 215

Heywood, Thomas, **II:** 19, 47, 48, 68, 83

"Hexagon" (Murphy), **V:** 328

Hibberd, Dominic, **VI:** xvi, xxxiii

Hide, The (Unsworth), **Supp. VII:** 354, 356

"Hide and Seek" (Gunn), **Supp. IV:** 272

Hide and Seek (Collins), **Supp. VI:** 92, 95

Hide and Seek (Swinburne), **V:** 334

"Hidden History, A" (Okri), **Supp. V:** 352

Hidden Ireland, The (Corkery), **Supp. V:** 41

"Hidden Law" (MacCaig), **Supp. VI:** 186

Higden, Ranulf, **I:** 22

Higgins, F. R., **Supp. IV:** 411, 413

Hockney's Alphabet (McEwan), **Supp. IV:** 389
Hodder, E., **IV:** 62n
Hodgkins, Howard, **Supp. IV:** 170
Hodgson, W. N., **VI:** 422, 423
Hoff, Benjamin, **Supp. V:** 311
Hoffman, Calvin, **I:** 277
Hoffman, Heinrich, **I:** 25; **Supp. III:** 296
Hoffmann, E. T. A., **III:** 333, 334, 345
"Hoffmeier's Antelope" (Swift), **Supp. V:** 432
Hofmeyr (Paton; U.S. title, *South African Tragedy: The Life and Times of Jan Hofmeyr*), **Supp. II:** 356–357, 358
Hogarth Press, **VII:** xv, 17, 34
Hogg, James, **IV:** xvii, 73
Hogg, Thomas Jefferson, **IV:** 196, 198, 209
Hoggart, Richard, **VII:** xx, xxxviii; **Supp. IV:** 473
Hold Your Hour and Have Another (Behan), **Supp. II:** 65–66, 70
Holiday, The (Smith), **Supp. II:** 462, 474, **476–478**
Holiday Romance (Dickens), **V:** 72
Holiday Round, The (Milne), **Supp. V:** 298
"Holidays" (Kincaid), **Supp. VII:** 220
Hollington, Michael, **Supp. IV:** 357
Hollis, Maurice Christopher, **VI:** xxxiii
Hollis, Richard, **Supp. IV:** 88
"Hollow Men, The" (Eliot), **VII:** 150–151, 158
Hollow's Mill (Brontë), *see* Shirley
Holloway, John, **VII:** 82
Holroyd, Michael, **Supp. IV:** 231
"Holy Baptisme I" (Herbert), **II:** 128
Holy City, The; or, The New Jerusalem (Bunyan), **II:** 253
"Holy Fair, The" (Burns), **III:** 311, 315, 317
Holy Grail, The, and Other Poems (Tennyson), **IV:** 338
Holy Life, The Beauty of Christianity, A (Bunyan), **II:** 253
"Holy Mountain, The" (Nicholson), **Supp. VI:** 215
"Holy Scriptures" (Vaughan), **II:** 187
Holy Sinner, The (Mann), **II:** 97n
Holy Sonnets (Donne), **I:** 362, 366, 367
Holy War, The: Made by Shaddai . . . (Bunyan), **II:** 246, 250, 251–252, 253
"Holy Willie's Prayer" (Burns), **III:** 311, 313, 319
"Holy–Cross Day" (Browning), **IV:** 367
"Holyhead, September 25, 1717" (Swift), **III:** 32
"Homage to a Government" (Larkin), **Supp. I:** 284
Homage to Catalonia (Orwell), **VII:** 275, 280–281
Homage to Clio (Auden), **VII:** 392
"Homage to Burns" (Brown), **Supp. VI:** 72
"Homage to the British Museum" (Empson), **Supp. II:** 182
"Homage to William Cowper" (Davie), **Supp. VI:** 106
"Home" (Ewart), **Supp. VII:** 37
Home (Storey), **Supp. I:** 408, 413, 417

Home and Beauty (Maugham), **VI:** 368–369
Home and Dry (Fuller), **Supp. VII:** 70, 81
"Home at Grasmere" (Wordsworth), **IV:** 3, 23–24
Home Chat (Coward), **Supp. II:** 146
"Home for a couple of days" (Kelman), **Supp. V:** 250
"Home for the Highland Cattle, A" (Lessing), **Supp. I:** 241–242
Home Front (Bishton and Reardon), **Supp. IV:** 445
Home Letters (Disraeli) **IV:** 296, 308
Home Letters of T. E. Lawrence and His Brothers, The (Lawrence), **Supp. II:** 286
"Home Thoughts from Abroad" (Browning), **IV:** 356
"Home Thoughts Abroad" (Newman), **Supp. VII:** 293
"Home [2]" (Thomas), **Supp. III:** 405
"Home [3]" (Thomas), **Supp. III:** 404
Home University Library, **VI:** 337, 391
Homebush Boy (Keneally), **Supp. IV:** 344, 347
Homecoming, The (Pinter), **Supp. I:** 375, 380, 381
Homecomings (Snow), **VII:** xxi, 324, 329, 335
"Homemade" (McEwan), **Supp. IV:** 389, 391, 395
"Homemaking" (Kincaid), **Supp. VII:** 229
Homer, **I:** 236; **II:** 304, 347; **III:** 217, 220; **IV:** 204, 215
Homeric Hymns (tr. Chapman), **I:** 236
"Homesick in Old Age" (Kinsella), **Supp. V:** 263
"Homeward Prospect, The" (Day Lewis), **Supp. III:** 129
Hone, Joseph, **VI:** 88
Hone, William, **IV:** 255
Honest Man's Fortune, The (Field, Fletcher, Massinger), **II:** 66
Honest Whore, The (Dekker and Middleton), **II:** 3, 21, 89
Honey for the Bears (Burgess), **Supp. I:** 191
Honeybuzzard (Carter), *see Shadow Dance*
Honeymoon Voyage, The (Thomas), **Supp. IV:** 490
Honorary Consul, The (Greene), **Supp. I:** 7, 10, 13, 16
Honour of the Garter, The (Peele), **I:** 205
Honour Triumphant; or, The Peeres Challenge (Ford), **II:** 88, 100
"Honourable Laura, The" (Hardy), **VI:** 22
Honourable Schoolboy, The (le Carré), **Supp. II:** 301, **313–314**, 315
Hood, Thomas, **IV:** xvi, xx, **251–267**, 311
Hood's (periodical), **IV:** 252, 261, 263, 264
"Hood's Literary Reminiscences" (Blunden), **IV:** 267
Hood's Own (Hood), **IV:** 251–252, 253, 254, 266
Hook, Theodore, **IV:** 254

Hooker, Richard, **I:** **176–190**, 362; **II:** 133, 137, 140–142, 147
"Hope" (Cowper), **III:** 212
Hope, A. D., **Supp. VII:** **151–166**
Hope for Poetry, A (Day Lewis), **Supp. III:** 117, 119
Hopes and Fears for Art (Morris), **V:** 301, 306
Hopkins, Gerard Manley, **II:** 123, 181; **IV:** xx; **V:** ix, xi, xxv, 53, 205, 210, 261, 309–310, 338, **361–382; VI:** 75, 83; **Supp. II:** 269; **Supp. IV:** 344, 345
Hopkins (MacKenzie), **V:** 375n 382
Hopkinson, Sir Tom, **V:** xx, xxxviii
Horace, **II:** 108, 112, 199, 200, 265, 292, 300, 309, 347; **IV:** 327
Horae Solitariae (Thomas), **Supp. III:** 394
"Horatian Ode . . . , An" (Marvell), **II:** 204, 208, 209, 210, 211, 216–217
"Horatius" (Macaulay), **IV:** 282
Horestes (Pickering), **I:** 213, 216–218
Horizon (periodical), **Supp. II:** 489; **Supp. III:** **102–103**, 105, 106–107, 108–109
Horne, Richard Hengist, **IV:** 312, 321, 322
Hornet (periodical), **VI:** 102
Horniman, Annie, **VI:** 309; **VII:** 1
"Horns Away" (Lydgate), **I:** 64
Horse and His Boy, The (Lewis), **Supp. III:** 248, 260
"Horse Dealer's Daughter, The" (Lawrence), **VII:** 114
"Horse–Drawn Caravan" (Murphy), **Supp. V:** 329
"Horse, Goose and Sheep, The" (Lydgate), **I:** 57
"Horses" (Muir), **Supp. VI:** 204–205"Horses" (Muir), **Supp. VI:** 204–205
Horse's Mouth, The (Cary), **VII:** 186, 188, 191, 192, 193–194
Hoskins, John, **I:** 165–166, 167
"Hospital Barge" (Owen), **VI:** 454
Hostage, The (Behan), **Supp. II:** 70, **72–73**, 74
Hot Countries, The (Waugh), **Supp. VI:** 272, 274
Hot Gates, The (Golding), **Supp. I:** 81
Hotel, The (Bowen), **Supp. II:** **82–83**
Hotel du Lac (Brookner), **Supp. IV:** 120, 121, 126–127, 136
Hotel in Amsterdam, The (Osborne), **Supp. I:** 338–339
"Hotel of the Idle Moon, The" (Trevor), **Supp. IV:** 501
"Hotel Room in Chartres" (Lowry), **Supp. III:** 272
Hothouse, The (Pinter), **Supp. I:** 377–378
Hothouse by the East River, The (Spark), **Supp. I:** 210
Hotson, Leslie, **I:** 275, 276
Houd–den–bek (Brink), **Supp. VI:** 51
Hough, Graham, **IV:** 323n, 339; **V:** 355, 359
Houghton, Lord, *see* Monckton Milnes, Richard
Hound of Death, The (Christie), **III:** 341

Life and Letters of Leslie Stephen, The
(Maitland), **V:** 277, 290
Life and Letters, The (Macaulay), **IV:**
270–271, 284, 291
Life and Loves of a She–Devil, The
(Weldon), **Supp. IV:** 537–538
*Life and Opinions of Tristram Shandy,
Gentleman, The* (Sterne), *see Tristram
Shandy*
"Life and Poetry of Keats, The"
(Masson), **IV:** 212, 235
*Life and Strange Surprizing Adventures
of Robinson Crusoe . . . , The* (Defoe),
see Robinson Crusoe
Life and the Poet (Spender), **Supp. II:**
489
Life and Times of Laurence Sterne, The
(Cross), **III:** 125
Life and Times of Michael K (Coetzee),
Supp. VI: 76, **82–83**
"Life and Writings of Addison"
(Macaulay), **IV:** 282
Life Goes On (Sillitoe), **Supp. V:** 411
"Life in a Love" (Browning), **IV:** 365
Life in Greece from Homer to Menander
(Mahafty), **V:** 400
"Life in London" (Egan), **IV:** 260
Life in Manchester (Gaskell), **V:** 15
*Life, Letters, and Literary Remains of
John Keats* (Milnes), **IV:** 211, 235,
351
Life of Addison (Johnson), **III:** 42
Life of Alexander Pope (Ruffhead), **III:**
69n, 71
Life of Algernon Charles Swinburne, The
(Gosse), **V:** 311, 334
*Life of Benjamin Disraeli, Earl of Bea-
consfield, The* (Monypenny and
Buckle), **IV:** 292, 295, 300, 307, 308
Life of . . . Bolingbroke, The (Goldsmith),
III: 189, 191
Life of Charlotte Brontë, The (Gaskell),
V: xii, 1–2, 3, 13–14, 15, 108, 122
Life of Christina Rossetti, The (Sanders),
V: 250, 260
Life of Cicero, The (Trollope), **V:** 102
Life of Collins (Johnson), **III:** 164, 171
Life of Crabbe (Crabbe), **III:** 272
Life of Dr. Donne, The (Walton), **II:** 132,
136, 140, 141, 142
Life of Dr. Robert Sanderson, The
(Walton), **II:** 133, 135, 136–137, 140,
142
Life of Dryden, The (Scott), **IV:** 38
Life of George Moore, The (Horne), **VI:**
87, 96, 99
Life of Henry Fawcett, The (Stephen), **V:**
289
Life of John Bright, The (Trevelyan), **VI:**
389
Life of John Hales, The (Walton), **II:** 136
Life of John Milton, The (Wilson), **Supp.
VI:** 301–302
Life of John Sterling (Carlyle), **IV:** 41–
42, 240, 249, 250
Life of Johnson, The (Boswell), **I:** 30;
III: 58, 114n, 115, 120, 234, 238, 239,
243–248; **IV:** xv, 280
Life of Katherine Mansfield, The (Mantz
and Murry), **VII:** 183

"Life of Ma Parker"(Mansfield), **VII:**
175, 177
Life of Man, The (Arden), **Supp. II:** 28
Life of Mr. George Herbert, The (Walton),
II: 119–120, 133, 140, 142, 143
Life of Mr. Jonathan Wild the Great, The
(Fielding), *see Jonathan Wild*
Life of Mr. Richard Hooker, The (Walton),
II: 133, 134, 135, 140–143
Life of Mr. Richard Savage (Johnson),
III: 108, 121
Life of Mrs. Godolphin, The (Evelyn), **II:**
275, 287
"Life of Mrs. Radcliffe" (Scott), **IV:** 35
Life of Mrs. Robert Louis Stevenson, The
(Sanchez), **V:** 393, 397
Life of Napoleon, The (Scott), **IV:** 38
Life of Napoleon Bonaparte, The
(Hazlitt), **IV:** 135, 140
Life of Nelson, The (Southey), **IV:** xvii,
58, 69, 71, 280
Life of Our Lady, The (Lydgate), **I:** 22,
57, 65–66
Life of Pico (More), **Supp. VII:** 233, 234,
238
Life of Richard Nash, The (Goldsmith),
III: 189, 191
Life of Robert Louis Stevenson, The
(Balfour), **V:** 393, 397
Life of Robert Louis Stevenson, The
(Masson), **V:** 393, 397
Life of Rudyard Kipling, The (Carrington),
VI: 166
Life of Saint Albion, The (Lydgate), **I:** 57
Life of Saint Cecilia, The (Chaucer), **I:**
31
Life of Saint Edmund, The (Lydgate), **I:**
57
Life of Saint Francis Xavier, The (tr.
Dryden), **II:** 305
Life of Samuel Johnson, The (Boswell),
see Life of Johnson, The
Life of Schiller (Carlyle), **IV:** 241, 249,
250
Life of Sir Henry Wotton, The (Walton),
II: 133, 141, 142, 143
Life of Sir James Fitzjames Stephen, The
(Stephen), **V:** 289
Life of Sterling (Carlyle), *see Life of John
Sterling*
"Life of the Emperor Julius" (Brontë), **V:**
113
"Life of the Imagination, The"
(Gordimer), **Supp. II:** 233–234
Life of the Rev. Andrew Bell, The
(Southey and Southey), **IV:** 71
Life of the Seventh Earl of Shaftesbury
(Hodder), **IV:** 62
Life of Thomas Hardy (Hardy), **VI:** 14–15
Life of Thomas More, The (Ackroyd),
Supp. VI: 12, 13
"Life of Thomas Parnell" (Goldsmith),
III: 189
Life of Wesley, The (Southey), **IV:** 68, 71
Life of William Morris, The (Mackail), **V:**
294, 297, 306
"Life Sentence" (West), **Supp. III:** 442
"Life to Come, The" (Forster), **VI:** 411
"Life with a Hole in It, The" (Larkin),
Supp. I: 284

Life's Handicap (Kipling), **VI:** 204
Life's Little Ironies (Hardy), **VI:** 20, 22
Life's Morning, A (Gissing), **V:** 437
"Liffey Hill, The" (Kinsella), **Supp. V:**
267
"Lifted Veil, The" (Eliot), **V:** 198
Light and the Dark, The (Snow), **VII:**
324, 327
"Light breaks where no sun shines"
(Thomas), **Supp. I:** 172
Light for Them That Sit in Darkness . . .
(Bunyan), **II:** 253
*Light Garden of the Angel King: Journeys
in Afghanistan, The* (Levi), **Supp. IV:**
159
"Light Man, A" (James), **VI:** 25, 69
Light Music, (Mahon), **Supp. VI:** 173
Light of Day, The (Ambler), **Supp. IV:** 4,
16–17
Light Shining in Buckinghamshire
(Churchill), **Supp. IV:** 180, 186–188
"Light Shining Out of Darkness"
(Cowper), **III:** 211
Light That Failed, The (Kipling), **VI:**
166, 169, 189–190, 204
"Light Woman, A" (Browning), **IV:** 369
Lighthouse, The (Collins), **Supp. VI:** 95
"Lighthouse Invites the Storm, The"
(Lowry), **Supp. III:** 282
Lighthouse Invites the Storm, The
(Lowry), **Supp. III:** 282
"Lights Among Redwood" (Gunn), **Supp.
IV:** 263
"Lights Out" (Thomas), **Supp. III:** 401
Like Birds, Like Fishes and Other Stories
(Jhabvala), **Supp. V:** 235
Like It Or Not (Ewart), **Supp. VII:** 47
*Lilac and Flag: An Old Wives' Tale of a
City* (Berger), **Supp. IV:** 93–95
Lilian (Bennett), **VI:** 250, 259–260
"Lilly in a Christal, The" (Herrick), **II:**
104
"Lily Adair" (Chivers), **V:** 313
Limbo (Huxley), **VII:** 199, 200
Lincolnshire poems (Tennyson), **IV:** 327,
336
Linda Tressel (Trollope), **V:** 102
Linden Tree, The (Priestley), **VII:** 209,
228–229
Line of Life, A (Ford), **II:** 88, 100
"Lines Composed a Few Miles Above
Tintern Abbey" (Wordsworth), **IV:** ix,
3, 7, 8, 9–10, 11, 44, 198, 215, 233
"Lines Composed in a Wood on a Windy
Day" (Brontë), **V:** 132
"Lines Composed While Climbing the
Left Ascent of Brockley Combe"
(Coleridge), **IV: 43–44**
"Lines for a Book" (Gunn), **Supp. IV:**
260, 261
"Lines for Cuscuscaraway . . . " (Elliot),
VII: 163
"Lines for Thanksgiving" (McGuckian),
Supp. V: 289
"Lines of Desire" (Motion), **Supp. VII:**
254, 260–261
"Lines on a Young Lady's Photograph
Album" (Larkin), **Supp. I:** 285
"Lines on the Loss of the *Titanic*"
(Hardy), **VI:** 16

Nashe, Thomas, **I:** 114, 123, 171, 199, 221, 278, 279, 281, 288; **II:** 25; **Supp. II:** 188
Nation (periodical), **VI:** 455
Nation Review (publication), **Supp. IV:** 346
National Observer (periodical), **VI:** 350
National Standard (periodical), **V:** 19
National Tales (Hood), **IV:** 255, 259, 267
"National Trust" (Harrison), **Supp. V:** 153
Native Companions: Essays and Comments on Australian Literature 1936–1966 (Hope), **Supp. VII:** 151, 153, 159, 164
"Natura Naturans" (Clough), **V:** 159–160
Natural Causes (Motion), **Supp. VII:** 254, 257–258, 263
Natural Curiosity, A (Drabble), **Supp. IV:** 231, 249–250
Natural History and Antiquities of Selborne, The, (White), **Supp. VI:** 279–284, **285–293**
Natural History of Religion, The (Hume), **Supp. III:** 240–241
"natural man," **VII:** 94
"Natural Son" (Murphy), **Supp. V:** 327, 329
Naturalist's Calendar, with Observations in Various Branches of Natural History, A (White), **Supp. VI:** 283
Naturalist's Journal (White), **Supp. VI:** 283, 292
"Naturally the Foundation Will Bear Your Expenses" (Larkin), **Supp. I:** 285
Nature of a Crime, The (Conrad), **VI:** 148
Nature of Blood, The (Phillips), **Supp. V:** 380, 391–394
Nature of Cold Weather, The (Redgrove), **Supp. VI: 227–229,** 236
"Nature of Cold Weather, The" (Redgrove), **Supp. VI:** 228,237
"Nature of Gothic, The" (Ruskin), **V:** 176
Nature of History, The (Marwick), **IV:** 290, 291
Nature of Passion, The (Jhabvala), **Supp. V:** 226
"Nature of the Scholar, The" (Fichte), **V:** 348
Nature Poems (Davies), **Supp. III:** 398
"Nature That Washt Her Hands in Milk" (Ralegh), **I:** 149
Natwar–Singh, K., **VI:** 408
Naufragium Joculare (Cowley), **II:** 194, 202
Naulahka (Kipling and Balestier), **VI:** 204
"Naval History" (Kelman), **Supp. V:** 250
"Naval Treaty, The" (Doyle), **Supp. II:** 169, 175
Navigation and Commerce (Evelyn), **II:** 287
"Navy's Here, The" (Redgrove), **Supp. VI:** 234
Naylor, Gillian, **VI:** 168
Nazarene Gospel Restored, The (Graves and Podro), **VII:** 262
Nazism, **VI:** 242
Neal, Patricia, **Supp. IV:** 214, 218, 223
Near and Far (Blunden), **VI:** 428

"Near Lanivet" (Hardy), **VI:** 17
"Near Perigord" (Pound), **V:** 304
Necessity of Art, The (Fischer), **Supp. II:** 228
Necessity of Atheism, The (Shelley and Hogg), **IV:** xvii, 196, 208
"Necessity of Not Believing, The" (Smith), **Supp. II:** 467
Necessity of Poetry, The (Bridges), **VI:** 75–76, 82, 83
"Necessity's Child" (Wilson), **Supp. I:** 153–154
"Neck" (Dahl), **Supp. IV:** 217
"Ned Bratts" (Browning), **IV:** 370
Ned Kelly and the City of the Bees (Keneally), **Supp. IV:** 346
"Ned Skinner" (Muldoon), **Supp. IV:** 415
"Need to Be Versed in Country Things, The" (Frost), **Supp. IV:** 423
Needham, Gwendolyn, **V:** 60
Needle's Eye, The (Drabble), **Supp. IV:** 230, 234, 241, 242–243, 245, 251
"Neglected Graveyard, Luskentyre" (MacCaig), **Supp. VI:** 182, 189, 194
Neizvestny, Ernst, **Supp. IV:** 88
"Nelly Trim" (Warner), **Supp. VII:** 371
Nelson, W., **I:** 86
Nerinda (Douglas), **VI:** 300, 305
Nero Part I (Bridges), **VI:** 83
Nero Part II (Bridges), **VI:** 83
Nesbit, E., **Supp. II:** 140, 144, 149
"Nest in a Wall, A" (Murphy), **Supp. V:** 326
Nest of Tigers, A: Edith, Osbert and Sacheverell in Their Times (Lehmann), **VII:** 141
Nether World, The (Gissing), **V:** 424, 437
Netherwood (White), **Supp. I:** 131, 151
"Netting, The" (Murphy), **Supp. V:** 318
Nettles (Lawrence), **VII:** 118
"Netty Sargent's Copyhold" (Hardy), **VI:** 22
"Neurotic, The" (Day Lewis), **Supp. III:** 129
Neutral Ground (Corke), **VII:** 93
New Age (periodical), **VI:** 247, 265; **VII:** 172
New and Collected Poems 1934–84 (Fuller), **Supp. VII:** 68, 72, 73, 74, 79
New and Collected Poems, 1952–1992 (Hill), **Supp. V:** 184
New and Improved Grammar of the English Tongue, A (Hazlitt), **IV:** 139
New and Selected Poems (Davie), **Supp. VI:** 108
New and Useful Concordance, A (Bunyan), **II:** 253
New Apocalypse, The (MacCaig), **Supp. VI:** 184
New Arabian Nights (Stevenson), **V:** 384n, 386, 395
New Atlantis (Bacon), **I:** 259, 265, 267–269, 273
"New Ballad of Tannhäuser, A" (Davidson), **V:** 318n
New Bath Guide (Anstey), **III:** 155
New Bats in Old Belfries (Betjeman), **VII:** 368–369

New Bearings in English Poetry (Leavis), **V:** 375, 381; **VI:** 21; **VII:** 234, 244–246
"New Beginning, A" (Kinsella), **Supp. V:** 270
New Belfry of Christ Church, The (Carroll), **V:** 274
New Characters . . . of Severall Persons . . . (Webster), **II:** 85
"New Cemetery, The" (Nicholson), **Supp. VI:** 219
New Cratylus, The: Notes on the Craft of Poetry (Hope), **Supp. VII:** 151, 155
New Country (ed. Roberts), **VII:** xix, 411
"New Delhi Romance, A" (Jhabvala), **Supp. V:** 236–237
New Discovery of an Old Intreague, An (Defoe), **III:** 12
New Dominion, A (Jhabvala), **Supp. V:** 230–231
New Dunciad, The (Pope), **III:** 73, 78
"New Empire Within Britain, The" (Rushdie), **Supp. IV:** 436, 445
"New England Winter, A" (James), **VI:** 69
New Essays by De Quincey (ed. Tave); **IV:** 155
New Ewart, The: Poems 1980–82 (Ewart), **Supp. VII:** 34, 44, 45
New Family Instructor, A (Defoe), **III:** 14
"New Forge" (Murphy), **Supp. V:** 328
New Form of Intermittent Light for Lighthouses, A (Stevenson), **V:** 395
New Grub Street (Gissing), **V:** xxv, 426, 427, 429, 430, 434–435, 437; **VI:** 377; **Supp. IV:** 7
"New Hampshire" (Reid), **Supp. VII:** 326
New Inn; The Noble Gentlemen (Jonson), **II:** 65
New Journey to Paris, A (Swift), **III:** 35
"New King for the Congo: Mobutu and the Nihilism of Africa" (Naipaul), **Supp. I:** 398
New Light on Piers Plowman (Bright), **I:** 3
New Lines (Conquest), **Supp. IV:** 256
New Lives for Old (Snow), **VII:** 323
New Love–Poems (Scott), **IV:** 39
New Machiavelli, The (Wells), **VI:** 226, 239, 244
New Magdalen, The (Collins), **Supp. VI:** 102
New Meaning of Treason, The (West), **Supp. III:** 440, 444
New Men, The (Snow), **VII:** xxi, 324, 328–329, 330
New Method of Evaluation as Applied to ∂, The (Carroll), **V:** 274
New Monthly (periodical), **IV:** 252, 254, 258
"New Novel, The" (James), **VI:** xii
New Numbers (periodical), **VI:** 420; **Supp. III:** 47
New Oxford Book of Irish Verse, The (Kinsella), **Supp. V:** 274
New Poems (Arnold), **V:** xxiii, 204, 209, 216
"New Poems" (Bridges), **VI:** 77
New Poems (Davies), **Supp. III:** 398

Roman Quarry and Other Sequences, The (Jones), **Supp. VII:** 167, 171

Romance (Conrad and Ford), **VI:** 146, 148, 321

"Romance" (Sitwell), **VII:** 132–133

"Romance of Certain Old Clothes, The" (James), **VI:** 69

Romantic Adventures of A Milkmaid, The (Hardy), **VI:** 20, 22

Romantic Agony, The (Praz), **III:** 337, 346; **V:** 412, 420

Romantic Image (Kermode), **V:** 344, 359, 412

Romantic Poetry and the Fine Arts (Blunden), **IV:** 236

"Romanticism and Classicism" (Hulme), **Supp. VI:** 135, 138, 142–145

"Romaunt of Margaret, The" (Browning), **IV:** 313

Romeo and Juliet (Shakespeare), **I:** 229, 305–306, 320; **II:** 281; **IV:** 218

Romola (Eliot), **V:** xxii, 66, 194–195, 200

Romulus and Hersilia; or, The Sabine War (Behn), **Supp. III:** 29

Rondeaux Parisiens (Swinburne), **V:** 333

"Roof–Tree" (Murphy), **Supp. V:** 329

Rookwood (Ainsworth), **V:** 47

Room, The (Day Lewis), **Supp. III:** 118, 129–130

"Room, The" (Day Lewis), **Supp. III:** 130

Room, The (Pinter), **Supp. I:** 367, 369

"Room Above the Square" (Spender), **Supp. II:** 494

Room at the Top (Braine), **Supp. IV:** 238

Room of One's Own, A (Woolf), **VII:** 22–23, 25–26, 27, 38; **Supp. III:** 19, 41–42; **Supp. V:** 36

Room with a View, A (Forster), **VI:** 398, 399, **403–404**

"Rooms of Other Women Poets, The" (Boland), **Supp. V:** 37

Rootham, Helen, **VII:** 129

Roots of Coincidence (Koestler), **Supp. I:** 39

"Roots of Honour, The" (Ruskin), **V:** 179–180

Roots of the Mountains, The (Morris), **V:** 302, 306

Roppen, G., **V:** 221*n*

Rosalind and Helen (Shelley), **IV:** 208

Rosalynde (Lodge), **I:** 312

Rosamond, Queen of the Lombards (Swinburne), **V:** 312–314, 330, 331, 332, 333

Rose, Ellen Cronan, **Supp. IV:** 232

"Rose, The" (Southey), **IV:** 64

Rose and Crown (O'Casey), **VII:** 13

Rose and the Ring, The (Thackeray), **V:** 38, 261

Rose Blanche (McEwan), **Supp. IV:** 390

Rose in the Heart, A (O'Brien), **Supp. V:** 339

"Rose in the Heart of New York, A" (O'Brien), **Supp. V:** 340–341

"Rose Mary" (Rossetti), **V:** 238, 244

Rosemary's Baby (film), **III:** 343

Rosenberg, Bruce, **Supp. IV:** 7

Rosenberg, Eleanor, **I:** 233

Rosenberg, Isaac, **VI:** xvi, 417, 420, **432–435; VII:** xvi; **Supp. III:** 59

Rosenberg, John, **V:** 316, 334

Rosencrantz and Guildenstern Are Dead (Stoppard), **Supp. I: 440–443,** 444, 451

Rosenfeld, S., **II:** 271

"Roses on the Terrace, The" (Tennyson), **IV:** 329, 336

"Rosiphelee" (Gower), **I:** 53–54

Ross (Rattigan), **Supp. VII:** 320, 321

Ross, Alan, **VII:** xxii, 422, 433–434

Ross, John Hume (pseud., Lawrence), **Supp. II:** 286, 295

Rossetti, Christina, **V:** xi–xii, xix, xxii, xxvi, **247–260; Supp. IV:** 139

Rossetti, Dante Gabriel, **IV:** 346; **V:** ix, xi, xii, xviii, xxiii–xxv, **235–246,** 247–253, 259, 293–296, 298, 299, 312–315, 320, 329, 355, 401; **VI:** 167

Rossetti, Maria **V:** 251, 253

Rossetti, William, **V:** 235, 236, 245, 246, 248–249, 251–253, 260

Rossetti (Waugh), **VII:** 291

Rossetti and His Circle (Beerbohm), **Supp. II:** 51

"Rossetti's Conception of the 'Poetic' " (Doughty), **V:** 246

Røstvig, Maren–Sofie, **I:** 237

"Rosyfingered, The" (MacCaig), **Supp. VI:** 186

"Rot, The" (Lewis), **VII:** 73

Rotting Hill (Lewis), **VII:** 72

Rough Shoot (film, Ambler), **Supp. IV:** 3

Round and Round the Garden (Ayckbourn), **Supp. V:** 2, 5

Round of Applause, A (MacCaig), **Supp. VI: 187–188,** 190, 194–195

Round Table, The (Hazlitt), **IV:** xvii, 129, 137, 139

Round Table, The; or, King Arthur's Feast (Peacock), **IV:** 170

Round the Sofa (Gaskell), **V:** 3, 15

Roundabout Papers (Thackeray), **V:** 34, 35, 38

Roundheads, The; or, The Good Old Cause (Behn), **Supp. III:** 25

Rousseau, Jean Jacques, **II:** 235, 236; **IV:** xiv, 207; **Supp. III:** 239–240

Rover, The (Conrad), **VI:** 144, 147, 148

Rover, The; or, The Banish'd Cavaliers (Behn), **Supp. III:** 26, 27–29, 31

Rowe, Nicholas, **I:** 326

Rowley, Hazel, **Supp. IV:** 459, 460

Rowley, William, **II:** 1, 3, 14, 15, 18, 21, 66, 69, 83, 89, 100

Roxana (Defoe), **III:** 8–9, 14

Roy, Arundhati, **Supp. V:** xxx, 67, 75

Royal Academy, The (Moore), **VI:** 98

Royal Beasts, The (Empson), **Supp. II:** 180, 184

Royal Combat, The (Ford), **II:** 100

Royal Court Theatre, **VI:** 101

Royal Hunt of the Sun, The (Shaffer), **Supp. I:** 314, **319–322,** 323, 324, 327

"Royal Jelly" (Dahl), **Supp. IV:** 221

"Royal Man" (Muir), **I:** 247

"Royal Naval Air Station" (Fuller), **Supp. VII:** 69

Royal Pardon, The (Arden and D'Arcy), **Supp. II:** 30

Rubáiyát of Omar Khayyám, The (FitzGerald), **IV:** xxii, 342–343, **345–348,** 349, 352, 353; **V:** 318

Rubin, Merle, **Supp. IV:** 360

Rudd, Margaret, **VI:** 209

Rudd, Steele, **Supp. IV:** 460

Rude Assignment (Lewis), **VI:** 333; **VII:** xv, 72, 74, 76

Rudolf II, Emperor of Holy Roman Empire, **Supp. IV:** 174

Rudyard Kipling, Realist and Fabulist (Dobrée), **VI:** 200–203

Rudyard Kipling to Rider Haggard (ed. Cohen), **VI:** 204

Ruffhead, O., **III:** 69*n*, 71

Ruffian on the Stair, The (Orton), **Supp. V:** 367, 370, 372, 373

"Rugby Chapel" (Arnold), **V:** 203

Ruined Boys, The (Fuller), **Supp. VII:** 74, 75

"Ruined Cottage, The," (Wordsworth), **IV:** 23, 24

Ruins and Visions (Spender), **Supp. II:** 486, 489

Ruins of Time, The (Spenser), **I:** 124

Rukeyser, Muriel, **Supp. V:** 261

Rule a Wife and Have a Wife (Fletcher), **II:** 45, 65

Rule Britannia (du Maurier), **Supp. III:** 133, 147

"Rule, Britannia" (Thomson), **Supp. III:** 412, 425

Rules for Court Circular (Carroll), **V:** 274

"Rummy Affair of Old Biffy, The" (Wodehouse), **Supp. III:** 455, 457

Rumors of Rain (Brink), **Supp. VI: 49–50**

Rumour at Nightfall (Greene), **Supp. I:** 3

"Run" (Motion), **Supp. VII:** 259

Running Wild (Ballard), **Supp. V:** 30–31

Rural Denmark (Haggard), **Supp. III:** 214

Rural England (Haggard), **Supp. III:** 214

Rural Minstrel, The (Brontë), **V:** 107, 151

Rural Sports: A Poem (Gay), **III:** 67

Rushdie, Salman, **Supp. IV:** 65, 75, 116, 157, 160, 161, 162, 170–171, 174, 302, **433–456; Supp. V:** 67, 68, 74

Rushing to Paradise (Ballard), **Supp. V:** 31

Ruskin, John, **IV:** 320, 346; **V:** xii, xviii, xx–xxii, xxvi, 3, 9, 17, 20, 85–86, **173–185,** 235, 236, 291–292, 345, 362, 400; **VI:** 167

Ruskin's Politics (Shaw), **VI:** 129

Russell, Bertrand, **VI:** xi, 170, 385; **VII:** 90

Russell, G. W. E., **IV:** 292, 304

Russell, John, **Supp. IV:** 126

Russia House, The (le Carré), **Supp. II:** 300, 310, 311, 313, **318–319**

Russian Interpreter, The (Frayn), **Supp. VII:** 52–53, 54

Russian Nights (Thomas), **Supp. IV:** 483–486

Rusticus (Poliziano), **I:** 240

"Ruth" (Crabbe), **V:** 6

Ruth (Gaskell), **V:** xxi, 1, 6–7, 15

VII: xvi; **Supp. III:** 59; **Supp. IV:** 57–58

"Satan in a Barrel" (Lowry), **Supp. III:** 270

Satan in Search of a Wife (Lamb), **IV:** 84, 85

Satanic Verses, The (Rushdie), **Supp. IV:** 116, 433, 434, 436, 437, 438, 445–450, 451, 452, 456

Satire and Fiction (Lewis), **VII:** 72, 77

Satire on Satirists, A, and Admonition to Detractors (Landor), **IV:** 100

Satires (Donne), **I:** 361

Satires (Wyatt), **I:** 100, 101–102, 111

Satires of Circumstance (Hardy), **VI:** 14, 20

Satires of Circumstance (Sorley), **VI:** 421

"Satiric Muse, The " (Hope), **Supp. VII:** 163

"Satisfactory, The" (Pritchett), **Supp. III: 319–320**

Saturday Life, A (Hall), **Supp. VI:** 120–122

"Saturday Night" (Gunn), **Supp. IV:** 269

Saturday Night and Sunday Morning (Sillitoe), **Supp. V:** 409, 410, 413, 416–419

Saturday Review (periodical), **V:** 279; **VI:** 103, 106, 366; **Supp. II:** 45, 48, 53, 54, 55

"Saturday; or, The Flights" (Gay), **III:** 56

"Saturnalia" (Gunn), **Supp. IV:** 269

"Saturnalia" (Wilson), **Supp. I:** 158

"Satyr Against Mankind, A" (Rochester), **II:** 208*n*, 256, 260–261, 270

"Satyrical Elegy on the Death of a Late Famous General, A" (Swift), **III:** 31

Saucer of Larks, The (Friel), **Supp. V:** 113

"Saul" (Browning), **IV:** 363

Saunders, Charles, **II:** 305

Sauter, Rudolf, **VI:** 284

Sauve Qui Peut (Durrell), **Supp. I:** 113

Savage, Eliza Mary Ann, **Supp. II:** 99, 104, 111

Savage, Richard, **III:** 108

Savage Gold (Fuller), **Supp. VII:** 70

Savage Pilgrimage, The (Carswell), **VII:** 123

Save It for the Minister (Churchill, Potter, O'Malley), **Supp. IV:** 181

Save the Beloved Country (Paton), **Supp. II:** 359, 360

Saved (Bond), **Supp. I:** 421, 422–423, 425–426, 427, 435

Saved By Grace (Bunyan), **II:** 253

Savile, George, *see* Halifax, marquess of

Saville (Storey), **Supp. I:** 419

Saviour of Society, The (Swinburne), **V:** 333

"Savonarola Brown" (Beerbohm), **Supp. II:** 5l, 56

Savonarola e il priore di San Marco (Landor), **IV:** 100

Savrola (Churchill), **VI:** 351

"Say not of me that weakly I declined" (Stevenson), **V:** 390

"Say not the struggle nought availeth" (Clough), **V:** 158–159, 165, 166, 167

Sayers, Dorothy L., **III:** 341; **VI:** 345; **Supp. II:** 124, 126, 127, 135; **Supp. III: 333–353**; **Supp. IV:** 2, 3, 500

"Scale" (Self), **Supp. V:** 403–404

Scandal (Wilson), **Supp. VI:** 302–303, 308

"Scandal in Bohemia, A" (Doyle), **Supp. I:** 173

Scandal of Father Brown, The (Chesterton), **VI:** 338

Scandalous Woman, A (O'Brien), **Supp. V:** 339

Scannell, Vernon, **VII:** 422, 423–424

Scapegoat, The (du Maurier), **Supp. III:** 136, 139, 140–141

"Scapegoat, The" (Pritchett), **Supp. III:** 312, 317–318

Scapegoats and Rabies (Hughes), **Supp. I:** 348

Scarcity of Love, A (Kavan), **Supp. VII:** 213, 214

"Scarecrow in the Schoolmaster's Oats, The" (Brown), **Supp. VI:** 71

Scarlet Tree, The (Sitwell), **VII:** 128–129

Scarperer, The (Behan), **Supp. II:** 67

Scarron, Paul, **II:** 354

"Scenes" (Dickens), **V:** 44–46

Scenes from Italy's War (Trevelyan), **VI:** 389

"Scenes from the Fall of Troy" (Morris), **V:** 297

Scenes of Clerical Life (Eliot), **V:** xxii, 2, 190–191, 200

Sceptick (Ralegh), **I:** 157

Schelling, Friedrich Wilhelm, **V:** 347

Scheme and Estimates for a National Theatre, A (Archer and Barker), **VI:** 104, 113

Schepisi, Fred, **Supp. IV:** 345

Schiller, Friedrich von, **IV:** xiv, xvi 173, 241

Schindler's Ark (Keneally), *see Schindler's List*

Schindler's List (Keneally), **Supp. IV:** 343, 346, 348, 354–357, 358

Schirmer Inheritance, The (Ambler), **Supp. IV:** 4, 13–16, 21

Schlegel, A. W., **I:** 329; **IV:** vii, xvii; **V:** 62

Schneider, Elizabeth, **V:** 366, 382

"Scholar and Gypsy" (Desai), **Supp. V:** 65

"Scholar Gipsy, The" (Arnold), **V:** xxi, 209, 210, 211, 216

School for Husbands (Mahon), **Supp. VI:** 175

School for Wives (Mahon), **Supp. VI:** 175

School for Scandal, The (Sheridan), **III:** 97, 100, 253, **261–264,** 270

School of Abuse (Gosson), **I:** 161

School of Donne, The (Alvarez), **II:** 125*n*

"School of Eloquence, The" (Harrison), **Supp. V:** 150, 151–157

"School Stories" (Wodehouse), **Supp. III:** 449

"School Story, A" (Trevor), **Supp. IV:** 502

Schoolboy Verses (Kipling), **VI:** 200

"Schoolboys" (McEwan), **Supp. IV:** 393

Schools and Universities on the Continent (Arnold), **V:** 216

Schopenhauer, Arthur, **Supp. IV:** 6

Schreber's Nervous Illness (Churchill), **Supp. IV:** 181

Schreiner, Olive, **Supp. II: 435–457**

Science and Poetry (Richards), **VI:** 207, 208; **Supp. II:** 405, 412, 413, 414, **417–418,** 419

Science of Ethics, The (Stephen), **V:** 284–285, 289

"Science of History, The" (Froude), **IV:** 324

Science of Life, The (Wells), **VI:** 225

Scilla's Metamorphosis (Lodge), **I:** 306

"Scipio, Polybius, and Panaetius" (Landor), **IV:** 94

Scoop (Waugh), **VII:** 297

Scornful Lady, The (Beaumont and Fletcher), **II:** 65

Scorpion and Other Poems (Smith), **Supp. II:** 463

Scorpion God, The (Golding), **Supp. I:** 82–83

Scot, William, **Supp. III:** 20, 22, 23

"Scotch Drink" (Burns), **III:** 315

"Scotland" (Reid), **Supp. VII:** 331

Scots Musical Museum (Johnson), **III:** 320, 322

Scott, Geoffrey, **III:** 234*n*, 238, 249

Scott, John, **IV:** 252, 253

Scott, Paul, **Supp. I: 259–274; Supp. IV:** 440

Scott, Robert Falcon, **II:** 273

Scott, Sir Walter **II:** 276; **III:** 146, 157, 326, 335, 336, 338; **IV:** viii, xi, xiv, **27–40,** 45, 48, 102, 111, 122, 129, 133–136, 167, 168, 173, 254, 270, 281; **V:** 392; **VI:** 412; **Supp. III:** 151, 154, 167

Scott Moncrieff, Charles, **VI:** 454, 455

Scottish Journey (Muir), **Supp. VI:** 198, 201

Scott–James, Rolfe Arnold, **VI:** x, xxxiv, 1

Scott–Kilvert, Ian Stanley, **VI:** xvi, xxxiv; **VII:** xxii

Scott–King's Modern Europe (Waugh), **VII:** 301

Scotus, Duns, *see* Duns Scotus, John

Scourge of Villainy, The (Marston), **II:** 25, 26, 40

Scrapbook (Mansfield), **VII:** 181

Screams and Other Poems, The (Richards), **Supp. II:** 407, 427

Screwtape Letters, The (Lewis), **Supp. III:** 248, 255, 256–257

"Script for an Unchanging Voice" (McGuckian), **Supp. V:** 292

Scriptorum illustrium maioris Britanniae catalogus (Bale), **I:** 1

Scrutiny (periodical), **VII:** 233, 238, 243, 251–252, 256; **Supp. III:** 107

Scudéry, Georges de, **III:** 95

Sculptura; or, The History . . . of Chalcography and Engraving in Copper (Evelyn), **II:** 287

Scum of the Earth (Koestler), **Supp. I:** 26

"Shrove Tuesday in Paris" (Thackeray), **V:** 22, 38

Shuttlecock (Swift), **Supp. V:** 429–431

"Sibylla Palmifera" (Rossetti), **V:** 237

Sibylline Leaves (Coleridge), **IV:** 56

"Sic Vita" (King), **Supp. VI:** 162

Sicilian Carousel (Durrell), **Supp. I:** 102

Sicilian Romance, A (Radcliffe), **III:** 338

"Sick King in Bokhara, The" (Arnold), **V:** 210

Sidgwick, Henry, **V:** 284, 285

Sidhwa, Bapsi, **Supp. V:** 62

Sidley, Sir Charles, *see* Sedley, Sir Charles

Sidney, Sir Philip, **I:** 123, **160–175; II:** 46, 48, 53, 80, 158, 221, 339; **III:** 95

Siege (Fry), **Supp. III:** 194

Siege of Corinth, The (Byron), **IV:** 172, 192; *see also* Turkish tales

Siege of London, The (James), **VI:** 67

Siege of Pevensey, The (Burney), **Supp. III:** 71

Siege of Thebes, The (Lydgate), **I:** 57, 61, 65

"Siena" (Swinburne), **V:** 325, 332

"Sierra Nevada" (Stevenson), **Supp. VI:** 254–255

"Sighs and Grones" (Herbert), **II:** 128

Sign of Four, The (Doyle), **Supp. II:** 160, 162–163, 164–165, 167, 171, 173, 176

Sign of the Cross, The (Barrett), **VI:** 124

Signal Driver (White), **Supp. I:** 131, 151

"Signpost, The" (Thomas), **Supp. III:** 403, 404

"Signs" (Stevenson), **Supp. VI:** 263

Signs of Change (Morris), **V:** 306

"Signs of the Times" (Carlyle), **IV:** 241–242, 243, 249, 324; **V:** viii

Sigurd the Volsung (Morris), *see Story of Sigurd the Volsung and the Fall of the Niblungs, The*

Silas Marner (Eliot), **V:** xxii, 194, 200

"Silecroft Shore" (Nicholson), **Supp. VI:** 216

Silence (Pinter), **Supp. I:** 376

Silence Among the Weapons (Arden), **Supp. II:** 41

Silence in the Garden, The (Trevor), **Supp. IV:** 505, 506, 515–516, 517

"Silent One, The" (Gurney), **VI:** 427

Silent Passenger, The (Sayers), **Supp. III:** 335

"Silent Voices, The" (Tennyson), **IV:** 329

Silex Scintillans: . . . (Vaughan), **II:** 184, 185, 186, 201

Sillitoe, Alan, **Supp. V:** **409–426**

Silmarillion, The (Tolkien), **Supp. II:** 519, 520, 521, 525, 527

"Silver Blaze" (Doyle), **Supp. II:** 167

Silver Box, The (Galsworthy), **VI:** 273, 284–285

Silver Bucket, The (Orton), **Supp. V:** 364

Silver Chair, The (Lewis), **Supp. III:** 248

Silver Spoon, The (Galsworthy), **VI:** 275

Silver Tassie, The (O'Casey), **VII:** 6–7

Silverado Squatters, The (Stevenson), **V:** 386, 395

"Silvia" (Etherege), **II:** 267

Simenon, Georges, **III:** 341

Simmons, Ernest, **V:** 46

Simmons, James, **Supp. IV:** 412

"Simon Lee" (Wordsworth), **IV:** 7, 8–9, 10

Simonetta Perkins (Hartley), **Supp. VII:** 122–123, 126

Simonidea (Landor), **IV:** 100

Simple and Religious Consultation (Bucer), **I:** 177

"Simple Susan" (Edgeworth), **Supp. III:** 153

Simpleton of the Unexpected Isles, The (Shaw), **VI:** 125, 126, 127, 129

Simplicity (Collins), **III:** 166

"Simplify Me When I'm Dead" (Douglas), **VII:** 440

Simpson, Alan, **Supp. II:** 68, 70, 74

Simpson, Percy, **I:** 279

Simpson, Richard, **IV:** 107, 122

Sinai Sort, The (MacCaig), **Supp. VI:** **186–187**

"Since thou, O fondest and truest" (Bridges), **VI:** 74, 77

"Sincerest Critick of My Prose, or Rhime" (Congreve), **II:** 349

Singer, S. W., **III:** 69

"Singing, 1977" (Fuller), **Supp. VII:** 79

Single Man, A (Isherwood), **VII:** 309, 316–317

Sing-Song (Rossetti), **V:** 251, 255, 260

Singular Preference, The (Quennell), **VI:** 237, 245

Sinjohn, John, pseud. of John Galsworthy

Sins of the Fathers and Other Tales (Gissing), **V:** 437

Sir Charles Grandison (Richardson), **III:** 80, 90–91, 92; **IV:** 124

"Sir Dominick Ferrand" (James), **VI:** 69

"Sir Edmund Orme" (James), **VI:** 69

"Sir Eustace Grey" (Crabbe), **III:** 282

Sir Gawain and the Carl of Carlisle, **I:** 71

Sir Gawain and the Green Knight, (Gawain–Poet), **I:** 2, 28, 69, 71; **Supp. VII:** 83, 84–91, 94, 98

Sir George Otto Trevelyan: A Memoir (Trevelyan), **VI:** 383, 391

Sir Harry Hotspur of Humblethwaite (Trollope), **V:** 100, 102

Sir Harry Wildair, Being the Sequel of AThe Trip to the Jubilee" (Farquhar), **II:** 352, 357, 364

Sir Hornbook; or, Childe Launcelot's Expedition (Peacock), **IV:** 169

Sir John Vanbrugh's Justificahon of . . . the Duke of Marlborough's Late Tryal (Vanbrugh), **II:** 336

Sir Launcelot Greaves (Smollett), **III:** 149, 153, 158

Sir Martin Mar–All; or, The Feign'd Innocence (Dryden), **II:** 305

Sir Nigel (Doyle), **Supp. II:** 159

Sir Proteus, a Satirical Ballad (Peacock), **IV:** 169

Sir Thomas More; or, Colloquies on the Progress and Prospects of Society (Southey), **IV:** 69, 70, 71, 280

Sir Thomas Wyatt (Dekker and Webster), **II:** 68

Sir Tristrem (Thomas the Rhymer), **IV:** 29

"Sir Walter Scott" (Carlyle), **IV:** 38

Sir Walter Scott: The Great Unknown (Johnson), **IV:** 40

"Sir William Herschel's Long Year" (Hope), **Supp. VII:** 164–165

"Sire de Maletroit's Door, The" (Stevenson), **V:** 395

Siren Land (Douglas), **VI:** 293, 294, 295, 297, 305

"Sirens, The" (Manifold), **VII:** 426

Sirian Experiments, The: The Report by Ambien II, of the Five (Lessing), **Supp. I:** 250, 252

Sirocco (Coward), **Supp. II:** 141, 146, 148

"Siskin" (Stevenson), **Supp. VI:** 256

Sisson, C. J., **I:** 178n, 326

"Sister Anne" (Potter), **Supp. III:** 304

"Sister Helen" (Rossetti), **IV:** 313; **V:** 239, 245

"Sister Imelda" (O'Brien), **Supp. V:** 340

"Sister Maude" (Rossetti), **V:** 259

Sister Songs (Thompson), **V:** 443, 449, 450, 451

Sister Teresa (Moore), **VI:** 87, 92, 98

Sisterly Feelings (Ayckbourn), **Supp. V:** 3, 6, 10, 11–12, 13, 14

"Sisters" (Kinsella), **Supp. V:** 261

Sisters, The (Conrad), **VI:** 148

Sisters, The (Swinburne), **V:** 330, 333

"Sitting, The" (Day Lewis), **Supp. III:** 128–129

Situation of the Novel, The (Bergonzi), **Supp. IV:** 233

Sitwell, Edith, **I:** 83; **III:** 73, 78; **VI:** 454; **VII:** xv–xvii, **127–141**

Sitwell, Osbert, **V:** 230, 234; **VII:** xvi, 128, 130, 135; **Supp. II:** 199, 201–202, 203

Sitwell, Sacheverell, **VII:** xvi, 128

Six Distinguishing Characters of a Parliament–Man, The (Defoe), **III:** 12

Six Dramas of Calderón. Freely Translated (FitzGerald), **IV:** 342, 344–345, 353

Six Epistles to Eva Hesse (Davie), **Supp. VI:** 111

"Six o'clock in Princes Street" (Owen), **VI:** 451

Six of Calais, The (Shaw), **VI:** 129

Six Poems (Thomas), **Supp. III:** 399

Six Stories Written in the First Person Singular (Maugham), **VI:** 374

"Six Weeks at Heppenheim" (Gaskell), **V:** 14, 15

"Six Years After" (Mansfield), **VII:** 176

"Six Young Men" (Hughes), **Supp. I:** 344

"Sixpence" (Mansfield), **VII:** 175, 177

Sixteen Self Sketches (Shaw), **VI:** 102, 129

Sixth Beatitude, The (Hall), **Supp. VI:** 120, 122, **130**

Sixth Heaven, The (Hartley), **Supp. VII:** 124, 125, 127

"Sixth Journey, The" (Graham), **Supp. VII:** 109

Sizemore, Christine Wick, **Supp. IV:** 336

"Skating" (Motion), **Supp. VII:** 251, 256

Skeat, W. W., **I:** 17

Stein, Gertrude, **VI:** 252; **VII:** 83; **Supp. IV:** 416, 542, 556, 557–558
Steiner, George, **Supp. IV:** 455
"Stella at Wood–Park" (Swift), **III:** 32
"Stella's Birth Day, 1725" (Swift), **III:** 32
"Stella's Birthday . . . A.D. 1720–21" (Swift), **III:** 32
"Stella's Birthday, March 13, 1727" (Swift), **III:** 32
Stella's Birth–Days: A Poem (Swift), **III:** 36
Stendhal, **Supp. IV:** 136, 459
Step by Step (Churchill), **VII:** 356
Stephen, Janus K., **IV:** 10–11, 268
Stephen, Leslie, **II:** 156, 157; **III:** 42; **IV:** 301, 304–306; **V:** xix, xxv, xxvi, **277–290,** 386; **VII:** xxii, 17, 238
Stephen Hero (Joyce), **VII:** 45–46, 48
Stephens, Frederick, **V:** 235, 236
Stephens, James, **VI:** 88
Steps to the Temple. Sacred Poems, with Other Delights of the Muses (Crashaw), **II:** 179, 180, 184, 201
Sterling, John, **IV:** 54
Stern, Gladys Bronwen, **IV:** 123; **V:** xiii, xxviii, 395
Stern, J. B., **I:** 291
Stern, Laurence, **III:** **124–135,** 150, 153, 155, 157; **IV:** 79, 183; **VII:** 20; **Supp. II:** 204; **Supp. III:** 108
Steuart, J. A., **V:** 392, 397
Stevens, Wallace, **V:** 412; **Supp. IV:** 257, 414; **Supp. V:** 183
Stevenson, Anne, **Supp. VI:** **253–268**
Stevenson, L., **V:** 230, 234
Stevenson, Robert Louis, **I:** 1; **II:** 153; **III:** 330, 334, 345; **V:** xiii, xxi, xxv, vxvi, 219, 233, **383–398; Supp. IV:** 61
Stevenson and Edinburgh: A Centenary Study (MacLaren), **V:** 393, 398
Stevenson Companion, The (ed. Hampden), **V:** 393, 395
Stevensoniana (ed. Hammerton), **V:** 393, 397
Stewart, J. I. M., **I:** 329; **IV:** xxv; **VII:** xiv, xxxviii
Stiff Upper Lip (Durrell), **Supp. I:** 113
Still Centre, The (Spender), **Supp. II:** 488, 489
"Still Falls the Rain" (Sitwell), **VII:** xvii, 135, 137
Still Life (Byatt), **Supp. IV:** 139, 145, 147–149, 151, 154
Still Life (Coward), **Supp. II:** 153
Stirling, William Alexander, earl of, *see* Alexander, William
"Stoic, A" (Galsworthy), **VI:** 275, 284
Stoker, Bram, **III:** 334, 342, 343, 344, 345; **Supp. III:** **375–391**
Stokes, John, **V:** xiii, xxviii
Stolen Bacillus, The, and Other Incidents (Wells), **VI:** 226, 243
Stone, C., **III:** 161n
"Stone Mania" (Murphy), **Supp. V:** 326
Stone Virgin (Unsworth), **Supp. VII:** 355, 356, 357, 360–361, 362, 365
Stones of Venice, The (Ruskin), **V:** xxi, 173, 176–177, 180, 184, 292

"Stony Grey Soil "(Kavanagh), **Supp. VII:** 189–190
Stoppard, Tom, **Supp. I:** **437–454**
Storey, David, **Supp. I:** **407–420**
Storey, Graham, **V:** xi, xxviii, 381
Stories, Dreams, and Allegories (Schreiner), **Supp. II:** 450
Stories from ABlack and White" (Hardy), **VI:** 20
Stories of Red Hanrahan (Yeats), **VI:** 222
Stories, Theories and Things (Brooke–Rose), **Supp. IV:** 99, 110
"Stories, Theories and Things" (Brooke–Rose), **Supp. IV:** 116
"Storm" (Owen), **VI:** 449
"Storm, The" (Brown), **Supp. VI:** 70–71
Storm, The; or, A Collection of . . . Casualties and Disasters . . . (Defoe), **III:** 13
Storm and Other Poems (Sillitoe), **Supp. V:** 424
"Storm Bird, Storm Dreamer" (Ballard), **Supp. V:** 26
"Storm is over, The land hushes to rest, The" (Bridges), **VI:** 79
"Stormpetrel" (Murphy), **Supp. V:** 315
"Storm–Wind" (Ballard), **Supp. V:** 22
"Story, A" (Thomas), **Supp. I:** 183
Story and the Fable, The (Muir), **Supp. VI:** 198
"Story in It, The" (James), **VI:** 69
"Story of a Masterpiece, The" (James), **VI:** 69
Story of a Non–Marrying Man, The (Lessing), **Supp. I:** 253–254
"Story of a Panic, The" (Forster), **VI:** 399
"Story of a Year, The" (James), **VI:** 69
Story of an African Farm, The (Schreiner), **Supp. II:** 435, 438, 439, 440, 441, **445–447,** 449, 451, 453, 456
Story of Fabian Socialism, The (Cole), **VI:** 131
Story of Grettir the strong, The (Morris and Magnusson), **V:** 306
Story of Rimini, The (Hunt), **IV:** 214
Story of San Michele, The (Munthe), **VI:** 265
Story of Sigurd the Volsung and the Fall of the Niblungs, The (Morris), **V:** xxiv, 299–300, 304, 306
Story of the Glittering Plain, The (Morris), **V:** 306
Story of the Injured Lady, The (Swift), **III:** 27
Story of the Malakand Field Force (Churchill), **VI:** 351
Story of the Sundering Flood, The (Morris), **V:** 306
"Story of the Three Bears, The" (Southey), **IV:** 58, 67
"Story of the Unknown Church, The" (Morris), **V:** 293, 303
Story of the Volsungs and . . . Songs from the Elder Edda, The (Morris and Magnusson), **V:** 299, 306
Story So Far, The (Ayckbourn), **Supp. V:** 2
"Storyteller, The" (Berger), **Supp. IV:** 90, 91

Story–Teller, The (Highsmith), **Supp. V:** 174–175
Storyteller, The (Sillitoe), **Supp. V:** 410
Story–Teller's Holiday, A (Moore), **VI:** 88, 95, 99
Stout, Mira, **Supp. IV:** 75
Stovel, Nora Foster, **Supp. IV:** 245, 249
Stowe, Harriet Beecher, **V:** xxi, 3
Strachey, J. St. Loe, **V:** 75, 86, 87
Strachey, Lytton, **III:** 21, 28; **IV:** 292; **V:** 13, 157, 170, 277; **VI:** 155, 247, 372, 407; **VII:** 34, 35; **Supp. II:** **497–517**
Strado, Famiano, **II:** 90
Strafford: An Historical Tragedy (Browning), **IV:** 373
Strait Gate, The . . . (Bunyan), **II:** 253
"Strand at Lough Beg, The" (Heaney), **Supp. II:** 278
Strange and the Good, The (Fuller), **Supp. VII:** 81
"Strange and Sometimes Sadness, A" (Ishiguro), **Supp. IV:** 303, 304
Strange Case of Dr. Jekyll and Mr. Hyde, The (Stevenson), **III:** 330, 342, 345; **V:** xxv, 383, 387, 388, 395; **VI:** 106; **Supp. IV:** 61
"Strange Comfort Afforded by the Profession" (Lowry), **Supp. III:** 281
Strange Fruit (Phillips), **Supp. V:** 380
"Strange Meeting" (Owen), **VI:** 444, 445, 449, 454, 457–458
Strange Necessity, The (West), **Supp. III:** 438
"Strange Ride of Morrowbie Jukes, The" (Kipling), **VI:** **175–178**
Strange Ride of Rudyard Kipling, The (Wilson), **VI:** 165; **Supp. I:** 167
Stranger, The (Kotzebue), **III:** 268
Stranger Still, A (Kavan), **Supp. VII:** 207–208, 209
Stranger With a Bag, A (Warner), **Supp. VII:** 380
Strangers and Brothers cycle (Snow), **VII:** xxi, 322, **324–336**
Strangers on a Train (Highsmith), **Supp. V:** 167, 168–169
Strapless (film), **Supp. IV:** 282, 291–292
"Strategist, The" (Saki), **Supp. VI:** 243
"Stratton Water" (Rossetti), **V:** 239
Strauss, Richard, **Supp. IV:** 556
"Strawberry Hill" (Hughes), **Supp. I:** 342
Strayed Reveller, The (Arnold), **V:** xxi, 209, 216
"Street in Cumberland, A" (Nicholson), **Supp. VI:** 216
Street Songs (Sitwell), **VII:** 135
"Streets of the Spirits" (Redgrove), **Supp. VI:** 235
"Strephon and Chloe" (Swift), **III:** 32
Strickland, Agnes, **I:** 84
Strictures on AConingsby" (Disraeli), **IV:** 308
"Strictures on Pictures" (Thackeray), **V:** 37
Striding Folly (Sayers), **Supp. III:** 335
Strife (Galsworthy), **VI:** xiii, 269, 285–286
Strike at Arlingford, The (Moore), **VI:** 95
Strindberg, August, **Supp. III:** 12
Stringham, Charles, **IV:** 372

Wood Beyond the World, The (Morris), **V:** 306

"Wooden Chair with Arms" (MacCaig), **Supp. VI:** 192

Woodhouse, Richard, **IV:** 230, 232, 233

Woodlanders, The (Hardy), **VI:** 1, 5, 7, 8, 9

Woodman, Thomas, **Supp. IV:** 364

Woods, Helen Emily, *see* Kavan, Anna

"Woods of Westermain, The" (Meredith), **V:** 221

"Woodsman" (MacCaig), **Supp. VI:** 192

"Woodspurge, The" (Rossetti), **V:** 241, 242, 314—315

Woodstock (Scott), **IV:** xviii, 27, 39

Woodward, Benjamin, **V:** 178

Woolf, Leonard, **VI:** 415; **VII:** 17

Woolf, Virginia, **I:** 169; **IV:** 107, 320, 322; **V:** xxv, 226, 256, 260, 281, 290; **VI:** 243, 252, 275, 411; **VII:** xii, xiv—xv, **17—39;** **Supp. II:** 341—342, 487, 501—502; Supp. **III:** 19, 41—42, 45, 49, 60, 103, 107, 108; **Supp. IV:** 231, 233, 246, 399, 407, 461, 542, 558; **Supp. V:** 36, 63

Woolley, Hannah, **Supp. III:** 21

Woolley, Leonard, **Supp. II:** 284

"Word, The" (Thomas), **Supp. III:** 406

Word Child, A (Murdoch), **Supp. I:** 228

Word for the Navy, A (Swinburne), **V:** 332

Word over All (Day Lewis), **Supp. III:** 118, 128

Word—Links (Carroll), **V:** 274

"Words" (Gunn), **Supp. IV:** 267

Words and Music (Beckett), **Supp. I:** 53, 60

Words and Music (Coward), **Supp. II:** 152

Words of Advice (Weldon), **Supp. IV:** 536—537

Words upon the Window Pane, The (Yeats), **VI:** 219, 222

Wordsworth, Dorothy, **II:** 273; **IV:** 1—4, 10, 19, 49, 128, 143, 146

Wordsworth, William, **II:** 188—189; **III:** 174; **IV:** viii—xi, **1—26,** 33, 70, 73, 95—96, 111, 137, 178, 214, 215, 281, 311, 351, 352; **V:** 287, 311, 331, 351—352; **VI:** 1; and Coleridge, **IV:** 43—45, 50, 51, 54; and DeQuincey, **IV:** 141—143, 146, 154; and Hazlitt, **IV:** 126—130, 133—134, 137, 138; and Keats, **IV:** 214, 215, 225, 233; and Shelley, **IV:** 198, 203, 207; and Tennyson, **IV:** 326, 329, 336; literary style, **III:** 304, 338; **IV:** 95—96, 154, 336; verse forms, **II:** 200; **V:** 224; **Supp. II:** 269; **Supp. IV:** 230, 252, 558

"Wordsworth" (Pater), **V:** 351—352

"Wordsworth and Byron" (Swinburne), **V:** 332

"Wordsworth's Ethics" (Stephen), **V:** 287

"Work" (Lamb), **IV:** 83

Work in Progress (Lowry), **Supp. III:** 280

Work in Progress (Redgrove), **Supp. VI:** 231

"Work of Art, A" (Warner), **Supp. VII:** 380

"Work of My Own, A" (Winterson), **Supp. IV:** 558

"Work of Water, The" (Redgrove), **Supp. VI:** 235

Work Suspended (Waugh), **VII:** 298—299

Work, Wealth and Happiness of Mankind, The (Wells), **VI:** 225

Workers in the Dawn (Gissing), **V:** 424, 435, 437

Workes of Edmund Waller in This Parliament, The (Waller), **II:** 238

"Workhouse Clock, The," (Hood), **IV:** 261, 264

Workhouse Donkey, The (Arden), **Supp. II:** 28, 30

Workhouse Ward, The (Gregory), **VI:** 315, 316

Working Novelist, The (Pritchett), **VI:** 290

Working of Water, The (Redgrove), **Supp. VI:** 235—236

Working with Structuralism: Essays and Reviews on Nineteenth— and Twentieth—Century Literature (Lodge), **Supp. IV:** 365, 377

Works (Congreve), **II:** 348

Works (Cowley), **II:** 195

Works (Swift), **III:** 24

Works of Art and Artists in England (Waagen), **III:** 328

Works of Charles Lamb, The, **IV:** 73, 81, 85

Works of Henry Fielding, The (ed. Stephen), **V:** 290

Works of Henry Vaughan, The (Martin), **II:** 184

Works of Max Beerbohm, The (Beerbohm), **Supp. II:** 45, 46, 47

Works of Morris and Yeats in Relation to Early Saga Literature, The (Hoare), **V:** 299, 306

Works of Samuel Johnson, The, **III:** 108n, 121

Works of Sir John Vanbrugh, The (ed. Dobrée and Webb), **II:** 323n

Works of Sir Thomas Malory, The (ed. Vinavier), **I:** 70, 80

Works of Thomas Lodge, The (Tyler), **VI:** 102

Works of Virgil, The (tr. Dryden), **II:** 304

Works of William Blake, The (ed. Yeats), **VI:** 222

World (periodical), **VI:** 103, 104

"World, The" (Vaughan), **II:** 185, 186, 188

World Crisis, The (Churchill), **VI:** 353—354

World I Breathe, The (Thomas), **Supp. I:** 176, 180—181

World in the Evening, The (Isherwood), **VII:** 309, 314—315

World of Charles Dickens, The (Wilson), **Supp. I:** 166

World of Difference, A (MacCaig), **Supp. VI:** 193—194

"World of Light, A" (Jennings), **Supp. V:** 210

World of Light, A (Sarton), **Supp. II:** 82

World of Light, The (Huxley), **VII:** 201

World of Love, A (Bowen), **Supp. II:** 77, 79, 81, 84, 94

World of Paul Slickey, The (Osborne), **Supp. I:** 333—334

World of Strangers, A (Gordimer), **Supp. II:** 227, 231, 232, 236, 243

World Set Free, The: A Story of Mankind (Wells), **VI:** 227, 244

World Within World (Spender), **Supp. II:** 482, 483, 484, 485, 486, 487, 488, 490

Worldliness (Moore), **VI:** 95, 98

Worlds, The (Bond), **Supp. I:** 423, 434

World's Desire, The (Haggard and Lang), **Supp. III:** 213, 222

"World's End, The" (Empson), **Supp. II:** 182

World's Room, The (MacCaig), **Supp. VI:** 192

"Worlds That Flourish" (Okri), **Supp. V:** 356

Worm and the Ring, The (Burgess), **Supp. I:** 186, 187, 188, 189

Worm of Spindlestonheugh, The (Swinburne), **V:** 333

Wormwood (Kinsella), **Supp. V:** 262—263

"Wormwood" (Kinsella), **Supp. V:** 262

Worst Fears (Weldon), **Supp. IV:** 538

"Worst of It, The" (Browning), **IV:** 369

"Worstward Ho" (Beckett), **Supp. I:** 62

Worthies of England (Fuller), **II:** 45

Wotton, Sir Henry, **II:** 132, 133, 134, 138, 140, 141, 142, 166

Wotton, William, **III:** 23

Wotton Reinfred (Carlyle), **IV:** 250

Woty, W., **III:** 170n

"Wound, The" (Gunn), **Supp. IV:** 259

"Wound, The" (Hughes), **Supp. I:** 348

"Wreath for Tom Moore's Statue" (Kavanagh), **Supp. VII:** 193

"Wreaths" (Hill), **Supp. V:** 186

"Wreck" (MacCaig), **Supp. VI:** 186

Wreck of the Archangel, The (Brown), **Supp. VI:** 71

"Wreck of the Deutschland, The" (Hopkins), **V:** 361, 362, **363—366,** 367, 369, 370, 375, 379, 380, 381

"Wreck of the Deutschland, The": A New Reading (Schneider), **V:** 366, 382

Wreck of the Mary Deare, The (film, Ambler), **Supp. IV:** 3

Wrecked Eggs (Hare), **Supp. IV:** 282, 293

Wrecker, The (Stevenson), **V:** 383, 387, 396

Wrens, The (Gregory), **VI:** 315—316

Wretched of the Earth, The (Fanon), *see Les Damnés de la terre*

Wright, William Aldis, **IV:** 343, 353

Write On: Occasional Essays, '65—'85 (Lodge), **Supp. IV:** 366

Writer and the Absolute, The (Lewis), **VII:** xv, 71, 72, 73—74, 76

Writers and Their Work series, **VII:** xi, xxii

Writer's Britain: Landscape in Literature, A (ed. Drabble), **Supp. IV:** 230, 252

Writer's Diary, A (Woolf), **V:** 226

"Writer's Friends, A" (Stead), **Supp. IV:** 461, 466